THE FRENCH REVOLUTION

fifth edition

THE FRENCH REVOLUTION
Conflicting Interpretations

selected & edited by

Frank A. Kafker
University of Cincinnati

James M. Laux
University of Cincinnati

Darline Gay Levy
New York University

KRIEGER PUBLISHING COMPANY
MALABAR, FLORIDA
2002

Cover illustrations taken from one pro-Revolutionary pair of caricatures of sans-culottes and one anti-Revolutionary pair, reproduced by permission of the Department of Prints and Photography, Bibliothèque Nationale of France, Paris, with a grant from the Office of the Dean of Humanities of the Faculty of Art and Science, New York University

First Edition 1968
Second Edition 1976
Third Edition 1983
Fourth Edition 1989, 1990 with corrections & Supplementary Bibliography
Fifth Edition, 2002

Printed and Published by
KRIEGER PUBLISHING COMPANY
KRIEGER DRIVE
MALABAR, FLORIDA 32950

Copyright © 2002 by Frank A. Kafker, James M. Laux, and Darline Gay Levy

Library of Congress Cataloging-in-Publication Data

The French Revolution : conflicting interpretations / selected and edited by Frank A. Kafker, James M. Laux, and Darline Gay Levy.
    p. cm.
Includes bibliographical references.
ISBN 1-57524-092-0 (pbk. : alk. paper)
    1. France—History—Revolution, 1789–1799. I. Kafker, Frank A., 1931.
II.   Laux, James Michael, 1927– . III. Levy, Darline Gay, 1939– .

DC142 .F69 2002
944.04—dc21   2001038116

10   9   8   7   6   5   4   3   2

CONTENTS

Contents

MAPS

PREFACE

Albert Camus has remarked that the modern age opens in a din of collapsing walls. He may have had in mind not only the walls of the conquered Bastille, but also those that sheltered kings, the clergy, and the nobles in France under the Old Regime.

Historians disagree about the results of this collapse. What actually fell because of the French Revolution? What motivated its leaders and supporters? Were they sensible idealists or fools and knaves? What did they envision to replace the old ways? How much did they really innovate? What were the unintended consequences of their actions? Did the Revolution do more harm than good in the short run? In the long run?

One of the primary aims of this anthology is to acquaint readers with the conflicting answers to these questions and to others provided by leading historians of the French Revolution—the great figures of the past as well as present-day scholars. We as editors have not sought to give special prominence to any one view or school of revolutionary studies. Instead, we have tried to include selections by historians of different political persuasions, religious beliefs, and historical methodologies. All we have asked is that they present their points of view clearly and informatively. In our search for such selections we have not limited ourselves to those easily accessible or already available in English. Twelve of the selections, for example, are our own translations from the French.

We have organized the readings around many of the important historical problems of the Revolution and the differing interpretations of them. The selections chosen are long enough to represent not only the authors' viewpoints, but also the main arguments they use to support them; and we have not confined ourselves to two contrasting interpretations when others might be considered equally cogent. We hope that readers will see that some of the explanations and analyses offered here have more validity than others, and that they can reach preliminary conclusions on at least some of the historical problems presented.

Of course, some noted historians are not represented and some major problems are not discussed. However, we believe that many of these gaps can be filled. For example, issues such as the long-range causes of the Revolution or the relation between the French Revolution and other revolutions of the eighteenth century have been treated elsewhere in paperback works.[1] In any event, given the vast historical literature on the French Revolution—an embarrassment of riches—gaps are inevitable. Some indication of this literature can be found in a bibliography that is much expanded from earlier editions.

For this fifth edition, we have also revised the chronological summary, the biographical sketches of historians, and the introductions to the chapters, but, more important, we have enlarged the book. Two chapters have been added: "Women, Gender, and Politics in Revolution and Counterrevolution: Gains and Losses"; and "The Revolutionary Legacy: Positive or Negative?" Moreover, although five previous selections have been omitted, ten selections were added. These new selections include one each by T. C. W. Blanning, William Doyle, François Furet, Olwen H. Hufton, Gary Kates, Laura Mason, Timothy N. Tackett, and David Gordon Wright, and a longer, more recent essay by Darline Gay Levy and Harriet Branson Applewhite replacing the one they contributed to the fourth edition. Furthermore, for the first time, we include the text in French and an English translation of "La Marseillaise," a popular song of the Revolution then and now.

As in the companion volume, *Napoleon and His Times: Selected Interpretations* (Malabar, Florida: Krieger, 1989), the spelling, capitalization, and punctuation of the individual authors have been retained. *Please note that we as editors have supplied titles for the selections.* When we have added explanatory material to any selection, such additions have been enclosed in brackets. To distinguish these brackets from the authors' brackets in the original text, we have italicized the contents of the authors' brackets.

We are pleased to acknowledge the help of Professor Charles McKay, who has made several useful suggestions for the improvement of this edition, Mr. Joseph Medici and Professor Gregory Robinson, who have provided technical assistance in the preparation of the bibliography, and Ms. Evelyn M. Schott, who has helped prepare the manuscript for publication.

F. A. K.

J. M. L.

D. G. L.

---

[1]See Peter Amann, ed., *The Eighteenth-Century Revolution: French or Western?* (Boston: Heath, 1963); William F. Church, ed., *The Influence of the Enlightenment on the French Revolution* 2nd ed. (Lexington, MA: Heath, 1974); Ralph W. Greenlaw, ed., *The Economic Origins of the French Revolution: Poverty or Prosperity* (Boston: Heath, 1958); Ralph W. Greenlaw, ed., *The Social Origins of the French Revolution: The Debate on the Role of the Middle Classes* (Lexington, MA: Heath, 1975); and Haydn T. Mason, ed., *The Darnton Debate: Books and Revolution in the Eighteenth-Century* (Oxford: Voltaire Foundation, 1998).

CHRONOLOGY

THE PRE-REVOLUTION (1786–1789).

1786

August 20   Chief minister Calonne notifies Louis XVI of the government's financial crisis.

September 26   Eden commercial treaty between France and Great Britain is signed. Effective May 1787, it brings economic hardship to a few areas in France.

1787

February 22   First Assembly of Notables is convened to raise taxes, but fails to agree and is dissolved on May 25.

April 8   Calonne leaves office, and Loménie de Brienne replaces him in May.

1788

August 8   Louis XVI agrees to call Estates General.

August 25   Loménie de Brienne resigns as chief minister, and Jacques Necker assumes the post.

July–August   Very poor harvest.

September 23 and 25   Parlement of Paris rules that the new Estates General will follow the precedents of the previous Estates General of 1614.

November 6–December 12   Second Assembly of Notables fails to agree on a tax plan.

December 27   Louis XVI orders that the Third Estate will have double the number of deputies as each of the other two orders.

1789

January   Abbé Sieyes publishes *What Is the Third Estate?*, an influential pamphlet attacking the conservatism of the nobility and clergy.

February   Elections to the Estates General begin; lists of grievances or *cahiers de doléances* are compiled.

April 27–28   Workers riot in Paris against the businessmen Réveillon and Henriot, who were thought to have suggested wage reductions. The riot is suppressed.

FROM THE ESTATES GENERAL TO THE END OF THE
NATIONAL ASSEMBLY (MAY 5, 1789–SEPTEMBER 30, 1791).

1789

May 5   First session of the Estates General at Versailles.

June 17   Third Estate assumes the title of National Assembly and calls on the deputies from other orders to join it.

June 19   Deputies from other orders start to break ranks and join the National Assembly.

June 20   When its hall is closed, the Third Estate, meeting at a nearby tennis court, defies the royal administration by declaring that it will remain in session until it approves a new constitution.

June 23   Louis XVI presents government's reform program to a combined session of the three estates, and the Third Estate rejects it.

June 27   Louis XVI orders the First and Second Estates to join the National Assembly, thereby acquiescing to the demands of the Third Estate.

July 1   Louis XVI increases the number of troops around Paris.

July 11   Louis XVI dismisses Necker.

July 12–14   Riots in Paris and the taking of the Bastille.

July 16   Necker is recalled to office.

July 20–August 6   Peasants riot, and there is a great fear of brigands in the countryside.

August 4–11   National Assembly decrees the abolition of "feudalism" by ending certain manorial dues, serfdom, hunting rights, clerical tithes, the sale of government offices, and other privileges.

August 26   Declaration of the Rights of Man and the Citizen is adopted by the Assembly.

September 10–11   Assembly votes against the creation of an Upper House and against allowing Louis XVI the power of a permanent veto. He is given a suspensive veto.

October 5–6   Parisian women lead a march on Versailles and force Louis XVI to move to Paris.

October 19   Assembly moves to Paris.

November 2   Assembly votes to expropriate church property.

December 14 and *22* Assembly begins to abolish old provinces and create new departments.

December 19 Government authorizes the issuance of assignats, interest-bearing securities acceptable in payment for expropriated church property.

December 22 Distinction between active and passive citizens is codified.

December 24 Religious liberty granted Protestants.

1790

February 13 Assembly votes to end all Catholic religious orders except those that teach and distribute charity.

June 19 Titles of hereditary nobility are abolished.

July Condorcet publishes *On the Admission of Women to the Rights of Citizenship.*

July 12 Assembly passes the Civil Constitution of the Clergy.

July 14 Festival of the Federation on the Champ-de-Mars, a celebration of the Revolution in which National Guard delegations from all over France, along with 300,000 men, women, and children, swear an oath of loyalty to Nation, Law, and King.

September 6 The parlements abolished.

September 29 Assignats are converted into paper money.

October Louis XVI starts to seek foreign help for a counterrevolution.

November 27 Public officials, including bishops and priests, are required to sign a loyalty oath to the nation.

1791

March 2 Guilds are abolished.

March 10 Pope Pius VI publicly condemns the Civil Constitution of the Clergy and the Declaration of the Rights of Man.

April 13 Pius VI disciplines those clergymen who have signed the Civil Constitution of the Clergy.

June 14 Le Chapelier Law prohibits labor unions and strikes.

June 20–25 Louis XVI attempts to flee France and raise a counterrevolution, but is captured at Varennes near the northeast border and returned to Paris.

July 17 Massacre of the Champ-de-Mars occurs as Lafayette's National Guard fires on demonstrators.

August Franchise is further restricted.

August 27 In the Declaration of Pillnitz, the rulers of Austria and Prussia pledge to crush the Revolution only if England and other powers sign an alliance with them.

September Publication of Olympe de Gouges's *Declaration of the Rights of Woman.*

September 14 Louis XVI accepts the new constitution.

September 27 All Jews are granted full citizenship.

THE LEGISLATIVE ASSEMBLY (OCTOBER 1, 1791–SEPTEMBER 20, 1792).

1792

February 7 Austria and Prussia ally against France.

March 1 Leopold I of Austria dies, and Francis II replaces him.

April 20 France declares war on Austria. Prussia sides with Austria. War of the First Coalition lasts from 1792 to 1797.

April 25–26 Rouget de Lisle writes the song that soon will become known as "La Marseillaise."

June 20 Rioters invade the Palace of the Tuileries.

July 25 Brunswick Manifesto warns Parisians not to disobey Louis XVI.

August 10 Palace of the Tuileries is invaded again. Louis XVI is suspended from his duties and soon imprisoned.

August 11 Assembly votes to have a National Convention elected by universal manhood suffrage.

August 16 Prussian, Austrian, and émigré army under the command of the Duke of Brunswick invades France.

August 19 Lafayette deserts to the Austrians.

September 2 Verdun capitulates to the Prussian army.

September 2–6 Massacres of more than one thousand prisoners in Paris and the provinces.

September 20 French defeat the Prussians at the battle of Valmy in northeastern France.

THE CONVENTION (SEPTEMBER 21, 1792–OCTOBER 26, 1795).

1792

September 21–22 Convention decrees the abolition of Monarchy and the creation of a Republic.

November 6 French victory in the battle of Jemappes.

December 11 Trial of Louis XVI begins.

December 15 Convention approves revolutionary policies in occupied territories.

1793

January 21 Louis XVI is executed after being tried before the Convention.

February–March Riots in Paris by men and women protesting high prices.

February 1 Convention declares war on Great Britain and Holland.

February 20–24 Convention votes for a military draft and conscripts 300,000.

March Vendée revolt begins.

March 7 Convention declares war on Spain.

April 1793–March 1794 Sans-culottes at height of their power.

April 5 French general Dumouriez deserts to Austrians after having lost a battle.

April 6 Committee of Public Safety is created by the Convention.

May The Society of Revolutionary Republican Women is formed.

May 4 Price of grain is fixed.

May 29 Revolt against central government begins in Lyon.

May 31–June 2 Mountain seizes power in a coup d'état. Brissot and other political opponents are arrested.

June 6 Marseille cuts ties to the central government.

July 13 Charlotte Corday assassinates Marat.

July 26 Hoarding of goods is made a capital crime.

August 1 Convention decrees a new system of weights and measures: the metric system.

August 23   General mobilization of the male population, a *levée en masse*, is ordered.

August 25   Revolt in Marseille is suppressed.

August 27   Toulon surrenders to the British.

September 5   Under the pressure of demonstrations and riots by men and women demanding more vigor in defense of the Revolution, the Convention authorizes strong measures, "terror," to quell opposition.

September 29   Convention passes a law of the Maximum, which puts a ceiling price on important goods and fixes wages.

October 5   Convention adopts the revolutionary calendar.

October 9   Revolt in Lyon is suppressed.

October 16   Queen Marie Antoinette is executed.

October 30   Convention outlaws the Society of Revolutionary Republican Women and all women's political clubs.

October 31   Girondins are executed.

November 10   Dechristianization reaches a peak with the Festival of Reason followed by the closing of Catholic Churches in Paris twelve days later.

December   Vendée revolt largely ends.

December 4   Revolutionary government is strengthened by the Law of 14 Frimaire.

December 4   Massacres of conservatives begin at Lyon.

December 19   British evacuate Toulon, and Napoleon Bonaparte distinguishes himself in the battle.

1794

February 4   Slavery is abolished in the French colonies.

February 26–March 3   Laws of Ventôse, which authorize the seizure of the property of suspects.

March 24   Hébertists are executed.

April–May   Military danger to France recedes.

April 5   Dantonists are executed.

June 8   Festival of the Supreme Being is celebrated.

June 10 Law of 22 Prairial reduces legal safeguards of suspects and contributes to an increase in imprisonments and executions.

June 26 French victory in the battle of Fleurus leads to the recapture of the Austrian Netherlands.

July 23 New Maximum on wages is instituted.

July 27–28 (9–10 Thermidor) Overthrow of Robespierre and his followers.

November 12 Jacobin club of Paris is closed.

December 24 Law of the Maximum is repealed.

1795

February 21 Convention decrees the separation of Church and State.

April–September Anti-Jacobin White Terror.

April–May Men and women revolt over food shortages and other grievances. They are suppressed.

April 5 Prussia signs a peace treaty with France.

May 16 France signs a treaty with the Netherlands (now the Batavian Republic).

July 22 France signs a peace treaty with Spain.

August 22 Institut de France is founded.

August 22 New constitution creates a bicameral legislature with executive Power vested in a five-man Directory.

October 4–6 Royalist insurrection in Paris is crushed by troops led by Napoleon and others.

THE DIRECTORY (NOVEMBER 2, 1795–NOVEMBER 10, 1799).

1796

February 19 Assignats, having lost most of their value, are discontinued.

March 27 Napoleon takes command of the Army of Italy at Nice.

1797

May 27 Conspirator Babeuf is executed.

September 4 (18 Fructidor) Directors purge the legislature of conservatives.

September 30 and December 14   Directors repudiate two-thirds of the public debt.

October 17   France signs peace treaty of Campo Formio with Austria.

1798

1798–1801   The War of the Second Coalition allies Russia, Great Britain, Austria, and other powers against France.

May 11 (22 Floréal)   Directors purge the legislature and other public institutions of opponents.

July 1   Napoleon lands his army in Egypt.

August 1   Admiral Nelson defeats a French fleet at Aboukir Bay, Egypt.

1799

June 18 (30 Prairial)   Legislature stages a coup d'état and excludes certain Directors from office.

August 23   Napoleon leaves his command in Egypt and returns to Paris on October 16.

November 9–10 (18–19 Brumaire)   Coup d'état by Napoleon.

French Provinces in 1789

THE NEW DEPARTMENTS IN 1790

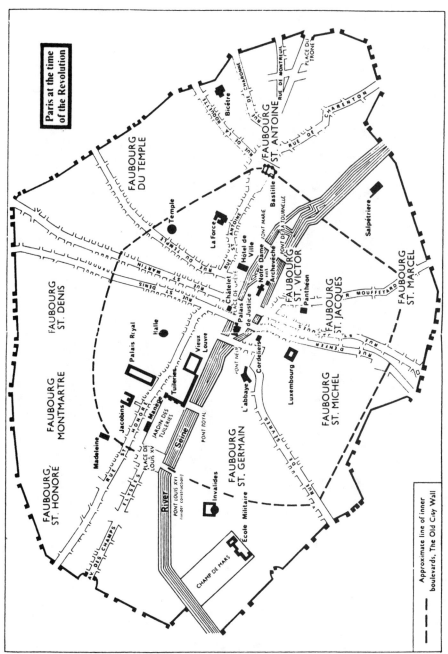

Paris at the time of the Revolution

FAUBOURG DU TEMPLE

FAUBOURG ST. ANTOINE

RUE DE MONTREUIL

PLACE DU TRÔNE

RUE DE CHARONNE

CHARENTON

Bicêtre

RUE DE

Temple

La Force

Hôtel de Ville

RUE ST. ANTOINE

PONT MARIE

Bastille

PONT DE LA TOURNELLE

Salpêtrière

FAUBOURG ST. DENIS

RUE ST. MARTIN

RUE ST. DENIS

Notre Dame

Archevêché

Châtelet

PLACE DE GRÈVE

Palais de Justice

FAUBOURG ST. VICTOR

Panthéon

FAUBOURG ST. JACQUES

R. MOUFFETARD

FAUBOURG ST. MARCEL

RUE ST. DENIS

FAUBOURG MONTMARTRE

Palais Royal

Halle

Jacobins

RUE ST. HONORÉ

Vieux Louvre

Tuileries

Manège

JARDIN DES TUILERIES

PONT NEUF

Cordeliers

L'abbaye

Luxembourg

RUE D'ENFER

FAUBOURG ST. MICHEL

FAUBOURG, ST. HONORÉ

Madeleine

AV. DES CHAMPS ELYSÉES

PLACE DE LOUIS XVI

PONT ROYAL

Seine

River

PONT LOUIS XVI (under construction)

Invalides

FAUBOURG ST. GERMAIN

Ecole Militaire

CHAMP DE MARS

— Approximate line of inner boulevards, The Old City Wall

from M. J. Sydenham, *The French Revolution* (New York: G. P. Putnam's Sons, 1965), pp. 52–53. Used by permission of M. J. Sydenham.

1
The Outbreak
of the Revolution
(1787–1789)

WHO led the overthrow of the Old Regime in France? Although every July 14 the French celebrate the victory of "the conquerors of the Bastille," historians long ago decided that the story was much more complicated. Some of them have accepted an interpretation popularized by Georges Lefebvre in his *Coming of the French Revolution:* "The first act of the Revolution, in 1788, consisted in a triumph of the aristocracy. . . . But, after having paralyzed the royal power which upheld its own social preeminence, the aristocracy opened the way to the bourgeois revolution, then to the popular revolution in the cities and finally to the revolution of the peasants—and found itself buried under the ruins of the Old Regime."[1] Thus, the outbreak of the Revolution occurred in four stages; it was carried out by four different social classes; and it was dominated by class conflict. We include here a short version of Lefebvre's interpretation from his survey *The French Revolution.*

Relying on the research of many historians since the 1950's, William Doyle marshals arguments to challenge Lefebvre's class interpretation. Doyle points out that aristocrats and bourgeois before 1787 belonged more to a common elite than to conflicting elites. Moreover, he argues that the Revolution was not the result of a long and inevitable historical development leading to the rise of the bourgeoisie. Rather, from 1787 to 1789, France experienced a financial, economic, and political crisis; and French political leaders, the educated public, and the common people had to improvise in order to deal with these unforeseen events. Revolution was the outcome. No one could predict, for example, the consequences of the calling of the Estates General, the election campaign of the deputies, the drawing up of the cahiers, and the deliberations of the Estates General. All of these accentuated the differences between the aristocracy and the bourgeoisie and aroused the common people.

Has Lefebvre's class interpretation been undermined by Doyle and

---

[1]Georges Lefebvre, *The Coming of the French Revolution,* trans. Robert R. Palmer (Princeton: Princeton University Press, 1947), p. 3.

1

other revisionist historians? Is his four-stage analysis of the coming
of the Revolution too neat? Is his main division of eighteenth-century
society into aristocrats, bourgeois, city masses, and peasants too im-
precise and too simple? Moreover does he exaggerate the importance of class to the neglect of the role of individuals?

In judging Doyle's interpretation, one may ask whether he provides nuances and complements to Lefebvre's class interpretation or
whether he demolishes it. What explains the reactions of individual
aristocrats and bourgeois to the unpredictable events of 1787–1789?
Were class interests more important than idealism or political maneuvering? Moreover, were the revolts in the cities actually led by class-
conscious workers and were the insurrections in the countryside led
by peasants with long-standing and clearly stated grievances?

In all times, men and women from similar social backgrounds have
chosen different political routes. For example, some aristocrats supported the King in 1788 and many Parisian workers did not riot on
July 14. Were such cases exceptional or common, inconsequential or
momentous? The answers to these questions have an importance
that extends far beyond the study of the French Revolution, for they
would illuminate to what extent human beings are shaped by their
class and to what extent they are free agents, powers in their own
right.

A SERIES OF CLASS REVOLTS

Georges Lefebvre

Georges Lefebvre (1874–1959) is considered one of the foremost twentieth-century historians of the French Revolution. The son of a clerk, he was born in the north of France and attended local public schools and the University of Lille. For twenty-five years he taught at provincial and Parisian secondary schools. At first he did research on medieval history, but after several years he turned to the study of the Revolution. In 1924, at the age of fifty, he presented his four-volume doctoral thesis on the peasants of the Department of the Nord during the French Revolution. This pioneering study of the life of the common people during the Revolution made his reputation. He then taught at various universities and published many books on such topics as the outbreak of the Revolution, the great peasant panic of 1789, and the revolutionary mentality, as well as highly regarded surveys of the revolutionary and Napoleonic epochs. In 1932 he succeeded Albert Mathiez as editor of the learned journal, the *Annales historiques de la Révolution française,* and from 1937 he was Professor of the History of the French Revolution at the University of Paris. Although he retired from teaching in 1945, his formidable energy, intelligence, and devotion to the study of the French Revolution continued to the end of his life. Many of his books have been translated into English.

The Aristocratic Revolution, 1787–1788

The French Revolution was started and led to victory in its first phase by the aristocracy. This fact is of primary importance, but for

From Georges Lefebvre, The *French Revolution from Its Origins to 1793,* trans. Elizabeth Moss Evanson (New York: Columbia University Press, 1962), pp. 97–130. Copyright © 1962 Columbia University Press. Reprinted with some minor changes in translation by permission of Columbia University Press, Inc., and Routledge and Kegan Paul.

differing reasons both the Third Estate and the aristocracy took pains to thrust it into the background. The immediate cause of the Revolution was a financial crisis originating with the war in America. Necker [the Finance Minister] had financed the war by borrowing, and his successor, Calonne, had used the same method to pay off arrears. The deficit grew to such proportions that on August 20, 1786, Calonne sent Louis XVI a note declaring state reform imperative.

Calonne and the Notables

The fiscal administration was so confused that the situation can be described only roughly. A statement of financial expectations drawn up in March, 1788, the first—and last—budget of the Old Regime, estimated expenditures at 629 million livres and receipts at 503 million, leaving a deficit of 126 million, or 20 per cent. Contemporaries attributed the deficit to court wastefulness and financiers' profits. Some economies could be and were made, but servicing the debt alone required 318 million, more than half of expenditures. The government could have reduced expenses only by repudiating the debt; raising taxes seemed out of the question, as taxes were already considered too high. At any rate there was one resource left. Certain provinces paid very little in taxes; the bourgeoisie less than the peasantry, the nobility and clergy least of all. From a technical point of view, the crisis could be easily resolved: equality of taxation would provide enough funds.

Calonne did not prove bold enough for fiscal equality, but he at least proposed to extend the [government's] salt and tobacco monopolies through the whole kingdom and to replace the *capitation* and twentieths[1] by a direct land tax, a "territorial subvention," to be levied without exception upon all landowners. At the same time he planned to stimulate economic activity and consequently swell treasury receipts by freeing the grain trade from all controls, by abolishing internal customs barriers, and by suppressing certain indirect taxes. Going even further, he intended to give responsibility for apportioning taxes to provincial assemblies elected by landowners without distinction as to order, and to relieve the clergy of its own debt by selling the Church's manorial rights [chiefly, its right to collect dues on land worked by others]. Financial stability would strengthen royal

---

[1][The *capitation* and the twentieth (*vingtième*), as well as the *taille*, were direct taxes levied by the Crown. During the course of the eighteenth century they came to fall most heavily on the peasants, while the privileged groups were able to avoid paying much of their share. —Eds.]

power, reducing opposition from the parlements to insignificance. Unity of the kingdom would be advanced. The bourgeoisie would be permitted to take part in government administration.

Although the sacrifices required of privileged groups were modest—they would still be exempt from the *taille* [a royal tax on land or income] and from the tax which Calonne proposed to substitute for road-service obligations (the *corvée des routes*)—he entertained no illusions as to how the parlements would receive his plans. He might have attacked them openly had he been able to count upon the king's support, but the fate of Turgot and Necker[2] gave him no encouragement. Moreover, although royalty still carried prestige, Louis personally had none. He was devoted to the hunt and liked to work with his hands; he drank and ate to excess; he liked neither high society, gambling, nor dancing; he was the laughing-stock of his courtiers; and rumours of the queen's conduct made him appear ridiculous. Marie Antoinette had gained the reputation of a Messalina and had lost face in the Diamond Necklace Affair of 1785. Calonne was therefore resigned to practise indirect methods. He thought out a plan to convoke an assembly of notables consisting primarily of various noble elements. By selecting them himself, and banking on administrative influence plus respect due the king, he expected that they would prove amenable and that their acquiescence would in turn impress the parlements. But the calling of an assembly was an initial surrender: the king was consulting his aristocracy rather than notifying it of his will.

When they convened on February 22, 1787, the notables were angered by the proposal to elect provincial assemblies without distinction as to order, by the restriction of their powers, and by the attack on the clergy's manorial rights. As could be expected, they censured the direct land tax and asked that they first be given a treasury report. They declared themselves desirous of contributing to the welfare of the state—but they intended to dictate their own terms. Louis saw that Calonne would get nowhere with the assembly, and dismissed him on April 8.

Brienne and the Parlements

At the head of those who opposed Calonne stood Loménie de Brienne, archbishop of Toulouse, who wanted to become [a govern-

---

[2][Both of these ministers had proposed reform programs which aroused opposition. Louis XVI had given neither of them wholehearted support. Turgot was dismissed in 1776; Necker resigned in 1781.—Eds.]

ment] minister and did so without delay. To soothe the notables he submitted the treasury accounts to them, promised to retain the three orders in the provincial assemblies and to leave the clergy's manorial rights alone. But he took over the plan for a territorial subvention and to it added an increase of the stamp duty. The notables replied that it was not within their power to consent to taxes, an allusion to the Estates-General. On May 25 their assembly was dissolved. Calonne's device had failed; it was obvious that Brienne had next to proceed to the parlements.[3]

The Parlement of Paris made no protest over registering freedom of the grain trade, commutation of the *corvée des routes,* and institution of provincial assemblies. But it drafted remonstrances against the stamp tax and rejected the territorial subvention, openly referring this to an Estates-General. A *lit de justice* was held on August 6; the parlement declared it null and void, then started proceedings against Calonne, who fled to England. On August 14 the magistrates were exiled to Troyes. Other sovereign courts supported them. Brienne quickly retreated, and on September 19 the reinstated parlement recorded restoration of the old taxes.

Brienne fell back on loans, but the same problem faced him: he had to have consent of the parlements to borrow. A few members agreed to negotiate and did not hesitate to set their decisive condition—that the government should promise to convoke the Estates-General. Brienne asked for 120 million livres to be raised over a five-year period, at the end of which—in 1792—the Estates-General would be convened. But, uncertain of a majority, he suddenly had an edict presented by the king himself on November 18 in a "royal session," that is, a *lit de justice* in which traditional ceremonies of convocation had not been observed. The duc d'Orleans protested and the registering of the edict was declared void. Louis retaliated by exiling the duke and two councillors [members of the Parlement]. The parlement came to their defence, condemning *lettres de cachet* and demanding that royal subjects be given personal freedom. To ward off an attack by force, on May 3, 1788, it published a declaration of fundamental laws of the king-

---

[3][During the reign of Louis XVI, an edict often became a law in the following manner: the royal administration prepared the edict, which was then sent to the leading law court of France, the Parlement of Paris. If the Parlement accepted the edict, it was registered. It if objected to parts of the edict, it drafted remonstrances. The king could override these objections by a *lit de justice,* that is, he could appear before Parlement in person or by proxy, sit on a pile of cushions (a *lit*), and order the registration. Then, according to the king, the edict had the force of law, but the Parlement frequently did not accept this interpretation.—Eds.]

dom, stating that the monarchy was hereditary, that the right to vote subsidies belonged to the Estates-General, that Frenchmen could not be arbitrarily arrested and detained, that their judges were irremovable, the customs and privileges of provinces inviolable.

The government had evidently resolved to imitate Maupeou.[4] On May 5 armed soldiers took up posts around the Palais de Justice until two members of the parlement who had been placed under arrest gave themselves up. On May 8 Louis succeeded in registering six edicts drawn up by Lamoignon, keeper of the seals [Minister of Justice]. According to them the power of registration was transferred to a "plenary court" composed of princes and crown officers, and at the same time the judiciary was reformed at the expense of the parlements—without, however, abolishing venality [the sale of government offices]. The *question préalable*—torture preceding the execution of criminals—was abolished (the *question préparatoire,* used to extract evidence during a judicial inquiry, had ended in 1780). Last of all, a fresh blow was dealt the aristocracy: a litigant could now refuse to accept the ruling of a manorial court by referring his case to royal tribunals.

This time resistance was more widespread and more violent. The provincial parlements and most of the lower tribunals protested. The assembly of the clergy, already annoyed by a recent edict granting Protestants a civil status, criticized the reforms and offered only a small contribution as its "free gift" [the Church's periodic grant of money to the government]. Riots broke out in Paris and several other cities. On June 7 the citizens of Grenoble rose and rained missiles upon the garrison from the rooftops in what was known as the "Day of Tiles." The provincial assemblies set up at the end of 1787 satisfied no one; several provinces clamoured for their old estates vested with the right to vote taxes. In the Dauphiné nobility and bourgeoisie met together at the château of Vizille on July 21, 1788, to convoke the Estates on their own authority. Brienne gave way.

The treasury was now empty. Pensions had had to be cut. Stockholders [owners of government securities] received nothing and notes from the Bank of Discount were made legal tender. Having no money, Louis had to leave it to the Prussians to invade Holland and support the Stadholder against his burghers. The Stadholder broke his alliance with France and joined with the English. Brienne yielded again, this occasion being the last: the Estates were to convene on

---

[4][A minister of Louis XV from 1768 to 1774, who had attempted to tame the parlements.—Eds.]

May 1, 1789. He resigned on August 24, 1788. The king recalled Necker, whose first act was to dismiss Lamoignon and reinstate the Parlement of Paris. On September 23 the parlement hastened to stipulate that the Estates-General would consist of three orders, as in 1614. Each order would have the same number of representatives, would make its decisions separately, and would have a veto over the others. The nobility and clergy were made masters of the assembly. This was the aristocracy's victory.

During these events privileged groups—especially those in Brittany—had acted together in forming propaganda and resistance organizations to protest royal authority; they had intimidated and sometimes won over the intendants and army leaders; occasionally they had roused sharecroppers and domestics. These revolutionary precedents were not to be forgotten. The parlements above all had taught a lesson: the Third Estate would duplicate their tactics when the Estates-General met. They had even presumed to indict a minister, making Calonne the first émigré.

The Bourgeois Revolution

To annoy the ministers a number of commoners, notably lawyers, had favoured the revolt of the nobility. Many others, such as the Rolands, expecting nothing, remained neutral. The summer of 1788 brought no evidence that bourgeois would take part in events. But news that an Estates-General was to be convened sent a tremor of excitement through the bourgeoisie: the king was authorizing them to plead their case. In this early stage accord with the aristocracy was not out of the question: the example set by the Dauphiné, where nobles granted commoners vote by head and equality of taxation, was welcomed enthusiastically. The atmosphere changed abruptly when the Parlement of Paris showed its true colours on September 23. Suddenly the popularity of the magistrates vanished. A clamour arose throughout the kingdom. "Public debate has assumed a different character," [the journalist] Mallet du Pan stated in January of 1789. "King, despotism, and constitution have become only secondary questions. Now it is war between the Third Estate and the other two orders."

Formation of the Patriot Party

The rupture was still not complete. Some of the liberal great lords joined the upper bourgeoisie to form the "National," or "Patriot," party. The "Committee of Thirty," which seems to have exerted considerable influence within the party, counted among its members the duc de La Rochefoucauld-Liancourt, the marquis de Lafayette, and the marquis de Condorcet, along with Talleyrand, bishop of Autun, and the abbé Sieyes. Mirabeau also appeared at its meetings. Sieyes and Mirabeau were in contact with the duc d'Orléans, who had at his disposal a large sum of money and who wielded unquestionable influence within his extensive appanage. Personal connections as well as bonds created by the many associations that had sprung up in the eighteenth century—academies, agricultural societies, philanthropic groups, reading circles, Masonic lodges—were utilized in the provinces as in Paris. Some have attributed to the Masonic Grand Orient, whose grand master was the duc d'Orléans, a decisive role. But the duc de Luxembourg, its administrator-general, remained devoted to the aristocratic cause, and the lodges were full of nobles. It is difficult to imagine that Masonry could have sided with the Third Estate without being split by conflicts, of which we have no evidence.

Although propaganda of the Patriots provoked counterarguments, the government raised no objection to controversy: the king had invited his subjects to air their thoughts and viewpoints concerning the Estates-General. Under pretext of replying to his appeal, a flood of pamphlets appeared, and their authors slipped into them whatever they wanted to say. The Patriots none the less used brochures with cautious skill—they limited themselves to requesting as many representatives for the Third Estate as for the nobility and clergy combined, invoking the example of the provincial assemblies and the Estates of the Dauphiné. The order of the day was to overwhelm the government with petitions, for which the municipalities assumed, willingly or not, full responsibility. Actually, all were counting on Necker.

Necker and the Doubling of the Third Estate

The minister of finance took care of the most urgent fiscal needs by drawing upon the Bank of Discount and by granting financiers, as security for their advances, "anticipations" on future tax receipts. He did this only to gain time until the Estates assembled, since he expected them to abolish fiscal privileges. If the nobility dominated the Estates the government would be at its mercy. Necker was therefore inclined to favour the Third Estate without being under its power. By doubling that order, and by limiting the vote by head to financial questions, all could be reconciled: equality of taxation would be adopted, while constitutional reform would bring conflict and require arbitration by the king. There can be no doubt about Necker's own view concerning the type of government to be instituted. He admired the British system—a House of Lords would soothe the aristocracy; admission to public office regardless of distinction by birth would satisfy the bourgeoisie.

He had no intention of revealing these plans. As an upstart financier, a foreigner, a Protestant, he had always been suspect in the eyes of the aristocracy, the court, and the king. Several of his colleagues—especially Barentin, the new keeper of the seals—opposed him. Determined above all else to preserve his power, he advanced with measured step. Like Calonne he hoped to persuade the notables to approve doubling of the Third. To this end he again convened them on November 6, 1788, but they disappointed him. On December 12 the royal princes sent Louis an entreaty which, by virtue of its clarity and moving tone, can be considered the manifesto of the aristocracy.

> The State is in danger . . . a revolution of governmental principles is brewing . . . soon the rights of property will be attacked, inequality of wealth will be presented as an object of reform: already the suppression of feudal rights had been proposed. . . . Could Your Majesty resolve to sacrifice, to humiliate, his brave, his ancient, his respectable nobility? . . . Let the Third Estate cease attacking the rights of the first two orders . . . let it confine itself to asking a reduction of the taxes with which it is perhaps overburdened; then the first two orders, recognizing in the third citizens dear to them, may renounce, in the generosity of their feelings, the prerogatives relating to pecuniary matters, and consent to bear public obligations in the most perfect equality.

But Necker went further and with the support of a few colleagues won the day—probably because Brienne's fall had displeased the queen and the nobility's rebellion had antagonized the king. An "Order of the Council" of December 27 granted doubling of the Third Estate. Louis XVI has since been criticized for not specifying the voting method at that time. This reproach is groundless, for in his report Necker mentioned that voting by order was to be the rule. But the decree failed to record this, and the minister had already hinted that the Estates-General might consider it appropriate to vote by head on tax questions.

The Third Estate cried victory and affected to consider the vote by head won. The nobility denied this interpretation and in Poitou, Franche-Comté, and Provence violently protested the doubling which had given rise to that conclusion. In Brittany class struggle degenerated into civil war; at Rennes fights broke out at the end of January, 1789. The Third Estate, annoyed, moved towards radical solutions. In a famous pamphlet issued in February, "What Is the Third Estate?" Sieyes described with cool rancour the hatred and scorn inspired in him by the nobility: "This class is assuredly foreign to the nation because of its do-nothing idleness." At the same time Mirabeau, in a speech which he had planned to deliver to the Estates of Provence, praised Marius "for having exterminated the aristocracy and the nobility in Rome." Fearful words, heralding civil war.

The Elections and the Cahiers

The electoral rules could have handicapped the bourgeoisie either by giving existing provincial estates the right to appoint deputies or by reserving a proportion of seats in the Third Estate to provincial delegates. Some of the nobles recommended these devices; Necker brushed them aside.

The method of election varied considerably, but the ruling of January 24, 1789, generally prevailed. It designated bailiwicks (*bailliages*) and seneschalsies (*sénéchaussées*) as electoral districts, even though these judicial areas were unevenly populated and differed widely in size. Contrary to precedent, whether or not he possessed a fief every noble was summoned to appear in the assembly of his order, but those ennobled by personal [nonhereditary] title only were relegated to the Third Estate—an error, for it wounded their pride. To elect clerical deputies, all parish priests met with the bishops, whereas [groups of] monks and canons were merely allowed to send representatives. Most parish priests were of the Third Estate and, commanding a majority, often neglected to elect their aristocratic bishops as delegates. The electors who chose the Third Estate's deputies assembled in bailiwick meetings after themselves being named by tax-paying heads of families within villages and parishes. They were elected directly in the villages, by two stages in the large towns. In each of the small bailiwicks designated "secondary" electoral districts, the meeting was allowed only to draw up a *cahier de doléances,* or list of grievances, and send one-quarter of its members to the assembly in the "principal" bailiwick to which it was attached. Peasants outnumbered all others at these meetings, but, lacking education, were incapable of expressing their opinions and were all the more intimidated because the meetings began with discussion of what should be included in the *cahiers*. They almost in-variably elected bourgeois deputies.

Among the representatives elected by clergy and nobility were able men who opposed reform, such as Calzalès and the abbé Maury, but owing to circumstances only the liberals—Duport, Alexandre de Lameth, and notably Lafayette—took a leading role. Deputies of the Third Estate were for the most part mature, often rich or well-to-do, educated, industrious, and honest men. Sometimes they had received special distinction—Bailly and Target were members of the Académie Française—but more often they had earned a reputation in their par-ticular province. Mounier and Barnave were well known in the Dauphiné, Lanjuinais and Le Chapelier in Brittany, Thouret and Buzot in Normandy, Merlin de Douai in Flanders, Robespierre in Artois. A telling characteristic of the bourgeoisie was that it had long idolized the marquis de Lafayette, noble deputy from Riom, and that the most celebrated of its own deputies, Sieyes and Mirabeau, came from the privileged classes. This foretells what position the nobility could have assumed in a reformed society by siding with the bourgeoisie.

Sieyes and Mirabeau were both from Provence. Sieyes, the son of a notary in Fréjus, had become canon of Chartres and was elected deputy from Paris. He guided the Third Estate during the early weeks. His pamphlets earned him a reputation as an oracle. It was he who developed the theory of "constituent power," declaring that sov-ereignty resided in the nation alone and that representatives of the nation were to be invested with dictatorial power until a constitution could be written and put into effect. He was the loyal interpreter of the bourgeoisie and later made the significant distinction between "active" and "passive" citizens. But, lacking application or special talent as an orator, he quickly shut himself off in isolation. Mirabeau, on the other hand, possessed the realistic foresight of a statesman, knew how to handle men, and was unexcelled in eloquent oratory. Unfortunately his scandalous youth and cynical venality made it im-possible to respect him; no one doubted that the court could buy him at will. Neither he nor Sieyes could direct the Third Estate. Its work remained a collective achievement.

Necker could have exerted considerable influence over the draft-ing of the *cahiers de doléances*. Malouet, an official in the naval min-istry and a deputy of the Third Estate from Riom, pointed out to him that he must draw up a royal programme to guide public opinion, im-press the nobility, and—most important—restrain the enthusiasm of the Third Estate. Necker very likely sensed the wisdom of this sug-gestion, but he had already been soundly criticized for permitting the doubling and was now inclined to consider his moves carefully. He rejected this additional risk, content with having persuaded the king to remain neutral.

The bourgeois were therefore free to participate in drafting lists of grievances from the parishes. Some model *cahiers* were sent out from Paris or were drawn up regionally; lawyers and parish priests sometimes set pen to paper for the cause. A number of *cahiers* were nevertheless original: indifferent to constitutional reform, they were content to criticize the overwhelming burdens laid upon the populace. But these should not necessarily be taken as an accurate reflection of what the lower classes felt most deeply, for in the presence of a manorial judge, peasants were not always likely to say what they thought. Moreover, the proletarians rarely participated in deliberations. Grievances sent out from the bailiwicks are even less representative, since bourgeois members simply eliminated from the original lists those demands which displeased or did not interest them. The popular classes of town and countryside were concerned not only with attaining fiscal equality and tax reduction, but with suppressing the tithe, manorial rights, and seigneurial authority, with gaining observance of collective usage [of common land in rural communities], regulating the grain market, and instituting controls to curb capitalist expansion. The people threatened aristocratic property along with aristocratic privileges, and bourgeois aspirations as well. But since the populace did not have access to the Estates-General, king, aristocrats and bourgeois were left alone to settle their triangular conflict.

In their *cahiers* the nobles and bourgeois were of one accord in expressing devotion to the monarchy, but they also agreed upon the need to replace absolutism with rule of law accepted by representatives of the nation; with reasonable freedom of the press and guarantees of personal liberty against arbitrary administrative and judicial ruling; with reform of various branches of the administration, including ecclesiastic reorganization. To the desire for national unity was joined a keen desire for regional and communal autonomy which would end ministerial despotism by loosening the grip of a centralized administration. Both classes agreed to religious toleration, but secularization of the state stopped at this point: they wished to leave the privilege of public worship to the Catholic Church and did not consider abolishing religious instruction or Church poor relief, nor did they deny clerics the right to register births, marriages, and deaths. The clergy was not satisfied with this much: it would not allow criticism of its doctrines through the press or the same treatment for heretics as for true believers. Even a recent edict granting legal status to Protestants had provoked protest. Except for these qualifications, not inconsiderable in themselves, the clergy agreed with the other two orders. More or less generally conceived, liberty was a national desire.

Class conflict was none the less evident. The privileged classes resigned themselves to financial sacrifices—with strong reservations as to the extent and method of contributions demanded of them—but they were generally opposed to the vote by head and expressly stipulated that the orders be preserved and honorific prerogatives and manorial rights be retained, whereas for the Third Estate equality of rights was inseparable from liberty.

But this did not mean that royal arbitration was destined to fail. No one challenged the king's right to approve legislation or the need to leave executive power intact. By renouncing the exercise of arbitrary will and by governing in accord with the Estates-General, the Capetian dynasty would only emphasize its national character; royal authority would not be lessened if reformed. There were many men among the aristocracy and bourgeoisie who, whether they actively desired it or not, might have leaned towards compromise. Among the nobles obedience to the princely will might have quelled opposition. Such bourgeois as Malouet and Mounier wanted above all to end despotism and judged that wrangling among the orders would perpetuate it. With little concern for the peasants, they were willing to respect the manorial authority and honorific primacy of the noble. Among each of the orders fear of civil war, already perceptible, secretly pleaded for conciliation.

A great king or a great minister might have taken the initiative towards a settlement. But Louis XVI was not Henry IV; Necker was clearsighted, but his background paralysed him. The nation was left to itself.

The Victory of the Bourgeoisie

Far from thinking of compromise, the court tried to get rid of Necker. The Parlement of Paris, repentant, gladly offered its assistance. In April rumour had it that a new cabinet would be formed and would promptly adjourn the Estates-General *sine die*. The issue of verifying powers aroused contention among the ministers: Barentin held that precedent accorded power of verification to the Council of State [the king's Cabinet]; Necker objected. Louis ended by supporting Necker, thereby averting a palace revolution but leaving the question of who was qualified to verify powers undecided. This conflict probably accounts for the postponement of the opening of the Estates from April 27 to May 5.

Prudence advised that the deputies should assemble far from Paris, but Versailles was the preferred choice—by the king so he could hunt; by the queen and her entourage for their own pleasures. The court also acted unwisely in clinging to a protocol that humiliated the Third Estate. Each order was assigned a particular dress, and they were segregated for presentation to the king on May 2. In the procession of the Holy Ghost, on May 4, they paraded in separate groups from Notre Dame to Saint Louis. Representatives of the Third, dressed in black, were indistinguishable except for the commanding ugliness of Mirabeau, but were applauded confidently by an immense crowd. The nobles were decked and plumed. The dark mass of parish priests came next, then the king's musicians, then bishops dressed in dazzling robes. This war of ceremony lasted until July 14: in royal sessions the Third affected to dress like the privileged orders; Bailly gave notice that deputations he led to the king would not kneel before the royal presence.

The Hôtel des Menus-Plaisirs on the Avenue de Paris, actually an ordinary storehouse, had been prepared for the meetings of clergy and nobility. Behind it, on the Rue des Chantiers, a room built for the notables was enlarged and redecorated for plenary sessions, which were presided over by the king. But because nothing else was large enough to hold the Third Estate, this "national hall" was turned over to it on ordinary occasions. Spectators sat on the speakers' platforms, thronged in and out, and were allowed to join in discussions, a habit which persisted until the end of the Convention [1795]. This careless arrangement increased the importance of the Third Estate and subjected the more timid to pressures of intransigent and rash opinions.

Louis opened the meeting on May 5. His brief address was applauded. Barentin, who could not be heard, followed. Then Necker, with the aid of an acting official who relieved him from time to time, harangued the anxious deputies. His listeners were soon disappointed and seriously annoyed. For three hours the minister of finance explained the detailed situation of the Treasury and the proposed improvements, made no allusion to constitutional reform, expressed confidence in the generosity of the privileged classes, then repeated the method of voting which had been announced in December. On the following day the nobility and clergy began to verify their powers separately. The Third Estate refused to follow suit. The Estates-General was paralysed.

Deputies from Brittany and the Dauphiné favoured outright refusal to vote by order, but that would have been an infringement of legality, and the politicians did not want to take chances so early in the game. The representatives were not yet familiar with one another, and no one knew how far each would agree to advance. Some found the ardour of the Bretons alarming. A delaying tactic was necessary, and Necker's refusal to grant the Council of State power of verification provided an escape. The Third Estate alleged that each order had to establish whether the two other orders were legally constituted, and that powers should therefore be inspected in common session. During this stalemate the Third refused to constitute itself as a separate order: no minutes were taken, no rules established; not even a steering committee was set up. They consented only to choose a "dean," who after June 3 was Bailly. At the beginning the Third had taken the name Commons (*communes*) for itself. Although no one other than a few of the more erudite knew exactly what the medieval communes were, the word evoked a vague memory of popular resistance to feudal lords, an idea strengthened by what knowledge they had of English history. To the Third Estate the name meant refusal to recognize a social hierarchy that had relegated it to third rank.

This attitude had its drawbacks. The people were told that the Third Estate was responsible for delaying the abolition of fiscal privileges. When Malouet tried to negotiate by offering to guarantee the rights and property of the aristocracy he was roundly criticized. Everyone, however, sensed the need for some new tactical issue, and it was the clergy which furnished them with just that. The nobility, in no way perturbed, on May 11 announced itself constituted as a separate order. Because a large proportion of the parish priests supported the Commons, the clergy instead proposed that designated members of the three orders meet in conference. To humour the other order, the Third Estate agreed. But the discussions of May 23 and 25 came to nothing: the nobles retreated behind precedents which the Third Estate either challenged or fought with arguments of reason and natural right. They next tried to get the clergy to agree that the three orders should be fused. The bishops sensed imminent defection from the parish priests and asked the king to intervene. On May 28 Louis asked that the conferences be resumed in the presence of his ministers, and on June 4 Necker drafted a conciliatory proposal: each order should first verify the powers of its own members, then announce the results to the others and consider any objections that were raised. If no agreement could be reached, the king was to deliver a final decision. Once more the Third found itself in a difficult position. This time it was the nobility that came to its rescue by rejecting royal arbitration except for the "complete" delegations—those which, as in the Dauphiné and in several bailiwicks, had been chosen in common by the three orders. This was the signal for revolutionary action.

On June 10 the Third Estate followed a proposal from Sieyes and invited the privileged members to join it. Those who did not appear to answer a roll call would be considered to have defaulted. The roll was begun on June 12 and finished on the 14th: several parish priests had responded, but not one noble. After two days' debate the Third Estate on June 17 conferred the title "National Assembly" upon the combined and enrolled orders. It immediately arrogated to itself the power to consent to taxation, confirming existing taxes provisionally. Had sovereignty passed to the nation? Not exactly. On June 20 Bailly acknowledged that these revolutionary resolutions required the king's approval.

Louis had no intention of approving them. The Dauphin had died on June 4, and the king had withdrawn to Marly, where the queen and royal princes instructed him. The nobility finally abdicated in favour of the throne and begged the king to make the Third Estate return to the path of duty. On June 19 the majority of the clergy declared itself in favour of fusing the three orders. The bishops hastily called for assistance. Royal ministers and even Necker agreed that intervention was necessary. The Council of State announced that a royal session would be held on June 22. But what would the king declare then? With the support of [the ministers] Montmorin and Saint-Priest, Necker hoped to manage the Commons by simply ignoring their decrees rather than by overriding them. At last he came out into the open, proposing to establish equality of taxation, to admit all Frenchmen to public office, and to authorize the vote by head in constituting future Estates-General, stipulating that the king would agree to this only if the Estates met as two houses and if he were granted full executive power with a legislative veto. Necker protected aristocratic prerogatives and property with the vote by order [in future Estates-General], but Barentin objected: did this mean they were to adopt the British system of government? Louis hesitated, postponing the decision. The royal session was put off until June 23.

On June 20 the Third Estate discovered its hall closed without notice or warning. It finally found asylum in a neighbouring tennis court, where, because there was talk of retiring to Paris and seeking the protection of the people, Mounier stepped in and proposed the famous oath, that they remain united until a constitution was established. A threatened *lit de justice* had provoked enough indignation to incite the deputies, with few exceptions, to sign the oath. The Third Estate, like the Parlement of Paris, rebelled in advance against the royal will.

On June 21 Louis admitted his brothers to the Council and, finally, withdrew his support from Necker, whose programme was defeated the next day. On the 23rd an impressive show of armed force surrounded the Hôtel des Menus-Plasirs, from which the public was excluded. Received in silence, Louis had Barentin read two declarations of capital interest in that they revealed quite clearly what was at stake in the struggle. They granted the Estates-General power to consent to taxes and loans and to various budget allocations, including the funds set aside for upkeep of the court. Personal liberty and freedom of the press would be guaranteed; decentralization would be carried out through the provincial estates; an extensive programme of reforms would be studied by the Estates-General. In sum, the proposals meant that a constitutional system, civil liberty, and achievement of national unity were to be the common inheritance of monarch and nation. Louis made an exception only for the clergy: its special consent was required for everything touching upon ecclesiastic organization and religious matters. Furthermore, he appeared as arbiter among the orders—if the Third Estate's decrees were overridden, so were the binding mandates that the privileged orders had invoked to compel voting by order and to postpone equality of taxation. Verification of powers would follow the system proposed on June 4. The orders were authorized to meet together to deliberate matters of general interest. The king strongly hoped that the clergy and nobility would agree to assume their share of public burdens.

But Louis failed to impose equal taxation and remained silent upon the question of admittance to public office; he expressly retained the orders and excluded vote by head from such matters as organization of future Estates-General, the manorial system, and honorific privileges. The throne thereby committed itself to preservation of the traditional social hierarchy and aristocratic pre-eminence. As a result of this decision, the Revolution was to mean conquest of equality of rights.

The king concluded by ordering the Estates to separate into orders and by giving them to understand that he would dissolve the assem-

bly if its members did not obey. He then departed, followed by the
nobility and most of the clergy. The Third Estate did not stir. Brezé,
grand master of ceremonies, repeated his sovereign's command, to
which Bailly replied: "The assembled nation cannot receive orders."
Sieyes declared: "You are today what you were yesterday." Ignoring,
as the Parlement of Paris had done previously, the existence of a
royal session, the Third Estate confirmed its own decrees and declared its members inviolable. The expressive and significant statements made by Bailly and by Sieyes deserve to be those remembered
by posterity, but Mirabeau's epigraph has proved more popular: "We
will not stir from our seats unless forced by bayonets." The Commons could not have carried out this challenge, but the court
thought itself in no position to find out, as agitation had already
reached menacing proportions. After this point, resistance to the
Third Estate disintegrated: a majority of the clergy and forty-seven
nobles joined the Commons; on June 27 the king asked the others to
follow suit.

The legal, peaceful revolution of the bourgeoisie, achieved by
lawyers who borrowed their methods from the Parlement of Paris,
was to all appearances victorious. On July 7 the Assembly appointed
a committee on the constitution and two days later Mounier delivered its first report. From that day, and for history, the Assembly was
the Constituent Assembly. On July 11 Lafayette submitted his draft
for a declaration of human rights.

Appeal to Armed Force

The Third Estate did not lose its composure. Dictatorship of the constituent power, advocated by Sieyes, was not instituted. Royal approval was still considered necessary. The modern idea that a constitution creates its own powers before it regulates them had not yet
been formulated; instead, Louis XVI, invested with his own power
rooted in history, would contract with the nation. On the other hand,
although the Third Estate fused the three orders, it did not proclaim
their disappearance within the nation, nor did it call for election of a
new assembly: the bourgeoisie therefore did not aspire to class dictatorship. On the contrary, it seemed possible that a moderate majority would be formed: the clergy, the liberal nobility, and a segment
of the Commons favoured a party of the middle. Most of the nobles,
however, made it known that they by no means considered the matter settled, and when troops were seen thronging around Paris and

Versailles the king was suspected of preparing a show of force. He had excuses: agitation was growing, hunger multiplied disturbances; at the end of June disorderly conduct of the French Guards [a regiment of royal troops] caused a riot in Paris.

The court had not yet fixed a plan of action. To draw one up, it had to get rid of Necker and his friends. The maréchal de Broglie and the baron de Breteuil had been called in. Wisdom commanded that a cabinet be formed secretly, ready to appear when sufficient forces were on hand. This was a game with fearful consequences. We can understand that the king regarded deputies of the Third Estate as rebels and that the nobility considered surrender a humiliation. But if a show of arms failed, the blood spilled would stain both king and aristocracy. Nevertheless, on July 11 Necker was hastily dismissed and banished from the kingdom; his friends were replaced by Breteuil and his cohorts. No further steps were taken. But the Assembly expected the worst, and the bourgeois revolution seemed lost. They were saved by popular force.

The Popular Revolution

Resort to arms transformed the struggle of social orders into civil war which, abruptly changing the character of the Revolution, gave it a scope that far surpassed what the bourgeoisie had intended or expected. Popular intervention, which provoked the sudden collapse of the social system of the Old Regime, issued from progressive mobilization of the masses [caused] by the simultaneous influences of the economic crisis and the convocation of the Estates-General. These two causes fused to create a mentality of insurrection.

The Economic Crisis

Starting in 1778, the surge in production which had followed the Seven Years War and which is known as the splendour of Louis XV, was checked by difficulties rooted in agricultural fluctuations, a continual problem of the old economy. These setbacks became established in cyclical depressions and caused what their historian[5] called the decline of Louis XVI. First, unusually heavy grape harvests pro-

---

[5][C.-E. Labrousse, *Esquisse du mouvement des prix et des revenus en France au XVIIIe siècle* (Paris: Dalloz, 1933) and *La Crise de l'économie française à la fin de l'ancien régime et au début de la Révolution* (Paris: Presses Universitaires de France, 1943).—Eds.]

voked a dreadful slump in the wine market. Prices fell by as much as 50 per cent. They rose somewhat after 1781 because of scarcity, but short supply then meant that the wine sector could not recoup its losses. Wine-growing was still practised in almost every part of the kingdom and for many peasants was the most profitable market product. They suffered cruelly; those who were sharecroppers found their income reduced to nothing. Grain prices were the next to fall, remaining relatively low until 1787. Finally, a drought in 1785 killed off much of the livestock.

Rural inhabitants constituted the majority of consumers, and because their purchasing power was reduced industrial production was in turn threatened after 1786. Traditional interpretation has laid primary blame for industry's troubles upon the commercial treaty with Britain [the Eden Treaty of 1786]. Although this was not the most important cause, it certainly did obstruct industry temporarily, since production had to modernize if it was to withstand foreign competition. Unemployment spread. The countryside, where domestic industry had developed, suffered as much as the cities.

The lower classes therefore had no reserves left when they faced the brutal prospect of famine after grain crops failed in 1788. The price of bread rose steadily. At the beginning of July, 1789, a pound of bread sold for four sous in Paris—where the government nevertheless sold its imported grains at a loss—and twice as much in some provinces. At that time wage earners considered two sous per pound the highest price they could possibly pay and still subsist, for bread was their staple food and average daily consumption ranged from one and a half pounds per person to two or three for an adult manual labourer. Necker ordered large purchases from abroad, and, as usual, labour centres [*ateliers de charité,* or public workshops] opened up, while measures were taken for distributing soup and rice. The previous winter had been severe, and the cruel effects of high prices did not lessen as the harvest season drew near. For over a half-century we have known, chiefly from the works of Jaurès, that the prosperity of the kingdom of France was responsible for the growing power of the bourgeoisie, and in this sense it is with reason that [the historian] Michelet's interpretation has been attacked, for the Revolution broke out in a society in the midst of development, not one crippled and seemingly threatened with collapse by nature's Providential shortages. But the social importance of this enrichment should not deceive us. Since colonial profits were realized mainly through re-exportation, the nation's labour force did not benefit as much as we might think, and, while a long-term rise in prices swelled the income of large landowners and bourgeoisie, wages failed to keep pace. We now know that production was dislocated and curtailed in the last decade before the Revolution, and we can justifiably state that the living standard of the masses was steadily declining. Famine, when it came, overwhelmed the populace.

"The people" (artisans, shopkeepers, hired help) as well as proletarians ("the populace"), peasants—small proprietors and sharecroppers who did not raise enough to support themselves or wine-growers who did not raise any grain—as well as townsmen unanimously agreed that the government and upper classes were responsible for these afflictions. Income declined but taxes did not. Tolls and duties on consumption became more hateful in times of high prices. If the wine market was restricted it was because excises limited consumption. There was no bread because Brienne removed controls on grain exports and shipments in 1787. True, Necker had stopped exports, subsidized imports, and reinstituted market sales. But he was too late. "Hoarders" had gone to work. Anyone in authority, all government agents, were suspected of participating in hoarding. The "famine plot" was thought to be more than a myth. Tithe collectors and lords were just as odious—they were hoarders because their levies cut into a poor harvest and consumed the peasants' supplies. The final blow was that collectors and lords profited even more from the high prices that increased poverty. And, finally, the solidarity of the Third Estate was shaken: the grain merchant, the baker, and the miller were all threatened; the bourgeois, partisan of economic freedom, clashed with popular hostility towards capitalism, since the people, of course, favoured requisitions and controls. In April Necker authorized requisitions to replenish the markets, but the intendants and municipal officials rarely used this power.

As the months of 1789 passed, riots kept the tired and frightened officials in a constant state of alert. On April 28 Parisian workers from the faubourg [district] Saint-Antoine sacked the manufactories of Réveillon and Henriot. Throughout the kingdom markets were the scenes of disturbances. Grain shipments, forced by milling and transportation conditions to use roads and rivers in plain view of famished hordes, were sometimes halted. The army and constabulary exhausted themselves rushing from one place to another, but were not inclined to deal harshly towards rebels whose privations they shared and unconsciously began to feel a common sympathy with them. The armour of the Old Regime was rapidly disintegrating.

Agitation was especially pronounced in the countryside. There the tax burden was crushing; tithes and manorial dues drove the peasants to desperation. Sentiment in the peasant community was divided among journeymen, sharecroppers, small proprietors, and large-scale tenant farmers, but on all matters of taxation it was solidly opposed to royal authority and the aristocracy. Tremors of agrarian revolt could be felt well before July 14—in Provence at the end of March, around Gap in April, in Cambrésis and Picardy in May. Near Versailles and Paris game had been exterminated, forests cleaned out. Moreover, the people were afraid of each other because begging, a regional trouble, spread before their eyes. Many journeymen and small landowners became mendicants. The poor left their villages to crowd into towns or else become vagabonds, forming groups which coursed through the country. They invaded farms even at night, forced themselves in by the fear of burning and of attacks on livestock, trees, the crops that were just beginning to grow, or by threatening to pillage everything. Officials had their own reasons for worrying about the crops and let the villagers arm themselves for protection. As fear of brigandage spread, panics broke out. The slightest incident was enough to put a timid person to flight, convinced that brigands had arrived, sowing fear wherever he fled.

The "Good News" and the Great Hope

But we cannot be sure that economic crisis would have driven the people to aid the bourgeoisie if the calling of the Estates-General had not deeply moved the populace. The goals appropriated by the bourgeois they elected scarcely concerned the lower classes, but an event so foreign was welcomed as "a good piece of news" presaging a miraculous change in men's fates. It awoke hopes both dazzling and vague of a future when all would enjoy a better life—hopes shared by the bourgeoisie. This vision of the future united the heterogeneous elements of the Third Estate and became a dynamic source of revolutionary idealism. Among the common people it gave to the Revolution a character that can be called mythical, if myth is taken to mean a complex of ideas concerning the future which generate energy and initiative. In this sense the Revolution in its early stages can be compared to certain religious movements in nascent form, when the poor gladly discern a return to paradise on earth.

Arthur Young [the British traveller and agricultural reformer] has recorded that on July 12, while walking up a hill near Les Islettes, in the Argonne Forest, he met a poor woman who described her misery to him. " 'Something was to be done by some great folk for such poor ones,' but she did not know who nor how, 'but God send us better, *car les tailles et les droits nous écrasent*'" (for the *taille* and [*manorial*] rights are crushing us).

Since the king consulted his people, he pitied their plight. What could he do if not remove their burdens—taxes, tithes, fees? He would therefore be content if they went ahead and helped him: after the elections aristocratic cries of alarm arose on all sides, for the peasants openly declared that they would pay no more.

At the same time this great hope inflamed fearful passions, from which the bourgeoisie was not exempt. The revolutionary mentality was imbued with them; the history of the period bears their deep imprint.

The Aristocratic Conspiracy and the Revolutionary Mentality

The Third Estate was at once convinced that the nobles would stubbornly defend their privileges. This expectation, soon confirmed by aristocratic opposition to the doubling and then to the vote by head, aroused suspicions that with little difficulty hardened into convictions. The nobles would use any means to "crush" the villagers; they would outwit their well-intentioned king to obtain dissolution of the Estates-General. They would take up arms, bar themselves in their châteaux, and enlist brigands to wage civil war just as the king's agents enlisted the poverty-stricken. Prisoners would be released and recruited. Nobles who had already hoarded grain to starve the Third Estate would willingly see the harvest ruined. Fear of the aristocracy was everywhere rapidly linked with fear of brigands, a connection that fused the results of the calling of the Estates with those of the economic crisis. Moreover, foreign powers would be called on to help. The comte d'Artois was going to emigrate and win over his father-in-law (the king of Sardinia), the Spanish and Neapolitan Bourbons, and the emperor, brother of the queen. France, like Holland, would be invaded by the Prussians. Collusion with foreign powers, which weighed heavily in the history of the Revolution, was assumed from the beginning, and in July an invasion was feared imminently. The whole Third Estate believed in an "aristocratic conspiracy."

The burden of royal centralization and the conflict of orders dominated the Third Estate's view of the crisis. Neglecting to accuse natural forces and incapable of analysing the total economic situation, the Third laid responsibility upon royal power and the aristocracy. An incomplete picture perhaps, but not inexact. The freeing of the grain trade, which Brienne had decreed, did favour speculators; to the argument that this would increase production the people replied that it would profit the aristocracy and bourgeoisie first, while they had to bear the costs. Similarly, if the Third Estate falsely imputed Machiavellian qualities to the aristocracy, it was true that the court, in agreement with the nobles, thought to punish the deputies for their insubordination; and it was true that the aristocratic conspiracy, although denounced prematurely, was soon to become a reality. In any case the mind of the Third Estate is of capital interest in showing the historian that events have their immediate roots not in their antecedents but in the men who intervene by interpreting those events.

If aristocratic conspiracy and "brigands" instilled many with enough fear to cause occasional panics, there were others who, although frightened, remained rational and faced danger resolutely. Consequently the labels "fears" and "Great Fear" unjustly imply that the whole Third Estate was struck dumb with terror. Actually the revolutionary mentality was capable of countering unrest with vigorous defensive reaction. The Third was kept informed by letters from its deputies and in turn encouraged its representatives with innumerable appeals. The bourgeoisie would gladly have pushed further: it wanted to take municipal control from the petty oligarchy made up of those who owned offices, many of whom had acquired noble titles. At Paris the electors who had chosen deputies organized a secret municipal council in the Hôtel de Ville at the end of June. Notables hoped to set up a "national militia" [soon to be called the National Guard]. This was proposed by Parisian electors to the Constituent Assembly, but deputies did not dare authorize it. A double purpose lay behind the desire to organize a militia: to resist royal troops should the occasion rise, and to hold the people in check. Meanwhile efforts were made to win over the army, not without success, since lower-ranking officers had no hope of advancement and the soldiers, who had to pay for part of their subsistence, were affected by high prices. The French Guards fraternized with crowds at the Palais Royal; at the end of June the people freed prisoners at the Abbaye [jail]. Several men are known to have distributed money among the soldiers or to have paid the July insurgents. Beyond doubt the agents of the duc d'Orléans did as much.

Finally, along with the defensive reaction there existed a punitive will either to cripple the aristocratic conspiracy, hoarders, and all enemies of the people, or to punish those enemies. From July on this took the form of imprisonments, acts of brutality, and popular massacres.

These three aspects of the revolutionary mentality—fear, defensive reaction, and punitive will—together constitute one of the keys to the unfolding narrative of the French Revolution. The conspiracy was to all appearances halted by the end of 1789, and repression slackened. The plot later reappeared, cloaked with many of the characteristics given it in advance, and foreign powers came to its aid. The resulting defensive reaction first stimulated the volunteers who poured in and then was responsible for the mass levy [military conscription]. Punitive will provoked the massacres of 1792 and, when danger again loomed in 1793, the Convention warded off further perils only by setting up the Terror. Fear and its accompaniments died out only, and gradually, after the uncontested triumph of the Revolution.

The Parisian Revolution

Against this background, Necker's dismissal was a torch set to a powder keg: it was taken as evidence that the aristocratic conspiracy had begun to act. News of the event circulated in Paris on Sunday, July 12. The weather was good and a crowd gathered at the Palais Royal, whose garden and arcades, recently opened by the duc d'Orléans, had become a centre of amusement. Groups clustered about extemporaneous orators; only one, Camille Desmoulins,[6] do we know by name. Soon processions of demonstrators reached the boulevards, then the Rue Saint-Honoré. The cavalry undertook to make them disperse and charged the crowd at the Place Louis XV. The French Guards in return attacked the cavalry. The baron de Besenval, military commander, mustered his whole following on the Champ de Mars that evening.

The Parisians did not think of rallying to the aid of the Assembly; they saved it, but only indirectly. They were concerned with their own fate, convinced that their city, surrounded by royal troops and brigands, would first be bombarded from Montmartre and the Bastille and then would be pillaged. Panics erupted continually during these "days," Act One of the Great Fear. The police were gone. Toll gates were burned. [The monastery of] Saint-Lazare was sacked. Person and property were seemingly endangered. Fright hovered over the capital, abandoned to its own resources.

---

[6][At that time a penniless young lawyer and writer, he was soon to become a polemical revolutionary journalist. By 1794 he was a supporter of Danton and was executed with other Dantonists on April 5, 1794.—Eds.]

A defensive reaction followed immediately. Barricades arose in the streets, and gunsmiths' stores were wiped clean. The electors appointed a permanent committee and set up a militia. To arm their forces, they took 32,000 guns from the Invalides[7] on the morning of July 14. In search of more, they went to the Bastille. Its governor, de Launay, parleyed. Commanding only a small garrison, he had ordered the outer courts evacuated. They were quickly filled by the crowd. Behind walls ninety feet high, surrounded by a water-filled ditch seventy-five feet wide, he had no cause to fear an attack. But he lost his nerve and opened fire. Several men fell; others drew back in disorder, crying treason, convinced that they had been permitted to advance only to offer better aim. Shots rang out from those who were armed, and battle was engaged, but on an entirely unequal basis: the assailants lost a hundred men, whereas one sole member of the garrison was hit. A census was later taken among the "conquerors of the Bastille," so we know a good number of the attackers. All classes of society were represented among them, but most were artisans from the faubourg Saint-Antoine.

The tide of battle was still uncertain when the French and National Guards arrived from the Hôtel de Ville. Led by a former non-commissioned officer named Hulin and by Lieutenant Élie, they entered the courtyard of the Bastille and under heavy fire aimed their canons at the gate. De Launay took fright and offered to give himself up. Élie accepted, but the attackers protested—No surrender! Amid total confusion the governor had the drawbridge lowered, and the crowd rushed across into the fortress. Efforts to save most of the defenders were successful, but three officers and three men were massacred. De Launay was with difficulty led to the doors of the Hôtel de Ville, where he lost his life. Shortly after, Flesselles, provost of the merchants [chief municipal official of Paris], was also killed. Their heads were paraded through the city on pikes.

Besenval ordered a retreat to Saint-Cloud. The electors took over municipal control, appointed Bailly mayor, and offered command of the National Guard to Lafayette, who soon afterwards gave the Guard a cockade of red and blue, the colours of Paris, between which he placed a white band, the king's colour. Through Lafayette the tricoloured flag, emblem of the Revolution, joined old France with the new.

No one considered the Bastille the stakes of the struggle, and at

---

[7][A large public building housing elderly war veterans and military equipment.—Eds.]

first no one thought that its fall would determine the outcome. Panics continued. But seizure of the Bastille, of mediocre importance in itself, broke the court's resistance. The forces Versailles had on hand were not enough to take Paris, especially since the loyalty of the troops was not certain. Louis hesitated. Would he try to flee? Against the urgings of the comte d'Artois he decided to give in. On July 15 he yielded to the Assembly and announced the dismissal of his troops. The next day he recalled Necker. On the 17th he went to Paris and accepted the cockade.

Few concluded from this that the aristocracy had laid down its arms, and wild rumours continued to circulate. The comte d'Artois and many others emigrated; according to one story an English squadron lay in wait off the coast of Brest. The permanent committee searched the edges of Paris for brigands. Finding only vagabonds, it sent them back where they had come from. The suburbs feared that they would be overrun with such wanderers, and panic spread. Bertier de Sauvigny, the intendant of Paris, his father-in-law, Foullon de Doué, and Besenval himself were arrested. Massacres began again: on July 22 Sauvigny and Doué were hanged at the place de Grève; Necker returned just in time to save Besenval on July 30. These murders provoked strong protest, but now part of the bourgeoisie, roused by the obvious danger, joined the people in their fury—"Is this blood then so pure?" cried Barnave before the Constituent Assembly. Nevertheless, they could hardly deny that summary executions ought to cease. On July 23 a notary from the Rue de Richelieu proposed, in the name of his district, that a popular tribunal be set up; and on the 30th Bailly made a similar request. The Assembly paid no heed. Only in October did it institute prosecution for crimes of *lèse-nation* [treason against the people], to be handled by the Châtelet of Paris—an ordinary court. In July the Assembly did at least establish a "committee of investigation," prototype of the Committee of General Security; and the municipality of Paris organized another which was the first revolutionary committee. While debating the issue of privacy of correspondence during the summer, deputies of all representation, from the marquis de Gouy d'Arsy and Target, member of the Académie Française, to Barnave and Robespierre, firmly maintained that one could not govern in time of war and revolution as in time of peace—in other words, that the rights they were proposing to grant to all citizens depended upon circumstances. This was to become the doctrine of the revolutionary government.

The Municipal Revolution

In the provinces, too, Necker's dismissal provoked strong feeling and an immediate reaction. The populace was no longer content only to send addresses, now often menacing, to its representatives. In several towns the public coffers were broken open and arsenals or military storehouses looted. One committee undertook to set up a militia and issued an appeal to neighbouring communes, even to the peasants. The governor of Dijon was arrested; nobles and priests were confined to their dwellings—this was the first example of detention of suspects. At Rennes the townsmen persuaded the garrison to desert and then rose up. The military commander fled.

When news came of the fall of the Bastille and of the king's visit to Paris—an event celebrated in some places—the bourgeoisie took heart and laid hands on the instruments of control in almost every area. The "municipal revolution," as it is known, was in most cases a peaceable one: the municipal councils of the Old Regime took on notables or stepped down for the electors.[8] Very often they had to create, or permit the formation of, a permanent committee. It was charged initially with organization of the National Guard, but gradually absorbed the whole administrative apparatus. Nevertheless, the people, having taken part in bourgeois demonstrations, demanded that bread prices be lowered. If this was not soon granted riots broke out, the houses of officials and those known as hoarders were sacked, and often the former municipal councils were ousted.

The municipal revolution thus differed from place to place and was often arrested half way. In every instance, however, the only orders obeyed were those of the National Assembly. The king no longer commanded authority. Centralization, too, was weakened: each municipality wielded absolute power within its own confines and over surrounding districts as well. From August on, towns started to conclude mutual-assistance pacts, spontaneously transforming France into a federation of communes. Local autonomy opened the field of action to a small group of resolute men who, without waiting for instructions from Paris, passed what measures they considered necessary to secure public safety. This was a basic stimulant to revolutionary defence.

Yet the other side of the coin was immediately visible. The Con-

---

[8][The electors were those in the cities and towns who had chosen deputies to the Third Estate. Often the electors had remained organized.—Eds.]

stituent Assembly enjoyed a prestige accorded none of its successors, but the populace observed only such decrees as suited it. What
did the people want above all else? Tax reform, abolition of indirect
levies, institution of controls over the grain trade. Tax collection was
suspended; the salt tax, excises, and municipal tolls were suppressed;
exchange of grains was either forbidden or continually thwarted.
Proclamations and decrees against this had no effect. At Paris the
populace went even further. Within the districts—divisions established for elections to the Estates-General—assembled citizens, like
the electors before them, claimed to supervise the municipal authority they set up to replace the electors. In their eyes national sovereignty entailed direct democracy, an idea that would remain dear to
the sans-culottes.

The Peasant Revolution and the Great Fear

The countryside had joined the towns, but revolution in Paris had
even greater effect on rural areas. Agrarian revolt broke out in several regions. In the woodlands of Normandy, in the Hainaut and
Upper Alsace, châteaux or abbeys were attacked by those seeking
to burn archives and force surrender of manorial rights. In Franche-
Comté and the Mâconnais peasants set fire to many châteaux,
sometimes laying them waste. The bourgeoisie was not always
spared: they, too, had to pay. In Alsace the Jews suffered. On the
other hand, there was clear evidence of rural hostility towards a
menacing capitalism whose instrument had become the manorial reaction: free pasturage was reclaimed, enclosures destroyed, forests
invaded, commons taken back or demanded for the first time—the
peasant revolution was a double-edged sword. Faced with this
threat, the notables drew closer together. Urban militias were used
to restore order. In the Mâconnais the bourgeoisie set up extraordinary tribunals beside the old provost courts, and thirty-three peasants were hanged. Revolt fired men's minds. Even more important,
however, was a passive resistance which everywhere interfered with
collection of the tithe or the *champart*[9] demanded from crops har-
vested. Only those who wished to pay did so. The Great Fear gave irresistible force to this movement.

Events in Paris strengthened fear of the aristocratic conspiracy, of
foreign invasion which could carry it out, of recruitment of brigands

---

[9][A manorial rent payable in kind by the peasant to the lord.—Eds.]

for its service. Brigands were the source of even greater fear now that the wheat was ripe, and Paris, along with other large towns, was expelling beggars and vagabonds. Grain riots and agrarian revolts heightened tension. So did forays by National Guards who left towns to pillage châteaux or demand grain. The Great Fear grew out of six localized incidents no different from those which had unloosed so many panics, but this time they set off currents which were fed along the way by new outbreaks acting as relay reinforcements. Some of these can be traced for hundreds of miles, with branches that covered entire provinces. This extraordinary diffusion in a chain reaction gives the Great Fear its distinctive character and illuminates the mentality that made it possible.

A "disturbance" at Nantes alarmed Poitou. At Estrées-Saint-Denis, in the Beauvais, another spread fright in all directions. A third in southern Champagne sowed terror through the Gâtinais, Bourbonnais, and Burgundy. A fourth, originating near the Montmirail forest, close to La Ferté-Bernard, alerted Maine, Normandy, Anjou, and the Touraine. From the edge of the Chizé forest fear struck Angoulême, spread into Berry and the central mountains, alarmed Aquitaine as far as the Pyrenees. In the east, agrarian revolts in Franche-Comté and the Mâconnais drove fear to the shores of the Mediterranean.

Revolutionaries and aristocrats accused one another of having contrived the Great Fear. The enemies of the Revolution, charged the revolutionaries, sowed anarchy in an effort to paralyse the National Assembly. The bourgeoisie, replied the aristocrats, alarmed the people to make them take up arms and rebel just when the lower classes desired to remain at peace. This last version met with success because the Great Fear provoked a defensive reaction which turned upon the aristocracy. Near Le Mans and in Vivarais three nobles were put to death, and peasants in the Dauphiné provided a formidable relay station for panic by burning châteaux.

It was therefore repeated afterwards that fear had broken out everywhere and at once, spread by mysterious messengers and engendering agrarian revolt. It did not, in fact, cover the whole kingdom: Brittany, Lorraine, lower Languedoc, among other areas, were unaffected. The Great Fear lasted from July 20 to August 6. Documents show that some propagated it in good faith, and one significant fact is that it never touched the districts which had previously witnessed insurrection. Only in the Dauphiné did it provoke a *jacquerie* [large-scale peasant revolt]. If it encouraged the revolution of the peasants it did not cause it. They were already on their feet.

The Night of August 4 and the Declaration
of the Rights of Man and the Citizen

While popular revolution spread, the Assembly's debates dragged on ineffectively. Was this the appropriate moment to publish a declaration of rights? Would it not be better to postpone any such action until the constitution was drawn up, so that the two could be reconciled? Arguments of a general nature were voiced with no mention of the reasons behind opposing views: the existence of orders and the privileges, both of which would be suppressed by the principles to be proclaimed. Aristocrats therefore favoured postponement, hoping to preserve a few of their prerogatives, while the Patriots, growing impatient, accused the nobles of undue obstruction, and the more clairvoyant suspected that privileges held by provinces and towns gave the nobility secret supporters within the Third Estate. On the morning of August 4 the Assembly ruled that it would begin by voting the declaration. But its members could expect discussion to provoke new resistance.

On the other hand, the popular revolution had to be resolved. The Assembly, which it had saved, had no choice but to endorse it, yet order had to be re-established, since the people were quietly waiting for the reforms their representatives would deem appropriate. The bourgeoisie in all probability could control townsmen, but the peasants were a different matter. They were destroying the manorial regime without concerning themselves about the Assembly. What course should be taken? If it resorted to the army and provost courts, the Assembly would break with the people and place itself at the mercy of king and aristocracy. The alternative was to grant satisfaction to the rebels—but then how would the parish priests and liberal nobles react? And it was their support which had assured the Third Estate's victory.

The terms of the decision and the tactics to carry it out were decreed during the night of August 3–4 by a hundred deputies meeting at the Café Amaury as a "Breton Club," which dated back to the end of April, when deputies from Brittany had, as soon as they arrived in town, adopted the custom of concerting their moves and had immediately opened their debates to colleagues from other provinces. They resolved to sway the Assembly by "a kind of magic." In matters involving the feudal system, the duc d'Aiguillon was to take the lead.

But on the evening of August 4 it was the vicomte de Noailles who made the first move, and there was no alternative but to support him. Without debate the Assembly enthusiastically adopted equality of taxation and redemption of all manorial rights except for those involving personal servitude—which were to be abolished without indemnification. Other proposals followed with the same success: equality of legal punishment, admission of all to public office, abolition of venality in office, conversion of the tithe into payments subject to redemption, freedom of worship, prohibition of plural holding of benefices, suppression of annates (the year's income owed the pope by a bishop upon investiture). Privileges of provinces and towns were offered as a last sacrifice. Nevertheless, the "magic" had worked its powers.

These resolutions had to be written up formally, so the debate opened again the next day and lasted until August 11. The final decree began: "The National Assembly destroys the feudal regime in its entirety." This was far from exact: they retained the law of primogeniture and honorific prerogatives, while requirement of an indemnity promised a long life to manorial fees. The tithe was suppressed without indemnity, but, just as fees could be collected until the method of redemption was determined, the tithe could be exacted until a law on public worship was passed.

Despite these qualifications, on the night of August 4 the Assembly achieved in principle the legal unity of the nation. It destroyed the feudal system and aristocratic domination over rural areas; it launched fiscal and ecclesiastical reform. The way was paved for discussion of a declaration of rights. This started on August 20 and continued without intermission until the 26th. Proclaiming liberty, equality, and national sovereignty, the text was in effect the "act of decease" of the Old Regime, which had been put to death by the popular revolution.

CHALLENGING THE LEFEBVRE THESIS

William Doyle

William Doyle (1942–), a Fellow of the British Academy, is a distinguished historian of the Old Regime and the French Revolution. He took his B.A., M.A., and Ph.D. at Oxford University and has taught European History at the University of York, the University of Nottingham, and, since 1986, at the University of Bristol. The author of many books and articles, he is best known for his provocative *Origins of the French Revolution* (3rd ed., 1999) and his colorful and informative *Oxford History of the French Revolution* (1989). His other publications include *The Parlement of Bordeaux and the End of the Old Regime, 1771–1790* (1974), *The Ancien Regime* (1986), *The Old European Order, 1660–1800* (2nd ed., 1992), *Officers, Nobles, and Revolutionaries: Essays on Eighteenth-Century France* (1995), *Venality: The Sale of Offices in Eighteenth-Century France* (1996) and *Jansenism: Catholic Resistance to Authority from the Reformation to the French Revolution* (2000).

The year 1939, which saw the outbreak of the Second World War, is also remembered among students of the French Revolution as the 150th anniversary of the storming of the Bastille. In France the occasion was marked by extensive celebrations and a spate of new writings on the Revolution and its significance. Undoubtedly the most distinguished product of this activity was Georges Lefebvre's concise account of the origins of the Revolution and its outbreak, *Quatre-Vingt-Neuf* [1789]. Unashamedly exulting in the achievements of 1789, Lefebvre's book itself had an eventful history in the years following its publication. Much of the edition was destroyed, as subversive literature, on the orders of the Vichy government. In 1947, however, it

Reprinted from *Origins of the French Revolution* by William Doyle (3rd edition, 1999) pp. 5–21, 194–196, 197 note 1 to 201 note 66, 225 notes 11 and 12, by permission of Oxford University Press.

was translated into English by the American scholar Robert R. Palmer; and under the title of *The Coming of the French Revolution* it rapidly became essential reading wherever the French Revolution was studied throughout the English-speaking world. By the time of Lefebvre's death in 1959 it had sold over 40,000 copies in English. It remains, and will remain, a model of historical writing by a master of his subject. For many years its analysis of the death throes of the old order in France, and the diseases which killed it, remained the definitive statement of what by the 1980s was beginning to be called the "classic" version of the Revolution's origins.

The ultimate cause of the French Revolution, Lefebvre believed, was the rise of the bourgeoisie.[1] A lifelong socialist, by 1939 he was falling increasingly under the influence of Marxism—a theory of history which assigns a central role to the bourgeoisie as the representatives and beneficiaries of capitalism.[2] According to Lefebvre, 1789 was the moment when this class took power in France, after several centuries of growing numbers and wealth. Medieval society had been dominated and ruled by a landed aristocracy, for land was the only form of wealth. By the eighteenth century, however, "economic power, personal abilities and confidence in the future had passed largely to the bourgeoisie," who were buttressed by "a new form of wealth, mobile or commercial" and a "new ideology which the 'philosophers' and 'economists' of the time had simply put into definite form." In 1789, the bourgeoisie overthrew the remnants of the aristocratic, landed order which had till then retained social predominance despite its economic eclipse, and established a regime which more closely reflected the new distribution of economic power. Yet there was nothing automatic in this development, at least in the short run. The bourgeoisie were able to overthrow the aristocracy because the political authority of the monarchy had collapsed. It had collapsed because the monarchy was unable to pay its way. And it was unable to pay its way because the aristocracy, the "privileged orders" of nobility and clergy, clung to their exemptions and privileges, and used their political power to prevent the king from making the necessary reforms.

Between 1787 and 1789, however, Lefebvre discerned not one revolutionary movement but four. First came the revolt of the aristocracy, which destroyed the monarchy, and was the climax of a century-long

---

[1] G. Lefebvre, *The Coming of the French Revolution* (paperback ed New York, 1957), Introduction.

[2] For a survey of Marxist writings on this subject, see G. Ellis, "The 'Marxist Interpretation' of the French Revolution," *Economic History Review* xciii (1978), 353–76.

aristocratic resurgence or reaction, in which the nobility had sought
to regain the pre-eminence in the state of which Louis XIV had deprived them. In order to effect their revolution, the nobility had recruited the support of the bourgeoisie, but the very success of the
movement gave the bourgeoisie ideas of their own. When in September 1788, the parlement of Paris, the very spearhead of the aristocratic reaction, declared that the Estates-General promised by the
government for 1789 should be constituted as they had been in 1614
(their last meeting), the bourgeoisie exploded with fury; for the
"forms of 1614" guaranteed aristocratic predominance. Thus began
the revolution of the bourgeoisie, a class struggle against the aristocracy which lasted until the creation of the bourgeois-dominated National Assembly in June 1789. The bourgeois aim was civil equality;
they wished to destroy the privileges of the nobility and the clergy
and establish a regime where all men obeyed the same laws, paid
taxes on the same basis, enjoyed the same career opportunities, and
owned property on the same terms. These ideals stemmed from the
Enlightenment, the intellectual product of the rise of the bourgeoisie.
The collapse of the monarchy in 1788 gave the bourgeoisie an opportunity of which they had long been dreaming to put them into practice. But, just as the aristocracy had marshalled bourgeois support to
defeat the monarchy, so the bourgeoisie needed other elements in
order to consolidate their own success. In July 1789, their precarious
victory was threatened by a noble-inspired royal attempt to dissolve
the National Assembly. The *coup* was only defeated by an uprising of
the Parisian populace, whose most spectacular achievement was the
storming of the Bastille. This third revolution, the popular revolution,
was a movement which sprang from hope that the new order would
resolve the growing economic problems of urban workers. These
same workers intervened decisively again in October 1789, when the
Estates-General once more seemed threatened by a royal-aristocratic
counter-*coup*. Before that happened, however, the economic crisis of
1788–9 had produced a fourth revolution, the peasant revolution—a
nation-wide uprising, fired by panic fears for the safety of ripening
crops—against the exaction of seignorial dues and labour services by
aristocratic landlords. This movement was only stilled by the abolition, on the night of 4 August 1789, of the whole apparatus of this
"feudalism," the last bastion of the old aristocratic order.

Such a brief summary inevitably distorts a work as subtle and skil-
fully written as *Quatre-Vingt-Neuf.* To appreciate its full flavour there
is no substitute for reading the book itself. In addition, Lefebvre's argument can be sampled in the general survey of the 1790s which he

wrote twelve years later.[3] The interesting problem is why his interpretation of the origins of the Revolution was able to command such
widespread support. After all, in the 150 years since it had occurred,
few historical events had aroused more sustained and impassioned
controversy.

One reason was that, by 1939, Lefebvre was the undisputed master of the subject. Professor of the History of the French Revolution
at the Sorbonne, he had built up a formidable scholarly reputation
through a series of monographs which had transformed understanding of the agrarian history of the Revolution.[4] His exact contemporary, and only possible rival, Albert Mathiez, had died prematurely in 1932. With him died a bitter, polemical tradition in
revolutionary historiography which Lefebvre, for all his commitment to many of the ideals and interpretations of Mathiez, avoided.
Another strength of Lefebvre's interpretation was that it took full account of the researches of Ernest Labrousse into the economic origins of the Revolution.[5]

Labrousse's analysis of price movements down to 1789 gave economic substance to the discontent expressed by all classes in 1789,
and lent impressive strength to the argument of Lefebvre. The publication of Labrousse's next study in 1944, which described in particular detail the crisis in wine production between 1778 and 1789, reinforced rather than modified Lefebvre's explanation of peasant
discontents.

The most bitter debates about the Revolution in the earlier part of
the century had had strong political overtones. Historians of the left,
like Jean Jaurès and Mathiez, believed that the Revolution was both
desirable and inevitable. Those of the right, like Pierre Gaxotte,
Bernard Faÿ, and Frédéric Braesch, saw it as abominable and something which, if the proper steps had only been taken, might, and
should, have been avoided.[6] The basic disagreement was about

---

[3]*La Révolution française* (*Peuples et Civilisations,* vol. XIII) (Paris, 1951), 1–2, 113–53.
Eng. trans. (London and New York, 1962–4).

[4]Notably, *Les Paysans du Nord pendant la Révolution française,* 2 vols (Lille, 1924), (new
edn, Paris, 1972), and *La Grande Peur de 1789* (Paris, 1932), Eng. trans. (London,
1973). On the personality and influence of Lefebvre, see the commemorative issue of
Annales historiques de la Révolution française xxxii (1960), and the sketch in R. C.
Cobb, *A Second Identity. Essays on France and French History* (Oxford, 1969).

[5]C. E. Labrousse, *Esquisse du mouvement des prix et des revenus en France au XVIIIᵉ siècle,* 2 vols (Paris, 1933); *La Crise de l'économie française à la fin de l'Ancien Régime et
au début de la Révolution* (Paris, 1944).

[6]P. Gaxotte, *La Révolution française* (Paris, 1928), Eng. trans. (London, 1932); B. Faÿ, *La
Grande Révolution* (Paris, 1959); F. Braesch, *1789: L'Année cruciale* (Paris, 1941).

democracy, democratic principles, and public order; and nobody could doubt where Lefebvre stood on this. He was a man of the left, a believer in popular power, and he thought that the Revolution of 1789 could not have been effected without violence. The Vichy regime which suppressed his book was well aware of the fact. And yet he propounded a view of what caused the Revolution that even the most conservative of French historians could broadly accept. For the quarrel between left- and right-wing historians was largely about the Revolution's consequences. On the question of its origins, the two sides did not fundamentally disagree at all. Both acknowledged that the rise of the bourgeoisie was the fundamental cause. Both agreed that the monarchy tried to reform itself, and that it was prevented from doing so by the selfish obstruction of the aristocracy. Both believed that the Enlightenment had sapped faith in traditional values (irrespective of whether they welcomed or deplored the fact). In these circumstances Lefebvre's interpretation passed largely unassailed by what might have seemed potentially its most vehement critics.

In fact, *Quatre-Vingt-Neuf* passed unassailed by almost anyone, thanks largely to the Second World War. Not only were most copies destroyed; scholarly activity in general came to a halt, and very few reviews appeared before that happened.[7] Even more important, hardly any new research was done during the war or for several years after it ended. Most work published in the 1940s was based upon research done during the previous decades.[8] All these circumstances combined to leave Lefebvre's account of the Revolution's origins unchallenged for the best part of twenty years after it appeared. The first major post-war history, a subtle, brilliant, and concise account by the Englishman Albert Goodwin, contained an analysis of the movement's origins that differed hardly at all from Lefebvre's, and plainly owed a good deal to him.[9] Almost a decade later, the first general work on the Revolution from a new generation of French historians,[10] by Albert Soboul, added little to Lefebvre's account except applause, and a more explicit bias towards Marxism than the latter had ever shown. Only in 1965 did François Furet and Denis Richet

---

[7]For the early impact of Lefebvre, see B. F. Hyslop's review of Palmer's translation in *American Historical Review* liii (1947/8), 808–10, and her earlier article, "Recent Work on the French Revolution," ibid. (1942), 489–90.

[8]e.g. A. Goodwin, "Calonne, the Assembly of French Notables of 1787 and the Origins of the *Révolte Nobiliaire*," *Economic History Review* lxi (1946).

[9]A. Goodwin, *The French Revolution* (London, 1953), chs I–V.

[10] A. Soboul, *Précis d'histoire de la Révolution française* (Paris, 1962), Eng. trans., 2 vols (London, 1975).

presume to challenge what had become a rigid orthodoxy in France; and even then their dissent was over the course of the Revolution rather than its origins. . . .[11]

Outside the narrow, then largely monolingual world of French scholarship, fundamental doubts had begun to arise much earlier. Alfred Cobban, newly appointed Professor of French History at the University of London, chose the occasion of his inaugural lecture in 1954 to attack what he called the "Myth of the French Revolution."[12] This myth, which he contended had dominated serious research on the history of the Revolution during the twentieth century, was that the Revolution was "the substitution of a capitalist bourgeois order for feudalism."[13] Cobban argued that anything that could conceivably be called feudal had passed away long before 1789, and that to use the term for the complex of rights and dues that were swept away on the night of 4 August 1789 (as had Lefebvre and other writers before him) was to confuse rather than clarify matters. Gleefully, Cobban picked out Lefebvre's own admission that many bourgeois in the National Assembly owned such rights and dues and were reluctant to relinquish them. This would have been awkward to explain if the revolutionary bourgeoisie had been, as Lefebvre contended, the representatives of mobile, industrial, and commercial wealth—capitalists, in a word. But Cobban argued that they were not. By analysing the social and professional background of the bourgeois elected to the Estates-General in 1789, he showed that only 13 per cent of them came from the world of commerce, whereas about two-thirds were lawyers of one sort or another. Goodwin had already dwelt on this,[14] but Cobban carried the analysis much further. He pointed out that 43 per cent of the bourgeois deputies were not only lawyers, but petty officeholders and government servants. And he went on to argue that it was the frustrations of such people, doing the work of government but receiving none of the credit, and seeing the value of the venal offices in which they had invested their money declining, which provided the reforming impetus of the revolutionary bourgeoisie, and its commitment to careers open to the talents. From this, major conclusions followed: the Revolution was not the work of a rising bourgeoisie at all, but rather of a declining one. The revolution-

---

[11] F. Furet and D. Richet, *La Révolution française,* 2 vols (Paris, 1965), Eng. trans. (London, 1970).

[12] A. Cobban, *The Myth of the French Revolution* (London, 1955), conveniently reprinted in his *Aspects of the French Revolution* (London, 1968), 90–111.

[13] *Aspects,* 106.

[14] *French Revolution,* 53–72.

aries of 1789 were not hostile to "feudalism," which the peasants, not they, destroyed; nor were they the standard-bearers of capitalism. Cobban incorporated these views into his own general survey of eighteenth-century France, published two years later.[15]

At first they did not make the impression they deserved. Inaugural lectures are seldom widely read, and to bury new ideas in a general survey is to risk many readers overlooking their importance. Besides, Cobban's "revisionism" was very rapidly dismissed by Lefebvre himself. Writing in the one journal read by all serious students of the Revolution, the *Annales historiques de la Révolution française,* which he himself edited, he declared that Cobban was trying to deprive the Revolution of its fundamental significance.[16] Cobban's strictures on the use of the term feudalism were a quibble about terminology, and although his analysis of the membership of the revolutionary assemblies was of value and interest, the conclusions he drew missed the point. Even if the men of 1789 were not capitalists, their actions favoured capitalism's future development, and that was the most significant thing. To suggest anything else was to denigrate the Revolution, and Lefebvre suggested that this was Cobban's true aim. As a representative of the twentieth century's ruling orders, the Englishman was frightened of revolutions, and sought to minimize the inspiring precedent and example of 1789. The "myth," if myth it was, was a necessary one.

But Cobban was not so easily disposed of, nor were the problems he raised. As so often in historical research, he had merely been the first to express views towards which other scholars were also working quite independently. As early as 1951, an American doctoral student, George V. Taylor, had argued in an unpublished thesis that those members of the bourgeoisie who were capitalists were largely uninterested in politics both before and during the Revolution, except as a possible vehicle for protecting their own commercial and industrial privileges.[17] The implication was that they did not share the aspirations of the reformers in the Assembly, and that therefore the bourgeoisie was far from the united, self-conscious and self-confident class that had often been assumed. The only important French historian besides Lefebvre to deign to notice Cobban's arguments in the late 1950s, Marcel Reinhard, also noted that commercial

---

[15] *A History of Modern France* (London, 1957), I, 140, 153, 167, 257.

[16] Review of *The Myth of the French Revolution* in *Annales historiques de la Révolution française* xxviii (1956), 337–45.

[17] At least according to P. Dawson, *Provincial Magistrates and Revolutionary Politics in France, 1789–1795* (Cambridge, Mass., 1972), ii.

and professional members of the bourgeoisie were often deeply suspicious of one another; he called for more research into such matters.[18] The few pieces of archival research into the bourgeoisie that now began to appear also concluded with the need for more research; but in their own limited fields of enquiry they emphasized the diversity of the eighteenth-century bourgeoisie, and the wide range and varied composition of its fortunes.[19] Only works based on literary sources rather than archival research continued to be more preoccupied with what bound the bourgeoisie together than with its inner divisions and contradictions.[20] In 1964, therefore, when Cobban returned to the attack, the atmosphere was more receptive—and Lefebvre, who had died in 1959, was no longer there to concert a defence of the accepted wisdom.

In *The Social Interpretation of the French Revolution,*[21] the published version of a series of lectures delivered in 1962, Cobban argued his case of 1955 in more detail. He now defined "feudalism" as seignorial rights and dues, but continued to argue that it was the peasants rather than the bourgeoisie who really opposed the system and overthrew it. Above all, he returned to his theme that "the revolutionary bourgeoisie was primarily the declining class of *officiers* [office holders who owned their posts] and the lawyers and other professional men, and not the businessmen of commerce and industry."[22] Far from promoting capitalism, the Revolution was to retard it; and that was, indeed, the fundamental aim of the various revolutionary groups in 1789:

> In so far as capitalist economic developments were at issue, it was a revolution not for, but against, capitalism. This would, I believe, have been recognised long ago if it had not been for the influence of an unhistorical sociological theory. The misunderstanding was facilitated by the ambiguities implicit in the idea of the bourgeoisie. The bourgeois

---

[18] M. Reinhard, "Sur l'histoire de la Révolution française. Travaux récents et perspectives," *Annales* xiv (1959), 557–62. [*Annales* is a short title for the periodical *Annales: Économies, sociétés, civilisations.* —Eds.]

[19] e.g. M. Vovelle and D. Roche, "Bourgeois, rentiers, propriétaires: éléments pour la définition d'une catégorie sociale à la fin du XVIIIᵉ siècle," *Actes du 84ᵉ Congrès national des sociétés savantes (Dijon, 1959), Section d'histoire moderne et contemporaine* (Paris, 1962), 483–512, Eng. trans. in J. Kaplow (ed.), *New Perspectives on the French Revolution. Readings in Historical Sociology* (New York, 1965), 25–46; A. Daumard and F. Furet, *Structures et relations sociales à Paris au milieu du XVIIIᵉ siècle* (Paris, 1961) 35–7, 39–40, 92.

[20] Elinor G. Barber, *The Bourgeoisie in 18th Century France* (Princeton, NJ, 1955).

[21] (Cambridge, 1964).

[22] *Social Interpretation,* 67.

of the theory are a class of capitalists, industrial entrepreneurs and financiers of big business; those of the French Revolution were landowners, *rentiers* [persons living off income from property] and officials.[23]

He added that the latter group was bitterly at odds with the former during the closing decades of "the old order." And what gave special piquancy to Cobban's onslaught on orthodoxy was the way he used the arguments and researches of its greatest champions, such as Lefebvre himself and Soboul, to support his own case and undermine theirs. How could Soboul, he asked, declare dogmatically that the triumph of the bourgeoisie was the essential fact of the Revolution, when in the same breath he admitted that the history of the bourgeoisie during the Revolution remained unwritten.[24] The final chapter of Cobban's book was an analysis of Lefebvre's last work,[25] which had just been posthumously published, in which he showed that Lefebvre's findings on the social structure of the pre-revolutionary Orléanais lent less support to the general views of their French author than to those of his English critic.

This time, Cobban's opinion made some impact in France, if only to invite indignant refutation from the established academic authorities. A totally hostile review by Jacques Godechot, one of the leading French authorities on the Revolution, provoked a series of spirited and entertaining replies from Cobban.[26] Even English-speaking reviewers had their breath taken away by the scale and range of Cobban's attack. Unlike the French, most of them seemed inclined to accept the destructive side of his argument, but they were deeply sceptical of what he proposed to put in place of the orthodoxies he had undermined. Most reviewers seemed to agree (for a wide range of reasons) that Cobban's arguments raised far more questions than they answered. The appearance of his book, in fact, signalled the beginning of a period of acute controversy in the historiography of the Revolution, not unlike the "storm over the gentry" which had already

---

[23] *Ibid.*, 172–3.

[24] *Ibid.*, 23.

[25] *Études orléanaises, i. Contribution à l'étude des structures sociales à la fin du XVIIIᵉ siècle* (Paris, 1962).

[26] Godechot's review was in *Revue historique* ccxxxv (1966), 205–9; the *Annales historiques de la Révolution française* did not deign to notice the book at all. Cobban's replies are most conveniently found in his *Aspects,* 264–87. A full account of the controversy can be found, with copious references, in ch. I of Dawson, *Provincial Magistrates.* See also Gerald C. Cavanaugh, "The Present State of French Revolutionary Historiography: Alfred Cobban and Beyond," *French Historical Studies* (1972).

been raging for almost two decades among historians of the English Revolution of the seventeenth century.[27]

The credit (or blame) for this did not lie with Cobban alone. By the mid-1960s it was evident that old views were crumbling in every direction. Norman Hampson, for example, who stigmatized Cobban for having produced nothing more than a "non-Marxist economic interpretation of the revolution,"[28] had already laid stress, in a new general survey published in 1963, on the ambiguities of the term bourgeoisie. He emphasized that social and economic motivations were not the same thing, and he stressed the importance of intellectual convictions in bourgeois hostility to the old order.[29] Cobban had, by contrast, always tended to belittle the role of the Enlightenment in the origins of the Revolution—another way in which he differed from Lefebvre.[30] Hampson still, however, saw a fundamental opposition between the "privileged orders" and their interests on one side, and the bourgeoisie and its interests on the other. Neither Cobban nor his French opponents would have disagreed. But the great development of the late 1960s was to call even this into doubt.

Nothing contributed more to a reappraisal of the revolutionary bourgeoisie than new work on its supposed antithesis, the nobility. Yet this was a subject on which Cobban was completely orthodox. He hardly ever expressed a view about the nobility with which Lefebvre would have wished to disagree. He believed that the nobility was a selfish, increasingly exclusive caste which used its political power, wielded through the parlements, to prevent the crown from attacking its privileges. Eventually, noble obstruction brought the old order down.[31] Unlike the traditional picture of the bourgeoisie, that of the nobility was to be slowly eroded rather than shattered by frontal attack.

The drift of two future decades of scholarly opinion was, indeed, foreshadowed in 1953 by John McManners. In an impressionistic essay buried in a collection devoted to European nobilities in the eighteenth century, he argued that money, not privilege, was the key to pre-revolutionary society in France. Wealth transcended all social

---

[27] See L. Stone, *The Causes of the English Revolution, 1529–1642* (London 1972), ch. II.

[28] *Irish Historical Studies* xiv (1964–5), 192.

[29] *A Social History of the French Revolution* (London, 1963), 20–2, 63–4, 80–1.

[30] See his essay, "The Enlightenment and the French Revolution," reprinted in *Aspects*, 18–28.

[31] See "The *Parlements* of France in the Eighteenth Century," *Aspects*, 68–82; *History of Modern France*, I, 253–4.

barriers and bound great nobles and upper bourgeois together into "an upper class unified by money."[32] This essay was not a work of original research, but the previous year Jean Egret had used new French material to argue that the exclusivism of the parlements, the supposed spearhead of the "aristocratic reaction" which preceded the Revolution, had been much exaggerated.[33] Such work suggested that the rigidity of the pre-revolutionary social structure had been overdrawn, and deserved further research; but as yet this was not forthcoming. The most influential work of the early 1950s, in fact, merely lent new arguments to established opinions. This was Franklin Ford's *Robe and Sword*,[34] which re-examined the customary division of the nobility into nobles of the sword and nobles of the robe. The former, according to tradition, were of old stock; they looked down upon the latter's recent ennoblement by judicial office. Ford now argued that by the early eighteenth century many of the robe nobility no longer owed their ennoblement to their offices, and that by 1748 they had captured the leadership of the nobility as a whole. The old antagonism between sword and robe was largely forgotten, as nobles united against commoners on one side and the crown on the other. Ford's book was widely acclaimed as a brilliant contribution to the understanding of eighteenth-century France, for it offered a convincing explanation of why the aristocratic reaction— which most authorities agreed took place in the later eighteenth century—occurred, and why it was such a powerful movement.

The first widely noticed blows to the traditional picture of the nobility did not fall until the early 1960s. In 1960, Robert Forster published a social and economic study of the nobility of Toulouse which showed that they were neither impoverished rustics nor debt-laden prodigals, but shrewd and careful managers of their estates. The key to their social and economic position was to be found in "adherence to the so-called bourgeois virtues of thrift, discipline and strict management of the family fortune."[35] A series of articles by the same author over the next few years[36] emphasized the lesson for other areas

---

[32] "France," in A. Goodwin (ed.), *The European Nobility in the Eighteenth Century* (London, 1953), 28.

[33] "L'Aristocratie parlementaire française à la fin de l'Ancien Régime," *Revue historique* ccviii (1952), 1–14.

[34] Subtitled, *The Regrouping of the French Aristocracy after Louis XIV* (Cambridge, Mass., 1953).

[35] *The Nobility of Toulouse in the Eighteenth Century* (Baltimore, Md., 1960), 177.

[36] "The Noble Wine Producers of the Bordelais in the Eighteenth Century," *Economic History Review* xiv (1961), 18–33; "The Provincial Noble: A Reappraisal," *American Historical Review* lxviii (1962–3).

of France. They suggested that in economic outlook the nobility and the bourgeoisie had much in common. Meanwhile, Betty Behrens had argued that the fiscal privileges of the nobility were not as great as the revolutionaries, and historians following them, had claimed. The French nobility, in fact, was perhaps the most highly taxed in Europe; and the really important tax exemptions were those enjoyed by the commercial bourgeoisie of the great mercantile cities.[37] Five years later, Behrens expanded on these views to argue that no social group in pre-revolutionary France had a monopoly of privilege. Most of society was privileged in some way or other, and among the most valuable privileges were those belonging to the bourgeoisie.[38] By this time, too, George V. Taylor was beginning to publish his long-awaited findings. In 1964, he produced a careful analysis of the types of capitalism that existed in France before the Revolution, concluding that they bore little resemblance to the industrial capitalism of the future. Above all, eighteenth-century capitalism was far from a bourgeois monopoly. One of its basic features was the heavy involvement of nobles.[39]

The effect of all this work, in demolishing, or at least challenging, the traditional picture of the pre-revolutionary nobility, was to reveal them as more and more like the bourgeoisie; and Taylor did not fail to see the implication. In 1967, he suggested, in an article second only to Cobban's book in its impact, that the wealth of all social groups in pre-revolutionary France was overwhelmingly non-capitalist in nature. "Proprietary," he suggested, would be a better word.[40] Capitalism had not, therefore, become the dominant mode of production in the French economy before 1789. Moreover, "even in the well-to-do Third Estate proprietary wealth substantially outweighed commercial and industrial capital. . . . [T]here was, between most of the nobility and the proprietary sectors of the middle classes, a continuity of investment forms and socio-economic values that made them, economically, a single group."[41]

---

[37] "Nobles, Privileges and Taxes in France at the end of the Ancien Régime," *Economic History Review* xv (1962–3), 451–75. Her arguments have not gone unchallenged; see G. J. Cavanaugh, "Nobles, Privileges and Taxes in France. A Revision Reviewed," *French Historical Studies* viii (1974), 681–92. Cavanaugh's criticisms, which seem valid, nevertheless do not diminish the importance of Behren's ideas in opening up the question of nobility.

[38] *The Ancien Régime* (London, 1967), 46–62.

[39] "Types of Capitalism in Eighteenth Century France," *Economic History Review* lxxix (1964), 478–97.

[40] "Noncapitalist Wealth and the Origins of the French Revolution," *American Historical Review* lxxii (1967), 469–96.

[41] *Ibid.*, 487.

Discussion in France, meanwhile, was proceeding on parallel lines. Roland Mousnier, a historian of the seventeenth century, had been provoked by Marxist analyses of popular uprisings during that century into formulating a new model of old regime society. Mousnier believed that before the eighteenth century society could not be separated as Marxists analysed it, into classes.[42] A society of classes, he argued, was one where supreme social value was placed upon the production of material goods; class was determined by productive role. But there were also societies of orders or estates, in which social position was determined by social function rather than by relationship to material production.[43] France in the seventeenth century was a society of orders. The highest order was the nobility, whose function was the supreme one of defending the state. The social position of lower orders was determined by their contribution towards supporting the state in lesser ways; thus administrators and magistrates, for example, enjoyed more power and prestige than merchants or tradesmen. Mousnier's explanation of the French Revolution was that, in the course of the eighteenth century, the consensus about social values that underlay the old society of orders began to break down. By the 1750s, production was coming to seem more important than the service of the state, and with the Revolution the new outlook triumphed. A class society replaced the old society of orders.[44]

Whatever we may think of this bold attempt to redirect thinking on social history, it made its mark in France—if only because the power of professors like Mousnier made it advisable for ambitious young academics to pay lip-service to his doctrines. Assertions that pre-revolutionary society was a society of orders began to appear in textbooks and even in more general, popular works.[45] By the late 1960s, historians beyond the reach of Mousnier's patronage were also beginning to emphasize what bound the nobility and upper bourgeoisie together into a single plutocratic élite.[46]

The guardians of the old orthodoxies were dismayed to see that

---

[42] For an introduction to this debate, see J. H. M. Salmon, "Venal Office and Popular Sedition in 17th Century France," *Past and Present* 37 (1967).

[43] See R. Mousnier, *Les Hiérarchies sociales de 1450 à nos jours* (Paris, 1969), Eng. trans., *Social Hierarchies* (1973).

[44] R. Mousnier, *La Société française de 1770 à 1789* (Paris, 1970), 1–2; see, too, his debate with Labrousse and Soboul in *L'Histoire sociale: sources et méthodes* (Paris, 1967), 26–31.

[45] e.g. S. Pillorget, *Apogée et déclin des sociétés d'ordres 1610–1787* (Paris, 1969).

[46] e.g. P. Goubert, *L'Ancien Régime I: La Société* (Paris, 1969), 235. Eng. trans. (1973).

denouncing or ignoring sceptical "Anglo-Saxons" was not enough to preserve their purity, and that their own compatriots were beginning to have doubts.[47] They took refuge in repetition. Soboul, elevated to Lefebvre's chair at the Sorbonne and to the editorship of the *Annales historiques de la Révolution française,* regularly produced surveys of various aspects of the Revolution which dogmatically reiterated the old line. And in 1970, Claude Mazauric roundly attacked the revisionism of Furet and Richet's survey, which had sold well since its publication five years before.[48] Furet and Richet, however, were no longer the isolated young iconoclasts of 1965; they were now among the leaders of an equally well-armed and well-entrenched scholarly phalanx, the *Annales* school of historians. The attention of this group had mainly been engaged by quantitative explorations of early modern history. They had largely left the Revolution alone. Now, however, Furet used the prestigious pages of *Annales* to defend his and Richet's approach, and to revise their account of the Revolution's origins in the light of recent work. In a witty and devastating attack on what he called the "revolutionary catechism,"[49] he denounced Soboul, Mazauric, and their ideological ancestors. Soboul's picture of eighteenth-century society, Furet argued, was a "neo-Jacobin" one: it accepted the revolutionaries' own myths about the order they had destroyed. In emphasizing antagonisms between the nobility and the bourgeoisie, the "catechism" ignored all that bound them together, the manifold interests that they had in common but which were increasingly threatened by the demands of a government over which neither had control. Richet had already used the pages of *Annales,* too, to elaborate on a long-term alienation of all property owners from the state.[50] Now at last Cobban received some praise in France for showing how few links the bourgeois revolutionaries of 1789 had with capitalism. Like Taylor, Furet concluded that nobles and bourgeois were economically members of the same class, and that the essence of their wealth was proprietary.

But all such analyses ran into a serious problem. If the nobility and

---

[47] In his survey of the historiography of the Revolution, *Un jury pour la Révolution* (Paris, 1974), Godechot nowhere mentions Cobban or Taylor.

[48] C. Mazauric, *Sur la Révolution française* (Paris, 1970).

[49] F. Furet, "Le catéchisme révolutionnaire," *Annales* xxvii (1971), 255–89, reprinted in his *Penser la Révolution française* (Paris, 1978), trans. Elborg Forster as *Interpreting the French Revolution* (Cambridge, 1981).

[50] D. Richet, "Autour des origines idéologiques lointaines de la Révolution française: Élites et despotisme," *Annales* xxiv (1969), 1–23. His ideas were further elaborated in *La France moderne: l'esprit des institutions* (Paris, 1973).

the bourgeoisie had so much in common, why did they become such implacable enemies in 1789? The most radical solution to this problem was suggested by Taylor. His analysis of the nature and distribution of wealth before 1789 implied that the Revolution could not be explained in economic terms, as a clash of opposed interests. Taylor declared himself unconvinced by Cobban's attempt to provide a new economic explanation through the declining bourgeoisie. It was time, he concluded, to revert to a purely political explanation of the Revolution's outbreak. The radical reforms of 1789 were products of a political crisis, and not the outcome of long-maturing social and economic trends. "It was essentially a political revolution with social consequences and not a social revolution with political consequences."[51] In a further article, five years later, Taylor underlined this point by demonstrating from the *cahiers* of 1789, the grievance lists drawn up by the electoral assemblies which chose the deputies for the Estates-General, that the mood of France in 1789 was deeply conservative. There was no demand from the grass roots for most of the reforms that were soon to take place—which again emphasized that revolutionary radicalism was a result rather than a cause of the political crisis.[52]

To deny the Revolution any social origins at all, however, proved too daring a step for most historians. They continued to seek, and to find, trends in the pre-revolutionary social structure that helped to explain what happened later. From the mass of important new material that appeared after the debate on the Revolution's social origins really got under way in the early 1960s, two particularly important conclusions suggested themselves. The first was the impossibility of drawing any clear contrast between the nobility and the bourgeoisie. Nobody challenged Taylor's contention that the wealth of the bourgeoisie was as overwhelmingly proprietary as was that of the nobility. And whereas nobody denied that the bulk of commercial and industrial wealth was in bourgeois hands, it was shown that there was extensive noble investment in these fields, too.[53] It was even argued that if any social group represented a restless, aggressive, innovatory capitalism before 1789, it was the nobility rather than the timid and conservative bourgeoisie.[54] There was equally little sign of the

---

[51] "Noncapitalist Wealth," 491.

[52] "Revolutionary and nonrevolutionary content in the *Cahiers* of 1789: an interim report," *French Historical Studies* vii (1972), 479–502.

[53] G. Richard, *Noblesse d'affaires au XVIII⁰ siècle* (Paris, 1974).

[54] G. Chaussinand-Nogaret, *La Noblesse au XVIII⁰ siècle. De la féodalité aux lumières* (Paris, 1976), 119–61.[Eng. trans. by William Doyle (Cambridge, Eng., 1985.—Eds.]

bourgeoisie's outstripping the nobles in wealth, whether in the countryside, in stagnant towns like Bayeux or Toulouse, or in major industrial centres like Lyons.[55] Only in booming seaports like Bordeaux had bourgeois fortunes equalled or surpassed those of the local nobility.[56] And even there, as everywhere else, there was a constant passage of the richest into the ranks of the nobility. This pattern of behavior had long been noticed, and is constantly emphasized by new research. For instance, between 1726 and 1791, 90 per cent of the Farmers-General of taxes, often considered the supreme example of bourgeois men of wealth, were noble.[57] And the logical implication of the bourgeoisie's abandoning of their status in order to become noble is that the nobility cannot have been a closed caste. So far from that, one estimate suggests that at least a quarter of all noble families in 1789 had been ennobled since the beginning of the century.[58]

The basis of these calculations has indeed not gone unchallenged; and until scholars can agree on how many nobles there were, the matter must remain speculative. The latest research, however, concludes that between 35 and 45,000 newcomers entered the French nobility between 1725 and 1789, equivalent to about two persons per day.[59] So it now seems quite incontestable that the nobility was an open élite, not a hereditary caste apart. Nor is it still possible to maintain that this élite grew less open as the eighteenth century went on, thanks to some exclusivist "aristocratic reaction." Most evidence suggests that institutions that were largely noble in composition in the 1780s had been so a century earlier, and that apparent attempts to discriminate against non-nobles were really signs of antagonism between different sorts of nobles.[60]

The second major theme to emerge from revisionism follows from this. If what divided nobles from bourgeois once received too much

---

[55] O. H. Hufton, *Bayeux in the Later Eighteenth Century. A Social study* (Oxford, 1967), 42, 57–80; J. Sentou, *Fortunes et groupes sociaux à Toulouse sous la Révolution* (Toulouse, 1969), 146; M. Garden, *Lyon et les Lyonnais au XVIIIe* (Paris, 1970), 358, 360, 362, 387–98.

[56] J. P. Poussou in G. Pariset (ed.), *Bordeaux au XVIIIe siècle* (Bordeaux, 1968), 351–2.

[57] Y. Durand, *Les Fermiers-Généraux au XVIIIe siècle* (Paris, 1971), 294–301.

[58] Chaussinand-Nogaret, *La Noblesse au XVIIIe siècle*, 48.

[59] W. Doyle, *Venality. The Sale of Offices in Eighteenth-Century France* (Oxford, 1996), 165.

[60] For a survey of this evidence, see W. Doyle, "Was There an Aristocratic Reaction in Pre-Revolutionary France?" *Past and Present* 57 (1972), reprinted in D. Johnson (ed.), *French Society and the Revolution* (Cambridge, 1976), 3–20; of fundamental importance, too, is D. D. Bien, "La Réaction aristocratique avant 1789: l'exemple de l'armée," *Annales* xxix (1974).

attention, what divided bourgeois from bourgeois and noble from noble did not receive enough. Research on various aspects of the bourgeoisie continues to confirm the suggestions of Cobban and Taylor about the lack of contact or sense of common interest between the bourgeoisie of the professions and that of trade.[61] It is also clear that even among the lawyers and *officiers* there was far from universal agreement about what reforms were desirable in 1789.[62] As to the nobility, earlier historians were always anxious to show how much it deserved its fate after 1789; accordingly, they were happy to repeat the old scornful dismissal of the noble order as a "cascade of disdain," in which every member despised the next. Yet they were equally willing to portray the nobility in 1788–9 as united and determined in pursuit of power. How, if this were the case, the nobility was so easily overthrown was not a question these historians chose to ask, let alone answer. If, however, attention is concentrated on divisions within the nobility, this problem becomes far less difficult, and revisionist research emphasized such divisions. A massive study of the Breton nobility in the eighteenth century revealed, for example, what deep antagonism there was in this noble-swamped province between rich and poor nobles, and how hostile were the resident nobility to the gilded absentees of Versailles.[63] The famous Ségur ordinance of 1781 was convincingly shown to be directed not against bourgeois aspirants to military commissions, but against new nobles and their offspring.[64] Despite Franklin Ford's famous argument, robe and sword nobles were still attacking each other in the 1780s.[65] Most striking of all, analysis of the *cahiers* of the nobility in 1789 showed them to be deeply divided ideologically, with large numbers of them won over to the political liberalism hitherto assumed to have been the monopoly of the bourgeoisie.[66]

How such findings affect the interpretation of the origins of the Revolution is not easy to assess, but attempts were soon made to incorporate them into new explanations. The most ambitious to appear in the English-speaking world was that of Colin Lucas, published in

---

[61] L. R. Berlanstein, *The Barristers of Toulouse in the Eighteenth Century (1740–1793)* (Baltimore, Md., 1975), 34 -5, 51–5.

[62] *Ibid.,* 149–60, 177–82; Dawson, *Provincial Magistrates,* 152–84, 200–40.

[63] J. Meyer, *La Noblesse Bretonne au XVIIIe siècle* (2 vols, Paris, 1966).

[64] Bien, "La Réaction."

[65] Bailey Stone, "Robe against Sword: The Parlement of Paris and the French Aristocracy, 1774–1789," *French Historical Studies* ix (1975).

[66] Chaussinand-Nogaret, *La Noblesse au XVIIIe siècle,* 181–226.

1973.[67] All recent work, Lucas argued, suggested that, "The middle class of the later Ancien Régime displayed no significant difference in accepted values and above all no consciousness of belonging to a class whose economic and social characteristics were antithetical to the nobility.[68] Bourgeoisie and nobles were all part of a single proper-tied élite. Why then did they not unite in 1788–9? Lucas found the an-swer in the declaration by the parlement of Paris in September 1788 that the Estates-General should meet according to the forms of 1614. For Lefebvre, too, this had been the crucial turning point, the moment when the bourgeoisie had seen that its interests were profoundly at odds with those of the nobility, the trigger which detonated the bourgeois campaign to capture control of the Estates.[69] This interpre-tation had been criticized in 1965 by Elizabeth L. Eisenstein on the grounds that the mysterious "Committee of Thirty," which largely or-chestrated the outburst of denunciatory pamphleteering which fol-lowed the parlement's ruling, had many noble members and therefore could hardly be considered the voice of the bourgeoisie alone.[70] In 1980 Daniel Wick went even further, arguing that the Committee of Thirty was largely driven in its attack on the old order by the resent-ment of Court nobles who had lost political influence over the reign of Louis XVI.[71] Despite rejoinders from American defenders of Lefeb-vre that in objective terms the Committee of Thirty was still doing the bourgeoisie's work, Eisenstein's arguments lent strength to the ten-dency, culminating with Lucas, towards regarding nobles and bour-geoisie as part of the same social élite. But for Lucas the essential point about the parlement's ruling was not that it represented the un-willingness of a noble élite to share power with the bourgeoisie; it was rather that the distinction between nobles and nonnobles, obsolete now for several generations, was arbitrarily resurrected by the elec-toral requirements of the Estates-General.

This has proved an insight of fundamental importance. Less happy

---

[67] "Nobles, Bourgeois and the Origins of the French Revolution," *Past and Present* 60 (1973), reprinted in Johnson (ed.) *French Society and the Revolution,* 88–131. All ref-erences are to this edition.

[68] Johnson, 95.

[69] Lefebvre, *The Coming,* 30–4.

[70] See E. L. Eisenstein, "Who intervened in 1788? A commentary on *The Coming of the French Revolution,*" *American Historical Review* lxxi (1965), 77–103, and the rejoin-ders of J. Kaplow and G. Schapiro, *American Historical Review* lxxii (1967), 498–522.

[71] D. L. Wick, *A Conspiracy of Well-Intentioned Men. The Society of Thirty and the French Revolution* (New York, 1987). This book expanded on an article first published in 1980.

was Lucas's suggestion that the antagonisms then created were exacerbated by the existence of "stress zones" within the single propertied élite where explosive social tensions had built up over preceding decades. Rooted in a conviction shared by perhaps most historians trained in mid-century that major historical phenomena must have social origins (if not necessarily those proposed by Marxists), the idea of stress zones was an attempt to integrate Cobban's "declining bourgeoisie" into the argument. Subsequent research by the present author, however, has demonstrated that such evidence as Cobban offered for a declining class of office-holders was either erroneous or irrelevant.[72] At best, this idea was a fruitful error. More recently, in an essay much anthologized (more perhaps for its knockabout humour than the cogency of its argument), Colin Jones attempted to resuscitate a revolutionary bourgeoisie with evidence from society's growing commercialization and the professionalization of public services.[73] But whatever their value, these arguments are more about the Revolution's long-term context than its social origins. Meanwhile, while even some who still call themselves Marxists have abandoned the idea of class conflict between bourgeois and nobles,[74] it has been suggested by one leading revisionist that the very term "noble" has little analytical value.[75] This, indeed, remains a step too far for most, and more recently still the starkness of nobles' continuing separate pretensions in 1789 has been re-emphasized as a crucial determinant of how the Revolution developed. It may not have been a class conflict, but a clash rooted in distinctions of status it certainly was.[76] And, if the essential achievement of 1789 can no longer be seen as the replacement of feudalism by capitalism, the abolition of privilege and later noble status was still the removal of the last obstacles to recognition of what had happened in French society during the economic expansion of the eighteenth century. What it meant was that France was now to be ruled not by men of birth but by men of property, not by nobles but by what soon afterwards would be called "notables." Under this umbrella both former nobles and former bourgeois found

---

[72] Doyle, *Venality,* ch. 7, esp. 227.

[73] C. Jones, "Bourgeois Revolution revivified: 1789 and social change," in C. Lucas (ed.), *Rewriting the French Revolution* (Oxford, 1991), 69–118.

[74] G. C. Comninel, *Rethinking the French Revolution. Marxism and the Revisionist Challenge* (London and New York, 1987).

[75] R. Forster, "The French Revolution and the new élite, 1800–50," in J. Pelenski (ed.), *The American and French Revolutions* (Iowa City, 1980), 182–207.

[76] T. Tackett, *Becoming a Revolutionary. The Deputies of the French National Assembly and the Emergence of a Revolutionary Culture (1789–1790)* (Princeton, 1996).

a common shelter.[77] Nor did the Revolution bring about this solution; it merely clarified it. . . .

The principles of 1789 . . . cannot be identified with the aspirations of any one of the pre-revolutionary social groups. It was not even clear, when the Estates-General met, what the principles of 1789 would turn out to be, and certainly much of what had been achieved by August, and even more that was to be done later, had no clear mandate in the *cahiers* of that spring. Indeed, as the conservative third estate deputy, Malouet, complained, without the abrogation of mandates no revolution of any consequence could have occurred.[78] The ragged, inconsequential, coincidental, and sometimes almost haphazard way in which the principles of 1789 were formulated is a typical enough reflection of how the Revolution itself originated.

It was neither inevitable nor predictable. What *was* inevitable was the breakdown of the old order. The ever-mounting strain of military expenditure on an inefficient financial system, together with the un-willingness of those in charge of the state to undertake any serious or at least sustained effort at structural reforms, made some sort of breakdown practically unavoidable. When it came, Louis XVI appealed to his subjects for help, but only on his own terms. By the 1780s, however, their faith in the system of government he represented had been so undermined that they refused to come to his aid except on terms of their own: the convocation of the Estates-General. It took eighteen months of bitter conflict to make the government accept this solution, and, even when it did, it collapsed under pressure of renewed financial difficulties rather than the strength of the opposition.

The government's collapse left a vacuum of power. It took the forces of opposition by surprise. They had known well enough what they were against, which could be summarized in the word "despotism." They knew, too, that the remedy was the Estates-General. Beyond that, however, nobody was clear what they wanted, and the winter of 1788–9 was spent in impassioned discussion of this question. By the time the Estates actually met, some degree of political consensus had emerged. All parties agreed on the need for a constitution embodying a representative form of government with guarantees for individual liberty and the rule of law. All agreed, too, that fis-

---

[77] G. Chaussinand-Nogaret, *Une histoire des élites, 1700–1848* (Paris and The Hague, 1975).

[78] P. V. Malouet, *Mémoires* (Paris 1874), I, 265–7. [Originally each cahier was supposed to be accompanied by a mandate that gave the representative instructions on what to vote for or against and on other matters. —Eds.]

cal privileges should have no place in the new order and that the time was ripe for a complete overhaul of the systems of finances, administration, and justice. All this the Revolution was to bring about—but not until other problems, unforeseen eighteen months before, had first been settled.

First among these problems came the integration of the bourgeoisie into the political nation. Until 1788, bourgeois had merely been increasingly well-informed spectators of public affairs, with no evident desire to participate. But the calling of elections, and indeed the very composition of the Estates-General, inevitably drew them into activity, and they found themselves wooed for their potential political weight. By the spring of 1789 they had conceived the desire, in Sieyès's phrase, "to be something."[79] The nobility was called upon to share political power in the new order. Unfortunately, the claim to share political power, which few nobles would have dismissed out of hand, became confused with attacks on their age-old social leadership, and by the time of the elections there was deep mutual suspicion and misunderstanding. The *cahiers,* by forcing people to transform vague feelings into words, compounded growing antagonisms. By the time the Estates actually met, nobility and bourgeoisie, who basically agreed on so much, had become competitors for power rather than partners in its exercise. Only when the right of nobles to separate treatment in anything had been destroyed could the new political élite of propertied "notables," an amalgam of former nobles and bourgeois, get down to the exercise of power.

This took until mid-July, and it might never have come about but for the coincidence of the economic crisis, which brought the populace into political activity. In the midst of the worst economic difficulties for generations, the ordinary people of France were led to expect unforeseen relief from the Estates-General. They, too, had their vision clarified by the *cahiers.* But when relief did not come they grew impatient and began to take the law into their own hands. They also accepted the claims of third estate deputies, their own deputies after all, that aristocratic obstructionism was responsible for the delay. When the government, bestirring itself at last, appeared poised to throw its weight behind those who were impeding progress, the people of Paris intervened to save the new-born National Assembly from destruction. Few deputies felt happy to have such an ungovernable ally, but when troops closed in on Paris and Versailles there seemed

---

[79] See W. H. Sewell, *A Rhetoric of Bourgeois Revolution. The Abbé Sieyes and "What is the Third Estate?"* (Chapel Hill, 1994).

to be no alternative. Even then it is not clear that Paris could have saved the situation if the king had not lost faith in his own army. But the matter was not put to the test; the Bastille fell; and Louis XVI capitulated. Power in France now lay unchallengeably with a proper-tied élite recognizing no special place for nobles, either at national or local level.

The National Assembly at last set about designing a constitution; but the ramifications of the economic crisis were not yet at an end. The peasantry as well as the people of Paris had been thrown into turmoil by the coincidence of economic adversity and political excitement, and they took advantage of uncertain times to throw off the most dispensable of their burdens, the "feudal" dues. The deputies were appalled at such wanton disregard for property, but there was no prospect of restoring order in the countryside without accepting what the peasants had done. And so, in spite of themselves, the men of 1789 acquiesced in the destruction of feudalism.

Only now could France's new ruling élite begin to assess what they stood for, and what they had achieved. As victors will, they soon convinced themselves that all had gone according to plan from the start. But there was no plan, and nobody capable of making one, in 1787. Nobody then could have predicted that things would work out as they did. Hardly anybody would have felt reassured if they could. For the French Revolution had not been made by revolutionaries. It would be truer to say that the revolutionaries had been created by the Revolution.

2

The Peasants:
Mentality and Behavior in 1789

HISTORIANS agree that peasant violence helped to overturn the old order in 1789, but disagree on why the protests occurred. According to Albert Soboul, eighteenth-century France was essentially a feudal country, and peasants were subject to oppressive feudal dues. He discusses many of these, including not only various payments in money and kind to the clergy and especially to the aristocracy, but also restrictions on hunting and fishing, the baking of bread, and the making of wine. Soboul claims that the main motive for the revolt of the peasants was to liberate themselves from feudal dues; and when they did, they helped destroy feudalism in France and thus prepare the way for capitalism.

François Furet argues that Soboul has greatly exaggerated the oppressiveness of the so-called feudalism of the Old Regime because Soboul seeks to impose a simplistic Marxist interpretation on the eighteenth century. Furet asserts that Soboul, in doing this, has misunderstood the cahiers of 1789 as well as Alexis de Tocqueville's *Old Regime and the French Revolution.* Furet also contends that Soboul has wrongly taken at face value peasant complaints about economic exploitation. On the other hand, Furet thinks that the aristocrats and clergy served as scapegoats for the peasants. The incidence of feudal dues varied widely in France; in some places they were light and in others heavy. Peasant violence can be better explained by their fear of economic change, whether it be feudal or capitalistic, by poverty resulting from overpopulation, by taxation by the king and the clergy, and by humiliation and wounded pride.

What are the grounds for this disagreement between Soboul and Furet? Is it based on insufficient historical knowledge of the extent of feudal dues throughout France? Would it therefore have been resolved if more research had been completed before Soboul died?[1] Or is this more a quarrel about words, especially the definition of feudalism? Do they divide because they have different views of how to

---

[1]But the research of Peter M. Jones, *The Peasantry and the French Revolution* (Cambridge, Eng.: Cambridge University Press, 1988) and John Markoff, *The Abolition of Feudalism: Peasants, Lords, and Legislators in the French Revolution* (University Park: The Pennsylvania State University Press, 1996) does not settle the question.

understand peasants—Soboul accepting what peasants say, Furet searching for unexpressed motivations? Finally, is this dispute caused by these scholars' different philosophies of history, political views, and social backgrounds?

AN ATTACK ON FEUDALISM

Albert Soboul

Albert Soboul (1914–1982) came from a peasant family that had moved from the south of France to Algeria. After his father had been killed in the First World War, he was raised by his mother and then by an aunt, the headmistress of a girls' school in southern France. In the 1930s he attended the elite Parisian secondary school, the Lycée Louis-le-Grand, and the University of Paris. His teaching career was interrupted during the Second World War when, in 1942, he was dismissed from his post for supporting Communism and opposing the Vichy government. From 1943 to 1945 he worked for a Parisian museum of popular culture doing research on peasant life. After the liberation of France, he resumed his teaching and writing. A student of Georges Lefebvre, he gained a reputation as the leading Marxist historian of the French Revolution with the publication, in 1958, of *Les Sans-culottes parisiens en l'an II* (of which there are two abridged English translations, 1964 and 1980). Among his many books are *Précis d'histoire de la Révolution française* (1962 and 1964; English translation, 1974), *La Révolution française* (1964 and 1967; English translation, 1977), *Paysans, sans-culottes et jacobins* (1966), *La Civilisation et la Révolution française* (3 volumes; 1970–1983), and, with others, the *Dictionnaire historique de la Révolution française* (1989). In 1960, he succeeded Georges Lefebvre as editor of the learned journal, *Annales historiques de la Révolution française;* and from 1967 until his death, Soboul was Professor of the History of the French Revolution at the University of Paris.

From Albert Soboul, *La Civilisation et la Révolution française,* I: *La Crise de l'ancien régime* (Paris: Arthaud, 1970), pp. 43–44, 63–69, 191–193. Printed by permission of Librairie E. Flammarion. Editors' translation.

During the Old Regime in France, the law was characterized by privileges accorded to various groups. It differentiated three "orders" or "estates." These were the Clergy and Nobility, or the privileged orders, and the Third Estate, comprising the commoners, the great majority of the population.

The legal foundation of these orders went back to the Middle Ages. The oldest was the Clergy, which possessed from its very beginning a special arrangement with the monarchy that was determined by church law. Later, among the laity, the Nobility came to form a social group. The third order, the commoners, developed more slowly. At first it consisted only of bourgeois, the free men of towns that had received charters of liberties from their rulers. Only in 1484 did commoners from the countryside enter the Third Estate, when, for the first time, they voted in the elections to choose deputies for this estate. Gradually, each of the three orders consolidated itself by custom, and they forced the monarchy to recognize them as distinct bodies, so that the separation of the people into three orders became one of the "fundamental laws" of the kingdom.

Actually, in the eighteenth century only one of the orders, the Clergy, was truly organized and had a representative system.[1] The Nobility, despite its efforts since the Fronde [1648–1653], never achieved such a structure. As for the Third Estate, it had only a legal existence, defined primarily by what it was not. This legal façade concealed the importance of the peasantry. France in the eighteenth century, like the rest of Europe, remained basically rural. Tilling the soil and agricultural production dominated economic and social life. In addition, although towns lived off the produce of the countryside, they rejected the dull monotony of its mental horizon. The peasantry, the social base on which the entire Old Regime rested, remained essentially outside the major ideological currents of the century.

If we accept the estimate of more than 26 million as the population of France in 1789, and if we judge the urban population to be about 15 per cent of the whole, then the peasants formed the great majority, certainly over 22 million. In 1846, when the census distinguished urban from rural population for the first time, the rural still comprised 75 per cent of the total.

This preponderance of the peasantry in the society of the Old

---

[1][The General Assembly of the Clergy of France began in 1561. It represented the clergy as a group. It met every five years. Its members were elected but in the eighteenth century almost no priests of non-noble background were chosen for the General Assembly. A useful account in English can be found in L. Greenbaum, *Talleyrand: Statesman Priest* (Washington: Catholic University of America Press, 1970), pp. 24–56.—Eds.]

Regime explains its fundamental role in the Revolution. The main motive for peasant action was the issue of feudal rights or dues and the
remnants of feudalism. The Great Fear [the peasant uprisings in the
summer of 1789] played a large part in bringing about the reforms of
the night of August 4, 1789, for this revolt led to a thorough, although
gradual, abolition of the feudal system. The acquisition of national
land [former Church and émigré property] would also attach the land-
owning peasants to the new order. Peasant affairs were at the center
of the bourgeois revolution.

The Old Regime formed the framework for the life and work of the
peasant masses, and the Regime remained in its essence feudal and
aristocratic. Over the last forty years or so, French historians have
investigated the action of economic forces, the rise of the bourgeoisie, and urban growth, but sometimes they have ignored the
real character of the Old Regime and consequently have lost sight
of the profound meaning of the Revolution. Economic changes, and
the undeniable social changes that arose from them, could not conceal the continuation of certain underlying realities. Europe and
France were essentially rural. The peasants—nearly all the population—were traditionally dominated by seigneurs [lords]. As a symbol of their right of "eminent" domain over the land, these seigneurs
were owed feudal obligations. Landed income, for the most part of
a feudal nature, was the main consideration in agricultural life and
therefore in the entire economy. This income controlled social relationships; it strongly affected the commercial and industrial bourgeoisie by the prestige it gave to owning land. It shaped ideology.
The priority that the Physiocrats gave to agriculture formed one
kind of defense of a land-based economy, even though Quesnay in
his fiscal theory attacked the tax privileges of certain groups.[2] His
Economic Table (1758) is closer to describing the reality of this
agrarian society than those schemes often outlined by present-day
historians who are too ready to emphasize features that foreshadow
the nineteenth century.

In the Old Regime, economic development and growth were held
back, if not threatened, by the persistence of old structures and
by the aristocratic model which captivated even bourgeois people
and which emphasized spending one's income for consumer goods

[2][François Quesnay was the founder and leader of a school of social philosophers
who came to be called Physiocrats. Physiocracy, which flourished in France from
1763 to the early 1770's, attempted to make France prosperous by formulating new
theories and policies. One of its chief tenets was that land is the only true source of
wealth.—Eds.]

and for display. At the close of the eighteenth century, feudal payments were at the heart of the economic problem and of social injustice. . . .

Seigneurs and Peasants

We begin with the words themselves. It is controversial to use the terms "feudalism," "feudal system," and "feudal dues" when describing the eighteenth century. Medieval historians refuse to countenance the word feudalism as applying in this period. Robert Boutruche in *Seigneurialism and Feudalism* (1959) scorned this "abuse of language," and in 1956 Georges Lefebvre at an important international meeting on "the transition from feudalism to capitalism" also rejected the use of this term.

One cannot deny that at the end of the Old Regime feudalism in the strict sense of the word had been for a long time a system that was "decrepit and had received extreme unction," to use Carlyle's phrase as cited by Boutruche. This was true even though the fees payable to rural seigneurs or lords remained vigorously enforced and all the burdens imposed by lords on peasants were still attributed to the feudal system. But we cannot stop with bloodless definitions from legal dictionaries or from the treatises of jurists. Often scornful of social realities, they provide only a static, sclerotic, and narrowly legalistic view of things. What interests us is the social dimension of this term feudalism at the end of the Old Regime—how it was understood by peasants, not by jurists. Words do not have intrinsic meanings; they have to be understood in context. As the institution of feudalism declined, the significance of the word quite naturally changed; and many notaries of the seventeenth and eighteenth centuries, through ignorance or in an effort at simplification, had for a long time confused feudal [military and political] obligations and seigneurial [economic] dues. For peasants and for others concerned with matters of landholding, feudalism was, in the rather exaggerated language of the eighteenth century, the "burden of the land" on which weighed the irremovable land rents, perpetual payments, property transfer fees, and also tithes, in short, the feudal complex of which the jurists spoke.

The word was used in this sense throughout the Revolution and for a long time afterward. A specialist in these matters, Merlin de Douai, explained this clearly in his report of September 4, 1789 to the National Assembly's committee on feudal dues. "Although the words feudal rights, in an exact sense, denote only the dues and the land tenure that derive from the feudal contract, in general usage the meaning has been extended to all dues ordinarily paid to seigneurs and which together form what Dumoulin has called the feudal complex.[3] Therefore, although the seigneurial rents of various kinds, the *champart* [a payment in kind], the labor services, the seigneurial monopolies [obligation to use only the seigneur's mill, wine press, or oven], the payments reflecting former serfdom, and so on, are not feudal dues strictly speaking, we cannot avoid dealing with them."

At that time the abstract term feudalism was helpful because of its broad meaning. Indeed, those who used the word understood its reality very clearly. In the narrow sense it included such feudal dues as the very heavy *franc-fief* payable when land owned by a noble passed into the hands of a commoner. It also included the seigneur's legal authority that allowed him to render justice and that gave him police power from which in turn came the seigneurial monopolies. Long after the end of feudalism in the strict sense of the word, the seigneur was still the first inhabitant of the village and would remain so because he was owner of the château. Finally, feudalism included the payments whose origins were derived from seigneurial or crown land such as the various kinds of perpetual rents.

For the peasants this was the reality of feudalism, still alive and kicking, originating from force and always bearing the marks of their bondage. The bourgeois of the National Assembly did not regard this popular understanding of feudalism as faulty. On the night of August 4, 1789 they abolished without compensation the *mainmorte* [a type of serf landholding] and the payments that were derived from it. These were considered contrary to individual liberty. They also abolished seigneurial dues, for they had been seized to the detriment of the state and collected by force. But because they had themselves acquired fiefs and established estates, they pretended that these seigneurial dues were payments owed for the original grant of land to peasant farmers. The peasants were not taken in, and the results were revolutionary. For the peasants, feudalism was not a myth, as some historians now maintain, nor was seigneurial domination a paternal and benevolent authority, as some people are eager to say.

Alexis de Tocqueville did not err on this point, and we cannot deny the testimony of this acute observer. He constantly used the term feudalism in his *Old Regime and the French Revolution* (1856). For him

---

[3][Philippe Antoine, comte Merlin (de Douai) (1754–1838), was elected a deputy to the Third Estate in 1789 and served in several of the revolutionary assemblies and as a prosecutor in the highest court of the Napoleonic empire. Charles Dumoulin (1500–1566) was a prominent scholar of the law and critic of feudalism.—Eds.]

the French Revolution was, in its essence, anti-feudal. Its effect "was to abolish those political institutions which for several centuries had held total sway over most of the European peoples, institutions that we ordinarily call feudal." The basic task of the Revolution was to destroy "everything that in the old society depended on aristocratic and feudal institutions, everything that even to the smallest degree bore their imprint." At the conclusion of the chapter that he devoted to feudal dues Tocqueville wrote, "feudalism had remained in 1789 the greatest of all our social and economic institutions, although it no longer had a political content. Reduced in power in this way, feudalism aroused even more hatred, and it would be correct to say that after the destruction of some parts of medieval institutions, those that remained became a hundred-fold more hateful."

All of rural life in the Old Regime seemed to be hemmed in and often paralyzed in this archaic straightjacket. To be sure there were regional differences. In a province such as Brittany the effects of feudalism remained visible; as to the Beauvais region [north of Paris], a vigorous seigneurial system presented a clear picture of the traces of a formal and old feudalism; and Languedoc [in the south] offered a still different view, a much faded feudalism. It also remains true that in all the various regions it is not easy to draw sharp distinctions between property and seigneurie, between feudalism and seigneurie, and between these three terms on the one hand and the concept of nobility on the other. Yet, the economic and social reality of feudalism continued to exist.

Until the coming of the Revolution ended the old legal framework, the legal system of landholding and its derivative, the social organization of the countryside, was based on the long-lasting foundations of feudal society. In regard to public law [law relating to the monarchy], royal authority had long since destroyed this system and assumed sovereignty from the seigneurs, but private law [law among individuals] still remained. Land was divided among a great number of seigneuries [comparable to medieval English manors], both secular and religious. These were of very different sizes. They belonged either to clergy, nobles, or bourgeois, for the former relationship between the legal status of land and that of its owners had disappeared [that is, non-nobles, commoners, could now own seigneuries].

In feudal law, the land on these seigneuries was divided between the demesne (*domaine proche*) and the tenures (*censives* or *domaine utile*). The demesne usually included a "reserve" or home farm, and various types of rented or sharecropped fields. On the reserve usually stood a château with its dependent buildings, wood-

lands, heaths, ponds, and so forth, and a certain amount of cultivated land. Sometimes the seigneur farmed this reserve himself with
the aid of his hired hands (which did not involve *dérogeance* [losing
his noble status]) and with additional help from unpaid labor service provided by the free peasants of the seigneurie. In other situations, the seigneur rented out the home farm or had it worked on a
crop-sharing basis.

The tenures usually included noble estates (fiefs) belonging to vas-
sals of the seigneur and non-noble holdings belonging to peasants
who paid the *cens* [perpetual rent due annually]. In the eighteenth
century, these tenures were considered the holder's property. The
peasant "held" the land on a hereditary basis. He could sell, be-
queath, or mortgage it. But still he did not own it in the fullest sense
of the word. The holder of land in the tenures had only an imperfect
and incomplete title to his land. The seigneur had the right of "eminent" domain over this property. It was said that he held it directly.
Because of this, the land of the tenures owed dues to the seigneur.
"Whoever possesses land in the tenures," wrote a feudal lawyer, "is
called the owner; the person who has a direct holding is its seigneur,
and the seigneur owns the right to collect dues." These dues included both regular and occasional payments.

Theoretically, a distinction should be made between strictly feudal
dues, which depended on the feudal contract, and the seigneurial
dues, which derived from certain rights and payments stemming
from the political authority formerly exercised by the seigneur. When
the king regained his political sovereignty over the land, he left these
latter rights and payments with the seigneurs.

Landed property was burdened by both feudal and seigneurial
dues, which limited the rights of ownership. As a feudal lawyer put
it, the peasant who held a piece of *censive* land owed an annual payment (*cens*), "the symbol of the seigneur's eminent domain" on non-
noble landholdings, "just as faith and homage are the mark of holding a feudal fief [a noble landholding]." The feudal fief, because it lost
its political character and no longer represented a type of social organization, was profoundly changed, but *censive* land still remained
a way for seigneurs to earn an income until the Revolution. It was the
most extensive type of tenure land and of land subject to the
seigneur's right of eminent domain. Peasants who paid the *cens* actually believed they themselves were nothing less than the real owners of their land; they understood nothing of feudal law and considered it monstrous to have to make payments.

In addition to *censive* landholding, serf landholding continued. The serf landholder had to make payments and provide services, but at a higher rate. The serf could not transfer his land by sale or bequest, a restriction called *mainmorte*. By the end of the eighteenth century many serf holdings had been converted to *censive* property. Yet other serf holdings remained, especially in eastern and central France.

In the midst of this complicated network of seigneuries and tenures, some land escaped the control of the seigneur. This was allodial or free property, which was exempt from all dues or payments. But this type of landholding was exceptional. Much allodial land had been converted to *censive* land in those areas where the rule provided that there was "no land without a seigneur." The allodial regions generally remained in those areas where written law applied and where the rule was "no seigneur without a title of nobility." But from the seventeenth century, the amount of allodial land decreased due to the efforts of aggressive royal officials. In order to increase tax revenue, they made as much land as possible subject to feudal charges and land payments. By virtue of the *directe universelle* [the king's alleged eminent domain], the royal officials tried to put under the monarch's feudal control all land of the kingdom that did not have a seigneur with the right of eminent domain. Still, until the end of the Old Regime, allodial land did remain in the Bordeaux region, Languedoc, Dauphiné, and Nivernais, but it was not at all typical. The feudal complex burdened almost all the land of the kingdom and thus its peasants.

If we try to make this entire system somewhat clearer (and even specialists on these matters in this period, the feudal lawyers, had a difficult time of it), we should distinguish feudal dues from seigneurial dues.

Feudal dues, in the narrow sense of the term, derived from the feudal contract, as Merlin de Douai pointed out in his report of September 4, 1789. They comprised a package of dues, "some fixed, some occasional, some having to do with substance and some with honorific forms." The payments due from noble landholdings—fiefs—did not concern peasants unless they had bought a piece of land that was considered noble. But this kind of purchase was rare except in the south, an area more advanced in this regard than the north. In such cases the non-noble buyer paid the *franc-fief*, an expense and a humiliation for those from the Third Estate. On the other hand, dues on *censive* land were either regular and payable in money (*cens*) or in kind (*champart, agrier*) or else they were occasional (*lods et ventes*) [on the occasion of a property transfer]. All these various dues, which in theory signified an original grant of land by a seigneur to a vassal or to a peasant, were designated "real" dues by the National Assembly and were declared repurchasable.

Seigneurial dues, unlike feudal dues, were derived from the political authority originally exercised by the seigneurs and concerned the relationships between the seigneurial landholder and the peasants. The right to dispense "high and low" justice remained fundamental. From it sprang honorific rights. These were taken quite seriously by the seigneur because they symbolized his preeminence. The judicial power also was the basis for certain dues that brought in revenue. These dues included such personal payments as the seigneurial tax (either so much per head or a variable rate), the hearth tax, guard service commuted to a cash payment, and labor services owed by persons or derived from certain pieces of land. Additional dues followed from the police power, which itself was associated with the right to dispense justice. From this, the seigneur had a monopoly of milling, baking, the wine press, and also livestock butchering, the forge, and breeding by bulls and boars. All of these were actually economic monopolies. The seigneur even held the *banvin,* a monopoly on the sale of wine. The regulations concerning the time for mowing and on the harvesting of grain or grape, all associated with "high" justice, were also derived from the police power. To these we add tolls, many kinds of fees to sell one's produce at markets or fairs, rights associated with hunting, keeping rabbits and pigeons, and finally, fishing rights.

Church tithes, although not legally part of this system, should be placed in the economic and social reality of the feudal complex. The tithe, paid in kind on field crops and on the growth of livestock herds, was in principle supposed to support the clergy, the maintenance of the Church, and the relief of the poor. "Feudalized," the tithe escaped the control of the Church and went to benefit a layperson. This happened usually by simple usurpation. Tithes were paid on agricultural output and not on the land itself, except in the case of woodland and often of pasture land. There were the "large tithes" on the four "large" grains—wheat, rye, barley, and oats—and on wine. "Small tithes" or "green" tithes were paid on the produce from gardens and orchards—vegetables and fruits—and on hemp and flax. The meat or blood tithe was assessed on herds and barnyards—lambs and wool, sucking pigs, and poultry. Lastly, there were the "novale" tithes paid on newly cleared land, but peasants considered these "novale" tithes unjustified.

"Picture for yourself," said Tocqueville in *The Old Regime and the French Revolution,* "the French peasant of the eighteenth century . . .

so hungry for land that he devotes all his savings to it and buys it at any price. To obtain it, he first makes a payment not to the government but to other landholders of the neighborhood, as far removed as he from the central administration. . . . Finally he takes possession of this land; he plants his heart in it along with his seeds. . . . Then along come these same neighbors; they drag him from his own field and force him to work elsewhere without payment. If he wants to protect his seedlings from the animals they hunt, they stop him; they also wait at the river crossing to levy a toll. He meets them again at the market where they make him pay for the right to sell his own products; and when, on returning home, he wants to use the rest of his grain for himself, grain that grew under his own eyes and through his own efforts, he can do this only after having it ground in the mill and baked in the oven of these same people. So part of the income from his small farm goes to support these people, and the fees he pays cannot be changed or redeemed. Whatever he does, he meets everywhere these annoying neighbors in his way, interfering with his pleasure and his work, eating up his produce. When he has finally taken care of them, others, dressed in black [the clergy], step up and take the best of his harvest. If you consider the peasant of the eighteenth century, his situation and his needs, his temperament and his passions, then you can calculate the great fund of hatred and envy built up in his heart."

No one has portrayed this hatred better than [the man of letters] Hippolyte Taine, certainly no friend of the Revolution. In *The Origins of Contemporary France* he described how the advance of the Prussian army and the émigrés in September 1792 profoundly shocked the peasant masses of France. Small farmers, share-croppers, laborers, and also poachers, vagabonds, and beggars "had no difficulty remembering the outrageous royal, church, and seigneurial taxes before 1789. . . . They had only to open their eyes to see the magnitude of their liberation. . . . A powerful anger swept from workshop to hovel. . . . This was the second flood of the Revolution, which rose and thundered, not as wide as the first [in 1789], since it hardly included more than ordinary folk, but much higher and much more destructive." This second flood carried off and finally destroyed feudalism. . . .

The mass of the peasants was energized to action in 1789 more by harsh living conditions than by the power of ideas. The peasants expressed their grievances in the parish cahiers for the Estates General of 1789. The objective historical value of these cahiers has been challenged, and of course one must check them against other contemporary documents. But the cahiers were prepared in the presence of persons representing seigneurial authority, and it would have been difficult for peasants to denounce a demand or an exploitation that was purely imaginary. Questions also have been raised about the subjective bias of the cahiers, but these doubts concern only the political requests. On these points some cahiers clearly reveal a bourgeois origin. On the other hand, regarding matters of social organization, the parish cahiers accurately reflect peasant grievances, although the poorest peasants could not always make themselves heard.

The peasantry was unanimous about feudalism and about dues paid on land. Of all the peasant obligations, feudal dues and Church tithes were the most detested—because they were heavy and irritating, because the peasants did not understand their origin, and because they appeared unjust. In one cahier from a parish of the Nord, feudal dues were said to have "their origin in the shadows of a contemptible mystery." If there were legitimate payments due, proof of this should be presented and in such cases they should be redeemable. Most parish cahiers stated quite clearly that the origins of these payments had to be verified and insisted that the original document should be produced in order to validate that these dues had been imposed in return for holding the land. If such documents were not produced, then the dues should be cancelled. The peasant believed that he was the only legitimate owner of the land and, unless there was proof to the contrary, ascribed seigneurial dues to no origin other than force. Sometimes the peasant expressed his bitterness quite sharply against the "bloodsucking" seigneurs. Let the tithe be paid in a fixed amount of cash, reasoned the peasant; for it would end up as a ridiculously small amount due to the declining purchasing power of money over time. Let the privileged people pay taxes. And so forth. The peasants harbored much more substantial complaints against the aristocracy than did townspeople, and the peasants, from 1789 on, struck a mortal blow against the aristocracy.

On the question of land the peasantry, united heretofore, divided. Many peasants lacked land, but rare were the cahiers that dared to request that property be taken from the clergy. They limited themselves to suggestions that part of the clergy's revenues be used to pay off the public debt and to fill the deficit. They seemed to regard property as untouchable, even that held by a privileged order. Peasant cahiers were less timid on the matter of how land was to be worked. A number of them called for the division of large farms. But here already emerged the split that permanently divided the peasantry once feudalism was abolished. Contradictions appeared be-tween the interests of the large-scale peasant farmers and the mass of peasants who held small parcels of land or none at all. The peasants were far from unanimous about the reforms attempted by the monar-chy before 1789—enclosure of open fields, free trade in grain, and the use of common land. In 1789 the more well-off peasants, the various kinds of "rural bourgeoisie," began to recognize that the mass of the peasants constituted a danger to their interests. Some cahiers, from the Nord region, called for a property qualification for voting so as to exclude from political affairs those who paid no taxes or who received charitable assistance; this was "the only way to keep political meet-ings from becoming too unruly." Already "well-to-do farmers," the "matadors" or "big shots of the village," were concerned to preserve their social authority.

In this manner were sketched out, at the end of the Old Regime, the future antagonisms within the French peasantry. Its unity came about only in opposition to privilege, in hatred for the aristocracy. By abolishing feudal dues, tithes, and privileges, the Revolution had the effect of permanently moving the landholding peasantry into the party of order [the conservatives]. As for the land, the Revolution multiplied the number of small property holders through the sale of national land, but it maintained, if it did not increase, the number of large estates too, with all the social consequences one might expect. The structure of the peasantry at the end of the Old Regime fore-shadowed the moderate agrarian reforms of the Revolution once feu-dalism had been abolished. As Georges Lefebvre once remarked, these reforms looked "like a compromise between the bourgeoisie and rural democracy."

MISDIRECTED RAGE

François Furet

François Furet (1927–1997) was a banker's son. A
Parisian, he attended the prestigious Parisian secondary
school, the Lycée Janson-de-Sailly, and the University of
Paris. He then held coveted appointments at the Centre
national de la recherche scientifique from 1956 to 1961
and at the École des hautes études en sciences sociales
from 1961. After serving as president of the latter school
from 1977 to 1985, he became Director of its Institut Raymond Aron while holding a joint appointment at the University of Chicago. Furet published many works. They
include *La Révolution française* (2 volumes; with Denis
Richet, 1965–1966; English translation, 1970), *Penser la
Révolution française* (1978; English translation entitled
Interpreting the French Revolution, 1981), *Marx et la Révolution française* (1986; English translation, 1988), *Dictionnaire critique de la Révolution française* (1988; edited
with Mona Ozouf; English translation, 1989), and *La
Révolution: De Turgot à Jules Ferry, 1770–1880* (1988;
English translation entitled *Revolutionary France 1770–
1880,* 1992). These works dissent from various points of
view put forward by Albert Soboul and several other
Marxist historians of the Revolution. Furet grew disillusioned with Marxism after having been a Communist
party member from about 1949 to 1956. In the shaping of
events, he stressed the importance of ideas and politics
rather than class conflicts.

$$\clubsuit\clubsuit\clubsuit\clubsuit\clubsuit$$

In Soboul's analysis [in his *Crise de l'ancien régime*], the peasants
have the lion's share and occupy almost half of the book. Two hundred pages are devoted to them, in my opinion the best part of the

volume. Albert Soboul gives us a synthesis of the many studies on the
peasantry under the Ancien Régime and produces a very full analysis
of the various aspects of rural life, including the social setting, tech-
nology, demography, everyday working habits, cultures and beliefs.

These pages, in conveying a concrete sympathy for the world of
the countryside and an insight into the life of humble people, have a
very special flavour. Yet when it comes to the basic interpretation,
the analysis raises one immense problem, with which it deals rather
too summarily: seigneurial rights and the burden of feudalism in the
French countryside of the eighteenth century.

Soboul has made up his mind. On the conceptual level, although he
is evidently aware of the distinction between "feudal" and "seigneurial," just as were the jurists of the Revolution,[1] he constantly mixes
the two notions in exactly the same way revolutionary ideology did.
Thus, in his historical analysis, he can speak of a "feudal complex" or
"régime" as defining what was essential in the economic and social
relationships of the countryside. At the price of a constant confusion
of words, between "feudal," "seigneurial" and "aristocratic," the historian, here again, takes his bearings from the contemporary perceptions of the event he describes[2] and once more he is imprisoned
in the sharp division made in 1789 between "old" and "new," a division in which "old" meant "feudal." Suddenly there he is, forced to
charge to "feudalism" all the negative and in the end "explosive" aspects of rural life, from the exploitation of the peasantry and its misery to the obstacles to agricultural productivity and the slow pace of
capitalist development. But since by the eighteenth century that
"feudal régime" had been under heavy attack for some four or five
centuries, the old idea of an "aristocratic reaction"[3] is brought in to
rescue the threatened concept. From Soboul's language and ideas,
the reader almost feels as if he were participating in the meeting held
on the famous night of 4 August 1789.

As everyone knows, the facts and figures for an analysis on a national scale of the relative weight of seigneurial dues in the total
landed revenue—and in the incomes of peasants and nobles—do not

---

[1]Cf. Merlin de Douai (whom Soboul cites on p. 66) and his reports to the Constituent
Assembly on behalf of the *Comité féodal* (Committee on feudalism) on 4 September
1789 and 8 February 1790.

[2]Claude Mazauric proceeds in the same manner in *Sur la Révolution française* (Paris:
Éditions sociales, 1970), pp. 118–34. Marxism is reduced to a device for justifying the
contemporary consciousness of the event.

[3]Here as elsewhere Soboul does not distinguish between aristocratic, seigneurial and
feudal.

exist. Nor will they exist very soon, because the dues were incredibly diverse, the sources are scattered, and the data to be gathered from the *terriers* [*seigneurial rent rolls*] do not lend themselves to being grouped into statistical series. Soboul writes: "Landed income, *for the most part of a feudal nature,* was the main consideration in agricultural life." This statement, in the part I have italicised, is patently false for eighteenth-century France, where leases, sharecropping and direct management unquestionably produced more income than seigneurial dues. And one is surprised to hear a specialist making it. The degree of his inexactness is what is important here. But just how wrong is he? The many monographs at our disposal testify to a wide variety of situations. Le Roy Ladurie's peasants in their relatively "unfeudalised" *Midi* [southern France] seem to have rid themselves of seigneurial payments quite early, that is, by the beginning of the sixteenth century.[4] In Paul Bois's Sarthe,[5] the level of seigneurial dues seems to have been very low, amounting to a tiny fraction of the total landed income in comparison with the income from leases. Nor did the revision of the *terriers* in the seventeenth century bring to light any supplementary dues. "It is only slightly exaggerated to say," concludes P. Bois, "that the matter of seigneurial dues did not concern the peasant." The same goes for Abel Poitrineau's Auverge[6] where seigneurial dues do not seem to have represented more than ten per cent of net landed income, although here they did rise in the course of the century. By contrast, in Jean Meyer's Brittany[7] and in Pierre de Saint-Jacob's Burgundy,[8] to which a new study was recently devoted by Régine Robin,[9] the seigneur's share deducted from the net yield of the land remained high, especially when it involved payments in kind. The *champart* levied in Burgundy and the rights attached to the *domaine congéable* in Brittany seem to have been, in the economic sense, truly burdensome seigneurial rights.

Given the present state of our knowledge, it is therefore impossi-

---

[4]Emmanuel Le Roy Ladurie, *Les Paysans de Languedoc* (Paris: S.E.V.P.E.N., 1966), cf. vol. 1, pp. 291–2.

[5]Paul Bois, *Paysans de l'Ouest* (Paris and The Hague: Mouton, 1960), cf. pp. 382ff.

[6]Abel Poitrineau, *La Vie rurale en Basse-Auvergne au XVIIIe siècle 1726–1789* (Paris and The Hague: Mouton, 1965), cf. vol. 1, pp. 342ff.

[7]Jean Meyer, *La Noblesse bretonne au XVIIIe siècle* (Paris: S.E.V.P.E.N., 1966). See in particular vol. 2. Meyer found relatively burdensome seigneurial levies in Brittany; yet he concluded that "seigneurial rights in the narrow sense, high though they were, represented a relatively small percentage of the nobles' income" (p. 1248).

[8]Pierre de Saint-Jacob, *Les Paysans de la Bourgogne du Nord au dernier siècle de l'Ancien Régime* (Paris: Les Belles Lettres, 1960).

[9]Régine Robin, *La Société française en 1789: Semur-en-Auxois* (Paris: Plon, 1970).

ble to speak of a "feudal reaction" in the eighteenth century as if it
were an objective process within the economy and rural society. It is
not even sure that landed dues (*droits réels*), which were above all a
burden to the landowner—since, like the Church tithe (*dîme*), they
were usually deducted from the owner's share—appreciably affected
the standard of living of the poorest of the peasants, those who
worked a small plot. But even if the opposite were true, even if a
growth in seigneurial levies as a share of agricultural output did
cause a pauperisation of the peasantry at the end of the eighteenth
century, it would still not follow that this trend was aristocratic and
"feudal" (by which Soboul means both noble and anti-capitalist).
Abel Poitrineau published in his work a very interesting curve showing the increasing commercialisation of the *seigneuries* of Auvergne
in the second half of the century, as well as their growing involvement in the market.[10] In the case of mid-eighteenth-century Burgundy, Pierre de Saint-Jacob—who, incidentally, seems to use the
term "seigneurial reaction" with a certain reserve[11]—has shown how
the *seigneurie*, through its dues collectors, who invested their receipts, took part in what he calls the "physiocratic revolution," that
is, the development of rural capitalism.[12] Perhaps we would be well
advised to speak, as Alfred Cobban suggested,[13] not of an "aristocratic reaction" but of an *embourgeoisement* of the *seigneurie*. Seen in
this light, the peasant's resistance against the *seigneurie* may well
have been not anti-aristocratic or "anti-feudal," but anti-bourgeois
and anti-capitalist. Hence the enthusiasm of the night of 4 August
would not be that of a battle-front rallying all classes of society to the
common interest, but the means to gloss over a disagreement or at
least a radical misunderstanding. Indeed, it is only too obvious that
the abolition of seigneurial rights and dues did not dispel the subsequent resistance in French rural society to the development of capitalism. As P. Bois's book suggests, the peasant's hostility toward the
seigneurie may simply have been the archaic form of his opposition
to economic change.

In this connection, a recent German article[14] suggests an interest-

---

[10] Poitrineau, *La Vie rurale*, vol. 2, p. 123.

[11] Saint-Jacob, *Les Paysans de la Bourgogne*, p. 434.

[12] *Ibid.* pp. 469–72.

[13] Alfred Cobban. *The Social Interpretation of the French Revolution* (Cambridge: C.U.P., 1964), p.47.

[14] Eberhard Weis, "Ergebnisse eines Vergleichs der grundherrshaftlichen Strukturen Deutschlands und Frankreichs vom 13. bis zum Ausgang des 18. Jahrhunderts," *Vierteljahrschrift fur Sozial-und Wirtschaftsgeschichte* (1970), 1–14.

ing hypothesis, based on a comparison between Bavaria and France. It shows the very different situation that existed in the German territories west of the Elbe, where the clergy and the nobility, while keeping their seigneurial rights (*propriété éminente*), had ceded all the old domain lands to perpetual leaseholders (*paysans tenanciers*), who thus had become virtual owners of 80–90 per cent of the income-producing land. In France, by contrast, the outstanding trait of the *seigneurie* was the retention of title to domain lands by seigneurs who "farmed out" those lands under a renewable money-lease, a practice that became increasingly widespread between the sixteenth and the eighteenth century. In France this was more important than the quit-rent (*censive*) [perpetual annual rent]; which the nobles detested because fixed payments did not keep pace with inflation and the devaluation of the currency. By the end of the eighteenth century, perpetual leaseholders in France held little more than a third of the soil, far less, therefore, than what has been generally believed. This comparative analysis of the evolution of the seigneurial system in France and western Germany has the advantage of explaining pauperisation in the French countryside on the eve of the Revolution, and the presence of a vast peasant proletariat without equivalent on the other side of the Rhine, where 90 per cent of the land was permanently in the hands of owner-occupiers. But it also underscores the fact that in France the development of rural capitalism was linked to the practice of "farming out" domain lands. Far from standing in its way, the *seigneurie,* with its stewards (*régisseurs*) and bourgeois middlemen, was the vehicle of that development.[15] And Paul Bois is quite probably correct when he claims that in protesting against residual and secondary seigneurial rights, which were psychologically all the more irritating as they represented a marginal drain on an already marginal operation, French peasants of the late eighteenth century were really attacking the spread of landed capitalism.

Yet if the hazy notion of an aristocratic reaction, characterised by an increased emphasis on seigneurial rights, has been accepted by historians for so long, it can only be because it fits perfectly into the simplistic vision of class struggle and alliances related to it. It also enables Albert Soboul to fall back on an elementary textbook Marxism and to write that "the changeover to a capitalist form of agriculture demanded the abolition of feudalism and privilege." Above all, that notion holds sway because it rests upon a series of eighteenth-

---

[15] Some remarkable examples of this fact can be found in Georges Lefebvre's *Etudes orléanaises*, 2 vols. (Paris: Bibliothèque Nationale, 1962–3), vol. 1, ch. 1, "Les campagnes orléanaises."

century literary documents, foremost among them the *Cahiers* of the Estates General. It should be recalled that the debate about the documentary value of the *Cahiers*—and Heaven knows that this debate has been animated since the beginning of the century—has so far turned essentially on whether and to what extent the writers of each *Cahier* faithfully expressed the true wishes of their respective communities. Supposing that the question can be answered in the affirmative—and it can, in most cases—a second and probably more fundamental problem must be solved before the *Cahiers* can be used. Should they be read as statements describing the actual situation or as documents reflecting the political climate and ideology prevailing in French society in 1789? I am inclined to opt for the second type of reading, along with R. Robin who, on this point, has opened a new perspective.[16] At the very least, the second question must be dealt with before the first; the content of the *Cahiers* at every sociological level must be described before they can be related to the real social circumstances from which they were issued.

It is true that the peasant *Cahiers* are often filled with grievances against seigneurial rights. Yet those grievances were expressed less frequently, it seems, than those against the tithe (*dîme*) and the royal income or property tax (*taille*), which together were the true bane of the rural community. Among the various seigneurial rights, the peasant *Cahiers* were often less opposed to landed dues (*droits réels*) than to personal rights, such as monopolies over mills and ovens (*banalités*), and hunting rights. The notion that these rights had become more onerous in the recent past can also be found, especially in the form of hostility toward the experts who brought the seigneur's *terriers* up to date. But even supposing—and this supposition is certainly unwarranted in this form—that the peasant *Cahiers* were unanimous in their complaints about a recent increase in the seigneur's share, what would that prove? Virtually nothing at all.

It is quite likely, for example, that if a consultation on the 1789 model, calling for written statements of grievances, were conducted in rural France today, these modern *Cahiers* would be unanimous against taxation, even though French farmers have been notoriously under-taxed for the last hundred and fifty years. It is in the very nature of a political text and of any political consciousness, however rudimentary, to place the blame for evil on men rather than on things; that is what Ernest Labrousse,[17] who is still the leading Marx-

---

[16] Robin, *La Société française,* pp. 255–343.

[17] Ernest Labrousse, *La Crise de l'économie française à la fin de l'Ancien Régime et au début de la Révolution* (Paris: P.U.F., 1943), Introduction, p. 47.

ist historian of the origins of the French Revolution, very aptly calls "placing the blame on politics." The pervasive poverty of the late eighteenth century, for which we have a great deal of undeniable evidence, may have been due to demographic growth; after all, the extra five or six million subjects of the king of France had to find a little niche for themselves somewhere. That poverty is also inscribed in Labrousse's admirable graphs, in which the price of leases, that is, landed income in its most "bourgeois" [capitalist] form, climbs ever so much faster than wages and even prices.[18] But how would the peasants, and even the local *notaire* [notary], know that? How could they fail to turn, almost spontaneously, against the château and its retainers, who represented the image of power at the local level? As R. Robin pointed out in connection with the *Cahiers* from the region of Auxerre,[19] the grievances of the rural community were not a matter of historical and economic analysis but of concrete everyday life: taxes, tithes, hunting; the things that were taken away and those that were no longer permitted. Moreover, the consultation took place in the spring of 1789, at the height of a short-term crisis. It was perfectly natural for the immense masses of poor peasants to seek reasons for their difficulties in the recent past and in increased deductions from the pay for their labours.

That the seigneur or, in the case of the tithe, the clergy was made to play the rôle of scapegoat for the crisis has been shown most convincingly by Paul Bois, who examines the case—a limited one to be sure—of the department of the Sarthe in the chapter of his book devoted to the analysis of the local *Cahiers*.[20] He demonstrates that there was simply no correlation between three things—the intensity of the peasants' objection to abuses by the privileged orders, the actual burden of deductions by the seigneur or the *dîme,* and the political behaviour of the communities studied. Far to the contrary, the attacks on the privileged orders, and especially on the clergy,[21] were harshest in the *Cahiers* of the western part of the department, even though no objective reasons for this hostility, such as a particularly

---

[18] Ernest Labrousse, *Esquisse du mouvement des prix et des revenus en France au XVIIIe siècle* (Paris: Dalloz, 1933), see Book 7, ch. 2. In fact, Labrousse clearly suggests, in *La Crise de l'économie française,* the idea I am developing here, i.e. that the "seigneurial reaction" was, economically speaking, essentially a matter of the increasing price of leaseholds in terms of their real value, that is, their net yield (Introduction, p. 45).

[19] Robin, *La Société française,* pp. 298–313.

[20] Bois, *Paysans de l'Ouest,* pp. 165–219.

[21] On the whole, the *Cahiers* of what was to become the department of the Sarthe were not particularly anti-noble.

large proportion of Church land or a particularly onerous tithe, can be found there. Moreover, that part of the department was later to be an area of counter-revolutionary activity (*chouannerie*), while the south-eastern part, whose *Cahiers* were particularly moderate with respect to the privileged, was to become a stronghold of republican loyalty. In other words, it is a mistake to seek to unlock the secrets of the peasants' frame of mind and their behaviour by setting up, *ex post facto,* an imaginary "anti-feudal" class front consolidated by a hypothetical "feudal reaction."

What, then, was the reason for the diffuse but fundamental and very intense frustration that eighteenth-century French society felt toward the nobility and the privileged orders? It seems to me that the "aristocratic reaction" was a psychological, social and political reality far more than a fact of economic life. The eighteenth century witnessed a kind of exacerbation of snobbery,[22] which as a backlash produced the exacerbation of *differences* all along the social spectrum. In one of the footnotes to his thesis, Jean Meyer cites a very amusing text that makes this point.[23] It is an anonymous pamphlet against the *présidents à mortier* [some of the leading judges] of the *Parlement* of Brittany, purporting to be a manual of etiquette for *présidents à mortier:*

> Since there are very few of us, we cannot always be together. We must learn how to be alone and to be bored in a dignified manner; we are working hard at learning it, but one does eventually develop the habit, and I now prefer the honour of being bored by myself or in the company of another *président* to the pleasure I might derive from the company of a few councillors or *gentilshommes* [lower-ranked judges or ordinary nobles]. That degree of perfection is attained only by the long practice of being a *président.*

There is no doubt that among nobles of the *robe,* finance and the sword—but these distinctions within the nobility became less and less meaningful with time, as if they were muted in order to emphasise the real distinction, the great social gulf between noble and non-noble status—a real exacerbation of noble "racism" had taken place. But the nobility's compulsive preoccupation with protocol and the trappings of power did not necessarily go hand in hand with increased economic demands on the peasantry. On the contrary, one can argue that the nobles, deprived of power by the absolutist

---

[22] Cf. in particular the article by Marcel Reinhard, "Élite et noblesse dana la seconde moitié du XVIIIe siècle," *Revue d'histoire moderne et contemporaine* 3 (1956), 5–37.

[23] Meyer, *La Noblesse bretonne,* vol. 2, p. 961.

State—or believing that they were so deprived, which in practice amounts to the same thing—harped on the outward signs of domination and the rituals of separation to the point of caricature.[24] Following the nobles' example, a whole society played out the psychodrama of dominance and subservience, setting nobles against nonnobles, great nobles against lesser nobles, rich against poor, Parisians against provincials, urban against rural dwellers. The problem thus involved not so much economic property as social dominance. As Tocqueville already realised,[25] eighteenth-century French society was a world that had been *deprived of its cohesion* by the cen-

---

[24] *Ibid.* vol. 1, p. 793, one finds the following assessment by the Estates of Brittany in 1772 of "feudal rights." "Although feudal rights are not usually very considerable with respect to their financial benefits, they are sweet and precious with respect to adornment and respectability."

[25] Tocqueville, *L'Ancien Régime et la Révolution,* Book 2, ch. 9, of his *Oeuvres complètes* (J.P. Mayer, general editor).

I must parenthetically note here that Soboul's references to Tocqueville are no more than pious gestures and almost always incorrect. For example: in support of his analysis of the burden of feudal rights and the "feudal system" on French rural life in the eighteenth century, he uses a page of *L'Ancien Regime* taken from chapter 1 of Book 2 devoted to the peasants' resentment of feudal rights. He thus repeats the misinterpretation he had already stated in an article published in *Annales historiques de la Révolution française* [(*July-September 1958), 294–7*], entitled "La Révolution française et la féodalité." For it must be clear to any attentive reader of *L'Ancien Régime* that Tocqueville's thesis was the following:

(a) "Feudal" rights were less burdensome to the French peasant turned landowner than to his neighbours in continental Europe, many of whom were still subject to labour services (*corvées*). If the rural population was strongly opposed to feudal rights, it was not because they were particularly burdensome, but because they were *vestigial* and no longer accompanied by their natural counterpart: local and "paternal" administration by the seigneur.

(b) If the French peasant was "sometimes" worse off in the eighteenth century than in the thirteenth, it was because the eighteenth-century peasant was at the mercy of arbitrary measures by the monarchy, especially with respect to taxation, and yet no longer able to count on the seigneur's mediation (Book 2, ch. 12).

(c) As in Marx's early writings (cf. especially *The Jewish Question*), feudalism is for Tocqueville a political as well as a civil and socio-economic institution: one of the causes of the Revolution was that the institution had ceased to exist politically, for it had been destroyed by the monarchy, and that it nonetheless survived in a vestigial and *therefore* intolerable form in civil society.

Much could also be said about the use of certain passages from Tocqueville, carefully removed from their context, in Soboul's afterword to Georges Lefebvre's *Quatre-vingt-neuf* (Paris, 1970), pp. 260, 263 and 283. Only on the basis of a careless reading of Tocqueville or a total indifference to the meaning of these texts is it possible to suggest that *L'Ancien Régime et la Révolution* can lead to the kind of interpretation that is proposed by Soboul. Exactly the opposite is the case.

tralisation of the monarchical State and the concomitant rise of individualism. Seen in this perspective, the Revolution can be considered a vast process of sociocultural integration, achieved through the "anti-feudal" patriotism of 1789 and the Jacobin ideology that succeeded it. Egalitarianism was the opposite side of humiliation, "republican" togetherness the opposite of "monarchical" isolation. Given those convictions, it is only natural that the nobility was made to pay the full price of national integration.

3

The Character of the National Assembly
(1789–1791)

FROM 1789 to 1791, the National or Constituent Assembly began overhauling French institutions. Very few legislatures have ever attempted such a transformation in so short a period. By the time the Assembly adjourned on September 30, 1791, the King could no longer consider himself an absolute monarch and had to share power with a legislature elected by a majority of Frenchmen twenty-five years of age and older. This Assembly granted full civil and political rights to many males, including Protestants and Jews, although not to women or propertyless males. The traditional administrative divisions of the country were abolished along with the parlements, the old provincial supreme courts; and these were replaced by a new administrative structure of eighty-three departments and a new legal system in which judges obtained their posts by election rather than by purchase. In addition, the Assembly passed laws that fundamentally changed economic and social life. France adopted a new paper currency, the assignat, which was based on expropriated Church land rather than on gold and silver; and freedom of domestic trade became the governing policy without the guilds or internal tolls and tariffs that so shaped the Old Regime. Moreover, tax privileges for the nobility and clergy were abolished, while labor unions and strikes were outlawed.[1] Given the extent of this transformation, it is not surprising that there has been disagreement about the political ability of the deputies to the National Assembly and the wisdom of their reforms. Did these men act sensibly and moderately or were they impractical and intolerant, too much influenced by the ideas of such thinkers of the Enlightenment as Jean-Jacques Rousseau? Were they moved by the humanitarian ideal of national regeneration or by personal and class interests? Were their policies mostly blunders or long overdue and necessary reforms?

---

[1] For a short survey of the Assembly's reforms, see Jacques Godechot, *France and the Atlantic Revolution of the Eighteenth Century, 1770–1799,* trans. Herbert H. Rowen (New York: Free Press, 1965), pp. 101–123. For a more detailed treatment of the actions of the Assembly, see Michael P. Fitzsimmons, *The Remaking of France: The National Assembly and the Constitution of 1791* (Cambridge, Eng.: Cambridge University Press, 1994).

A classic attack on the deputies appeared early in the Revolution. Watching from London, Edmund Burke was appalled by the Assembly's destruction of French traditions. Replacing provinces by departments, making the legislature almost omnipotent, abolishing the parlements, issuing new currency, and seizing church lands were for Burke the most extravagant follies. Men are civilized by their religions, traditions, and prejudices; and to deride these or to seek to change them quickly for the sake of abstract ideals is to cause want and theft, anarchy and brutality. The deputies were incompetent and dangerous political neophytes.

Timothy N. Tackett defends the deputies from the charges of Burke, as well as from those of the historians François Furet and Norman Hampson. Tackett argues that most deputies were not neophytes, for they had had experience in various local, regional, and national political and religious bodies before 1789; and that while in office, most were not captured by Enlightenment ideologies bent on reform at any price. Only at times driven by imaginary plots, they generally consulted with constituents and valued negotiation and compromise. Moreover, their reforms were workable and could have been successful if the King had cooperated more with the legislature.

Of the Assembly's many reforms, perhaps none caused more upheaval or had such far-reaching consequences than its attempt to reorganize the Gallican (French Catholic) Church. For this reason, we have included three contrasting views of the Civil Constitution of the Clergy. In his description of the conflict between the revolutionaries and the Church, the Catholic historian André Latreille shows that both sides erred, the Church perhaps less than the State. But he prefers to explain rather than to blame, and his account is quite moderate. It indicates that Church-State relations by mid-twentieth-century France had become much less acrimonious than at any time since 1789. The selection from Jean Jaurès also suggests the atmosphere in which it was written: the beginning of the twentieth century, when Jaurès and others were striving to weaken the political influence of the Catholic Church in France and to separate it from the State. Here one encounters a vehement anticlerical defense of the Assembly's religious policies—the deputies salvaged as much as possible from an inevitable divisive conflict with a powerful, conservative, and outdated institution. They preserved the Revolution while weakening the Church, and they enlarged the people's intellectual freedom while diminishing their reliance on the supernatural. William H. Sewell, Jr., however, denies that the divisive conflict between the revolutionaries and the Church was inevitable. He argues that when the

deputies required a loyalty oath from clergymen, the motivation behind the demand was more ideology than practical politics.

One may ask whether the Assembly had the moral or legal right to
reform the Gallican Church. Did the deputies blunder? Should they
have taken for granted that the Church would acquiesce as it had
earlier when the Assembly abolished manorial dues and clerical
tithes on August 4–11, 1789, when it expropriated Church property
on November 2, 1789, and when it dissolved most monasteries and
convents on February 13, 1790? Should the deputies have negotiated
with Pope Pius VI on the drafting of the Civil Constitution of the
Clergy? Should the deputies have required loyalty oaths from clergymen? On the other hand, was the Pope so dilatory, inflexible, and unaware of French conditions that he himself precipitated the break?
Was the Gallican Church so disunited and unsure of its way that it
stumbled into a schism?

Is it possible to make an impartial and dispassionate historical
judgment on the accomplishments and failures of the National Assembly? Or is this one of those questions where a historian must be
more advocate than social scientist? In addition, was Benjamin
Franklin right to question the concept of inevitability in history when
he remarked that "in this world nothing is certain but death and
taxes"?

I THE DEPUTIES

IMPRACTICAL ZEALOTS

Edmund Burke

Edmund Burke (1729–1797), often styled the founder of modern conservatism, was born in Dublin. His father was a Protestant lawyer; his mother was a Catholic; and the boy was brought up as a Protestant. He trained for the law, but found his calling in English politics, where he became a spokesman for the aristocratic Whig magnates in the House of Commons. Unlike most politicians, Burke espoused a consistent political philosophy: the rule of an enlightened aristocracy against challenges from absolute monarchy and democracy. He was also a man of letters. His impassioned *Reflections on the Revolution in France,* published in November 1790 in the form of a letter to a Frenchman, sold thirty thousand copies in two years and was a very influential contemporary indictment of the Revolution.

You [Frenchmen] might, if you pleased, have profited of our example, and have given to your recovered freedom a correspondent dignity. Your privileges, though discontinued, were not lost to memory. Your [ancient] Constitution, it is true, whilst you were out of possession, suffered waste and dilapidation; but you possessed in some parts the walls, and in all the foundations, of a noble and venerable castle. You might have repaired those walls; you might have built on those old foundations. Your Constitution was suspended before it was perfected; but you had the elements of a Constitution very nearly as good as could be wished. In your old states you possessed that variety of

From Edmund Burke, *Reflections on the Revolution in France, Works* (4th ed.; Boston: Little, Brown, & Co., 1871), III, 276–278, 280, 282–284, 299–301, 331–332, 344–348, 524–525, 560–561.

parts corresponding with the various descriptions of which your community was happily composed; you had all that combination and all that opposition of interests, you had that action and counteraction, which, in the natural and in the political world, from the reciprocal struggle of discordant powers draws out the harmony of the universe. These opposed and conflicting interests, which you considered as so great a blemish in your old and in our present Constitution, interpose a salutary check to all precipitate resolutions. . . .

You had all these advantages in your ancient states; but you chose to act as if you had never been molded into civil society, and had everything to begin anew. You began ill, because you began by despising everything that belonged to you. You set up your trade without a capital. If the last generations of your country appeared without much luster in your eyes, you might have passed them by, and derived your claims from a more early race of ancestors. Under a pious predilection for those ancestors, your imaginations would have realized in them a standard of virtue and wisdom beyond the vulgar practice of the hour; and you would have risen with the example to whose imitation you aspired. Respecting your forefathers, you would have been taught to respect yourselves. You would not have chosen to consider the French as a people of yesterday, as a nation of low-born, servile wretches until the emancipating year of 1789. . . .

Compute your gains; see what is got by those extravagant and presumptuous speculations which have taught your leaders to despise all their predecessors, and all their contemporaries, and even to despise themselves, until the moment in which they became truly despicable. By following those false lights, France has bought undisguised calamities at a higher price than any nation has purchased the most unequivocal blessings. . . .

Laws overturned; tribunals subverted; industry without vigor; commerce expiring; the revenue unpaid, yet the people impoverished; a church pillaged, and a state not relieved; civil and military anarchy made the constitution of the kingdom; everything human and divine sacrificed to the idol of public credit, and national bankruptcy the consequence; and, to crown all, the paper securities of new, precarious, tottering power, the discredited paper securities of impoverished fraud and beggared rapine, held out as a currency for the support of an empire, in lieu of the two great recognized species [gold and silver] that represent the lasting, conventional credit of mankind, which disappeared and hid themselves in the earth from whence they came, when the principle of property, whose creatures and representatives they are, was systematically subverted.

Were all these dreadful things necessary? Were they the inevitable results of the desperate struggle of determined patriots, compelled to wade through blood and tumult to the quiet shore of a tranquil and prosperous liberty? No! nothing like it. The fresh ruins of France, which shock our feelings wherever we can turn our eyes, are not the devastation of civil war: they are the sad, but instructive monuments of rash and ignorant counsel in time of profound peace. They are the display of inconsiderate and presumptuous, because unresisted and irresistible authority. . . .

This unforced choice, this fond election of evil, would appear perfectly unaccountable, if we did not consider the composition of the National Assembly: I do not mean its formal constitution, which, as it now stands, is exceptionable enough, but the materials of which in a great measure it is composed, which is of ten thousand times greater consequence than all the formalities in the world. If we were to know nothing of this assembly but by its title and function, no colors could paint to the imagination anything more venerable. In that light, the mind of an inquirer, subdued by such an awful image as that of the virtue and wisdom of a whole people collected into one focus, would pause and hesitate in condemning things even on the very worst aspect. Instead of blamable, they would appear only mysterious. But no name, no power, no function, no artificial institution whatsoever, can make the men, of whom any system of authority is composed, any other than God, and Nature, and education, and their habits of life have made them. Capacities beyond these the people have not to give. Virtue and wisdom may be the objects of their choice; but their choice confers neither the one nor the other on those upon whom they lay their ordaining hands. They have not the engagement of Nature, they have not the promise of Revelation for any such powers.

After I had read over the list of the persons and descriptions elected into the *Tiers État,* nothing which they afterwards did could appear astonishing. Among them, indeed, I saw some of known rank, some of shining talents; but of any practical experience in the state not one man was to be found. The best were only men of theory. But whatever the distinguished few may have been, it is the substance and mass of the body which constitutes its character, and must finally determine its direction. . . .

It is said that twenty-four millions ought to prevail over two hundred thousand. True; if the constitution of a kingdom be a problem of arithmetic. This sort of discourse does well enough with the lamp-post for its second: to men who *may* reason calmly it is ridiculous. The will of the many, and their interest, must very often differ; and great will be the difference when they make an evil choice. A government of five hundred country attorneys and obscure curates is not good for twenty-four millions of men, though it were chosen by eight-and-forty millions; nor is it the better for being guided by a dozen of persons of quality who have betrayed their trust in order to obtain that power. At present, you seem in everything to have strayed out of the high road of Nature. The property of France does not govern it. Of course property is destroyed, and rational liberty has no existence. All you have got for the present is a paper circulation, and a stock-jobbing constitution: and as to the future, do you seriously think that the territory of France, upon the republican system of eighty-three independent municipalities (to say nothing of the parts that compose them), can ever be governed as one body, or can ever be set in motion, by the impulse of one mind? When the National Assembly has completed its work, it will have accomplished its ruin. These commonwealths will not long bear a state of subjection to the republic of Paris. They will not bear that this one body should monopolize the captivity of the king, and the dominion over the assembly calling itself national. Each will keep its own portion of the spoil of the Church to itself; and it will not suffer either that spoil, or the more just fruits of their industry, or the natural produce of their soil, to be sent to swell the insolence or pamper the luxury of the mechanics of Paris. In this they will see none of the equality, under the pretence of which they have been tempted to throw off their allegiance to their sovereign, as well as the ancient constitution of their country. There can be no capital city in such a constitution as they have lately made. They have forgot, that, when they framed democratic governments, they had virtually dismembered their country. The person whom they persevere in calling king has not power left to him by the hundredth part sufficient to hold together this collection of republics. The republic of Paris will endeavor, indeed, to complete the debauchery of the army, and illegally to perpetuate the Assembly, without resort to its constituents, as the means of continuing its despotism. It will make efforts, by becoming the heart of a boundless paper circulation, to draw everything to itself: but in vain. All this policy in the end will appear as feeble as it is now violent. . . .

It is now sixteen or seventeen years since I saw the queen of France, then the Dauphiness, at Versailles; and surely never lighted on this orb, which she hardly seemed to touch, a more delightful vision. I saw her just above the horizon, decorating and cheering the elevated sphere she just began to move in—glittering like the morning-star, full of life and splendor and joy. Oh! what a revolution!

and what a heart must I have, to contemplate without emotion that elevation and that fall! Little did I dream, when she added titles of veneration to those of enthusiastic, distant, respectful love, that she should ever be obliged to carry the sharp antidote against disgrace concealed in that bosom! Little did I dream that I should have lived to see such disasters fallen upon her in a nation of gallant men, in a nation of men of honor, and of cavaliers! I thought ten thousand swords must have leaped from their scabbards to avenge even a look that threatened her with insult. But the age of chivalry is gone. That of sophisters, economists, and calculators has succeeded; and the glory of Europe is extinguished forever. Never, never more, shall we behold that generous loyalty to rank and sex, that proud submission, that dignified obedience, that subordination of the heart, which kept alive, even in servitude itself, the spirit of an exalted freedom! The unbought grace of life, the cheap defense of nations, the nurse of manly sentiment and heroic enterprise, is gone! It is gone, that sensibility of principle, that chastity of honor, which felt a stain like a wound, which inspired courage whilst it mitigated ferocity, which ennobled whatever it touched, and under which vice itself lost half its evil by losing all its grossness![1] . . .

Thanks to our sullen [English] resistance to innovation, thanks to the cold sluggishness of our national character, we still bear the stamp of our forefathers. We have not (as I conceive) lost the generosity and dignity of thinking of the fourteenth century; nor as yet have we subtilized ourselves into savages. We are not the converts of Rousseau; we are not the disciples of Voltaire; Helvétius has made no progress amongst us. Atheists are not our preachers; madmen are not our lawgivers. We know that *we* have made no discoveries, and we think that no discoveries are to be made, in morality—nor many in the great principles of government, nor in the ideas of liberty, which were understood long before we were born altogether as well as they will be after the grave has heaped its mold upon our presumption, and the silent tomb shall have imposed its law on our pert loquacity. In England we have not yet been completely emboweled of our natural entrails: we still feel within us, and we cherish and cultivate, those inbred sentiments which are the faithful guardians, the active monitors of our duty, the true supporters of all liberal and manly morals. We have not been drawn and trussed, in order that we may be filled, like stuffed birds in a museum, with chaff and rags, and

---

[1][This particular paragraph of Burke's has been called a landmark in the beginning of English literary romanticism.—Eds.]

paltry, blurred shreds of paper about the rights of man. We preserve the whole of our feelings still native and entire, unsophisticated by pedantry and infidelity. We have real hearts of flesh and blood beating in our bosoms. We fear God; we look up with awe to kings, with affection to Parliaments, with duty to magistrates, with reverance to priests, and with respect to nobility. Why? Because, when such ideas are brought before our minds, it is *natural* to be so affected; because all other feelings are false and spurious, and tend to corrupt our minds, to vitiate our primary morals, to render us unfit for rational liberty, and, by teaching us a servile, licentious, and abandoned insolence, to be our low sport for a few holidays, to make us perfectly fit for and justly deserving of slavery through the whole course of our lives.

You see, Sir, that in this enlightened age I am bold enough to confess that we are generally men of untaught feelings: that, instead of casting away all our old prejudices, we cherish them to a very considerable degree; and, to take more shame to ourselves, we cherish them because they are prejudices; and the longer they have lasted, and the more generally they have prevailed, the more we cherish them. We are afraid to put men to live and trade each on his own private stock of reason; because we suspect that the stock in each man is small, and that the individuals would do better to avail themselves of the general bank and capital of nations and of ages. Many of our men of speculation, instead of exploding general prejudices, employ their sagacity to discover the latent wisdom which prevails in them. If they find what they seek (and they seldom fail), they think it more wise to continue the prejudice, with the reason involved, than to cast away the coat of prejudice, and to leave nothing but the naked reason; because prejudice, with its reason, has a motive to give action to that reason, and an affection which will give it permanence. Prejudice is of ready application in the emergency; it previously engages the mind in a steady course of wisdom and virtue, and does not leave the man hesitating in the moment of decision, skeptical, puzzled, and unresolved. Prejudice renders a man's virtue his habit, and not a series of unconnected acts. Through just prejudice, his duty becomes a part of his nature.

Your literary men, and your politicians, and so do the whole clan of the enlightened among us [the English supporters of the French Revolution], essentially differ in these points. They have no respect for the wisdom of others; but they pay it off by a very full measure of confidence in their own. With them it is a sufficient motive to destroy an old scheme of things, because it is an old one. As to the new, they are in no sort of fear with regard to the duration of a building run up in haste; because duration is no object to those who think little or nothing has been done before their time, and who place all their hopes in discovery. They conceive, very systematically, that all things which give perpetuity are mischievous, and therefore they are at inexpiable war with all establishments. They think that government may vary like modes of dress, and with as little ill effect; that there needs no principle of attachment, except a sense of present conveniency, to any constitution of the state. They always speak as if they were of opinion that there is a singular species of compact between them and their magistrates [government officials], which binds the magistrate, but which has nothing reciprocal in it, but that the majesty of the people has a right to dissolve it without any reason but its will. Their attachment to their country itself is only so far as it agrees with some of their fleeting projects: it begins and ends with that scheme of polity which falls in with their momentary opinion.

These doctrines, or rather sentiments, seem prevalent with your new statesmen. . . .

It is besides to be considered, whether an Assembly like yours . . . is fit for promoting the obedience and discipline of an army. It is known that armies have hitherto yielded a very precarious and uncertain obedience to any senate or popular authority: and they will least of all yield it to an Assembly which is to have only a continuance of two years. The officers must totally lose the characteristic disposition of military men, if they see with perfect submission and due admiration the dominion of pleaders—especially when they find that they have a new court to pay to an endless succession of those pleaders, whose military policy, and the genius of whose command (if they should have any), must be as uncertain as their duration is transient. In the weakness of one kind of authority, and in the fluctuation of all, the officers of an army will remain for some time mutinous and full of faction, until some popular general, who understands the art of conciliating the soldiery, and who possesses the true spirit of command, shall draw the eyes of all men upon himself. Armies will obey him on his personal account. There is no other way of securing military obedience in this state of things. But the moment in which that event shall happen, the person who really commands the army is your master—the master (that is little) of your king, the master of your Assembly, the master of your whole republic. . . .

But am I so unreasonable as to see nothing at all that deserves commendation in the indefatigable labors of this Assembly? I do not deny, that, among an infinite number of acts of violence and folly,

some good may have been done. They who destroy everything certainly will remove some grievance. They who make everything new
have a chance that they may establish something beneficial. To give
them credit for what they have done in virtue of the authority they
have usurped, or to excuse them in the crimes by which that authority has been acquired, it must appear that the same things could
not have been accomplished without producing such a revolution.
Most assuredly they might; because almost every one of the regulations made by them, which is not very equivocal, was either in the
cession of the king, voluntarily made at the meeting of the Estates-
General, or in the concurrent instructions to the orders. Some usages
have been abolished on just grounds; but they were such, that, if
they had stood as they were to all eternity, they would little detract
from the happiness and prosperity of any state. The improvements
of the National Assembly are superficial, their errors fundamental.

MOST DEPUTIES PRACTICAL, TOLERANT, AND EXPERIENCED POLITICIANS

Timothy N. Tackett

Timothy N. Tackett (1945–) received his B.A. from Pomona College and his Ph.D. from Stanford University. He has taught at several American and foreign universities and is currently professor of history at the University of California, Irvine. He has published three well-researched and informative monographs on eighteenth-century French history: *Priest and Parish in Eighteenth-Century France: A Social and Political Study of the Curés in a Diocese of Dauphiné, 1750–1791* (1977); *Religion, Revolution, and Regional Culture in Eighteenth-Century France: The Ecclesiastical Oath of 1791* (1986); and *Becoming a Revolutionary: The Deputies of the French National Assembly and the Emergence of a Revolutionary Culture (1789–1790)* (1996). He is also the editor with Michel Vovelle and Claude Langlois of the *Atlas de la Révolution française. Vol. 9. Religion* (1996).

●●●●●●

Anyone who has examined the biographies of the deputies to the Estates General of 1789 is invariably impressed by the impact of the Terror on their subsequent careers. Without a doubt the overwhelming majority of the members of that Assembly found their lives profoundly disturbed between 1792 and 1794. Indeed, no less than ninety-two met early deaths during this period: most through execution, others through murder, death in battle, death in prison, or suicide. The ninety-two in question included nearly one in twenty of all deputies from the Third Estate, one in fourteen from the Clergy, and

Reprinted from Timothy N. Tackett , "The Constituent Assembly and the Terror," in *The French Revolution and the Creation of Modern Political Culture*, Vol. 4, *The Terror*, ed. Keith Michael Baker (Oxford: Pergamon, 1994), pp. 39–54, with permission from Elsevier Science.

one in eight from the Nobility.[1] It also included a substantial proportion of the Constituent Assembly's most prominent speakers and leaders: Barnave, Bailly, Thouret, the duc de La Rochefoucauld, Rabaut-Saint-Etienne, Pétion, Robespierre, Fréteau de Saint-Just, Duval d'Eprémesnil, Le Chapelier, the comte de Clermont-Tonnerre. In considering the sad fate of individuals such as these, one cannot but wonder whether the Revolution they had begun somehow contained the seeds of their own destruction; whether violence and Terror were inherent in their actions and positions in 1789.

In fact, an affirmative response to this question stands as a common thread through much of French Revolutionary historiography, from Edmund Burke to Hippolyte Taine, Frédéric Braesch, and more recently, François Furet, Norman Hampson, and Keith Baker. To be sure, none of the recent proponents of this position would link the first National Assembly directly to the concept of state-sponsored violence. That the overwhelming majority of the deputies of 1789 abhorred the use of violence per se is rarely put into question.[2] But to what extent was there a more fundamental link between Constituents and Terrorists in their underlying political assumptions, in their ideology, in their language? To what extent, in other words, did they share a common political culture? In their general interpretations, both François Furet and Norman Hampson would argue that there was indeed such a link. Deprived of any direct experience in the exercise of power, the leaders of the Constituent Assembly had, as Hampson would phrase it, "nothing to fall back on but first principles": the abstract political theories of the philosophes, and primarily those of Rousseau—to which most of the Revolutionaries were said to have been enthusiastic con-

---

[1]Thirty-two (4.8%) of the 663 members of the Third Estate; 23 (7%) of 330 members of the Clergy; and 37 (11.5%) of the 322 members of the Nobility. In all, there were 62 executions, 18 murders (including 11 during the September Massacres), 4 killed in battle (in Federalist or counter-revolutionary actions), 5 deaths in prison, and 3 suicides (in prison or under threat of execution). Statistics based on Edna Hindie Lemay, ed., *Dictionnaire des Constituants, 1789–1791*, 2 vols. (Paris, 1991), and on a variety of other sources.

[2]Whatever their flexibility in condoning the Parisian uprisings of mid-July [1789] in the name of the salvation of the National Assembly, all but a handful of the deputies expressed shock and consternation in their letters and diaries when confronted with the 22 July lynchings of Foulon and Bertier in Paris and with the popular violence of the October Days. For each of these incidents we have found only about ten deputies—virtually all of them future Jacobins—prepared to justify the actions of the crowds. Cf. Barry M. Shapiro, *Revolutionary Justice in Paris, 1789–90* (Cambridge, 1993), esp. pp. 221–26, who emphasizes the generally mild and tolerant attitudes toward opponents of the Revolution taken by the Committees on Research in the National Assembly and the municipality of Paris.

verts. It was through Rousseau that they came widely to accept the concept of a unitary general will, by which political opposition and disagreement were viewed as intrinsically pernicious and "counter-revolutionary," undermining the public good through the workings of egotistical private motives. Such a conception led directly to a rejection of both political pluralism and the idea of a loyal opposition. It also led naturally to a veritable obsession with plots—for how else could one explain popular opposition to the general will?—plots which were, in the view of Norman Hampson and François Furet, usually more imaginary than real.[3]

The present paper can make no pretense of resolving all these issues. It proposes only to offer certain reflections, based on recent empirical research, pertaining to the lives and careers of the Constituent deputies during the first year of the Revolution. In its documentation, it will rely primarily on two types of materials: first, a new and fairly extensive collective biography of the deputies to the Estates General and the Constituent Assembly[4]; and, second, the testimonies of the Constituent deputies themselves, preserved in diaries and series of letters written during the first year of the Assembly's existence, and of which over 120 sets have been identified to date.[5] In particular, it will examine the three major contentions on which the interpretations of Hampson and Furet are based: first, that the ideas of the philosophes, and particularly of Rousseau, were dominant elements in the political culture of the deputies of 1789; second, that the deputies in question were inexperienced in politics; and third, that they were preoccupied with conspiracies to a degree out of all proportion to reality.

The problem of the influence of the Enlightenment on the deputies

---

[3]Norman Hampson, *Prelude to Terror: The Constituent Assembly and the Failure of Consensus* (Oxford, 1988), pp. 1–5, 42, 61–62; François Furet, *Interpreting the French Revolution,* trans. Elborg Forster (Cambridge, 1981), pp. 55, 62–63. For a rather different linkage of the Constituent and the Terror, see the analysis of Keith Michael Baker, *Inventing the French Revolution* (Cambridge, 1990), esp. the conclusion to the final chapter.

[4]A substantial data base has been constituted on the backgrounds and careers of the 1,315 individuals who sat at any time in the Constituent Assembly. This data base was subsequently complemented by information drawn from Lemay, ed., *Dictionnaire des Constituants.* May I express my appreciation to Edna Lemay for allowing me to consult her work while it was still in proofs.

[5]A full bibliography of these sources will be published subsequently. The letters were written to a wide variety of correspondents. Some were directed to local municipal leaders and were intended to be read in public; others were written privately for friends and family. Obviously, the intended audience must be taken into account when interpreting the letters.

of 1789 is particularly daunting and difficult to resolve. It is especially complex in that the Enlightenment itself is so multifaceted. Even in those instances where we know the pre-revolutionary libraries of individual deputies or their participation in literary or philosophical societies, it is often all but impossible to determine the real impact of such experiences: to ascertain which, if any, of the various strands of the Enlightenment had the most profound effect on the deputies; and to what extent individuals had actually integrated such ideas into their working assumptions about the world in which they lived.[6]

It is clear that only a handful of the deputies might be designated "philosophes" in the eighteenth-century sense of the word: men of letters, closely and self-consciously linked to one or another strand of the Enlightenment, and consecrating all or a substantial portion of their time to writing. Among these, one would probably need to include the comte de Mirabeau, Volney, Bergasse, Démeunier, Bailly, Dupont de Nemours, the chevalier de Boufflers, Delandine, the younger Garat, and perhaps—even though he had never published before 1788—the abbé Sieyès. In fact, a number of others—Condorcet, Marmontel, Suard, for example—had participated in the electoral process in Paris or elsewhere but had failed to win election. Bailly, who felt that his own election in Paris had been extremely unusual, took note of "the general disfavor in the [electoral] assembly for men of letters and academicians." He attributed this attitude to the dominant presence of merchants and lawyers in the assemblies—the first group generally unfamiliar with the intellectuals, the second traditionally their rivals.[7]

In order to assess the intellectual positions and range of interests of a somewhat broader sample of the deputies, it is useful to focus on those who had written for publication prior to the revolutionary era. In all, this group includes some 116 deputies publishing before 1787: slightly under one-fourth from the Clergy, slightly over one-fourth from the Nobility, and somewhat over fifty percent from the Third Estate—roughly the breakdown one might expect, given the composition of the Assembly.[8] In fact, the works produced by these deputies

---

[6] On the multiple discourses of the Enlightenment, see especially Baker, *Inventing the French Revolution,* chaps. 1 and 5.

[7] Jean-Sylvain Bailly, *Mémoires,* 3 vols. (Paris, 1821–22), 1:27, 51. See also, Keith Michael Baker, *Condorcet: From Natural Philosophy to Social Mathematics* (Chicago, 1975), pp. 266–67.

[8] The 116 include all those deputies whose writings are preserved in the Bibliothèque Nationale, or who are otherwise known—usually through individual biographies—to have written for publication prior to 1787. A detailed bibliography and a fuller analysis of individual examples will be given in a subsequent publication. Of the 116, 23

spread across the entire range of literary and scholarly genres. While the largest single category was in the arts and letters, respectable numbers of publications were also to be found on economics, law, science, politics and society, history and geography, and religion and theology.[9] Those writings most closely linked to the Enlightenment represent virtually all of the diverse tendencies within that tradition. There were disciples of Rousseau and disciples of Voltaire. There were deputy-physiocrats and deputy-scientists; there were former associates of enlightened bureaucrats and substantial contingents from both the Catholic Enlightenment and what might be termed the "mystical Enlightenment" of Mesmerism and Free Masonry. But there were a great many more who partook of several strands at once, or of none in particular. And there was a small but influential number, primarily but not exclusively among the Clergy and the Nobility, whose writings were quite in contradiction with, even explicitly hostile to, the spirit or the major tenets of the Enlightenment—particularly in their defense of religion and of a hierarchical and authoritarian view of society.

The great majority of such publications, however, were essentially of a literary or scholarly nature. While many revealed a familiarity with elements of Enlightenment thought and vocabulary, such elements were usually only peripheral or tangential to the authors' principal concerns. Few, if any, conveyed the fire and anger, the corrosive wit and sarcasm, the social criticism commonly associated with the more famous philosophes. Their plays and novels and their copious poetry were infused with a mild and pleasing rococo esthetic that might have been written in almost any decade of the eighteenth century. A certain number, in their prose eulogies in praise of great men, placed a premium on "Enlightened" rule and a concern for public welfare, but the general emphasis was on reform engineered from above. Particularly prominent within the Third Estate was that ample group of deputies for whom Enlightenment seemed to signify—if it

---

(20%) sat in the Clergy, 31 (27%) in the Nobility, and 62 (53%) in the Third Estate. These were approximately the same proportions as those found among the authors inventoried for the entire nation in the 1784 edition of *La France littéraire.* See Robert Darnton, "The Facts of Literary Life in Eighteenth-Century France," in Keith Michael Baker, ed., *The French Revolution and the Creation of Modern Political Culture,* vol. 1, *The Political Culture of the Old Regime* (Oxford, 1987), pp. 261–91.

[9]Since some deputies wrote in more than one category, the following statistics consider the total number of subjects (153) treated by the corps of deputy-authors. Thus, 14 (9%) were in theology-religion; 42 (27%) in *belles lettres;* 24 (16%) in history; 17 (11%) on economics; 20 (13%) on law; 22 (14%) on political or social questions; and 14 (9%) on science, mathematics or "pseudoscience."

signified anything at all—research, scholarly inquiry, and practical problem solving: in law, in history, in science, or in economic and social analysis. Indeed, in no single area did the deputies have a more distinguished publishing record than in law and legal theory. Camus, Merlin de Douai, Lanjuinais, Bouche, Target, Durand de Maillane, and Mourot were all nationally known within the legal community and might well be ranked among the most eminent scholars in the National Assembly. Though somewhat lower in preeminence, Creuzé-Latouche, Bonnemant, Turckheim, Baudouin de Maisonblanche, Moreau de Saint-Méry, Emmery, Gaultier de Biauzat, Hell, Mathieau de Rondevelle, and Tuault de La Bouvrie had all won substantial local or regional reputations. The publication record of these deputy specialists in the law is all the more significant in that they would rank among the most active and influential speakers and committee workers in the entire National Assembly—far more so, in most cases, than the deputy-philosophes.[10]

If we focus more specifically on the writings of the future deputies during the "pre-revolutionary" period, between 1788 and May of 1789, we discover much the same diversity of perspectives and ambiguity of vision. That a "Revolution of the mind" had already occurred for a few of the future deputies before the meeting of the Estates General can scarcely be doubted. This was almost certainly the case for several of the Breton deputies, whose attitudes had been formed through months of intense provincial struggle with a highly organized and intransigent local nobility and upper clergy. The same could surely be said of that former Breton resident and sometime philosophe, the abbé Sieyès, whose writings now strike us as an exceptionally articulate manifesto for a new concept of sovereignty and a new prescription for social relations—formulations in which the thought of Rousseau clearly played an important role. In this sense,

---

[10] For a rough measure of the participation of the deputies in debates, I have counted the number of speeches given by each individual on the floor of the Assembly over the entire course of the Constituent, as indicated in *AP,* 33—containing the index to vols. 8–32 (the Constituent Assembly). Though the *Archives parlementaires* are undoubtedly incomplete, they constitute the best single indication of debates in the Assembly. Of those we have dubbed "philosophes" only Mirabeau (439 speeches), Démeunier (435 speeches), and Dupont (215 speeches) played major roles in the Constituent—compared to an average of about 17 speeches per deputy in the overall Assembly. Sieyès, Volney, Bergasse, Boufflers, Delandine, and Garat averaged only 22 speeches each, and most of these were made before October 1789, after which they rarely or never spoke. Bailly rarely attended after he became mayor of Paris in July 1789. By contrast, the first group of lawyers mentioned averaged 254 speeches each. The second group averaged 61 speeches.

as Keith Baker has noted, "the decisive conceptual break with the past that lay at the heart of the revolutionary political culture had already occurred before the actual meeting of the Estates General."[11]

But to what extent was such a unified vision, strongly marked by the Enlightenment, shared by the majority of the future deputies? An examination of a sample of pamphlets published by future Third Estate deputies in the months before the Estates General suggests that this was anything but the case.[12] In their attitudes toward the king and toward the nobility, in their positions on the role of the masses and on the question of sovereignty, they displayed an enormous spread of frequently contradictory opinions, ranging from the liberal or radical to the generally conservative. And as they differed in their individual demands, so too in the fundamental rationales mobilized to sustain those demands, in their grounds for judgment, in their justifications for choices, they often found themselves substantially at variance. Diverse lines of logic and epistemology were commonly mixed pell-mell not only among the different writers, but within the corpus of individual future deputies. Though a few seemed to believe that France could be remade from the ground up on the basis of reason, most assumed that all transformations must be linked to the history and past practices of the kingdom, and several cautioned specifically against any "esprit de système" [system building] that would cut France off from its traditions. The great majority subscribed to a multidimensional approach that might include the "abstract" rational assessments of the philosophers, but that relied even more heavily on history, experience, and custom. In this curious and often inconsistent composite of ideas and value systems, in this general lack of a unified thread of argument, of a predictable "discourse," the future deputies seemed to be scrambling to make sense of their transforming world, to improvise new constructs appropriate for the extraordinary series of events which they were forced to confront. Indeed, one is tempted to argue that the ideological mix, the conceptual frameworks were present among the men of '89 for any number of political options, for any number of revolutions—or counter-revolutions or reform movements.

---

[11] *Political Culture of the Old Regime,* p. xxi. Baker is here commenting on the conclusions of Lynn Hunt.

[12] A detailed bibliography and a much fuller analysis of examples will be given in a subsequent publication. The sample represents the works of 30 Third-Estate deputies and has been constituted primarily of those publications easily accessible in the Bibliothèque Nationale. Cf. also Harriet Applewhite, "Political Legitimacy in Revolutionary France, 1788–1791," *Journal of Interdisciplinary History* 9 (1978): 245–73.

In all likelihood many of the deputies were familiar with the "conceptual breakthroughs" of Rousseau and Sieyès and the other great social and political critics of the Enlightenment—at least in second- or third-hand versions. But clearly there is a great difference between knowledge of and contact with ideas, on the one hand, and the reception and interiorization of those ideas, on the other; between familiarity with programs for political change, and the belief that such "abstract" and "utopian" plans were feasible in the real world. The case of one deputy, Michel-René Maupetit, is suggestive in this regard. In mid-June, Maupetit announced to a friend that he had read Sieyès's famous tract *What Is the Third Estate?* the previous February and that at present he found it a veritable guidebook to the events unrolling in Versailles: "Just read this work," he wrote, "and you will see the plan of our previous conduct and the road which we are about to take." And nevertheless, only a few weeks earlier the same deputy had strongly disapproved of the proposals of the Breton Club which so clearly embodied Sieyès's ideas. And he had seen no difficulty whatsoever in accepting a plan for the Estates General based on the permanent existence of separate orders. Clearly it was only in June 1789 that Maupetit came truly to "understand" and discover the significance of Sieyès's writings.[13]

Much the same conclusions can be drawn from a reading of the deputies' letters and diaries written during the first weeks after May 1789. Though it would be impossible in the present context to pursue a systematic content analysis of the language employed, it seems clear that the use of Enlightenment *mots clefs* [key words] was generally quite unusual. Indeed, a surprising number of deputies—including even some patriots on the Left—revealed themselves to be positively hostile to certain Enlightenment concepts. During the great debates in August 1789 on the Declaration of Rights, many of the deputies made derogatory comments on the "philosophical" or "metaphysical" nature of certain arguments, arguments which were not only difficult to understand, but a waste of precious time and in danger of being misunderstood by the population in general. The generally liberal comte de Lablache, for example, made such remarks and was harshly critical of abbé Sieyès for having "drawn almost entirely on the *Social Contract.*"[14] Particularly during the early months

---

[13] Michel-René Maupetit, "Lettres de Maupetit (1789–91)," in E. Quéruau-Lamérie, ed., *Bulletin de la Commission historique et archéologique de la Mayenne*, 2nd ser., 18 (1902): 157.

[14] Alexandre-Joseph de Lablache to marquis de Viennois: Archives of the Château d'Avauges, reproduced in AD Isère, 1 Mi 461ᴬ (letter of 29 July 1789). See also, e.g.,

of the Revolution, many deputies, in their diary entries and letters home, referred far more often to history and to God than to reason or the general will or Rousseau and Voltaire.[15] In any case, a strong argument could be made that the specific ideological choices that eventually emerged dominant among the patriots developed after the fact, as a function of specific political contingencies and sociopolitical interactions within the Assembly and between the Assembly and the population as a whole.

But it is also clear that the men of 1789, confronting the tasks of regenerating the nation, could count on much more than ideas and "first principles," that many of them, in fact, had significant exposure to politics prior to the Revolution. In most cases, to be sure, the exposure in question came from municipal or corporate affiliations. Rare were the Constituents without experience in the meetings of self-governing corporate bodies, whether guilds, academies and lodges, professional associations, chambers of commerce, or corps of judges, lawyers or university professors.[16] Perhaps more important, at least one in five of the Third Estate deputies are known to have held functions in the Old Regime municipal governments. No less than sixty-two were serving or had previously served as mayors

---

Laurent de Visme, ms. "Journal des Etats généraux": BN, Nouv. acq. fr. 12938 (entry of 9 July 1789); Claude-Jean-Baptiste de Garron de La Bévière to his wife: AD Ain, 1 Mi 1 (letter of 12 July); Claude-Pierre Maillot to an unnamed municipal official of Toul: AC Toul, JJ 7 (letter of 29 July); Jean-Bernard Grellet de Beauregard, "Lettres de M. Grellet de Beauregard," ed. Abbé Dardy, *Mémoires de la Société des sciences naturelles et archéologiques de la Creuse,* 2e sér., 7 (1899): 71–72 (letter of 3 July 1789); Nicolas-Théodore-Antoine-Adolphe de Lasalle, "Les archives municipales de Sarrelouis," ed. René Herly, *Bulletin de la Société des amis du pays de la Sarre* 4 (1927): 214–15 (letter of 1 August 1789); Maupetit, "Lettres," *Bulletin de la Commission historique et archéologique de la Mayenne* 19 (1903): 209 (letter of 29 July 1789).

[15] Among 46 Third-Estate deputy witnesses, whose correspondence during the first year of the Revolution has been read with care in this regard, 31 (67%) made at least one reference to God or to Divine Providence, and 15 (33%) made frequent references throughout their letters to the Deity and to their personal belief in God. See, for example, La Salle, 244; Jean-François Campmas to his brother, vicaire in Carmaux: BM Albi, Ms. 177 (entry of 12 July 1789); Guillaume Gontier de Biran to the municipality of Bergerac: AC Bergerac, Fonds Faugère, carton 1 (letter of 9 October 1789); Jean-François-Marie Goupilleau to his cousin, sénéchal in Rochefervière: BM Nantes, Collection Dugast-Matifeux, no. 98 (letter of 11 January 1790).

[16] André Castaldo, *Les méthodes de travail de la Constituante* (Paris, 1989), pp. 53, 69–70. See also, Baker, *Inventing the French Revolution,* pp. 20–23; and David Bien, "Offices, Corps, and a System of State Credit: The Uses of Privilege under the Ancien Régime," in Baker, *Political Culture,* pp. 89–114.

of their communities and an additional seventy had been elected to other municipal positions.[17] Moreover, since virtually all the commoner deputies were "notables" in their local communities, even those not formally linked to municipal administrations often found themselves swept up in the lively town and village politics which persisted throughout the eighteenth century—and which were notably invigorated by royal edicts after 1787.[18] Thus, at the local level, the great majority of the commoner deputies—and many of the nobles and clergy as well—were probably familiar with the forms and procedures of political action and collective political processes.

But even at the national and regional levels a significant number had held judicial, administrative, or ecclesiastical positions which gave them experience in government and politics. This was certainly the case of the contingent of twenty-three robe nobles, members of the sovereign courts, many of whom were veterans of decades of political wrangling and maneuvering in disputes with the monarchy. It was also the case of the fifty-odd episcopal deputies, most of whom had served in the General Assembly of the Clergy. But even among the Third Estate delegates, a small but highly influential group had held positions entailing substantial political experience and access to the highest levels of government and lines of power: Dupont de Nemours, Lebrun, Anson, D'Ailly, Malouet, Le Couteulx de Canteleu, and to some extent Target and Treilhard. Such experience was particularly significant in that all of the latter individuals would play leadership roles in the development of policy under the Constituent.[19]

Yet above and beyond the political initiation of the future deputies through their professional activities and their involvement in civic affairs under the Old Regime, a great many were marked by the veritable political mobilization which swept over France in the years be-

---

[17] Figures based primarily on the manuscript "biobibliographical" card file constituted by a team of researchers led by Georges Lefebvre and presently held, uncatalogued, in the *salle des imprimés* of the Bibliothèque Nationale; complemented by the *Dictionnaire des Constituants.* We have found a total of 70 mayors or ex-mayors among the deputies, 62 from the Third (89%) of the total) and 8 from the Nobility. Another 70 commoners and 1 noble are known to have held other municipal functions. Such figures are invariably incomplete.

[18] On the lively politics in the town of Vannes—in which commoners were particularly active—see T.G.A. Le Goff, *Vannes and Its Region: A Study of Town and Country in Eighteenth-Century France* (Oxford, 1981), chap. 4.

[19] The robe nobles in question gave an average of 72 speeches each during the Constituent Assembly—compared to the overall average of 17 per deputy. The Third-Estate deputies mentioned gave an average of 152 speeches.

fore the Revolution.[20] Among that older generation already holding positions of power in 1770, several had taken aggressive roles in opposition to Maupeou's judicial reforms [to tame the parlements in 1771]. Notable within this group were nine of the most influential future deputies from Paris: the lawyers Target, Treilhard, Tronchet, Hutteau, Camus, and Martineau; the duc de La Rochefoucauld; and the *parlementaires* Fréteau de Saint-Just and Duval d'Eprémesnil.[21] In the period after 1786, well over two hundred future Constituents took part in various of the pre-revolutionary regional assemblies and estates. Of these, no less than fifty sat on the powerful *commissions intermédiaires,* and twenty-three served as *syndics,* the principal regional executive officials in the new system.[22] The vast majority of the future commoner and curé deputies probably participated in the municipal assemblies of 1787 and 1788,[23] and many from all three Estates took part in the ad hoc provincial and municipal political organizing of the fall and winter of 1788–89. As a result, a substantial number were sent to Paris during this period to represent local demands and grievances to the king and his ministers. In this way many future deputies would become acquainted with one another and set up informal correspondence networks before the Revolution.[24] Thus, well before the electoral assemblies of the spring, numerous individuals

---

[20] This mobilization and its impact on the revolutionary generation remains to be studied. The analysis here is based largely on a reading of a wide variety of secondary materials.

[21] Jean Egret, *La pré-Révolution française,* 1787–1788 (Paris, 1962), p. 214; the previously mentioned fichier organized by Georges Lefebvre; Lemay, *Dictionnaire des Constituants;* and Paul-Louis Target, *Un avocat du XVIIIe siècle* (Paris, 1893), p. 15. Of the Parisians listed, all but Hutteau were important leaders in committees and in debate on the floor of the National Assembly, averaging 261 speeches each. Similar actions by future deputies outside Paris are presently much more difficult to document.

[22] From a wide variety of biographic sources, especially the Lefebvre fichier and Lemay, *Dictionnaire des Constituants.* The total given is almost certainly incomplete. See also Pierre Renouvin, *Les assemblées provinciales de 1787* (Paris, 1921), passim; and Egret, *La pré-Révolution,* p. 111. Of the future deputies participating in the regional assemblies, at least 31 were on *commissions intermédiaires* of the provincial assemblies, 19 on those of the *élection* assemblies. A total of 12 were syndics at the provincial level, 11 at the *élection* level.

[23] All curés and all inhabitants paying over ten livres in taxes had the right to participate in the new municipal elections created by the minister Calonne—thus including almost all future Third Estate deputies.

[24] Note, for example, the experience of Boissy d'Anglas during his trip to Paris as delegate of the region of Vivarais. He encountered so many compatriots from his province of Languedoc that he set up a Club du Languedoc which met twice a week: François-Antoine Boissy d'Anglas, "La Révolution vue de Paris et d'Annonay," *La revue universelle* 139 (1988): 50 (letter of 12 January 1789).

had already established reputations as regional political leaders. Altogether, perhaps half of all future deputies, and two-thirds of the Third Estate deputies, found themselves involved in one or another of these pre-revolutionary roles.[25] Such activities would have given them valuable practice in the process and techniques of collective meetings, factional negotiations, constituent relations, petitions, bargaining with ministers and royal officials, and, to some extent, in the electoral process itself.

But what real impact did such experiences have on the actual operations of the Constituent? In fact, there can be no doubt that certain elements of the Assembly, motivated by ideological imperatives and convinced of the truth and righteousness of their positions, would find negotiation and compromise unpalatable or unacceptable. Many deputies complained bitterly in Versailles of the "intolerance" and "spirit of domination" of certain individuals linked to the Breton club. "Our Breton deputies," wrote the Alsatians Schwendt and Turckheim, "good citizens, but still bitter, . . . want to exert a kind of domination over the opinions of everyone. They are unjustly suspicions of all those who prefer a conciliatory approach." "You cannot imagine the vehemence and passion of the inhabitants of this province," added Maupetit. "Whoever rejects their ideas is weak and degraded and an advocate of slavery."[26] Certain members of the Breton group and the early Jacobin Club assumed an elitist attitude toward the electorate as a whole, viewing themselves as the necessary tutors for the instruction of public opinion. With the undoubting conviction that they alone understood the general will, they set out to cultivate and, if necessary, incite and engender popular support for that general will; to create a market, as it were, for the Revolution as they conceived it. "Our enemies have been forced to yield," wrote

---

[25] Generalization based on biographic information (from a wide variety of sources) for the "sample" of the 120 principal "witnesses" for whom diaries and letters are preserved. Within this sample, 6 of 21 clerical deputies (29%), 13 of 25 noble deputies (52%), and 52 of 74 Third Estate deputies (70%) were found to have been involved in municipal governments or provincial estates or assemblies, or to have written pamphlets between 1787 and 1789.

[26] Etienne-François Schwendt and Jean de Turckheim, in Rodolphe Reuss, ed., *L'Alsace pendant le Révolution française,* 2 vols. (Paris, 1880–94), 1:108 (letter of 17 June 1789); Maupetit, "Lettres," *Bulletin de la Commission historique et archéologique de la Mayenne* 18 (1902): 151 (letter of 30 May 1789). See also Jean-Baptiste Poncet-Delpech, *La première année de la Révolution vue par un témoin 1789–90* ed. Daniel Ligou (Paris, 1961), pp. 21–22 (letter of 9 May); Pierre-François-Balthazar Bouche to municipality of Forcalquier: AC Forcalquier, Series D, "Correspondance 1789" (letter of 31 May 1789); and Pierre-Paul Nairac, ms. "Journal": AD Eure, 5 F 63 (letter of 19 May 1789).

Barnave in mid-July in an oft-cited letter, but "only the force of the general will can defeat them. . . . We must not lose a minute in ensuring that correct ideas are circulated throughout the provinces." "It is only by establishing this kind of correspondence in every region of the country," concurred Claude-Pierre Maillot, "that a civic spirit can be formed . . . and that the Third can be supported through the strength of the general will."[27]

But the testimonies of the letters and diaries would also suggest that the number of deputies strongly driven by ideology was relatively small. Throughout most of the Assembly, the great majority was ready and able to compromise and eager to negotiate solutions for their differences. For the most part they seemed to develop their opinions not on the basis of abstract thought but on pragmatic common sense and the expressed opinions of their constituents. The recent study by André Castaldo on *Les méthodes de travail de la Constituante* demonstrates the real success of the Assembly in developing practical methods for problem solving and the resolution of conflicting opinions.[28] Nor should we underestimate the growing professionalization of the legislative process. Committees manned primarily by individuals with appropriate experience and expertise rapidly replaced the "democratically" (i.e., randomly) chosen *bureaux* of the early weeks of the Assembly. Already, by the beginning of 1790, the committee system had come increasingly to dominate the work of the Constituent.[29] Throughout this process, the deputy men of law and legal theorists—far more than the deputy philosophes—continued to exercise a major influence.

Moreover, the great majority of the Constituents—even among the early Jacobins—carefully cultivated an image of service and responsibility to their constituencies, actively seeking the opinions of their

---

[27] Quotation from Barnave cited in Jean Egret, *La révolution des notables: Mounier et les monarchiens* (Paris, 1950), p. 91; and in Georges Michon, *Essai sur l'histoire du parti Feuillant: Adrien Duport* (Paris, 1924), p. 57. Also, Maillot, AC Toul, JJ 7 (letter of 3 June 1789).

[28] Cited above, note 16.

[29] I have analyzed the committee assignments based on *AP,* 32:545–70. Thus, for example, seventeen medical doctors sat on the Comité de Salubrité; Herwyn and the vicomte de Hertaut de Lamerville—both noted students and practitioners of experimental agriculture—sat on the agricultural committee; Gabriel de Cussy and Louis Naurissart, directors of the royal mints in Caen and Limoges, respectively, played major roles in committees dealing with coinage and minting. See also Norman Hampson, "The *Comité de la marine* of the Constituent Assembly," *The Historical Journal* 2 (1959): 132; Bertrand Barère, *Mémoires,* ed. Hippolyte Carnot, 4 vols. (Paris, 1842–44), 1:280–81; and the Lefebvre fichier.

home districts as part of their decision-making process. Their responsibility to the electors who sent them to Versailles is a common theme in almost all of the deputies' correspondence, both in letters written to be read in public and private letters addressed to family and friends. "I will dedicate my life to demonstrating that I am worthy of the confidence and respect of my fellow citizens" (Alquier, a radical from La Rochelle); "Never doubt the zeal with which we pursue your interests; we will do everything necessary to ensure that we obtain them" (the moderates Schwendt and Turckheim from Strasbourg); "I beg you to support me with your advice and assist me with your wisdom in attaining the success which I so ardently seek" (the Breton, Delaville Le Roulx).[30] Indeed, several deputies were quite insistent that the opinions of their constituencies would take precedence over their own views. "I beseech you," wrote Gaultier de Biauzat, "to let me know your ideas on the matter, so that my own opinions may be either supported or modified." Whenever it is a question of your interests," observed Maillot, "I will always ignore or put aside my own."[31] Whatever the theories of Sieyès and Talleyrand, whatever the deputies' earlier grand declarations about the independence of their conscience and the end of imperative mandates, most of the commoners—and a great many of the noble and clerical delegates as well—had a clear conception of the need for close deputy-constituents relations as part and parcel of the new phenomenon of representative democracy.

As for the obsession with conspiracies, a rapid perusal of the deputies' diaries and letters, written during the first year of the As-

---

[30] H. Perrin de Boussac, *Un témoin de la Révolution et de l'Empire: Charles-Jean-Marie Alquier* (Paris, 1983), p. 35; Reuss, *L'Alsace pendant le Révolution,* 2:117; Joseph Delaville Le Roulx to municipality of Lorient: AC Lorient, BB 12 (letter of 15 May 1789). See also, André-Marie Merle to the municipality of Mâcon: AC Mâcon, D(2) 13, carton 21 bis (letter of 21 October 1789); Guillaume Bonnemant to municipality of Arles: AC Arles, AA 23 (letter of 8 March 1790); Jean-Marie Baudouin de Maisonblanche, "Correspondance des députés des Côtes-du-Nord à l'Assemblée constituante," in D. Tempier, ed., *Bulletin et mémoires de la Société d'émulation des Côte-du-Nord 27* (1889): 28, 32 (letters of 16 and 24 October 1790); and Claude Gantheret to Pierre Leflaive, his brother-in-law: private collection of Françoise Misserey (letter of 26 June 1789): "I wish only to be the organ by which you manifest your will."

[31] Jean-François Gaultier de Biauzat, *Gaultier de Biauzat, député du Tiers état aux Etats généraux de 1789. Sa vie et sa correspondance,* ed. Francisque Mège, 2 vols. (Clermont-Ferrand, 1890), 2:200, 203 (letters of 24 and 25 July 1789); Maillot, AC Toul, JJ 7 (entry of 25 September 1789). See also, Reuss, *L'Alsace pendant la Révolution française,* 1:234–35; and Lepoutre (letter of 27 September 1789).

sembly, would seem to confirm the contention of Norman Hampson and François Furet. Such testimonies reveal a widespread and tenacious assumption that plots were afoot almost everywhere. Increasingly, in late 1789 and early 1790, all public disturbances, all recalcitrance to authority, virtually all occurrences with potentially negative consequences for the Revolution were construed by a great many representatives as part of a generalized conspiracy. Visiting Paris in January 1790, Arthur Young was struck by the omnipresence among his deputy friends of rumors of impending invasions, designs on the lives of the deputies, or threats to kidnap the king. All the riots and lynchings in Paris had been fomented, so it was argued, by secret opponents seeking to create anarchy (Pierre-François Bouche); the Parlement of Metz's challenge to the Assembly's authority in November 1789 was but "a single element in the general effort to bring the destruction of the Revolution" (Barnave); the rise in grain prices in the spring of 1790 "was too sudden, too unexpected, too systematic throughout the kingdom not to have been the fruit of a secret maneuver" (Fricaud). There were theories that the collapse of the spectators' balcony in the Assembly's temporary meeting hall on 26 October was part of a hidden plan to assassinate the deputies. Even the generally cynical and levelheaded Duquesnoy clearly felt the Assembly to be beleaguered and under siege: "attacked from all directions by the opposition, threatened from every side by insurrections and factions, the final efforts of the aristocracy."[32]

But if there can be no denying this peculiar state of mind shared by a great many deputies, how is that state of mind to be explained and what is its significance for later revolutionary history? To what extent was it the consequence of an ideological propensity on the part of the patriot deputies, a propensity directly related to a Rousseauist belief in a single and unified general will? Though it would be impossible to attempt a comprehensive solution in the context of this paper, three general observations are in order. In the first place, while the obsession with plots was perhaps most pervasive among the patriot deputies, it was by no means confined to them alone. A

---

[32] Arthur Young, *Travels in France during the Years 1787, 1788, and 1789* (Gloucester, Mass., 1976), pp. 222–23 (entries of 10 and 11 January 1790); Bouche, AC Forcalquier (letter of 2 February 1790); *AP*, 10:84 (speech of Barnave, 17 November 1789); Claude Fricaud to Jean-Marie Gelin, avocat in Charolles: copies of the originals kindly loaned me by Doctor Robert Favre (letter of 31 May 1790); Adrien Duquesnoy, *Journal d'Adrien Duquesnoy*, ed. R. de Crèvecoeur, 2 vols. (Paris, 1894), 2:272 (letter of 12 January 1790); Boullé, 16 (1889): 80 (letter of 26 October 1789). See also Campmas, BM Albi, Ms. 177 (letter of 1 November 1789); and Jean-Paul Rabaut-Saint-Étienne, *Précis historique de la Révolution française* (Paris, 1807), pp. 241–46.

similar mode of analysis was also in evidence among conservative and reactionary factions within the National Assembly. On the eve of the [5–6] October Days, for example, many of the participants in the Monarchien alignment—Bergasse, Mounier, Turckheim, etc.—were convinced that the growing unrest in Paris was part of a general plot conceived by the Left to attack their position and perhaps overthrow the king. And similar convictions were expressed during the winter and spring of 1789–90 by the Monarchiens' successors, the "Imparti-aux."[33] Indeed, the attraction to plot explanations probably came less from an ideological discourse associated with the Left than from a general cultural inclination characteristic of early modern European society in general. Under the Old Regime plot theories were a common mode of explanation among all classes of society for a wide variety of social and economic phenomena which otherwise seemed quite incomprehensible. This was clearly the case with the famous "famine plot persuasion," so widely embraced in eighteenth-century France and whose workings have been explored by Steven Kaplan.[34]

In the second place, we should not overlook the existence of real "plots" posing genuine or potential threats to the Revolution—even if those plots never took the form of the monolithic conspiracies commonly imagined. To a considerable degree, the penchant for paranoia seems first to have arisen in the wake of the events of mid-July 1789. Prior to that period, most of the deputy letters were infused with a strong measure of confidence and a remarkably optimistic assessment of the probable outcome of events. While suspicions of the motives of the ministers and the courtiers were common enough, almost all of the representatives of the Third Estate seemed convinced of the king's support for the reforms they envisioned. But this mood of confidence was shattered at the beginning of the summer, first by Louis XVI's speech to the Estates General on 23 June, and second, and more importantly, by the very real conspiracy to overthrow the Revolution organized in early and mid-July.

---

[33] See the depositions by numerous of the Monarchiens in *Procédure criminelle instruite au Châtelet de Paris, sur la dénonciation des faits arrivés à Versailles dans la journée du 6 octobre 1789* (Paris, 1790). Also, François-Henri de Virieu to the marquis de Viennois: Archives of the Château d'Avauges, reproduced in AD Isère, 1 Mi 461 (letter of 22 January 1790); Louis Verdet to Guilbert, curé of Saint-Sébastien of Nancy: Arch. du Grand Séminaire de Nancy, MB 17, folios 1–113 (letter of 6 February 1790); Jean-Félix Faydel to the municipality of Cahors: AM Cahors, unclassed box of letters from revolutionary deputies, held in BM Cahors (letter of 9 January 1790).

[34] Steven L. Kaplan, *The Famine Plot Persuasion in Eighteenth-Century France* (Philadelphia, 1982). See also the comments of Lynn Hunt, *Politics, Culture, and Class in the French Revolution* (Berkeley, 1984), pp. 38–43.

The massing of troops around Paris and Versailles and the "coup d'État," which replaced Necker and his liberal allies in the ministry with a team of reactionaries, enormously shook the deputies' confidence and transformed the tone of their letters, leaving many individuals far more receptive to conspiracy theories. The extraordinary and unprecedented circumstances of the Great Fear in late July and the complex events of early October could only confirm them in their suspicions. In December and January, moreover, a series of apparent conspirators were uncovered by various of the National Assembly and Parisian surveillance committees, conspirators of whom the marquis de Favras is probably the best known. Several of the deputies, both Jacobins and moderates, wrote at length and with evident anguish of the [counterrevolutionary] Favras affair, of the popular uprisings in central Paris, and of a revolt of the national guard on the Champs-Élysées: all of which emerged within a period of three weeks [in December 1789–January 1790] and were widely believed to be related.[35] It is important not to underestimate, moreover, the continued presence of a conservative opposition in the National Assembly. Patriots were daily compelled to face a vociferous and well-organized coalition of the Right and the Extreme Right, a coalition which remained strong enough through the spring of 1790 to organize victories not only in the election of Assembly officers but also in a certain number of votes on the floor, and whose rhetoric frequently flaunted counter-revolutionary threats. Indeed, there long persisted the very real menace of a counter-revolution engineered through the legal process of the Constituent Assembly itself.[36]

In the third place, it is evident that the intensity of patriot suspicions varied considerably over time. To rely once again on the diaries and letters, it would seem that the sense of insecurity reached a peak during the winter of 1789–90. At no other period did more deputies make more frequent references to their fear of developing conspiracies. There is evidence that this insecurity can be attributed not only to the fear engendered by the specific events described above, but also to the breakdown and virtual collapse of the Old Regime bureau-

[35] Merle, AC Mâcon, D(2), 13 (letter of 28 December 1789); Jean-Pierre Boullé to municipality of Pontivy: AC Pontivy, on microfilm in AD Morbihan, 1 Mi 140 (letter of 12 January 1790); Théodore Vernier to the municipality of Lons-le-Saunier: AC Bletterans (*non-classé*), "Lettres de Vernier" (letter of 12 January 1790); Duquesnoy, *Journal,* 2:276–77 (letter of 12 January 1790); Charles-Guillaume Dusers to the municipality of Vannes: AD Morbihan, 262 (E(s) (letter of 29 December 1789). On the Favras affair, see Shapiro, *Revolutionary Justice,* pp. 124–50.

[36] See the author's article, "Nobles and Third Estate in the Revolutionary Dynamic of the National Assembly, 1789–1790," *American Historical Review* 94 (1989): 271–301.

cracy throughout the country. For a period of several months, communication links between the Assembly and the provinces were tenuous at best and were frequently maintained through the personal contacts of individual deputies. Aware of the difficulty, the Constituents gave top priority to the establishment of a new administrative structure. "In general, we flatter ourselves," explained Antoine Durand from Quercy, "that as soon as the administrative assemblies are established, our constitution will be consolidated and safe from the plots of our enemies."[37] But the creation of new municipal and regional administrations invariably took time, and the departments—the linchpins of the revolutionary system—would not begin functioning before the late spring of 1790 at the earliest. In the meantime, in order to implement their decrees in the provinces, and to obtain information on the success or failure of those decrees, the deputies could only rely on the patriotism and good will of the unpredictable and sometimes uncontrollable municipal governments, provincial clubs, and National Guard units.

Yet by the spring and summer, as evidence mounted for a generally favorable reception of most of their decrees, the fears and suspicions of the patriot deputies appeared to subside. Tensions had run high when the Right seized on Dom Gerle's motion of 12 April to launch a public campaign against the Assembly's reputed antireligious position.[38] But the apparent failure of this campaign and the outpouring of letters and petitions supporting the Constituent's position, greatly reassured the patriots. They were likewise encouraged by the generally favorable reception of the assignats and the obvious interest and enthusiasm for the sale of church lands, which seemed to put an end to the long-standing fiscal crisis. Finally, the rapid formation of the departmental and district administrations, coupled with the earlier reorganization of the municipal governments, seemed to offer a hope of genuine bureaucratic ties linking the revolutionary legislature with

---

[37] Antoine Durand to his cousin: AM Cahors, unclassed box of letters from revolutionary deputies, held in BM Cahors (letter of 23 May 1790). See also Merle, AC Mâcon, D(2), 13 (letter of 16 December 1789); and Pierre-François Lepoutre to his wife: family archives of Adolphe Lepoutre-Dubreuil, Montignac-sur-Vezère (letter of 16 January 1790).

[38] Vernier, AC Bletterans (letters of 4 May and 15 June); Antoine-René-Hyacinthe Thibaudeau, *Correspondance inédite,* ed. H. Carré and Pierre Boissonnade (Paris, 1898), p. 82 (letter to Piorry, 10 May); Campmas, BM Albi, Ms. 177 (letter of 16 May); Thomas Lindet, *Correspondance de Thomas Lindet pendant la Constituante et la Législative (1789–1792),* ed. Armand Montier (Paris, 1899), pp. 146–47 (letter to Munic. Bernay, 5 May 1790); Maupetit, "Lettres," *Bulletin de la Commission historique et archéologique de la Mayenne* 20 (1904): 447, 450 (letters of 24 and 25 April).

the hinterlands. The deputies were quick to note that many of the statements of adhesion to the Assembly's religious stance came precisely from the new district and department administrators.[39] The marks of support of Louis XVI for the activities of the patriots—from his visit to the Assembly on 4 February through his participation in the Fête de la Fédération [of July 14, 1790]—only further boosted their morale and self-confidence. While new sources of disquiet continued to arise—most notably the Montauban and Nîmes [counter-revolutionary] uprisings and a brief threat of war with England—most of the letters and diaries of the spring and early summer were no longer obsessed with conspiracies and counter-revolution and seemed distinctly more positive and optimistic. Even the inveterate pessimist and staunch Jacobin, Théodore Vernier, appeared sanguine and positive: "everything's fine," he wrote in early May. "If our enemies cry out in rage, it is their last convulsions of despair." With only a few exceptions, the opposition "has announced that, following the old adage, they will make a virtue of necessity and yield to circumstances."[40] In short, then, historians must be wary of postulating a linear continuity between 1789 and 1791, between the patriot anxiety of the early months of the Revolution and the renewed fears engendered by the dramatically different configuration of circumstances which followed the [King's] Flight to Varennes.

In the end, our assessment of the links between the Constituent Assembly and the Terror must remain complex and somewhat ambiguous. That a few deputies arrived in Versailles as true believers in the political philosophy of Rousseau, and that others were converted to that philosophy in the first months of the Assembly, can scarcely be denied. It seems plausible to argue that many of the actions of these individuals were indeed based on "first principles." There were, as we have seen, sufficient instances of real and verifiable conspiracies to arouse the deputies' fears. Yet the unbounded confidence of such ideologues in their own understanding of the best interests of the nation, and their impatience and indignation with all those who opposed them, may also have contributed in raising their suspicions. In this sense, we may perhaps detect a link between the positions of one element of the Constituent and the political culture of the Terror.
    Nevertheless, it is also evident that this one element represented

---

[39] See the author's *Religion, Revolution and Regional Culture* (Princeton, 1986), pp. 211–15.

[40] Vernier, AC Bletterans (letters of 4 and 18 May 1790).

only a tiny minority of the deputies in the Assembly as a whole. Even among the patriots, the majority arrived in Versailles substantially more uncertain and ambivalent in their intellectual views. It was probably only in the context of the Assembly itself—in the "school of the Revolution" as one deputy put it[41]—that they found themselves forced to weigh and choose and hone more coherent positions. But it is by no means certain that the ideas of Rousseau formed the principal elements of those positions.[42] Most of the deputies remained decidedly elitist in their preconceptions and fearful of the more humble elements of society. If there was one area in which the pre-revolutionary ideology of the Enlightenment most affected the deputies' decisions—and led them afoul of a large segment of French popular opinion—it was probably in the formulation of religious policy and the Civil Constitution of the Clergy. Under the Constituent, a Voltairian passion to *écraser l'infâme*[43] was probably far more influential than a Rousseauist obsession with *la volonté générale* [general will].

Yet the vast majority of the deputies' actions were not driven by ideology at all, but by a strong strand of pragmatism. A great many, as we have seen, were practical men, steeped in a culture of the law and possessed of a considerable store of experience in local and regional politics. Despite the enormous challenges and difficulties they faced, they set to work with a great deal of energy, a willingness to compromise if necessary, and a sensitivity to constituency opinion—even though the constituency in question was usually limited to the urban elites. And after twenty-eight months of extraordinary intensity, they managed to complete a constitution that was altogether credible and viable. Though the question could be debated endlessly, a good case can be made that, under normal circumstances, the Constitution of 1791 might very well have worked. But obviously the circumstances were anything but normal. The failure of that Constitution under the Legislative Assembly is a subject that goes well beyond the limits of the present paper. Yet it seems likely that no such constitutional monarchy could hope to have been successful

---

[41] François-René-Pierre Ménard de la Groye, *François Ménard de La Groye, député du Maine aux Etats généraux. Correspondance, 1789–1791,* ed. Florence Mirouse (Le Mans, 1989), p. 161 (letter of 22 December 1789).

[42] Insofar as the deputies were fascinated with Rousseau, it was perhaps more with the lyrical prose of the *Nouvelle Héloïse* than the political philosophy of the *Social Contract.* This was certainly the case with Théodore Vernier, AC Bletterans (letter of 5 August 1789).

[43] [A slogan by Voltaire probably meaning either crush religious fanaticism or crush Christianity.—Eds.]

when it was repudiated not only by a large and powerful segment of the nobility, but by the monarch Louis XVI himself. Perhaps the critical and fundamental contradiction which emerged from the experience of the Constituent Assembly—the tragic contradiction which most linked that Constituent to the period of the Terror—was not a question of language or ideology; it was rather the inability of the executive, the key figure in the whole constitutional edifice, to reconcile himself to—perhaps even to understand—the new role which the Revolution had offered him.

II THE CIVIL CONSTITUTION OF THE CLERGY

TRAGIC ERRORS

André Latreille

André Latreille (1901–1984) was, like his father, a professional historian. Born and raised at Lyon, he studied at the local university. Then he taught at various French secondary schools and universities until his retirement from the University of Lyon in 1971. He also served in Charles de Gaulle's Provisional Government as Director of Religious Affairs in the Ministry of Interior from 1944 to 1945 and as a regular reviewer of historical works for the eminent Paris newspaper *Le Monde.* A specialist in French religious history, he published *Napoléon et le Saint-Siège* (1935), *L'Eglise catholique et la Révolution française* (new edition, 2 vols., 1970), *De Gaulle, la Libération et l'église* (1978), and, in collaboration with others, the *Histoire du Catholicisme en France* (1957–1962). His other works include *La Seconde guerre mondiale* (1966) and *L'Ère napoléonienne* (1974).

The Civil Constitution of the Clergy

On July 12, 1790, the National Assembly approved the measures that formed the *Civil Constitution of the Clergy.* It was called a constitution because it was intended as an essential part of a national regeneration and it was called civil because the assembly wanted to make clear that it dealt only with temporal issues. The idea was not to

From André Latreille and René Rémond, *La Période contemporaine,* Vol. III of *Histoire du Catholicisme en France* (3 vols.; Paris: Éditions Spes, 1957–1962), pp. 83–94, 96. These pages, written by A. Latreille, are printed by permission of the publisher. Editors' translation.

change the national religion, but to cleanse the ecclesiastical body of those abuses universally censured by the national will.

By-passing the Concordat of 1516,[1] which was the oldest of our treaties and actually represented a bilateral agreement with the Holy See, the assembly decided, by its own authority, to regulate the appointment, functions, and salary of the higher clergy.

The boundaries of the dioceses were altered so that henceforth there would be one diocese for each department. Instead of 135 there would be only 85; their size would be much less unequal than in the past; and they would be grouped in ten metropolitan provinces. In drawing up parish boundaries, the assembly ruled that each one had to contain at least 6,000 souls. A considerable reduction in the number of religious positions resulted from these two principles. In addition, all claims to ecclesiastical incomes other than those for bishops and parish priests were abolished. Consequently, clergymen with administrative functions, but who did not care directly for the souls of the faithful, lost their positions.

In the future all the Church's clergy would be elected. Bishops and priests would be elected exactly in the same manner as deputies and government officials—by the *active* citizens (those who paid the required amount of taxes) in the departmental or the district electoral assemblies. When elected, a bishop would request canonical institution from the metropolitan bishop of his province. As evidence of the unity of faith and communion, he would then notify the pope of his appointment; but he did not have to obtain Rome's confirmation of his powers. In the administration of all diocesan affairs, the bishop would be assisted by episcopal vicars, who would form a council and would have to be consulted before he could take any action based on his jurisdiction.

The clergy's salaries would be the responsibility of the state, which would every year (quarterly) pay in cash 20,000 livres to bishops, 1,200 to parish priests, and 700 to country vicars. In return, religious ceremonies would be performed without charge; special fees would disappear.

Such spokesmen for the assembly's Ecclesiastical Committee as the Abbés Goutte and Expilly (one might note that Protestant deputies refrained from commenting) insisted that they had only obeyed the needs of society without ever going beyond the incontestable

---

[1][The Concordat of 1516 between Francis I of France and Pope Leo X served as the basis of relations between the French Crown and the papacy until 1789. Among other things, it recognized the right of the king to choose bishops and other officials of the Church, who would then receive papal confirmation.—Eds.]

rights of state authority. Boisgelin, archbishop of Aix-en-Provence, and the Abbé Maury replied skillfully for the right-wing in the assembly. They carefully pointed out the inevitable dangers: the claim that the cooperation of the spiritual power could be dispensed with when revising ecclesiastical districts; the establishment of a system of popular election of bishops, which would result in allowing non-Catholics to vote for clergymen; and the separation introduced between the bishops and the head of the Church, which "would harm that unity so essential to religion." Despite the conciliatory attitude of Boisgelin, they received nothing from the assembly, but instead aroused some alarming replies. Armand-Gaston Camus [a lawyer specializing in Church matters] declared that the time had come for the French Church to be freed from "its servitude" to the bishop of Rome; and Mirabeau declared that "all the members of the clergy are public officials" and that "performing religious services . . . is a government function."

Controversy Over the Civil Constitution

Ever since the countless investigations and studies which flourished in 1790 and 1791, the birth and significance of the Civil Constitution of the Clergy have been examined frequently. The amount of influence particular groups had in the Ecclesiastical Committee will always be arguable. We agree with Edmond Préclin[2] that the measures were the result of "the not always harmonious efforts of several sponsors": we see first of all the Gallican and Caesarian legists;[3] also the Richerists (that is, the champions of the movement for the autonomy of the lower clergy) rather than the Jansenists (although these two movements had largely merged); and finally the *philosophes.* In any case, Canon Pisani is right to say that the Civil Constitution did not represent an unnatural conception "springing from the brains of some Jansenists and then violently imposed on a declining

---

[2][Some of the works by the historians mentioned in this selection are as follows: Edmond Préclin, *Les Jansénistes du XVIIIe siècle et la constitution civile du clergé* (Paris: Gamber, 1929); Canon Paul Pisani, *L'Église de Paris et la Révolution* (4 vols.; Paris: Picard, 1908–1911); Albert Mathiez, *Rome et le clergé française sous la Constituante* (Paris: Colin, 1911); Dom Henri Leclerq, *L'Église constitutionnelle* (Paris: Letouzey, Ané, 1934); Frédéric Masson, *Le Cardinal de Bernis* (Paris: Plon, Nourrit, 1884); Abbé Fernand Mourret, *Histoire générale de l'Église,* Vol. VII: *L'Église et la Révolution (1775–1823)* (Paris: Bloud, Gay, 1913).—Eds.]

[3][A Gallican favored the almost total freedom of the French Church from the ecclesiastical authority of the pope; and a Caesarist espoused the supremacy of the state in ecclesiastical matters.—Eds.]

France by Machiavellian tactics." It was the inevitable outcome of a religious situation for which no one could find a solution in time, as well as the result of some rather confused and contradictory forces that did not consciously aim at schism. Does this mean (as is still said by modern historians writing since the appearance of Albert Mathiez's work) that it was not unacceptable to Catholics, that the Gallicans recognized this, and that it was Pope Pius VI's malevolence toward the French Revolution that made it unacceptable? Certainly not. What pervades the whole Civil Constitution is the statist postulate that the secular authority alone has the right to make changes which it deems wise not only in ecclesiastical organization but also concerning religious worship. Although there were in the Gallican Church some theologians and canon lawyers quite willing to make any effort to reach a compromise, willing to accept, for example, the changes in the ecclesiastical districts or the election of bishops, they continually warned the assembly that it was necessary to consult with the spiritual authority, according to the prescriptions of canon law, "or else religion would be fundamentally harmed."

Earlier, the first chairman of the Ecclesiastical Committee, Bishop de Bonal, had commented about the monastic reform of 1790: "What I believe to be illegitimate in the exercise of this authority is that the assembly alone tears down obstacles that it has not erected . . . before we hear a pronouncement from the only power in the spiritual realm that has the authority to tie and untie on this earth." All the bishops who were deputies took the same position regarding the Civil Constitution of the Clergy. Three months after the vote, in a notable pamphlet entitled an *Exposition of Principles Concerning the Civil Constitution of the Clergy,* the thirty bishops who still sat in the Constituent Assembly (except for Talleyrand and Gobel, who had kept apart from the others) made the following declaration.

> If the civil authorities want to make changes in religious matters without the cooperation of the Church, they contradict the principles of the Church, but they do not destroy them; they contradict the principles and destroy the means that could help them carry out their opinions.
>
> We want to know the desires of the Church so as to reestablish a necessary agreement between the civil and religious authorities and by their concord put consciences at rest and maintain public tranquility. . . .

Where did this religious authority rest? The Gallican bishops could not go astray. Since the High Middle Ages the papacy had never admitted that the secular authority could determine the choices of bishops without its consent. More and more since the Council of Trent

[1545–1563], it had required bishops to recognize their subordination to the successor of Saint Peter; and it had established and organized dioceses, sometimes with the approval of secular princes and sometimes on its own. To be sure, Boisgelin urged that the Gallican Church be consulted in a national council, but only because the Gallican bishops considered it a point of honor to state their views before informing the Pope of them. The two archbishops who sat in the King's Cabinet advised him to ratify the Civil Constitution, but only because they judged open resistance to be impossible and because they still clung to the hope of a compromise *with* the Holy See. So, before knowing the opinion of either the French episcopate or the Pope, Louis XVI ratified the Civil Constitution on August 24, 1790. However, neither the precepts, nor the traditions of the Roman Curia, nor the attitudes of the reigning Pope made it likely that the Holy See would acquiesce.

By the end of October 1790 the Gallican bishops had accepted their responsibilities. To the *Exposition of Principles,* which had been the work of the bishops who were deputies, almost all the other bishops (ninety-three to be exact) associated themselves—they explicitly referred the determination of the dispute about the Civil Constitution to the successor of Saint Peter. Placed in the center of Catholic unity and communion, he had to be the interpreter and spokesman of the universal Church's wishes. They had to wait eight months before Pius VI announced his decision on March 10, 1791. Eight interminable months, at a time when his silence left the faithful in France uncertain, at a time when the assembly multiplied the decrees designed to speed up the implementation of the Civil Constitution, eight months of irretrievable delays!

The Constitutional Oath

Fortified by its first victory over the King, the Constituent Assembly quite naturally felt in no way inclined to reduce its claims to legislate independently on religious problems. To rush matters, on November 27, 1790, it decided to require, under the threat of dismissal, that "all bishops, former archbishops, parish priests, and other public officials" take an oath that they would "be loyal to the nation, to the law, and to the king, and would uphold with all their power the Constitution decreed by the National Assembly and accepted by the king." This was the historically famous constitutional oath that unleashed dissension within Church and State and brought about the breakdown of a harmony between the two powers so often extolled as indispensable to the success of the Revolution.

Of 160 prelates, only 7 decided to take the oath; 4 of these—Bri-enne, Jarente, Savine, and Talleyrand—were heads of dioceses, but because of their disbelief and their morals they were completely dis-credited. All the other bishops refused to take the oath after a ma-jority of the deputies had killed every proposal that would have def-initely allowed the clergy to exclude anything dependent on the spiritual authority from the oath.

But to what extent would the lower clergy and the faithful follow the example of the bishops? The path to take was less clear than it would be for us today. Rome's silence was not the difficulty: the good country priest ordinarily did not look so far, and the voice of the First Shepherd did not reach him easily. Often he was estranged from his own bishop by many legitimate resentments and by a very different manner of understanding the political situation. He looked for "en-lightenment from those whose way of life he shared and whose learn-ing he admired, without seeking his doctrines outside the diocese" (Dom Leclerq). He would ask some canon lawyer or some canon from a neighboring city, but very contradictory views were expressed. Even if he ignored the material and spiritual advantages that the ec-clesiastical reorganization promised him and even if he ignored the threat of being treated as "a disturber of the peace" and an enemy of national regeneration should he refuse to take the oath, he still hesi-tated to cut himself off from his flock, to abandon his post, his parish, and his rectory, to which he was bound by so many ties. This was es-pecially true when the local officials, desirous of keeping him, were willing to ignore the reservations that he added to the oath. As well as can be determined from innumerable local studies and general statistical accounts, we can estimate that half of the parish clergy or even a little more than that—in other words, a third of the entire clergy—accepted the Civil Constitution immediately. A high average, but like all averages the result of extreme divergencies on both sides: in the Vendée or Bas-Rhin departments 90 per cent refused to take the oath; in Var 96 per cent accepted it. And the average conceals many inexplicable "cases": in the Haute-Saône department, four re-fused to take the oath and 178 surely took it; but it has been deter-mined that 352 priests in Haute-Saône, two-thirds of the total, took it with reservations or later retracted their pledge.

The adherence of this rather large number of clergymen and lay-men thereby allowed the "Constitutional Church" to organize. Every Sunday from the end of January to the end of March 1791, in the cap-itals of the new departments, there were meetings of the active citi-zens responsible for electing the new bishops who were to replace the "refractory" ones. As no requirement of religious faith was stipulated, unbelievers took part in the elections, while those who were scrupulously faithful abstained. At Le Puy in the Haute-Loire department, 150 active citizens who were Catholics failed to attend the electoral assembly, while Protestants came from Yssingeaux [thirteen miles away]. With some exceptions these electoral activities took place in a calm atmosphere. The voice of the people chose as bishops eighteen of the priests who were members of the Constituent Assembly. When the final stage was reached everything almost came to nought, for someone had to consecrate these newly elected bishops so as to confer the apostolic succession on them, and even the bishops who had taken the oath shunned that task. Talleyrand finally agreed to assume this role: on February 24, 1791, the former bishop of Autun (just fifteen days earlier he had given up his authority there) took up the crosier again to consecrate Expilly as bishop of Finistère and Marolles as bishop of Aisne. Observers noticed that the liturgical ritual was followed exactly except that the reading of papal bulls was omitted, as was the oath of loyalty to the pope. Thereafter consecrations occurred in rapid succession, since by April 25 some sixty bishops were at their places in the new dioceses.

Precisely at this point the news began to spread in France that Pius VI had just condemned the Civil Constitution of the Clergy.

The Papal Condemnation

Historians have thoroughly investigated the motives for Pius VI's surprising delay in announcing his decision on the Civil Constitution. Frédéric Masson stresses the forbearance that he showed toward King Louis XVI, whose embarrassing position was explained to him by the French ambassador at Rome, Cardinal de Bernis. The Abbés Mourret and Richard insist on the Pope's uncertainty about the intentions of the Gallican bishops. Mathiez and Canon Leclerq emphasize the political considerations behind his delay and in particular his concern with saving [the papal territories of] Avignon and the Comtat Venaissin from the covetousness of the revolutionaries. More attention must certainly be directed toward the customary slowness of the Roman Curia. The cardinals who surrounded Pius VI were highly indignant at the actions of the Constituent Assembly. Its measures exceeded in scope and boldness anything so far attempted by the most radical reformers and enlightened despots—like Joseph II for example. But, for one thing, we must consider the clumsy machinery of the papal government and the traditional prudence of its advisers, elderly men anxious not to commit the "Throne of Truth" rashly. Then, too, there was the feeling that in a European situation where papal authority found enemies everywhere, it had to refrain from providing any pretext for a Gallican schism, something always dreaded by the ultramontanes [those favoring papal supremacy within the Church]. Together, these factors had led and almost always would lead the popes to act slowly and, only after great care, to come to a decision on the fearful problems raised by the Revolution. From 1789 to 1815, throughout the twenty-five years of almost uninterrupted crisis between Paris and Rome, again and again we gain the impression that the Holy See was falling behind. In reaction to the hasty moves of a young and dynamic political group, it took its positions only belatedly.

The pontifical decision finally appeared, on March 10, 1791, in an important document, the papal brief *Quot Aliquantum,* which was sent to Cardinal de La Rochefoucauld and to the bishops who had signed the *Exposition of Principles.* Pius VI declared that the Civil Constitution had "as its goal and consequence the destruction of the Catholic religion." By its provisions concerning the consecration of bishops, the election of priests, and the operation of diocesan councils, it mortally wounded the divine constitution of the Church. Although it was an article of faith that the Roman Pontiff had the highest authority over the whole Church, the Civil Constitution claimed to upset this fundamental concept. While scrutinizing the doctrinal and disciplinary matters that had been decided illegitimately by the assembly, the Supreme Pontiff took the occasion to pronounce a severe judgment on the principles that this legislature had proclaimed earlier. And so he publicly condemned the Declaration of the Rights of Man. (He had already done the same thing a year earlier in an unpublished consistorial address.) He said that the Declaration was wrong to have granted to the citizen "that unconditional liberty which guarantees not only the right of being left undisturbed for one's religious opinions, but which also grants the right to think, to write, and even to publish with impunity anything on religious matters that may be the product of the most disordered imagination—a shocking right, which the assembly, however, seems to believe is the result of everyone's natural equality and liberty." But what could be more senseless than to establish among men this unbridled equality and liberty which seem to destroy reason? . . . What can be more opposed to the rights of God the Creator—who limits man's liberty by forbidding him to commit evil—than "this liberty of thought and action that the National Assembly grants to man in society as an imprescriptible natural right?" Thus, with a terrible solemnity, the theses of the Roman Church and the principles of modern liberalism confronted each other. We shall see them clash very often after 1789.

Responding to the brief, the Gallican bishops, with much dignity and moderation, tried to explain their conduct; they distinguished between the area of natural law and that of political action. Using the same words as the Holy Father, they condemned a liberty and an equality contrary to the truths of reason and dogma; but as citizens desirous of not opposing popular aspirations in the civil sphere, they had believed it possible to set up the true dominion of public liberty in a hereditary monarchy: ". . . And we recognized without any difficulty that there is a natural equality whereby no citizen is excluded from the positions to which Providence calls him because of his talents and his virtues. Political equality can be extended or limited by different forms of government; and we believed that we were free to express ourselves, as was any other citizen, concerning those more or less extensive areas that God himself declares as given over for men to dispute." Having preceded the Pope in denouncing the Civil Constitution, the Gallican bishops had no difficulty in following the line of conduct he prescribed for them.

On April 13, 1791, Pius VI declared those consecrations of bishops already carried out to be criminal and sacrilegious, forbade all religious functions to the consecrators and those consecrated, threatened to suspend all priests who had taken the oath and did not retract it, and exhorted the misguided to repent and the faithful to a resolute firmness. It is and always will be impossible to judge the effects of these disciplinary measures. We know that the publicity given to the papal briefs by the loyal bishops brought about in certain dioceses a relatively large number of retractions of the oath, but of course many of these remained secret. The Constitutional bishops, however, were rather persuasive, whether in challenging the authenticity of the papal documents whose circulation was forbidden by the assembly, or in taking shelter behind the Gallican liberties in order to claim that the Pope, having no direct jurisdiction over the French people, could pronounce no canonical punishment in this matter.

Soon diplomatic relations between Paris and Rome were broken. When the French government ended Cardinal de Bernis' mission as ambassador, the Pope refused to receive a new ambassador. Turbulent demonstrations in Paris (during which the mob burned an effigy of "the Ogre of the Tiber" at the Palais Royal) led to the departure of Dugnani, the papal nuncio. At a time in France when it was especially important for an authorized representative of the Holy See to keep in touch with the loyal clergy, only a semiofficial chargé d'affaires stayed behind, and his position was unclear and indefinite.

The Two Churches

Henceforth there were two churches in the kingdom face to face. There were even frequent instances of two bishops or two priests in the same locality hurling anathemas at each other in front of a divided population which had its own way of interpreting the opposing issues. In fact the public did not understand much about the distinctions concerning ecclesiastical discipline: so long as the Mass was said as usual in the parish church and the sacraments were administered, it hardly cared whether the priest who officiated had legal jurisdiction or whether the taking of a political oath had made him a schismatic. The public was rather inclined to rate priests according to its own personal likes or dislikes and according to its support of the Constituent Assembly and the revolutionary cause. On one side were those clergymen who took the oath [*assermentés*], on the other were those who refused [*insermentés*]—contemptuously called *jurors* or *refractories,* approvingly called *civic priests* or *good priests.* Under such conditions, the antagonists had to fight for the favor of the public authorities and compete, with heated polemics, for the support of the faithful. . . .

Looking at the religious issue from a modern standpoint, it is rather hard to understand why the Constituent Assembly did not stand by its principles on the freedom of religious belief and quite simply adopt total freedom of religion, as it almost did during the last months of its existence. But one must clearly understand that this was impossible to do. All the Constituent Assembly's work had been based on the idea of a national religion serving the new political and social system. It had placed all its prestige behind the formation of the Constitutional Church, which it could not abandon, defenseless, to the relentless attacks of counterrevolutionaries. If the Constituent Assembly at the end of its term forbade refractory priests from preaching or opening new churches, at least it did have the merit of not banishing them.

NECESSARY AND ADMIRABLE DECISIONS

Jean Jaurès

Jean Jaurès (1859–1914) was one of the most eloquent and influential political figures of his day. A meridional, or southern Frenchman, he came from a middle-class family. At the Ecole normale supérieure in Paris he studied philosophy and gave promise of a brilliant academic career. But in the early 1890s he left teaching to enter politics full time and for the rest of his life he devoted himself to the cause of democratic socialism. He served as a leader of the Socialists in the Chamber of Deputies and in 1904 founded the French Socialist Party's newspaper, *L'Humanité*. He also edited the thirteen-volume *Histoire socialiste* (1901–1908), for which he wrote the four volumes on the French Revolution up to the fall of Robespierre. On the eve of the First World War a demented nationalist assassinated him.

The French Revolution was bolstered by a great increase in wealth. And though the vigor of mind and soul, the passion for liberty and knowledge, the spirit of audacity and inventiveness which great crises produce all contributed a good deal to this growth of national wealth, it had its first and principal source in the revolutionary expropriation of Church property.

But the National Assembly could not restrict itself to seizing and distributing the Church's landed property. It had to regulate all the relations between the Church and the new society created by the Revolution, and we are going to witness the tragic encounter of Christianity and the Revolution.

The assembly could not ignore the ecclesiastical organization. In the first place, the temporal power of the Old Regime, the king, played

From Jean Jaurès, *La Constituante (1789–1791)*, Vol. I of *Histoire socialiste (1789–1900)*, ed. Jean Jaurès (13 vols.; Paris: Rouff, 1901–1908), pp. 521–522, 532–533, 535, 539, 541, 543–544, 546–548. Editors' translation.

a role in the proceedings of the spiritual power. The pope confirmed bishops, but it was the king who nominated them. To a great extent the Revolution substituted the power of the nation for the power of the king. It therefore had to decide what it was to do with that aspect of royal power. In the second place, a very large number of monks and nuns, who were bound to the cloister by perpetual vows upheld by civil law, petitioned the assembly requesting it to strike off their chains. Finally, by seizing the Church's landed property, the assembly, in order to give a legal pretext for that magnificent revolutionary expropriation, had taken on the responsibility of providing for the administration of the cult and the support of its clergy. The assembly was therefore completely involved in ecclesiastical problems. . . .

A great many details of the Civil Constitution of the Clergy seem bizarre to us, and a great many historians have said that it failed miserably. False. In the first place, it lasted in its original form until February 21, 1795, that is to say four years, and it was, at least for three years, really in operation. The electors charged with choosing parish priests and bishops took their duties seriously. The religious ceremonies which were a part of the electoral procedure were attended without any ill will, even by the freest thinkers among them; and very far from believing that by so doing they compromised themselves with the Church, the electors believed instead that they were acting as good revolutionaries.

But the Civil Constitution survived especially in the Concordat of 1801, although bastardized and debased. There are two great differences between the Concordat and the Civil Constitution: in the first place, the Concordat reestablished the papal right of intervention [in the life of the French Church]. Whereas the Revolution had nothing to do with the pope and confidently affirmed the sovereignty of popular suffrage in the appointment of Church officials as well as other national officials, the Concordat was the result of negotiations with the pope and it restored his supreme right of canonical institution. The other difference is that, according to the Concordat, bishops and parish priests were to be selected by the executive branch of the French government and not by popular vote.

From the Civil Constitution to the Concordat there is, therefore, a diminution of the revolutionary spirit. The Civil Constitution is much more laic, national, and democratic than the Concordat. The Civil Constitution recognizes no foreign power, and, in the last analysis, no theocratic power: it is the nation, in its absolute sovereignty and by means of popular suffrage, that chooses and installs the officers of the Church.

But what is retained of the Civil Constitution in the Concordat is the right of a sovereign with a revolutionary and laic origin to appoint bishops and priests even though it receives its legitimacy not from the Church but from the people. In the Civil Constitution, those electoral assemblies in which everyone—even Protestants, even Jews, even nonbelievers—took part in naming the bishop and the priest seem a little bizarre to us; but in fact the situation is much the same under the Concordat, where the minister of religion in the Cabinet, who might be a Protestant, a deist, or an atheist, chooses the bishops and priests. The essential thing is that a power that does not emanate from the Church and that represents the rights of man—a conception absolutely opposed to that of the Church—takes part in the functioning and recruitment of the Church. This is what survives of the Civil Constitution in the Concordat and this principle is, despite everything, a grave defeat for theocracy.

Those, like us, who desire not only the complete separation of Church and State, but even the disappearance of the Church and Christianity, those who impatiently await the day when the authority of the state will be freed from all contact with the Church and when individual consciences will be freed from all contact with dogma, may believe that the Civil Constitution of the Clergy was an inferior product and a bastardized mixture. Nevertheless, for its time it was basically an act of revolutionary boldness and not, as some have said, an uncertain gesture. In fact, when subjected to the pressure of reactionary and clerical forces, it suffered, as did most revolutionary institutions, a terrible diminution in value; but there still remained in it an intangible part of the Revolution, which survives to this very day. . . .

But why didn't the Constituent Assembly immediately proclaim the separation of Church and State? Why didn't it say that religion was a purely private matter and that the nation should not pay the salaries of the clergy nor persecute, support, or regulate any sect? Why didn't it, according to the famous formula of the positivists, bring about then and there the separation of the spiritual and temporal powers? In his very substantial studies of the religious movement in Paris during the Revolution, [Jean-François-Eugène] Robinet vehemently reproaches the assembly for this. . . .

But, actually, taking into account the forces of the year 1790, could the assembly, at that instant, have declared the separation of Church and State? *At that time, the question was not even raised;* it did not exist. None of the legislators, none of the journalists, none of the thinkers or *philosophes* suggested this idea to the assembly. . . .

It was not . . . from the philosophy of the eighteenth century that

the politics of separation or of a systematic and immediate dechristianization could reach the Constituents. And the assembly (where
Jansenists and legists were much more numerous than *philosophes*)
was infinitely more concerned with freeing the French Church from
the domination of Rome and with applying the public law of the Revolution to ecclesiastical organization than with intentionally precipi-
tating the dissolution of Christian belief or breaking all legal bonds
between Church and State.

Besides, for the state to cut all ties with the Church and proclaim
that religion was simply a private matter would not have been tolerated by the overwhelming majority of the people in 1789 and 1790. In
religious matters there is a world of difference between the working
class today [1901], a part of which is resolutely nonbelieving, and the
people of 1789. Not to recognize this vast difference and to be severely critical of the religious achievements of the assembly is to ignore the real significance of the Revolution itself.

The traditions of many centuries had accustomed the people of
1789 to consider public life impossible without the monarchy or religion. It cannot have been expected that the assembly could undo in
a moment the results of centuries of servitude and passivity. It took
innumerable shocks—the flight to Varennes, the repeated treasons of
their leaders, the invasion by foreign hordes requested and aided by
the court—to separate the people (I mean the revolutionary people)
from the monarchy and the king.

It would take frightful ordeals—the underhanded and violent battle
of the clergy against the Revolution, its obvious complicity with the
enemies of liberty and the nation, its crimes in the Vendée, its fanatical appeals for civil war—to separate the revolutionary people first
from the clergy and then even from Christianity. And still the breach
was only superficial. Whoever does not take this into account is incapable of understanding history, incapable also of judging the real
stature of those great bourgeois revolutionaries who in four years not
only enacted the Civil Constitution, but began the dechristianization
of that France so unquestioningly religious for centuries. . . .

One must admire the assembly for its great audacity in bringing
the Church within the administrative framework of the Revolution
and in placing it under the jurisdiction of popular suffrage, where it
became one of many civil institutions.

Furthermore, how would the assembly have been able to separate
the Church from the State and refuse all public subsidy to religion at
the very moment when it was moving toward the general expropriation of Church property? I do not in the least imply by this that the

budget for religion was a debt the State owed to the expropriated Church. There is no debt that the State, the Revolution, owes to the Church. . . .

What most concerned the *philosophes* of the assembly was how to regulate the difficult relationships between the Church and the Revolution without too much commotion and at the least possible risk. They did not abdicate responsibility, they were not indifferent. They hoped that little by little Catholicism as an institution, once taken into the framework of the Revolution, would be permeated by the dissolvent influence of revolutionary thought. And when they pretended to believe that there was no contradiction between the principles of Christianity and those of the Revolution, *in practice* they did not deceive the country, for nations, like individuals, have the admirable faculty of not feeling immediately the contradiction between opposing principles that they sometimes hold.

It took several generations and the painful experience of numerous events before people came to feel that contradiction to the point where it became intolerable; for, thanks to the power of the illogical in life, mankind comes under the influence of a new principle without suffering immediately the anguish and sadness of a total and conscious repudiation of the past.

Thus the Constituents hoped that pure reason would little by little free itself from the unnatural compound of Christianity and the Revolution which formed the base of the national consciousness in 1789. At that time the essential thing for them (and they were right) was that the revolutionary stamp be imprinted on the organization of the Church, that the latter not be treated as a special institution, but subject to the same conditions as all civil institutions.

In that way the Church, at the same time as it found its property expropriated, also found its spiritual primacy expropriated. It was above all deprived by its mystery: how long would the people revere as the interpreters of a supernatural power those men whom they chose themselves, whom by their own votes they put into office like any local administrator? . . .

I do not say that this intellectual mixture of Christianity and rationalism is very attractive; furthermore, it is a very mediocre and very unstable philosophical compound. But the people had been kept in ignorance and in Christian dependency as much by the disdain of the *philosophes* as by the Church's will to dominate. And even though they were beginning a Revolution, they could not attain all at once the pure philosophy of knowledge and reason. In the religious sphere, therefore, this first revolutionary period was necessarily a period of compromise. The essential thing once again is that this compromise, while it imposed disagreeable rituals and unpleasant posturing on free thought, did not impair the essential power of reason; on the contrary, by diminishing the masses' spirit of passivity and dependency, it struck at the essence of the Church's power. The four million active citizens who yesterday greeted the bishop as a double incarnation of God and the king now elected that bishop. The Church was in the position of a candidate before the electors. In the last analysis, popular suffrage must decide, popular suffrage becomes pope, and, to a certain extent, by the transfer of sacerdotal power, popular suffrage becomes God.

Such an exalting of the people causes the abasement of the Church, and dogma loses the halo of power which made it truth. In any case, having lived under the Civil Constitution, the people would find it easier to look point-blank at the altar, where the priest stood thanks to them. I am convinced that the Civil Constitution, so disdained by some haughty spirits, contributed a good deal to the intellectual liberty of the people in religious matters today. It was a first step in the secular accommodation of religion and it accustomed the people to the wide-ranging audacities of free thought.

The Church felt the gravity of the blow; for under the Pope's direction it immediately began a furious resistance to the Civil Constitution. It claimed that the new arrangement of dioceses was absolutely counter to canon law. It claimed that the Constituent Assembly could not rightfully avoid consulting the leader of the universal Church. We can dispense with these claims. . . .

In its long life the Church has accepted too many different constitutions, it has adapted itself to too many diverse political and social conditions for it to be able to oppose revolutionary innovations with the authority of an unchanging tradition. The problem is summed up in a word. The Church aspires to domination; therefore, it declares as contrary to principle anything which hampers its domination; but since it is not obstinate before the inevitable and since it prefers to evolve rather than to disappear, it ends up by resigning itself to what it cannot destroy and by readjusting its principles to what exists.

If the Revolution had triumphed completely, if political liberty and popular suffrage had not been submerged in the despotism of the Napoleonic Empire, if the electoral principle had continued to function everywhere, and if the triumph of the Revolution and democracy had given France a vigorous national purpose, the clergy and the Pope himself would have been forced to accept the Civil Constitution. The Pope certainly would not have cut off revolutionary France from the universal Church; he would have confined himself as much as possible to maintaining "the unity of the faith" between the elected bishops and the Holy See. Therefore, the controversy did not concern a question of canon law. It was a political question. The issue was whether the Revolution would have the power to prevail in all its works and in the Civil Constitution itself.

I sometimes hear "moderates" regret that the French Revolution created so many enormous difficulties for itself by bestowing a Civil Constitution on the clergy. But truly they reason as if it were possible for the Revolution to ignore the existence of a Church which had dominated and molded France for centuries. They reason as if it were possible for the Revolution, by feigning ignorance, to abolish the profound conflict between the Catholic principle and revolutionary principles. There was not a single question on which the Revolution had to take a stand where it would not meet the Church in its path.

To raise only the question of the dioceses: at a time when the constitution abolished the old provincial boundaries and made France uniform, should it have allowed the dioceses to continue as a reminder of the old France superimposing itself on the lines of the new France and encouraging a universal hope of reaction? At a time when the nation took power from the king, surely it was necessary for it to decide what to do with that part of his authority which concerned the Church; or should it have left the Church for an indefinite period master of everything, of its recruitment, of its preaching, of schools, of the registers of vital statistics?

Again, the dramatic encounter of Christianity and the Revolution could not be postponed. The only task of the Constituent Assembly was to arrange that encounter in such a way that it would wound as slightly as possible the prejudices of the masses who would have turned against the Revolution and also arrange it in such a way that it would give the people new habits of freedom on religious matters. As much as possible, that is what the Civil Constitution provided. In fact the Revolution did find Constitutional priests for every parish, Constitutional bishops for every diocese. It could thus divide the Church against itself; it prevented a unanimous uprising of religious fanaticism in which it would have foundered; and it gave itself time to render the essential part of its work unassailable and irrevocable.

REVOLUTIONARY IDEOLOGY

William H. Sewell, Jr.

William H. Sewell, Jr. (1940–), born at Stillwater, Oklahoma, received his B.A. from the University of Wisconsin, Madison and his M.A. and Ph.D. in history from the University of California, Berkeley. He has taught at the University of Chicago, the University of Arizona, and the University of Michigan; and he has returned to teach once more at the University of Chicago, where he is a Professor of History and Political Science. He is the author of *Work and Revolution in France: The Language of Labor from the Old Regime to 1848* (1980), an award-winning account of the life of French workers, *Structure and Mobility: The Men and Women of Marseille, 1820–1870* (1985), and *A Rhetoric of Bourgeois Revolution: The Abbé Sieyes and "What is the Third Estate?"* (1994).

🎩🎩🎩🎩🎩🎩

The role of ideology was important in the National Assembly's disastrous attempt to reform the Church. On the night of August fourth [1789], representatives of the clergy renounced tithes and tax privileges, thus necessitating important reforms in Church organization. But it was by no means inevitable that these reforms would drive the Church into counterrevolution. The reform of the Church revolved around three issues: finances, church government, and oaths.[1] The financial issues were the most practically exigent, but also gave rise to the least controversy. Since tithes had been abolished, some new means of supporting the clergy had to be devised. The Assembly's solution was to make clergy paid state officials. This new demand on the public budget was more than compensated for by expropriation

From William H. Sewell, Jr., "Ideologies and Social Revolutions: Reflections on the French Case," *Journal of Modern History* 57 (March 1985), 79–81. Reprinted by permission of the author.

[1]For an excellent brief discussion of these reforms, see M. J. Sydenham, *The French Revolution* (New York, 1965), pp. 74–78.

of the Church's vast landholdings. Since the old taxes were virtually uncollectible and new taxes had not yet been imposed, sale of Church lands was the only practical means available to the state to finance the costly reforms of the early Revolution. The expropriation of Church land was accepted with surprisingly little protest—in part, perhaps, because the state salaries for parish priests were considerably more generous than their prerevolutionary earnings.

Reforms in Church government were derived more from ideological than from practical political necessity. Their essential features were a redefinition of parishes and episcopal sees to make them correspond to the communes and departments of the new civil administrative system, and the provision that priests and bishops, like other governmental officials, were to be elected by popular suffrage. The reasoning of the National Assembly on this issue is clear enough: if priests and bishops were to become public servants, they should be chosen by the same methods as legislators, judges, mayors, and councilmen. This proposal posed serious problems for priests, however, since it seemed to require an obedience to popular will that contradicted their obedience to bishops and the pope. Reforms of Church government, therefore, threatened to drive a wedge between the Church and the Revolution in a way that expropriation of Church lands did not.

The issue that precipitated an open break, however, was the far more abstract, purely ideological, issue of oaths. This issue went straight to the core of the metaphysical transformation of 1789. The religious vow or oath had been an essential metaphysical constituent of Old Regime society. An oath was a crucial part of the royal coronation; guild members swore an oath upon entering the body of guild masters; it was the vows taken in ordination that transformed laymen into members of the First Estate. These oaths were sworn to God, and were therefore permanent; as the metaphor put it, they made an indelible impression on the soul of the swearer. It was largely through the medium of religious oaths that spirit structured the social order of the Old Regime. The Revolution based the social order on reason and natural law rather than divine spirit, on dissoluble contracts rather than permanent religious oaths. It therefore could not tolerate oaths that claimed to establish perpetual obligation or that recognized an authority superior to the French nation. Thus it dissolved all monasteries and convents and released monks and nuns from their "perpetual" vows. (It was this same impulse that led to making marriage a purely civil and dissoluble contract rather than a sacrament.)

Finally, the National Assembly, in 1791, imposed a civic oath—a kind of public vow of adherence to the social contract—on all priests. The civic oath was a simple and superficially innocuous affair: "I swear to be faithful to the Nation and the Law, and the King, and to maintain with all my power the constitution of the kingdom."[2] The problem was that it seemed to a majority of the clergy to contradict the oath of obedience to ecclesiastical authority, and therefore ultimately to the pope, which they had sworn upon ordination. They therefore refused to take the oath, were suspended from their parishes, and were driven either into exile or into open defiance of the Revolution. The attempt to impose the civic oath on the clergy was one of the greatest political disasters of the Revolution. The alienation of the clergy, whose prestige and influence in many rural parishes was enormous, also alienated much of the rural population. It created a continual source of disorders—clandestine masses, baptisms, and marriages performed by nonjuring priests, riots when "constitutional" priests were introduced into parishes, and so on. In the west of France, these conflicts led to the famous Vendée rebellion of 1793, which plunged the Republic into civil war at the same time that the allied monarchical forces were advancing on Paris.[3] The attempt to reform the Church, hence, set in motion one of the major dynamics that led to political polarization, radicalization, and the Terror. More clearly than any other episode of the Revolution, perhaps, it demonstrates the importance of ideology as a determinant of the course of Revolutionary history.

---

[2] John Hall Stewart, *A Documentary Survey of the French Revolution* (New York, 1951), p. 233.

[3] The best account is Charles Tilly, *The Vendée* (Cambridge, Mass., 1964).

4
Who Was Responsible
For The War Of 1792?

THE War of 1792 was one of the most momentous and tragic events of the French Revolution. It lasted off and on until 1815, resulted in the death of millions, and demanded such sacrifices from the French people that it helped provoke the Terror, counterrevolution, and ultimately military dictatorship.

Who was responsible for causing the war? Some historians, such as Albert Goodwin, distribute the blame on both sides: influential members of the French cabinet and legislature sought war; on the other hand, émigrés and some European monarchs were determined to crush the Revolution by force of arms. Other historians, such as Hippolyte Taine, blame the French assembly and especially the deputy Brissot and his supporters for using justifiable grievances against émigrés and foreign rulers as a pretext for war. T. C. W. Blanning discusses these interpretations plus others: the inevitable collision of the ideologies of the old versus the new order and the misperceptions by both sides.

In analyzing this controversy, one may ask if we hold those who declared war solely responsible? Or those who uncompromisingly sought ends prejudicial to their neighbors? Or those who misunderstood other powers and blundered into war without foreseeing the consequences? Or those who had any part in causing the tension? War "guilt" is difficult to assess, as anyone who has studied the events leading to the First World War well knows.

REVOLUTIONARIES AND COUNTERREVOLUTIONARIES BOTH RESPONSIBLE

Albert Goodwin

Albert Goodwin (1906–1995), from northeastern England, studied modern history at Oxford University and the University of Paris and then taught the subject at the University of Liverpool, Oxford University, and the University of Manchester until his retirement in 1969. For many years he was one of the outstanding British historians of the Old Regime and the French Revolution. He edited *The European Nobility in the Eighteenth Century* (revised edition, 1967); and *The American and French Revolutions, 1763–1793* (1965), which is Volume VIII of *The New Cambridge Modern History.* He also published many articles, a short survey, *The French Revolution* (revised edition, 1983), notable for its clarity and good sense, and *The Friends of Liberty: The English Democratic movement in the Age of the French Revolution* (1979), which describes in detail late eighteenth-century English radicalism in relation to American, Irish, Scottish, and especially French affairs.

The possibility of war with Europe had existed ever since the king's escape to Varennes, if only for the reason that the stricter confinement of the sovereigns in the capital confirmed Marie Antoinette in her views that the sole hope of salvation for the monarchy lay in foreign intervention. The king's acceptance of the constitution in September [1791] was a formal act, the effective results of which remained to be seen. For the moment, it merely stimulated further the reactionary fervour of the *émigrés.* By her continued intrigues the

From Albert Goodwin, *The French Revolution* (2nd ed. rev.; London: Hutchinson and Co., 1956), pp. 112–113, 114–120. Reprinted by permission of Hutchinson Publishing Group, Ltd.

queen early aroused the suspicions of the Legislative Assembly and provoked a wave of anti-Austrian feeling, which did much to impair good relations with the Emperor and to undermine the influence of the Feuillants.[1]

In contrast with the Feuillants' efforts to reconcile the refractory priests and to conciliate the Emperor [Leopold II], the Brissotins set out to repress the ecclesiastical counter-revolution and to intimidate the *émigrés*. Their first move in this direction was the passing of a decree on 31st October, summoning the count de Provence [one of the king's brothers] to return to France within three months, upon pain of forfeiting his rights to the succession. This, however, only produced a belated and evasive reply from the prince in December. The next step was taken on 9th November, when the Assembly decreed that all *émigrés* who had not repatriated themselves by 1st January, 1792, would be treated as traitors. Their goods would thus be subject to confiscation and, if caught, their lives would be forfeit. Though the *émigré* Court at Coblentz, now guided by Calonne, had undoubtedly been partly responsible for the Declaration of Pilnitz [August 27, 1791], and though the military forces of counter-revolution under the Prince de Condé at Worms were assuming greater coherence, it can hardly be considered that the threat represented by the *émigrés* was in itself a serious one. On the other hand, the effect of the emigration on the financial and commercial situation in France and on the discipline in the army could not be ignored. More disturbing were the administrative and political results of the religious schism. . . .

Though the decrees of 9th and 29th November[2] were vetoed by the king in December on the advice of the Feuillant leaders, the Brissotins continued with their policy of legislating against the agents of counter-revolution. Under pressure from this quarter and on the advice of [the Minister of War] Narbonne, the king announced in the Assembly on 14th December that he would summon the elector of Trèves to disband the armed gatherings of *émigrés* at Coblentz before 15th January, 1792, and that he would declare war on the elector if he refused to give satisfaction. To show that this was not an empty threat, Narbonne announced that three French armies would be formed under the command of Rochambeau, Lückner and Lafayette.

---

[1][A loose-knit group of anti-Jacobin deputies and ministers who favored a peaceful foreign policy and constitutional monarchy in 1791. Its leading members included Lafayette, Sieyes, Adrien Duport, Barnave, and Alexandre de Lameth. Their club often met at a former convent of the Feuillants, hence their name.—Eds.]

[2][These decrees provided for severe penalties against émigrés and those clergymen who refused to take an oath of loyalty to the nation.—Eds.]

The elector of Trèves, glad of the excuse of ridding himself of his un-welcome guests, and conscious of the Emperor's lukewarm support of the *émigrés,* replied without delay that he was willing to carry out Louis' wishes.

That these events did not bring about a relaxation of the tension between France and Austria may be attributed, on the one hand, to a sudden stiffening of the Emperor Leopold's attitude and, on the other, to the military and political schemes of Narbonne. Even before the French pressure on the elector of Trèves, Leopold had revived the question of the feudal rights of the imperial princes in Alsace. In accordance with the decrees of 4th–11th August, 1789, the feudal dues of the German princes with possessions in Alsace had either been abolished or made subject to redemption. In reply to this uni-lateral action taken by the Constituent Assembly, the German princes had refused to discuss the matter of compensation and had appealed to the Imperial Diet. After long hesitations, the Frankfort Diet had finally issued, on 21st July 1791, a decree or *conclusum,* up-holding the claims of the princes. On 3rd December the Emperor in-formed Louis XVI in a dispatch that he intended to ratify the decision of the Imperial Diet, which he did a week later. This issue, which had seemed likely to become extinct, was thus revived. More provocative was an imperial dispatch, dated 21st December, 1791, in which the Emperor, while approving the dispersal of the *émigrés* at Coblentz, announced that he had ordered Marshal Bender, commander-in-chief of the Imperial troops in the Netherlands, to protect the elector of Trèves, if the need arose, from any incursions on his territory by undisciplined French forces. This action was supported by the argu-ment that the French government was no longer master of the situ-ation on its own soil.

That there was some substance in these contentions is shown by the fact that, on 21st December, Narbonne had set out on a tour of the north-eastern frontier districts in order to tighten up the disci-pline of the troops. In three weeks, Narbonne practically put a stop to emigration in the army, raised its morale and returned to the As-sembly with plans for raising 50,000 new recruits by fusing the Na-tional Guards with the regiments of the line. These plans, however, proved premature, and Narbonne soon concluded that the army could only be cured of the evils with which the revolution had af-flicted it if it were tested in a limited war with the Rhineland electors. The protection offered by the Emperor to the elector of Trèves, how-ever, threatened to transform the punitive expedition which Nar-bonne had in mind into a more general conflict. This situation forced

Narbonne into an alliance of convenience with the Brissotins, with whom he had come to agree in thinking that France's real enemy was not the *émigrés* but Austria. It also induced him, at the suggestion of Madame de Staël, to set on foot negotiations with the idea of ensuring Prussian neutrality and an alliance with Great Britain. At the end of December 1791 the count de Ségur was dispatched on an official mission to Berlin with instructions to dissuade the King of Prussia from supporting the Emperor. Meanwhile, the son of Marshal Custine was commissioned to pay a secret visit to Frederick II's great captain, the duke of Brunswick, in order to offer him the post of generalissimo of the French armies. In January 1792 Talleyrand, a personal friend of Narbonne's, was sent on an unofficial mission to London to prepare the ground for a Franco-British understanding. All these overtures were rebuffed. Ségur's mission was wrecked by the agents of the *émigrés* and by Louis XVI's secret repudiation of his envoy, Custine's by the caution of the duke of Brunswick, and Talleyrand's by his intrigues with the parliamentary opposition and by the British Government's mistrust of his proposals.

The secret political design upon which these diplomatic manœuvres hinged was that the constitutional revision envisaged by the Feuillants should be effected by means of an army victorious in war, which could then be employed in the interest of the monarchy. Narbonne was thus the first to contemplate ending the revolution and restoring order by a military dictatorship. These plans, however, involved the minister in a situation which soon got out of control. His scheme for a limited war against the elector of Trèves alienated Barnave, who early in 1792 finally realized the hopelessness of his attempts to guide the queen and retired from the political scene. Narbonne's alliance with the Brissotins also had the effect of stimulating the rising demand in the country, not for a military promenade in the Rhineland, but for a fullscale war with Austria. Ever since October 1791 Brissot had been preaching an ideological war of peoples against sovereigns, and the war with Austria was envisaged as one in which France would be assisted by the subject races of the Habsburg dominions. In this illusion the Brissotins were encouraged by refugee patriots from Belgium, Liège, Holland and Switzerland. In January 1792 Robespierre, at the Jacobin club, did his best to expose the preparations for a military dictatorship made by Narbonne and to dissuade the war-mongers from becoming "armed missionaries," but he only succeeded in widening the breach between the Brissotins and his own followers. It is perhaps worth noting, in passing, that Robespierre, at this point, was neither an unqualified pacifist, nor a covert collaborationist. He was merely contending that counter-revolution should be defeated in France before its protectors abroad were assailed. Marat, too, argued in the same sense, but his influence was diminished by the fact that his popular newspaper, *L'Ami du Peuple,* had temporarily ceased to appear in the middle of December 1791.

A fresh stage in the events leading to war opened in the middle of January 1792 when [the deputy] Gensonné, in the name of the diplomatic committee of the Assembly, raised the question whether the Emperor's orders to Marshal Bender could be reconciled with the Franco-Austrian treaty of 1756. On 25th January, the Assembly decided to challenge the Emperor on this point. It invited Louis to ask Leopold whether he still regarded himself as an ally of the French nation and whether he renounced all engagements directed against French sovereign independence and the stability of the French constitution. If no answer were received to this inquiry before 1st March, France would feel compelled to declare war on Austria. From this point, all de Lessart's efforts, as Foreign Minister, to tone down the asperity of the notes which subsequently passed between Paris and Vienna only played into the hands of the Brissotins, who now determined to overthrow the Feuillant government by exposing the almost criminal weakness of its diplomacy. Meanwhile, on 7th February, the Emperor had succeeded in procuring the King of Prussia's signature to a treaty of defensive alliance, the preliminaries of which had been concluded in the previous July. In this treaty the two powers agreed to afford each other mutual aid and assistance and to promote a concert of other powers for the settlement of French affairs. Though the question of a possible further partition of Poland continued to divide the allies, and though the treaty did not protect the most vulnerable parts of Austrian and Prussian territory, it persuaded the Austrian chancellor, Kaunitz, that France could safely be hectored into submission. Hence it was that Franco-Austrian diplomacy in February and March of 1792 consisted merely of an exchange of mutual recrimination and abuse.

The final phase of these rapidly deteriorating relations opened on 10th March, when Louis XVI abruptly dismissed Narbonne and news was received in Paris of the death of the Emperor Leopold. Narbonne had virtually brought about his own fall by intriguing against the king's favourite minister, de Molleville, and by threatening Louis with the combined resignations of Rochambeau, Lückner and Lafayette. The king's action, however, provided the Brissotins with the excuse for impeaching de Lessart, and for denouncing the other members of the Feuillant administration. In this way, the ministry was overthrown and the Brissotins were left to construct one of their own. The Department of Foreign Affairs was given to Dumouriez, that of Finance to Clavière, a Swiss banker and former collaborator of Mirabeau, the Ministry of the Interior to Roland de la Platière, a civil servant, the Navy and Colonies to Lacoste, and the Ministry of Justice to Duranthon. Narbonne's place was taken by de Grave—a nonentity. The chief figure in the new government was Dumouriez, a fanatical opponent of Austria, ambitious and determined on war. The change of Austrian rulers also brought war nearer, for the successor of the cautious and pacific Leopold was Francis II, young, impetuous and with a taste for military adventure. His very youth threw him into the hands of the Imperial Chancellor Kaunitz, who was determined to humiliate France by threatening her with the newly concluded alliance with Prussia. It soon became clear, moreover, that Francis had made up his mind to champion the cause of the Alsatian princes and of the Pope, and to secure some guarantee of strong government in France.

In some respects, the policy of Dumouriez proved to be identical with that of his predecessor. He had the same conviction that Austria could be isolated by means of understandings with Prussia and Great Britain, and hoped that he might even be able to induce the German princes not to elect Francis as emperor. Like Narbonne, he secretly regarded war as an effective means of restoring the monarchical authority of Louis XVI.[3] As a former agent of Louis XV's secret diplomacy, however, Dumouriez inherited from the *ancien régime* a bitter hatred of the Austrian alliance, and was convinced that the German powers intended to treat France as a second Poland. As soon as he became Foreign Minister, Dumouriez adopted a challenging and uncompromising attitude towards Vienna and pushed on with active preparations for war. Whereas, however, Narbonne had contemplated a French offensive on the Moselle and the Rhine, directed on Trèves and Mayence, Dumouriez laid plans for overrunning the Low Countries. His object there was not formal annexation, for that would have antagonized Great Britain, but the establishment of a Belgian federal republic. The attack was to be justified to the British ministers on the ground of military necessity, and it was intended that the French armies should live on the country and thus relieve the pressure on French finances. One of Dumouriez's first acts was to dis-

---

[3][For a differing account of Dumouriez in 1792—as a republican rather than a royalist—see Patricia Chastain Howe, "Charles-François Dumouriez and the Revolutionizing of French Foreign Affairs in 1792," *French Historical Studies* 14 (1986), 367–390.—Eds.]

patch Maret—the future duke of Bassano—as an agent to incite the Belgians to revolt. Custine was once again charged with the duty of separating Prussia from Austria, and Talleyrand was entrusted with the task of preparing the way for a prospective alliance with England. The suggestions which were put to the British Government were bold and imaginative. As the basis of the alliance, Dumouriez offered to draw up a new commercial treaty, to surrender Tobago and to co-operate in the liberation of the Spanish American colonies. Great Britain, France and possibly the United States were together to share the opportunities for great commercial ventures, which would thus be opened up. The aggressive continental ambitions of Austria, Prussia and Russia could be checked, and the peace of Europe guaranteed by means of a balance between the liberal powers of the West and the autocratic monarchies of the East. It was the same policy which Talleyrand was to champion with success after a quarter of a century of conflict at the Congress of Vienna in 1815.

These grandiose plans and calculations, however, soon came to grief. Custine's mission in Berlin was futile from the start, since the King of Prussia was obsessed with the danger from revolutionary France. Throughout Europe, Dumouriez's diplomacy was frustrated by the secret agents employed by the baron de Breteuil, who was now working in close association with Fersen and the count de Mercy-Argenteau.[4] The Austro-Prussian combination proved unbreakable, while the duke of Brunswick showed his real sympathies by accepting the post of commander-in-chief of the combined anti-French forces. As the interchange of notes between Paris and Vienna degenerated in the course of March into a series of ultimata, war became inevitable. On 20th April, 1792, war on the "King of Hungary and Bohemia" [Francis II] was declared on the proposition of Louis XVI in the Legislative Assembly, before Talleyrand had set out for London. Only seven votes were cast against the motion.

---

[4][Breteuil, Louis XVI's unofficial adviser; Fersen, Marie Antoinette's Swedish admirer; and Mercy-Argenteau, the Austrian Ambassador to France, were all three avowed counterrevolutionary confidants of the royal family.—Eds.]

THE FRENCH DEPUTIES PRIMARILY RESPONSIBLE

Hippolyte Taine

Hippolyte Taine (1828–1893) was one of France's best-known men of letters in the second half of the nineteenth century. After having attended the École normale supérieure in Paris and the Sorbonne, this son of a Protestant lawyer from Ardennes built his reputation with works of literary criticism, esthetics, art history, and philosophy. Then, very distressed by the Franco-Prussian War and the Commune of 1871, he directed his powerful intellect to French history and published his multivolume *Origins of Contemporary France* (first French edition, 1876–1894). Although Taine has been criticized by historians for such faults as inadequate research and a biased presentation of evidence, his *Origins* nevertheless has been influential in France and elsewhere, especially among those who deplore the Revolution.

🎩🎩🎩🎩🎩🎩

War, like a black cloud, rises above the horizon, overspreads the sky, thunders and wraps France filled with explosive materials in a circle of lightning, and it is the Assembly which, through the greatest of its mistakes, draws down the bolt on the nation's head.

It might have been turned aside with a little prudence. Two principal grievances were alleged, one by France and the other by the Empire. On the one hand, and very justly, France complained of the gathering of *émigrés,* which the Emperor [Leopold] and Electors tolerated against it on the frontier. In the first place, however, a few thousands of gentlemen, without troops or stores, and nearly without money, need not excite much fear, and, besides this, long before the decisive hour came these troops were dispersed, at once by the

From Hippolyte Taine, *The French Revolution,* trans. John Durand (2nd ed. rev.; New York: Henry Holt and Co., 1892), II, 96–102. Some of the footnotes have been omitted or clarified. This volume is part of Taine's *Origins of Contemporary France.*

Emperor in his own dominions, and, fifteen days afterwards, by the Elector of Trèves in his electorate. On the other hand, according to treaties, the German princes, who owned estates in Alsace, made claims for the feudal rights abolished on their French possessions and the Diet forbade them to accept the offered indemnity. But, as far as the Diet is concerned, nothing was easier nor more customary than to let negotiations drag along, there being no risk or inconvenience attending the suit as, during the delay, the claimants remained empty-handed.

If, now, behind the ostensible motives, the real intentions are sought for, it is certain that, up to January, 1792, the intentions of Austria were pacific. The grants made to the Comte d'Artois, in the Declaration of Pilnitz, were merely a court-sprinkling of holy-water, the semblance of an illusory promise and subject to a European concert of action, that is to say, annulled beforehand by an indefinite postponement, while this pretended league of sovereigns is at once "placed by the politicians in the class of august comedies."[1] Far from taking up arms against new France in the name of old France, the Emperor Leopold and his prime minister Kaunitz, were glad to see the constitution completed and accepted by the King; it "got them out of trouble,"[2] and Prussia likewise. In all state management political interest is the great mainspring and both powers needed all their forces in another direction, in Poland, one for retarding, and the other for accelerating its divisions, and both, when the partition took place, to get enough for themselves and prevent Russia from getting too much. The sovereigns of Prussia and Austria, accordingly, did not yet entertain any idea of delivering Louis XVI, nor of conducting the *émigrés* back, nor of conquering French provinces, and if anything was to be expected from them on account of personal ill-will, there was no fear of their armed intervention.

On the side of France it is not the King who urges a rupture; he

---

[1]Jacques Mallet du Pan, *Mémoires et correspondance . . . pour servir à l'histoire de la Révolution française* (Paris: Amyot, 1851), I, 254 (Feb. 1792). Mirabeau and the Comte de La Marck, *Correspondance . . . pendant les années 1789, 1790, 1791 . . .* (Paris: Vve Le Normant, 1851), III, 232 (note of M. de Bacourt). On the very day and at the moment of signing the treaty at Pilnitz, at eleven o'clock in the evening, the Emperor Leopold wrote to his prime minister, M. de Kaunitz, to this effect: "The agreement he had just signed does not really bind him to anything. The declarations it contains, extorted by the Count d'Artois, have no value whatever." He ends by assuring him that "neither himself nor his government is in any way bound by this instrument."

[2]Words of M. de Kaunitz, Sept. 4, 1791, as quoted in Alfred von Vivenot, *Quellen zur Geschichte der deutschen Kaiserpolitik Oesterreichs . . .* (5 vols.; Vienna, 1873–1890), I, 242.

knows too well what mortal danger there is to him and his in the chances of war. Secretly as well as publicly, in writing to the *émigrés,* his wishes are to bring them back or to restrain them. In his private correspondence he asks of the European powers not physical but moral aid, the external support of a congress which will permit moderate men, the partisans of order, all owners of property, to raise their heads and rally around the throne and the laws against anarchy. In his ministerial correspondence every precaution is taken not to apply the match or let it be applied to gunpowder. At the critical moment of the discussion[3] he entreats the deputies, through M. Delessart, his Minister of Foreign Affairs, to weigh their words and especially not to send forth a challenge on a "fixed term of delay." He resists to the very last as far as his passive will lets him. On being compelled to declare war he requires beforehand the advice of all his ministers, over their signatures, and, only at the last extremity, utters the fatal words "with tears in his eyes," dragged on by the Assembly which has just cited M. Delessart before the supreme court at Orléans, under a capital charge, and which qualifies all caution as treachery.

It is the Assembly then which launches the disabled ship on the roaring abysses of an unknown sea, without a rudder and leaking at every seam; it alone slips the cable which held it in port and which the foreign powers neither dared nor desired to sever. The Girondists are the leaders and hold the axe; since the last of October they have grasped it and struck repeated blows. As an exception, the extreme Jacobins, Couthon, Collot d'Herbois, Danton, Robespierre, do not side with them. Robespierre, who at first proposed to confine the Emperor "within the circle of Popilius"[4] [that is, to give him an ultimatum], fears the placing of too great power in the King's hands, and, growing mistrustful, preaches distrust. But the great mass of the party, led by clamorous public opinion, impels on the timid marching in front. Of the many things of which knowledge is necessary to conduct successfully such a complex and delicate affair, they know nothing; they are ignorant about cabinets, courts, populations, treaties, precedents, timely forms and requisite style.

Their guide and counsellor in foreign relations is Brissot, whose pre-eminence is based on their ignorance and who, exalted into a

---

[3]*Réimpression de l'ancien Moniteur . . .* (Paris: Plon, 1847–1850), XI, 142 (session of Jan. 17, 1792). Speech by M. Delessart. Decree of accusation against him Mar. 10, 1792. Declaration of war, Apr. 20, 1792. . . .

[4]B.-J. Buchez et P.-C. Roux, *Histoire parlementaire de la Révolution française . . .* (Paris; Paulin, 1834–1838), XII, 402 (session of the Jacobin Club, Nov. 28, 1791).

statesman, becomes for a few months the most conspicuous figure in Europe.[5] To whatever extent a European calamity may be attributed to any one man, this one is to be attributed to him. It is this wretch, born in a pastry-cook's shop, brought up in an attorney's office, formerly a police agent at 150 francs per month, once in league with scandal-mongers and black-mailers,[6] a penny-a-liner, busybody, and intermeddler, who, with the half-information of a nomad, scraps of newspaper ideas and reading-room lore, added to his scribblings as a writer and his club declamation, directs the destinies of France and starts a war in Europe which is to destroy six millions of lives. From the garret in which his wife washes his shirts, he enjoys the snubbing of potentates and, on the 20th of October [1791], in the tribune,[7] he begins by insulting thirty foreign sovereigns. This keen, intense enjoyment on which the network fanaticism daily feeds itself, Madame Roland herself delights in, with evident complacency, the two famous letters in which, with a supercilious tone, she first instructs the King and next the Pope.[8] Brissot, at bottom, regards himself as a Louis XIV, and expressly invites the Jacobins to imitate the haughty ways of the Great Monarch.[9]

---

[5]Gustavus III, King of Sweden, assassinated by Ankarström, says: "I should like to know what Brissot will say."

[6]On Brissot's antecedents, cf. Edmond Biré, *La Légende des Girondins* (Paris: V. Palmé, 1881). Personally Brissot was honest, and remained poor. But he had passed through a good deal of filth, and bore the marks of it. He had lent himself to the diffusion of an obscene book, *Le Diable dans un bénitier,* and, in 1783, having received 13,355 francs to found a Lyceum in London, not only did not found it, but was unable to return the money.

[7]*Moniteur,* X, 174. "This Venetian government, which is nothing but a farce. . . . Those petty German princes, whose insolence in the last century despotism crushed out. . . . Geneva, that atom of a republic. . . . That bishop of Liège, whose yoke bows down a people that ought to be free. . . . I disdain to speak of other princes. . . . That King of Sweden, who has only twenty-five millions income, and who spends two-thirds of it in poor pay for an army of generals and a small number of discontented soldiers. . . . As to that princess (Catherine II), whose dislike of the French constitution is well known, and who is about as good looking as Elizabeth, she cannot expect greater success than Elizabeth in the Dutch revolution." (Brissot, in this last passage, tries to appear at once witty and well read.)

[8]Letter of Roland to the King, June 10, 1792, and letter of the executive council to the Pope, Nov. 25, 1792. Letter of Madame Roland to Brissot, Jan. 7, 1791. "Briefly, adieu. Cato's wife need not gratify herself by complimenting Brutus."

[9]Buchez et Roux, XII, 410 (meeting of the Jacobin Club, Dec. 10, 1791). "A Louis XIV declares war against Spain, because his ambassador had been insulted by the Spanish ambassador. And we, who are free, we give a moment's hesitation to it!" [Until late 1792 Brissot and many of his followers were members of the Jacobin clubs. That is why Taine can speak of them as Jacobins.—Eds.]

To the mismanagement of the interloper, and the sensitiveness of the upstart, must be added the rigidity of the sectary. The Jacobins, in the name of abstract right, deny historic right; they impose from above, and by force, that truth of which they are the apostles, and allow themselves every provocation which they prohibit to others. "Europe must know," exclaims Isnard,[10] "that ten millions of Frenchmen, armed with the sword, with the pen, with reason, with eloquence, might, if provoked, change the face of the world and make tyrants tremble on their thrones of clay." "Wherever a throne exists," says Hérault de Séchelles, "there is an enemy."[11] "Honest capitulation between tyranny and liberty," says Brissot, "is impossible. Your Constitution is an eternal anathema against absolute monarchs. . . . It places them on trial, it pronounces judgment on them; it seems to say to each—to-morrow thou shalt pass away or shalt be king only through the people. War is now a national benefit, and not to have war is the only calamity to be dreaded."[12] "Tell the King," says Gensonné, "that war is necessary, that public opinion demands it, that the safety of the empire [France] makes it a law."[13] "The state we are in," concludes Vergniaud, "is a veritable state of destruction that may lead us to disgrace and death. To arms! to arms! Citizens, freemen, defend your liberty, confirm the hopes of that of the human race. . . . Lose not the advantage of your position. Attack now that there is every sign of complete success. . . . The manes of past generations seem to me crowding into this temple to conjure you, in the name of the evils which slavery has compelled them to endure, to preserve future generations from similar evils, the generations whose destinies are in your hands! Let this prayer be granted! Be for the future a new Providence! Ally yourselves with eternal justice!"[14]

There is no longer any room for serious discussion with those Marseilles orators. Brissot, in response to the claim made by the Em-

---

[10] *Moniteur,* X, 503 (session of Nov. 29 [1791]). The Assembly orders this speech to be printed and distributed in the departments.

[11] *Moniteur,* X, 762 (session of Dec. 28 [1791]).

[12] *Moniteur,* XI, 147, 149 (session of Jan. 17 [1792]); X, 759 (session of Dec. 28 [1791]). Already, on the 16th of Dec., he had declared at the Jacobin Club: "A people that has conquered its freedom, after ten centuries of slavery, needs war. War is essential to it for its consolidation." (Buchez et Roux, XII, 410). On the 17th of Jan. [1792], in the tribune, he again repeats: "I have only one fear, and that is, that we may not have war."

[13] *Moniteur,* XI, 119 (session of Jan. 13 [1792]). Speech by Gensonné, in the name of the diplomatic committee, of which he is the spokesman.

[14] *Moniteur,* XI, 158 (session of Jan. 18 [1792]). The Assembly orders the printing of this speech.

peror in behalf of the princes' property in Alsace, replies that "the sovereignty of the people is not bound by the treaties of tyrants."[15] As to the gatherings of the *émigrés,* the Emperor having yielded on this point, he will yield on the others.[16] Let him formally renounce all combinations against France. "I want war on the 10th of February [1792]," says Brissot, "if we do not receive advices of this renunciation." No explanations are to be listened to; we want satisfaction; "to require satisfaction is to put the Emperor at our mercy."[17] The Assembly, so eager to start the quarrel, usurps the King's right to take the first step and formally declares war, fixing the date.[18]

The die is now cast. "They want war," says the Emperor, "and they shall have it." Austria immediately forms an alliance with Prussia, threatened, like herself, with revolutionary propaganda.[19] By sounding the tocsin the Jacobins, masters of the Assembly, have succeeded in bringing about that "monstrous alliance," and, from day to day, this tocsin sounds the louder. One year more, thanks to this policy, and France will have all Europe for an enemy and for an only friend, the regency of Algiers, whose internal system of government is about the same as her own.

---

[15] *Moniteur,* X, 760 (session of Dec. 28 [1791]).

[16] *Moniteur,* XI, 149 (session of Jan. 17 [1792]). Speech by Brissot.

[17] *Moniteur,* XI, 178 (session of Jan. 20 [1792]). Fauchet proposes the following decree: "All partial treaties actually existent are declared void. The National Assembly substitutes in their place alliances with the English, the Anglo-American, the Helvetic, Polish, and Dutch nations, as long as they remain free. . . . When other nations want our alliance, they have only to conquer their freedom to have it. Meanwhile, this will not prevent us from having relations with them, as with *good-natured savages.* . . . Let us occupy the towns in the neighborhood which bring our adversaries too near us. . . . Mayence, Coblentz, and Worms are sufficient." *Ibid.,* p. 215 (session of Jan. 25). One of the members, supporting himself with the authority of Gelon, King of Syracuse, proposes an additional article: "We declare that we will not lay down our arms until we shall have established the freedom of all peoples." These stupidities show the mental condition of the Jacobin party.

[18] The decree is passed Jan. 25 [1792]. The alliance between Prussia and Austria takes place Feb. 7. (François de Bourgoing, *Histoire diplomatique de l'Europe pendant la Révolution française [Paris: Lévy, 1865–1885],* I, 457.)

[19] Albert Sorel, "La Mission du Comte de Ségur à Berlin" (published in the *Temps,* Oct. 15, 1878). Dispatch of M. de Ségur to M. Delessart, Feb. 24, 1792. "Count Schulenburg [the Prussian cabinet minister] repeated to me that they had no desire whatever to meddle with our constitution. But, said he with singular animation, we must guard against gangrene. Prussia is, perhaps, the country which should fear it least; nevertheless, however remote a gangrened member may be, it is better to cut it off than risk one's life. How can you expect to secure tranquillity, when thousands of writers every day . . . mayors, office-holders, insult kings, and publish that the Christian religion has always supported despotism, and that we shall be free only by destroying it, and that all princes must be exterminated because they are all tyrants?"

Behind their *carmagnoles* we can detect a design which they will avow later on. "We were always opposed by the Constitution," Brissot is to say, "and nothing but war could put the Constitution down." Diplomatic wrongs, consequently, of which they make parade, are simply pretexts; if they urge war it is for the purpose of overthrowing the legal order of things which annoys them; their real object is the conquest of power, a second internal revolution, the application of their system and a final state of equality.

A REVIEW OF DIFFERING INTERPRETATIONS

Timothy Charles William Blanning

T. C. W. Blanning (1942–), a Fellow of the British Academy, took his B.A., M.A., and Ph.D. at the University of Cambridge, where he has taught Modern European History since 1968. An authority on eighteenth-century German and French history, he has written many books, including *The French Revolution in Germany: Occupation and Resistance in the Rhineland, 1792–1802* (1983), *The Origins of the French Revolutionary Wars* (1986), *The French Revolutionary Wars, 1787–1802* (1996), and *The French Revolution: Class War or Culture Clash?* (2nd ed., 1998). He has also edited *The Rise and Fall of the French Revolution* (1996), *The Eighteenth Century: 1688–1850* (2000), and other works.

🐞🐞🐞🐞🐞🐞

On 20 April 1792, less than three years after the fall of the Bastille, the National Assembly voted to declare war on Austria.[1] The war was expected to be short, decisive and victorious. In the event, it dragged on for more than two decades, punctuated by truces masquerading as peaces, inflicting permanent social, economic and political damage and ending with the destruction of the Revolution. As that primal Austro-French war swelled to embrace almost every other European country, it became incomparably the great conflict in the history of the world until that time. If some earlier wars had been longer, none had ranged so widely, required such intense exertion, caused such domestic and international upheaval, or inflicted such casualties. It

From T. C. W. Blanning, *The Origins of the French Revolutionary Wars* (London: Longman Group Limited, 1986), pp. 69–73, 89 note 1 to 91 note 26, reprinted by permission of Pearson Education Limited.

[1] *Archives parlementaires de 1787 à 1860: Recueil complet des débats législatifs et politiques des chambres françaises,* 127 vols. (Paris 1879–1913), vol. 42, pp. 217–18. Technically, war was declared on Francis King of Hungary. He did not become the Emperor Francis II until elected Holy Roman Emperor in July 1792.

has been estimated that France alone lost 1.4 million of her inhabitants as a direct result of the war.[2] No wonder then, that this elemental struggle attracted the concern of so many nineteenth-century scholars living in its shadow and generated such fierce controversy. In terms of personal animosity and political axe-grinding, the disputes over the origins of the revolutionary wars were in no way inferior to present-day controversies over the origins of twentieth-century world wars. But once the First World War had set new standards for military carnage, socio-economic dislocation and political upheaval, interest in that earlier conflict did not so much wane as collapse. With the exception of Karl Otmar Freiherr von Aretin's study of the Holy Roman Empire,[3] no monograph of any substance bearing on the war of 1792 has been published since.[4] So any historiographical review not only has to begin with the literature of the second half of the nineteenth century but has to be largely confined to it.

A central concern has been the role played by ideology. For Ranke and his numerous pupils, the war was a clash not so much between states as between principles: between the monarchical conservatism of the old regime and the republican liberalism of the Revolution. As the master put it in one of his characteristically sonorous passages: "The question of war and peace became identical with the question of whether the constitution reserving prerogatives for the King should be maintained or not. It was a dual dispute which contained within it the future of the world: monarchy or republic, war or peace with Europe."[5] So it was argued that through the welter of conflicting aims and considerations ran the essential antagonism between old and new. The precise occasion for and timing of open conflict might remain open to chance, but sooner or later it was inevitable. For that reason, Ludwig Häusser identified 1789 rather than 1792 as the real beginning of the war: "Compared with this inner necessity of things, all those events outside France, such as Pilnitz and Koblenz, were of

---

[2]Richard Cobb, *Death in Paris 1795–1801* (Oxford 1978), p. 7, n. 1.

[3]Karl Otmar Freiherr von Aretin, *Heiliges Römisches Reich 1776–1806. Reichsverfassung und Staatssouveränität*, 2 vols. (Wiesbaden 1967).

[4]The wars of 1793 and 1798–99 have fared rather better in this regard. A bulky American dissertation of 1971 has a promising title—*The Girondists and the "Propaganda" War of 1792: a re-evaluation of French Revolutionary Foreign Policy from 1791 to 1793* (Princeton 1971)—but disappointing contents. Its author, Frank L. Kidner, cites nothing in the German language and also appears to be unaware of such important English-language publications as R. H. Lord's *The Second Partition of Poland* (Cambridge, Mass. 1915).

[5]Leopold von Ranke, *Ursprung und Beginn der Revolutionskriege, 1791 und 1792* (Leipzig 1879) p. 131.

subsidiary importance; the Revolution had destroyed not only the old laws of France on 4 August [*1789*] but also existing international law; it proceeded aggressively—and had to proceed aggressively if it were not to deny its innermost nature."[6] This view of the war as an inevitable collision of principles (*Prinzipienkrieg*) has had a long life and is still being repeated. A. J. P. Taylor, for example, has described the war of 1792 as "in some ways the most modern of all wars, a war brought about by rival systems of political outlook."[7] An even more recent general survey has also concluded that the war had "primarily ideological causes."[8]

Significantly, those who have adopted this interpretation have also usually (but not invariably) taken a long-term perspective. Their wide-angle lens has stressed salient features at the expense of detail. However, those historians familiar with the day-to-day conduct of policy, especially with the day-to-day conduct of Austrian policy, were much less impressed by the ideological dimension. One of the most able of them, Heinrich von Sybel, explicitly took his old master, Ranke, to task for demoting individuals to the status of unconscious tools of impersonal ideas.[9] He preferred to stress the paramount role of *raison d'état* [power politics], which kept Austria and Prussia out of French affairs for two years after the outbreak of the Revolution and would have kept them at peace in the long term too—if the Girondins had not forced them into war. Without that pernicious Girondin intervention, Sybel argued, revolutionary France could have been absorbed into the European states-system just as easily as the United States of America had been.[10] Albert Sorel chose to dilute the ideological content of revolutionary foreign policy by stressing its continuity with old-regime opposition to the Austrian alliance of 1756 and thus with French traditions which stretched back to Francis I [1515–1547] and beyond.[11]

---

[6]Ludwig Häusser, *Deutsche Geschichte vom Tode Friedrichs des Großen bis zur Gründung des deutschen Bundes,* 3rd edn, vol. 1 (Berlin 1861) p. 341. For an almost identical view, see Hans Glagau, *Die französische Legislative und der Ursprung der Revolutionskriege 1791–1792, mit einem Anhang politischer Briefe aus dem Wiener K. und K. Haus-, Hof- und Staatsarchiv,* Historische Studien, vol. 1 (Berlin 1896) p. 271.

[7]A. J. P. Taylor, *How Wars Begin* (London 1980) p. 18.

[8]Derek McKay and H. M. Scott, *The Rise of the Great Powers 1646–1815* (London 1983) p. 275.

[9]Heinrich von Sybel, *Geschichte der Revolutionszeit von 1789 bis 1795,* 4th edn, vol. 1 (Düsseldorf 1877) p. v.

[10]*Ibid.,* pp. iv, 325, 340–4, 366.

[11]Albert Sorel, *Europe and the French Revolution,* vol. 1: *The political traditions of the old régime,* eds. Alfred Cobban and J. W. Hunt (London 1969) pp. 338–42.

The culpability of Brissot and the Girondins has been stressed repeatedly, by such diverse scholars as Heinrich von Treitschke and Albert Soboul.[12] The reason for this odd coincidence of opinion between German nationalist and French Marxist is not difficult to fathom: for the former, the Girondins personified French aggression; for the latter they personified bourgeois capitalism. The predominantly neo-Jacobin tone of most French historical writing on the Revolution has cost Brissot and his supporters dear in terms of reputation. Georges Michon, whose detestation of Brissot was matched only by his adulation of Robespierre, delivered the definitive indictment: "The war," he stated baldly, "was desired and provoked by the Girondins."[13] But not even he supposed that they bore the sole responsibility for the war. All of his hero's numerous enemies inside France—with the Feuillants, the Lafayettistes and the court in the van—played their part. It is a fine paradox (albeit one very familiar to students of the First World War) that the most unequivocal statement of French responsibility for the war of 1792 should stem from a Frenchman:

> There was no question of any threat from outside or of any aggression on the part of the foreign powers. War was willed solely to act as a diversion from the social problems which were becoming more serious with every day that passed. For six months several methods had been employed in an attempt to destroy the democratic party and not one had succeeded; so this time the extreme remedy—war—was to be tried, for it would give the government dictatorial powers and would allow it to eliminate its detested enemies. For these groups the war was a grand manœuvre of domestic politics.[14]

Albert Soboul added some economic ingredients to this loathsome stew of social imperialism: in his view, the commercial bourgeoisie also sought war to re-establish the credit of the *assignats* (the Revolution's paper money) and to secure lucrative contracts to supply the army.[15] Yet he—like most other neo-Jacobin historians—has been unable to accept that the war was just the work of one or more political factions. However selfish the intrigues which preceded its outbreak, the war itself was a grand affair of principle: "simultane-

---

[12] Heinrich von Treitschke, *Deutsche Geschichte im neunzehnten Jahrhundert,* vol. 1 (Leipzig 1927) p. 119. Albert Soboul, "La Révolution française 1789–1815," in *Histoire économique et sociale de la France,* eds. Fernand Braudel and Ernest Labrousse, vol. 3: *L'avènement de l'ère industrielle (1789—années 1880),* pt 1 (Paris 1976) pp. 28–9.

[13] Georges Michon, *Robespierre et la guerre révolutionnaire* (Paris 1937) p. 9.

[14] Georges Michon, *Essai sur l'histoire du parti Feuillant* (Paris 1924) p. 359.

[15] Soboul, "La Révolution francaise," pp. 28–9. Michel Vovelle, *The Fall of the French Monarchy 1787–1792* (Cambridge 1984) p. 220.

ously national and revolutionary, simultaneously a war of the Third
Estate against the aristocracy and a war of the nation against the
united powers of old regime Europe."[16]

The role played by those old-regime powers, especially by Austria
and Prussia, has also been sharply disputed. At one extreme, Pierre
Muret argued that the war was part of a great Prussian-led conspiracy to conquer Alsace and Lorraine—and it comes as no surprise to
discover that he was writing while those two provinces were part of
the German Empire.[17] But that sort of view has not been confined to
French nationalists; A. J. P. Taylor has also asserted that the revolutionaries "were forced into war by the declared intention of the conservative powers to destroy the French Revolution."[18] Such a view
must be seen as wishful thinking bred by chronic Germanophobia,
for the reluctance of the Austrians to go to war is as well documented
as anything can be. Indeed, it was von Sybel's main achievement to
demonstrate beyond question Leopold II's preoccupation with eastern Europe until 1791 and his aversion to taking any positive action
against the Revolution in France.[19] In the course of a long and bitter
polemical dispute, he was able to discredit the view of his arch-
enemy Ernst Herrmann that Leopold was an arch-reactionary who
plotted the destruction of the French Revolution right from the
start.[20] Sybel's line has been given authoritative, not to say definitive,
confirmation by Leopold's most recent biographer, Adam Wandruszka. Indeed, the central theme of his massive study is the sincerity and consistency of his subject's attachment to constitutional-

---

[16] Albert Soboul, "La Révolution francaise. Problème national et réalités sociales,"
*Actes du Colloque Patriotisme et Nationalisme en Europe à l'époque de la Révolution
française et de Napoléon. XIIIe Congrès international des sciences historiques (Moscou,
19 août 1970)* (Paris 1973) p. 38.

[17] Pierre Muret, "L'affaire des princes possessionnés d'Alsace et les origines du conflit
entre la Révolution et l'Empire," *Revue d'histoire moderne et contemporaine,* 1 (1889–
1900) pp. 448, 591.

[18] Taylor, *How Wars Begin,* p. 14.

[19] Sybel, *Geschichte der Revolutionszeit, passim.* It is essential that this fourth edition
be used, for it was the first in which von Sybel incorporated the fruits of his researches in the Austrian archives.

[20] Herrmann did, however, gain the upper hand over Leopold's participation in the Polish "revolution" of 3 May 1791, being able to show that Leopold had had no prior
knowledge of the affair, let alone had instigated it. Sybel, on the other hand, argued
convincingly that Leopold had been much more sympathetic towards the new
regime in Poland than Herrmann had allowed. For representative samples of this
protracted and tedious dispute, see Ernst Herrmann, "Die polnische Politik Kaiser
Leopold II," *Forschungen zur Deutschen Geschichte,* 4 (1864) and Heinrich von Sybel,
"Noch einmal über Leopold II gegen E. Herrmann," *Historische Zeitschrift,* 12 (1864).

ism. Far from seeking to extirpate the Revolution, Leopold sympathised with and himself sought to realise many of its aims. On the very eve of a war he had neither sought nor relished, he was still seeking to liberalise the constitutional arrangements of his own dominions and was still insisting that there should be no total counter-revolution inside France.[21]

Complementary to this exculpation of the Austrians was the indictment of the Prussians as being far more eager for counter-revolutionary intervention. Once the Prussian and Austrian archives had been opened, the full extent of Frederick William II's restless search for territorial gains became apparent and Ranke's emphasis on Prussian caution had to be modified, if not abandoned. In 1874, for example, Adolf Beer revealed that the Prussians were promoting a scheme for the annexation of French territory as early as September 1790.[22] That was no momentary aberration; at all important stages during the next eighteen months Prussia was consistently the most acquisitive and aggressive of the two German powers. In one of the last and one of the best diplomatic studies of the period, R. H. Lord stressed that the Prussians entered the war not because the French attack on Belgium had activated their defensive alliance with Austria but because they were eager to pick up the rich territorial pickings they erroneously thought would drop into their laps.[23] Such was the weight of evidence that even Prussian historians had to concede the point. In the same year that Lord published his work, Otto Hintze's classic survey of Prussian history—*Die Hohenzollern und ihr Werk*—appeared. In the section dealing with the origins of the war of 1792, Hintze confirmed that Frederick William II had been much more bellicose than his Austrian counterpart.[24]

The dispute about the relative aggressiveness of Austria and Prussia was concerned with intentions rather than consequences. As such, it was rather unreal, for it was the perception of those intentions by the various parties concerned—especially by the French revolutionaries—which did more to determine the course of events.

---

[21] Adam Wandruszka, *Leopold II. Erzherzog von Österreich, Großherzog von Toskana, König von Ungarn und Böhmen, Römischer Kaiser,* vol. 2 (Vienna and Munich 1965) pp. 372, 381.

[22] Adolf Beer (ed.), *Leopold II, Franz II und Catharina. Ihre Correspondenz. Nebst einer Einleitung: Zur Geschichte der Politik Leopold II* (Leipzig 1874) pp. 36–7. It was proposed that Austria should take part of French Flanders, Prussia should take Jülich and Berg and the Elector of the Palatinate and Bavaria should take part of Alsace.

[23] Lord, *The Second Partition of Poland,* pp. 269–70. Unusually, this masterly work delivers much more than its rather narrow title suggests.

[24] Otto Hintze, *Die Hohenzollern und ihr Werk,* 8th edn (Berlin 1916) p. 417.

No matter how acquisitive the Prussians may have been, they were in no position to conduct a policy alone. In fact, as was usually the case at the fissiparous court of Frederick William II, more than one policy was being pursued simultaneously. So the question of Prussian intentions is really neither here nor there. A judicious selection of quotations could be made to allow them the appearance of indifference towards the Revolution as well as of bellicosity. The same applies to Austria. Consequently certain historians have chosen very sensibly to concentrate on the way in which policies were perceived rather than on the policies themselves. That perception was usually misconception. Denied reliable information and working from entirely different premises, the old-regime powers and revolutionary France held quite erroneous notions of each other's position and intentions. Writing about the period leading up to the outbreak of war, Kurt Heidrich observed: "They [*the French revolutionaries*] and their opponents no longer understood each other. They were breathing, as it were, in different political atmospheres."[25]

This was not a case of myopia, for the image was seen clearly; nor was it a case of distortion, for the image was seen in what were apparently its correct proportions. It can be termed the "Coppelia effect" (after the magic spectacles which Dr. Coppelius gave to the wretched Hoffmann and which for him turned Spalanzani's doll Olympia into a beautiful woman [in the opera *Tales of Hoffmann* by Jacques Offenbach]). Frederick William II and [his advisor] Bischoffwerder, Leopold II and [his foreign minister] Kaunitz, *thought* they knew what was happening in France and acted accordingly. Yet because their image did not correspond to reality, the actions they took had the opposite of the desired effect. The intimidatory exercise launched by Kaunitz with his note of 21 December 1791 was designed to prevent war; thanks to the Coppelian effect, it only served to make it more certain. Moreover, it afflicted the revolutionaries every bit as much as their enemies. The confident belief that the old regime powers were teetering on the brink of collapse and that one tap on the door would demolish the whole edifice played a major part in sweeping the National Assembly along in the wake of the Girondin warmongers. It is this approach, concentrating on the miscalculations of the two sides, which has yielded the most cogent analyses of the origins of the war.[26]

---

[25] Kurt Heidrich, *Preußen im Kampfe gegen die französische Revolution bis zur zweiten Teilung Polens* (Stuttgart and Berlin 1908) p. 45.

[26] See, for example, Jacques Droz, *Histoire diplomatique de 1648 à 1919*, 3rd edn (Paris 1972) p. 184.

5

The Causes
of the Vendée Revolt
# of 1793

THE Vendée uprising in Western France was a civil war in the midst of a revolution, one of the most violent events in a violent period. Estimates of the number of deaths owing to this counter-revolution and its repression vary. Such historians as Reynald Secher place the number at more than a hundred thousand from 1792 to 1802 and describe the quelling of the revolt as genocide.[1] Other historians argue that there was a smaller number of deaths and reject the term genocide as anachronistic and unjustified.[2] No one denies, however, that both sides in the revolt committed atrocities and that thousands of civilians as well as combatants were massacred.

The revolt began on a large scale in 1793 and continued sporadically throughout Napoleon's rule. Historians, as well as such novelists as Honoré de Balzac, Victor Hugo, and Alexandre Dumas, have been attracted to this dramatic and tragic episode. One of the questions they have asked, and may still be asked, is what brought tens of thousands to fight against the Revolution?

Jacques Godechot considers that the geography of the region, religious passion encouraged by the clergy, and social differences all helped to cause the revolt, and he also points to that bête noire of republican historians, the aristocratic conspiracy. Émile Gabory denies the importance of aristocratic and clerical plots and argues instead that religious feeling among the peasants was the main underlying cause of a revolt triggered by other provocations. Finally, John McManners reviews several interpretations and concludes that abject poverty, social tension, and religious fervor all played a significant role helped along by the geography of the region and the shortage of pro-revolutionary troops needed to re-establish order quickly.

How do we decide why people embark on civil war and counter-

---

[1]See Reynald Secher, *Le Génocide Franco-Français & La Vendée-vengé*, with a Preface by Jean Meyer and an Introduction by Pierre Chaunu (Paris: Presses universitaires de France, 1986), especially pp. 253, 293–306.

[2]See Charles Tilly, "State and Counterrevolution in France," in *The French Revolution and the Birth of Modernity*, ed. Ferenc Fehér (Berkeley: University of California Press, 1990), pp. 58–63.

revolution? Should we rely on what the rebels say are the reasons for their actions? Do we search for unexpressed or subconscious motivations? Which of the many forces—social, economic, political, military, geographical, or religious—do we stress?

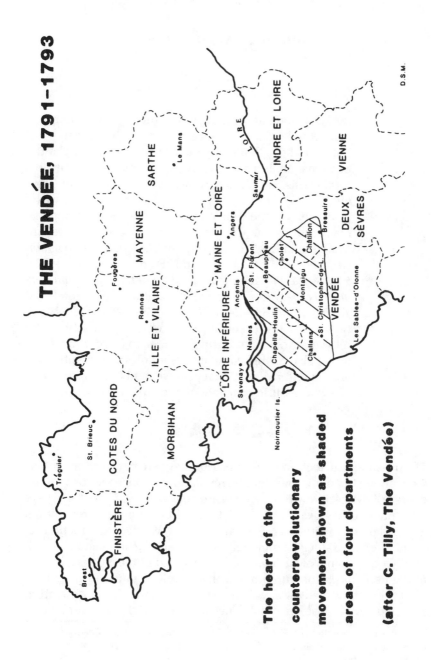

THE VENDÉE, 1791–1793

FINISTÈRE

Brest

Tréguier

St. Brieuc

CÔTES DU NORD

MORBIHAN

ILLE ET VILAINE

Rennes

Fougères

MAYENNE

SARTHE

Le Mans

LOIRE INFÉRIEURE

Savenay

Nantes

Ancenis

Noirmoutier Is.

Chapelle-Heulin

Challans

St. Florent

MAINE ET LOIRE

Angers

Saumur

LOIRE

Beaupréau

Cholet

Montaigu

Châtillon

St. Christophe-de-L.

VENDÉE

Bressuire

DEUX SÈVRES

Les Sables-d'Olonne

INDRE ET LOIRE

VIENNE

D.S.M.

The heart of the
counterrevolutionary
movement shown as shaded
areas of four departments

(after C. Tilly, The Vendée)

157

A REPUBLICAN INTERPRETATION

Jacques Godechot

Jacques Godechot (1907–1989), the son of a business-man from Lorraine, studied history at the University of Nancy and the University of Paris. While teaching at the École navale in Brest, he published his important doctoral thesis, *Les Commissaires aux armées sous le Directoire* (1937). For most of his academic career, he was a professor at the University of Toulouse. Among his many books on the revolutionary period, three are available in English translation: *The Counter-Revolution* (revised edition, 1981; first French edition, 1961), *France and the Atlantic Revolution of the Eighteenth Century, 1770–1779* (1965; French edition, 1963), and *The Taking of the Bastille: July 14th, 1789* (1970; French edition, 1965). Professor Godechot was an authority on the reforms carried out during the French Revolution. He is noted also for his comparative studies of revolutionary and counterrevolutionary movements in France and elsewhere during the late eighteenth century.

The peasant insurrections in western France were but the first of their kind among the numerous counterrevolutionary insurrections. In the course of the period with which we are concerned [1789–1804], there were many other peasant insurrections directed against revolutionary leaders or institutions. For example, the Vendée insurrection revived after 1795, then reappeared in 1799, and again even as late as 1830. The peasants of Normandy, Brittany, and of the western fringes of the Paris basin took up arms against the Revolution from 1793 to 1799. This movement was called the *Chouannerie*. In southwestern France peasants rose up in the name of the king in 1799. Several peas-

From Jacques Godechot, *La Contre-Révolution: Doctrine et action, 1789–1804* (Paris: Presses universitaires de France, 1961), pp. 216–229. Printed by permission of the publisher. Editors' translation.

ant insurrections took place in Italy from 1796 to 1799, especially in Calabria [the "toe" of the Italian boot], in the Papal States, and in Tuscany. In Belgium there was a "peasant war" in 1798, which was also a counterrevolutionary insurrection. German and Swiss peasants took up arms against the Revolution on several occasions between 1796 and 1799. After 1800 numerous peasant insurrections of a counterrevolutionary nature broke out in different areas of Europe. The most famous such uprising, and the one which had the most important consequences, was that of the Spanish peasantry, known as the Spanish War of Independence. The German wars of "liberation" in 1813 and 1814 also were, in part, peasant insurrections.

All these insurrections belonged to the same family, and we can ask if they sprang from similar causes. Historians disagree considerably about the causes of the insurrections in western France. There are a great many books dealing with the subject, but most are apologetic and hagiographic works written by royalists who eulogize the Vendeans or *Chouans.*

In their studies of the causes of the insurrections in western France, historians are divided between two points of view, depending on their political sympathies. Those hostile to the Revolution favor the thesis of a spontaneous uprising: the Constitution of 1791 and the institutions of the Revolution contradicted the natural order of things; and so the peasants, shocked by the aberration, revolted spontaneously. They also rebelled against atheism, against all religious innovations, and against unjustified reforms. On the other hand, historians favorable to the Revolution support the thesis of an insurrection incited either by the actions of the clergy and the nobility, or by the agents of the émigrés, or by the countries at war with France.

Because of insufficient research, we do not know enough about the economic or social structure of the insurgent areas in either western France or the other regions where peasant uprisings occurred. Only two works have sketched the social structure of the insurgent regions—for France, Léon Dubreuil's book, *Histoire des insurrections de l'Ouest,* and for Italy, that of Gaetano Cingari.[1] Other works are more anecdotal, describing the course of events without really analyzing their causes. Moreover, Dubreuil's study of the social structure of the

---

[1] *Giacobini e sanfedisti in Calabria nel 1799* (Messina, 1957). [Marcel Faucheux's *L'Insurrection vendéenne de 1793: aspects économiques et sociaux* (Paris: Commission d'histoire économique et sociale de la Révolution, 1964) and Charles Tilly's *The Vendée* (Cambridge, Mass.: Harvard University Press, 1964), among other works, have appeared since the present selection was originally published.—Eds.]

insurgent regions is quite brief. But at the present moment, new research is attempting to add to our knowledge of this question.

General Characteristics of Counterrevolutionary
Peasant Insurrections

We may ask if the peasant insurrections can be explained by geographical determinism. Upon examining the insurrections in western France, we see that they occurred in the *bocage* areas, where small fields were surrounded by hedgerows through which winding roads ran and where it was easy to hide. The peasants' fields were scattered, and they lived in isolated hamlets. But, an analysis of other peasant insurrections reveals that they took place in regions of a different character. In southern Italy, Calabria was an area of rather wild scrub land where the peasants lived in very large villages, actually rural cities which sometimes contained more than twenty thousand inhabitants. Yet, communications were as difficult as in western France. In Spain the 1809 insurrection occurred on the Castilian plateau as well as in the *huerta* [irrigated fruit lands] of Valencia and in the Aragonese plains. Communications were difficult in the Spain of the Old Regime too. Therefore, it is hard to identify a geographical determinism underlying the peasant revolts.

Can we speak of a sociological determinism, of a certain social structure which predisposed people to revolt? We must mention that in all insurgent areas during the revolutionary era, in France, Italy, Spain, and elsewhere, insurrections occurred most often in regions where the peasants were very submissive to their lords and landowners. Even today [1961] in the Vendée the peasants speak of the landowner as "our master," perhaps a vestige of their former submissiveness. In these areas the peasants either respect the landowner, the lord, and submit to him, or they hate him. The landlord exercises his authority in the secular sphere by collecting the rents due him, and in the religious sphere by requiring his peasants to attend mass, receive the sacraments, and send their children to Catholic school.

It has been pointed out that in these areas, the authority of the clergy, especially that of the local priests, was very great. In the Vendée as well as in Calabria, when the priest was a partisan of the new regime the local population followed him; when, on the contrary, he opposed it, so did the population. The influence of the clergy appears to predominate in all the areas where peasant insurrections have been observed, whether in western France, southern or eastern Italy, Spain, Belgium, or Switzerland.

Are we dealing here with a matter of religious faith or of custom? It is difficult to say. In these regions where communication was difficult and where formal education was rare and hardly developed, superstition was widespread. It appears that the clergy incited the peasants to resist changes in religious ritual rather than arousing them to fight for basic tenets of faith. We also can wonder about the role played in the preparation and development of the insurrections by a secret religious organization, the Aa, a group still very little understood. This association, growing out of the Congregation of the Holy Sacrament, which in turn was linked with the Society of Jesus, grouped together refractory priests, especially in southwestern France. It is possible that it also promoted the Vendée rebellion.[2] Signor Cingari states that in Calabria there were believers and nonbelievers in both the revolutionary and the opposing camps.

It appears, therefore, that the peasant insurrections were caused to some degree by geography—the difficulty of communication that hindered new ideas from spreading. Peasant insurrections were also a consequence of the social structure. They developed in regions where the peasants—sharecroppers or tenants—were very dependent on the landlords, as well as frequently in areas where the peasant was hostile to the bourgeois. The peasant was best acquainted with the bourgeois in his capacity as a tax collector, either for the state or the lord, or as a merchant exploiting the countryside and often lending money at usurious rates of interest. In addition, the effect of religion, of religious practice, is undeniable; the influence of the clergy is certain.[3]

Turning to the particular conditions that affected the insurrections in western France, we must first point out the attitude of the peasants toward the Revolution. At the beginning of the Revolution the re-

---

[2]On the Aa, see B. Faÿ, *La Grande Révolution* (Paris, 1959), as well as P. Droulers, *Action pastorale et problèmes sociaux sous la Monarchie de Juillet chez Mgr d'Astros, archevêque de Toulouse* (Paris, 1954). Consult also the article on the Aa in the *Dictionnaire de spiritualité*. More probing studies of the Aa are in progress. [Other historians have pointed to the influence of the Missionaires du Saint-Esprit founded by Louis-Marie Grignion de Montfort. See François Furet, "Vendée," in *A Critical Dictionary of the French Revolution,* ed. François Furet and Mona Ozouf, trans. Arthur Goldhammer (Cambridge, MA: Harvard University Press, 1989), pp. 173–174; Simon Schama, *Citizens: A Chronicle of the French Revolution* (New York: Knopf, 1989), p. 697; and Charles Tilly, *The Vendée* (2nd printing, Cambridge, MA: Harvard University Press, 1968), p. 103—Eds.]

[3][For more on the clergy of western France, see Timothy N. Tackett, "The West in France in 1789: The Religious Factor in the Origins of the Counterrevolution," *Journal of Modern History* 54 (December 1982), 715–745.—Eds.]

gions that were to rebel so extensively and violently were not hostile to reforms. The peasants, on the contrary, favored them. In 1789 they greeted the abolition of tithes and feudal dues enthusiastically—they already had requested such actions in their cahiers of grievances. In the Old Regime the salt tax had aroused much discontent among the peasants and they were happy that it was abolished. They also had been very hostile to the drawing by lot for *militia service,* even though this did not weigh very heavily on them.

There were some peasants, however, whose demands were not satisfied by the reforms of the revolutionary era. In western France there were tenant farmers in a special category—tenants on cancellable leases or *colons partiaires* [a type of sharecropper]. These particular kinds of land tenure existed only in this region. Peasants who were fettered by these especially onerous types of land tenure generally were loyal to the Revolution; in spite of everything, they hoped for changes in their land tenure.

Therefore, the peasant did not, a priori, oppose the revolutionary regime. On the other hand, he was frequently hostile to the bourgeois. He knew the bourgeois only as an employee of the lord, an agent of the noble. It was the bourgeois who collected feudal dues for the lord. It was the bourgeois who sold essential goods to the peasant, and the peasant believed that he was being exploited. Among the peasants, the bourgeois had a reputation for being miserly, grasping, and selfish. Peasants generally were hostile to him. The same attitude can be seen in Italy, Belgium, and Spain. The alliance between the bourgeoisie and the peasantry allowed the Revolution to succeed, but in France, as elsewhere, in those regions where this alliance could not be achieved, the Revolution miscarried.

The religious attitudes of the peasantry of western France have not yet been examined by recently developed methods of sociological analysis. But, in general, the peasant of the West was very attached to religious practices, if not to religion itself. He was very loyal to the forms, rituals, and ceremonies, to which he tended to attach a magical value. The closing of churches and the interruption of normal religious practices certainly caused discontent. He would not tolerate such innovations. In Calabria and Spain there were similar reactions.

The peasantry in western France was subject to the clergy's leadership. Before the Revolution, the clergy was divided into two categories. The lower clergy, poorly educated and very close to the common people, were obliging, charitable, and loved by their flocks. The upper clergy were usually very haughty. In sharp contrast to the poor parish priests, they were recruited from the nobility, often belonged to Masonic lodges, and were wealthy. The richest bishop was that of Bayeux. He had an income of 90,000 livres per year. The poorest bishop, that of Saint-Brieuc, had an income of 12,000. The lower clergy in western France warmly welcomed the meeting of the Estates General. In the elections very few bishops were chosen. Only two out of seven bishops were elected from the archdiocese of Rouen; from that of Tours, only two out of twelve; and Brittany sent no bishops to the Estates General. But from Bordeaux, seven out of ten were elected (the Bordeaux archdiocese was the one least troubled by revolutionary insurrections).

We see, then, that the clergy welcomed the Revolution enthusiastically. But, after the very first measures, they grew dissatisfied. Although pleased with the abolition of the old method of paying priests, they opposed the abolition of tithes, which was decided during the night of August 4, 1789, and they opposed even more the nationalization of Church property, which was voted November 2, 1789. Religious liberty, as set forth in the Declaration of the Rights of Man and later even more clearly by various laws, also offended this region that was almost entirely Catholic (there were only a few Protestants). The clergy was irritated above all because the revolutionary reforms placed religion and its ministers in a subordinate position instead of keeping them in the top rank, as was true before 1789. On September 12, 1789, Bishop Le Mintier of Tréguier, Brittany, published a statement very hostile to the Revolution. It attacked the thought of the Enlightenment, condemned freedom of the press, warned the faithful against dangerous innovations which put "the essence of royal authority in the hands of the multitude." He deplored "the weakened military discipline and the fact that citizens were taking up arms against each other. . . ." "The Church," he said, "is falling into degradation and servility; its ministers are threatened with being reduced to the status of appointed clerks. Also, the highest courts are ignored and humiliated." Le Mintier went on to protest against the substitution of state welfare for charity and against the abolition of certain very wise old laws. Finally, he warned the peasant against buying nationalized Church lands, even though they had not yet been put on sale. Le Mintier's statement had a very great impact. All the nobles of the region approved of it, and it marked the beginning of the break between the people of the western area and the Revolution.

The publication of the Civil Constitution of the Clergy heightened the discontent, especially because it reduced the number of dioceses. Seven dioceses were abolished in the western region, and in an area of such poor communications this could have resulted in very serious inconveniences. Many priests, perhaps encouraged by the Aa, refused to take the oath required by the Civil Constitution. In the diocese of Angers over 50 per cent of the priests were refractory; in the Vendée and in Brittany more than 80 per cent. Nevertheless, this was not the major reason for the outbreak of the insurrection; for there was an equal or even a greater proportion of refractory priests in other areas of France where insurgency did not develop. For example, around the Massif Central over 80 per cent of the priests were refractory and in the departments of Moselle and Bas-Rhin, 92 per cent.

The replacement of refractory priests by those who took the oath and who were alleged to be bad priests began to arouse some opposition. Arrests of refractory priests made matters worse. Refractory priests then held clandestine services, and religious processions marched at night. Such nocturnal ceremonies awakened the mystical spirit characteristic of the people of western France. The Bretons, who believed in goblins prowling the moors at night, were attached to their legends. Their fears and superstitions were aroused, and this created an attitude hostile to the Revolution. Hatreds were inflamed.

The bourgeoisie's attitude, on the other hand, was generally favorable to the Revolution. The bourgeoisie in western France, as everywhere else, was a composite class—it included merchants, lawyers, and lower government officials. But added altogether, the bourgeoisie was less numerous in the West than elsewhere. In 1789 it actually was large only in Nantes.

From the beginning of 1789 the bourgeoisie gained entry into the municipal councils of the large cities. When Church property went on sale, most of the purchasers were bourgeois. We should not believe, however, that all the bourgeois had the same point of view. Though many of them supported the Revolution, others were quite hostile. An entire group of the bourgeoisie had connections with the nobility by family ties and aspired to noble rank. Nobles and bourgeois mingled in the "literary societies" and Masonic lodges. For example, the lodges of Le Mans included nobles, merchants, and government officials.[4] Yet, in general, the bourgeoisie went along with the revolutionary movement. The majority of the western peasantry, on the contrary, grew more and more hostile to the reforms.

The Origins of the Insurrection

Certainly, the general conditions just analyzed played a very important part in the origin of the western insurrections, but a catalyst was

---

[4]A. Bouton, *Les Francs-maçons manceaux et la Révolution française* (Le Mans, 1958).

necessary. The thesis of republican historians—that the insurrection originated in plots organized either by refractory priests or by the nobility—cannot be dismissed out of hand. Clearly, the actions of the nobility and the clergy played a decisive part in the preparation of the insurrection. In this regard, it appears that a plot organized by a noble, the Marquis de La Rouairie, had a great impact.[5]

The Marquis de La Rouairie was born at Fougères, Brittany, in 1750. He had a wild adolescence, with numerous duels and remarkable love affairs, and gained notoriety by an attempt at suicide. He took part in the American War for Independence: under the name of Colonel Armand he led a band of irregulars, which made him a celebrity. He came back from America very enthusiastic for liberty, but he had neither the intelligence nor the social rank of Lafayette; on his return to France, he was received rather coldly. It appears that the comparison between his reception and that given to Lafayette displeased and embittered him.

In 1788, during the agitation which preceded the calling of the Estates General, he passionately favored the Parlement of Brittany and he was chosen to transmit to Paris the grievances of the Breton nobility, who were hostile to the recent decisions of the King. La Rouairie was arrested and thrown into the Bastille. Released at the fall of the Brienne ministry, he returned in triumph to his birthplace, Fougères. He protested against the ordinance regulating the methods of election for the Estates General because it disregarded the laws and customs of Brittany. He was particularly hostile to the doubling of the Third Estate; and when the Constituent Assembly was created, he opposed the first reform measures. It appears that by the beginning of 1790 he was thinking of organizing a counterrevolutionary movement: he gathered a number of his aristocratic friends in his château near Saint-Brieuc; and at this time some of them already suggested appealing to England for aid in supporting a counterrevolutionary movement.

La Rouairie left France in May 1791. Furnished with an ordinary passport, he reached Coblenz. There he claimed to represent the Breton Association, which was composed of émigrés from this region. The Association had as its aim a restoration of a monarchy "checked" by the ancient constitution of France, a monarchy respectful of the traditional Breton liberties and of "the religion of our forefathers." As a striking force, La Rouairie hoped to provide the As-

---

[5]See on this subject A. Goodwin, "Counter-Revolution in Brittany: The Royalist Conspiracy of the Marquis de La Rouërie, 1791–1793," *Bulletin of the John Rylands Library,* 1957, pp. 326–355. The name can be spelled either La Rouairie or La Rouërie.

sociation with guerrilla bands similar to those he had led in the United States. The Breton Association soon established branches in all the provinces of the West—Brittany, Normandy, Anjou, and Poitou. It was based on a whole series of committees organized in every city that had been an official seat of a diocese before the Revolution. Each committee was composed of six members and a secretary. There were less important committees in other cities. The committees received orders from their leader, the Marquis de La Rouairie himself. Article 6 of the manifesto distributed to the committees defined the Association's object: to contribute with "the least possible violence" to the restoration of absolute monarchy and to the recognition of "the prerogatives of provinces, landowners, and Breton honor." Association members were urged to do their best to win over National Guardsmen. Article II stated, "The military organization will be established later." Clearly, the Association was preparing to create a true counterrevolutionary militia.

In June 1791, the Comte d'Artois [the émigré brother of Louis XVI] recognized La Rouairie as the head of the Breton Association. For financing he went to see Calonne,[6] but received only a small subsidy in the devaluated paper currency of the Paris Discount Bank and in counterfeit assignats. Later, the Comte de Provence confirmed La Rouairie's powers. La Rouairie had many supporters in Brittany, among them his mistress Thérèse de Moëlien, his brother Gervais de La Rouairie, and other nobles, including Boisguy, the soon-to-be-notorious Pictot de Limoëlan, as well as the Chevalier de Tinténiac, a cashiered naval officer. It appears that the Breton Association also included Jean Cottereau, who would soon take the pseudonym Jean Chouan, from which the word *Chouannerie* seems to be derived.

The rank and file was made up of former salt-smugglers who had lost their livelihood now that the salt tax had been abolished; Breton émigrés who had gone to England, the island of Jersey, or Germany; those who had lost their jobs as a result of revolutionary reforms; and some members of the officer corps of the National Guard.

Large cities, such as Nantes and Brest, lent little support to the Association, but it had some success in the small ones. The Association charged the members of the conspiracy dues equal to a year's income, but many members did not pay them. It was never financially well-off. Nevertheless, at the beginning of 1792 the Association possessed over six thousand guns, some powder, and four cannon.

---

[6][The former Controller-General of Finances from 1783 to 1787 became a leader of the émigrés early in the Revolution.—Eds.]

The plotters of the Breton Association hoped to seize Rennes at the same time as an émigré corps landed in Brittany and counter-revolutionaries aroused opposition in the Cévennes, Lozère, and Ardeche departments in southcentral France. But the coordination of all these movements could not be fully assured. In addition, the victory of the Revolution at the battle of Valmy disconcerted the plotters. They had expected to revolt at the moment when the Prussian and Austrian armies approached Paris. The defeat of the invaders completely changed their plans.

As early as May 1792 the revolutionary authorities learned of the plot. On the night of May 31–June 1, 1792, one of La Rouairie's secretaries, as well as several other plotters, were arrested and their papers seized. Others talked, especially a man named Chévetel. Still, before the fall of the monarchy, the authorities dared not act against the conspirators. Only after August 10, 1792, did the new Minister of Justice, Danton, order an urgent investigation of the plot. The order to arrest the leading members of the conspiracy was issued. La Rouairie managed to escape the police, but he fell seriously ill and on January 30, 1793, he died in a château in the Côtes-du-Nord department.

Some of the plotters were arrested. Twelve were tried, convicted, and on June 18, 1793, guillotined. So the conspiracy failed. Yet it appears to have played an important role in preparing the insurrection of the West. It trained leaders and organized counterrevolutionary committees; it established contacts among those who were or might become the principal leaders of the counterrevolutionary movement.

The Breton Association sought, it appears, an insurrection not only in Brittany, as its name suggests, but also throughout the West between the estuary of the Gironde and the estuary of the Seine. The conversations of the Vendean leader d'Elbée with General Turreau on Noirmoutier Island shortly before d'Elbée's execution seem to reveal the aim of the Breton Association. In fact, d'Elbée said to Turreau, "Since the Vendée insurrection had broken out ahead of the time set for a general uprising, I did all I could to restrain and prevent any premature action because the whole organization was not completely set up and I foresaw the danger of a piecemeal movement."

In addition, among the documents about the émigrés in the Archives of the Ministry of Foreign Affairs in Paris, there is a paper containing the following question written by an agent of the Comte de Provence: "Who decided the moment for the Vendeans to revolt?" and the response, "Jeopardized by the death of M. de La Rouairie and the seizure of his papers, the coalition of counterrevolutionaries was forced to take action and its first move was to gather 150 men and disarm the National Guard of a small village." These documents prove that there were indisputable connections between La Rouairie's plot and the Vendée insurrection, which in turn marked the beginning of the general insurrections in the West. In fact, it even appears that the seizure of the papers of the Breton Association at the time of its leaders' arrest brought on the Vendée insurrection. The Vendean leaders, already compromised by their part in the Breton Association, feared arrest; and to forestall it, they decided to revolt in early March 1793.

Such was the immediate origin of the Vendée insurrection. But it profited from a whole series of earlier armed uprisings. Some small riots and insurrections already had occurred in the region. In the tiny village of La Croix de la Viollière, in the Vendée department, the peasants took up arms during a village fête in September 1790, but this riot was easily quelled. A government official wrote in October 1790, "The aristocrats have bent all their efforts . . . to bring on a civil war and they have hired men to take up arms against the friends of the people." Near Les Sables-d'Olonne a peasant riot broke out in February 1791, and local officials were roughly handled. On March 1, 1791, armed peasants attacked gendarmes at Saint-Christophe-de-Ligneron. Dumouriez, commander of the military district, was charged with reestablishing order. Again in 1791 another lord, the Marquis de La Lézardière, joined with other notables of his area to organize a plot. The authorities were informed. Before the uprising could break out, it was stopped. The plotters, meeting at La Lézardière's château, were imprisoned; while the peasants, on their way to assemble at the château, were dispersed. Thirty-six persons were prosecuted in the court at Les Sables-d'Olonne and were convicted. But since these actions were soon followed by the amnesty of September 15, 1791 (declared after the King had accepted the new constitution), this plot was not so severely repressed as that of the Marquis de La Rouairie. Nevertheless, the plot of the Marquis de La Lézardière played a part in unleashing the Vendée insurrection.

In 1792 there was another uprising in the Vendée. On August 20, a few days after the fall of the monarchy, the former mayor of Bressuire, Delouche, organized some peasants and occupied the small city of Châtillon. These peasants came from eighty different villages and were led by such nobles as La Béraudière and de Béjarry, who later headed the Vendeans. The National Guard of Bressuire managed to arrest the armed peasants and their leaders. If the Vendeans had been able to take Bressuire at this time, their insurrection might have begun in August 1792 rather than in March 1793. After their march on

Bressuire, most of the nobles and peasants were arrested, but then released. No one was punished.

Such were the plots and riots that preceded the Vendée revolt. They seem to have been fostered by the social structure of the region, by the poor communications, by the influence of landowners, nobles, and clergy, by the discontent resulting from the Civil Constitution of the Clergy, and by the actions of refractory priests.

But one more factor played a decisive part. At the end of February 1793, the Convention decided on a levy of 300,000 men in order to resist the military coalition which now included nearly all the countries of Europe. But the peasants of western France always had been very hostile to military service. In the Old Regime volunteers filled the regular army, but it was supplemented by a militia comprised of peasants chosen by lot. This was not a heavy burden for them; only a small number were drawn, and they were subject to just a few training periods a year. Still, the militia was very unpopular throughout France and especially in the West. The peasants always made great efforts to escape being drawn for militia service.

The volunteers raised by the Constitution and Legislative Assemblies in 1791 and 1792 had really joined the colors spontaneously, but by 1793 the number willing to volunteer had been exhausted. The Convention was forced to decide that if there were not enough volunteers to fill the quota of 300,000 men, additional soldiers would be chosen by local authorities or by any other means. In practice, local officials could either designate those whom they wished or choose them by lot. So, the militia reappeared under another form. There can be no doubt that the 300,000-man levy considerably aggravated the discontent in the western region.

The insurrection's chronology is quite clear. The decree ordering the levy of 300,000 men was dated February 24, 1793. It was known at Angers on March 2 and published in the communes of the western region on March 10. On March 11, to the cries of "No conscription!" and "Down with the militia!," insurrection broke out along the left bank of the Loire. On March 12, peasants shouting these slogans seized Saint-Florent-le-Vieil, an especially important town on the left bank of the Loire, a crossing point that allowed one to go from the Vendée to Normandy and Brittany.

What tends to prove, however, that the insurrection was not spontaneous and not caused by conscription alone, was that nobles assumed leadership and organized the peasants from the very beginning. For example, d'Elbée led a band of peasants and occupied Beaupréau. Lescure and La Rochejacquelein took the leadership of peasant bands. However, peasant leaders also appeared, for such men as Cathelineau and Stofflet emerged during the Vendée War. But, at the beginning, on March 12, 13, and 14, noblemen were the most effective leaders.

Actually, the Vendée War presented two distinct features from the start. On the one hand, it was a peasant insurrection. Caring little about forms of government, the peasants wanted to keep their religion and their "kindly priests"; and they especially disliked the militia, the draft. On the other hand, it was a counterrevolutionary movement. The nobles wanted to profit from the peasant revolt; to use a contemporary phrase, they wanted "to restore the throne and altar."

A RELIGIOUS EXPLANATION

Émile Gabory

Émile Gabory (1872–1954) was born in the Vendée. Trained at the École nationale des chartes in Paris, he served as a professional archivist in his native region and devoted much time to writing about its colorful and exciting history. His major works include *Napoléon et la Vendée* (1914), *Les Bourbons et la* Vendée (1923), *La Révolution et la Vendée* (1925–1928), and *L'Angleterre et la Vendée* (1930).

The Uprising

The civil war in the Vendée broke out when the Convention called up 300,000 men to protect the *patrie en danger*. The death of Louis XVI [January 21, 1793] had brought about a general coalition. After Austria and Prussia, the English, Russians, Spanish, and Dutch had struck at the frontiers with waves of soldiers. In three decrees issued between February 20 and 24, 1793, all single Frenchmen from the age of eighteen to forty were declared eligible for military service, and then 300,000 were called to the colors. Eighty members of the Convention were ordered to oversee these operations in the provinces. For the patriotic republicans this provided a new opportunity for emotional demonstrations. But among embittered souls, whose highest aims in life were far beyond personal and mundane goals, there arose a unanimous feeling of protest. However, the draft quota fixed for each department of western France was very small: for the department of the Vendée, 4,197 men out of a population of 305,610; in Maine-et-Loire, 6,202 men, of which 752 were to come from the Cho-

From Émile Gabory, *La Révolution et la Vendée* (Paris: Librairie académique Perrin, 1925), I, 146–148, 195–199, 201–206, 214–217. Printed by permission of the publisher. Editors' translation. Wherever possible, the author's citations of sources in footnotes have been clarified.

let district and 701 from that of Saint-Florent; and in Loire-Inférieure 7,327 from a population of 430,000.

If there had been time to prepare the public and to explain the decrees, opposition certainly would have been less vehement; but the orders had to be carried out immediately. . . .

One detail of the draft procedure was especially exasperating. Article 20 of a decree dated March 4 exempted most public officials from military service. To be sure, the militia of the Old Regime had also exempted royal officials, as well as most manorial officials. Moreover, those peasants who were at all well-to-do had known how to slip through the net. But in the new regime, where that glorious word equality rang out in every sentence, why, exclaimed the peasants, were these old distinctions kept for the benefit of the privileged class? When all this was added with electrifying rapidity to the underlying causes, one of the most awful political tempests in human memory was unleashed throughout a part of the West. It was like a sudden growth of every bad seed, like the unexpected sprouting of gigantic plants under a tropical sun. . . .

The Circumstances of the Uprising Clarify Its Causes

In the crackling of volleys, the thunder of cannon, the incitements to massacre, and the imploring wails, one can recognize the signs of all the remote and immediate causes that provoked and then launched the uprising. The rebels shouted their various rancors and individual resentments; they insistently proclaimed their motives. One cannot misread them.

What does not appear is "the plot," the celebrated and legendary plot that several writers have seen as the origin of the movement. No doubt, it would take a bold man to deny any significance to the instigations of the nobility and especially the clergy. To deny the existence of agitation by these suspected persons would be to misunderstand the situation. After having desired a new order or at least acquiesced in it, they had come to loathe a regime of which they had much to complain; and they did not hide their opinions. But no tie among all these dissatisfied people can be found, nor can any expressed or secret intention to overthrow the government by force of arms be found. Although some blood had flowed since 1791, there was no general pattern. In many other departments, the installation of Constitutional priests had also been carried out by gunfire; yet no plot or concerted plan is suggested.

In an oppressive atmosphere the storm could be felt building up:

"We are having disturbances in our district, and we are afraid of seeing the germs of a general insurrection develop here," said a report from the town of Montaigu in the Vendée department. A dispatch dated March 10, 1793, from Chapelle-Heulin in Loire-Inférieure, noted the arrival "of men known to be disloyal; they have influenced the citizens to such a point that most of the commissioners of the sections [elected officials of small administrative units] have resigned." But these individual agitators obeyed no single watchword—they were moved to action by their own passions. The officials of the Maine-et-Loire department wrote to the Convention, "The servants of clergymen and of former nobles were the first agitators and many of them are leading crowds."[1] Could it have been otherwise? Was it not natural that the leaders of the movement would be those whose masters had suffered the most, those who had listened to their masters utter the most violent recriminations? These servants were the best prepared and often were former noncommissioned officers. The plot? It was denied even by those supporters of the revolutionary government who were intimately acquainted with the disorders. One of them wrote, "I realized that these events could not be considered the result of a concerted plan."[2] Later, the republican General Travot, always so acute and fair in his judgments, asserted that although the peasants had to be forced and coerced to march in the year VIII [fall 1799], the movement of March 1793 was spontaneous.

Some authors have tried to connect the pseudo-plot to the real one of Armand, Marquis de La Rouairie, in Brittany,[3] but the facts shout out against such an assertion. No one has been able to uncover the mysterious network which was supposed to have joined Brittany to the other provinces of the West. If some nobles in Anjou or Poitou were acquainted with the schemes of La Rouairie, which is possible, none were caught having any direct or indirect relation with him. No

---

[1]François Grille, *Lettres, mémoires et documents . . . sur . . . l'esprit du Ier bataillon des volontaires de Maine-et-Loire . . .* (Paris: Amyot, 1850), IV, 215, 218, concerning March 17, 1793; F.-A. Aulard (ed.), *Recueil des actes du Comité de salut public avec la correspondance officielle des représentants en mission . . .* (26 vols.; Paris: Imprimerie nationale, 1889–1923), III, 432; the plot is mentioned in *Mémoires d'un ancien administrateur,* p. 10; on the causes cf. Dom François Chamard, *Les Origines et les responsabilités de l'insurrection vendéenne* (Paris: Savaète, 1898); and Henry Jagot, *Les Origines des guerres de Vendée* (Paris: Champion, 1914).

[2]Célestin Port, *La Vendée angevine* (Paris: Hachette, 1888), II, 202; Desmazières, *Précis des évènements dans le district de Cholet.*

[3]Charles-Louis Chassin, *La Préparation de la guerre de Vendée, 1789–1793* (Paris: Dupont, 1892), III, 285. [For biographical information on La Rouairie, see the selection on the Vendée revolt by Jacques Godechot.—Eds.]

letter gives proof of such an association, no revelation to a friend, no admission before a court of law. Not one emissary of the Bourbon princes was arrested at this time while making his way toward the Vendée. There is total agreement in the statements of Vendean nobles carried along, despite themselves, by the popular flood and in the statements of peasants whose tongues were undoubtedly loosened by being so near the scaffold. All denied any prior agreement and insisted on the spontaneity of the movement's outbreak.

It has been asserted that d'Elbée[4] knew of the Breton plans, but neither at meetings nor among close friends did he ever mention them. "If the Vendeans had taken part in La Rouairie's plot," Madame de La Bouëre has wisely pointed out, "they would have obtained weapons and ammunition; they did not do so; instead they had to fight with sticks."[5]

The insignificant part played by those Vendeans who, according to the scheme of the Breton plotter La Rouairie, were to lead his artificial uprising, is quite revealing. The region had been split up and assigned to various leaders. If we can trust the historian Alphonse de Beauchamp[6] (who, as an employee of the Ministry of Police under the Napoleonic Empire, had access to documents that have since disappeared), the principal agents of La Rouairie in the Nantes region were Palierne and Gaudin-Bérillais. Palierne, however, appeared on the scene only after the uprising had occurred—he asked for a military post under General Bonchamps. Gaudin-Bérillais showed himself to be mainly interested in calming the fervor of the insurgents. In Poitou Prince de Talmont was supposed to be the head of the uprising. But Talmont had emigrated to Germany. He joined the rebel army at Saumur only after the tumult of the Vendean hurricane attracted him. Paris was not fooled: on May 30, 1793, the Provisional Executive Council, which the deputies accused of not having foreseen the revolt, drew up a brief account of the measures taken to deal with the disturbances in the Vendée. It flatly declared that the La Rouairie affair had no connection with them. . . .

The peasants, and not the agents of La Rouairie, succeeded in igniting the general conflagration. The Breton agitator thought the nobles would begin and the peasants would follow, but in fact it was the peasants who led and the nobles who obeyed. This was the reverse

---

[4][Maurice Gigost d'Elbée, a former army officer, emigrated in 1791, returned to France in 1792, became a leader of the Vendeans in 1793, and was executed in 1794.—Eds.]

[5]Comtesse de La Bouëre, *Souvenirs* (Paris: Plon, Nourrit, 1890), pp. 30–31; also see M.-J.-N. Boutillier de Saint-André, *Mémoires* (Paris: Plon, Nourrit, 1896), p. 51.

[6]Author of *Histoire de la guerre de Vendée* . . . (Paris: Giguet and Michaud, 1806).

of the plan. As soon as the first shots were fired, the rustics recognized the seriousness of their action. If they gave up, it meant the gallows. Fighting was their safest bet, but they lacked leaders. The republicans were commanded by career officers; they had to have some also. Logic clearly pointed to the manor houses. "If we had some nobles to lead us," one of them cried out, "we could march on Paris."[7] The nobles had served in the army; they had learned strategy and tactics. Because of their social standing, they had gained an authority which they would know how to exercise and which could quiet the rivalries among the commoners who were vying for leadership. Finally, the rebels had the very natural thought—almost instinctive among peasants who had fallen into an unfavorable situation—that of appealing to those more powerful than themselves, to those whose châteaux had stood for centuries amidst their cottages, protecting or menacing them. . . .

Nor did the black robes of the clergy appear in front of the red glare of the early fighting. Can one seriously believe that they contrived a plot, but discreetly left it to the peasants to carry out? The clergy had suffered even more than the nobles. Outlawed in 1792 for refusing to take a schismatic oath, individual priests stirred up their faithful and fought back at the thresholds of their churches. But it is a long step from this kind of resistance to a general conspiracy. The day that the uprising broke out, the priests were not to be found amidst the crash and thunder leading the insurgents. No hidden thread bound the rectory to the parishioners. Studying the investigations made of those dramatic days, one can find no instance of a group led by clergymen. The priest of Saint-Martin de Beaupréau, tears in his eyes, rushed in front of his parishioners and begged them to return to their homes. It was too late, for they had already manhandled the government's recruiting agents. The bridges were burned between them and repentance. . . .

The older, underlying cause of the Vendée revolt, that of religion, was soon evident. Though rebels in the districts of Challans, Savenay, and Ancenis mentioned the call up of the three hundred thousand men in their manifestoes of March 14, 15, and 19, they especially emphasized their desire for the old religious arrangements and their vision of liberty. They complained of the many kinds of oppression. They boasted of bringing back "the good priests." They forced

---

[7]Port, III, 271, the words of Julien Chauvat; C.-L. Chassin, *La Vendée patriote, 1793–1800* (Paris: Dupont, 1893–1895), I, 209, where Guerry du Cloudy wrote to Boulard, "Soon . . . the people felt that they had to organize; willy-nilly, they chose peaceful men and forced on them the difficult and paramount duty of command."

republicans to shout "Long live the Pope, down with the nation." "God will end up being stronger than the devil," asserted the young women of the village of La Chèze. On March 24 Joly's insurgent army issued a declaration of justification while en route to Les Sables-d'Olonne. It sought to reestablish, so the army said, the throne and religion, order and peace. In this declaration the military draft was no longer an issue.

"Yes, we are defending the religion of our forefathers," declared the leaders of the Vendean army a little later, "and we shall defend it to the last drop of our blood, as did our divine Master, who did not fear to give His own life to establish it among us." And General Bonchamps, in the peroration of a speech, vehemently criticized republican officials for religious persecution, for hunting down priests, and for profaning churches. He did not refer to military service. Still later, replying to requests contained in M. de Gilliers' dispatch, sent by the Bourbon princes, the leaders of the revolt said the same thing: "The peasants took up arms mainly to reestablish the Catholic and Roman religion." Nothing about military service. Some rebels are even supposed to have said—and we learn this from the republican General Kléber: "Give us back our good priests and we will let you have the King." They were supposed to have added, "And we will let you have our nobles too." But that was not the way a Vendean thought.[8]

All the peasants who were arrested insisted on their Catholicism before their judges. Their enemies called this attitude a delirium: "They are really fanatical, as in the fourth century. Every day they are executed and every day they die while singing hymns and professing their faith. The use of capital punishment . . . only has the effect of rendering odious the power that employs it." This comes from a statement by the deputy Volney, on mission from the Convention to Loire-Inférieure. The republican General Berruyer wrote, "Death is the beginning of happiness for them." Turreau [on mission from the Convention] compared them to crusaders.[9]

No doubt, some nobles did say that they wanted to restore the King. The Vendean leader Sapinaud died crying out, "I die happy, for

[8]*Kléber en Vendée (1793–1794). Documents publiés . . . par Henri Baguenier Desormeaux* (Paris: Picard, 1907), p. 29.

[9]Port, II, 330, statement of Pierre Davy and similar accounts, pp. 232 *et seg.,* and p. 260; Vicomte B. d'Agours (ed.), *Documents inédits pour servir à l'histoire des soulèvements de mars 1793 . . .* (Saint-Nazaire, 1883), p. 123; Chassin, *La Vendée patriote,* I, 358, a report to Minister Lebrun dated May 20; Jean Savary, *Les Guerres de Vendéens . . .* (Paris: Baudouin, 1824–1827), I, 170, dated April 28; Louis Turreau, *Mémoires pour servir à l'histoire de la guerre de la Vendée . . .* (Paris: Baudouin, 1824).

I am dying for my King." When the Vendean General Beauvollier was asked by his judges, "What was your aim?" he replied, "My aim was to have a king." On August 18, 1793, the Vendean generals wrote to the Comte d'Artois, "We have revolted in the defense of Louis XVII, a child so worthy and so unfortunate." But all these people had forgotten the truth. They were plunged into the struggle by the sinewy arms of the peasants and only later did they recognize the interests of the monarchy.

Not all of them so misrepresented the real cause of the revolt. While dying, d'Elbée confessed, "I swear on my honor that although I sincerely and truly wanted a monarchical government, I had no specific plan in mind, and I would have lived as a peaceful citizen under any regime as long as it assured my tranquillity and the free exercise of the religious beliefs that I have always practiced." On the republican side, Choudieu [a deputy on mission in the Vendée] asserted that the monarchical cause had no effect on the revolt. An Angevin, Joseph Clemenceau, insists in his *History of the Vendée War* (1909) that the military draft simply provided an opportune excuse. The views of the deputy Turreau do not differ from this.

The ridiculous has even been claimed—that the Vendeans wanted to revive the feudal dues. Why should they? In their cahiers they had requested abolition of these payments. Immediately after the abolition of these dues, why would they feel regret? What they really wanted was the restoration of property to its former owners—to churches, to monasteries, and to individuals; but they were not so stubborn as to want it returned still covered with the feudal moss that these properties had accumulated over centuries.

Such interpretations of the causes are errors made by republicans. Now to deal with a royalist error that can be quickly refuted in the light of events: some writers, more interested in edifying their readers than in instructing them, have characterized all the insurgent peasants as men of angelic sweetness. But this was a war, a religious war, not a war of religion—a religious war upholds liberties, a war of religion tries to impose beliefs. This was a war, and no war, even if made by the best of Christians, can be won by the cross alone without other weapons. The crusaders also used swords, and the old chronicles tell us how terribly they used them on entering Jerusalem. In the fire of battle the ethereal zephyrs of Christianity are not always enough to temper hatreds—icy breaths which rise from the inner depths of men. This is even more true in civil wars, so open to the interplay of resentment and hatred. The uprising was a peasant revolt, as were previous uprisings against the nobles in other provinces.

The insurgents wore their rosaries around their necks, but they carried their scythes with them. Woe to the one who refused to join their ranks! The popular flood uprooted by brute strength anyone who hesitated.

Insurgent parishes forced their neighbors to march with them. Peasants placed convinced republicans at their head when they recognized their abilities. Menaced by grape pickers' knives, Citizen Gelligné, a well-known patriot of Saint-Aignan, was forced to command the rioters. They needed not only leaders but also rank and file. This caused recruitment to be extremely brutal. The rebels "scoured the countryside, forcing all the inhabitants to join them—everyone marched, even ten to twelve-year-old boys."[10] Unless the peasant could furnish proof of a severe wound making it impossible for him to march, he was liable to be recalled. If he could not fight, but was able to do such work for the army as kneading dough, then he was forced to do so. If he could perform no service, he had to give money. Often curiosity led the peasant to follow the crowd. Once committed, he rallied to succeeding musters without difficulty. Woe to those who were known to oppose this conscription against conscription! . . .

It should not be imagined that the two sides in the war corresponded without exception to particular social classes: all peasants did not become insurgents; all nobles were not carried away by the uprising; nor were all bourgeois favorable to republican ideas. In the most patriotic cities, such as Cholet and Segré, there were strong movements against national conscription. On the other hand, one has only to glance through the lists of refugee patriots (to be found in the Archives in Nantes) to be struck by the preponderance of peasants. While many petty bourgeois from rural areas marched at the heads of rebel groups, nobles could be found in the front ranks of the republican forces in the Vendée or on the national frontiers. . . .

From the same peasant family some went to the Right, others to the Left. The two Bernard brothers from Vézins turned up in opposing camps: one was a city official who saw his workshop burned by rioters; the other joined the Vendean army and was shot after the battle of Savenay. Charles Davy des Nauroy, a surgeon at Saint-Étienne-du-Bois, took part in the insurrection and became a major in General Charette's army; his brother stoutly proclaimed his republican sentiments. One bloody example of family hatreds deserves special notice.

---

[10] Henri Gilbert, *Précis historique de la guerre de Vendée, publié par Baguenier Desormeaux;* see also Boutillier de Saint-André, p. 48; and the *Documents inédits* of Vicomte d'Agours.

At the taking of Legé, Joly, commander of one of Charette's divisions, learned that one of his sons had just received a mortal wound. He ran to him; just then he was told that his other son, who was fighting on the republican side, had been captured. "What shall we do with him?" he was asked. "Shoot him," spat out the inexorable father. The two sons died at the same moment.

[The nineteenth-century republican historian] Edgar Quinet posed this question: if the land of the nobles and priests had been divided among the peasants, would they have revolted? He did not think so. But this is still an open question. For one thing, human self-interest seemed to be minimal in the uprising—rewards in the next world predominated over material desires. Some well-to-do peasants and some rich bourgeois, who would have been able to draw up chairs at the huge banquet of national property taken from the Church and the émigrés, refused to increase their fortunes by acquiring these confiscated properties. We do not hear from the mouths of rebels any regrets that they did not receive the government's manna in return for a little handful of depreciated assignats. But another point has to be made: those who are acquainted with the greediness of the farmer and his frantic desire for land would naturally think that a free gift, a total partitioning of the land, as was to be carried out in Russia, would have won over enough peasants to hinder the others, the great majority, from acting.

There are other unanswerable questions. Would the uprising have broken out without the draft of three hundred thousand men, that drop of water in a pitcher filled to overflowing, that spark in a building crammed with combustible materials? We do not know. Perhaps another cursed event would have occurred to unite all the discontented in one unanimous act. Or if religion had not been a factor, would the Vendée have obeyed the draft call? All we can say is that when complete religious liberty was granted under the Consulate, the conscription issue lost its sharp edge. A valuable piece of evidence, but in this kind of speculation, analysis loses its power and any attempt to see through the shadows is only vanity.

A SYNTHESIS

John McManners

John McManners (1916–), a clergyman's son, was educated at Oxford and Durham Universities before entering military service during the Second World War. After
the war he became an Anglican priest and a teacher of
history at universities in Australia and Great Britain. In
1984 he retired as Regius Professor of Ecclesiastical History, Oxford University. At present, he is Chaplain and
Fellow of All Souls College, Oxford University. His writings on French history include *French Ecclesiastical Society under the Ancien Régime: A Study of Angers in the
Eighteenth Century* (1960), *The French Revolution and
the Church* (1969), and *Church and Society in Eighteenth-
Century France* (1998). These books combine sound
scholarship with a sympathetic understanding of the
Catholic Church and its clergy. Another of his books,
*Death and the Enlightenment: Changing Attitudes to
Death among Christians and Unbelievers in Eighteenth-
Century France* (1981), is a judicious and thorough in-
vestigation of the subject.

🎩🎩🎩🎩🎩🎩

What part did religion play in the atrocious civil war that was waged
in the Vendée? We must distinguish here between the motives of the
rising as contemporaries saw them and as they appear today in the
light of analyses of the social structure of the insurrectionary areas,
and between the causes of the original outbreak and the forces which
kept rebellion going once it had started, like draughts fanning a blaz-
ing torch. To their republican opponents the Vendéans were a cruel
peasant rabble wearing pious images in their hats and chaplets
round their necks, obeying the orders of royalist agents and fanatical
churchmen. It was true enough that the rising, once started, was

From John McManners, *The French Revolution and the Church* (London: The Society
for Promoting Christian Knowledge, 1969), pp. 81–84. Reprinted by permission of the
publisher.

taken over by supporters of the *ancien régime*—nobles, or ecclesiastics like Bernier, ex-*curé* of Saint-Laud of Angers. But this was not how the insurrection had begun. About its origins there is a legend with a dual bias, for clerical historians have depicted pious peasants marching to defend their good *curés,* while anti-clerical historians have improved upon the same theme with a fable of a plot of priests who, in [the nineteenth-century historian] Michelet's words, "devised a work of art, singular and strange, a revolution against the Revolution, a republic against the Republic."

There is something (within limits) to be said for the clerical version and nothing at all for the anti-clerical one. The revolt began on the fringes of no less than five ecclesiastical dioceses—Luçon, La Rochelle, Angers, Nantes, Poitiers—and not a single bishop or ecclesiastical official made any attempt to organize resistance to the Revolution. The earliest leaders of the rioters were not priests or nobles, but an itinerant vendor of fruit and fish and a ruined *perruquier* [wigmaker]. True, the clergy of the heartland of the rebellion were overwhelmingly on the refractory side (though the proportion varied oddly from one locality to another: almost all refractories in the "Mauges" area of southern Anjou, but no less than ninety-six *curés* and five *vicaires* among the constitutionals, as against 134 *curés* and seventy-two *vicaires* remaining orthodox, in the insurrectionary area of the actual department of the Vendée). Many of the clergy dispossessed by the Civil Constitution were popular with their flocks—we know that some of them were remarkably generous with their alms in hard times—while those who were not popular were at least influential, for in such an isolated rural *milieu* they were indispensable in all local business. It is clear too that the reorganization of parishes by the District authorities under the Civil Constitution legislation was bitterly resented. There were riots to preserve [church] bells from confiscation and petitions to keep well-loved churches open. Envious clamour was raised against the intriguing "patriots" who stood well with the revolutionary officials and pulled strings to ensure that their own parishes were preserved while others were suppressed. Yet, all this could be said about many areas of Brittany, and Brittany remained comparatively quiet, passively accepting the revolutionary settlement of the Church. Why was the Vendée so different?

If an answer in one word is required that word is "poverty." Ever since the beginning of 1789 the peasants of the rough, infertile country of the rising had been on the verge of starvation. They had been unfairly taxed under the *ancien régime* in comparison with other areas. Their *cahiers* had made simple requests—lower taxation, the repair of their miserable roads, and help for the infirm and indigent, who abounded. What, in fact, they received from the Revolution was a new consolidated land tax based on the same unjust assessment, and so arranged that the cultivator had to pay it all directly, instead of some falling on the proprietor, as in the days before the reform. "In the special case of the Vendée," writes Faucheux, "there was a demoralizing impression that they were paying more out of a diminished revenue—as indeed they were."[1] So the revolutionary government was hated. When it introduced a conscription law (Sunday 10 March was the date of enrolment) the rising began. In proportion to the population few conscripts were being called up. This made no difference. The point had been reached at which starving and disillusioned men would obey no longer. The broken nature of the country, the lack of urban rallying points for republican forces, the fact that troops were not available for quick suppressive action meant that isolated riots could combine into a full scale, wide-spread rebellion, and once it had begun those who had committed themselves were doomed if they surrendered.

But the Vendéan rising was more than an attack upon a hated government: it was also an attack upon a specific social class which was identified with the revolutionary régime—the bourgeoisie of the country towns, the officials, and the richer farmers. These were the men with capital who had bought the lion's share of ecclesiastical property when it came onto the market. Earlier historians had noticed the division between town and country and the peasants' envious hatred of the acquirers of the *biens nationaux* [expropriated Church and émigré lands], but the study of these social tensions upon a detailed statistical and geographical basis is a recent development, inspired by Paul Bois' *Paysans de l'Ouest* (1960). Bois' problem was to explain the motives of the *chouans,* the catholic-royalist brigands of the Sarthe, to the north of the main Vendéan war zone. In 1789 the peasants of the west of the Sarthe had been more hostile to nobles and clergy than their fellows in the rest of the department, yet from 1793 they furnished the recruits for a sinister guerrilla feud against the revolutionary bourgeoisie. The paradox is explained once the destination of the *biens nationaux* is analysed. In most of the department there was little ecclesiastical property for sale, and the peasants were too poor to buy it; in the west, there was more property for sale and the peasants were prosperous enough to have ob-

---

[1][Marcel Faucheux, *L'Insurrection vendéenne de 1793: aspects économiques et sociaux* (Paris: Commission d'histoire économique et sociale de la Révolution, 1964).—Eds.]

tained it—had not the bourgeoisie outbid them at the auctions. A similar analysis, more straightforward in this case, has been made of the areas of the Vendéan rising by Charles Tilly[2] and later by Marcel Faucheux. In the District of Sables d'Olonne, for example, out of 217 buyers of *biens nationaux,* only fifty-seven were small peasants or artisans; in the District of Cholet only 156 out of a total of 640. Those who were able to buy ecclesiastical property, one might conclude, became enthusiasts for the Revolution, which was their guarantee that they could keep it: those who were defeated at the auctions became acutely conscious of the religious loyalties which reinforced their hatred of their richer and victorious rivals.

That there is a sociological explanation for the role played by religion in the Vendéan rising does not mean that the religious motivation has been explained away. Collectively and statistically these obscure, grim fighters can be added together in groups acting in patterns which explain, in retrospect, why they were the ones to rebel, while other peasants with similar religious convictions did not carry their dissatisfaction to the point of civil war. But, taken individually, there is little doubt what their inspiration in battle will be, for the forefront of men's minds is filled by their most avowable motives. In their own eyes the "Whites" [Vendeans] who lay in ambush for the "Blues" [Revolutionaries] along the sunken lanes and dense hedgerows of the Bocage, and who were shot and guillotined in droves by republican military commissioners, were fighting for their families, for the Virgin and the saints, for their own local ideal of "liberty"—liberty to contract out of the nation's unjust wars and taxation, and to stay at home and hear mass said by their old familiar priests.

---

[2][Charles Tilly, *The Vendée: A Sociological Analysis of the Counterrevolution of 1793* (Cambridge: Harvard University Press, 1976, orig. 1964).—Eds.]

6
Why Terror in 1793–1794?

"MAKE terror the order of the day!" "Deliver a last blow against the aristocracy of merchants!" "Punish not only traitors, but even the indifferent!" These slogans were proclaimed in 1793 by Barère, Collot d'Herbois, and Saint-Just, members of the most powerful executive body in France.[1] It was clear that France had now entered the period historians call "The Reign of Terror."

The Committee of Public Safety had been created in April 1793 as a committee of the Convention. At first it guided the Convention by issuing provisional regulations and by overseeing ministers. But during the next seven or eight months, it acquired new and vast powers: to make arrests, to staff parts of the bureaucracy, to name and remove generals, and to control the government's emissaries to the troops and the provinces. The legislators of the Convention, jealous of their powers and prerogatives, delegated this authority only reluctantly. But could the unwieldy assembly itself have directed the armies combating most of the countries of Europe? Could it have quashed the many revolts in the French provinces? In Paris, could it have held prices down, fed the starving, and restrained, if not satisfied, the disaffected?

There can be little doubt that, at least from September 1793 to July 1794, the Committee with its emissaries and supporters resorted to coercion. The number of those executed reached over ten thousand, and tens of thousands more were killed without trial in the Vendée and elsewhere. Others were imprisoned—hundreds of thousands, perhaps as many as half a million, in a population of fewer than thirty million.

Why there was such coercion is a matter of great controversy. Some historians defending the Revolution stress that the Terror was the product of conditions—especially civil and foreign wars—and that most of the Terrorists were neither bloodthirsty brutes nor impractical theorists. Albert Mathiez is concerned with how events affected the revolutionary leaders, and Richard Cobb describes the impact of circumstance on the rank and file.

Other historians are less favorably disposed to the revolutionaries

---

[1]The nine other members of the Committee of Public Safety from September 1793 to July 1794 were Billaud-Varenne, Carnot, Couthon, Hérault de Séchelles, Lindet, Prieur of the Côte-d'Or, Prieur of the Marne, Robespierre, and Saint-André.

of the year II. Crane Brinton and François Furet do not deny that trying circumstances helped shape the Terror, but they claim that these
alone were not sufficient. Brinton finds that, for a few months, the
leaders of the Revolution, the Jacobins, attempted to create a kind of
heaven on earth; rigid and puritanical in their faith and zeal, they
often killed or imprisoned those whom they could not convert. Furet
searches for the roots of this Terrorist mentality and finds it in a political culture that had existed since 1789. Influential revolutionaries
reacted against some of the forces of the Old Regime: the monarch's
pretensions to absolute rule and the aristocrats' claims to privilege
and superior social status. Heavily indebted to Jean-Jacques Rousseau's idea of the general will, they sought to regenerate the nation
by instituting an all-powerful government that would foster equality
and virtue. They rejected compromise and checks and balances; instead they demonized their foreign and domestic opponents as trai-
torous plotters who deserved severe punishment, including imprisonment and even execution.

Were very difficult circumstances more important than the temperament and ideas of the revolutionaries in explaining the Terror?
Mass arrests often coincided with threats to the Republic. Also, most
executions and assassinations took place in the regions of civil war.[2]
On the other hand, even in those regions, the extent of coercion depended upon the revolutionaries in charge. Some, like Mathieu Jouve,
known as Jourdan the Decapitator, were brutes; other leading local
politicians were much more moderate. One also notes that the Terrorists themselves did not always justify their deeds by claiming they
acted out of necessity, that they had no choice.[3]

In addition, if a violent and intolerant revolutionary political culture was more important than circumstances, did this culture arise
during the Terror or was it evident from the beginnings of the Revolution, as Furet argues?[4] Were the summary executions and obsession with plotters that arose as early as 1789 of long lasting significance or were they only occasional and ephemeral?

Is it possible for us to decide dispassionately whether the Reign of

---

[2]Donald Greer, *The Incidence of the Terror During the French Revolution: A Statistical Interpretation,* Cambridge, MA: Harvard University Press, 1935.

[3]Mona Ozouf, "War and Terror in French Revolutionary Discourse," *Journal of Modern
History,* 56 (December 1984), 579–597.

[4]See the article by Timothy N. Tackett in Chapter 3 above, "The Character of the National Assembly (1789–1791)," in which he differs from Furet on this point. So does
Barry M. Shapiro. See especially his *Revolutionary Justice in Paris, 1789–1790* (Cambridge, Eng.: Cambridge University Press, 1993).

Terror was largely justifiable or reprehensible? Has our judgment been clouded by comparisons with the twentieth-century dictatorships and the horrors of Communism, Nazism, and Fascism? On the other hand, have these movements illuminated the reasons for the Terror? One thing is certain, we need to grapple with the great complexity of the Terror and the difficulties in interpreting it.

A REALISTIC
NECESSITY

Albert Mathiez

Albert Mathiez (1874–1932) came from a peasant family in eastern France. He combined great ability with energy and aggressiveness to gain entrance to the prestigious École normale supérieure in Paris. A student of Alphonse Aulard, who was one of the first professional historians of the French Revolution, Mathiez was also strongly influenced by the historical works of the socialist Jean Jaurès. Mathiez first began writing mostly about the religious history of the Revolution. Eventually he went on to study its political and, to a limited extent, its economic and social aspects. Three of his books have been translated into English: *The French Revolution* (1929; French edition, 1922–1927); *The Fall of Robespierre and Other Essays* (1927; French edition, 1925); and *After Robespierre: The Thermidorian Reaction* (1931; French edition, 1929). His attempt to rehabilitate the character and policies of Robespierre and to denigrate those of Danton launched a famous quarrel with his former teacher, Aulard. In addition to writing many monographs and a survey of the Revolution, Mathiez started editing the scholarly journal *Annales révolutionnaires* in 1908. The journal's name was changed to *Annales historiques de la Révolution française* in 1924, and he continued as its editor until his death.

♣♣♣♣♣♣

The Montagnards, a minority in the National Convention, based their power on the big city governments and on the Jacobin clubs from which they quickly expelled their rivals. Since the Montagnards had opposed the War of 1792, the common people could not blame them

From Albert Mathiez, "La Révolution française," *Annales historiques de la Révolution française* 10 (1933), 13–18. Printed by permission of the editor of the *Annales historiques de la Révolution française.* Editors' translation.

for the frightful economic crisis the war caused; and they kept in contact with the masses by their social welfare program. The military defeats in the spring of 1793, General Dumouriez's treason, and the revolt of the Vendée finally allowed them to take power. This was done by force of arms during the three days from May 31 to June 2, 1793. They purged their adversaries from the Convention and very soon organized a dictatorship, a collective dictatorship by two committees—the Committee of Public Safety and the Committee of General Security—both supported by a Convention temporarily in the hands of the Mountain. These events constituted a new revolution. . . . The dictatorship by the committees was really a dictatorship by the Montagnard party and to some degree by the sans-culottes.

This dictatorship, which lasted a little more than a year, was much less the result of a well-thought-out ideology than of inescapable pressures brought on by civil and foreign war. The enemy had to be repulsed, the royalist and Girondin revolts crushed. The cities and the armies, starving because of the English blockade, had to be fed, while the million soldiers going to the frontier needed supplies and arms. Terror became the order of the day, and the regime set up the guillotine to deal with its enemies. It suspended elections and sent emissaries with full powers to crush resistance in the provinces. The watchword went out to the generals—victory or death! The statue of liberty was veiled, and authority replaced it in ascendancy. The revolution of the Mountain rested on premises opposed to the individualistic revolution of 1789. In the name of public safety, as formerly in the name of the king, conformity was enforced and property rights were limited when circumstances required. To further the defense of the nation and the Revolution, all provisions were pooled and all kinds of merchandise and food requisitioned. The regime established price ceilings on the most important commodities and opened municipal bakeries and butcher shops. In short, a sort of forced experiment in collectivism was set up. I say a forced experiment, since even those who attempted it considered it only temporary and hoped that it would soon disappear without leaving a trace.

The new dictatorship differed greatly from that of the Constituent Assembly of 1789–1791. The people had accepted and had even desired the earlier one; they merely submitted to this one and even detested it. Public opinion, while supporting the deputies of the Constituent Assembly, pushed them into taking more and more severe actions against the enemies of the Revolution. The assembly's committees were obeyed docilely by elected officials who accepted their authority. But now there was a marked shift, with a civil war to match a foreign war. The Vendée and federalist revolts, the execution of the King, the military defeats, the requisitions, the impoverishment caused by inflation, as well as the dechristianization campaign and the closing of the churches, the arrest of suspects, and the continuing use of the guillotine—all these formidable manifestations of crisis discouraged a large number of Frenchmen and created an opposition that desired peace at any price, even at the cost of restoring the Old Regime.

It was no longer possible to justify this new dictatorship, as the Abbé Sieyes had the earlier one, simply by referring to the theory of constitutional authority. It was only too noticeable that the new dictatorship was no longer an application of the sovereignty of the people but rather its opposite. Therefore, responding to an attack by the Dantonists, Robespierre justified the dictatorship by making the significant distinction between a state of war and a state of peace, a revolutionary government and a constitutional government. His two speeches, of 5 Nivôse [December 25, 1793] and 17 Pluviôse [February 5, 1794], based on this theme, express the theory of revolutionary government that foreshadows the future Marxian Dictatorship of the Proletariat. Constitutional government can function, he said, only in peacetime. It has to be suspended in wartime—otherwise it would cause liberty to perish. "The aim of constitutional government is to preserve the Republic, that of revolutionary government is to establish it. The Revolution is liberty at war against its enemies; the Constitution is the regime of a victorious and peaceful liberty." The Revolution is essentially a civil war; and therefore "its government has to be extraordinarily active precisely because it is at war, . . . because it is forced to employ unremittingly new and speedy measures so as to meet new and pressing dangers."

Whereas the theory of constitutional authority established dictatorship solely on the basis of the will of the people, the theory of the revolutionary regime based dictatorship on political and patriotic necessities stemming from the war!

Besides, Robespierre himself had seen and admitted the dangers of such a regime. What would become of the state if the dictators used their omnipotence to gain their own ends? A single remedy, a moral one, suggested itself—the dictators must be virtuous.

The French revolutionaries had believed that seizing political power would be enough to resolve the economic and social problems. Rather quickly they perceived their error. Their work crumbled under the weight of the wealthy. The rich, united against the revolutionary laws, made them inoperable. However, the revolutionaries did not think of modifying their principles. It did not cross their minds to found society on a consistent and permanent limitation of property rights, and they continued to regard individual property as untouchable. Their only intent was to correct momentary abuses, and they considered the revolutionary dictatorship merely a temporary expedient. They imagined that all they had to do to resolve the social problem—which in their eyes remained a political issue, a moral issue—was to frighten the aristocrats, imprison them, or exile them. This attitude can be understood if one bears in mind that a large number of the revolutionaries were landowners, well-to-do bourgeois, merchants, or professional men with some landed property. The Terrorist dictatorship was meant to answer the needs of the people, but it was run by bourgeois.

Only a small minority of the bourgeoisie learned from experience and understood that the continuation of the sans-culottes in power would be possible and durable only at the cost of a gradual and permanent limitation of individual property rights. Robespierre, Saint-Just, and Couthon sought in the Ventôse Laws to expropriate the property of suspects and to distribute it to the poor. But their colleagues secretly resisted these efforts. The Committee of Public Safety had already been unwilling to nationalize civilian food distribution. Carnot had opposed government operation of factories, even those created by the representatives on mission. The Committee of General Security, with the concurrence of some members of the Committee of Public Safety, blocked the operation of the Ventôse Laws, and their sponsors were overthrown on 9 Thermidor.

The great majority of the deputies to the Convention were individualists, very hostile to anything resembling communism. The true communists, those who believed that the Fourth Estate [the common people] could reign only by the suppression of private property, were isolated and without influence; in any case, most of these men thought only of a collectivization of food and consequently of collectivizing only the land which produced the food. When Babeuf, after Thermidor, sought to unite them into a strong party, it was too late. The dictatorship had collapsed, and Babeuf was powerless to reestablish it. His attempt, which cost him his life, was both behind and ahead of its time. Behind its time because it occurred after the Montagnard party had been thrown out of power and had been already decimated by the proscriptions of Thermidor; ahead of its time because society was not yet prepared for communist ideas.

The revolution of July 1789, which had brought the bourgeoisie to power, was the offspring of the philosophy of the eighteenth century, a philosophy fundamentally liberal and individualistic. The revolution of June 1793, which raised the Montagnards to dictatorial power, was the product of circumstance and necessity. It was not the result of either intellectual training, systematic thought applied to the principles of government or society, or a profound investigation of economic development. And how could it be otherwise when machine production was only coming into being, when industrial concentration (which is the inevitable consequence of it) was not yet apparent? The boldest of the revolutionary thinkers, Babeuf himself, conceived only of agricultural communism. Most of the communists of the time made a careful distinction between industrial property, which, having been the product of work, was worthy of respect, and agricultural land, the only property that they wanted to collectivize.

One must keep this situation in mind to understand how the Jacobin dictatorship fundamentally differs from more recent dictatorships and to comprehend the underlying reasons for its failure.

If the Bolshevik dictatorship, like the Jacobin dictatorship, sought to justify its conduct by the necessities of war, it was, unlike the Jacobin, at least based on a coherent doctrine, Marxism, which it tried to put into practice. The Bolsheviks were quick to abolish not only private ownership but even the very structure of the state which they had seized. The Jacobins, on the other hand, touched only with trepidation and reluctance the regime established by the Constituent Assembly. They superimposed their economic dictatorship on the individualistic legislation without destroying the legislation. Their requisitions and their price controls did not abolish private property rights, but only hindered their exercise. Their communism, temporary and incomplete, was only an expedient for which they felt they had to apologize.

In the political domain, the same differences appear. The Russian Communists, faithful to Marx's thought, sought from their first days to give all power to the proletariat. The government they formed is basically a government of one class. On the contrary, the Jacobin Montagnards, although they had to rely on the sans-culottes, to govern in their name, and to benefit them, never arrived at the concept of class. They pursued the royalists, the Feuillants, and the Girondins not because they thought them class enemies but because they were considered to be political adversaries and accomplices of the enemy. The reason for this is clear. The leaders of the Mountain sitting in the committees and in the Convention were not proletarians but only the friends and allies of the proletarians. They had not rejected the philosophy of the eighteenth century. Its political aspect, which continued to inspire them, is the negation of the existence of classes—it ignores social groupings and stresses the individual.

That is why, unlike the Bolshevik dictatorship (which is based on class antagonism), the dictatorship of the Mountain (which remained fundamentally individualistic) was never a total or full-scale dictatorship. Lenin and his associates understood that in order to establish a dictatorship of the proletariat and to make it permanent, the separation and division of the State's powers would act as an impediment. The Council of People's Commissars legislates and administers at the same time. Such was not the case during the Terror in France, for unity was never entirely achieved within the revolutionary government. No doubt the Convention was purged and in theory it combined legislative and executive power. But actually the Committee of Public Safety took charge of the war effort, diplomacy, and administration, while the Committee of General Security took charge of the repression of plots and the secret police. Thus in France the legislative and executive powers were separated—the Convention retaining the one and the Committees the other. And there was even a separation within the executive branch, since two distinct committees shared its powers. The revolutionary machine of the Montagnards was infinitely more complicated and therefore its operation more delicate than the revolutionary machine of Soviet Russia.

A MENTALITY SHAPED BY CIRCUMSTANCE

Richard Cobb

Richard Cobb (1917–1996) has characterized his own family background and schooling as typical of the English upper middle class—his father was a colonial civil servant, and Cobb himself was educated at boarding schools and at Oxford. Before and after the Second World War he lived in France. In 1955 he returned to teach at various British universities, most notably at Oxford from 1962 to 1987. His earliest books were written in French and include *Les Armées révolutionnaires* (2 volumes, 1961–1963, English translation entitled *The People's Armies,* 1987). In this study of the paramilitary forces whose main task was to insure that the cities and towns of France were adequately provisioned, he argues that their reputation for bloodthirstiness and rapine is undeserved. Among his later publications are *Terreur et subsistances, 1793–1795* (1965), *A Second Identity: Essays on France and French History* (1969), *The Police and the People: French Popular Protest, 1789–1820* (1970), *Reactions to the French Revolution* (1972), *Paris and Its Provinces: 1792–1802* (1975), *Death in Paris . . . : October 1795–September 1801* (1978), and *People and Places* (1985). He also edited, with Colin Jones, *Voices of the French Revolution* (1988). As a historian, he rejected and criticized the stress on elites, Marxist-inspired analyses of social classes, and statistical studies in the manner of the historical journal *Annales: Économies, sociétés, civilisations.* Instead he wrote vivid, impressionistic accounts, drawn largely from archival material, of ordinary people in Paris and the provinces caught in the revolutionary whirlwind.

From Richard Cobb, "Quelques aspects de la mentalité révolutionnaire," *Revue d'histoire moderne et contemporaine* 6 (April–June 1959), 86–87, 96–104, 116–120. Printed by permission of the author and the Secretary General of the Société d'histoire moderne. Editors' translation.

We have spoken elsewhere of the revolutionary sans-culotte during the period of his greatest activity, between April 1793 and Germinal year II [March–April 1794], and we have been especially interested in describing his personal attitudes and his emotional life.[1] These men were puritans for whom vice went hand in hand with counterrevolution. They therefore condemned celibacy, gastronomy, gambling, prostitution, obscenity, finery, and luxury; but on the other hand, they showed a marked indulgence for drunkenness. Such then was the essence of their private behavior. It now remains to describe some aspects of their collective behavior, their "public" life. . . .

The revolutionary was not an evil man, still less a professional informer or writer of anonymous letters. So if he occasionally did denounce someone, the main reason was his political credulity . . . caused by his belief in the dangers, the plots of all kinds, which he continuously saw about him. It must be said that the enemies of the regime certainly managed to strengthen his sense of always being "in danger of an assassin's sword"; for they were incredibly indiscreet, and this was certainly not because of drunkenness alone. The evidence is unmistakable: in spite of the Terror, in spite of the sight of the guillotine prominently displayed in the busiest places, in spite of the informers who might be anywhere, especially in the cafés and the public squares, those Frenchmen who disliked the revolutionary regime had no qualms about expressing their dissatisfaction as loudly and publicly as possible, reproaching the Revolution and its works in the most vulgar language. They were the Pères Duchesne[2] in reverse, as noisy as street vendors. Even very young women in Lyon, waitresses in the cafés patronized by the troops of the garrison, did not hesitate to justify the [counterrevolutionary] events of May 29 [1793] right in front of the government soldiers; and they added that they were proud to have helped the federalist troops by bringing them food and ammunition and that, if the insurrection were to resume, they would again aid "our brave lads of Lyon."[3] Common people and fashionable people alike were not satisfied with muttering to themselves, and if the men from Paris trusted only what they heard, they would not have had any difficulty in persuading themselves that they

---

[1]Richard Cobb, "The Revolutionary Mentality in France," *History*, XLII (1957), 181–196.
[2][A reference to the inflammatory revolutionary newspaper edited by Jacques-René Hébert.—Eds.]
[3]Archives départementales, Rhône 42 L 149 (Commission temporaire, série alphabétique, dossier de Franchette Mayet, an eighteen-year-old girl whose fiancé had been killed during the siege of Lyon). She was denounced by the artillerymen of the Paris Revolutionary Army. See also 42 L 151 (concerning the woman Miou).

were in a completely royalist region. It was not in Lyon alone that people were so indiscreet in what they said; a similar garrulousness is to be noted among the enemies of the regime and the discontented at Nantes, Brest, Rouen, and especially in the countryside, where farmers did not hesitate to say what they thought about a Republic they viewed mainly in the forbidding light of price controls, requisitions, and the closing of churches. Avowed counterrevolution marched in the open; royalism was on display; and even at the height of the Terror, federalism still sought converts, especially in such areas as Lyon, where it could be identified with local patriotism.

A denouncer on occasion, a denouncer in spite of himself, the average revolutionary supported the great measures of repression; he had, besides, called for them insistently in the political clubs during the autumn of 1793. At least in his public statements and collective actions he was even harsher on domestic enemies than was the government itself. In particular, he demanded that it legalize the Terror. Repression in the year II followed the rules of "revolutionary legality"; but repression in the year III [the anti-Jacobin terror after the fall of Robespierre], even when carried out by criminal courts, was largely a matter of undisguised murder, individual violence, and class vengeance. The revolutionary of 1793 wanted to punish domestic enemies according to the rules of a justice that was summary to be sure and that was administered of course by the sans-culottes. This was therefore a political justice, but it was justice which nevertheless permitted certain rights to the accused. In the year III there was a reversion to [acts like the massacres of] September 1792, the difference being that this time the Terrorists were the victims; for even in the courts, justice revolved around class and social background. In 1795, in the Midi [southern France], people claimed that the "bloodthirsty sans-culottes" could be recognized by their dress; that is, they were clothed like artisans, like workers. The repressive justice of the year III was marked therefore by a class bias scarcely present in the revolutionary repression of the preceding year.[4] In the year III a goldsmith of Salon-de-Provence was accused "of having called for the death of citizens who powdered their hair and wore shirt cuffs

---

[4]Arraigned before the tribunal of Aix, some Terrorists from Marseille, accused of having participated in the riot of Vendémiaire year III [September–October 1794], challenged some of the jurors: "In behalf of his co-defendants, one declared that they did not want merchants, clerks, and property owners as jurors, but workers like themselves . . ." (Archives nationales de France, D III 31 (3) (405), Comité de Législation, Marseille; report made by the criminal tribunal of Bouches-du-Rhône, Ventôse year III [February–March 1795]).

with ruffles,"[5] which is also a way of making justice a class matter; but we think this was mostly just talk. Certain frivolous dress had been much denounced by the sans-culottes, but bewigged members of society did not persecute them because of this.

These *buveurs de sang,* these *mathevons,*[6] were they therefore so fierce? Their language certainly was. Here, for example, is what they said and wrote about Lyon and the Lyonnais. Marcillat, a former parish priest of Jaligny in Allier and a member of the Temporary Commission [set up to pacify Lyon and punish the rebels there], wrote the following to his colleagues on the Revolutionary Committee of Moulins: ". . . Our Commission has sworn to revive public spirit; but what am I saying, comrades, there isn't any, it is gone. Villeaffranchie [the name the revolutionaries gave Lyon] is composed of aristocrats and the selfish: the former we will send to the guillotine; we will make the latter pay and we will make them recognize that poor unfortunates are their equals." We notice, in passing, this didactic aspect of the repression, a repression which people at the time also called a "regeneration." The former priest went on to say, "Blood must be shed in order to consolidate the Republic and to have it recognized in the city where we are living." And he concluded rather unexpectedly: "The people of this city (which had once been called Lyon) are fools. . . ."[7] A member of the Society of Valence [a revolutionary political club] even proposed that all federalists be expelled from Commune-affranchie [Lyon] and from Ville Sans Nom (Marseille), which would really mean the expulsion of nearly all the inhabitants, and that the two cities be repopulated with sans-culottes who would move into their homes. A statement to this effect was sent to the National Convention.[8] Rather often similar sentiments came from the pens of Parisian revolutionaries when referring to Lyon, whose population was accused of being both counterrevolutionary and "crassly mercenary."[9] In public and, more important, in

---

[5]Archives nationales, D III 29 (2) (61), Comité de Législation, Aix; sentence handed down 3 Thermidor, year III [July 21, 1795], against twenty-four Terrorists from Arles and Salon.

[6][Two terms of disparagement directed against militant revolutionaries.—Eds.]

[7]Archives départementales, Allier, L 879, Comité de Moulins, correspondence (Marcillat to the Committee, 29 Brumaire, year II [November 19, 1793]).

[8]Archives départmentales, Drôme, L 1086*, Société de Valence; meeting of 5 Pluviôse, year II [January 24, 1794].

[9]See, for example, Friedrich Christian Heinrich Laukhard, *Un Allemand en France sous la Terreur,* trans. Wilhelm Bauer (Paris, 1915), p. 267: ". . . They claim that almost all the people of these areas are crassly mercenary and shamelessly rob poor artisans, workers, and laborers of their pay. . . . Here the aristocracy of money rides high. . . ."

private, they, like Marcillat, approved of rigorous repression that struck, with little regard for social distinctions, sometimes nobles, sometimes the upper middle class, and sometimes silkworkers. A proprietor of a gift shop on the Rue Saint-Denis in Paris, a loyal republican who was to be outlawed twice (after the affair at the Camp de Grenelle and again in the year IX),[10] wrote to his section: "In my last letter, I told you that the guillotine is taking care of some *dozens* of rebels every day and that about the same number are shot. Now I want to inform you that several *hundreds* are to be shot every day so that we will soon be rid of those scoundrels who seem to defy the Republic even at the moment of their execution. . ."[11] Officers from Montpellier, at the time also stationed at Lyon, revealed the same kind of unqualified approval; and since their sentiments were expressed in letters to their personal friends, they are all the more reliable as evidence of sincerity. One of them noted that "every day the Holy Guillotine cleanses the soil of liberty of all federalists in the department of the Rhône and Loire; so it goes, so it will continue. . . ." Another officer from Montpellier, in an almost jovial tone, wrote to someone back home that "everything continues to go well here, all rebels are being guillotined and shot. . . ."[12]

However, these men were neither professional executioners, nor naturally bloodthirsty. But they felt no pity for the people of Lyon, federalists who attacked the indivisibility of the Republic, an unpardonable crime deserving capital punishment. Their hatred for the population of Lyon, already strongly conditioned by a Parisian press that unanimously called for quick reprisals against federalists, was undoubtedly reinforced on the spot by the state of isolation imposed on them by a silent and hostile people. A tour of duty at Lyon in the year II was not a laughing matter, and the troops complained bitterly about the ill-will and the unfriendliness of the city. Whether Parisians or men of Nivernais and Allier, they were disliked even though *they* were the good sans-culottes, the real revolutionaries. This is therefore one more piece of evidence that "the stupid Lyonnais" lacked the republican spirit. It is true that a few soldiers, on seeing the extreme poverty of the inhabitants and on talking to some women of

---

[10] [These two events concern abortive plots against the government, the first quelled by the Directors in 1796 and the second by Napoleon and his Minister of Police Fouché in 1800–1801.—Eds.]

[11] Archives nationales, F7 4767 d 2, Lassagne (Réaume to the president of the Revolutionary Committee of the Bonne-Nouvelle section).

[12] Archives départementales, Seine-et-Oise, IV Q 187 (confiscated material, papers of Mazuel) (Fayet à Mazuel, 2 Pluviôse, year II [January 21, 1794]; Penelle à Mazuel, 27 Frimaire, year II [December 17, 1793]).

the lower classes, did feel compassion; and there was one revolutionary officer who even dared to denounce the repression by declaring that "in a Republic no one should be singled out for proscription."[13] But these examples are rare. Most soldiers did not mingle with a population they distrusted—the bodies of soldiers were sometimes fished out of the Rhône River—and the local imitators of the *Père Duchesne,* Dorfeuille and Millet, made it their business to encourage the zeal for repression by sounding the trumpet for revolutionary vengeance.[14]

It is very easy to condemn the repression at Lyon straight off. Not only can it be considered a horrible crime, but also an incredible political blunder which succeeded only in turning all Lyon against a Republic that, in its eyes, seemed inseparable from the guillotine and the firing squad. Couthon saw this quite clearly. But we must also recapture the life of the year II; do not forget the great federalist revolts of the summer and how they had almost swallowed up the Republic in a terrible civil war. No doubt little effort was made to understand the causes of these revolts, but what was remembered was the critical situation in which they had placed France by June and July 1793. That is why the revolutionary, whether he was a small shopkeeper, a professional soldier, a former priest, a physician, or an artisan, approved the use of force against the people of Lyon, Marseille, the Vendée, and Toulon. He favored it also when it struck at refractory priests and more generally when it struck at those whom he accused of being "fanatics," for he could not forgive the latter for having caused "small Vendées" in various regions. Moreover, the soldiers, who had everywhere helped develop a definite revolutionary mentality, were especially hostile to the Catholic people of the countryside, whom they regarded as allies of the *Chouans* and the other avowed enemies of the regime. In their hatred of the "fanatics," there was also something more personal; for many of the soldiers had witnessed atrocities committed against republicans by the peasants, both men and women, of the Vendée.

But the revolutionary demanded even harsher measures against the hoarder, the economic criminal, and the disobedient, "selfish"

---

[13] See my study *L'Armée révolutionnaire parisienne à Lyon et dans la région lyonnaise* (Lyon, 1952), p. 31. Also Archives départementales, Rhône 31 L 50, Société de Lyon; meeting of 16 Frimaire, year II [December 6, 1793].

[14] *Le Père Duchesne* [of Lyon] (Dorfeuille and Millet), No. XX (17 Pluviôse, year II [February 5, 1794]) and No. XXVIII (24 Ventôse, year II [March 4, 1794]). Referring to the "embroidery merchants," they said quite delicately: "We are going to send over our dragoons . . . to make them dance the carmagnole to the tune of the commander of the garrison, and he will, with all due respect, shoot their faces to bits."

farmer and tried to show that these acts of repression had an economic basis. If the Parisians and the little people of Moulins and Nevers so favored the use of force in Lyon, it was primarily because they saw the city as that "big business capital" where even the workers were unworthy of liberty.[15] For similar reasons, Hébert and members of the Paris sections demanded that the machinery of terror and the temporary commissions of popular justice be sent to that other business capital, Rouen; for the revolutionaries also had a very low opinion of the population there.[16] Some people even wanted to extend repressive measures to every rural area and terrorize the farmers, but on this occasion government policy did not go so far as the one advocated by the urban sans-culottes.

This approval of force and the Terror was therefore the result of a combination of very diverse elements. With regard to the measures taken against the people of Lyon and Marseille, there were intermingled the economic prejudices of the small shopkeeper and the small merchant against the big merchants, the shipowners,[17] and the big firms; there was the condemnation of the "special interests" who had placed themselves between the citizen and the sovereign people and who had dared to strike a sacrilegious blow against the Convention; and of course there was the desire to conform to the customs of the time, as well as a vivid memory of what dangers the federalist crisis had inflicted on the Republic. Moreover, the press was ingenious in keeping public opinion at a fever pitch favorable to severe acts of repression; and the revolutionaries themselves, living as if in combat, as an occupation army, as strangers amidst hostile populations, were easily persuaded that only terror and repressive force saved them from the blows of their enemies. If they did not strike first, they would be "struck down by the assassin's sword." Such was the part fear and credulity played, and it was amply fed by the unbelievably imprudent remarks of the enemies of the regime, who did not hesitate to shout at Parisians their hatred for the Republic and the capital.

---

[15] Dorfeuille and Millet, editors of the Lyon *Père Duchesne,* wrote on the 17 Pluviôse [February 5, 1794]: "The workers of Lyon seem to think they have lost everything because they have lost their rich merchants." Almost all the men from Paris were indignant about the "federalist" spirit of the entire population of Lyon (article "Grande colère," *Père Duchesne* of Lyon, No. XX).

[16] See my article, "La Campagne pour l'envoi de l'armée révolutionnaire dans la Seine-Inférieure," *Annales de Normandie,* August 1952.

[17] Thus at Le Havre the merchants and shopkeepers who composed the Committee of Surveillance pursued the shipowners with special vigor, so much so as to hinder their business dealings with the shipowners of Lübeck, Altona, and Copenhagen, even though these had been undertaken for the Food and Supply Commission.

A taste for blood and vengeance does not seem to have played an important part; still it is very difficult to distinguish between what may have been a political and group attitude and what reveals a personal bent for violence and brutality. In the affair of the *noyades*,[18] some members of the Marat Company and of the Revolutionary Committee of Nantes were extremely cruel. They persecuted their prisoners, chased the wives of the *Chouans* while clubbing them with their musket butts, pulled girls by the hair, and shoved and cursed everyone. But according to witnesses, drunkenness could explain this especially odious example of brutality, just as it had fortified so many of the murderers at the Carmes prison in September 1792. To be sure, at the trial of Carrier, there was one witness, a young man of twenty, who not only admitted taking part in the "drownings," but who added that he had no regrets and that, if he had it to do over, he would again volunteer to carry out similar acts. But he was a young soldier of the first Nantes battalion and he had seen his comrades tortured by the wives and daughters of Breton peasants when the soldiers were captured by the *Chouans* in the countryside around Nantes; and he had himself escaped torture and mutilation thanks to a wound that was more horrible to look at than it was serious.[19] During the trial, most of the witnesses almost became sick while recalling the horrible scenes that had taken place on the small boats when the trap doors installed in the holds were opened. The men of the eighteenth century were somewhat accustomed to brutality, but this did not make them sadists. It is true that the revolutionary regime did allow some sadists to use their deplorable talents under exceptionally favorable circumstances, and everyone has heard of Mathieu Jouve Jourdan [called Jourdan the Decapitator] and other bloodthirsty brutes of his ilk, but these monsters were, we think, the exceptions. The revolutionaries were often violent, especially in speech; they were hot-tempered and fanatical; when they drank to excess they must have appeared at times terrifying and obscenely brutal in the manner of the *Père Duchesne*. Some civilian officials were hotheaded and violent, their fiery temperaments being most apparent in the years of proscription after the fall of Robespierre. No one would be so bold as to claim that a Collot-d'Herbois and a

---

[18] [The *noyades* of Nantes were mass executions by drowning conducted by the deputy on mission Jean-Baptiste Carrier, who had been sent to the city in October 1793 to suppress the revolt there.—Eds.]

[19] Archives de la Préfecture de Police, Paris, A A 269; notes of Topino-Lebrun on the trial of Carrier.

Javogues[20] were normal, sensible men, and many must have resembled them. But even this sort of violence was to be temporary; it was connected with the recent dangers brought on by the federalist crisis. The Revolution had its professional fiends, its murderers, its sadists; and in the cities of the Midi, some of the assassins of the years II and III were also to be the perpetrators of the bloody brutalities of 1814 and 1815. But the average revolutionary was neither a sadist nor a brute.

Finally, there was an educational aspect: the work of "regeneration" had to be undertaken, and the use of force was a part of a general program of civic education. A revolutionary in the Yonne department insisted that "all youths from seven to ten be brought together in order to watch all public punishments, including executions."[21] Now this *Émile* of repression was not a *buveur de sang;* and neither were the revolutionaries of the year II, despite all efforts of Thermidorean propaganda to identify them with the murderers. Actually, the epithet is much more appropriate for those young dandies of the year III who attacked individual Terrorists or men of modest appearance and poor dress and who could not even claim that they acted from fear. It is just as wrong to label the revolutionary a killer as it is to call him a denouncer. Because of certain circumstances, to be sure, at times he had to be both, but the revolutionaries with whom we are familiar—shopkeepers, small merchants, physicians, former priests, lawyers—do not resemble in the slightest those "sanguinary brutes" of Thermidorean and royalist iconography.

It would be equally wrong, I believe, to try to explain the origins of the Terror and the revolutionaries' approval of the great repressive measures by stressing hidden psychological motives in the traditional mentality of the common people, a mentality in which the fear of plagues aroused a climate of panic and mutual fear in bourgeois and artisan alike.[22] The revolutionary of the year II did not have the

---

[20] [Claude Javogues, deputy of the Convention, was an ultrarevolutionary who accused the Committee of Public Safety of counterrevolution and when on mission used terror against the rich, the priests, and others. See Colin Lucas, *The Structure of the Terror: The Example of Javogues and the Loire* (New York: Oxford University Press, 1973).—Eds.]

[21] Archives nationales, D III 306, Comité de Législation, Yonne; petition to the Convention by Héry, 1 Pluviôse, year III [January 20, 1795].

[22] René Baehrel, "Epidémie et terreur: histoire et sociologie," *Annales historiques de la Révolution française,* April–June 1951, pp. 113–146, and "La Haine de classe en temps d'épidémie," *Annales: Économies, sociétés, civilisations,* July–September 1952. The first of these studies provides very interesting information on the spread of the great plague of 1720 in Marseille and on the social and "terroristic" consequences of other

slightest need of very old historical memories in order to demand a pitiless outlawing of all those who, at the time, menaced the existence of the Republic. It was not a question of proscription based on class or even of a tradition of violence. The danger was there, it was obvious, and when the danger passed, it had to be prevented from recurring by "striking a mighty blow." From the year III on, all this seemed quite unreal even to the revolutionaries themselves when they recalled the crisis. This is so because the atmosphere had already changed, the time of extreme measures had passed. The justification for the Terror is that it was a response to circumstance, not a permanent state of mind or one act of a naturally violent temperament. It was just as transitory as the revolutionary man himself. . . .

plagues in French cities during the sixteenth, seventeenth, eighteenth, and nineteenth centuries. In particular, the author has analyzed the reactions of the common people to the measures taken by health officials and by "Boards of Health" to halt the spread of epidemics and to isolate the victims, measures which the poor especially—the probable sources of the infection—had to bear, while the well-off frequently went to their country homes. But doubtless Monsieur Baehrel is a little hasty when he identifies these measures and the very violent social conflicts they provoked with the executions and the Great Terror of the year II. Surely these two series of events had in common only the fear they aroused (fear of "conspiracies," fear of the spread of infection) and the rumors and panic they also aroused, especially among the common people of the cities and countryside. Fear, panic, and rumor are, however, evident throughout the history of the common people, but they do not always cause the same reaction. The people are often afraid, but only in 1792, 1793, and 1795 did fear set off a great outburst of anger and popular violence resulting in massacres, drownings, and mass shootings. And the great institutions of terror in the year II, the special commissions responsible for carrying out the repressive policies, were in no way instruments of any one class or any very distinct social group. The Terror was directed against almost every group that composed French society during the revolutionary period. To claim, as does Monsieur Baehrel, that "Frenchmen in 1792 inherited a long tradition of terrorism" and that the memory of the great plague of 1720, of the periodic famines during the eighteenth century, of the epidemic—the most recent occurring in 1775—helped create a climate of terror and helped inculcate among the French common people a class hatred, a use of terror against other social groups, is to argue abstractly and to advance some very speculative theories. We prefer to say that the Terror of the year II sprang from the special circumstances of that year—the civil war, the foreign war, the treasons, the victories of the coalition, the common people's suspicions of prison plots, the fear of prison breaks, federalism, etc. These seem to us to explain adequately why a terrorist mentality appeared that was as brief and fleeting as the revolutionary man himself. To suggest that there is no need to look for the origins of the terrorist mind in the memories of the plague of 1720 in no way detracts from the originality of Monsieur Baehrel's thesis. As for the rest, the author is certainly right to stress the importance of plagues and epidemics in the development of class hatred and sometimes in the outbreak of insurrectionary events. But such considerations are not relevant for 1793.

Our "revolutionary man," if he existed at all, is only known to us
by a kind of historical documentation unique to the revolutionary
period, and it reveals at least the public attitudes of a whole social
group, a complete cross section of the common people of the cities
and even of the towns. All of this is entirely hidden from us in other
periods of history. It is therefore difficult for us to distinguish
clearly between the public and the private man, since we know him
only at that one time, and then only for one year or eighteen
months, a unique time in the life of the individual and in the history
of France.

Let us try nevertheless to draw the essential features of our portrait. I believe we are concerned especially with a matter of temperament; and it seems to me that to rely solely on studies of social
structure will not furnish us with the basis for a satisfactory answer. The revolutionary man seldom behaved the way he did because of social struggles, except to the extent that he typified the
world of the small property owner, the small tradesman, and the artisan. His predominant characteristics were incontestable political
and physical courage, strong beliefs, also of course a certain love
for power, and finally an undeniable fondness for speech-making
and display. Public life in the year II, we must remember, was an opportunity for many of these small tradesmen to play the role of men
of importance, of "politicians," of Roman Senators, while at the
same time meddling in their neighbor's affairs. The rewards? Well,
they were not to be sneered at: first of all there was the presidency
of a political club, or much more influential though less conspicuous, a position on its executive committee. Any prominent place
in one of these clubs could sometimes provide excellent free publicity for one's business. Think for example of the club member at
Vaison, a painter by trade, who when asked to paint the tree of liberty in three colors, declined the honor. (He was not to be paid for
the job.) But after the society had asked another of the local
painters, the first changed his mind and declared that he would be
delighted by the club's confidence.[23] These posts and honors, furthermore, caused bitter personal strife and dispute often having
nothing to do with republican propriety, but this proves that they
were worth a lot of effort and ingenuity. We know little about the
elections of officers and noncommissioned officers in the National

---

[23] Archives départementales, Vaucluse, L VI 12; Register of the Société populaire de
Vaison.

Guard stationed in the cities, but we surely can guess that the competition was just as acrimonious.[24] The revolutionary was all the more avid for honors, sashes, and stripes, since they compensated for years of obscurity and insignificance.

But in the final analysis, in spite of these material incentives, the revolutionary temperament was mostly a product of faith, enthusiasm, and generosity. The poet Coleridge was not the only one who, recalling the enthusiasms of his youth, remarked how glorious it was to be alive at that time. How many mature men, settled in occupations as obscure as they were honorable, recalled in their old age the *Radiant Days of '93!* For the revolutionaries were mostly young men or men in the prime of life, and their enthusiasm must have been in part the enthusiasm of youth.[25]

In the birth of such a mentality of battle and crisis, the role of the war must also be stressed. The revolutionaries thought of themselves as always standing in the breach, and this was not merely a figment of the imagination. Those at Nantes knew that they were surrounded by almost universal hatred; those in Lyon, even more isolated, could never forget the head of Chalier, and most of the *mathevons* were to die in the terrible massacres of the year III.[26] Like the leaders of the great revolutionary committees, they were absolutely sure that Pitt had put their names on his death lists. It is true, in general, that nothing happened to them in the year II, but the Thermidorean proscription, owing to its blind vengeance against anyone, without exception, who had held power in the year II, certainly played a large part in causing this revolutionary temperament to survive somewhat, thanks to persecution. A political club in Vaucluse asked the following question when screening candidates for admis-

---

[24] My friend Rémi Gossez has told me that during the Revolution of 1848 there was fierce competition for promotions in the National Guard. Unfortunately we know little about the way such elections were conducted during the period of the French Revolution.

[25] A general study of lower-echelon revolutionary personnel would certainly demonstrate that men between twenty-five and forty were in the majority. Regarding the famous Temporary Commission of Lyon, thirty was the average age among some forty members. Revolutionary France was a country offering innumerable opportunities to young men of talent.

[26] Renée Fuoc, *La Réaction thermidorienne à Lyon (1795)* (Lyon, 1957).[Marie-Joseph Chalier was the leader of the Jacobins of Lyon. During the city's counterrevolution, he was arrested, tried, and on July 16, 1793, guillotined. After the revolt was quelled, he became a martyr; and a model of his decapitated head was publicly displayed, even carried to Paris, where it was presented to the Convention.—Eds.]

sion: *What have you done for which you would be hanged if the coun-terrevolution should triumph?*[27] This was not simply rhetoric. The rev-olutionaries had to face such an eventuality, especially in a region like the former Comtat Venaissin, where they constituted a very small minority isolated from the rest of the people.[28] They were, in every sense of the word, embattled.

Yet to maintain this spirit of combat, danger had to be constant. But beginning in Floréal year II [April–May 1794], it receded more and more from a France which until then had been besieged and invaded. The great victories of the summer of 1794, which made the threat of invasion and the military triumph of the counterrevolution more re-mote, inevitably resulted in some relaxation of tension. The feeling of urgency waned. It was also at this very time that the Robespierrist government chose to attack the political institutions of the common people. And then with the coming of summer, daily affairs demanded attention, and a great deal of it, since they had been neglected for so long. This was not only true for the country people, whose revolu-tionary temper did not usually survive the resumption of work in the fields. The urban sans-culotte also had to make a living, to think of his business. His wife kept reminding him of that. But the political clubs met almost every evening from five to ten o'clock, sometimes until midnight; and his life as an active revolutionary, which included guard duty and many other obligations, encroached not only on his leisure, but also resulted in long absences from his shop, which, how-ever, still had to be kept open sixteen hours a day. Such obligations, of course, also took time from billiards. Thus gradually normal life, banal existence, regained the upper hand. We can see quite well what constituted the drama in these men's lives. One from Anduze said in protest, *The bow breaks if bent too far.*[29] In fact, for most of the club members, politicians only for the moment, the bow did break; revo-lutionary enthusiasm and activity ended. In general, their billiards and wives had the last say.

---

[27] Archives départementales, Vaucluse, L VI 12; Register of the Société populaire de Vaison, meeting of 28 Messidor, year II [July 16, 1794].

[28] Archives nationales, D III 292 (2) (4), Comité Législation, Vaucluse, Avignon: ". . . The department of Vaucluse, which is largely inhabited by men who lived under the dom-ination of the Roman priesthood, has a great number of those opportunists . . . who call themselves patriots so that they will be able to get rich with impunity at public expense . . ." (to the Committee of Public Safety from Barjavel, Public Prosecutor of the Revolutionary Tribunal of the department, 25 Frimaire, year II [December 15, 1793]).

[29] Archives nationales, F7 4609 d 2, Borie (letter of Cavalié from Anduze to the Com-mittee of Public Safety, 25 Pluviôse, year II [February 13, 1794]).

Furthermore, the Robespierrist Republic was far from amusing. It oozed boredom and virtue, just like the insipid and pedantic speeches of Robespierre the Incorruptible. Think of those vapid and interminable celebrations of the Supreme Being, after which one sat down to eat the "republican plate," a single course, sometimes served without wine! It was useless to say to these men, *Look out; don't slacken; above all, don't miss club meetings; we still need you; the hidden enemies have not been defeated, victory is not yet won.* It was a waste of words if all they were called upon to do was vote on congratulatory speeches delivered in a bombastic and trite style. One grew weary. This is proven by the sharp drop in attendance at meetings of provincial clubs beginning in Germinal year II [March–April 1794]. Long before the fall of Robespierre, the revolutionary man began to fade away, to resume his anonymity. The time "to make revolution" was already long past.

To summarize, the revolutionary man was only a temporary phenomenon. A product of exceptional circumstances, he did not resist time, wear and tear, fatigue, and boredom. He was not a professional in the art of revolution. Anyway, what is a professional revolutionary if not a bureaucrat like all the others, a bureaucrat solidly installed in a petrified revolution; or else a half-baked conspirator, a romantic, a "cardboard revolutionary." Except in the imagination of the policemen and the informers reporting to the Ministry of Police, the followers of Babeuf had very little in common with the revolutionaries of the year II. Our men of 1793 were neither "cardboard revolutionaries," nor ideologists and professors of revolutionary theory. And the very moment they put on their slippers and relaxed, their role as politicians ended. Thus, after the great hopes and dangers had passed, they returned to their everyday banal existence. In the year III, when inequality became more marked and one's daily bread became the biggest problem, the matter was settled. The revolutionaries were less the victims of the *muscadins,* of those young assassins in fine shoes, than of an economic crisis and a food shortage which struck their families and which, in many cases, reduced them to wretchedness, to the anonymity of the beggar.

Something survived of the revolutionary mentality, of course, especially in the army, where it often took the form of violent anticlericalism. It also was to reappear in the political sphere beginning with the elections of the year IV [October 1795], which saw numerous attempts at regroupment among the former Terrorist cadres. But these efforts were confined to a handful of leaders. As for the conspirators among the revolutionaries, they constituted a very small minority—

the tough and pitiless, the totally convinced, perhaps also the *violent;* for the revolutionary temperament certainly included a dash of violence. Among the others, silence descended as before 1789. The revolutionaries vanished along with the extraordinary circumstances that had given them an intense but fleeting existence; so did those institutions whose extant records allow us to uncover a few months of the submerged history of the common people and thus to see the attitudes and prejudices of a world of stores and workshops. These voices would be heard again only through the very distorted screen of police reports.

A KIND OF
RELIGIOUS FAITH

Crane Brinton

Crane Brinton (1898–1968) was one of America's most notable historians. He studied at Harvard and Oxford universities and then taught at Harvard from 1923 to 1968. His numerous studies of intellectual and political history delight many readers with their spritely and sophisticated style. On the French Revolution he wrote, among other works, *A Decade of Revolution* (1934), an admirable survey; *The Jacobins: An Essay in the New History* (1930), an original attempt at sociological history; and *The Anatomy of Revolution* (revised edition, 1952), a provocative comparison of the French, English, American, and Russian revolutions.

The Jacobins unquestionably held their political philosophy as a matter of faith. It is possible to sketch from the proceedings of the clubs the outlines of a polity held together by concepts primarily theological. Grace, sin, heresy, repentance, regeneration have their place in these records. Of course, no one individual is assumed to go through this cycle. The theological parallel is not a literal one; but it is not a forced nor an imaginary one.

That Robespierre and his more sincere followers conceived themselves to be the small band of the elect is of course a truism. The conception of election, however, like so much else in the Terror, goes back surprisingly far in the Revolution. Desmoulins speaks at the Jacobin club in Paris in 1791 of "the very small number of those *to whom only the witness of their conscience is necessary,* the small number of men of character, incorruptible citizens."[1] This insistence on an inner, emotional conviction or righteousness rather than on external rules—the very old opposition of faith and works—comes out

From Crane Brinton, *The Jacobins: An Essay in the New History* (New York: Macmillan Co., 1930), pp. 218–222, 231–242. Reprinted by permission of the author.
[1] A. Aulard, *La Société des Jacobins* (Paris, 1889–1897), II, 103.

again in the proceedings in the Paris club. "One must distrust," says
the speaker, "liberty unaccompanied by virtue"; and by virtue he understands "not the mere practice of moral duties, but also an exclusive attachment to the unalterable principles of our constitution."[2]
The club at Limoges was told "It is not enough, in order to belong to
a truly republican society, to call oneself republican, to have done
guard duty, to have paid one's taxes; one must have given sure indications of hatred for kings and nobles, for fanaticism; one must have
passed through the crucible of perilous circumstance." The idea of
grace is actually complemented, in this same club, by the addition of
a new Jerusalem, the city of the elect. Paris, for its work in the revolution, is to be "that holy city."[3]

There are also the damned. The Jacobins did not feel of their opponents merely that they were wrong, or inconvenient; but that they
had sinned. A member at Rodez recalled to the society that just a
year before, a deputation from the Tarn had "soiled the precincts of
the society with venom of federalism." The society therefore decided
"as *expiation* for that scandalous session, to consecrate a portion of
the present session to patriotic songs."[4] At Bergerac the society
burned the papal bull condemning the civil constitution of the clergy,
in order to purify the paper from "the outrageous blasphemies which
insult our sublime Constitution."[5] The club of Toulouse delegated six
members, and asked the "peuples des tribunes" [the spectators in
the public gallery] (always that distinction, so out of place in an ideal
republic!) to delegate six more, to help burn and lacerate certain evil
journals.[6] At Beauvais, the club was delighted with a circular from
the Committee of Public Safety asking for lists of Jacobins eligible for
government places, and especially at the words, "Keep from these
lists all these cold, selfish, or indifferent men. . . . The law of Athens
would have inflicted death upon them. National opinion among us in-
flicts upon them political death."[7] The club of Le Havre was told by
that of Harfleur "not to receive in its bosom a certain Duclos, priest
of the protestant religion. He tried to compromise this society with
that of Gaineville, and to ruin the reputation of several patriots."[8]

---

[2]*Ibid.*, II, 235.
[3]A. Fray-Fournier, *Le Club des Jacobins,* (Limoges, 1903), pp. 246, 169.
[4]B. Combes de Patris, *Procès-verbaux de la Société populaire de Rodez* (Rodez, 1912), p. 347.
[5]H. Labroue, *La Société populaire de Bergerac,* (Paris, 1915), p. 118.
[6]Archives départementales, Haute-Garonne, L 746, April 19, 1793.
[7]Archives départementales, Oise, L IV, unclassified papers of the club of Beauvais.
[8]Archives départementales, Seine-Inférieure, L 5647, 24 Germinal, year II [April 13, 1794].

Some aristocrats at Vesoul having kissed the tree of liberty in mockery, the local club decided to purify it. So, with the president at its head, and with four members carrying vases of pure water and braziers of incense, the club marched in procession to the tree, where, after everyone had sworn to preserve it forever after from all contamination, "the tree was purified with the lustral water, and the president threw on the heated tripods generous handfuls of the most exquisite perfumes."[9] The club at Auch had so strong a conviction of sin that it adapted for its own use the attitude of the Church toward burial in consecrated ground. It proposed to have two town cemeteries, one for good citizens, the other for bad.[10]

Heresy is, of course, one of the easiest ways of falling into sin. The word itself was by no means shunned by the Jacobins. Even under the monarchy, Brissot is found at the Paris club objecting that an opinion of Barnave's is "a great heresy."[11] The rejections of members at the various *épurations* [weeding-out sessions] are, of course, usually for heresy of some sort. One man was excluded at Thann because, although at first he had been a good *patriote,* "the corrupting contact of his brother-in-law had completely perverted him"; another, though himself pure, because his maid was not.[12] At Carcassonne one of the questions put was: How long did you lack confidence in Marat and the Mountain? Several were excluded for honestly confessing that they had had a period of doubt on this subject.[13] The pressure of foreign and civil war made the Jacobins more than usually exacting towards their proselytes. One society at least penalized those converted after 1792 by not allowing them to hold office.[14] That of Moulins decided in the spring of 1794 never to admit a new member, except from other towns, and then only when such persons could prove membership in some clubs before September, 1793.[15] Heretics were apparently not even allowed to repent. Collot d'Herbois at Paris was seeking to get readmitted to the society some of those who had followed the *feuillants* [constitutional monarchists]

---

[9] *La Vedette, ou journal du département du Doubs,* No. 68 (June 29, 1792).

[10] F. Brégail, "La Société populaire d'Auch," *Bulletin du comité des travaux historiques* (1911), p. 152.

[11] Aulard, II, 189.

[12] H. Poulet, "L'Esprit publique à Thann pendant la Révolution," *Revue historique de la Révolution française,* XIII (1918), 544.

[13] J. Mandoul, "Le Club des Jacobins de Carcassonne," *Révolution française,* XXV (1893), 326.

[14] A. Fray-Fournier, p. 243.

[15] Archives départementales, Allier, L 901.

in the schism. "Many of these," he said, "are exceedingly repentant, and would like to efface from their lives the days they spent at the *feuillants.*" Yet at Robespierre's insistence they were rejected.[16] And, along with heresy, there is the concept of blasphemy. This is from a report of a session of a Paris club: "An officer, an exchanged prisoner, gives an account of the condition of the French and Austrian armies. But as he reports some violent words used by the enemy general, he is interrupted. Billaud-Varenne reminds the orator that he is repeating expressions which ought not to soil the mouth of a republican."[17]

A little club in Savoy took a milder, and perhaps more modern attitude towards those who disagreed with it. The majority of their fellow citizens they called "the sick ones we have to treat."[18] The club of Toulon, withdrawing its affiliation from the heretics of Pignans, wrote and warned other clubs of this *brebis galeuse* [black sheep].[19] But the best indication of the theological state of the Jacobin mind is to be found in a circular of the club of Montauban. The class of *émigrés* is to be composed, not merely of those who have gone off, *émigrés de fait,* but also of *émigrés d'opinion.*[20]

No less thoroughly religious a concept than that of regeneration is evident in these proceedings. The taking of the Bastille became the symbolic date, the moment when man was born anew, washed clean of the evils of the old régime. A little provincial society, accordingly, when it celebrates the "holy festival" of July 14, refers to it as the day "when man is resuscitated and born anew in his rights."[21] The society of St. Jean-de-Luz held a festival to celebrate the "abolition of royalty and the *resurrection* of the republic."[22] It is hard to see how the word resurrection can here be taken in any but a theological sense, as the French Republic had never existed on this earth. Finally, the society at Saverne gave proof of the most extraordinary faith in the completeness of the rebirth brought about in 1789, for its secretary refers to "les ci-devant Juifs" [the former Jews].[23]

---

[16] Aulard, III, 313.

[17] *Ibid.,* V, 618.

[18] A. Gros, *Le Club des Jacobins de St. Jean-de-Maurienne* (St. Jean-de-Maurienne, 1908), p. 70.

[19] H. Labroue, "Le Club jacobin de Toulon," *Annales de la Société d'Études provençales* (1907), p. 45.

[20] J. Bellanger, *Les Jacobins peints par eux-mêmes* (Paris, 1908), p. 123.

[21] H. Labroue, "La Société populaire de la Garde-Freinet," *Révolution française,* LIV (1908), 155.

[22] J. Annat, "La Société populaire de St. Jean-de-Luz," *Revue du Béarn* (1910), 170.

[23] D. Fischer, "La Société populaire de Saverne," *Revue d'Alsace,* XX (1869), 181.

The Jacobins, then, were a band of the elect, thoroughly aware of their election, and determined to rule on earth as well as in heaven. The club of Ervy was told, "You must suffer but one caste of men, that of Republicans, Sans-culottes, Montagnards."[24] At Le Havre, the club voted that those of its members who belonged to any kind of corporation or brotherhood must choose between the Jacobin club and such other corporations.[25] The club of Besançon indignantly refused to open its doors to all, as "the wicked, mixed with the good, would predominate."[26] The club of Chablis hesitated before accepting affiliation with the club of the Ursulines at Tonnerre, and then turned it down on the grounds that there couldn't possibly be two clubs in a small town like Tonnerre.[27] The secretary at Gerberoy apologized to the club of Beauvais, because everybody passed the *épuration*. Three—their names are duly sent on to Beauvais—should have been expelled. But the mayor formed a party among the "little enlightened," packed the club, and notwithstanding their vices, these three were passed "by the multitude." The whole letter is filled with a consciousness of being right and being few.[28]

Finally, it was evident even to some of their number that the Jacobins were a sect. A member at Ars-en-Ré remarked that "the moral discourses delivered on *décadis* [every tenth day of the French republican calendar] are so many dogmas, and consequently, so much religion." He was, it is true, immediately suspended.[29] The Jacobins held firmly to their final superiority; theirs was no fanaticism. . . .

The fall of Jacobinism . . . can be quite plausibly accounted for; an explanation of its rise is a far more difficult matter. It is not that the actual triumph of the Jacobins over other groups during the Revolution is at all hard to understand. Given Jacobin organization and Jacobin faith, their triumph was almost inevitable. . . . Indeed, it is tempting to assert that the ultimate, if brief, victory of well-organized extremists can be accepted as a kind of sociological law applicable to all great revolutions. The really interesting and subtle problem is, how did the Jacobins themselves come to be what they were? . . . The Jacobins were not predominantly failures before 1789, frustrates, vic-

---

[24] H. Destainville, "Les Sociétés populaires du district d'Ervy," *Annales historiques de la Révolution française,* I (1924), 446.

[25] Archives départementales, Seine-Inférieure, L 5644, September 19, 1793.

[26] *La Vedette,* No. 54 (May 11, 1792).

[27] Archives départementales, Yonne, L 1140, August 18, 1793.

[28] Archives départementales, Oise, L IV, unclassified papers of the club of Gerberoy.

[29] M. de Richemond, "Délibérations de la Société des Amis de la Liberté et de l'Égalité d'Ars-en-Ré," *Archives historiques de la Saintonge et de l'Aunis,* XXXIV (1904), 205.

tims of maladjustment; nor were they members of a lower class struggling against oppression by their masters, and held together by economic solidarity. They were in the main ordinary, quite prosperous middle-class people. And yet they behaved like fanatics. The Reign of Terror was marked by cruelties and absurdities which the greatest of misanthropes will hardly maintain are characteristic of ordinary human beings. The heart of our problem then, is this: how did the Jacobins come to produce, at least to accede to, the Terror?

Augustin Cochin saw with admirable clearness that all explanations of the Terror have fallen into two classes: that represented by Taine, which Cochin calls the *thèse du complot* [the conspiracy thesis], and that represented by Aulard, which he calls the *thèse des circonstances* [the circumstance thesis].[30] Taine in a famous metaphor asks what a spectator must think if he sees a man in apparently sound health take a drink, and suddenly fall down in a fit. The drink, obviously, contained a poison. The drinker was the Jacobin, and the poison was the philosophy of Rousseau. The Jacobins, then, were a group of madmen bent on realizing an impossible Utopia. The Revolution was plotted by these men, made irresponsible by fanatic devotion to their ideal. Their lack of principle made it easy for them, though in a minority, to overcome the good sense of the majority, and establish themselves in power. Once in power, they could maintain themselves only by the Terror. Cochin himself accepts a variant of this explanation. According to him, the Jacobins formed a "petite ville," a society of unpractical idealists, fanatics bent on imposing upon their fellows of the "grande ville" a rigid code governing all human actions, a code quite inconsistent with normal human conduct, as we know it from tradition and from observation.[31]

Now it is impossible not to accept much of this explanation. The Jacobins were certainly fanatics of the religion of humanity. It is tempting to maintain that the acceptance of certain tenets of eighteenth-century philosophy—the essential equality of men, the natural goodness of men—lead in action straight to the Terror. The trouble is that the acceptance of just these tenets by Thomas Jefferson, for instance, led to consequences so very different from those following their acceptance by Maximilien Robespierre. Moreover, granting to Cochin that the Jacobins formed a "petite ville," where are we to look for the "grande ville"? Cochin himself probably thought of decent, non-socialist Frenchmen of the Third Republic as

---

[30] A. Cochin, "La Crise de l'histoire révolutionnaire," in *Les Sociétés de pensée et la démocratie* (Paris, 1921).

[31] Jacobin virtue, for instance, is not attainable by ordinary human beings.

the citizens of the "grande ville." But even in the fairly stable nation-state of the nineteenth century, the realist will discern numerous "villes," numerous groups of men with different aims and different ways of life struggling to maintain themselves, and achieving only a precarious equilibrium. And during the Revolution, when this equilibrium was completely destroyed, this "grande ville" did not exist in France. Surely it was not the royalists, nor the Catholics, nor the Feuillants, nor the Girondins. And if the citizen of the "grande ville" is simply the ordinary man who acts reasonably, and in accordance with traditional ways, then he hardly exists in the French Revolution. Any study of the various groups just mentioned should convince the impartial observer that their state of mind was almost as abnormal, as much inclined towards extremes of cruelty or absurdity as the Jacobins'. The White [counterrevolutionary] Terror was as real as the Red.

It is perhaps too easy here to make a synthesis of Taine and Aulard. The Jacobins were an organized minority bent on imposing their way of life on their fellow Frenchmen; so much for the *thèse du complot.* But circumstances—the inheritance of the *ancien régime,* the pressure of war from without, of civil disturbances and food scarcity from within—put such obstacles in their way that they were driven to extremes. In order to exist at all, they were obliged to be cruel and intolerant. Even in their factitious ritual, their republican catechisms and decalogues, the Jacobins appear beleaguered; the touch of Hebraic fury one finds from time to time in their records is not wholly artificial. The revolutionary government was a government of national defense. No fair-minded person need deny the value of Aulard's life-work. The war, at least as much the product of traditional European high politics as of anything Jacobin, made the Jacobin more righteous, and more bitter, and saved him from any chance of appearing ridiculous in his own eyes. Moreover, the introduction of circumstances at least disposes of the difficulty with Thomas Jefferson. But it gives little comfort to the sociologist seeking from history laws permitting human beings to adjust their actions to conditions in the present—little comfort, in short, to the new historian. For the circumstances of a great event like the French Revolution are unique—unique, if not to omniscience, at least in their extreme complexity unique to the historian. The fatal "ifs" of history in the conditional—if Mirabeau had not died, if the king had not fled to Varennes—enter in, and make scientific induction impossible. Men's beliefs are, for a given group, held in common and relatively easy to arrive at; so too a given group may have certain similar and perfectly describable characteristics in common—rank, occupation, social standing, wealth. Yet we have no right to assume that their actions can be predicted from these data.

For the whole point of our study is just this: when one considers the material facts about the Jacobins—their social environment, their occupations, their wealth—one finds sufficient evidence of their prosperity to justify predicting for them quiet, uneventful, conservative, thoroughly normal lives. When one studies the records of their proceedings, one finds them violent, cruel, intolerant, and not a little ridiculous. The antithesis, it must be insisted, is real. Where material evidence indicates normality, we find abnormality. Rightly enough, no doubt, this material evidence seems real and important. Therefore the Jacobins present a genuine paradox. Their *political* being seems quite inconsistent with their *real* being. Their words and their acts *qua* members of the clubs are not what we should expect from them *qua* members of civil society. Or to put it as crudely as possible, the Jacobins present for a brief time the extraordinary spectacle of men acting without apparent regard for their material interests.

This of course, will never do. The economic interpretation of history would tell us that we are either mistaken in our facts (which is always possible) or that there is an explanation which will show men properly and decently following their material interests. Yet perhaps after all the economic interpretation of history is not the whole explanation of the Terror. We are in a realm of thought where the professional psychologist could no doubt add greatly to the precision of our argument. But to a layman it would appear that voluntary human action must have either a more or less directly physical, bodily source (desire, habit, desire partly intellectualized into interest) or a more or less immaterial and intellectual source (principle, idea, desire thoroughly intellectualized into ideal) or finally, must have its source in mere chance. Now if certain important Jacobin actions did not originate from interest, they must have originated from principle or from chance. The first alternative suggests the old-fashioned belief that men act on principle, and leads us back to the school of Taine. If it can be shown that Jacobin ideas logically produce Jacobin actions in 1794, then we need not worry because Jacobin interests and Jacobin habits would not produce such actions. There is just the possibility that the old-fashioned belief about the importance of ideas is justified, at least for certain historical crises, and for certain groups of men. It is not even necessary to refer to such examples of corporate madness as the Children's Crusade; one need only reflect on how much the *interests* of the average man were at stake in the late highly popular war [World War I]. But to accept this explanation world lead to the restoration of ideas to their active role in human life, and would put the history of ideas, at least during times of crucial change, on a level with the history of institutions, customs, commerce, and the rest of man's material environment. This will hardly content the new historian, for whom intellectual history is largely a reflection of social history, for whom ideas are most decidedly born of, and consistent with, material interests.

There is the final possibility of accepting chance as the determining factor in human conduct. This need not be as shocking as it seems. Chance may merely stand for a complexity unfathomable to human beings; or it may mean that historical events—that is, of course, human actions—are really unique and exempt from the play of cause and effect as nineteenth-century science understood it. That would still leave the play of cause and effect as the artist, and perhaps even the philosopher, have always understood it. It would still leave narrative history; it would merely destroy the new history.

Our enterprise in retrospective sociology has not perhaps been altogether satisfying. The kind of information about the Jacobins available to the social scientist has not provided us with any fashionable explanation of why men take part in revolutions. The Jacobins seem not to have been crudely at odds with their environment before the Revolution; they certainly were not starving; they were hardly a social or an economic class. They were certainly a collective body—a group—of more than ordinary cohesion, reasonably well disciplined, active, with a definite program, a ritual of their own, a faith charged with emotion, and a pertinacity, a vitality that has enabled the group to survive under changing forms into the Third Republic. Yet so disparate were the social and economic origins of these revolutionaries that we have been driven to the conclusion that large numbers of them, by espousing the Jacobin cause, acted against what they must have been aware were their true selfish interests. Before so surprising a conclusion sociology rightly recoils. The exploded intellectualist fallacy is obviously trying to creep in, and we had better not open the door any wider.

But if we have not got far with applications to the French Revolution of a science of social dynamics, can we not at least give a clearer definition of Jacobin at the end of this enquiry than at the beginning? Here, however, as with so much of modern history, the trouble is that we know too much. A fragment of the rules of one of the clubs would be illuminating to the historian at work in the dark; the records of hundreds of them are blinding. Where statistics fail—and they fail very soon—there is no way of arriving at what is common to the Jacobins. No classification of the complete records of these clubs can be so made that the members of each class can be counted. One might count the number of references to Rousseau; but would such a count serve to weigh the influence of Rousseau on the clubs? The historian must fall back on the normal functioning of his mind, which classifies loosely and pragmatically enough what he experiences in daily life, and which with urging can so classify the matter of his historical studies. But no matter how honest he is, into the making of this classification will come much of his own personal history. What one finds in the Jacobin clubs is what one finds important; and importance, when it is not mathematical, is as subjective as good and bad or sweet and sour.

And yet perhaps the true Jacobin is the rare and perfect Jacobin of the imagination—the Jacobins, let us say, of Anatole France's [novel] *Les Dieux ont soif.* One rarely meets an American like Uncle Sam or an Englishman like John Bull, and never a Frenchwoman like the cartoonist's Marianne. Indeed, just as a mass of unbarbered and untailored human animals, Englishmen, Frenchmen, and Americans are probably more alike than we are apt to think. Yet national types do exist, if only in our minds and aspirations. To define them is in a measure to create them; whether we create scarecrows or flesh-and-blood will perhaps not suffer ultimate determination.

This true Jacobin, who may be a scarecrow, but who we hope will be of flesh and blood, is then of no one occupation, of no one social class, of no determinable rank and wealth. He has no ordinary, daily, selfish human interests. He is a religious fanatic, a man inspired and possessed, a man bent on changing overnight this earth into his heaven. What his notion of heaven was we have tried to learn. It was not an uncommon notion of heaven, not one that many men of modern times, if they entertained at all the notion of heaven, would reject—a place where pain and strife could not exist, where the traditional Christian virtues had banished forever the traditional Christian vices, where men were free and equal, and contented with their freedom and equality. The Jacobin was not a revolutionary in that he believed in heaven, or even in that he believed in a special kind of heaven, but in that he attempted to realize his heaven here on earth. That attempt led to the Terror. You cannot have disagreement in heaven. When the Jacobin found he could not convert those who disagreed with him, he had to try to exterminate them. *La sainte guillotine* was not so christened in the spirit of Villon or of Rabelais, but in the spirit of Calvin.

Now common sense, to say nothing of the social sciences, would tell us that most of our five hundred thousand Jacobins were not of this heroic mold. Yet the Terror was a reality, a reality not to be diminished by statistical proof that even in 1794 violence was the exception, not the rule. The slightest document of the period—a theater program, a fashion plate—is no ordinary document, but a sign from another world. Most men in 1794 no doubt ate, drank, slept, and went about most of their business as they had in 1784; most men were no doubt as stupid, as selfish, as kindly, as good in 1794 as in 1784. But into the whole lives of some Frenchmen, into some part of the lives of all Frenchmen, had come this indefinable, incredible pattern of action and feeling we have called Jacobinism. Very real, very earthly grievances had gone into making the pattern; wise, selfish, ordinary men had helped make the pattern to achieve wise, selfish, ordinary purposes. But a few foolish, unselfish (as the world uses the term) and extraordinary men—with circumstances aiding—had by 1794 turned the pattern into the madness of true Jacobinism. Yet still most Jacobins were normal men. They were still of respectable middle class origins. What had happened to them? Were 499,000 of them hypocrites, trembling before a thousand fanatics? Probably not. It seems more likely that, for a few short months, these ordinary men were possessed by a faith, a contagion, an unearthly aspiration. Jacques Dupont, the man in the street, the economic man, the sociological man, the psychological man, ceased for a brief while to behave in the orderly fashion laid out for him by these sciences, and took instead to the ways of Carlylean heroes or Emersonian representative men.

Jacobinism is, then, first of all a faith. Were they not believers, the Jacobins would be unintelligible to us. As it is, the Jacobin may be strong or weak, tall or short, rich or poor, gentleman or vagabond; what makes him a Jacobin is none of these varying and individual attributes, but a fixed faith. "Liberty, Equality," Fraternity," as words, may be subject to definition and contain the seeds of infinite dispute; as symbols, they were to the Jacobins a common property above logic. The emotions which they evoked allowed the Jacobins to form, for the moment, one body; they provided a common fund of pooled emotions, an inexhaustible and immaterial fund.

Now, in time, this very immateriality of the fund began to pall on many Jacobins. Tough-minded philosophers who, from the utilitarians to the economic interpretationists have perhaps thought a little too highly of their fellow men, would of course maintain that the fund must have been material, or held out the promise of materiality, ever to have held human beings at all. To them, there must somehow be a connection between the individual's standing, and the position he takes in politics. Perhaps they are right as a general rule, right in the long run and in normal times. Yet our study of the Jacobin clubs has failed to establish such a connection for the French Revolution. Neither the class struggle theory nor the maladjustment theory seems in itself to account for the extraordinary diversity of membership in the clubs, nor for the extraordinary variety of things the clubs endeavored to do.

What was meant sincerely as a study in the new history has come to a conclusion strangely like that of very old-fashioned history indeed. If the subject matter of the social sciences be natural man, then the Jacobin appears to have a touch of the supernatural. The French Revolution appears, as it did to Maistre, to Wordsworth, and to Carlyle, as utterly inexplicable in terms of daily life, of common sense, of scientific causation. Yet perhaps we need not call the Revolution a miracle. Only if man is wholly at the mercy of his simpler appetites need we have recourse to the miraculous to explain Jacobin aberrations. If the incredibly complex world which human thought has added to the world of our simpler appetites can at times give ordinary men motives for action even stronger than these simpler appetites, then the French Revolution is explicable. It seems too bad to have to conclude that sometimes some men—or even many men—believe for no more apparent reason than that they want to believe, that their beliefs have, at least in part, independent and immaterial lives. Yet, if only in his capacity for adjusting his conduct to illusion and not to fact, man is most obviously an animal apart. Surely there is nothing surprising if a study of the Jacobins forces us to the conclusion that man cannot live by bread alone?

A DEEP-ROOTED IDEOLOGY
AS WELL AS CIRCUMSTANCE

François Furet

For biographical information on François Furet,
see Chapter 2, "The Peasants: Mentality and Behavior
in 1789."

🎭🎭🎭🎭🎭🎭

There exists a history of the history of the Terror, associated with the
vicissitudes of French political history over the past two hundred
years. But that history can also be written in a less chronological
mode by attempting to reconstitute the various types of interpretation to which the Terror has been subjected.

The most common strategy is to relate the Terror to circumstances
external to the Revolution; we are told, then, that the Terror was
merely the product of the tragic situation in which the Republic
found itself in 1793 and was a terrible yet necessary instrument of
public safety. Surrounded by enemies foreign and domestic, the Convention allegedly had no choice but to rely on fear of the guillotine to
mobilize men and resources. We find this interpretation being advanced by the Thermidorians in the period immediately following
Robespierre's fall, and it was destined to enjoy a brilliant future, for
it can also be found in most French public school texts for reasons
that are easy to understand: it has the advantage of offering to the ultimately victorious republican tradition a Revolution exonerated of
guilt for the terrorist episode, responsibility for which is shifted to its
adversaries. That is why this interpretation is favored by many who
consider themselves heirs of 1789, for it is a way of escaping the
dilemma of contradiction or denial.

The "circumstantial" thesis is often associated with another idea,
according to which the Terror coincides with a period during which
social strata other than the cultivated bourgeoisie were gaining ac-

cess to power: specifically, the class of urban artisans and tradesmen from which the sans-culotte activists were recruited and which [Auguste] Mignet, for example, setting the tone for liberal historiography, dubbed the "plebs" or the "multitude" to distinguish them from the bourgeoisie of 1789. Thus circumstances presumably brought to the fore a second revolution, which lacks the historical dignity of the first because it was neither bourgeois nor liberal; its necessity was merely circumstantial, that is, subordinate to the principal course of the event, which continued to be defined by the principles of 1789 and the rise of the bourgeoisie. But the plebian nature of this episode makes it possible to understand how the Terror was also the product of elementary political reflexes, at once egalitarian and punitive, triggered by military reverses and internal insurrections. The Ancien Régime had not known how to educate its people, and for this it paid a heavy price at the moment of its downfall.

It is not difficult to find elements of historical reality to support interpretations of this type. The Terror did in fact develop in the course of the Revolution at a time of foreign and domestic danger and out of obsession with "aristocratic" treason and an "aristocratic" plot." It continually justified itself in these terms as indispensable to the salvation of the fatherland. It was "placed on the order of the day" and exercised in the name of the state and the Republic only under pressure from sans-culotte militants. The Paris prison massacres of September 1792 showed the extremes to which the punitive passions of the people might go. A year later, it was in part to channel those passions that the Convention and the Committees turned the Terror into a banner of government.

Nevertheless, neither the circumstances nor the political attitudes of the *petit peuple* [common people] are enough to account for the phenomenon. The "circumstances," too, have a chronology. The risks for the Revolution were greatest at the beginning and in the middle of the summer of 1793, at a time when the activity of the Revolutionary Tribunal was relatively minimal. By contrast, the Terror intensified with the improvement of the situation and the victories, starting in October. It reached a peak during the winter, in a Lyons that had been vanquished for several months and in a defeated Vendée that had to be put to the torch, as well as in countless other places where there were violent clashes as a result of initiatives on the part of local militants or envoys of the Convention. There was indeed a connection between the civil war and the Terror, but it was not that the Terror was an instrument for ending a war; it followed and actually prolonged rather than shortened the war. One cannot credit it with patriotic devotion without falling into inconsistency, because to do so would be to assume—incorrectly, by the way—the existence of a counterrevolutionary France. Nor can one credit it with saving the fatherland or maintaining the Republic, since it came after the victory. "The Great Terror," wrote the republican [Edgar] Quinet as long ago as 1867, "nearly everywhere revealed itself after the victories. Can we maintain that it caused them? Can we argue that, in our systems, effect precedes cause?" (*Critique de la Révolution*).

The explanation involving the role of popular attitudes accounts for only some of the facts. It is indeed true that the pressure to establish a terrorist dictatorship came chiefly from sans-culotte militants. But it is not a simple matter to establish a dividing line between the "people" and the political elites, between "popular" culture and "high" culture. What about Marat, for example, who may be considered one of the purest ideologues of the Terror? To which group did he belong? This demi-savant, who since 1789 had been denouncing the aristocratic plot and tirelessly calling for scaffolds to be erected, straddled both "cultures." The same can be said of Hébert and the Hébertists, who extended his influence in Paris and played so important a role in the republican repression in Vendée. In fact, in 1793 terrorist discourse was in the mouths of nearly all the leaders of the Revolution, including those who had no special relation to sans-culotte activism, the legists and bourgeois of the committees and the Convention. Barère's demand in the summer of 1793 for the total destruction of the Vendée is enough to make clear the grip of terrorist fanaticism on all the Montagnard deputies.

Of course this call for widespread extermination grew out of the civil war, even if that was not its only cause. But, as Mona Ozouf has demonstrated, from the autumn of 1793 to the spring of 1794 the case for the necessity of the Terror abandoned the circumstantial grounds of the war in favor of a more fundamental justification: nothing less than the Revolution itself. After the end of March and the liquidation of the Hébertists, which put an end to the bloody escalation of what remained of sans-culottism, the Terror, by this point the exclusive instrument of the Robespierrist clan, had ceased to be a matter for learned and sometimes philosophical rationalization. It was less a part of the arsenal of victory than of an ambition for regeneration.

Nor was the climate any longer that of a besieged city, since the frontiers had been liberated and the civil war extinguished. The most obvious use of the guillotine was no longer the extermination of avowed enemies but rather that of "factions": the Hébertists followed by the Dantonists. The Terror raged all the more fiercely because the

Robespierrist group had no further support either on its left, among the activists, or on its right, in public opinion; it was a government of fear, which Robespierre portrayed in theory as a government of virtue. Conceived in order to exterminate aristocracy, the Terror ended as a means of subduing wrongdoers and combatting crime. From now on it coincided with and was inseparable from the Revolution, because there was no other way of someday molding a republic of citizens.

Hence the Terror cannot be reduced to circumstances, whether the emergency situation or pressure from the *petit peuple,* surrounding its birth. Not that circumstances played no role; obviously they provided an environment in which ideology developed and allowed terrorist institutions to be gradually put in place. But this ideology, present in the Revolution of 1789, predated the circumstances and enjoyed an independent existence, which was associated with the nature of French revolutionary culture through several sets of ideas.

The first of these ideas was of man's regeneration, in which respect the Revolution was akin to a religious annunciation but in a secularized mode. The actors in the events actually conceived of their own history as an emancipation of man in general. The issue was not to reform French society but to reinstitute the social pact on the basis of man's free will; France represented only the first act of this decisive development. This truly philosophical ambition was unusual, however, in that it was constantly caught up in the test of actual history, as though the truth of a religious promise had been left to empirical verification by the facts. In the gap between facts and promise was born the idea of a regeneration, to reduce the distance between the Revolution and its ambition, which it could not renounce without ceasing to be itself. If the Republic of free citizens was not yet possible, it was because men, perverted by their past history, were wicked; by means of the Terror, the Revolution—a history without precedent, entirely new—would make a new man.

Another idea said roughly the same thing, or arrived at the same result: that politics could do anything. The revolutionary universe was a universe populated by wills, entirely animated by the conflict between good intentions and evil plans; no action was ever uncertain, no power ever innocent. As first Hegel and later Marx recognized, the French Revolution was the theater in which the voluntarism of modern politics revealed itself in all its purity. The event remained ever faithful to its original idea, according to which the social contract could be instituted only by free wills. This attribution of unlimited powers to political action opened a vast field to radicalization of conflicts and to militant fanaticism. Henceforth each individual could arrogate to himself what had once been a divine monopoly, that of creating the human world, with the ambition of recreating it. If he then found obstacles standing in his way, he attributed them to the perversity of adverse wills rather than to the opacity of things: the Terror's sole purpose was to do away with those adversaries.

In the end, the Revolution put the people in the place of the king. In order to restore to the social order the truth and justice ignored by the Ancien Régime, it returned the people to its rightful place, usurped for so long by the king: the place of sovereign. What the Revolution, following Rousseau, called the general will was radically different from monarchical power in the manner of its formation yet identical to it in the extent of its jurisdiction. The absolute sovereignty of the king presaged the sovereignty of democracy. Wholly obsessed with legitimacy, having thrown off divine guidance without establishing reciprocal checks and balances in the American manner, the Revolution was unwilling to set limits to public authority. It had lived since 1789 on the idea of a new absolute—and indivisible—sovereignty, which excluded pluralism of representation because it assumed the unity of the nation. Since that unity did not exist—and Girondin federalism showed that factions continued to plot in the shadows—the function of the Terror, as well as of purging elections, was invariably to establish it. As early as 1795, in the discussion of the Constitution of Year III, Sieyès would blame the Terror on the Revolution's errors regarding the concept of sovereignty (speech of 2 Thermidor); somewhat later this idea was adapted and systematized by Mme. de Staël, Benjamin Constant, and finally Guizot.

This explanation of the Terror is not incompatible with a more sociological type of interpretation, which incidentally can also be found in the work of Constant and Staël. An enthralling chapter of the latter's *Considérations sur la Révolution française* (book 3, chap. 15) in fact suggests that the Ancien Régime bequeathed to posterity not only its conception of sovereignty but also the harshness of its social relations. Aristocratic society, composed of castes created by the monarchy and fiercely jealous of their privileges, left the embers of its violence to the Revolution, which fanned them into conflagration: "Because the various classes of society had almost no relations among themselves in France, their mutual antipathy was stronger . . . In no country were nobles as much strangers to the rest of the nation. When they touched the second class, it was only to give offense. . . . The same scene was repeated from rank to rank; the irritability of a very sensitive nation inclined each person to jealousy toward his neighbor, toward his superior, toward his master; and all individuals not content to dominate humiliated one another." In part, therefore, the "Terror" may have stemmed from an egalitarian fanaticism born of an inegalitarian pathology in the old society. For there is no reason not to think that in the genesis of the bloody dictatorship of Year II, Ancien Régime and Revolution combined their effects.

7
The Revolutionary
Common People of Paris

MANY present-day historians try to see events from the point of view of the common people rather than from the perspective of political, social, religious, or intellectual elites. Three of the best practitioners of "history from below" have written about the revolutionary common people of Paris. George Rudé has made a social analysis of those who took part in the great revolutionary insurrections from 1787 to 1795; and he has found that a large majority of the participants were women, shopkeepers, craftsmen, and wage earners, usually protesting high food prices and shortages. Albert Soboul has concentrated on the Parisian sans-culottes from 1793 to 1794—those political militants active in the forty-eight sections or wards of Paris during that period of mass radicalism. He describes, among other things, their image of themselves, their political ideals, their democratic political practices, their violence, and their lack of social class cohesiveness. Richard Cobb has preferred to depict vividly the lives of common people, both men and women, who became revolutionaries in Paris and the provinces.[1]

The research of these and other historians has sparked controversies about the revolutionary common people. One problem is whether they were, in general, admirable or detestable human beings. Were they plain-spoken, unpretentious patriots defending popular sovereignty, as they often claimed themselves to be? Or ordinary people driven to acts of desperation because of food shortages and other specific economic and political grievances or, more broadly, because of a sense of being treated unfairly?[2] Or boastful, mindless, vengeful, violent sadists, including in their ranks shiftless beggars, vagrants, and criminals? Moreover, did they have a similar enough social background and lifestyle to be considered a social class? Soboul denies that they constituted a social class, but some historians suggest that they were.[3] Finally, did they cooperate with

---

[1]See also the selection by Cobb in Chapter 6 above, "Why Terror in 1793–1794?"
[2]For research on the motivations of rioters, see Robert Darnton, "Reading a Riot," *New York Review of Books,* October 22, 1992, pp. 44–46.
[3]See, for example, Robert R. Palmer, "Popular Democracy in the French Revolution: Review Article," *French Historical Studies* 1 (Fall 1960), 468–469.

each other and act together so that one can speak of "the popular movement"? And if they were so united, was it a democratic mass movement or a movement of small, intolerant groups of militants grasping for power?[4]

---

[4]See Richard M. Andrews, "Social Structures, Political Elites and Ideology in Revolutionary Paris, 1792–94: A Critical Evaluation of Albert Soboul's *Les Sans-Culottes Parisiens en l'an II*," *Journal of Social History* 19 (1985): 71–112; and William H. Sewell, Jr., "The Sans-Culottes Rhetoric of Subsistence," in *The French Revolution and the Creation of Modern Political Culture*, Vol. 4, *The Terror*, ed. Keith Michael Baker (Oxford: Pergamon, 1994), especially pp. 249–252.

THE RIOTERS

George Rudé

George Rudé (1910–1993), a descendant of a governor of
Gibraltar, the son of an engineer, and a graduate of Cambridge University, first taught French and German in secondary schools. He changed fields in his thirties and
completed a Ph.D. in history at the University of London
in 1950. From 1960 he taught at various universities,
with his last appointment at Concordia University,
Montreal, from 1970 to 1987. He was an authority on
eighteenth-century riots and the social background of
the participants. Among his many books are *The Crowd
in the French Revolution* (1959), *Wilkes and Liberty*
(1962), *Paris and London in the 18th Century* (1970), *The
Crowd in History: A Study of Popular Disturbance in
France and England, 1730–1848* (revised edition, 1981),
Robespierre: Portrait of a Revolutionary Democrat (1975),
Ideology and Popular Protest (1980), *Criminal and Victim:
Crime and Society in Early 19th century England* (1985),
and *The French Revolution After 200 Years* (1988).

One aspect of the French Revolution that has been largely neglected
by historians is the nature of the revolutionary crowd. It has, of
course, long been recognized that the Revolution was not only a political, but a profound social upheaval, to the course and outcome of
which masses of ordinary Frenchmen, both in the towns and countryside, contributed. Not least in Paris; and, in the history of revolutionary Paris, a particular importance has been justly ascribed to the
great *journées,* or popular insurrections and demonstrations, which,
breaking out intermittently between 1789 and 1795, profoundly affected the relations of political parties and groups and drew many
thousands of Parisians into activity.

Reprinted from *The Crowd in the French Revolution* by George Rudé (Oxford: Clarendon Press, 1959), pp. 1–4, 184–190, 207–209, 232–233, by permission of Oxford University Press. All footnotes are included except for those that refer to appendixes or are
cross-references. Quotations originally in French have been translated by the editors.

So much is common knowledge and has long been commonly accepted. But how were the crowds composed that stormed the Bastille in July 1789, marched to Versailles to fetch the king and queen to the capital in October, that overthrew the monarchy in August 1792, or silently witnessed the downfall of Robespierre on 9 Thermidor? Who led them or influenced them? What were the motives that prompted them? What was the particular significance and outcome of their intervention? It is not suggested that the great historians of the Revolution have had no answers to these questions: far from it; but, for lack of more precise inquiry, they have tended to answer them according to their own social ideals, political sympathies, or ideological preoccupations. In this respect we may distinguish between those writers who, like Burke and Taine, adopted a distinctly hostile attitude to the Revolution and everything that it stood for; Republican historians like Michelet and Aulard, for whom the Revolution marked a great regenerative upsurge of the French people; and, again, a Romantic like Carlyle who, while broadly sympathetic to the "Nether Sansculottic World," was torn between admiration for its "heroism" and fascinated horror at the "World-Bedlam" or "anarchy" that it appeared to unleash.

To Burke the revolutionary crowd was purely destructive and presumed to be composed of the most undesirable social elements: the crowds that invaded the *château* of Versailles in October 1789 and "a band of cruel ruffians and assassins, reeking with . . . blood"; and the royal family, on their return journey to Paris, are escorted by "all the unutterable abominations of the furies of hell, in the abased shape of the vilest of women." The National Assembly, having transferred to the capital, is compelled to deliberate "amidst the tumultuous cries of a mixed mob of ferocious men, and of women lost to shame."[1] Yet Burke's invective is far outmatched by Taine, the former Liberal of 1848, soured by his experiences of [the French defeat and the Commune of] 1871, whose vocabulary of expletives has served the conservative historians of the Revolution ever since. The provincial insurgents of the early summer of 1789 are presented as "smugglers, dealers in contraband salt, poachers, vagabonds, beggars, ex-convicts." The Paris revolutionaries and the captors of the Bastille are the lowest social scum:

> The dregs of society came to the top . . . the capital seems taken over by the lowest of the low and by bandits . . . Vagabonds, ragamuffins, several "almost naked," most armed like savages, with terrifying faces,

---

[1] E. Burke, *Reflections on the Revolution in France* (London, 1951), pp. 66–69.

they are "among those that one does not remember having met in broad daylight."

The market women and others who marched to Versailles in October are thus described:

> The prostitutes of the Palais Royal . . . add to their number laundresses, beggars, women without shoes, fishwives recruited several days before for pay . . . [T]he troop absorbs women it meets, janitresses, dressmakers, charwomen, and even some bourgeoises. To these join vagrants, street prowlers, bandits, thieves, all those dregs crammed into Paris and who surface at each disturbance . . . Here is the muck which, back and forth, moves with the flood of the masses.

The insurgents of 10 August 1792, who drove Louis XVI from the Tuileries, become:

> Almost all the lowest of the low or people supporting themselves by disreputable trades, bullies and pimps, blood-thirsty . . . fearless and ferocious adventurers of any origin, men of Marseille and foreigners, Savoyards, Italians, Spaniards, expelled from their own countries.[2]

Following Taine, such terms as "la canaille [the rabble]," "la dernière plèbe," "bandits," and "brigands" have been commonly applied to the participants in these and similar events up to the present day.[3]

On the other hand, Michelet and the upholders of the Republican tradition have presented the revolutionary crowd in entirely different terms. Whenever it advanced, or appeared to advance, the aims of the revolutionary *bourgeoisie,* it has been presented as the embodiment of all the popular and Republican virtues. To Michelet the Bastille ceased to be a fortress that had to be reduced by force of arms: it became the personification of evil, over which virtue (in the shape of the People) inevitably triumphs: "The Bastille was not captured . . . it surrendered. Its bad conscience troubled it, drove it crazy, and made it lose its courage." And who captured it? "The people, all the people." Similarly, on 5 October, while the revolutionary leaders are groping for a solution to the crisis: "The people alone find a remedy: they go to look for the King." The role of the women takes on a more than merely casual significance: "The women are, assuredly, the most people-like among the people, that is, the most in-

---

[2]H. Taine, *Les Origines de la France contemporaine. La Révolution* (3 vols., Paris, 1876), i. 18, 53–54, 130, 272.

[3]See, for example, L. Madelin, who freely uses the terms "bandits" and "brigands" in relation to the Paris insurgents of July 1789 (*La Révolution [Paris, 1914]*), pp. 60, 66, 68); and P. Gaxotte, *La Révolution française* (Paris, 1948), *passim.*

stinctive, the most inspired."[4] Louis Blanc, though lacking Michelet's exaltation, follows him closely;[5] and Aulard, the Radical professor of the Sorbonne, for all his sobriety of language and wealth of documentary learning, is in the same tradition: "Paris, all of Paris, rose up, took arms, and seized the Bastille."[6]

Great as has been the influence of these two rival schools on the historiography and teaching of the Revolution in France, in this country [Great Britain] perhaps an even greater influence has been exerted on generations of students, teachers, and textbook writers by the striking imagery of Carlyle. The social forces unleashed by the Revolution and composing the active elements in each one of its decisive phases are variously described as an "enraged National Tiger"; "the World Chimera, bearing fire"; "Victorious Anarchy"; and "the funeral flame, enveloping all things . . . the Death-Bird of a World." With all this, it is perhaps not surprising that he should gravely warn his readers against attempting a more precise analysis: "But to gauge and measure this immeasurable Thing, and what is called account for it, and reduce it to a dead logic-formula, attempt not."[7]

Yet, widely different as these interpretations are and the influences they have exerted, there is one common thread running through them all: whether the revolutionary crowd is represented as "la canaille" or "vile multitude" by Taine and Burke; as "Victorious Anarchy" by Carlyle; or as "le peuple" or "tout Paris" by Michelet and Aulard—it has been treated by one and all as a disembodied abstraction and the personification of good or evil, according to the particular fancy or prejudice of the writer. . . .

We may note both the common feature and certain significant differences in the composition of the rioters and insurgents of this period. The common feature is, of course, the predominance of *sans-culottes*[8] in all but one of these *journées*. Yet other social elements

---

[4]J. Michelet, *La Révolution française* (9 vols., Paris, 1868–1900), i. 248, 377- 9. The original edition dates from 1847 to 1853.

[5]L. Blanc, *Histoire de la Révolution française* (12 vols., Paris, 1868–70), ii. 352–3; iii. 184. The first edition is dated 1847–62.

[6]A. Aulard, *Histoire politique de la Révolution française [1789–1804]* (Paris, 1905), p. 37.

[7]T. Carlyle, *The French Revolution* (3 vols., London, 1869), i. 226, 258, 264–6, 303. It is of some interest to note that Carlyle's first edition of 1837 bore the subtitle "A History of Sansculottism."

[8][In the glossary of *The Crowd in the French Revolution,* Rudé says he has used the expression sans-culottes "in its purely social sense as an omnibus term to include the small property-owners and wage-earners of town and countryside: in its Parisian context, the small shopkeepers, petty traders, craftsmen, journeymen, labourers, vagrants, and city poor. Contemporaries tend to limit its application to the more

played some part: overwhelmingly so in Vendémiaire of the Year IV [October 4–6, 1795]; but there were also small groups of *bourgeois, rentiers* [persons of independent means], merchants, civil servants, and professional men engaged in the destruction of the *barrières* [toll gates in the city walls] (possibly as direct agents of the Orleanist faction at the Palais Royal[9]), in the capture of the Bastille, the Champ de Mars affair, the assault on the Tuileries, and in the outbreak of Prairial [May 20–23, 1795]. Women . . . were particularly in evidence in the march to Versailles, the food riots of 1792–3, and in Prairial. This is, of course, not altogether surprising, as in these episodes food prices and other bread and butter questions were well to the fore; we find women playing a less conspicuous part in such an essentially political movement as that culminating in the "massacre" of the Champ de Mars—less still, of course, in largely military operations like the assaults on the Bastille and the Tuileries and in the expulsion of the Girondin deputies from the Convention. Again, while wage-earners played a substantial part on all these occasions, the only important outbreak in which they appear to have clearly predominated was the Réveillon riots in the Faubourg Saint-Antoine. The reason for this is not hard to find: though it cannot be termed a strike or a wages movement (Réveillon's own workers do not appear to have been engaged), it was the only one of these actions in which there is the slightest trace of a direct conflict between workers and employers. It is also no doubt significant that craftsmen—whether masters, independent craftsmen, or journeymen—were more conspicuously in evidence in some of the *journées* than in others. This seems particularly to have been the case when a district of small crafts became substantially involved—like the [Île de la] Cité in the riots of 1787 and 1788 or the Faubourg Saint-Antoine on various other occasions; but it also appears to have been a feature of the more organized, political movements—such as the Champ de Mars affair and the armed attacks on the Bastille and the Tuileries—when the driving element was no doubt the small shopkeepers and workshop masters who, in many cases, brought their *garçons* [helpers], journeymen, and apprentices along with them. In this connexion it is perhaps of interest to note the sustained militancy of members of certain trades such as furnishing, building, metalwork, and dress. Most conspicuous of all

politically active among these classes or to extend it to the 'popular' leaders, from whatever social class they might be drawn. Historians have frequently used the term in this political sense."—Eds.]

[9][The Orleanist faction consisted of the political followers of the Duc d'Orléans, Louis XVI's cousin, who lived in the Palais Royal.—Eds.]

were the locksmiths, joiners and cabinet-makers, shoemakers, and tailors; others frequently in evidence were stone-masons, hair-dressers, and engravers; and, of those engaged in less skilful occupations, wine-merchants, water-carriers, porters, cooks, and domestic servants. Workers employed in manufactories (textiles, glass, tobacco, tapestries, porcelain) played, with the exception of the gauze-workers, a relatively inconspicuous role in these movements.

A study of these records confirms the traditional view that the parts of Paris most frequently and wholeheartedly engaged in the riots and insurrections of the Revolution were the Faubourgs Saint-Antoine and Saint-Marcel. This is strikingly borne out in the case of Saint-Antoine, whose craftsmen and journeymen initiated and dominated the Réveillon riots, the capture of the Bastille, and the overthrow of the monarchy, and played an outstanding part in the revolution of May–June 1793 and the popular revolt of Prairial; the police reports suggest, in fact, that it was only in the events of 1787–1788 and in the Champ de Mars affair that Saint-Antoine played little or no part. The Faubourg Saint-Marcel, on the other hand, while it contributed substantially to the commotions of September–October 1788 and was represented by a score of volunteers at the siege of the Bastille, only began to play a really conspicuous role in the spring and summer of 1791. After this the part it played was second only to that of Saint-Antoine in the revolutions of August 1792 and May–June 1793, and in the days of Prairial. In Vendémiaire, of course, the pattern was quite different. Although property-owners and "moderates" had by now taken charge of even the popular Sections, it was not they but the traditional *bourgeois* Sections of Lepeletier (Bibliothèque) and Butte des Moulins (Palais Royal) that took the lead and held the initiative, while—characteristically—it was the [Section of] Quinze Vingts in the Faubourg Saint-Antoine which alone dispatched a contingent of armed volunteers to oppose the counter-revolutionary rebels.

But even if it can be demonstrated that the overwhelming majority of the participants in all but the last of the revolutionary *journées* were Parisian *sans-culottes,* how far can they be considered typical of the social groups from which they were drawn? Taine and his followers, while not denying the presence in revolutionary crowds of trades-men, wage-earners, and city poor, insisted, nevertheless, that the dominant element among them were *vagabonds, criminals,* and *gens sans aveu* [tramps].[10] In view of the panic-fear engendered among

---

[10] Taine, op. cit. 18, 41, 53–54, 81, 130, 135; P. Gaxotte, *La Révolution française,* pp. 122, 133–4, 146.

large and small property-owners by vagrants, petty thieves, and unemployed at different stages of the Revolution, it is perhaps not surprising that such a charge should be made: it was certainly voiced on
more than one occasion by hostile journalists, memorialists, and police authorities of the day. Yet, in its application to the capital at
least, it has little foundation in fact. Among the sixty-eight persons arrested, wounded, and killed in the Réveillon riots for whom details
are available, there were only three without fixed abode—a cobbler,
a carter, and a navvy [ditch-digger].[11] Of nearly eighty scheduled for
arrest after the burning of the *barrières* and four arrested for breaking the windows of the Barrière Saint-Denis, all were of fixed abode
and occupation.[12] Of some sixty persons arrested at the time of the
looting of the Saint-Lazare monastery in July 1789, nine were unemployed workers without fixed abode, who were caught up in the general drag-net directed against vagrants, *gens sans aveu,* and dwellers
in lodging-houses at the time of the July revolution, and probably had
no direct connexion with this affair at all.[13] Every one of the 662 *vain-
queurs de la Bastille* [conquerors of the Bastille] and of those claiming compensation for themselves and their dependents in August
1792 was of fixed abode and settled occupation.[14] In the weeks preceding the Champ de Mars demonstration one beggar was arrested
for abusing the king and queen, another for applauding their flight
from Paris, and two more for causing a disturbance and insulting the
National Guard; three other persons are described as being *sans état*
[without livelihood]; the rest of the 250 arrested during this period
appear to have been of settled abode.[15] Nor is there any mention in
the records of vagrants or beggars among those arrested in Germinal
and Prairial of the Year III; nor, even more surprisingly perhaps,
among those implicated in the grocery riots of 1792 and 1793. Doubtless these elements mingled with the rioters and insurgents on such
occasions, and we know that they caused concern to the Paris Electors during the revolution of July 1789;[16] but they appear to have
played an altogether minor role in these movements.

---

[11] Arch. Nat., Y 18795, fols. 444–62. [Arch. Nat. is the abbreviation used by the author
to designate the French Archives nationales.—Eds.]

[12] Arch. Nat., Z^{la} 886; Y 10649, fol. 18.

[13] *Ibid.,* fols. 20–21.

[14] Arch. Nat., T 514[1]; F[15] 3269–74; F[7] 4426.

[15] Archives de la Préfecture de la Police, Aa 167, fol. 51; 157, fol. 134; Ab 324, pp. 28–29,
32, 36, 37.

[16] *Procès-verbal des séances . . . de l'assemblée générale des Électeurs de Paris* (Paris,
1790), ii. 156 ff.

This does not mean, of course, that unemployed workers or workers and craftsmen living in furnished rooms or lodging-houses (the
often despised *non-domiciliés*) did not form a substantial element in
revolutionary crowds. This was particularly the case in the early
years of the Revolution, when, quite apart from the influx of workless
countrymen, there was considerable unemployment in a large number of Parisian crafts; this, however, became a declining factor after
the autumn of 1791. We find that eight of some fifty workers arrested
or wounded in the Réveillon riots were unemployed and that the proportion was somewhat higher among those arrested in connexion
with the Champ de Mars affair. In July 1789, too, there is circumstantial evidence to suggest that unemployed craftsmen, journeymen,
and labourers (only a handful of whom were from *ateliers de charité*
[public workshops]) were among those that took part in the assault
on the Bastille: we know, for example, that substantial sums were
raised after the fall of the fortress to relieve the distress of the
faubourg [Saint-Antoine] and that, of 900 stone-cutters who later petitioned the Assembly for unemployment relief, several claimed to
have been present at its capture.[17]. . . Unemployed workers from
neighbouring *ateliers de charité* played a certain part in the destruction of the *barrières* and the raid on the Saint-Lazare monastery. The
non-domiciliés formed a substantial proportion of the wage-earners,
small craftsmen, and petty traders of the capital, by no means limited
to the unemployed or casual labourers, though it was a fiction of the
time that the *hôtel* or *maison garnie* [cheap boarding house] provided only for provincials, foreigners, cut-throats, thieves, and *gens
sans aveu:* indeed, the *logeurs* or tenants [lodging-house keepers] of
such premises were compelled by law to keep a daily check and to
give a daily report to the police on all their lodgers.[18] In view of their
numbers[19] it is hardly surprising to find them fairly well represented
among those taking part in these disturbances—perhaps one in four
of those arrested in the Réveillon affair, one in ten among the *vain-
queurs de la Bastille,* one in five of those most actively concerned
with the Champ de Mars movement, and one in six of those arrested

---

[17] Arch. Nat., C 134, doss. 6, fols. 14–15; S. Lacroix, *Actes de la Commune de Paris* (2nd
series, 8 vols., Paris, 1900–14), v. 260.

[18] H. Monin, *Paris en 1789* (Paris, 1889), pp. 21, n. 5; 419, n. 4.

[19] In the census of 1795-the only census of the period in which the *non-domiciliés* are
accounted for—they number 9,792 for 25 Sections (P. Meuriot, *Un recensement de
l'an II,* p. 32); but this was a period of mass exodus, which was draining the hotels
and lodging-houses of a large part of their residents (J. de la Monneraye, *La Crise du
logement à Paris pendant la Révolution [Paris, 1928],* pp. 12–13).

and jailed in the grocery riots.[20] But this is, of course, a quite separate question from that of Taine's *gens sans aveu* and gives no further
indication of the number of vagrants involved.

The further contention that criminals and bandits played a significant part in the revolutionary *journées* collapses no less readily when
looked at more closely. The police in cross-examining their prisoners
habitually inquired whether they had served previous terms of imprisonment and it was easy enough to verify whether, as in the case
of more serious offences, they had been branded with the notorious
V [for *voleur*] of the thief or G of the galley-convict. The eight commissioners examining the Réveillon prisoners were able to find only
three who had incurred previous convictions of any kind—in two
cases these had involved short terms of detention in the Hôtel de la
Force on minor charges, whereas the port-worker Téteigne was
found to be branded with a V.[21] Yet such a case is exceptional. Of
those arrested for looting the Saint-Lazare monastery only one had
served a prison sentence—the butcher's boy Quatrevaux, who had
spent seventeen days in the Force on a previous conviction.[22] Not
one of the twenty-one arrested for the murder of Châtel, lieutenant to
the mayor, during a food riot at Saint-Denis in August 1789, appears
to have had a criminal record; and only three of fifteen arrested in a
similar disturbance at Versailles in September had served previous
sentences—one for stealing four pieces of wood in 1788 and two for
minor breaches of army discipline.[23] Of some 150 persons arrested in
the Paris Sections for political offences during the months preceding
and following the Champ de Mars affair, only four appear to have
served previous sentences, and these, again, were of a trivial nature.[24] Not one of the thirty-nine tried in the Year IV for alleged complicity in the September massacres had appeared in court before.[25]

---

[20] To take a random sample from Maillard's list of the *vainqueuers de la Bastille:* J. A.
Lamoureux, a tinsmith, lodged with one Boichamp, lodging-house keeper of the rue
de Lappe; Marc-Antoine Saint-Paul, a master fisherman, lived in a lodging-house in
the Faubourg Saint-Marcel; Jean Gabriel, a printer, lodged with a wine-merchant of
the rue de Plâtre, off the Place Maubert; and Gambi and Semain, riverside workers,
lodged at the Hôtel de Châlons in the rue du Figuier in the parish of Saint-Paul (Arch.
Nat., T 514¹).

[21] Arch. Nat., Y 15101, 13454.

[22] Arch. Nat., Z² 4691.

[23] Arch. Nat., Y 10497; Archives départementales Seine-et-Oise, series B, Prévôte de
l'Hôtel du Roi. Procédures, 1789, fols. 7–21.

[24] Archives de la Préfecture de la Police, Aa 137, fols. 177–8; 173, fols. 24, 25–26; 215,
fols. 451–2.

[25] P. Caron, *Les Massacres de septembre* (Paris, 1935), p. 111.

Such information is, unfortunately, not available for the other great *journées* of the Revolution; yet this evidence, as far as it goes, is overwhelming and should prove conclusive. By and large it does not appear, in fact, that those taking part in revolutionary crowds were any more given to crime, or even to violence or disorder, than the ordinary run of Parisian citizens from whom they were recruited. . . .

We must avoid the temptation, to which some historians have succumbed, of presenting the popular insurrections of the Revolution as being almost exclusively dominated by short-term economic considerations—as though each of these movements were, in essence, an "émeute de la faim" [hunger riot]. This was, of course, far from being the case. Not only [did] the *sans-culottes* [identify] themselves fully with a wide and varying range of political ideas and calls to action as the Revolution advanced; but we noted in particular the essentially political nature of the Champ de Mars demonstration and the whole preparatory movement leading up to it, not to mention the active support of the *sans-culottes* for such exclusively military-political actions as the assault on the Bastille and the Tuileries and the expulsion of the Girondins from the Convention. In the case of the Champ de Mars affair at least, the threat of famine or of rising prices played no part whatsoever. One the other hand, we have noted the abstention of the *sans-culottes* from any direct political intervention in the events of Vendémiaire of the Year IV—in striking contrast with their active participation, a few months earlier, in the days of Germinal and Prairial, though popular concern with bread-shortage and inflation was as acute in the one case as in the other. The essential difference lay of course in the changed political conditions and in the very differing aims of the rebels of Vendémiaire from those of Prairial:[26] in spite of continuing inflation and near-famine conditions, the active *sans-culottes* were not prepared to carry their hostility to the Thermidorian Convention to the point of giving comfort to the declared enemies of the Republic. The point is of interest: for one thing, it serves to disprove the contention that the *menu peuple* [common people], for lack of political maturity, were prepared to follow the lead of any demagogue irrespective of their own interests or inclinations; for another, it shows that a satisfactory explanation of popular participation in, or abstention from, these movements cannot be given without proper account being taken of both political and eco-

---

[26] It is true that there were other factors involved, of which the most important was the purely technical difficulty of staging a concerted action after the crushing defeat of Prairial; but this does not invalidate the argument in any way.

nomic factors and that concentration on the one to the exclusion of the other will only produce a distorted picture.

Yet, when all is said and done, the inescapable conclusion remains that the primary and most constant motive impelling revolutionary crowds during this period was the concern for the provision of cheap and plentiful food. This, more than any other factor, was the raw material out of which the popular Revolution was forged. It alone accounts for the continuity of the social ferment that was such a marked feature of the capital in these years and out of which the great political *journées* themselves developed. Even more it accounts for the occasional outbreaks of independent activity by the *menu peuple,* going beyond or running counter to the interests of their *bourgeois* allies and castigated by them as "counter-revolutionary"—such outbreaks as the blind fury of the Réveillon rioters or the more constructive efforts of Parisians to impose a form of popular price-control in the grocery riots of 1792 and 1793. Yet without the impact of political ideas, mainly derived from the *bourgeois* leaders, such movements would have remained strangely purposeless and barren of result; and had the *sans-culottes* not been able to absorb these ideas, as claimed by some writers, their influence on the course and outcome of the Revolution would have been far less substantial than in fact it was. . . .

We return to our central question—the nature of the crowds that took part in the great events of the Revolution in Paris. From our analysis these crowds have emerged as active agents in the revolutionary process, composed of social elements with their own distinctive identities, interests, and aspirations. Yet these were not at variance with, or isolated from, those of other social groups. In fact . . . the Revolution was only able to advance—and, indeed, to break out—because the *sans-culottes,* from whom these elements were largely drawn, were able to assimilate and to identify themselves with the new political ideas promoted by the liberal aristocracy and *bourgeoisie.* But, even when revolutionary crowds were impregnated with and stimulated by such ideas, they cannot for that reason be dismissed as mere passive instruments of middle-class leaders and interests; still less can they be presented as inchoate "mobs" without any social identity or, at best, as drawn from criminal elements or the dregs of the city population. While these played a part, it was an altogether minor one and on no occasion corresponded to the unsympathetic picture of the all-prevailing *canaille* painted by Taine and other writers.

Michelet's use of *le peuple* corresponds, of course, far more closely to the facts: we have seen Barnave, for one, applying the term to those participants in revolutionary events who were neither of the aristocracy nor of the *bourgeoisie*. Yet it is too indefinite; for while the *menu peuple,* or *sans-culottes,* taken collectively, formed the main body of rioters and insurgents, the part played by their constituent elements—women, wage-earners, craftsmen, journeymen, petty traders, or workshop masters—varied widely from one occasion to another. This, of course, merely emphasizes the point that revolutionary crowds, far from being social abstractions, were composed of ordinary men and women with varying social needs, who responded to a variety of impulses, in which economic crisis, political upheaval, and the urge to satisfy immediate and particular grievances all played their part.

THE SANS-CULOTTES

Albert Soboul

For biographical information on Albert Soboul, see Chapter 2, "The Peasants: Mentality and Behavior in 1789."

From June 1793 to February 1794, the Parisian sans-culotte movement played a major role in the political struggle leading to the consolidation of the Revolutionary Government and the organization of the Committee of Public Safety. During the same period, it imposed economic measures upon a reluctant Assembly intended to improve the living standards of the masses. If we wish to study the motives which explain the attitude of the people at this time, some kind of social definition of the Parisian sans-culotterie, some assessment of its composition is required.

This is not an easy task, for the economic or fiscal documents which could provide us with detailed analyses are missing, and what little statistical evidence we have is both vague and misleading. It is mainly through the political documents that we can explore the social characteristics of the sans-culotterie, particularly the dossiers dealing with the anti-terrorist repression of the Year III [1794–1795]. The true image, the mentality and behaviour of the Parisian sans-culotte, only emerges by comparing the attitudes of two social groups. Not particularly conscious of class distinctions, the sans-culotte reveals himself most clearly in relation to his social enemies. This absence of class-consciousness is reflected in the social composition of the Parisian population—in so far as it is possible to analyse it—and even more strikingly in the social composition of the political personnel of the Sections.

If we attempt to delimit the social contours of the sans-culotterie, we should, first of all, discover how the sans-culotte defined himself. There are enough relevant documents available for us to make, at least, an approximate definition.

Reprinted from *The Parisian Sans-Culottes and the French Revolution, 1793–1794* by Albert Soboul translated by Gwynne Lewis (Oxford: Clarendon Press, 1964), pp. 18–22, 23–24, 37–38, 99–100, 159–162, 254–260, by permission of Oxford University Press.

The sans-culotte was outwardly recognizable by his dress, which
served to distinguish him from the more elevated classes of society.
Trousers were the distinctive mark of the popular classes; breeches
of the aristocracy and, generally speaking, of the higher ranks of the
old Third Estate. Robespierre used to contrast the *culottes dorées* with
the *sans-culottes*—those who wore fancy or embroidered breeches
with those who simply wore trousers. The sans-culottes themselves
made the same distinction. The police-agent Rousseville, listing the
intrigues which had undermined the *comité de surveillance de Sceaux*
in his report of 25 Messidor Year II [July 13, 1794], emphasized the
hostility which existed between the *bas-de-soie* and the *sans-culottes*.[1]
Dress also distinguished the latter from the *muscadins*. Fontaine, a
gunner in the Section de la Réunion, was arrested on 5 Prairial [May
24, 1794] for repeating that he wished to revenge himself on the *muscadins,* defining the latter as "those (citizens) in the National Guard
who appeared to be better dressed than himself."

With the dress went a certain social comportment. Here again, it
is in his opposition to accepted social behaviour that the sans-
culotte asserts himself. The manners of the *ancien régime* were no
longer fashionable in the Year II; the sans-culottes no longer accepted a subordinate position in society. Jean-Baptiste Gentil, a
building-contractor and timber-merchant, arrested on 5 Pluviôse
Year II [January 24, 1794] for having failed to fulfil his obligations towards the Republic, was criticized by the *comité révolutionnaire* of
the Section des Quinze-Vingts for his manners: "People had to take
their hats off before they could approach him. The expression 'Monsieur' was still used in his house, and he always affected an air of importance." As a result, he had never been regarded as a good citizen.[2]

The sans-culottes readily judged a person's character from his appearance; his character then decided what his political opinions
would be. Everyone who offended their sense of equality and fraternity was suspected of being an aristocrat. It was difficult for a former
noble to find favour in their eyes, even when no definite accusation
could be levelled against him, "because such men cannot rise to the
heights of our Revolution. Their hearts are always full of pride, and
we will never forget the air of superiority which they used to assume,

---

[1]A.N., F[7] 4708. Concerning the origin of the word *sans-culotte,* and how its usage spread,
see Ferdinand Brunot, *Histoire de la langue française,* ix, 715. [*A.N.* is the abbreviation
used by the author to designate the French Archives nationales. *Bas-de-soie*—literally,
a silk stocking—was a term of disparagement used by the sans-culottes to describe
their more genteel enemies.—Eds.]
[2]*A.N.,* F[7] 4721.

nor the domination which they exercised over us." It was for these reasons that the *comité révolutionnaire* of the Section de la République arrested the duc de Brancas-Cérests on 16 October 1793, pointing out that he still enjoyed a yearly income of 89,980 *livres*.[3] The sans-culottes could not endure pride or disdain, since these feelings were thought to be typically aristocratic and contrary to the spirit of fraternity which should reign amongst citizens equal in rights: they obviously implied a political attitude hostile to the kind of democracy which the sans-culottes practised in their general assemblies and popular societies. For this reason, such personal defects are frequently mentioned in the reports justifying the arrest of suspects.

On 17 September 1793, the committee of the Section Révolutionnaire decided to arrest Étienne Gide, a wholesale merchant in watches and clocks, because he had given his allegiance to the Brissotin party, but also because he was of a "haughty and proud" disposition, and had often been heard to speak "ironically." On 28 Brumaire [November 18, 1793], the committee of the Section des Marchés arrested a music-dealer named Bayeux. It was alleged that he had said in a meeting of the general assembly that "it was disgusting to see a cobbler acting as president, particularly a cobbler who was so badly dressed." In the Section du Contrat-Social, the crime of the watchmaker Brasseur, who was arrested on 23 Floréal [May 12, 1794], was his remark "that it was very disagreeable for a man like himself to be in a guard-room with the sort of people whom, in the old days, one had nothing to do with." In extreme cases, a mere attitude of indifference towards a sans-culotte was enough for a person to be charged with harbouring "aristocratic feelings." Explaining the arrest of a former banker, Girardot-Marigny, on 12 Brumaire [November 2, 1793], the committee of the Section de Guillaume-Tell simply observed that it was a case of "one of these rich citizens who would not deign to fraternize with Republicans."[4]

Even more incriminating in the eyes of the sans-culottes than an attitude of pride, contempt, or plain indifference, was an insinuation of their social inferiority. In its report of 9 Frimaire [November 29, 1793] upon Louis-Claude Cezeron, arrested as a suspect, the committee of the Section Poissonnière referred in particular to some remarks he had made at a meeting of the general assembly in the preceding May, "that the poor depended upon the rich, and that the sans-culottes

---

[3]*A.N.*, F⁷ 4615, d. 3.
[4]*A.N.*, F⁷ 4584, pl. 5; 4615, pl. 4; 4726.

had never been anything but the lowest class of society." Bergeron, a dealer in skins from the Section des Lombards, "when he saw the sans-culottes fulfilling their obligations as citizens . . . said that it would be better if they got on with their own affairs instead of meddling in politics": he was arrested as a suspect on 18 Pluviôse [February 8, 1794]. The sans-culottes also had no time for the type of person who took advantage of his social position, wealth, or even his education, to impress or influence those beneath him. Truchon, a lawyer from the Section de Gravilliers, who had been denounced on several occasions by [the Enragé] Jacques Roux in his *Publiciste,* was finally arrested on 9 Prairial in the Year II [May 28, 1794]: the *comite révolutionnaire* accused him of having influenced citizens of "little discernment," and of expressing the opinion that "positions of authority should be filled by enlightened men with private means, since they alone had the time to spare."[5]

It is true that the sans-culottes had an egalitarian conception of social relationships. But beneath the general theory, there were more clearly defined factors which help to explain their behaviour, and it is interesting to consider to what extent they themselves were conscious of, and able to express, this deeper motivation.

Above all, the sans-culottes were conscious of the social antagonism which divided them from the aristocracy. The aristocracy had been the real enemy from 14 July 1789 to 10 August 1792, and it was against the aristocracy that they continued to struggle. The address of the *société des Sans-Culottes de Beaucaire* [in the department of the Gard] to the Convention on 8 September 1793 is significant in this respect: "We are sans-culottes . . . poor and virtuous, we have formed a society of manual workers and peasants . . . we know our friends— those who have delivered us from the clergy, the nobility, feudalism, the *dîme* [tithe], royalty and all the evils which accompany it. They are the same people who are called anarchists, troublemakers and followers of Marat by the aristocrats."[6] The idea of a class struggle emerges more clearly in the address of the *société populaire de Dijon* [in the department of the Côte d'Or] on 27 Nivôse Year II [January 16, 1794] which stated that "in future, we must be a united people, not two nations in opposition." To achieve this the society advocated the death penalty "for everyone, without exception, who is known to be an aristocrat."[7]

---

[5]*A.N.,* F[7] 4775[35].
[6]*A.N.,* C 271, pl. 666, p. 37.
[7]*A.N.,* C 289, pl. 394, p. 9.

The aristocrat was such a figure of hatred to the sans-culotterie that it was not long before the expression was being used to describe all their enemies, irrespective of whether they belonged to the former nobility or to the higher ranks of what had been the Third Estate. This failure to distinguish between the real aristocrat and a member of the upper bourgeoisie—which was peculiarly sans-culotte—helps to underline the separate and distinct character of their contribution to the Revolution. . . .

The economic crisis helped to sharpen these social conflicts, and as the crisis developed and the *patriote* party of 1789 began to disintegrate, differences of opinion between the sans-culottes and the upper classes of the old Third Estate were added to the fundamental sans-culotte—aristocrat antagonism. A note intended for the Committee of General Security in Pluviôse Year II [January–February 1794] referred to the existence of two parties in the Section de Brutus: one representing the people—*sans-culottisme*—and the other composed of "bankers, stock-brokers and moneyed-people." An address to the Convention on 27 Ventôse [March 17, 1794] contrasts with the "brave sans-culottes," not only the clergy, the nobility and the sovereign heads of Europe, but also solicitors, barristers, notaries, and particularly "well-to-do farmers, selfish citizens and all these fat, wealthy merchants. They are fighting against us instead of our oppressors."[8] Is this simply a struggle between citizens who owned property, and those who did not, a struggle between *possédants* and *non-possédants?* One cannot really say that it is, for we find craftsmen and shopkeepers amongst the sans-culotterie who were themselves property-owners. It is rather a conflict between those who favoured the idea of restricted and limited ownership, and those who believed in the absolute right of property as proclaimed in 1789; and even more clearly, a conflict between the defenders of a system of controls and fixed prices, and those who preferred an economic policy of *laissez-faire*—in general terms, a struggle between consumers and producers.

The sources enable us to probe fairly deeply into the social antipathies and preoccupations of the sans-culotterie. They denounced *honnêtes gens*—those citizens who, if not rich, enjoyed at least a comfortable and cultured life, and also those who were conscious, if not necessarily proud, of being better dressed and better educated than themselves. They denounced *rentiers*—citizens who lived off unearned incomes. And finally they denounced "the rich"; not just

---

[8]*A.N.,* C 295, pl. 994, p. 27.

property-owners or *possédants,* but the *gros* as opposed to the *petits*—the wealthy, big business-men as compared with those of their own kind who possessed but limited means. The sans-culottes were not hostile towards property so long as it was limited; they accepted property of the kind which artisans and shopkeepers already owned, and which many *compagnons* [journeymen] dreamed of owning themselves in the future. . . .

The sans-culotte . . . is defined by his political behaviour as much as by his place in society—the latter is more difficult to ascertain than the former.

A document dated May 1793 attempts to answer part of this difficulty, at least, in replying to "the impertinent question—what is a sans-culotte?"[9] The sans-culotte ". . . is someone who goes everywhere on foot . . . and who lives quite simply with his wife and children, if he has any, on the fourth or fifth floor." Jacques Roux also referred to the sans-culottes living in attics, and the *Père Duchesne* wrote, "If you wish to meet the cream of the sans-culotterie, then visit the garrets of the workers (ouvriers)." The sans-culotte is useful "because he knows how to plough a field, how to forge, to saw, to file, to cover a roof and how to make shoes. . . . And since he works, it is certain that you will not find him at the café de Chartres, nor in the dens where people gamble and plot, nor at the théatre de la Nation where they are performing *l'Ami des lois* . . . [10] In the evening, he goes to his Section, not powdered and perfumed, not elegantly dressed in the hope of catching the eye of the [female] citizens in the galleries, but to give his unreserved support to sound resolutions. . . . Besides this, the sans-culotte always has his sword with the edge sharpened to give a salutary lesson to all trouble-makers. Sometimes he carries his pike with him, and at the first beat of the drum, he will be seen leaving for the Vendée, for the *armée des Alpes* or the *armée du Nord.*"

The modest social condition of the sans-culotte is clearly of importance here; but, as we can see from the above document, a definition of the sans-culotte would not be complete without a statement of his political conduct. . . .

Although the sans-culotte militants were unable to devise an original and effective social programme, the coherent pattern of political ideas which they adopted distinguishes them as the most progressive group to emerge during the Revolution. Their demands for the autonomy and permanence of the Sections, the right to approve leg-

---

[9] *A.N.,* F[7] 4775[48].

[10] The café de Chartres was a favourite royalist meeting-place; *l'Ami des lois* was a comedy by Jean Laya performed in 1793.

islation, the exercise of control over their elected representatives and the power of revoking their mandate, based upon a wide interpretation of the expression "popular sovereignty," moved the sans-culotterie nearer the exercise of direct government and popular democracy.[11] But could the bourgeois conception of democracy and the exigencies of the Revolutionary Government be reconciled with the political leanings of the sans-culotterie?

The political behaviour of the militant sans-culotte can only be explained by his unqualified acceptance of the principle that sovereignty resides in the people. For the sans-culotte, this was not an abstract idea, but a concrete reality of the people gathered together in the assemblies of the Sections exercising the totality of their rights.

Popular sovereignty was "imprescriptible and inalienable; a right which could be delegated to no one," and on 3 November 1792, the Section de la Cité announced that "anyone who claims that he is invested with this right will be regarded as a tyrant, a usurper of the people's freedom who deserves to be punished by death." On 13 March 1793, after a citizen in the general assembly of the Section du Panthéon-Français had stated that "people are threatening us with a dictator," the assembly rose to its feet and swore to kill "any director, protector, tribune, triumvire, or any other kind of ruler, whatever title he chooses for himself, who attacks the principle of the people's sovereignty." This anxiety to defend the sovereignty of the people clearly explains why so many proposals by Marat to nominate a tribune of the people, or a dictator, were so unsuccessful, as well as the importance of the accusation that Hébert and others were planning to create an office of *grand juge,* a charge designed to weaken their popularity in the eyes of the people. . . .

Violence was adopted as a last resort by the sans-culotterie against anyone who refused to unite with them in their struggle: it became one of the most characteristic features of their political behaviour. Popular violence had enabled the bourgeoisie to launch their first attacks against the *ancien régime,* and there was never any question of the aristocracy being completely crushed without it. In 1793 and in the Year II, the sans-culotte adopted violent tactics, not only against the aristocracy, but against the moderates who refused to accept the idea of an egalitarian republic.

To understand this violence, and the feeling of exaltation which accompanied it, we would doubtless have to look sometimes for bio-

---

[11] The expression "popular republic" can be found in Étienne Barry's *Essai sur la dénonciation politique.*

logical reasons: temperament often explains many reactions which would otherwise remain obscure. The reports of Prairial Year III [May–June 1795] on the terrorists of the previous year often stress the quick-tempered or violent sides of their nature. As one informer stated, a man with such a temperament was subject to fits of passion "which might have led him to make exaggerated statements without foreseeing or even thinking about their consequences." Reactions were more immediate and more extreme because the sans-culottes were often rough and crude, lacking any real education, their lives inflamed by misery.

In the Year III, terrorists were indiscriminately described as *buveurs de sang* [bloodthirsty men], and although we must be careful not to generalize, or to take police reports and denunciations literally, it would be very difficult to deny that violence for some actually meant the spilling of blood. Arbulot, a cloth-shearer from the Section des Gardes-Françaises, arrested on 9 Prairial [May 28, 1795], was reputed to have been a very dangerous husband and neighbour, with a fierce and unyielding nature: it was said that he had taken great pleasure in the September massacres. Bunou from the Section des Champs-Elysées, arrested on 5 Prairial [May 24, 1795], was alleged to have asked for a guillotine for the Section in the Year II, "and that if they could not find an executioner, he would take the job on himself." Similar statements were supposed to have been made by Lesur from the Section du Luxembourg who was arrested on the following day. He was convinced "that the guillotine was not doing its work quickly enough; that there should be a bit more blood-letting in the prisons; and that if the executioner was tired, he would mount the scaffold himself, even if it meant soaking the two-pound loaf he had just bought with blood." In the Section des Gardes-Françaises, Jayet was arrested on 6 Prairial [May 25, 1795] because he had said in the Year II "that he wanted to see streams of blood flowing until they had reached ankle-height." Another citizen on leaving the general assembly of the Section de la République stated: "The guillotine is hungry; it has been fasting for too long."[12]

Temperament alone, however, does not explain why practically all the militant sans-culottes should have justified, if not exalted, a recourse to violence and the use of the guillotine. For many, brutal force appeared to be the only answer in times of acute crisis. Yet these same men, who did not hesitate to spill blood on these occasions, were quite peaceable citizens in the ordinary course of their daily

---

[12] *A.N.*, F7 4581, pl. 1; 4627, d. 2; 4636, d 2; 4749; 4774[86].

lives; good sons, husbands, and fathers. Duval, a shoemaker from the Section de l'Arsenal, was condemned to death on 11 Prairial Year III [May 30, 1795] for his part in the rising of the first of the month. His neighbours described him as a good father, a good husband, and a good citizen—"a man of good morals." The awareness of the danger facing the nation, the belief in the aristocratic plot, the atmosphere of the great insurrections, the tocsin, the warning cannon-shot and the parade of arms all played their part in lifting these men outside themselves, completely altering their characters. According to the *comité civil* [the political or administrative committee] of the Section du Faubourg du Nord, Joseph Morlot, a house-painter arrested on 5 Prairial [May 24, 1795] had two distinct natures: "The one, when governed by his natural disposition, is gentle, honest, and kind; it presents a combination of all the social virtues which he practises discreetly in his everyday life. The other, awakened by momentary dangers, produces the worst possible evils presented in their most lurid form which he parades in the most indiscreet manner."[13]

But violence was not adopted simply for its own sake: it had a political aim which was not devoid of a vague consciousness of class differences, forced upon the sans-culotterie by the continued resistance of the aristocracy. The *comité révolutionnaire* of the Section Poissonnière was alleged to have planned the arrest in Brumaire Year II [October–November, 1793] of a citizen named Charvin, well known for his moderation "which weakens the people's confidence in revolutionary acts and leads to a deterioration of public morale in the Section." Moussard, a teacher employed by the Executive Commission of Public Instruction, was arrested on 5 Prairial Year III [May 24, 1795]. "I was often over-enthusiastic," he wrote in his defence statement, "What person does not go a little beyond himself in a revolution? . . . I am too exalted in my opinions, they say. Yes, the passion for good burns inside me; I respond to the joys of freedom, and my blood will always boil when I hear of the enemies of my country."[14]

The guillotine was popular because the sans-culottes regarded it as the avenging arm of the nation, accounting for such expressions as "national hatchet," and "the people's axe"; the guillotine was also "the scythe of equality." Class hatred against the aristocracy was exacerbated by the widespread belief in the "aristocratic plot" which, since 1789, had represented one of the motivating elements of popular violence. Foreign and civil war helped to strengthen the convic-

---

[13] *A.N.* W 546; F[7] 4774[53].
[14] *A.N.,* F[7] 4776; 4774[54].

tion of the sans-culotterie that the only way of crushing the aristocracy completely was by terror, and that the guillotine was necessary
if the Republic was not to be overthrown. Becq, a clerk in the Admi-
ralty who, according to the *comité civil* of the Section de la Butte-des-
Moulins, a good husband and father and generally well thought of but
extraordinarily exalted [passionate] in his attitude towards the Revolution, directed his fanaticism against priests and nobles for whom he
prescribed, as a rule, assassination. Jean-Baptiste Mallais, a shoemaker and *commissaire révolutionnaire* from the Section du Temple,
sympathized wholeheartedly with these views. When he began one of
his many arguments, the subject would inevitably be his hatred of
priests and nobles whom he considered to be enemies of the people;
and when he spoke of arming the wives of patriots, it was "so that
they, in their turn, could cut the throats of aristocrats' wives." Bar-
rayer from the Section de la Réunion was alleged to have stated in the
Year II "that they had to kill the young devil in the church" because if
they did not, then "one day he would massacre the people." More significant still of the political significance which the sans-culottes attached to violence and the Terror were the remarks taken down by
the police-agent Perrière on 6 Ventôse Year II [February 24, 1794]:
"Are there any executions today? a small well-dressed moderate
asked.—Without any doubt, replied an honest patriot, since we are
still surrounded by treason."[15]

In the year III, the recourse to violence had an even greater significance for the sans-culotterie. The Terror had also had an economic
aspect: it had enabled the General Maximum to be applied which
had guaranteed the people their daily bread. Reaction coincided
with the end of price-fixing and the most acute food-shortage. Some
sans-culottes naturally identified the Terror with a well-stocked
larder, as they associated popular government with the Terror. The
shoemaker Clément from the Section de la République was denounced on 2 Prairial [May 21, 1795] for having said "that they could
not build the Republic without blood." A citizen named Denis from
the Section Brutus was arrested on 5 Prairial [May 24, 1795] because
in his opinion there were not so many "good republicans to be found
as when they used to guillotine people." Chalandon, a wife from the
Section de l'Homme-Armé, used to say "that things would never improve until they erect permanent guillotines on all the public thor-
oughfares of Paris." The remarks made by Richer on 1 Prairial [May
20, 1795], a carpenter from the Section de la République, were more

---

[15] *A.N.*, W 112.

precise. Richer was convinced "that the only way to get bread is to spill a little blood," adding "that during the Terror there was no shortage of it."[16] . . .

The contradictions peculiar to the Parisian sans-culotterie were equally as important in explaining the collapse of the system of the Year II as the conflicts which divided the Revolutionary Government and the popular movement.

There was a social contradiction between the Jacobins, drawn almost exclusively from the ranks of the lower, middle, and even the upper bourgeoisie, and the sans-culottes, if we accept [the revolutionary politician] Pétion's description of the latter as day-labourers and *compagnons de métiers* [journeymen artisans]. But it would be wrong to identify the sans-culotte with the wage-earner, despite the fact that wage-earners formed the largest section of the sans-culotterie. The reality is far more complex. The sans-culotterie did not constitute a class, nor was the sans-culotte movement based on class differences. Craftsmen, shopkeepers and merchants, *compagnons* and day-labourers joined with a bourgeois minority to form a coalition but there was still an underlying conflict between craftsmen and merchants, enjoying a profit derived from the private ownership of the means of production, and *compagnons* and day-labourers, entirely dependent upon their wages.

The application of the maximum [price ceilings] brought this contradiction into the open. Craftsmen and shopkeepers agreed that it was a sound and reasonable policy to force the peasantry to feed the population of the towns; but they protested immediately [when] the provisions of the maximum began to affect their own interests. *Compagnons* reacted in much the same way. By creating a shortage of labour, the *levée en masse* and the civil war led to a rise in wages: if producers and "middlemen" refused to observe price-fixing, why should the workers offer themselves as victims? The demands of the revolutionary struggle had welded the unity of the Parisian sans-culotterie and momentarily pushed the conflict of interests into the background: there was no question, however, of suppressing them altogether.

Differences in social outlook complicated the problem even further. The contradictions within the ranks of the sans-culotterie were not simply those which separated the *possédants* and producers from the salaried workers. Amongst the latter we find, in particular, those who belonged to the clerical and teaching professions, who,

---

[16] *A.N.,* W 548.

because of their way of life, regarded themselves as bourgeois, not to be identified with the *bas-peuple* [common people], even if they embraced the same cause. On the other hand, many citizens recognized as being members of the bourgeoisie described themselves as "sans-culotte" and acted as such.

The sans-culottes, recruited from so many different levels of society, could not, therefore, have been really conscious of belonging to a certain class. Although they were generally hostile to the new methods of production, it was not always from the same motives— the craftsman was afraid of being reduced to the status of a wage-earner; the *compagnon* detested the monopolist because he held him responsible for the rising cost of living. As for the *compagnons* alone, it would be anachronistic to speak of them as being class-conscious, since their mentality was still conditioned by the world of the craftsman in which they lived and worked. The capitalist concentration of industry, by bringing them into daily contact through the factory, had not yet created the mentality which would awaken the feeling of class solidarity.

However, if class-consciousness cannot be attributed to the sans-culotterie as a body, it is possible to detect a certain awareness of class amongst the wage-earners. Entirely dependent upon their employers, they regarded themselves as a distinct social group, not only because of the manual nature of their work and their place in the system of production, but also on account of the clothes which they wore, the food they ate, their pastimes, social habits and, in particular, their living accommodation. The fact that they were mostly uneducated—education being reserved solely for citizens privileged by birth and wealth—also tended to distinguish them from their fellow citizens, creating a feeling of inferiority and, sometimes, of powerlessness amongst the lower classes. Militant sans-culottes frequently reveal their hostility towards *hommes-à-talent,* but, by raising themselves to the same level, longed to play a decisive part in controlling their destiny.

Composed of diverse elements, not constituting a class and, therefore, devoid of class-consciousness, the Parisian sans-culotterie, despite a few hesitant attempts to co-ordinate their activity, lacked a really effective weapon of political action—a strictly disciplined party which could only have been created by a drastic purge followed by recruitment on a class basis. This was equally true of the Revolutionary Government, since the Jacobins themselves were not representative of any one social class. The entire régime of the Year II rested upon an abstract conception of political democracy which largely explains its weakness. The consequences of this were particularly disastrous for the popular movement.

Although there were many militants who tried to discipline the general assemblies and popular societies, leading figures in a number of the Sections aggravated the situation by disputing power amongst themselves, occasionally by abusing it when they eventually succeeded in gaining control. As for the mass of the sans-culotterie, apart from hatred of the aristocracy and the summary methods envisaged for dealing with the problem—chiefly massacre—they do not appear to have been gifted with any degree of political insight: they were simply waiting to receive the benefits which the Revolution would inevitably bring. They campaigned for the maximum, not so much in order to defend the *assignat* and guarantee the production of war supplies, but because they believed that price-controls would help to maintain their standard of living. When they realized that, in many respects, a controlled economy did not meet this requirement, they abandoned it in favour of a new policy. Would the sans-culottes have agreed to drop their demand for higher wages if—an untenable hypothesis—*possédants* and producers had agreed to respect the provisions of the maximum by accepting a margin of profit which the Revolutionary Government considered to be reasonable. The possibility appears to be extremely remote. The war made certain sacrifices inevitable—one of them was that no section of the community should try and profit from the circumstances it created in order to further its own particular interests.

From this point of view, the 9 Thermidor was, indeed, a *journée de dupes* [day of deception] for the sans-culottes. Disillusioned by the effect of the maximum, discontented with the Revolutionary Government, they failed to realize that its collapse would also involve their own ruin. Ten months later, their resistance weakened by the effects of famine and the high cost of living, realizing at last what they had lost, they demanded a return to a controlled economy, rose in insurrection for the last time only to be completely crushed and swept from the stage of history.

The internal contradictions of the sans-culotterie, however, do not entirely explain the collapse of the popular movement: its gradual disintegration was inscribed in the dialectical march of history itself. The indirect attacks of the Committees and the consolidation of the Revolutionary Government, the drama of Germinal and the feeling of deception which followed, only partly explain its weakness. It was, in fact, inevitable that the popular movement should have lost momentum: its development, its very success, only strengthened those factors which finally contributed to its defeat.

There was, in the first place, a reason of a biological nature. Most of the militants had been actively engaged in the revolutionary struggle since 14 July 1789; they had participated in every insurrection. Since 10 August 1792, they had redoubled their activity. But the enthusiasm and excitement of the great *journées* involved a certain expenditure of nervous energy which, after the victory, increased the tension and strain involved in the daily life of the militant. Five years of revolution had drained the physical resources of the sectionary personnel who provided the cadres of the popular movement. It was only natural that this physical exhaustion which, at different times, forced many of the leading figures of the Revolution—Robespierre himself in Messidor [June–July 1794]—to retire momentarily from the political scene, should not also have affected the militants always in the thick of the battle. Robespierre had predicted that as the war dragged on, the people would begin to "show signs of apathy." This apathy communicated itself to the popular movement, depriving it of its vigour and initial enthusiasm.

There was also a psychological reason arising out of the events of the Year II. The end of the civil war, the halt to the invasion, and, finally, the realization of victory, led to an understandable relaxation of tension. This was true of the population as a whole, although the relief felt by the bourgeoisie cannot be explained by the end of the Terror alone—there was also the prospect of an end to the economic policy of controls and fixed prices, as well as the return of administrative and governmental authority into the hands of the *notables.* The people were anxious to reap the benefits of all their effort. The opening of a register in the Section de la Montagne for new adherents to the Constitution cannot be regarded simply as a political manœuvre: in the eyes of the militants,the *Acte constitutionnel* of June 1793 was the symbol of social democracy; they had continuously campaigned for the right to receive public relief and the right to instruction. But the majority of the people were primarily concerned with their right to subsist. Since victory was at last in sight, they expected, if not exactly abundance, then, at least, less difficulty in being provided with food as well as a guaranteed daily supply of bread. In fact, victory led to the demobilization of the popular movement.

The Parisian sans-culotterie were also weakened from month to month by the dialectical effect of the war effort. The conscription of 300,000 men, the recruitment for the Vendée, then for the Eure, the *levée en masse* and the creation of the Revolutionary Army, deprived the Sections of a considerable number of the youngest, most active, often the most conscientious and enthusiastic patriots who regarded the defence of the nation as their first civic duty. In order to assess the vitality of the popular movement, an exact calculation of the number of men who enlisted for the various campaigns would clearly be of the greatest possible advantage. But, if we cannot attempt a general study, we can, at least, gain some idea of the significance of the loss of human energy suffered by the Parisian Sections in 1793. In the Section des Piques, which had 3,540 voters aged 21 and over in the Year II, 233 volunteers enrolled for the Vendée from 3 to 17 May 1793 alone—mainly sans-culottes in the prime of life. The lists of citizens capable of carrying arms drawn up by the Sections underlines this sapping of the armed strength of the Sections: men of over 50 and, occasionally, of 60 years of age represent a large proportion of the companies formed. Out of the 3,231 men in the Section de Quatre-Vingt-Douze, 767 (23.7 per cent) were over 50 years of age. In the Section des Arcis, the companies totalled 2,986 men "of whom, a quarter would have to be subtracted" of men aged over 60.[17] The popular movement grew old as a result of these successive enrolments: the inevitable effect on the revolutionary enthusiasm and combative keenness of the Parisian masses can readily be appreciated.

Finally, the dialectical effect of success led to a gradual disintegration of the framework of the popular movement. Many of the sectionary militants, even if they were not motivated by ambition alone, regarded an official position as the legitimate reward for their militant activity. The stability of the popular movement largely depended upon the satisfaction of these personal interests which happened to coincide with the need for purging the various committees. But, in such cases, success breeds a new conformity, as the example of the *commissaires révolutionnaires* illustrates. At first, their revolutionary ardour had distinguished them from the other members of the political organizations of the Sections. But since they had been recruited chiefly from the lowest social ranks of the sans-culotterie, it became necessary, even for the success of the Revolution, for them to be paid a salary. The fear of losing their position, just as much as the strengthening of the Revolutionary Government, soon turned them into willing instruments of the central power. Throughout the Year II, many of the militants were transformed into salaried civil servants as a result of this process, which was not only a necessary outcome of the inter-

---

[17] *A.N.*, AA 15, d. 783. Lists by Section of citizens capable of carrying arms.

nal evolution of the sans-culotterie, but also of the intensification of
the class struggle within France and on her frontiers. The really
politically-minded elements of the sans-culotterie became part of the
administrative machinery of the State; the sectionary organizations
suffered a corresponding loss of political activity, allowance having
been made for the accumulated demands of national defence. At the
same time, the democratic ideal was being weakened in the Sections,
the process of bureaucratization gradually paralysing the critical
spirit and activity of the masses. The eventual outcome was a relaxation of the control exercised by the popular movement over the
Revolutionary Government which became increasingly authoritarian
in character. This bureaucratic encroachment deprived the sans-
culottes of many of the channels through which the popular movement had operated.

These various considerations—which have a far wider application
than to the events of the Year II—account for the weakening of the
popular movement, and clearly precipitated its collapse.

It would be wrong, however, to draw up a purely negative balance
sheet of the popular movement in the Year II. Doubtless it was impossible for it to attain its particular objective—the egalitarian and
popular republic towards which the sans-culottes were moving without any clearly defined programme—prevailing circumstances as
well as its own contradictions raised far too many obstacles. Nevertheless, the popular movement has still contributed towards historical progress by its decisive intervention in support of the bourgeois
revolution.

Without the Parisian sans-culotterie, the bourgeoisie could not
have triumphed in so radical a fashion. From 1789 to the Year II, the
sans-culottes were used as an effective weapon of revolutionary combat and national defence. In 1793, the popular movement made possible the installation of the Revolutionary Government and, consequently, the defeat of the counter-revolution in France and the allied
coalition in Europe. It was the Thermidoreans who really benefited
from this victory; and if they failed to use their advantage to secure
peace, it was because the decision to abandon a controlled economy,
added to the demoralization of the troops totally deprived of supplies, paralysed the army and gave the enemy the necessary time to
prepare new campaigns. This contrast helps us to appreciate the
work of the Revolutionary Government as well as the importance of
the popular movement of the Year II.

A CRITIQUE

Richard Cobb

For biographical information on Richard Cobb, see
Chapter 6, "Why Terror in 1793–1794?"

🎩🎩🎩🎩🎩🎩

Both contemporaries and several generations of liberal or reactionary historians were shocked by the spectacle of popular violence during the French Revolution. Contemporaries feared that these new, unexpected, and unpredictable forms of violence might be used against property-holders and respectable people, rather than against poachers and lawbreakers. In fact, what seems to have shocked contemporaries and historians alike is that the violence should have been popular (and, by implication, lawless, brutish, chaotic, undirected). [The writer Louis-Sébastien] Mercier, in 1797, frequently refers to the violent language of the common people, rich in incitation to murder, varied too in cannibalistic metaphor—"I would like to eat your liver," "I would like to open up your belly and eat your guts," "I would like to eat a bourgeois' head," "let's eat a good hunk from an aristocrat," and so on—and he describes the evolution of this popular violence in its verbal expressions: "The words *carnage, blood, death, vengeance,* that ABC of the Jacobin idiom [*vengeance, in fact, belongs by right to the Thermidorian period, even on the admission of the Thermidorian local authorities*] is repeated, shouted, roared . . . by the *Mob.* The *Mob* has ruled for nearly fifteen months, has tyrannized the city. . . ." Referring to the verb *lanterner,* he observes: "Previously that word had meant to waste time by doing nothing . . . at the beginning of the Revolution, it meant to hang a man from a lamppost. The words *guillotiner* and *guillotine* have become so popular in usage that these words have completely driven out the words *lanterne* and *lanterner.* . . ."

Reprinted from *The Police and the People: French Popular Protest, 1789–1820* by R. C. Cobb (1970), pp. 87–90, 120–127, by permission of Oxford University Press. All footnotes included except for cross-references to notes in the appendix. Quotations originally in French have been translated by the editors.

I heard [*he claims to recollect*] screamed in my ear: "Let the French perish so long as liberty triumphs!" I heard someone else cry out in a section meeting: "Yes, I would grab my head by the hair and lop it off, and offering it to the despot, I would say to him: 'Tyrant, this is the action of a free man.'" This sublime degree of extravagance was created for the revolutionary common people, it was heard, it was a success. . . .

We may recall the women of the people, as depicted by *La Lanterne Magique,* eating the "naked and quivering bodies of their victims"; and this was the language which, in the year III [1794–1795], changed sides, to be used by former terrorists when describing the horrors of the White Terror; in Pluviôse of that year [January–February 1795], the survivors of the first wave of massacres at Nîmes—and the future victims of the next—describe the scene: "Each of these unfortunate people suffered a thousand deaths before finally expiring; they were mutilated, and the murderers, covered with blood, carried and raised as trophies the still throbbing limbs that they had just cut off. . . ." There is by then a standard vocabulary of massacre. A jeweller from the Lombards Section in Paris is accused, in a Thermidorian report, "of boasting that he had cut off eighteen heads" in September 1792, and, whatever we make of this popular boastfulness, there is no doubt as to the intentions of the man who made the report. They are as clear as those of Mercier and the lantern slide lecturer. All conveniently forgot the violence of others—of the old royal government, of the old royal army, and of *la Royale* [a prison off the coast of French Guiana], with its barbarous punishments; of the old penal system and the *bagne* [a forced-labor prison] with its ball and chain and similar refinements; of the old police ordinances and the language of the old administration, which, when addressed to the common people, could express itself only in threats and in the promise of retribution; of the treatment of Protestant children, especially in the Généralité de Rouen; of the old ruling class, and of their servants; of the Parlements, and of the *basoche* [law clerks]; of the cavalier of the *maréchaussée* [mounted police]; of the *Garde française* [a member of an army regiment stationed in Paris], so proud of his proficiency in killing quickly and hardly admissible into the inner sanctum of regimental solidarity until he had a corpse or two to his credit; of the hussar and the dragoon; of the sailor, and of the *guet* [the night police in Paris]—just as everyone often tends to ignore the violence of 1795 and the years following and to forget that Terror could be White as well as Blue. Nor do they ask themselves how else the people could exercise their will and get their grievances seen to.

Certainly an enraged crowd, a group of rioters in full cry, the repeated invitation of À *mort!* [Put him to death!] screamed like a litany, the bestiality of massacre and lynching, the near-cannibalism of some women and a very few male rioters, are repellent, dreadful, hideous, and above all depressing, just as the corpses that are strewn so copiously in every print, patriotic or counter-revolutionary, of the great revolutionary *journées* or of the great massacres are absolutely inadmissible, whatever their clothing, whichever their uniform, just as severed heads and headless bodies cry out endlessly against the Revolution and all its works.

Certainly, too, what is so often clothed over and "historicized" as something called the "popular movement" (how much is the historian's terminology dominated by thought of syllabus or by the search for a chapter heading?) was frequently cruel and cowardly, base and vengeful, barbaric and not at all pretty to watch. Professor Rudé's Crowd is somehow altogether too respectable; one hesitates to credit all these worthy shopkeepers and all these honest apprentices, family men too, with such horrors, and, in identifying the assailants, one is in danger of leaving the assailed out of the picture. Any honest historian of popular movements—and especially those of the French Revolution—must at times be seized with doubts. Is he not attempting to steer away from a violence that, on close inspection, becomes unbearable? Is he not trying to find excuses for brutality and murder? Is he not taking refuge in the convenient jargon of collective behaviourism to explain, to rationalize, massacre? Is there not something indecent, obscene, on his part, thus to pause, for so long, among yellowed sheets that describe, in the stilted language of French law, the details of a village lynching, or of a Christmas Day brawl ending in bloodshed? Is he not trying to get it both ways—the exhilaration of riot, experienced in the safety of a record office? Is he not making his *homme révolutionnaire* gentler, kinder, more tolerant, more whimsical, than he really was? Is he not trying to take the sting out of the *massacreur* by emphasizing the conceit, the *naïveté,* and the credulity of the *sans-culotte,* even if the one is not, in a particular instance, the other? Should not he, who, in fact, would never march behind the banner, would always stay at home, or who would be the first to run at the sound of firing, keep away from popular protest altogether and take refuge in the History of Parliament? Most historians of the French Revolution must have asked some of these questions, at one time or another, and especially in moments when they have been glutted with horror. And it would of course be both dishonest and misleading to represent the "popular movement" as a study in rumbustious good fellowship, enthusiasm, generosity, fra-

ternity, and hope, or as an early groping towards various forms of socialism, while leaving out of account the violence.

Yet this violence is not so odious and inadmissible as that of war
or of diplomacy; it was never gratuitous, nor was it ever exclusive to
any one class—or any one party: all classes, all parties were enthusiastic advocates of violence when there was a good chance of using
it against their immediate enemies, though they tended to discover
the advantages of mercy when they looked like being on the losing
side. . . .

Most historians are now familiar with Albert Soboul's rather for-
malized account of the relations between the classes—especially the
urban classes—in the course of the revolutionary period, both from
his *Précis*[1] and from his even shorter *Que sais-je?*[2] A *pas de deux* or
sometimes a *pas de trois,* that might be set to music as a historical
ballet. Opening scene: bourgeoisie and people, hand in hand, dancing on the prone figure of Privilege. Scene Two: (the people having
done their stuff) bourgeoisie and monarchy, hand in hand, dancing
on the prone figure of the people. Scene Three: bourgeoisie and people, hand in hand, dancing on the prone body of monarchy. Scene
Four: an intermezzo between bourgeoisie and people, only occasionally hand in hand, more often hands vainly extended, both playing
hard to get. Scene Five: bourgeoisie dancing alone, on the prone bodies of people and monarchy. One knew it would turn out like this all
along, for that is the rule of a particularly rigorous choreography that
will not allow a step to be taken out of place (and, if necessary, the
sans-culotte may have to be nudged and reminded of his part: "Get
back into line, you are part of the Popular Movement"; the bourgeois,
too, forgetting that he is either a Girondin, or Jacobin, or Montagnard, or Thermidorian, may have to be recalled rather roughly to realities, and not be allowed to wander off on his own to look at the
shops or enjoy a walk in the country). It is admirably done, the actors know their parts, sink to the ground on the appropriate note,
rise again when summoned. The prompter is very discreet and
hardly at all in evidence.

Yet one has doubts; it all seems too well rehearsed. And the doubts
are confirmed by the same author's definitive account of the *mouvement sectionnaire* in Paris and of its relations with the Revolutionary

---

[1]Albert Soboul, *Précis d'histoire de la Révolution française* (Paris, 1962).
[2]Albert, Soboul, *La Révolution française (Que sais-je?)* (Paris, 1963).

Government. For in this great work[3] the ballet steps are only briefly remembered, as a matter of form, at the opening and closing of chapters that in their massive middle disclose a much more confusing scene: uncertainties of contour, difficulties of definition, lack of clear objectives, shifting loyalties, internal contradictions, personal squabbles, the role of personalities and of militant minorities, preliminary committee work, the "fixing" of an agenda, passion, confusion, credulity, myth, anarchy, noise. It is not even certain whether the two tentative partners are, at all times, aware of each other's existence, and there is much more groping and shuffling and searching and backturning than anything like an ordered movement. This, in its always complicated, detailed narrative, looks much more like the real thing. Soboul's great merit is to have explored that narrative, recreated it, and put it end to end, so that, in the long-drawn-out and complicated process of gradual divorce between a very varied, highly decentralized *mouvement sectionnaire* and a Revolutionary Government that contains a wide range of revolutionary fervour, one is guided by a day-to-day chronology. . . .

Albert Soboul is describing a mass movement that operated, for a limited period, through certain institutions. The movement did not create the institutions, but the institutions, which already existed, created the movement and imposed upon it certain inbred structural weaknesses. These weaknesses necessitated forms of organization that were tentative and strongly federalist [decentralist], and that in turn involved a great deal of preliminary negotiation. It is often stated that the popular movement during the French Revolution tended towards extreme forms of decentralization, and Soboul's Paris *sectionnaire* is taken as the obvious example. But the *sectionnaire* is federalist because the Section is; thus the institutions model the movement, and the Section forms the *sectionnaire.* The Section was an urban village, the Quarter, a world to itself. Of course, when confronted with threats from outside, the Sections would seek to work together, and to impose a common programme. But the peril had to be very great; and much time and energy were taken up by quarrels between different Sections and by personal bids for power within the Section itself. The movement, all forty-eight Sections lumped together as a *mouvement sans-culotte,* may reasonably be described as a mass one comprising some two hundred thousand Parisians; but within each Section, effective power is exercised by small minorities of revolutionary mili-

---

[3]Albert Soboul, *Les Sans-culottes parisiens et le mouvement sectionnaire* (Paris, 1958).

tants—twelve or twenty men at the most,[4] who, thanks to their skill, to the strength of their vocal organs, to their physique,[5] to the time they are prepared to devote to militancy, to their own prestige, to their own patronage (for a number were important employers of labour), are able to manipulate the proceedings of the larger assemblies *en petit comité* and push through their proposals well in advance. (Later their opponents made much of this, in their efforts to isolate the *dominateurs,* the *aboyeurs* [those who were domineering and noisy], from the general mass of *sectionnaires,* and suggested that the experiment in "direct democracy" disguised what was in fact the workings of a "secret committee" manipulated by a handful of men. This is a constant theme in Thermidorian *enquêtes* [investigations] and propaganda, and all the more convincing in that it corresponded to a certain degree with the reality, as recalled by people of many shades of opinion, a year later.)

Soboul's own account shows that a great deal of preliminary work went into preparing Sectionary business, that there was often a lot of lobbying, that matters were seldom left to the chance of a free vote, and that the *sans-culotte movement* could hardly be described as spontaneous or even as particularly democratic unless we admit that there existed a degree of super–*sans-culottisme* which placed some *sectionnaires* over their fellow citizens, in a category apart, élitist and unassailable. For there existed, at least in the *bureaux* [executive committees], an inner ring of self-taught militants who, though political amateurs, were soon learning how to manipulate an assembly and prepare business from within a *comité*. In time, they would have become professionals. Already, by the first months of the year III, when in *commune* after *commune* they were dislodged from their entrenched positions, generally by the outside intervention of a *Représentant en mission*—it would take nothing less to prise them out of their hold on a *comité* or a municipality—they had acquired a professional mentality, considering themselves indispensable to the

---

[4]Mercereau, a policeman in the Panthéon Français Section, comments on the manner in which the Section committee was run: "I declare that the committee is the source of all kinds of hatred, it is composed of at most 60 men and the same number of women and with this small minority they would like to lead the Section which is composed of 8 to 9,000 men. I do not accuse all the members of the committee, but really 6 or 8 individuals . . ." (Archives Nationales, F7 4774 d 3 [*Mercereau*]).

[5]One *meneur* [ringleader], who is also an *inspecteur,* is accused, in the year III, of having terrorized his fellow *sectionnaires* by attending all the meetings of the *assemblée générale* and of the *société,* accompanied by an enormous and very fierce dog (Cobb and Rudé, "Le Dernier Mouvement populaire de la Révolution à Paris," *Revue historique,* October–December 1955).

forward march of the Revolution and to the particular interests of their own town or village. So much was this the case that, right up to the summer of 1795, their one thought was that they would soon get back, as their fellow citizens were bound to realize, sooner or later, that they could not do without their valuable services. But they were, of course, removable, even in the circumstances of the year II, and many of the bitter personal squabbles that take up so much space in Sectionary minutes—sometimes for weeks on end, to the exclusion of all else—arose out of attempts to dislodge the reigning clan that had, for one reason or another, made itself generally intolerable—and most of these *meneurs* were loud-mouthed, arrogant, intolerant, some of them were impossible little tyrants, constantly boasting of how they disposed of the power of life and death, gaily talking of the heads that would fall and taking an obvious enjoyment in sending shudders down the backs of those whom they were seeking to impress or to cow—and to replace it by people who were popular in the assemblies or in the *sociétés,* areas in which the virtues of the proverbial "good committee man" were likely to be less appreciated.

Even at this level, there were bound to be conflicts between the general mass of *sectionnaires,* for whom politics could only be very much of a part-time evening occupation, and the small groups of committed men, who claimed to do their thinking for them. Sectionary politics are full of clans, and so are those of provincial *sociétés;* for these were mostly people who knew each other well—that is to say, who knew much that was damaging about one another—and posts in the *bureaux,* especially those which raised their holders to a prominent position, above most of their fellows, on a *tribune* or in the president's high chair, were objects of as much envy and backbiting as an officer or non-commissioned rank in the *Garde nationale.* The butcher, the grocer, the shoemaker of the Quarter or of the *bourg* are bound to live in conceit. Their wives lived even more so and it was because of the corroding influence of feminine jealousies that some popular assemblies sought to exclude women, even as onlookers. The greatest glory was that which was visible to the whole street, to the whole village. The soldier decorated for gallantry and the scholarship boy will hurry home to exhibit themselves. And, though women did not vote in the assemblies, they did much to blow on the furnaces of neighbourly discord if they felt that their husbands or companions were not getting the recognition that they deserved for their patriotism and long service to the Revolution. If the *patriotes de 93* were in control, then the whole syndicate of the *patriotes de 89*—and the *sans-culottes* could generally muster a few of

these—would be grumbling in the wings about newcomers, dema-
gogues, and so on, in sulky deprivation. Revolutionary patriotism,
they suggested, should be calculated in terms of length of service to
the Cause.

To this the newcomers might reply that the first in the field had
fallen by the wayside, having compromised themselves on one of
the many occasions between July 1789 and May–June 1793 when it
was possible to plump for the wrong side. There was much to be
said, in the conditions of the year II, for having been out of public life
till 1793. It might, in fact, more often be a conflict between the April
men and the September men, for not a great many *sans-culottes*
could show service much before 1792, and the great internal revolutions within the Sections occurred between the spring and the late
summer of 1793. Many *meneurs* (*aboyeurs* as the Thermidorians
were to call them) made themselves intolerable by their insolent
bearing, and, at the beginning of the year III, there was a genuine and
very wide-spread revulsion against the former *dominateurs*. They
had at best been meddlesome, "superior," and impatient of criticism, at worst tyrannical, heartless, brutal, and insufferable. Militancy is not likely to breed fraternal love; the militant had few
friends and many toadies; and in the year III such people would have
no friends at all, those whom they had once obliged or protected
being the first to keep their distances. But already in the year II it is
possible to distinguish between a minority of activists and the general mass of good, middling, or indifferent *sans-culottes*. As popular
institutions everywhere declined, after Floréal [April–May 1794],
this distinction would already have become more marked, with a
vast increase in this last category, so that the militants would become members of a tiny *cénacle* [coterie], devoted to keeping going
a "movement" that no longer existed—an act of revolutionary piety
that was to be the principal concern of those who survived for the
next twenty years.

Perhaps one of the greatest weaknesses of the popular movement
of the year II was this reliance on very small groups of individuals,
easily isolated and immediately identifiable, who through impru-
dence, conceit, or the foolish notion that their power would endure
for ever, had made themselves and the movement with which they
had become identified (and Thermidorian propaganda was devoted
to "personalizing" *la sans-culotterie* in a handful of names and character sketches) thoroughly disliked by a wide section of the community that included many people of their own condition. The hatred so

often shown to them in the conditions of the year III cannot only have been the result of intelligent vilification; in some cases at least, particularly in Lyon and the Midi, they were hated because they had been hateful. Nothing very terrible happened to the former terrorists of the Upper Norman Departments. The most surprising thing about these zealous servitors of Terror and Repression was that they should have taken so many risks and offered themselves up so completely as hostages to the future. For few of their victims, real or potential, ever made the mistake of calculating that the Terror and the "popular movement" would go on for ever, or that they could be anything other than temporary and accidental. Perhaps the enjoyment of power and genuine revolutionary patriotism were stronger inducements than common prudence. If one is to judge at all from Thermidorian reports—and these are, of course, heavily loaded—it is amazing how suicidal many of these militants had been, though more in speech than in action. Many of them were to pay with their lives for words uttered as boasts, to demonstrate that there was nothing that they could not, or would not, do.

In principle, Soboul is writing about a mass movement—this is his own approach—but in fact his celebrated thesis is mostly concerned with the role of élites and the methods employed by individual militants. He does name the militants, but he does not give any of them the benefit of a personality. The result is that we can see how they operated, but we gain virtually no impression of what they were like, whether they were sincere or were time-servers, whether they were out for publicity or for the fruits of office, whether they had sound sense or were crackpots. We just have to accept that they were militants and that something, whether ambition or sincerity, distinguished them from the general mass of their neighbours. He introduces us to *les sectionnaires*—that small core of six or seven hundred, sometimes even fewer, twenty or thirty in places like Le Havre or Dieppe, ten or fifteen in small towns like Salon or Martigues—upon whom was to fall the weight of future successive proscriptions; but we do not meet *le sectionnaire,* the man himself, swimming in the history of the Revolution, fighting to keep his head above tormented and fast-flowing waters.

This is partly the author's own choice, for he is dealing with so large a team that, in a study of this kind, there could hardly be room for portraits of individuals. It might be objected too that recourse to personal "case histories" puts too great a burden on the historian's imagination or on his powers of selection, that such a method is "unscientific," and even borders on the anecdotal.[6] Even so, the impression remains that there is an element missing: Soboul has lived with his *sans-culottes,* but, perhaps, not very intimately—they are there to serve a purpose, and can then be dismissed. He gives only a cursory glance at their domestic arrangements and makes little attempt to track them down into non-political leisure; and, after 1795, they enter the night of time—unless they are lucky enough to have attracted the approving attention of Babeuf and his Revolutionary Selection Board.

This is a pity. The *sans-culottes,* particularly the more extravagant figures who, especially in small towns far from Paris, emerged at the head of them for a few months, were often intense individualists. They regarded the revolutionary movement as their own personal property and were unwilling to take orders from any man, however high placed and however covered in sash and ribbon. It is quite possible to add that further dimension by extending the time limit of research, as far as the Paris *sans-culottes* are concerned—hence the interest of following the "popular movement" in Paris into the Slough of Despond from 1795 to 1816 or beyond, not so much to discover why the popular movement failed as to discover what happened to its leaders after the year III. The scope of research can also be extended by, for instance, investigating the "pauperization" of the former *sans-culotte* cadres in the years IV and V, through petitions to the *Commission des Secours* [Welfare Office], in order to justify indigence and so qualify for relief, at least in the form of free bread.

Another method is to choose a smaller canvas and to study the *sans-culotte* milieu and certain dominant traits of the "revolutionary temperament" in a provincial setting.[7] For the real terrain of "ultra-revolutionism"—a "movement," if the term can be used for anything so individualistic and anarchical, far more extreme and less calculating than that of the Paris *sectionnaires*—was not in the capital, for the Parisians had the Revolutionary Government on their doorsteps and could not make a move without provoking threatening rumblings from the Committee of General Security. The opportunity for the "ultra-revolutionary," a man who might be described, according

---

[6]The present author has been criticized for having, in his *Armées révolutionnaires,* allowed certain of his characters too long an audience, simply because they had a lot to say for themselves, or because they were attractive, or amusing, or curious. See the review article by Hr. Kåre Tønnesson, in *Past & Present,* No. 27, 1964.

[7][For an example, see the selection by Richard Cobb in Chapter 6, "Why Terror in 1793–1794?"—Eds.]

to tastes, as *le révolutionnaire intégral,* as *un grand exaspéré,* or as *un grand naïf* [a complete revolutionary, an absolutely outraged person, a total innocent] and a fool of suicidal proportions, was in the Departments.

8
The Media and Revolutionary Political Culture

THE revolutionaries hoped not only to change French institutions, but also to regenerate the French people. They reacted against a society that they regarded as dominated by the monarchy, the church, and the aristocracy, and that they believed promoted tyranny, superstition, and inequality. In place of this old regime, they sought a society with a new democratic political culture that valued liberty, virtue, fraternity, and equal opportunities for males.

The revolutionaries used various means of communication to further their cause. This chapter will examine four of these—engravings, festivals, language, and music—to understand and evaluate this attempt to create a new democratic culture. Lynn Hunt's study of engravings and Michel Vovelle's study of festivals find that each had authentic roots in the past and mass appeal. Furthermore, Hunt thinks that the prints, when used as propaganda, were not so crudely manipulative as many twentieth-century examples of propaganda; and Vovelle regards the festivals as innovative and often useful in advancing the Revolution. On the other hand, Richard Cobb argues that the chief revolutionaries, at least during the Reign of Terror, adopted a public language that was out of touch with reality and with the people they claimed they wanted to regenerate. Laura Mason maintains that music and revolutionary political culture in general presented a very mixed message—always discordant—and which was also ineffectual during the Directory. However she thinks this democratic revolutionary culture did enjoy a revival in the nineteenth and twentieth centuries. This chapter also includes the text of the "Marseillaise," an influential song of the Revolution and now the French national anthem.

Were revolutionary media creative and uplifting or crude and debasing? Were they very important in shaping political beliefs and behavior, and, if so, during all periods of the Revolution? Or were they so changeable and contradictory that they contributed to the Revolution's downfall and were more important for enriching the popular democratic culture of the nineteenth and twentieth centuries?

ENGRAVINGS

Lynn Hunt

Lynn Hunt (1945–) was born in Panama and raised in St.
Paul, Minnesota. She received her B.A. from Carleton
College and her Ph.D. from Stanford University. She has
taught at the University of California, Berkeley and the
University of Pennsylvania and she teaches now at the
University of California, Los Angeles. One of the pio-
neers of the new cultural history, she uses insights
gained from the study of art, anthropology, literature,
sociology, psychology, and gender studies to under-
stand revolutionary politics and culture. She is the au-
thor of *Revolution and Urban Politics in Provincial
France: Troyes and Reims, 1786–1790* (1978), *Politics,
Culture, and Class in the French Revolution* (1984), *The
Family Romance of the French Revolution* (1992), and,
with Joyce Oldham Appleby and Margaret C. Jacob,
Telling the Truth about History (1994), and, with Jack R.
Censer, *Liberty, Equality, Fraternity: Exploring the French
Revolution* [Text and CD Rom] (2001). She is also the ed-
itor of *The New Cultural History* (1989), *Eroticism and the
Body Politic* (1991), *The Invention of Pornography: Ob-
scenity and the Origins of Modernity, 1500–1800* (1993),
*The French Revolution and Human Rights: A Brief Docu-
mentary History* (1996), and other works.

Propaganda first became associated with politics during the French
Revolution. The revolutionaries had propaganda, propagandists, and
even propagandism, which one dictionary of the time defined as a
"new political malady," which consists of "wanting to propagate the
system of equality and liberty." In this, as in so many other things,

From Lynn Hunt, "Engraving the Republic: Prints and Propaganda in the French Revolution," *History Today* 30 (October 1980), 11–17. Article reprinted by permission of the
author and by the editor of *History Today* with illustrations supplied by the editors of
this anthology.

the French revolutionaries were replacing religion with politics. Propaganda had a religious origin in the *propaganda fide,* a special religious congregation established in Rome in the seventeenth century to oversee missionary work. In 1792, French radicals began to call for "Apostles" and "Propagators" of Reason, who would form the cadres of "la propagande révolutionnaire." Propaganda in this new political sense was part of an ambitious programme of public instruction that aimed at nothing less than the total regeneration of the French people. The Revolution required a new man, republican man. And every possible means was mobilised in the national effort to produce a people of virtue: festivals, songs, medals, ribbons, speeches, newspapers, prints, posters, even the design of plateware and playing cards could carry the revolutionary gospel.

In 1789, at the beginning of the Revolution, there were no systematic plans for public instruction in revolutionary virtue. What is interesting about this early period is the spontaneous way in which new symbols and images were created. The deputies deliberating in Versailles, and then in Paris, had little time for thought about new rituals of public life; they were too busy debating the fundamental principles of the new constitution. As a consequence, the first revolutionary symbols were popular productions. The liberty tree [see illustration 1], for example, was first planted as a maypole of celebration or even warning by peasants who were eager to declare their freedom from seigneurial dues and restraints. It was then taken up by political leaders in the towns who converted the planting of liberty trees into public ceremonies of revolutionary affirmation. By May of 1792, 60,000 liberty trees had been planted in France.

Other revolutionary symbols combined popular and middle-class impulses. The liberty cap [see illustration 1], which appeared almost immediately on official seals and engravings, recalled the cap of Roman times that was worn by freed slaves; members of the middle class might associate it with its classical heritage or with its medieval tradition, for it was donned then by students who passed their degree examinations and by apprentices who were admitted to guild masterships.

Yet it was the popular movement that gave the bonnet of liberty real currency; in mass demonstrations after the fall of the Bastille, rude hats decorated the pikes and poles carried by the marchers. The pike and bonnet soon became the standard accessories of the goddess of liberty [see illustration 2], who was pictured on medals, letterheads, and prints, and who later was represented in 'living tableaux' in revolutionary processions and festivals. Christian, masonic, and classical sources all fed into the growing stream of revolutionary images: the masonic eye of watchfulness, the level of equality, the Book or Tables of the Law, the fraternal bread, the altar of the fatherland, and the relics of the Bastille—all of them appealed in different ways to a wide variety of groups and classes. The very eclecticism of revolutionary symbols made them attractive and accessible to large numbers of people.

Revolutionary iconography was more visible in the streets and in political meeting rooms than in the exhibition hall. During the Revolution, the fine arts responded slowly and somewhat reluctantly to new political enthusiasms. In part, this was a consequence of lack of time. A proclamation, a speech, or a newspaper could be printed in a few hours and widely distributed. A play or a gigantic spectacle, such as one of the many revolutionary pageants, could be mounted in a few weeks or even days when necessary. But paintings and sculptures required months of planning and execution, and in the Revolution, months could mark breathtaking changes in the political situation. Still, the possibility of a political or revolutionary art was recognised: art critics, governmental leaders, and many artists advocated the use of art for patriotic propaganda.

The Constituent Assembly ordered the conversion of one of Paris' newest churches into a national Pantheon of revolutionary heroes; sculptors and craftsmen removed Christian imagery from the church and replaced it with revolutionary symbols, figures, and scenes. Radical artists in Paris succeeded in breaking the stranglehold of the Royal Academy of Painting and Sculpture, and through their membership in the newly-formed Popular and Republican Society of the Arts they urged the government to fund national monuments and patriotic works of art. The finest example of this politically-inspired art was Jacques-Louis David's painting of "Marat Assassinated" [see illustration 3].

David's success in combining fine art and politics was exceptional, however, and most of the grandiose projects for revolutionary art never materialised. There were hundreds of models in plaster and sketches on paper, but no buildings, few busts in stone, and not even very many paintings to show. For the most part, political unity and fine art could only be forced into an unhappy, sterile, and brief marriage. David himself continued to paint neo-classical pictures as he had before the Revolution, and as he would under Napoleon later. Other artists went on painting landscapes, portraits, and scenes from ancient history, ignoring the tumultuous events of the time. Less than one-tenth of the paintings exhibited in the official salons between 1789 and 1799 can be classified as explicitly political.

1. Liberty tree topped by a liberty cap.

2. Seal of the Republic, with goddess, pike, and liberty cap (1792–1804).

Popular art in the form of cartoons, caricatures, and simple engravings offered more potential for political propaganda. They were
easily reproducible and therefore were capable of reaching a sizeable
audience. Prints adorned many of the hundreds of new newspapers
that popped up everywhere after mid-1789. In Paris, individual engravings were hawked along the Seine, and either singly or in collections they were sold by newspaper offices and print-shops. Some
prints were available by subscription. Images of various sorts appeared as well on dishes, medals, proclamations, letters, calendars,
school books, political tracts, snuffboxes, fans, jewellery, even but-
tons—any piece of paper, clothing, or furniture might carry the revolutionary message through imagery.

3. The Assassination of Marat, painting by David, 1793.

To some extent, the market for printed images was a carry-over from the Old Régime. In the Rue St. Jacques on the Parisian Left Bank and in several provincial cities, print-makers had turned out illustrated proverbs, almanacs, calendars, scenes from the lives of saints or royalty, and humorous vignettes of daily life by the thousands. These prints were sold along with inexpensive chapbooks by colporteurs [peddlers] who roamed the kingdom's highways and backroads. In a society of relatively low literacy, especially in rural areas, the printed image was a treasure within the means of the popular classes. Engravings embellished the walls of the local notary's office, and cheap prints decorated many a peasant cottage.

The revolutionary government could not overlook the propaganda possibilities of the medium. In 1793, the National Convention commissioned a series of prints from David "which would arouse public feeling, and make people aware how hateful and ridiculous are the enemies of the Revolution." Direct governmental intervention should not be exaggerated, however, since officials were too preoccupied with raising money for cannons, ships, and food supplies to spend much on the diffusion of prints. The political effects of the prints were more indirect and oblique.

The prints of the revolutionary era have never been systematically studied by either art historians or historians of France. There are several good reasons for this neglect. Although the collections of the Bibliothèque Nationale and the Musée Carnavalet include thousands of prints (certainly over 20,000 of them), most of them were not dated either by the artists or by the original collectors. In addition, the prints suffered from a succession of political vicissitudes: at the height of the Terror, for example, few engravers were willing to risk their heads to produce new prints which might displease a rapidly shifting government, and after the Terror many previously published prints were destroyed. Prints of lesser artistic quality or little obvious political interest no doubt escaped the curiosity of collectors altogether. Yet even with this pre-selection, the prints that have been assembled are of uneven quality and difficult to classify either chronologically or stylistically.

Print-making was too heterogeneous to be classified simply as a popular art. A few engravers, who belonged to the circles of academic and fine art before 1789, continued to produce pieces for the salons of the revolutionary period. During the Revolution, doctors, lawyers, and merchants subscribed to the publication of relatively expensive collections of "historical tableaux," which depicted major events. The popular classes bought prints of *sans-culottes* and soldiers [see illustration 4], of caricatures or battlescenes. Needless to

4. A republican placard of 1793. Soldier, sans-culotte, symbols, and slogans.

say, the amount of skill involved varied enormously. The principal tools used for engraving had not changed much over the centuries, but they were still the province of specialised craftsmen. And even the most hastily produced prints required access to the machinery of reproduction, however crude. Thus, like the supposedly popular newspapers, prints could be designed for the popular classes but they were not produced by them.

All such qualifications granted, the prints come closer to popular or mass art than any other form associated with the Revolution. They were reproducible in large quantities and comprehensible even to those who could not read. Moreover, since they were produced by so many different artists of such varied skill and standing, and since they were engraved or etched in the heat of the political moment, the prints offer a wealth of information about political attitudes. Although they cannot be relied upon as barometers of lower-class political opinions, they can provide clues about the process of propaganda. For even though the government did not have the means to use the prints for direct manipulation of opinion, it could encourage some themes and set the limits on criticism. The print-makers balanced this governmental pressure against the demands of their nonofficial (and much larger) popular and middle-class markets. The choice of certain subjects and the avoidance of others, the use of iconography, the differences in composition and style—all of these entered into the subtle process of shaping and expressing political attitudes.

Despite the uncertainties of classification, it is possible to discern significant shifts in the subjects of the prints. In 1789–90, prints of great events such as the fall of the Bastille and the Festival of Federation predominated [see illustrations 5 and 6]; in 1791–92, ribald burlesques of the court and clergy appeared in large numbers; in 1793–94, the focus shifted to representations of the new Republic; after the fall of Robespierre in July, 1794, satirical prints reappeared but this time their target was either the preceding "reign of Terror" or the new morality of the Directory era; finally, between 1795 and 1799, pictures of soldiers and portraits of generals became favourite subjects.

There was, to be sure, always a rich mixture of themes in the prints: every period saw its share of engravings of individual legislators and of memorable political turning-points; and after the war began in 1792, battle scenes found a ready market. Nevertheless, in the midst of continuing themes, a variety of styles and great disparity of quality, there were distinct trends in print-making which exemplify broader political changes.

5. An engraving of the attack on the Bastille.

6. Festival of the Federation, Paris, July 14, 1790, print by Girard the younger.

One of the most telling of such trends is the change in depiction of revolutionary heroism between 1789 and 1799. At the beginning of the Revolution, a large number of prints showed mass scenes of the French people claiming their liberty, defending it once won, and showing their allegiance to the new order. Implicit in these prints was the view that the whole nation and even the most ordinary people were the heroic founders of the new state. After the Republic was established in September, 1792, allegorical representations began to displace the crowd scenes; feminine representations of the Republic, of Liberty, Equality, Nature, Reason, and Victory replaced the crowd or the ordinary citizen as the central revolutionary figure in the print [see illustration 7]. This displacement signalled a major change in political attitude: the collective violence of seizing liberty and overthrowing the monarchy were effaced behind the tranquil visage and statuesque pose of an aloof goddess. The appearance of the feminine allegorisation was momentous, for it became associated with the Republic ever after. By examining it in greater detail, it is possible to see how prints serve the purposes of propaganda in unexpected ways.

The feminine allegorisation of political values was not invented by the Revolution; the goddess of liberty, for example, appeared in French painting in the 1770s along with many other revived classical images. From the very beginning of the Revolution, allegorical representations of liberty, the city of Paris, the monsters of feudalism and the like were commonly used on engravings and medallions. When the Republic was declared, the problem of representation became more urgent; what was to replace the King, his person, his portrait, and his crown as the affective centre of national political life? The National Convention immediately chose the Goddess of Liberty for the official seal, and even after Robespierre fell from power and a new constitution was enacted, the official symbol remained much the same. Government and army letterheads, seals, medals, and prints by the thousands propagated the emblem of the Republic, a young woman draped in a Roman tunic [see illustration 2].

The choice of a feminine allegory is susceptible to many different kinds of interpretation. What could have stood in starker contrast to the paternal figure of the King than the young, fragile, almost always virginal image of the Republic? The King had a particular, very individual face as father of his people; the visage of the Republic was as abstract and multifaceted as the new state she incarnated. Within the iconographic limits set by the Goddess of Liberty—and the limits were rather wide—every artist could imagine his own republic; and yet all referred to *the* Republic. The King was an actual, living person

7. Goddess of Liberty during the Terror, printed by Debucourt, 1793.

who might exercise his beneficence or wrath at any time; the Republic was an idealised figure, a goddess who stood for various civic values, but who herself exercised power only in the imagination.

The sexual imagery of power in the Revolution combined familial, religious, and political metaphors. In the old system of values, the King had been the father, immediately linked to God in the great chain of being, and his political authority was inextricably bound up with those analogies. The new Republic was the sister—iconographically—of liberty, nature, and reason. By implication, the fraternity of revolutionaries had rescued her and her sisters from the dark tyranny of the father, at first, they tried only to restrain him, but in the end they felt compelled to commit the ultimate national act of patricide-regicide.

Then they had to protect her against the revenge of the uncles, the other monarchs of Europe. On the battlefield, republicans waged a real war against the dead King's relatives; with the prints, as with the other forms of propaganda, republicans struggled for control of the hearts and imaginations of their fellow citizens. No one was very explicit about the imagery of this other, equally vital, campaign. The stakes were too high, and the enormity of the act too frightening: hence there were hundreds of depictions of the antique sisters and almost none of the King's actual death.

The figure of the Republic was compelling for different, even contradictory reasons. To some she no doubt evoked the Virgin Mary with her innocence and concern for the "enfants de la Patrie" [children of the Fatherland]. To others, the Republic with her antique accoutrements recalled a purer time supposedly free of fanatical superstition and the machinations of an overweening clergy. In either case, these were visions free of any but the most stylised and thus distant conflict. It was the counter-revolution that published descriptions of the royal family's agonies. And it was the counter-revolutionaries who derided the Republic as a "fille," a prostitute, a "Marianne" of the commonest extraction.

Although there was a definite unity in conception behind the feminine allegorization of the Republic, there were also some consequential modifications in the imagery between 1792 and 1799. An official engraving commissioned by the Directorial government in 1798 showed the Republic seated like a statue and surrounded by a host of other symbols. There were so many different symbols in the vignette that the government felt it necessary to publish a long description which explained the meaning of the allegory. How else were viewers to know that the crown of oak and laurel was a "symbol of the rewards given by the government to those citizens who distinguished themselves," or that the shield was a symbol "of the paternal solicitude of the magistrates," or that the thunderbolt in the claws of the Gallic cock was an "emblem of the fate being prepared for the enemies of the Republic?"

After the heady radical months of late 1792 and 1793, representations of the Republic became increasingly staid and composed. Many of the early engravings showed a Republic in action, striking down the Hydras of tyranny, feudalism, aristocracy and monarchy. Those Republics had a vigorous look about them, and their limbs and gestures conveyed energy and youthful determination. Those were the days, too, of the living representations, of women dressed as goddesses of liberty and marching in processions or overseeing the inauguration of temples of Reason. When Robespierre and his colleagues eliminated their political opposition, they also clamped down on such demonstrations as unseemly and subversive. The Republic was to be a distant icon, and her image was cleaned up; henceforth she was more matronly, and most often she was seated rather than standing. She might still be trampling the monsters of various forms of tyranny (now including "anarchical" tyranny), but this was accomplished by the weight of her presence rather than her active energy.

The engravings of the Republic have little in common with the trumpet blasts and cynical pronouncements of much modern propaganda. Yet there is no denying that they conveyed critical political and social messages. In the feminine allegory the violence of the Revolution was conventionalised and to a large extent repressed. The violence in the scenes of 1789–92 [see illustration 8] had seemed liberating; after that it no doubt felt oppressive. At the zenith of the Terror in the first months of 1794, few prints of any sort were produced, and most depictions of revolutionary violence came from abroad. The projection of the Republic onto a feminine figure allowed French revolutionaries to idealise and utopianise their political goals while living in the midst of life-and-death struggles that had nothing pretty about them.

The feminine allegory might have served any social group or class interest; Delacroix's "Liberty," for example, has the look of a woman of the people. But that was the 1830 revolution. The First Republic was rarely personified as a woman of the people; she was after all a goddess of antique lineage. Since she was dressed in the Roman style, the Republic, like her prototype, the Goddess of Liberty, was not identified with any one political faction or group. Like the spoken

8. The murder of Flesselles, a leader in the Paris city government, July 14, 1789. An engraving by Verthault after a drawing by Prieur.

and written rhetoric of the revolutionaries, the visual image of the Republic represented universalistic values. Yet behind the universalism, there was a certain social content. The Republic was neither a woman of the people, wrathful and avenging, nor a queen linked by marriage or motherhood to a traditional male power. She might appeal to anyone, but she was surely most attractive to the lay middle classes, who established the new government and picked out its emblem. The engravings of the Republic do not tell a story of naked manipulation; they show rather the halting, groping efforts of that class to define itself and its revolution while attempting to win the allegiance of the nation.[1]

---

[1]Notes on further reading: Hannah Mitchell, "Art and the French Revolution: An Exhibition at the Musée Carnavalet," *History Workshop*, 5 (1978), 123–45; Maurice Agulhon, *Marianne au combat: l'Imagérie et la symbolique républicaines de 1789 à 1880*, Flammarion (Paris, 1979); and especially, *L'Art de l'estampe et la Révolution française*, catalogue of the exhibition at the Musée Carnavalet, 1977.

FESTIVALS

Michel Vovelle

Michel Vovelle (1933–), the son of schoolteachers, was born in the town of Gallardon, near Chartres. He studied at the Lycées Marceau at Chartres, Louis-le-Grand and Henri IV in Paris, and the École normale supérieure at Saint-Cloud before attending the University of Paris. Most of his teaching career was at the University of Provence until 1983, when he succeeded Albert Soboul as Professor of the History of the French Revolution at the University of Paris. In 1989 he was the director of the scholarly events commemorating the two hundredth anniversary of the French Revolution. He retired in 1993. In addition to several books investigating European attitudes toward death since 1400, he has published *The Fall of the French Monarchy, 1787–1792* (1984; French edition, 1972), *Ideologies and Mentalities* (1990; first French edition, 1982, revised in 1992), *The Revolution Against the Church: From Reason to the Supreme Being* (1991; French edition, 1988), and many other books on the religious, social, cultural, intellectual, and political history of France from 1715 to 1820.

❧❧❧❧❧❧

The revolutionary festival occupies a special place in the dream of a regenerated society and an ideal world. As a historical subject it is attractive these days, and justly so. In the brief moment of a festival are concentrated all the dreams of a particular point in time. Yet it is astonishing that the discovery of this subject has taken so long, although during the period of positivism—around 1900—such aspects of the festival as its music were not neglected. Should we say that the events of 1968 [when there were widespread student and worker demonstrations against the de Gaulle regime], by associating the fes-

From Michel Vovelle, *La Mentalité révolutionnaire: Société et mentalités sous la Révolution française* (Paris: Éditions sociales, 1985), pp. 157–168. Printed by permission of Messidor-Éditions sociales. Editors' translation.

tival with a fleeting mirage of a revolution, "launched" the topic? Such an explanation would reduce to a matter of fashion the exploration of a historical field that has in the last dozen years produced a number of books that together constitute one of the major currents of the "new kind of history."

Mona Ozouf, in her book, *Festivals and the French Revolution,* has analyzed the elements of a "transfer of sacrality," and I, for my part, in *The Metamorphosis of the Festival* have studied the festival from 1750 to 1820 in Provence seeking to investigate the relationship between short term and long term attitudes. Over the long term, the attachment to the festival in this province of southern France is confirmed by eighteenth-century travelers and belongs to a tradition fashioned over centuries by a series of urban or rural festivals (the *romérages* or votive festivals), festivals diverse and rich while at the same time lively. In certain respects, even before the Revolution, festivals were becoming a part of folklore when seen through the eyes of the elite, who already considered them as having an ethnographic character. In the short term, the revolutionary festival appeared, and it was quite different in many ways. At first glance the newer kind of festival seems less plebeian, bringing a Rousseauist kind of model that was quite novel—a festival with uniform scenarios throughout the nation, carefully structured and apparently more rational, but less lively than the kind it supplanted. Therefore the question emerging from a narrow study can be posed for the whole of revolutionary France. In the transition from the one to the other kind of festival, what was the relationship between the old and the new?

The accepted wisdom derived from the counterrevolutionary historical tradition spoke unhesitatingly. Generalizing from conclusions based on the festivals of the Directory, it emphasized the failure of these dismal spectacles that were deserted by the masses. Even before this cliché became established, the historical writing of the Romantic period, in which Michelet took part and which had its roots in the Revolution itself, presented an interpretation that was only a little more nuanced. It stressed the progressive mummification of the festivals by contrasting such allegedly unanimous fraternal celebrations as the Festival of the Federation on July 14, 1790 with the celebrations that began with the Festival of the Supreme Being on 20 Prairial, year II [June 8, 1794].

In both interpretations the dominant image was exemplified by the dechristianizing masquerade that occurred in the winter or spring of the year II [December 1793–June 1794]. These manifestations of dechristianization were considered shameful, or were at best misunderstood, and even pro-revolutionary historians preferred to treat them with embarrassed silence.

We shall reopen the question of revolutionary festivals using current approaches taken by historians. This can be done not only by a fundamental review of the record—by exploiting such unused sources as reports, minutes of meetings, and narratives—but also by investigating without preconceptions. Are we dealing with a graft that did not take, or on the contrary, an authentically popular phenomenon, or even a third kind, a dialectical mixture of two kinds of festivals, old and new, local and national? And perhaps there may be a fourth interpretation: between the two kinds of festivals—the official one and the subterranean one found in the villages—was there not at times a peaceful co-existence and at other times conflict? Given the complexity of the revolutionary period and the outburst that it provoked in the realm of feeling, we are led to formulate the problem of festivals in different terms from those proposed at the colloquium held in the city of Clermont-Ferrand in 1974. There, some of the researchers, mainly scholars in literature, saw the authentic revolutionary festival as epitomized by the days when revolutionary action took place or even by massacres and executions, with all the immediate purging of collective passion and spontaneous theatricality that these events brought. Historians, on the other hand, although not denying the importance of such spontaneous actions (which have been badly misinterpreted up to now), have also been willing to take seriously the officially organized spectacles. Two contrasting models of the festival confront each other—either a violent catharsis or the establishment of a new order in which, as Mona Ozouf says, a "transfer of sacrality" took place. Historians accept the risk that certain people will criticize the alienating, and even more, the mystifying and "totalitarian" character of this transfer.

It is premature to try to resolve the question. Certainly it is more legitimate to consider the festival within the context of its own history and within the ample breadth of the Revolution, for the festival reflected the various stages of the Revolution.

If there is a subject where we can speak of a change already prepared by an earlier reconsideration, a reconsideration that took place during the second half of the eighteenth century, then it certainly was the festival. From Diderot to Rousseau, everyone confronted the problem: what should the new festival be like so as to correspond with a time that was already felt to be new? They denounced the aristocratic pageants at the royal court and even at the Opera or the Italian theater in Paris; for these sought, as Diderot put it, "to amuse a few hundred people in a small obscure place." "We should not adopt these exclusive entertainments," said Rousseau in his *Letter on the Theater*. He was followed by many others, including Sébastien Mercier, who assailed the elitism of those who sat in the best box seats. As an alternative, Rousseau had already bequeathed to the French Revolution what would be its ideal reference point, the abolition of the festival and at the same time its magnification to glorify a unanimous exaltation. "No, happy peoples, these are not your festivals at all. Instead, you must gather in the open air, under the sky, and devote yourselves to the sweet sentiment of happiness. . . . Let the sun illuminate the innocent entertainments that you will create yourselves, the worthiest that ever can be illuminated. . . . But what then will be the objects of these entertainments? What will be shown there? Nothing, if you so wish. With liberty, wherever the masses congregate, well-being will reign also. In the middle of a public square set up a pole topped by flowers, gather the people about, and you will have a festival. Better yet, let the spectators become the spectacle; let them be their own actors; let each examine himself and love himself by looking at others so that unity will prevail."

The abolition of the old festival made everybody a participant, as Jean Starobinski writes, "everybody is spectator and actor at the same time." As a consequence, the "spectacle is everywhere and nowhere." The abolition of décor in the name of a virtue that does without images carries a germ of the iconoclasm of the Revolution.

To this theoretical body of writing on the conception of the festival, available from the Old Regime, the Revolution added a few, even many, sequels. These took several forms during the course of revolutionary events. We seek here only to make understandable the major steps so that the most innovative, dominant traits of the festival become clear.

The Metamorphoses of the Revolutionary Festival

The first sequence was from 1789 to 1792. This was a transitional step where the languages of the revolutionary festival were searching for a form and where the ceremonies of the old type (the religious, monarchical, municipal, or plebeian ones) continued while at times adapting to the new order. But the intrusion of important innovations, either "wild" or highly controlled, destabilized this traditional system. The religious festival—votive or folkloric—persisted from the beginning of the Revolution until a date that varies depending on the region, the summer of 1792 in the most anti-clerical, the winter of 1792 and even the spring of 1793 in the most conservative or traditional areas. Popular ideas were added to the symbolism or the structure. For example, during the festival of Corpus Christi at Aix-en-Provence, certain traditional games questioned the hierarchy in the parade of the traditional society of orders. But the celebrations that honored the first events of the Revolution—the greeting of a deputy from the Estates General returning to his province and the installation of the new public authorities—still followed the tried and true recipes. They joined together religious ceremonies and parades in the manner of the entrance of a new monarch to a city in medieval times. When Mirabeau died in 1791, solemn religious services honored this unbeliever in both Paris and the provinces. But even within this apparent continuity tensions and rifts occurred. In the south those publicly doing penance were challenged. Also, the first tremor caused by the constitutional schism [between the priests who accepted the Civil Constitution of the Clergy and those who did not] resulted in disputes that would grow more and more serious, although they did not immediately lead to a radical break. In particular, during the height of the bloody days at the beginning of the Revolution, a new festive language began to be heard which at times contained incongruous terms. For example, in Marseille in 1790, despite everything, a true festival took place when, after the capture of the Saint-Nicolas Fort, one of the Marseille "Bastilles," men and women danced the farandole throughout the city while carrying on the end of a stick the intestines of Major Beausset, the commander of the fort, and shouting, "Who wants refreshment?"

The popular "wild" festival was not simply these unplanned and uncontrolled events. In Avignon in 1791, the local patriots, called "Icemen" (a reference to a massacre that took place in the icehouse tower of the Palace of the Popes), returned to the city after having served a brief exile imposed by their enemies. Then they held a carnivalesque parade that included floats (for example one of Bacchus, the god of wine and revelry, in which young men clinked their wine glasses) which brought up to date the revenge expressed by a popular culture long kept on the margin of things. The most developed expression, the one which held the most promise in the long run for creating a union between popular culture and the revolutionary movement, was the planting of trees of liberty, or as was said often of them, with a turn of phrase that evokes more explicitly the ancient roots of the custom, the "Maypoles of liberty." From January 1790 in Périgord, they used live trees or poles decorated with emblems. This practice spread throughout France in the following years, a pattern of diffusion that would be very interesting to study. (The Provençal Midi does not seem to have been affected before the spring of 1792.)

In these years, however, alongside this spontaneous outburst and partly as a continuation of it, a more elaborate (shall we say more elitist?) model of the festival appeared. The Festival of the Federation of July 1790 is the perfect expression of this. We should not artificially cut this kind of festival off from its "popular" or semi-popular roots in the provinces. We know very well, for example, that it was in the town of Étoile, near Valence, on November 29, 1789, that the first such celebration joined national guard units from both sides of the Rhône river and that this inspired similar actions from Dole to Pontivy in the winter of 1790, then from Lille to Strasbourg in the spring. Still, the one in Paris, on the Champ-de-Mars, July 14, 1790, had the greatest appeal and served as the example for all the provinces. A year later, the Federation celebration became an anti-Great Fear demonstration as well as an act of confidence and of faith in national solidarity. It united the population around the new regime. In this respect, the Federation reflected exactly the dream of unanimity sought by the bourgeoisie of the National Assembly. They aspired not only to stop the Revolution from going any further, but also to endow it with an ethic and a civic spirit for which the festival would provide the cement and the symbolic expression. In order to transform this dream into reality, the point of reference was derived from the ideas of Jean-Jacques Rousseau, ideas with which the deputies of the National Assembly, like the assemblies that followed, were imbued. In 1790–1791, Cabanis, one of the members of the brain-trust around Mirabeau, a man of considerable importance in his own right as the learned theorist of the *Physical and Moral Report* [*on Man,* 1802], prepared an *Essay on National Festivals* which is of fundamental importance for our discussion. It was the first outstanding theoretical essay on a theme that the Parisian Festival of the Federation seemed to typify in a striking way.

Since the Festival of the Federation came about through the collective will of thousands of Parisians whose volunteer efforts prepared the Champ-de-Mars for July 14, 1790, it is understandable that the Festival appeared to such witnesses as Mercier and others who have left us descriptions of it as the epitome, the ideal, that they would refer to later with nostalgia. On the whole, it fit Rousseau's model: an open-air festival, in a definite place, where the tiers of seats arranged around the altar of the Fatherland made the immense audience both spectators and actors in an elaborate liturgy. It resembled the old festivals in certain respects (for example there was a religious service), but it was also innovative in other ways. The oath ["to be faithful forever to the nation, the law, and the king"] which the King took, as did the delegations drawn from everywhere in France, inaugurated what would become one of the essential characteristics of succeeding celebrations. It was of little importance that behind the fiction of a wholesome solidarity, cracks appeared. While some sang together, "Frenchmen, let us go to the Champ-de-Mars," a more plebeian verse was hummed by others:

Aristocrat you now are done for,
The Champ-de-Mars has kicked you in the ass,
We will sleep with your wives
And you will be hanged.

This split in the festival celebrations could be detected a year later, in 1791, when one could see both festival and antifestival: the royal family's return from Varennes in April [actually on June 25] was a procession of shame in the midst of the silence of the Parisian people, quite the opposite of a joyous entry; and the counterpoint to this was the transfer of Voltaire's remains to the Pantheon [July 11]. Then on July 17, at the altar of the Fatherland on the Champ-de-Mars, some petitioners were fired upon when they sought the dethronement of the King.

In 1792 the festivals came in competing pairs, a reflection of the shattered unity. At the same place where the Feuillants [a club of constitutional monarchists] honored by an official procession the memory of Simonneau, mayor of Étampes who had been killed by the people asking for a fixed price on grain and who was therefore a martyr in the defense of Law and Order, very progressive democrats several weeks before had held a popular festival to rehabilitate the Châteauvieux Swiss regiment unjustly condemned at Nancy a year earlier for their patriotic action [of mutinying against their officers]. Procession versus procession; from the spring of 1792 on, sides were chosen.

From 1793 to the spring of 1794 there definitely appeared a burst of festivals that sought a new form. Was there a new language for the "official" festivals? Can one find a more grandiose illustration, and in certain respects a more surprising one, than that festival inaugurating the Constitution [of 1793] on August 10, 1793? At the head of the procession marched the deputies of the National Convention who proceeded as a body to the Fountain of Regeneration on the site of the destroyed Bastille. There the President of the Convention symbolically filled his glass with the pure water streaming from the breasts of an enormous Egyptian statue. A new symbolism searching for supporting images. Elsewhere in the parade there was an equally enormous Hercules representing "the French people crushing the Hydra of Federalism" [the provincial uprisings of 1793 directed against Paris].

Throughout France, however, there was also an irresistible desire to revive the traditional secret language of the carnivals. In the winter of 1793–1794, from Nièvre [in the center] to the four corners of France, processions took place with donkeys dressed up in a bishop's headdress and carrying the remains of superstitious fanaticism. This dechristianizing masquerade resembled the old charivaris. It was a purifying sacrificial funeral pyre of the vestiges of the Old Regime that recalled the bonfires of Saint John's Day [Midsummer's Day]. In addition, there were processions of goddesses of Reason, living personifications of the new cults. In these subversive processions, which flaunted conventions and often combatively, aggressively, and scornfully challenged the rules of the previous period, do we not see a resurgence of a very old-style popular festival that long ago had been pushed aside and relegated to folklore? There is also more to it than that. When we analyze, as we have begun to do, the order of march within the processions staged in the winter of 1793 to celebrate the military victories, the martyrs of liberty, and the first anniversaries of a Revolution that now started to commemorate its own past, then we see on display a complete symbolic presentation whose parts were arranged in a clear language designed to educate. In the rich and often disconcerting festivals of 1793–1794, we meet a precarious but dangerous equilibrium, the remains of the very old popular carnivalesque festival mixed with newly coined language.

The next turning point of this history probably consists of those festivals of the Supreme Being on 20 Prairial, year II [June 8, 1794]. The many records of these events coming from everywhere in France demonstrate that it was an immense collective success, despite what has been written about it. [The painter] David's scenario, used for the Paris celebration, was not completely accepted in all places. Without going to the extreme of those villagers of Fontvieille near Arles, who in order to pay their respects to equality decided to march in alphabetical order, the local organizers of the Festival of the Supreme Being elsewhere followed their own inspiration and made the festival both the apogee of the great popular celebrations and the forerunner of the disciplined affairs that would be imposed under the Directory.

In fact, from 1795 to 1800, that is from the Thermidorean Convention to the end of the Directory, there appeared one of the most characteristic periods in the adventurous history of the revolutionary festival. It was then that the Thermidorean bourgeoisie in power tried to construct in systematic and synthetic festivals—which Robespierre earlier had dreamed about—the symbolic expression of its view of the world. [The Director] La Revellière-Lépeaux was the theoretician par excellence of this Thermidorean and Directorial model of the festival. He systematized the new ideal in very different terms from those of Cabanis at the beginning of the Revolution. Whereas Cabanis associated himself with the legacy of Rousseau and Condillac and stressed the spontaneity of the masses seeking and finding in the festival their own enjoyment, La Revellière proposed a more organized system to generate a collective conditioning. The post-Thermidorean bourgeoisie, having lost its illusions, revealed its new pedagogical strategies. From the year IV of the Republic [1795–1796], these ceremonies, which aimed to convince and instruct, belonged to a cycle that juxtaposed various kinds of festivals: those on the anniversaries of January 21, 1793 [the execution of Louis XVI], July 14, 1789 [the taking of the Bastille], 9 Thermidor [the fall of Robespierre, July 27, 1794], with those in Ventôse celebrating the sovereignty of the people and those in Vendémiaire commemorating the founding of the Republic; also festivals stressing morality—those for the young, for the old, for agriculture, and for expressing gratitude, and all those were in addition to the funeral ceremonies for dead heroes. Relying on the past while organizing the future, projecting an ideal community whose moral ceremonies were supposed to reflect it, the period of the Directory was only partially successful in its festivals. It was very dependent on shifts in the political winds. There was a burst of festivals in the years IV [1795–1796] and VI [1797–1798], but they were inhibited in the years III [1794–1795] and V [1796–1797] by stronger counterrevolutionary attitudes. In the final analysis, these new kinds of festivals failed. The ceremonies of the Directory were dashed by the return of the traditional festivals, the non-religious ones as much even as the religious. Few people supported the festivals on every tenth day of the revolutionary calendar, and these festivals were unable to stop the restoration of Sunday. In the villages of the Midi [southern France], as elsewhere, the votive festival—the *romérage* in Provence—was at first only tolerated but had regained its strength by the end of the Directory.

From the inevitably brief discussion just presented, we feel that it is arbitrary to suggest a general blueprint of the revolutionary festival, for there were in fact several "models" that came one after another and at times overlapped.

The Faces of the Festival: An Attempt at Analysis

Regarding the characteristics of the festival, at least a certain number of generalizations can be made. The festival evolved over time, and what we can reconstitute by extrapolating a little from those in Provençal Midi leads us to detect a general expansion in the number of festivals and the increasing importance of their role from 1790 to 1792, the first notable outburst of them. Then in 1793 (a year very much marked by the Federalist episode) there was stagnation until the eruption of festivals from the year II [1793–1794] until Thermidor. Finally, during the Directory there were the phases when the counterrevolution triumphed and festivals were shunned (year III and year V) and phases when they prospered—the year IV and especially the year VI during a temporary, yet effective, Jacobin revival.

Within this general expansion that can be perceived from an analysis of about one thousand festivals, there are some striking differences based on the sizes of the communities. The urban areas remained predominant until the end of the year II (despite the impact in the villages of such celebrations as that of the Supreme Being), but during the Directory, especially in the year VI, there occurred a real penetration of the festival into the fabric of the villages, into a rural world which seemed at that time to grow accustomed to it. Such a study, in the single region that has been intensively researched [southern France], leads one to note a varied geography, where the urbanized and much stirred-up areas of the western sections of lower Provence and of the Comtat around Avignon contrast with upper Provence, noticeably less influenced by revolutionary innovations. These kinds of variations would probably be found elsewhere without much difficulty.

By following the transitions, one cannot avoid differentiating festivals by type: the spontaneous ones; the occasional or unique celebrations (a victory, an heroic death) or commemorative or yearly festivals by a Revolution that annually celebrated its anniversaries; and lastly those organized spectacles every tenth day of the revolutionary calendar from the year II on, as well as the moral festivals of the Directory. The "spontaneous" festivals, typified by the dechristianizing masquerades, played an important role in 1792 and in the winter of 1793–1794, then grew weaker and finally disappeared; however, the commemorative festivals became more and more important, and, in the years VI and VII, the moral festivals had some short-lived favorable moments. Combinations also developed that modified the

appearance of the festival from year to year and made ritual dominate over creation.

Moreover, we can follow the changing mode of the festival. At the
beginning, in the Festival of the Federation, it was held in one place;
then there were processions with a new style; and finally, at the end
of the Revolution, festivals were sometimes enclosed in a public
building or in a "green room" surrounded by foliage.

In addition to this tentative description of the form and structure,
can we risk speaking about a sociology of the revolutionary festival?
This is an arduous task, which depends on the records of the festivals and the eyewitnesses. There are the false claims of unanimity
and later, in contrast, the counterrevolutionary stereotype of the un-
attended festivals. But we can at least—which is not exactly the same
thing—follow the evidence from the attendance and roles of certain
groups in the history of the festival. Women played an increasing
part from 1792 until the beginning of 1794; this was the period of the
depiction of Amazons and the goddesses of Reason. Then they returned to a subordinate position. As to children, they also were valued in the time of the young heroes Bara and Viala,[1] but they re-
gressed to the modest role of schoolboys at the end of the Directory.
At still another level, there was in the discourse or the symbolism of
the festival a dream or an ideal consciously or unconsciously perplexing: in identifying social groups in the processions, the largely
urban festivals cultivated the picture of the country plowman even
when the picture very often departed from reality.

Furthermore, we should recall, as Mona Ozouf has pointed out,
that until the appearance of the festivals celebrating morality during
the Directory, the symbols of age played an increasingly important
part as a way of introducing an ideal order into a homogeneous society which had extinguished its tensions and all references to actual
hierarchies.

Always the bearer of a discourse or a language, either conscious or
unconscious, the revolutionary festival expressed itself in various
ways, whether it be verbal (the speech), singing, and even writing.
The essential role of written statements on placards and banners is
frequently stressed in this popular education. Thus, there was a system of changing images and symbols conveyed by the festival, a
storehouse of accessories, to put it disrespectfully, which included
the pike [the weapon of the common people], the carpenter's level [a

---

[1] [F.-J. Bara and J.-A. Viala were two youngsters who became revolutionary martyrs:
Bara was killed in 1793 by Vendeans when he refused to shout, "Long live the King!";
and Viala died in the same year fighting against royalists in Provence.—Eds.]

symbol of equality and of a sacred object], the liberty cap, the eye of vigilance, and the representation of the Mountain. But these imaginative images could also be depicted by living heroines symbolizing liberty or reason, by groups of old people in Spartan dress, or by vestal virgins of the cult of the nation. Karl Marx called all this, "the cheap finery of the Romans," a short way of describing the ancient style of these neo-classical liturgies.

Passing, if I may say, from vocabulary to syntax, from the elements of the processions to their arrangement, the discourse used in the festival was also organized in stages. First in time was the traditional—the religious procession or the parade of the orders in the old manner. Then from 1791 to 1792 there was what has been called the fixed-location festival, which led to the birth of a standard arrangement where such actors in the great revolutionary drama as the public authorities, the political club, and the national guard played their parts. This arrangement burst apart in the subversive explosion that occurred from late 1792 until early 1794. We can see this in the disconcerting mixture of the thirty-three groups that were deployed in the fraternal festival of 1 Germinal, year II [March 21, 1794] at Marseille:

1. A cavalry detachment and two trumpeters
2. A Hercules carrying the pennant of the Republic
3. Twelve drummers playing tambourines
4. The departmental fasces [symbol of unity]
5. Flags and paintings of August 10, 1792 [when Louis XVI was overthrown]
6. Six military drums
7. A float with Hercules carrying the remains of Federalism
8. The Genoese nation and its flag joined to that of the French Republic
9. The directors of the hospital
10. The plow and farmers
11. A float with Abundance and the Four Seasons
12. The Committee of Public Welfare
13. Six military drums
14. A float with Mars and warriors
15. A company of disabled veterans
16. A model of the Bastille
17. A troup of musicians, actors, and actresses
18. A float with Apollo and his Nine Muses
19. Representatives from the public schools carrying symbols of the arts

20. A group of old people
21. A group of women citizens wearing tricolor ribbons
22. The bust of Le Peletier [a deputy assassinated by a royalist]
23. The bust of Marat
24. The bust of Brutus
25. A statue depicting Reason
26. The political club
27. A float of great men who have died for the Fatherland
28. A band of musicians
29. A float of the Mountain followed by the decree that gave Marseille its name back [for a few weeks Terrorists had called Marseille "Sans Nom," to signify that it had lost its name as punishment for being the first city in southern France to rebel against the central government]
30. The representatives of the people and the civil and military authorities
31. The revolutionary workshops
32. The people and the military garrison unarmed
33. A squadron of cavalry to end the parade

This is an astonishing assemblage, put together before the establishment of the staged scenarios characterizing the festivals of the Directory, especially those from the year IV on. The latter organized the rhythm and order of appearance on the program as well as the meeting place. But the Festival of the Supreme Being in Prairial, year II [June 8, 1794] and the speech of Robespierre for the national festivals of 18 Floréal, year II [May 7, 1794] had already furnished an outline that was never truly repudiated.

Let us avoid the facile remarks of those critics who have seen in these staged festivals, with their pedagogic purposes, only lifeless and labored exercises. They were at least partially successful, which proves that they had an influence on people. They are especially important because it is from them that one can analyze this different reading of the sacred—civic or patriotic—which is based on a certain number of simple symbolic gestures: the oath, the fraternal greeting, the exchange, the triumph, the representation [of an event or a quality], but also (although restrained and codified) the execution. But if the scenario was so simple that it could be immediately understandable, the accompanying events were no less important: the banquet or the farandole dance of the year II, which expressed the overflow of spontaneous popular enthusiasm; then in the last years of the Directory, there was the more ambiguous irregular festival, parallel to the official one, which saw the return of games, the ball, and in southern France, the traditional ceremony of the *bravade* [a parade of youths bearing arms], a step toward the restoration of the old festival.

This leads us to conclude with a question at once naive and unavoidable: was the revolutionary festival unsuccessful or successful, sterile or creating both a temporary phenomenon and a forerunner of the future? Neither completely innovative, nor without contradictions or obvious tensions, it dipped into the inherited treasures of popular "folklore" and also into the storehouse of accessories supplied by the ancient world and made available by the humanist education of the intellectual leaders of the Revolution. In this respect, we may agree with the rather severe judgment of Jean Starobinski, who in a certain way repeats the comments of Karl Marx about the "cheap finery of the Romans." The Revolution failed to achieve the Rousseauist dream of the abolition of the theatrical performance, an abolition which would result from the abundance of the festival: "Far from giving rise to an authentic presence [of the people], the festival fell into the old trap of a performance. Reason turned out to be an actress from the Opera. It was still a play, still a representation. The artificiality of the production, when applied to such a ceremony, gave a true measure of the lack of spontaneity." Was the revolutionary festival even worse than sterile, because it was led astray by the contradictory weight it bore? For my part, I remain not only impressed by its passionate creativity and spontaneity so evident in 1793, but also by the boldly original character of the enterprise. Not everything about it was forgotten, and a return to the traditional festival became impossible. Buried for a time under the Restoration, the revolutionary festival remained in people's memories and helped originate the civic ceremonies of the nineteenth century.

REPUBLICAN LANGUAGE

Richard Cobb

For biographical information on Richard Cobb, see
Chapter 6, "Why Terror in 1793–1794?"

🎩🎩🎩🎩🎩🎩

In terms of vocabulary, the Year II [the Reign of Terror, 1793–1794],
was a vast charade in which the official nomenclature and the official
costumes contrasted quite horribly with the ugly realities that they
may have been designed to disguise. Or perhaps this is rather a
jaded view of the contemporary scene. Some people may have really
believed in the charade and may have persuaded themselves that a
vocabulary of hope, innocence, and utility would condition a new
race of citizens distinguished by their optimism, their purity and
their skills. It is easy to mock; and it may even have been fun to have
been a child in such exciting times. No school, and plenty of spectacles. Plenty of opportunity too for a new race of little *Émiles, Brutuses*
and *Guillaume Tells* to denounce their parents, though goodness
knows what happened to such little zealots of Virtue in the very different conditions of the Year III [1794–1795], when parents no longer
had anything to fear from that quarter. There is certainly no evidence
to suggest that people were any *better* in the Year II than in the years
preceding such collective regeneration. In Paris, both murders and
suicides were a little above the annual average; so were divorces (but
there was a long backlog on which to catch up, and many of the divorces of the Year II concerned couples long since alienated). Ban-
ditry was down, but embezzlement was up.

Evidence, in terms of absenteeism, the declining attendance figures
at clubs, would suggest that, by the summer of 1794, by *Floréal*
[April–May 1794] more and more people, among the literate and the
politically committed, had begun to turn their backs on the charade,
on symbolism, myth and fantasy, had become *bored* with such insis-

From Richard Cobb, "Thermidor or the Retreat from Fantasy," in *History and Imagination: Essays in Honor of H. R. Trevor-Roper,* ed. Hugh Lloyd-Jones, Valerie Pearl, and
Blair Worden (New York: Holmes and Meier, 1981), pp. 279–283, 295. Reprinted by
permission of Gerald Duckworth & Co. Ltd., and Holmes & Meier Publishers, Inc.

tent collective pressures, and had sought solace in more conventional refuges: the family, the *billard,* the enjoyments of leisure, the extreme privacy of love, the private world of greed and lust, even in *prome-nades solitaires* so oddly recommended by the originator of the cha-rade, Rousseau. By the summer of the Year II, the fantasies had worn very thin, and a vocabulary of abundance could not conceal the visi-ble and daily evidence of penury. What a derision to call a *décadi* [every tenth day of the revolutionary calendar] *CHEVAL* [horse], when there was not a horse to be had up and down the country, al-most all having been requisitioned for the Army! To call a *quintidi* [every fifth day] *COCHON* [pig], when in cities at least, all pigs and, in-deed, most other livestock, had been slaughtered for sale on the black market! Why call a *décade CHARRUE* [plough], when the only hands to a plough were those of women and children and old men? Why give a *quintidi* to *CHIEN* [dog] when, all over the Republic, urban bow-wows had been put down, as providing bad sexual examples to young citizens, or had been eaten? Why award a *quintidi* to *TRUITE* [trout] at a time when rivers had been fished dry, generally at night, often with the help of explosives (one of the few articles of which there was no shortage)? And so why make mouths water at the mention of *CARPE*? Where would one encounter a *DINDON* [turkey] or a *PINTADE* [guinea hen], other than in the pages of the revolutionary calendar? One could not eat the revolutionary calendar, a document that laid out a rich menu that did not exist. It is easy to see how people might turn away, in disgust and fury, from a fantasy that must have seemed a cruel provocation in existing conditions. One could not expect mira-cles such as those that occurred in [the twentieth-century novelist Marcel] Aymé's story in *le Vin de Paris,* when a painter of still life, dur-ing the Occupation [of the 1940s], all at once discovered that his paintings of game, meat, fruit and vegetables were actually eatable.

The régime of the Year II was offering its citizens a whole range of objects that it could not provide, many of which had become little more than memories, *names,* thus lending to the new calendar and the new vocabulary a sort of ironical reality. It was all very well for Robespierre to ask why he should have to bother himself with "vul-gar groceries" when he had the Happiness of Mankind to work on; on his table, as we know, there appeared, regularly, *real* tomatoes and oranges, peaches, small birds and pastries. He might—and did—live in a fantasy world, but he did not have to eat his own fantasies, tast-ing as they would of cheap, coarse, yellowish revolutionary paper. His Golden City was not one conjured up by a delirious, starving man. But then, Robespierre kept away from the window, looked inwards, and only received the sort of people who talked his own language. It is doubtful if he ever even *noticed* the queues outside the shops in his own street, he had no eyes for that sort of thing, and, of course, he would not know about queuing, something that could be left to women and servants. By Thermidor [late July 1794]—perhaps long before it—in Germinal [March–April] or, at the latest Floréal [April–May]—people who took the trouble to read had got fed up with Virtue. It was not an edible commodity. They had got tired, too, of the endless reiteration of the words Unanimity and Indivisibility, because, like Abundance (illustrated in pretty pictures of cows, trees and farmyard animals, windmills, waterfalls, canals, bridges), they too flew in the face of evidence. Most people knew that the France of the Year II was endlessly divisible, whether into 83, or into 10,000 separate components; and Unanimity was like a game of Musical Chairs, with fewer and fewer players, as one rigged trial after another removed more and more of those who were *not* unanimous. By Thermidor it might indeed have seemed that it would all end with the Unanimity of one. That would remove the problem. It was the same with Plots; there had been too many of them, they had all followed the same recipe, they had all been served up several times, both hot and cold, according to a menu as repetitive and as improbable as that advertised in *l'Almanach National.* Nor could Supreme Beings contribute to the food shortage. Much of the execration heaped over the memory of the recently murdered Robespierre, in no way a really bad man, rather a boring, self-righteous one full of good intentions, was that reserved for someone who had been, rightly, shown up as a *marchand d'illusions* [seller of pipe dreams.]

Robespierre had been the principal victim of his own fantasies, at least in the last month of his life, for, earlier, he had managed to combine Virtue, *le Bonheur Commun* [public well-being], with a healthy sense of political realism. In this case, there had been a retreat into make-believe, provoked possibly by increasing despair. Saint-Just is a more complex case. In his missions to the Armies of the North and the East, he had shown quite remarkable qualities of military leadership and conciliation, had taken a sensible middle-of-the-road line, lashing out at the extremists, the out-and-outers, the impossibilists. Yet he had also contemplated putting the population—or at least the male half of it—into white, as worthy members of a new Sparta. All were to wear linen togas. What this would have meant in terms of the mud, dust and filth of the Paris streets and of the almost total lack of soap—the selfish city of Marseille taking care to hold on to this precious commodity—is not hard to imagine. It would certainly have made of the Year II a (somewhat shivering) Republic of *blanchis-seuses, repasseuses,* and *amidonniers* [laundresses, ironers, starchers], and would have drawn on the brawny, watery support of the *garçons baigneurs* [bath attendants] of the public baths—*Bains Chinois, Bains Poitevin,* and so on. Historically, there must be some lingering interest in such unpublished fantasies of Saint-Just, as perhaps the first revolutionary theorist to have equated political orthodoxy with personal cleanliness. Certainly an illusion as great as any of Robespierre's, as there is ample evidence to suggest that, the more a *sans-culotte* was orthodox, the more he smelt. But, unlike Robespierre's, Saint-Just's fantasies were only made known a number of years after his death, when his secretary, Gateau, published extracts from his *Fragments.*

Thermidor [July 9–10, when Robespierre was arrested and executed], the most accidental of all the revolutionary *journées,* the most unexpected, save by a narrow circle of politicians that included Robespierre himself and his most consistent enemies: Amar, Vadier, Rühl, Fouché, Châles, Thuriot, Bourdon de l'Oise, Léonard Bourdon, Lecointre de Versailles, Tallien, and the most widely and spontaneously welcomed, for once on a truly national scale, has not ceased to be an object of discussion among historians, both as to its causes and its consequences. The Thermidorians [those who dismantled the Terror], a very mixed bag, are themselves not easy to define, even in the simple statement that they were all those who survived Thermidor, for some of these were to survive only to Germinal or Prairial of the following year [dates of insurrections of April–May 1795]; and the Thermidorian régime (should one not say régimes) is so fragmented as to defy any simple analysis. But the most positive effect of this momentous *journée* was to bring a sense of physical relief and an end to fear; and, up and down the country, as the news of what had happened in Paris; in Rouen, on the 12th; in le Havre and Dieppe, on the 13th; in Dijon, on the 14th; in Lyon, on the 16th; in Marseille, on the 19th; in Toulouse, on the 22nd; in Perpignan, on the 24th; in Bayonne, on the 25th; in Nice, outside the month which had given its name to the *journée,* at the beginning of Fructidor [mid–August 1794], the same thing happened without any orders having been given by higher authority: the prisons were opened, and the prisoners, both political and criminal, poured out. There may have been some sort of chain reaction, the Narbonnais benefiting from the news of what had happened in Montpellier, the Perpignannais emulating the Toulousains, though there is no firm evidence for such transmission of news. It seems more likely that, everywhere, municipalities and National Guards bowed to irresistible and spontaneous public pressure. And those who expressed incredulity, or who suggested that it would be best to wait for further orders, were at once brushed aside. So Thermidor opened, as the First Restoration was to open in March 1814, as a day of national reconciliation and forgiveness, a mood, however, that was not to last, soon giving way to unrestrained vengeance. In this respect, Thermidor represented a return to the type of local initiative that had so much marked the early stages of the Revolution; and this was a process that rapidly proved irreversible. Thus Thermidor also represented the decisive defeat of Paris and of Parisian dictatorship, an event to which the *journées* of Germinal, Prairial, and Vendémiaire [insurrections in April, May, and October 1795] merely provided the epilogue.

But there is another aspect of Thermidor that has received scant attention. It represented a deliberate escape from fantasy and illusion, a rejection of boring and meaningless orthodoxies on such subjects as Indivisibility, Unanimity, Vigilance, a revolt against a public language that had become totally divorced from private discourse. So it signified a conscious attempt to put meaning back into words and to lessen the gap between intention and reality, and the rejection of a vocabulary weighed down and obscured by hints and allusions. For instance, whereas in the spring of 1794, at the time of the crisis of Ventôse-Germinal [February–April], the official line had been that there *was* no food shortage, denying the evidence of the queues, and that indeed there *would* be no food shortage, provided people did not talk about such a possibility (so that anyone who *did* talk about such a possibility could be seen as deliberately seeking to bring about a *disette factice* [an artificial famine]), *after* Thermidor, the authorities, both municipal and national (though the former were the more candid) referred openly to the existence of a famine crisis, which, by the autumn of 1794, was real enough, and suggested practical remedies by which it might be alleviated: the purchase of grain on the Baltic markets, of rice in the United States, public subscriptions for the relief of the starving, the expulsion from the cities of those who could not justify the proof of a year's residence. Thermidor brought to an end hints and silence, releasing a cacophony of dissent, discussion, denunciation and argument, giving momentary vigour to a quarrelsome press, and even raising hopes among ultra-revolutionaries. It also bridged the gap that had grown up between public and private language, to the advantage of the latter, in the same way that it represented the assertion of long-contained private aspirations, private enjoyments, and private pleasures (including every possible form of vice). Thermidor was a public assertion of privacy, both in language and in priorities. . . .

We should not make fun of Robespierre and those of his kind for their rather touching attachment to words and symbols; they probably believed in the regenerative power of both, and no doubt their greatest error was overoptimism, the naïve, but generous, belief that others would be willing to share their pretty dreams and to participate in their redeeming allegories. After Thermidor, the evocative months, Robespierre's cherished playthings, his brightly-coloured butterflies, lie like broken toys, or insects with their brilliant wings fading, adding to the bitter pathos of a life hardly lived, and then largely in fantasy, that had seen so little, neither the sea, or the bright Midi, nor the Alps, nor the green Pyrenees, nor even very much of Paris, and terminated at 36. Of course, it should not have ended thus; he should have been allowed to wander on into old age, with his butterfly net and his water-colour pad, his chalks and his lined notebooks for delicately turned poems about bright flowers and rosy-cheeked girls with the pale blue eyes of the Pas-de-Calais. But here am I making the same mistakes as he did, and giving metaphors and fancies the force of realities. 1794, the year of illusions, was followed by 1795, the year of the loss of illusions. After 1984, what of 1985?

MUSIC AND REVOLUTIONARY POLITICAL CULTURE IN GENERAL

Laura Mason

Laura Mason (1959–), who received her B.A. from the University of California, Santa Cruz, and her Ph.D. from Princeton University, teaches history at the University of Georgia. She is the author of *Singing the Revolution: Popular Culture and Politics, 1787–1799* (1996). She has also edited with Carla Hesse the *Catalogue of the Pamphlets, Songsheets and Periodicals of the French Revolutionary Era in the Princeton University Library* (1989), and with Tracey Rizzo *The French Revolution: A Document Collection* (1998).

🎩🎩🎩🎩🎩🎩

Few doubt any longer that one of the distinctive innovations of French revolutionaries was their elaboration of a wholly new political culture. In the past two decades, Maurice Agulhon, Mona Ozouf, François Furet, Lynn Hunt, and others, have shifted attention away from social interpretations of the French Revolution by arguing that the Revolution was distinctive not because it brought a loosely defined bourgeoisie to power but because it created new political language, practices, and symbolism.[1] Drawing upon the evidence of festivals, rhetoric, and iconography, these scholars have advanced powerful analyses that affirm the importance of linguistic and cultural practices to the development of revolutionary politics. As Lynn

From Laura Mason, *Singing the French Revolution: Popular Culture and Politics, 1787 - 1799* (Ithaca, NY: Cornell University Press, Copyright ©, 1996), pp. 5, 212–215, 222 notes 6 and 7. Used by permission of the publisher, Cornell University Press.
[1]Mona Ozouf, *Festivals and the French Revolution,* trans. Alan Sheridan (Cambridge, Mass., 1989); Lynn Hunt, *Politics, Culture, and Class in the French Revolution* (Berkeley, 1984); Maurice Agulhon, *Marianne into Battle: Republican Imagery and Symbolism in France,* trans. Janet Lloyd (Cambridge, 1981); François Furet, *Interpreting the French Revolution,* trans. Elborg Forster (Cambridge, 1981); *The French Revolution and the Creation of Modern Political Culture,* vol. 2, *The Revolution,* ed. Colin Lucas (Oxford and New York, 1987–1989).

Hunt has explained, such work reveals, "the ways in which 'the Revolution' took shape as a coherent experience. . . ."[2]

The evolution of song culture between 1789 and 1799 suggests that
we revise our current notions of revolutionary political culture.
Above all, we can no longer assert that republican culture was a coherent entity which meant roughly the same thing to all members of
revolutionary society. The festivals, ideologies, and symbolism described by Ozouf, Furet, Hunt, and others made up only a tiny fraction of the more general phenomenon that we call political culture.
Compositions, singing practices, and changing attitudes toward
songs indicate the degree to which song culture in particular, and
revolutionary political culture more generally, emerged haphazardly,
pieced together by a mobilized and heterogeneous populace whose
members engaged in almost perpetual struggle among themselves as
well as against their royalist opponents. The consensus that some
revolutionaries forged during the first years of the Republic was temporary, more the product of political circumstances than a master-
piece fashioned by legislators.

Because revolutionary society was irretrievably fragmented, neither legislators nor even a broad cross-section of republican society
was able to create a lasting and homogeneous republican culture.
French society was divided by politics, by changing definitions of appropriate expression and behavior, and by ongoing tensions between
an emerging bureaucratic state and an unruly populace. All these divisions favored the creation of a mobile and effervescent culture.
Each fault line that traversed revolutionary society shaped not only
the kinds of songs that citizens chose to write or sing but also how
they sang and how they interpreted the performances, or silences, of
others. At any given moment, songs and singing served multiple purposes. Even when all voices seemed to be united in a single chorus—
as they were when they praised republican singing in 1793 and
1794—individual goals remained disparate or even diametrically opposed. The Revolution as a whole had scarcely any uniformity, for
opinions, alliances, and aspirations shifted repeatedly, winning new
partisans and evoking novel kinds of behavior as the years passed.

The fluidity that was visible within song culture suggests a great
deal about political culture more generally. Certainly songs and
singing were more accessible than almost any other expressive form
during the Revolution, but song culture was not isolated. Rather,
songs and singing throw into relief trends that were apparent else-

---

[2]Hunt, *Politics, Culture, and Class,* p. 14.

where. The heterogeneity that characterized song culture, and revolutionary society more generally, suggests the limits of genres that were less accessible than singing and song writing. Such genres as newspapers, pamphlets, plays, novels, and paintings, all of which were more restricted at the level of production or consumption, tell us less about the Revolution than songs do precisely because they represented the hopes and aspirations of a smaller fraction of the population.[3]

Besides suggesting the heterogeneity and conflict that characterized revolutionary political culture, the development of song culture also underscores the importance of the directorial period for song in the nineteenth century. Certainly 1793–94 marked the zenith of song culture and of the broader republican culture of which it was a part. These years witnessed an extraordinarily intense level of cultural activity and the production of many broadly shared symbols. But it was in the years after Thermidor [the fall of the Robespierrists on July 27–28, 1794] that the government began to fix the content of revolutionary culture and institutionalize the symbols that it hoped to promote as signs of the Republic. It was also in the years after Thermidor that the vestiges of activist republican culture moved indoors to bars and cafés: protected arenas in which that culture would persist and, eventually, again flourish.

Finally, the ongoing conflicts and frictions that were inherent in the constitution of revolutionary song culture help explain not only the intensity with which revolutionaries treated cultural matters but also the failure of republican culture at the end of the eighteenth century, a failure that contributed to the slow, steady decline of French politics into the authoritarian regime of Napoleon Bonaparte. It was the revolutionaries' failure to create a successful and pluralistic republican political culture that contributed to the Revolution's decay after 1795. Unable to find homogeneity without coercion and believing themselves unable to sustain political pluralism without violence or instability, few protested the Directory's efforts to freeze republican culture and promote it from above in the same heavy-handed manner with which it orchestrated electoral life. At the same time, many private citizens sought new avenues of activity and worked to achieve a cultural consensus that they believed to be apolitical and nonrevolutionary. It was this abandonment of an activist and engaged repub-

---

[3][For the history and words of one of the popular songs of the Revolution, "La Marseillaise," see the following selection. "La Carmagnole" and "Ça ira" are other popular songs of the period—Eds.]

licanism that helps to explain the success of Napoleon's coup in 1799, for Napoleon was prepared to foster a culture in which the citizenry would find domestic peace and unity: a supply of frozen political icons, an entertainment culture emphasizing wit and style over substance, and foreign wars that would nourish national unity as domestic politics could not.

Song Culture as Popular Culture

Although revolutionary political culture may be said to have failed in the short term, it was a rousing success in the long run. Why was this so? Republican political culture survived and flourished in the nineteenth century in part because of its ability to incorporate forms of what had been, and would again be considered "popular culture." The visible adoption of the objects and practices of popular culture stands as one of the most radically novel dimensions of revolutionary political culture; it was the iconic equivalent of universal male suffrage. Furthermore, in drawing on the "popular," republicanism gave new life to the notion of popular culture itself. Just as republicanism might be represented as the property of all members of the polity, so particular forms of popular culture—songs among them—acquired a distinct political identity. This identity persisted throughout the nineteenth and into the twentieth centuries, as radical republicans and the proponents of a self-conscious working-class culture adopted and expanded it.

"LA MARSEILLAISE"

Claude-Joseph Rouget de Lisle

Claude-Joseph Rouget de Lisle (1760–1836), an army captain in the Royal Engineering Corps stationed at Strasbourg in 1792, was also a poet and musician. At the request of the mayor of the city, Philippe Frédéric, baron de Dietrich, he wrote the words and music for a war song for the French Army of the Rhine ("Chant de guerre pour l'armée du Rhin"). Consisting of six stanzas, it was reportedly written during the night of April 25–26, 1792, less than a week after France had declared war on Austria. By the summer, this gory, patriotic, and idealistic song denouncing counterrevolutionaries had widespread appeal throughout France. A battalion of volunteers from Marseille sang it at about the time of the storming of the Tuileries Palace on August 10, 1792, and Parisians adopted the song and renamed it "La Marseillaise." Sung by the French troops as they went into various battles, it was decreed the national anthem by the Convention on July 14, 1795. But many French men and women came to associate the song with the Terror and refused to sing it. Later, Napoleon and some of the other nineteenth-century French rulers discouraged the singing of the song. The National Assembly of the Third Republic, on February 14, 1879, formally declared it the French national anthem.

Editors' translation of the original Strasbourg edition of May or June 1792 as quoted in *A. Rouget de Lisle, la vérité sur la paternité de la Marseillaise* (1865). It has often been parodied, and some later versions change a few of the lyrics and add stanzas.

French lyrics

1

Allons enfants de la patrie!
Le jour de gloire est arrivé.
Contre nous de la tyrannie
L'étendart sanglant est levé,
L'étendart sanglant est levé.
Entendez-vous dans les campagnes.
Mugir ces féroces soldats?
Ils viennent jusque dans vos bras,
Égorger vos fils, vos compagnes! . . . .
Aux armes, citoyens! formez vos
    bataillons:
Marchez, Marchez, qu'un sang
impur abreuve nos sillons.

2

Que veut cet horde d'esclaves,
De traîtres, de Rois conjurés?
Pour qui ces ignobles entraves,
Ces fers dès longtemps préparés?
Ces fers dès longtemps préparés?
Français! Pour nous, ah! quel
    outrage!
Quels transports il doit exciter?
C'est nous qu'on ose méditer
De rendre à l'antique esclavage! . . .
Aux armes . . . [etc.]

3

Quoi des cohortes étrangères
Feraient la loi dans nos foyers!
Quoi! ces phalanges mercenaires
Terrasseraient nos fiers guerriers!
Terrasseraient nos fiers guerriers!
Grand Dieu! . . . par des mains
    enchaînées,
Nos fronts sous le joug se
    ploiraient!
De vils despotes deviendraient
Les maîtres de nos destinées!
Aux armes . . . [etc.]

4

Tremblez Tirans! et vous, perfides,
L'opprobre de tous les partis,
Tremblez! . . . vos projets parricides
Vont enfin recevoir leur prix.
Vont enfin recevoir leur prix.
Tout est soldat pour vous
    combattre.
S'ils tombent nos jeunes héros,
La terre en produit de nouveaux
Contre vous tout prêts à se battre.
Aux armes . . . [etc.]

5

Français! en guerriers magnanimes
Portez ou retenez vos coups.
Épargnez ces tristes victimes
À regret s'armant contre nous.
À regret s'armant contre nous.
Mais le despote sanguinaire!
Mais les complices de Bouillé!
Tous ces tigres qui sans pitié
Déchirent le sein de leur mère.
Aux armes . . . [etc.]

6

Amour sacré de la patrie
Conduis, soutiens nos bras
    vengeurs!
Liberté, liberté chérie,
Combats avec tes défenseurs.
Combats avec tes défenseurs.
Sous nos drapeaux que la victoire
Accoure à tes mâles accents:
Que tes ennemis expirans
Voient ton triomphe et notre
    gloire . . .
Aux armes . . . [etc.]

English translation

1

Onward, children of the fatherland!
The day of glory has arrived.
Against us
Tyranny's bloody flag has been
  raised,
Tyranny's bloody flag has been
  raised.
Do you hear in the countryside,
The howls of those fierce soldiers?
They come, as close as they can,
To cut the throats of your sons,
  your wives! . . . .
To arms, citizens! form your
  battalions:
March on, March on, so that an
  impure blood waters our fields.

2

What do these hordes of slaves,
traitors, conspiratorial kings want?
For whom are these vile shackles,
These chains readied a long time
  ago?
These chains readied a long time
  ago?
Frenchmen! for us, ah! What an
  outrage!
What transports should they excite?
They dare to consider
Returning us to the old slavery! . . .
To arms, citizens! form your
  battalions:
March on, march on, so that an
  impure blood waters our fields.

3

What, some foreign cohorts
Would decide the law in our land!
What, these mercenary phalanxes
Would strike down our proud
  warriors!
Would strike down our proud
  warriors!
Great God! . . . by shackled hands,
Our brow would yield under the
  yoke!
Vile despots would become
The masters of our destiny!
To arms, citizens! form your
  battalions:
March on, march on, so that an
impure blood waters our fields

4

Tremble tyrants! and you perfidious
  ones,
The shame of all parties,
Tremble! . . . your parricidal projects
Are finally going to reap their just
  desserts.
Are finally going to reap their just
  desserts.
Everyone is a soldier against you.
If our young heroes fall,
The land will bear new ones.
Everyone is ready to fight against
  you.
To arms, citizens! form your
  battalions:
March on, march on, so that an
  impure blood waters our fields.

5

Frenchmen! as magnanimous
   warriors
Strike or withhold your blows.
Spare those sad victims
Reluctantly bearing arms against us.
Reluctantly bearing arms against us.
But the bloody despot!
But the confederates of [the counter-
   revolutionary soldier] Bouillé!
All those tigers who, pitilessly
Tear their mother's breast.
To arms, citizens! form your
   battalions:
March on, march on, so that an
   impure blood waters our fields.

6

Sacred love of the fatherland
Guide, uphold our avenging arms!
Liberty! cherished liberty,
Fight alongside your defenders.
Fight alongside your defenders.
Under our flags let victory
Rush to your male voices:
Let your enemies while dying
See your triumph and our glory . . .
To arms, citizens! form your
   battalions:
March on, march on, so that an
   impure blood waters our fields.

9
Women, Gender, and Politics in Revolution And Counterrevolution: Gains and Losses

HISTORIANS now know enough to assert emphatically that the French Revolution was a revolution by women as well as men, for women participated in a large number and variety of political practices. But was the Revolution a revolution *for women?*

The selection by Darline Gay Levy and Harriet Branson Applewhite concentrates on revolutionary women activists in Paris. The authors offer a generally positive answer to the question. To be sure, male revolutionary political culture was gendered, even misogynist, and male political leaders excluded women from voting and holding political office. On the other hand, women in revolutionary Paris practiced citizenship in politically significant numbers. They actively participated in revolutionary insurrections, demonstrations, club meetings, and festivals, signed petitions, and wrote in support of the Revolution. Moreover, they contributed to shaping new ideas of citizenship, democracy, popular sovereignty, and universal human rights, although more than two centuries later these rights, as they pertain to women, remain incompletely realized and enforced.

The selection by Olwen H. Hufton provides a generally negative answer to the question of whether the Revolution was a revolution for women. Hufton focuses mostly on the counterrevolutionary practices of peasants and other women in provincial villages. Attached to traditional Catholicism, they were outraged by the Civil Constitution of the Clergy of 1790, by the dechristianization campaigns, and by such disruptive changes as the economic downturn, the disappearance of the old forms of poor relief, the introduction of paper money and price fixing, and the drafting of loved ones. Therefore, they came to oppose local and national revolutionary initiatives. Their resistance took varied forms, including boycotting state schools and the state religion, worshipping with outlaw priests, and rioting in defense of their religious beliefs. Male revolutionaries responded by castigating them as counterrevolutionaries who eroded the allegiance to the Revolution in the countryside.[1]

By what standards do we evaluate the gains and losses women experienced because of the Revolution? Do we compare their lives to those of women under the Old Regime in France?[2] Or to the lives of women in other countries during the revolutionary decade?[3] Or to present-day women in the United States, Western Europe, or elsewhere? Do we differentiate by social class as well? Women of the upper class, middle class, and lower class did not share the same life styles before, during, or after the Revolution. In addition, how do we evaluate the legacy of the Revolution as it affected women? Do we stress revolutionary principles, including declarations of human rights, which in the long run were extended to women in France and proclaimed throughout the world as the universal rights of women? Or do we underscore the revolutionary heritage of anti-clericalism that alienated a majority of women in nineteenth-century France from liberal and republican regimes?

---

[1] In other writings on women during the Revolution, Professor Hufton also interprets the politics of Parisian women revolutionaries. See, for example, her *Women and the Limits of Citizenship in the French Revolution* (Toronto: University of Toronto Press, 1992), pp. 3–50.

[2] See, for example, a comparison of women's significantly increased role in public debate during the French Revolution with their role in the decades before it. Carla Hesse, "French Women in Print, 1750–1800: An Essay in Historical Bibliography," in *The Darnton Debate: Books and Revolution in the Eighteenth Century,* ed. Haydn T. Mason (Oxford: Voltaire Foundation, 1998), pp. 65–82.

[3] See Harriet B. Applewhite and Darline G. Levy, eds., *Women and Politics in the Age of the Democratic Revolution* (Ann Arbor: University of Michigan Press, 1990).

A POLITICAL REVOLUTION FOR WOMEN? THE CASE OF PARIS

Darline Gay Levy and Harriet Branson Applewhite

Darline Gay Levy (1939–) received the Ph.D. from Harvard University. She teaches history at New York University and has published *The Ideas and Careers of Simon-Nicolas-Henri Linguet: A Study in Eighteenth-Century French Politics* (1980). Harriet Branson Applewhite (1940–) received the Ph.D. from Stanford University. She is a member of the Department of Political Science at Southern Connecticut University and has published *Political Alignment in the French National Assembly, 1789–1791* (1993). Professors Levy and Applewhite have authored and co-authored articles on women, gender, and French revolutionary politics. They have also co-edited *Women and Politics in the Age of the Democratic Revolution* (1990) and, with Mary Durham Johnson, *Women in Revolutionary Paris, 1789–1795: Selected Documents Translated with Notes and Commentary* (1979). They are currently completing an interpretive study, *The Impossible Citizenship: Women, Gender, and Power in Revolutionary Paris.*

The French Revolution was arguably the most democratic of all the revolutions in the eighteenth-century Western world. Although the revolutionaries did not live in a world of modern democratic government, with its mass suffrage, political parties, and interest groups, the institutions and principles that the revolutionaries modified and created laid the foundations of the republican tradition in French politics and established the most important precedents for modern democracy. Revolutionaries developed and spread doctrines of human rights, redefined citizenship, and established popular sovereignty both in principle and in practice. They established legislatures, local governing bodies, political clubs, a popular press, and other institutions for political participation; and they involved millions of individuals throughout French society in political conflict and civil and international war.

Women involved themselves in these transformations in many ways: as members of revolutionary crowds, as radical leaders, and as supporters of the French government. Some donated their jewels to the treasury, knitted stockings, made bandages for the armies, or joined revolutionary festivals. Others were victims of revolutionary change: noblewomen who lost rank and privilege, and deeply religious women whose world fell apart when their churches were attacked and their faith declared unpatriotic. Women edited, printed, and distributed journals and political tracts and thereby contributed to both revolutionary and counterrevolutionary ideology. Their revolutionary allegiances were complex and their roles staggeringly diverse. Just as for men, women's experiences and their contributions were conditioned by their situations and their beliefs: Did they live in Paris or the provinces? Were they noblewomen or domestic servants? Did they keep market stalls or write plays? Were they devout Catholics or did they resent the wealth and power of the Church?

As historians have reflected on the meaning of revolutionary democracy for women, they have sharpened the lines of historiographic debate. Did the Revolution irreversibly establish precedents for women's involvement in the public sphere, in political contestations and rights issues? Or did it irrevocably and fundamentally separate women from the arena of political power in ways that normalized their domestic roles? Were "universal" principles in fact fundamentally masculinist ideological formulations that point to the exclusion and marginalization of women? Were these principles necessary and sufficient conceptual foundations for women's claims to equal civil and political rights?

Recently a number of scholars—such as Madelyn Gutwirth and Joan Landes—have interpreted women's revolutionary political activism as heroic but ultimately futile struggles doomed to failure because conducted in a cultural field determined by masculinist values and interests. They argue that as Enlightenment philosophes chal-

lenged the hierarchical world of old regime privilege, they undermined the influence of noble and bourgeois women at court and in the
salons. They established the model of a society of rational autonomous individuals understood to be male, with interests that the
sovereign power was obligated to protect. They either believed
women were biologically limited in reasoning capacity and physical
strength or argued that their interests were adequately represented
by fathers, husbands, or sons.[1] Other historians have questioned this
deterministic reading and have emphasized multiple and competing
Enlightenment theories about gender roles, including the Marquis de
Condorcet's ringing claims for universal political rights that were
grounded in the human capacity to reason and to feel and that dissolved gender differences in the political world. Joan Scott has argued
recently that when revolutionary feminists connected their interests
to universal rights, they opened a complex and continuing dialogue
about the necessary and sufficient conditions of liberty, equality, and
autonomy for women as political selves, citizens in the modern world.
She views the revolutionary legacy for women in terms of irresolvable
paradoxes that nonetheless allow some room for maneuvering:
women necessarily must emphasize sexual difference in order to
claim the applicability of universal rights to themselves; and they also
must deny differences in order to claim equality.[2] In several articles,
Lynn Hunt has backed away from the cultural determinism that informed her *Family Romance and the French Revolution* to emphasize
women's self-conscious political organization within "surprisingly
open political spaces" to demand their rights.[3]

We argue that links between women's revolutionary political practices and rights issues place the woman question permanently in the
modern French political tradition and in modern political culture. We
focus here on what women meant when they claimed and practiced
citizenship; how those claims were received by their contempo-

---

[1]Madelyn Gutwirth, *The Twilight of the Goddesses: Women and Representation in the
French Revolutionary Era,* Rutgers University Press, New Brunswick, 1992; Joan B.
Landes, *Women and the Public Sphere in the Age of the French Revolution,* Cornell University Press, Ithaca, 1988.
[2]Joan Wallach Scott, *Only Paradoxes to Offer: French Feminists and the Rights of Man*
Harvard University Press, Cambridge, 1996.
[3]Lynn Hunt, "Forgetting and Remembering: The French Revolution Then and Now,"
American Historical Review 100 (1995),pp. 1119–1135; quote from p. 1131; "Introduction: The Revolutionary Origins of Human Rights," in *The French Revolution and
Human Rights: A Brief Documentary History,* ed. Lynn Hunt, Bedford Books of St. Martin's Press, Boston, 1996.

raries; and what their posterity made of those claims. The political language and the acts of women in the revolutionary capital—their political performances—cannot be dismissed simply because the implications of these words and deeds were not realized in French revolutionary politics, or even with the establishment of women's suffrage in 1944 at the beginning of the Fourth Republic, and still have not produced equality in positions of political power.[4] Rights claims, once defined and defended, become indelibly imprinted in a political culture. Revolutionary writers like Olympe de Gouges and Etta Palm d'Aelders formulated their claims as human rights. In doing so they showed that a revolutionary and democratic recasting of relationships between governors and governed dictated a recognition of difference as a condition and ground of common claims for equal rights of citizenship. Other women whose words and thoughts were never recorded made their mark on the Revolution by marching, demonstrating, signing or marking petitions, attending revolutionary meetings, and participating in neighborhood self-government. Thousands of women marched to Versailles from Paris in October 1789, signed petitions concerning the future of the constitutional monarchy on the Champ de Mars in July 1791, and paraded through the halls of the Legislative Assembly and the king's residence in the Tuileries in the summer of 1792. Through these practices, they forged a link between their identities and behaviors as citizens, on the one hand, and new concepts of popular sovereignty, citizenship, and political legitimacy, on the other—the touchstones of modern democratic practices.

The Challenge to Royal Legitimacy and the Invention of Women's Citizenship

During the 1770s and 1780s, as journalists and other publicists communicated political news and shaped public opinion, they also focused attention on despotic and tyrannical acts of government authorities and thus contributed to narrowing the frames through which the public viewed political issues. In part, the involvement of women of the popular classes in public discourse at this juncture developed out of sociability fostered by their daily routines, like hauling water together and purchasing bread; but it also developed out of their participation in ceremonial functions that both reinforced

---

[4]See the comments of Joan Scott concerning 1990s proposals for gender quotas in the French National Assembly, in Scott, *op. cit.,* p. 2.

and subverted order, sometimes simultaneously. The *poissardes* (fishwives) of Paris were required to attend the childbirth of a reigning queen in order to certify the legitimate birth of the royal heir, and were present later when the infant dauphin was presented in a ceremony at the Hôtel de Ville [City Hall]. In the patriarchal society of the old regime, ruled by a monarchy in which a woman could not inherit the throne, this women's occupational group played a central role in validating the future king on behalf of the people; the *poissardes* contributed an important plebeian presence to rituals that legitimated the monarchy.

The legitimacy of Louis XVI and his authority to govern were under challenge from the very beginning of his reign in 1774. These challenges came from many institutions: the parlements whose power to register laws gave them the power to delay or block royal decrees; provincial estates and assemblies, which had some regional authority over law, administration, and taxes; the Church, with its power to tax, censor, and regulate behavior; and many specially privileged groups of people—army officers, judges, and local administrators—who exploited various opportunities for oppositional political maneuvering.

In addition to these institutional challenges, Enlightenment thinkers had long been questioning, debating, and reformulating theories about the nature and limits of legitimate authority. Enlightenment writers broadcast new doctrines of natural law, natural rights, and social contract. They demanded reforms in civil and criminal law; they challenged the legitimacy of a monarchy based on hereditary right and divine right; and they questioned defenses of privilege based on models of a hierarchical corporate society. Their discourse contributed to eroding the foundations of traditional authority and generating doubts about the legitimacy of one of the strongest monarchies in Europe. Enlightenment debates opened up opportunities for women to participate and, in the process, to acquire new civic identities. Women who presided over Paris salons promoted an antihierarchical sociability reflecting their influence in managing male discourse, but the *salonnières* also heightened male anxieties about women's exercise of real political power.[5]

As ministers and defenders of monarchy joined in the struggle to shape opinion, public opinion itself became a resource available to all parties; inevitably those who formed and exploited it, both elites

---

[5]Dena Goodman, *The Republic of Letters: A Cultural History of the French Enlightenment*, Cornell University Press, Ithaca, 1994.

and plebeians, women along with men, in effect were subverting the traditional foundations of authority. The manuscript journal of Siméon-Prosper Hardy, the Parisian bookseller, provides one window onto women's deployment of oppositional strategies. Hardy reported events like the crowd's failure to shout "Vive le Roi!" ("Long live the King!") as Louis XVI and his queen, Marie Antoinette, reviewed the French Guards and the Swiss Guards on May 8, 1787.[6] He noted that during the Feast of the Assumption in 1787, authorities had to present the *poissardes des Halles* (the fishwives of the Halles market) with a police order to force them to go through with their customary ceremonial offering of bouquets to the queen.[7] In recent close studies of daily life in eighteenth-century Paris, historians have brought into relief a plebeian public sphere and documented circumstances in which women of the popular classes contributed to the erosion of royal legitimacy, particularly in escalating attacks on the person and character of the king.[8]

In May 1788, after failing in a number of attempts to gain support for new taxes from various groups of notables, the king and his ministers decided to convoke the Estates General, an assembly of deputies representing the clergy (First Estate), the nobility (Second Estate), and the common people (Third Estate). The king hoped that the Estates, which had last met in 1614, would consent to the levying of taxes. The announcement generated great excitement and an outpouring of political pamphlets proposing a broad agenda of institutional reform. After the dates for elections to the Estates General had been fixed for the spring of 1789, electors at the local and provincial level drafted *cahiers de doléances* [lists of grievances]. The Paris electoral assemblies and the *cahier*-drafting process mobilized women along with men. Some working-class women authored *cahiers* in which they defended their economic interests by demanding protection for their crafts and occupations; others made

---

[6]Siméon Prosper Hardy, "Mes Loisirs, ou Journal d'événements tels qu'ils parviennent à ma connoissance," vol. 7, May 8, 1787, fol. 475, in Bibliothèque nationale, MSS, fonds français, no. 6687.

[7]Henri Monin, *L'Etat de Paris en 1789: Etudes et Documents,* Jouaust, Noblet, et Maison Quantin, Paris, 1889, p. 637.

[8]Nina Gelbart, *Feminine and Opposition Journalism in Old Regime France: Le Journal des Dames,* University of California Press, Berkeley, 1987; Arlette Farge and Jacques Revel, *The Vanishing Children of Paris: Rumor and Politics Before the French Revolution,* trans. Claudia Miéville, Harvard University Press, Cambridge, 1991; Arlette Farge, *Subversive Words: Public Opinion in Eighteenth-Century France,* trans. Rosemary Morris, Pennsylvania State University Press, University Park, 1994.

dramatic political claims for rights to political representation.[9] On April 20, 1789, the lieutenant general of police in Paris, Thirout de Crosne, reported the following incident to the king: "I have been assured that women presented themselves for admission to the [electoral] assembly of the Abbaye Saint-Germain. When they were turned down by the Swiss Guards, they asked to see one of the members of this assembly who came to assist them and brought them in. They are twelve in number."[10] No record exists of what these women did or said inside the assembly; nonetheless, the police report documents their striking determination to be included in the process of electing political representatives.

The legal initiatives of the Revolution of 1789 began with the June 17 transformation of the Estates General into a National Assembly whose deputies charged themselves with drafting a constitution. The king initially resisted this legal revolution and then acceded to it, but then, just prior to dismissing Jacques Necker, his popular finance minister, he began massing troops around Paris and Versailles. Parisians, fired up by the writings and speeches of revolutionary leaders and certain that they were about to be invaded by royal armed forces, rushed to arm themselves, seizing weapons from caches all over the city. Women cast themselves as ringleaders in attacks upon the tollgates surrounding Paris where duties were levied; they blamed the king's collectors for raising prices and creating bread shortages in the markets. On July 14th, a crowd of National Guardsmen and other citizens, heavily supported by neighborhood crowds, including women, attacked and conquered the Bastille; immediately afterward, the public, seizing upon the symbolic importance of the deed, proclaimed this victory a triumph of liberty over despotism. In an all-night session on August 4, the National Assembly abolished feudal privileges, and on August 26 passed, and sent to the king, a Declaration of the Rights of Man and of the Citizen.

During August and September, in the aftermath of these revolutionary events, hundreds of women from the central markets of Paris participated as principal players in nearly daily marches that wound

---

[9]See, for example, *Doléances particulières des marchandes bouquetières fleuristes chapelières en fleurs de la Ville et faubourgs de Paris* (1789), in Charles-Louis Chassin, *Les Élections et les cahiers de Paris en 1789*, 4 vols., Paris, 1888–89, vol. II, pp. 534–537; translated in *Women in Revolutionary Paris, 1789–1795*, ed. Darline Gay Levy, Harriet Branson Applewhite, and Mary Durham Johnson, University of Illinois Press, Urbana, 1979, pp. 22–26.

[10]Letter from Thirout de Crosne to Louis XVI, 20 April 1789 in Archives nationales, C 221/160/146, fol. 67.

through Paris. Ostensibly, these marches were acts of thanksgiving for the liberation of the Bastille, the withdrawal of royal troops from the environs of Paris, the establishment of the National Guard as the city's protective force, and the creation of a reformed municipal administration accountable to electors. The women, accompanied by contingents from the National Guard, marched in formation and to drumbeat. Typically, they proceeded to the Église Sainte Geneviève (now the Panthéon), Nôtre Dame, and the Hôtel de Ville (seat of the municipal government of Paris). In passing through these spaces, the participants linked themselves with both traditional and newly designated protectors of the city: Sainte Geneviève, patron saint of Paris; Nôtre Dame, the national church; the Hôtel de Ville, locus of the new elected representative government; and the National Guard, the newly constituted military force composed of property-owning men. Observers detected subversive elements in these ceremonies, and with good reason. The Marquis de Lafayette, commander of the National Guard, the mayor Jean Sylvain Bailly, representatives of the city government, and by extension national authorities and the king himself, were put on notice that women of the popular classes were holding them accountable for provisioning the city and safeguarding its liberty. The bookseller Hardy found these imposing demonstrations of popular allegiance patently ridiculous, but they also made him nervous.

> Many people found there was something terrifying in [*the procession's*] arrangement, composition, and immensity. Sensitive people found these public acts, which could not be interrupted and of which piety was unfortunately not the full motive, ridiculous. They thought it would have been infinitely wiser for each man and woman citizen to thank the Almighty individually . . . rather than collectively.[11]

These processions continued until a few days before the women's march to Versailles in October 1789. For some weeks, radical leaders and the people of Paris had been concerned about the king's failure to ratify the Declaration of Rights and also about the unresolved constitutional question of a royal veto and the summoning of additional troop reinforcements. All these issues came to a head over news of soldiers' insults to the revolutionary tricolor cockade (a hat decoration with the three revolutionary colors, red, white and blue) at a banquet held for royal bodyguards at Versailles. Just after dawn on October 5, a rainy Monday, the tocsin (alarm bell) began to ring from the Hôtel de Ville, and then from most churches all over the city. We

---

[11] Hardy, *op. cit.* vol. 8, fol. 475, September 14, 1789.

can hear the stomp of the *poissardes' sabots* (wooden shoes) and imagine the smell of their damp skirts as they swarmed into the Hôtel de Ville and forcibly kept men out. They were looking for ammunition, but also (according to Stanislas Maillard, a National Guardsman) for administrative records; they said that all the revolution had accomplished so far was paperwork. Another eyewitness heard them say that "men didn't have enough strength to avenge themselves and that they [the women] would demonstrate that they were better than men."[12] Late in the morning, they left the Hôtel de Ville and returned to the streets; they drummed the *générale* (a military call to arms), recruited thousands of additional women, then marched off en masse to Versailles. Hardy noted that they left "allegedly with the design of . . . asking the king, whom they intended to bring back to Paris, as well as the National Assembly, for bread and for closure on the Constitution."[13]

When the first group of women reached Versailles, a small delegation was granted an audience with the king. After leaving the royal apartments and returning to the palace courtyard with news of Louis XVI's promise to provision Paris, this delegation was threatened by waiting crowds of women who sent back two among them to obtain a written document sealing the king's commitment. Louise Chabry, one of those who had been granted the royal audience, and thirty-nine other women marchers returned to Paris at 3:00 A.M. in royal carriages; they reported that Stanislas Maillard and women with him were returning to Paris with signed decrees on provisionment.[14] Chabry, allegedly forced to march that morning, took it upon herself (or was assigned) to act as a spokesperson for the royal audience and principal courier bringing the news back to the Paris Commune. Furthermore, Chabry presented the mayor with the orders that the king had given her. This young lace worker had assumed a quasi-official position as emissary for her city and its government.

Other women who marched to Versailles entered the National Assembly and occupied it throughout the night, disrupting procedures, voting on motions, and occupying the speaker's chair. Such political dramaturgy draws upon the French tradition of role reversals on carnival days; however, these were not carnival days. The women's ac-

---

[12] *Procédure criminelle instruite au Châtelet de Paris*, Baudouin, Paris, 1790, Part I, witness 81, p. 118.

[13] Hardy, *op. cit.*, no. 6687, fol. 502, October 5, 1789.

[14] *Ibid.*, and testimony of Chabry, No. 183, *Procédure criminelle*, Part II, pp. 23–25. In her account, Chabry says she and the other women arrived back in Paris at 2:00 A.M.; the secretary of the Commune puts it an hour later.

tions were direct interventions in the legislative process and symbolic replacements of representatives who did not represent.

Early on the morning of October 6, the crowd, including women and Guardsmen, broke into the château and killed two royal bodyguards. Fearing more violence, the king agreed to go with his family to reside in Paris. A bizarre procession was formed for the march from Versailles to Paris: the women, some mounted on gun carriages and carrying loaves of bread mounted on pikes; National Guardsmen intermingled with royal bodyguards; the royal family in a carriage from which they could view the heads of the murdered guards impaled on pikes; delegations of deputies; and a host of others.

After October 6, authorities moved to suppress collective demonstrations of popular force. City officials decreed martial law in Paris after the lynching of a baker whom a woman had accused of reserving bread for deputies to the Assembly (the charge implied that deputies had subordinated the public good to their private interests). This event suggests that women and men in the crowd held deputies directly accountable to the people for their actions. Following the proclamation of martial law, two Paris districts protested the prohibition of public gatherings; they also protested the failure of city officials to consult with them before decreeing martial law. These protests amounted to an unequivocal demand for the right of referendum, which authorities did not grant, although they did permit delegations of up to six persons to submit grievance petitions.[15]

The National Assembly, relocated in Paris, began to work in the late fall of 1789 on the details of the new constitution. On December 22, 1789, the assembly set up electoral assemblies and defined the limits of the franchise. Abstract debates about citizenship now yielded a concrete and codified definition. Active citizens were men who could meet a tax qualification: the payment of "a direct tax equal to the local value of three days' labor."[16] The decree did not define a category for those not qualifying as active citizens; however, the question had been discussed in the National Assembly during the October 1789 debates on citizenship.[17] Other people—women, foreigners, domestic servants, and men who did not meet the tax qualification—were considered passive citizens. The deputies construed their definitions to allow for the possibility that men classified as passive citizens might

---

[15] Archives nationales, C 32, no. 271.

[16] John Hall Stewart, *A Documentary Survey of the French Revolution,* Macmillan, New York, 1951, p. 129.

[17] J. Mavidal, E. Laurent, et al., eds., *Archives parlementaires, de 1787 à 1860,* First Series (34 vols., Paris; Imprimerie nationale, 1867–1890), 9, (October 20, 1789), p. 470.

become active citizens should their tax payment reflect an increased income. No such possibility existed for women.

The exclusion of women from the status and political rights of full legal citizenship was never remedied in any revolutionary code or constitution. Nonetheless, many thousands of women in all socio-professional categories pushed past the legal boundaries to claim citizenship in words and acts, to erode acceptance of the constitutional monarchy even as it was being established, and to take their place alongside men in the ranks of the sovereign people, inextricably combining democratic practices with political empowerment and rights claims. In the absence of any preponderant political or administrative authority willing or able to pronounce upon the legality of this de facto citizenship, all these practices together sufficed to keep the question of women's status open and indeterminate.

Publicists and observers promoted this openness as they assigned competing meanings to the October Days. Aristocratic publicists on the extreme right wrote off the October women as mistresses of the former French guards; one pamphleteer called them "the vilest toads from the dirtiest street in the most disgusting city in the universe."[18] Some supporters of the Paris revolution expressed uneasiness about women's initiatives—however strongly they approved the political outcomes of the October Days. Shortly after the insurrection, the radical newspaper *Révolutions de Paris* printed a letter from a priest recounting the classical story of the Spartan mother who, informed that her five sons had all died in battle, refused to mourn her loss since Sparta had won, saying she loved her *patrie* a thousand times more than she loved her sons—indeed she loved them more than she loved her own life.[19] For the journalist, this story taught that women's patriotic responsibilities—their roles as citizens—centered on the rearing of sons and the cultivation of a willingness to sacrifice them, if necessary, for the higher cause of the nation. The Declaration of the Rights of Man and a constitution would not produce good citizens automatically; women must accept responsibility for educating their sons in valor and their daughters in habits of self-sacrifice.

Other pamphleteers celebrated women's achievements on October 5 and 6 in more exalted language; but they assigned women curiously mundane tasks, such as overseeing quality control in the markets. One anonymous polemicist praised the women's daring move

---

[18] Bibliothèque nationale, 39 2412. *Relation très exacte des événemens du 5 et 6 octobre,* Paris, 1789.

[19] *Révolutions de Paris,* no. 19 (November 14–21), p. 46.

to bring the king to Paris, but admonished them to restrain themselves henceforth: they must remain sober, avoid questionable popular entertainers, and keep watch at the tollgates to prevent the importation of spoiled fruit and grain into Paris. In brief, they should abandon insurrectionary politics and limit themselves to narrowly circumscribed surveillance activities.[20]

Some women authors appropriated the language of heroism on women's behalf and demanded their plenary empowerment. In November 1789, the editors of a short-lived journal, the *Étrennes nationales des dames,* published a letter from a "Madame la M. de M," a writer who may have been a man speaking in a woman's voice and who apparently was a collaborator in their enterprise. In a light, bantering tone, teasingly but also pointedly, this writer directly linked the bravery and enterprise of the October women to women's demands for political rights: "Let us return men to the right path, and let us not tolerate that, with their systems of equality and liberty, their declarations of rights, they leave us in a condition of inferiority—let us tell the straight truth—slavery—in which they have kept us for so long."[21] "Madame la M. de M" conjures up scenarios in which women demand representation in the National Assembly, undertake surveillance activities at the Hôtel de Ville, and assume posts in the voluntary National Guard as "amazons of the Queen." The writer holds out to women subscribers the promise of a complete political education—political news, legislative decrees, judicial decisions, extracts from foreign newspapers, military and economic news, and happenings in the world of letters, science, and the arts. For this writer, the achievements of the women of the October days heralded new conquests—plenary rights of citizenship for all women.

During the course of 1790 and 1791, power struggles pitted radicals in the Paris districts and clubs against the municipal leadership and the National Assembly, whose leaders were trying to contain the potential force of the sovereign people by limiting the suffrage, prohibiting collective petitions, and outlawing strikes.

Nonetheless, the Paris sections (neighborhood governing bodies that replaced the districts) met regularly; political clubs actively recruited members and took on an educational mission. Women vigor-

---

[20] Anonymous, *Les Héroïnes de Paris ou l'entière liberté de la France, par les femmes . . . police qu'elles doivent exercer de leur propre autorité. Expulsion des charlatans &c. &c., le 5 octobre 1789* (n.p., n.d.).

[21] *Étrennes nationales des dames,* no. 1 (November 3, 1789).

ously challenged restrictions on popular sovereignty, not only as gallery spectators and wives, but also as active members of clubs and popular societies, printers, journalists, political organizers, petitioners, and delegates. Together with men classified as passive citizens, women of the popular classes involved themselves centrally in the spring 1791 crisis over the legitimacy of the constitutional monarchy—a crisis that escalated as Parisians became increasingly suspicious of Louis XVI. As they challenged royal legitimacy, these activists linked the meanings of their protests to rights, sometimes construed as individual rights and sometimes as the collective rights of the sovereign people.

The published minutes of the Cordeliers Club (a radical political club) for February 11, 1791, contained an exhortation to club members by several *citoyennes* [women citizens] from the Rue de Regard. The *citoyennes* characterized themselves as good Rousseauian mothers who taught constitutional principles to their children; but they also threatened to become militant if men did not fight hard enough for the right to liberty.

> We have consoled ourselves for not having been able to contribute anything toward the public good by exerting our most intense efforts to elevate the spirit of our children to the heights of free men. But if you were to deceive our hope, if the machinations of our enemies were to dazzle you to the point of lulling you at the height of the storm, then indignation, sorrow, despair would lead and propel us into public places. There, we would fight to defend liberty; until you conquered it [*liberty*], you were not men. Then [*under these conditions*], we would save the Fatherland, or dying with it, we would uproot the memory of having seen you unworthy of us.[22]

On the night of June 21, 1791, members of the royal family, in disguise, were smuggled out of the Tuileries palace into a waiting coach and driven east toward the Belgian border, where they were scheduled to meet up with several French generals, rejoin the Austrian army, and unleash a counterrevolution. At the town of Varennes, local officials recognized them; they were forced to return to Paris, escorted by deputies from the National Assembly. They entered the city surrounded by an escort of National Guards and rode past a silent, largely hostile crowd lining the route.

The National Assembly temporarily suspended the king's executive authority and debated what to do with him. Paris radicals were

---

[22] Club des Cordeliers, Société des amis des droits de l'homme et du citoyen, *Extrait des délibérations du 22 février 1791*, Paris, 1791, in Bibliothèque historique de la Ville de Paris, 10,065, No. 67.

not so hesitant. Clubs like the Cercle Social and the Cordeliers reached out to other popular societies, many of whose members were men and women of humble rank, and recruited them to sign petitions challenging the legitimacy of both the king and the National Assembly. Women directly involved themselves in this political mobilization. One Mlle. Le Maure, a regular participant in activities of the Cordeliers Club, presented before the assembled club members an address "to the representatives of the French Nation," a systematically argued defense of the right of collective petitioning, a right that the National Assembly had just recently outlawed. The Cordeliers adopted the address, and it was printed in a number of the radical journal *Le Creuset*. Le Maure argued that all individuals of the French nation (a deliberately all-inclusive formulation) had delegated their powers to the National Assembly; however, they had done so without renouncing their rights: ". . . without annihilating the declaration of the rights of man, you could not state as a principle that the right of petition can be exercised only individually. . . ." She argued that the new legislation violated several articles of the Declaration of the Rights of Man, including Articles 3 and 6 (which stated that the source of all sovereignty was in the nation and that the law was the expression of the "general will").[23]

Women were charged with surveillance activities (exposing an arms cache, for example); they incited Parisians to acts of vandalism against statues of the king in Paris, and signed petitions demanding consultation on the future of executive authority in the new constitution.[24] Forty-one "women, sisters, and Roman women" appended their signatures to the "Petition of the 100" delivered to the National Assembly on July 14, 1791. The text of this petition stated: ". . . make this sacred commitment to await the expression of this public voice before pronouncing on a question [*the fate of the king*] which affects the entire nation and which the powers you have received from [*the nation*] do not embrace."[25] On this fundamental question of political legitimacy, the petitioners asked the legislators to defer to the will of the nation, expressed concretely in a national vote. They had transformed acts of petitioning from deferential pleas into forceful expressions of the will of the sovereign people.

On July 17, thousands of commoners, women and men of all socio-professional ranks, met on the Champ de Mars [a Paris parade ground]

---

[23] *Le Creuset*, no. for June 9, 1791.

[24] *Ibid.;* Levy, Applewhite, and Johnson, *op. cit.,* pp. 78, 79, 83, 84.

[25] *Ibid.,* p. 79, taken from Albert Mathiez, *Le Club des Cordeliers* . . . (Geneva: Slatkine-Megariotis Reprints, 1975; reprint of 1910 edition), pp. 223–224.

and directly challenged the deputies in the National Assembly as well as the Constitution of 1791 that had authorized only the legislature to act in the name of the sovereign nation. They gathered peaceably to sign a petition demanding a national referendum on the question of monarchical authority. The text of the petition read: ". . . the decree [*of the National Assembly, reinstating Louis XVI*] is null in fact because it is contrary to the will of the sovereign. . . ."[26] The language of these petitioners, and particularly the reference to the "will of the sovereign," again echoes Article 3 of the Declaration of the Rights of Man and Citizen, which located the source of all sovereignty in the nation, and Article 6, which defined the law as the expression of the general will.[27] Late in the afternoon, the municipality declared martial law, following the crowd's summary execution of two men suspected of spying on the petitioners. National Guard battalions, dispatched to the Champ de Mars, fired on the assembled crowds, killing and wounding several dozen people. The mass demonstration had ended in a bloody confrontation between the political leaders of Paris and the crowd of petition signers acting on their claim to the right to express the will of the sovereign in the name of the nation.

Following this violent suppression, authorities arrested a number of participants, including several women. One of them, Anne Félicité Colomb, was the owner of the print works that produced the radical journals the *Ami du Peuple* and the *Orateur du peuple* and a future member of the radical women's political club, the Society of Revolutionary Republican Women. More than half a year before the massacre on the Champ de Mars, Colomb already had made an extraordinary contribution to the practice and defense of republicanism and radical democracy. Her story points to critically important alliances shaping up among political clubs, popular societies, and the printers and editors of radical journals as they stepped up pressure on constituted authorities. On December 14, 1790, Colomb was visited in her shop by a police commissioner and a publicist named Étienne. Étienne had obtained a police order from municipal officers authorizing Colomb's interrogation as well as the removal of copies of the journals she was printing, at Étienne's own risk. On the spot, Colomb protested the search of her lodgings and print works as "illegal, damaging to the rights of citizens, whose domiciles could be inspected only by a duly authorized court." She declared that she was reserving the right to initiate proceedings "before the appropriate courts

---

[26] Petition of July, 17, 1791, in Stewart, *op. cit.,* pp. 219–220.
[27] "Declaration of the Rights of Man and Citizen," in Stewart, *op. cit.,* p. 114.

and in full view of the Nation, which is concerned about preserving the liberty of all its members." Furthermore, she stated that she would name the authors of the *Ami* and the *Orateur* "only at the appropriate time and place and to the appropriate persons."[28] On December 18, the court decided against Colomb and ordered her to stop printing and distributing any and all papers. On January 10, 1791, with the Cordelier activist Buirette de Verrières representing her, Colomb appealed before the Tribunal of Police at the Hôtel de Ville. Buirette de Verrières restated Colomb's earlier arguments; asked that Étienne be assessed for 10,000 livres in costs and damages to Colomb's good name and the reputation of her print works; and requested that the sum she demanded be distributed among the poor of the Sections Henry IV and Théâtre Francais. Through her lawyer, Colomb also asked the court to invoke Article 11, the free press guarantee in the Declaration of the Rights of Man, and demanded that her print works as well as the authors of the *Ami* and the *Orateur* and her distributors all enjoy protections accorded to them under law, with the understanding that they would be held responsible for abuses of freedom of the press. The court vindicated Colomb and ordered Étienne to pay a small fine.[29]

On July 20–21, 1791, following the events on the Champ de Mars, authorities arrested and jailed Colomb and others at her print works. The prisoners proceeded to appeal directly to the National Assembly, and on August 16 the Committee on Investigations of the Assembly wrote to the tribunal of the sixth *arrondisement* (an administrative ward) concerning the prisoners' provisional release, claiming that, in at least some cases, arrest and interrogation records did not appear to warrant the court's long delay in reaching a decision. The committee informed the court that it had learned that the grievance of the detained parties would be aired before the National Assembly at any moment. On August 17, an officer of the tribunal replied that he was awaiting the results of further investigation.[30]

Colomb was an extraordinarily sophisticated political activist; during her interrogation of December 14, 1790, that is, even before the

---

[28] Dossier of Anne Félicité Colomb, Archives nationales, F[7] 2624. plaq. 1, fols. 52–69.

[29] *Ibid.*

[30] Section de la Place Vendôme, 20–21 July 1791, Procès-verbal of the seizure of manuscripts and printed works by Marat and others . . . arrest and imprisonment of Dlle. Colomb, Redelé de Fl [*illeg.*] and Verrières, in Archives nationales, W. 357, no. 750; Letter of the Comité des recherches to the Tribunal of the 6th Arrondissement, 16 August 1791 in Archives nationales, DXXIX[bis]31b, no. 324; letter from the Interim President of the Tribunal of the 6th Arrondissment to the Comité des Rapports, 17 August 1791, in DXXIX[bis]34, no. 352.

Cordeliers club member Buirette de Verrières took on her case, Colomb herself invoked the freedoms and rights of citizenship to defend her professional activities. She and others arrested with her in July 1791 were prepared to go beyond the courts, indeed to go directly to the National Assembly, to do battle for their rights. They may in fact have been trying to discredit the assembly by demonstrating that these newly guaranteed constitutional rights were being violated in investigations ordered by the assembly after the events on the Champ de Mars.

Also detained by the authorities, on the charge of insulting and threatening a member of the National Guard, was Constance Évrard, a cook, later a member of the Society of Revolutionary Republican Women, and a close friend of Pauline Léon (the proprietor of a chocolate shop who cofounded the society in the spring of 1793). The minutes of Évrard's interrogation by the police show that this "passive citizen" and political activist interpreted the National Guardsmen's acts on the Champ de Mars as a betrayal of a new, critically important bond of trust that had been developing between the nation's armed forces and citizens in the Paris sections. The wife of the Guardsman reported that Évrard, Pauline Léon, and Léon's mother had denounced her husband as "an assassin, a hangman, a scoundrel, who was killing everyone on the Champ de Mars"; Évrard had threatened to knife him within three days. Évrard herself admitted that she had returned from the Champ de Mars on July 17 "outraged at the conduct of the National Guard against unarmed citizens," and that, seeing the Guardsman with his battalion passing by en route to the Champ de Mars, she reproached him for going there.[31]

The interrogation of Constance Évrard highlights her extraordinary sensitivity to the potential disaster that the National Guard's treachery could cause. In addition, she identified herself with new concepts, responsibilities, and practices of citizenship and popular sovereignty that the crises of the summer of 1791 had crystallized. She told her interrogators that she had gone to the Champ de Mars and had "signed a petition like all good patriots." While admitting that she did not have the petition read to her on the Champ de Mars, she declared that she "believes that this petition tends to have the executive power organized in another way." She acknowledged that she sometimes went with groups of people to the Palais Royal and the Tuileries gardens (public places where political news was circu-

---

[31] Procès-verbal of the interrogation of Constance Évrard and witnesses, Section de la Fontaine de Grenelle, Sunday, 17 July 1791, in Archives, Préfecture de la Police, Paris, Series Aa, 148, fol. 30.

lated); she also attended the Cordeliers Club, although she was not a member. She reported subscribing to the radical journal *Révolutions de Paris;* she had complimented the editor, Prudhomme, on his article on tyrannicides, and told him how enthusiastic she was about this piece, adding that "had she been a man, she did not know how far patriotism would have led her." She also stated that she read the journals of Marat, Audouin, Desmoulins, and "very often the *Orateur du Peuple*"—all radical journals.[32]

During the summer of 1791, revolutionary activists in Paris, with women prominent among them, legitimated their practice of popular sovereignty by linking it to Article 3 of the Declaration of the Rights of Man and Citizen. Equally significantly, revolutionary leaders, determined to demonstrate the full weight of opposition to the constitutional monarchy, accepted and even recruited women as equal participants. For example, one of the men arrested for sedition on July 16 was accused of carrying a petition to the National Assembly and of reading an invitation to all citizens that included the statement "that all women and children who had attained the age of reason would be received to sign the petition."[33]

Notwithstanding their exclusion from such constitutional rights of citizenship as voting and holding office, the passive citizenry, men and women, identified themselves as citizens. They participated in revolutionary ceremonies; attended political meetings as discussants, petitioners, and delegates; wrote political tracts; formulated and communicated revolutionary ideology; and involved themselves centrally in revolutionary insurrections. They wore symbols of their patriotic commitment like tricolor cockades. These acts escalated pressures on authorities and contributed to transforming the French monarchy into the First Republic. At the same time, these revolutionary actors were crafting civic identities for themselves.

Women and the Triumph of Popular Sovereignty

Between September 1791 and August 1792, revolutionary leaders in Paris tolerated and even encouraged the involvement of women in open challenges to the constitutional monarchy, acts of popular sovereignty expressive of a progressively more democratic understanding of the meaning of citizenship.

---

[32] *Ibid.*
[33] Mathiez, *op. cit.,* p. 363.

The collapse of the constitutional monarchy on August 10, 1792, was the outcome of a battle in the courtyard of the Tuileries between the king's Swiss Guard and a popular armed force. However, it was prepared by a complex series of events that strengthened revolutionary forces and weakened resistance in the king's camp and in the legislature. On April 20, 1792, with the nation threatened with invasion, the Legislative Assembly voted a declaration of war against Austria; that event ushered in twenty-three years of nearly continuous war in Europe. Other principal developments were the king's alienation from revolutionary authorities with whom he was required to work under the Constitution of 1791, and the growing appeal of republicanism. Both of these widened the breach between king and people and sharpened the confrontation between the ministers, deputies, and municipal authorities, who continued to operate within constitutional limits, and the fully mobilized insurgents, who claimed legitimate sovereign authority for the people.

Between March 9 and June 20, 1792, thousands of men, women, and children from all over Paris participated in armed processions through the halls of the Legislative Assembly. In each procession, the participants demanded that the legislature recognize their legitimate power as the sovereign people; they received that recognition from the legislature. In the accompanying speeches, and through signs, exclamations, gestures, images, symbols (like the red cap of liberty and ribbons in revolutionary colors), and the line of march, participants expanded the significance of their actions and linked them to new definitions of citizenship, national sovereignty, and the legitimacy of rulers. Finally, they conspicuously paraded pikes and sabers, which carried the threat that they would deploy armed force. This display of military force, in combination with concrete demands and the symbols and words that colored them with a general significance, produced a second revolution, during which the constitutional monarchy collapsed and a republic was established.

The people in arms reclaimed and rebuilt an alliance with official armed forces that had been shattered by the gunfire on the Champ de Mars in July 1791. Astonishingly, radical leaders as well as authorities first questioned, but in the end tolerated, the presence among the Guardsmen of men and women armed with pikes, the real and symbolic weapons of the sovereign people.

In an editorial, "Des Piques," appearing in a February 1792 number of his *Révolutions de Paris,* the journalist Prudhomme called attention to the symbolic and military significance of the pike: "Universally accessible, available to the poorest citizen," the pike was an em-

blem for independence, equality under arms, vigilance, and the recovery of liberty. "The pikes of the people are the columns of French
liberty." Prudhomme explicitly denied the right of women to bear
these arms: "Let pikes be prohibited for women; dressed in white and
girded with the national sash, let them content themselves with
being simple spectators." In his calculations Prudhomme eliminated
the female portion of the 24 million potential pike bearers of
France.[34] In fact, women continued to claim and exercise the right to
arm themselves with pikes and with other weapons as well. They
constructed political identities for themselves that mirrored Prudhomme's definition of the revolutionary citizen: independent, free,
equal, vigilant, and armed.

On March 6, less than a month after Prudhomme's article appeared, a delegation of "*citoyennes* from the city of Paris," led by
Pauline Léon, presented to the Legislative Assembly a petition with
more than 300 signatures concerning women's right to bear arms.
The petitioners grounded their claim in an appeal to the natural right
of every individual to defend his or her life and liberty. "You cannot
refuse us and society cannot remove from us this right which nature
gives us, unless it is alleged that the Declaration of Rights is not applicable to women and that they must allow their throats to be slit,
like sheep, without having the right to defend themselves." The delegation requested permission for women to arm themselves with
pikes, pistols, sabers, and rifles; to assemble periodically on the
Champ de Mars; and to engage in military maneuvers. The assembly,
after debate, decreed a printing of the petition and honorable mention in the minutes and passed to the order of the day.[35]

While the Legislative Assembly hesitated between dismissing and
tolerating women's demands for the right to bear arms, the Paris
Commune and the mayor, Jérôme Pétion, took action to honor
women's militancy publicly, to reward it officially, and to instate it
as a model of women's citizenship. In his speech of April 5 to the
commune, Pétion endorsed a petition on behalf of Reine Audu, one
of the few participants in the women's march to Versailles in October 1789 who had been arrested and imprisoned. He argued that although French customs generally kept women out of combat, it also
was the case that "in the moment of danger, when the *patrie* is in
peril," women "do not feel any the less that they are *citoyennes*."
The Council of the Commune, acting on the petition, decreed a cer-

---

[34] Prudhomme, "Des Piques," *Révolutions de Paris,* vol. 11, February 11–18, 1792, pp.
293–298.

[35] *Archives parlementaires* 39 (March 6, 1792), pp. 423, 424.

emony in which the mayor would honor and decorate "this *citoyenne*" with a sword as "an authentic testimony to her bravery and her patriotism."[36]

During the weeks preceding the armed procession of April 9, 1792, a concept of female citizenship emerged that dissolved distinctions between active and passive, male and female citizens; combined women's right of self-defense with their civic obligation to protect and defend the nation; and placed both directly in the center of a general definition of all citizens' rights and responsibilities. Thus the armed women, who in spring 1792 marched in imposing processions, giving dramatic and forceful expression to the potent image of a united national family in arms, at the same time embodied militant citizenship, a driving force in the process of revolutionary radicalization. This moving picture is the clean, sharp inverse of the radical journalists' earlier depictions of unarmed families brutally gunned down by Lafayette's troops as they gathered on the Champ de Mars in July 1791 to sign the petition on the fate of the king. In the weeks following the events of July 17, 1791, Jean-Paul Marat had filled the pages of his *Ami du peuple* with provocative images: "The blood of old men, women, children, massacred around the altar of the fatherland is still warm, it cries out for vengeance."[37] The arming of passive citizens, including women, in the spring of 1792 turned upside down this picture of helpless martyrs; it empowered the powerless, and it activated an involuntarily pacific (because legally "passive") citizenry, including the potential force of women within the radical leadership's escalating estimates of the strength of the national family in arms.

The armed procession of June 20, 1792, reflected turmoil in Paris over the king's dismissal of liberal ministers and his vetoes of two decrees, one authorizing harsh sanctions against clergy who had refused to swear an oath of loyalty to the constitution and another establishing a camp for 20,000 French troops beneath the walls of Paris. Four days earlier, on June 16, a delegation from two militant neighborhoods informed municipal authorities of plans to commemorate the fourth anniversary of the Tennis Court Oath—an oath sworn by deputies in the National Assembly not to disband until they had given France a constitution. The key event was to be an armed procession before the assembly and the king to present petitions. The authorities tried to prevent the march, but the mayor, Pétion, realized that nothing could stop it. He developed a

---

[36] *Extrait du registre des délibérations du Conseil général de la Commune de Paris,* Vendredi, 5 avril 1792, Paris, 1792.

[37] Marat, *Ami du peuple,* no. 524, July 20, 1791, p. 2.

strategy of putting all armed citizens under the flags of the National Guard battalions and under the authority of battalion commanders, thereby legitimating a force composed of National Guardsmen and all citizens, passive along with active, women and children along with men.

On the morning of June 20, thousands of marchers were granted permission to parade through the meeting hall of the Legislative Assembly. Marchers included National Guardsmen, light infantrymen, grenadiers, and troops of the line—all interspersed with women ("*dames* and *femmes du peuple*" [ladies and ordinary women]), men (porters, charcoal burners, priests with swords and guns, veterans), and children. The marchers carried long pikes, guns, axes, knives, paring knives, scythes, pitchforks, sticks, bayonets, great saws, and clubs. Armed women were described as wearing liberty caps and carrying sabers and blades. The marchers' signs and banners proclaimed loyalty to the constitution,[38] and they meant what they said. In addition, their actions made it clear that the constitution, along with the government, was only the instrument of the will of an armed sovereign people.

Through these practices of citizenship, the insurrectionary crowds symbolically subverted the king's legally sanctioned executive authority, his right to veto laws, and his role as representative of national sovereignty. The marchers, constitutionally prohibited from exercising sovereignty, were doing just that.[39] When the marchers left the assembly, they charged into the Tuileries Palace and for six hours paraded, armed, before the king, displaying the banners and symbols that identified them as the sovereign nation. The king, in turn, refused to bend his will to that of this "sovereign people," and the mayor and other officers finally persuaded the demonstrators to leave the palace.[40]

Several witnesses were quick to seize the larger import of the day's events. An official of the Department of Paris (the national administrative unit for Paris) commented: "The throne was still standing but the people were seated on it, took the measure of it; and its

---

[38] *Archives parlementaires* 45 (June 20, 1792), pp. 406 ff, and esp. 411–419. [*Madame Rosalie Jullien*], *Journal d'une Bourgeoise pendant la Révolution, 1791–1793*, published by Edouard Lockroy, Calmann-Lévy, Paris, 1881, pp. 134–147. *Le Mercure universel*, June 21, 1792, as cited in Laura B. Pfeiffer, "The Uprising of June 20, 1792," *University Studies of the University of Nebraska* 12, no. 3 (July 1912), pp. 84, 85.

[39] Stewart, *op. cit.*, p. 234.

[40] Pfeiffer, *op. cit.*, pp. 284–323.

steps seemed to have been lowered to the height of the paving stones of Paris."[41] These armed marches, repeatedly legitimized by the assembly's votes to permit and honor them, were successful ceremonial demonstrations of the breadth, scope, and power of a fully mobilized democratic force in revolutionary Paris. The alliance between the women and men of the radical faubourgs (neighborhoods) and their National Guard battalions, an alliance shattered on the Champ de Mars in 1791, was reforged on foundations of rebuilt trust and restored unity of purpose. On June 21, a police commissioner reported that in the Faubourg Saint-Antoine people were saying that ". . . the people is the only sovereign, it must make the law WITHOUT CONSTITUTION AND WITHOUT SANCTION [*from any higher authority*]."[42]

Pétion, the mayor, called particular attention to the significance of women's involvement in the events of June 20. Under attack for having failed to use force to prevent or disperse the procession, Pétion rushed into print with a self-defense: *Conduct of the Mayor of Paris on the Occasion of the Events of June 20, 1792.* Pétion insisted that neither he nor anyone else could have commanded the force capable of stopping the march of "such an immense crowd of citizens." "Where was the repressive force capable of stopping the torrent? I say it did not exist." All battalions from the two faubourgs had marched with cannon and arms, followed by large numbers of armed citizens and a multitude of unarmed citizens, Pétion explained. Any force mobilized against the marchers could only have been composed of National Guardsmen who, in that case, would have been opposing fellow Guardsmen; combating fellow citizens armed with pikes; opposing unarmed men, maybe even their neighbors; confronting women— their sisters, their wives, their mothers; and battling with children, possibly their own. "Who would have been able to answer for the lives of these persons who are the most precious to the nation [*and*] whom it is most important to preserve?" On whom and where would this attacking force have fired? "The very idea of this carnage makes one shiver." "And to whom would this bloody battlefield have been left?" Three-quarters of the National Guard would have refused to fire on their fellow citizens, given that they all shared the marchers' mo-

---

[41] P.L. Roederer, *Chronique des cinquante jours du 20 juin au 10 août 1792,* Paris, 1832. p. 63.

[42] Dumont, commissaire de police, Section de la Rue Montreuil, to the Directory of the Department of Paris, June 21, 1792, in "Journée du 20 juin 1792," *Revue Rétrospective, ou Bibliothèque historique,* 2nd series, vol. 1 (1835), p. 180.

tives, and given that the Legislative Assembly already had set precedents when it "tolerated" earlier processions.[43]

The officials of the Department of Paris, who suspended Pétion
from office for his failure to prevent the march, acknowledged that he
was right about June 20: the presence of women and children in the
ranks of the National Guard had paralyzed it.[44] In short, authorities
of all convictions, that is, those who would have had to give the orders, perceived that the participants in the processions of June 20—
precisely this particular combination of National Guardsmen and
their commanders, armed and unarmed men and women and children, their relatives, friends and neighbors—symbolized a new political and military force, a national family in arms, that could be vanquished only at unthinkable cost.

Furthermore, the conjunction of women's claims to the rights of
citizenship, especially the right to bear arms, with their incorpora-
tion into the marching revolutionary "nation" endorsed by radical
male leaders, ran radically counter to the Rousseauian model of the
woman citizen as a civic educator. Women had appropriated radical,
alternative discourses of rights and responsibilities as well as dramatically broadened agendas of political action.

After the fall of the monarchy on August 10, the new republican authorities moved quickly to regulate the women and men who had
helped bring them to victory, yet even those controls illustrated
recognition of women's full political and military engagement. The
General Assembly of one neighborhood government printed a decree
that all male citizens aged 15 and over and all female citizens over
the age of 13 had to take an individual oath before the section assembly. The wording of the oath was similar to one decreed by the
Legislative Assembly on August 14: "To uphold liberty and equality
and to die, if necessary, for both. . . ." The section assembly declared
that it would regard as "bad" citizens and *citoyennes* those who
would not swear it, and that it would refuse entry into its sessions to
anyone who had not fulfilled this "civic duty." These authorities recognized that the armed men and women who had just brought down
the monarchy could not be dissolved or repressed. The administrative requirement was to regulate them: "It is important to know who

---

[43] Jérôme Pétion, *Conduite tenue par M. le Maire de Paris à l'occasion des événements
du 20 juin 1792*, in "Journée du 20 juin 1792," *Revue Rétrospective, ou Bibliothèque historique*, 2nd series, vol. 1 (1835), pp. 233–234.

[44] *Extrait des Registres des délibérations du Conseil du Département de Paris*, 6 juillet
1792, Paris, 1792.

are the good citizens and *citoyennes* who want to bring about liberty and equality, and who are the cowards and traitors who still would dare to yearn for despotism.[45]

In the spring of 1793, a group of *citoyennes*, petit-bourgeois and sans-culotte women who wanted to "bring about liberty and equality," organized themselves into the first exclusively female interest group in Western politics, the Society of Revolutionary Republican Women. Pauline Léon, who had been involved in the violent events on the Champ de Mars in 1791, and Claire Lacombe, an actress from the French provinces, were among the organizers; Constance Évrard and Anne Félicité Colomb, whose radical political activities in 1791 we review above, were members. Initially the society met under the aegis of the Jacobin Club, which provided a meeting hall; it formed close ties with the Enragés, radical men active in neighborhood politics. Members of the society were instrumental in helping to evict the Girondins (a loosely organized "party" of liberal deputies) from the National Convention in late May 1793. Throughout the summer, they pressured the Convention to apply more extreme curbs on aristocrats and to pass decrees regulating supplies and prices in Paris and supporting revolutionary armies. They strongly supported the Constitution of 1793 decreed by the National Convention on June 24. In the summer of 1793, a group of women describing themselves as *citoyennes* of the Section Droits de l'Homme came to the society to present a martial standard. Their speech, honoring the society's members, explicitly stated that "the Declaration of Rights is common to both sexes. . ."[46] In late summer, the society's radicalism evoked protests from market women, who opposed price controls and who accused the society of ruining their commerce.

Despite heroic defensive maneuvers by Claire Lacombe and others, the Convention voted to close the society in October 1793 on the grounds that its members threatened public order. Jacobin leaders who presented and debated the proposed repression of the society and the more general question of women's place in the new republican regime also exposed serious tensions and fissures in republican ideology. André Amar, who spoke for the Committee of General Security before the Convention on October 28, began with specific com-

---

[45] *Extrait des Registres des délibérations de la Section du Pont Neuf, Réunie en Assemblée permanente, le 15 août 1792, l'an 4e de la liberté, le 1er de l'égalité.* Paris, n.d. See also F. Braesch, ed., *Procés-verbaux de l'Assemblée générale de la Section des Postes, 4 décembre 1790–5 septembre 1792,* Paris, 1911, pp. 198, 199, no. 2.

[46] Pauline Léon, Police Dossier, Archives nationales, F7 4774 9, translated in Levy, Applewhite, and Johnson, *op. cit.,* pp. 158–160.

plaints about market disorders near Saint-Eustache, which the Revolutionary Women allegedly incited, and reported the request of the Section des Marchés (a self-governing municipal unit) for a prohibition of popular societies of women. Amar then posed the general question: Should women exercise political rights and meddle in political affairs? His negative answer no longer addressed the specific issue of the society's responsibility for market disorders; rather, in his rationalization of the legislation, Amar cited women's reproductive responsibilities, their moral weakness, their inadequate political education, and their nervous excitability. He thus developed a full-blown misogynist theory of the biological, psychological, and moral determinants of women's incapacity for political action. In contrast, another deputy, [Charles] Charlier, identifying and separating out from one another principles of universal rights and matters of public security, argued that the police ought to be able to deal with disorder and that women should not be denied their right to assemble peaceably: "Unless you are going to question whether women are part of the human species, can you take away from them this right which is common to every thinking being?" The deputy [Claude] Bazire brought the debate to a close; he declared that he did not want to hear any more about principles; public order was endangered; that situation called for the absolute prohibition of women's associations.[47] Bazire was not endorsing Amar's argument; he was being pragmatic: every political system had the authority to suspend rights in times of dire emergency. These deputies were fully aware of the political implications of defining gender roles either narrowly or broadly; women's status and rights were one factor in the power equation in a city and nation that was caught up in the throes of revolution and war and where the locus of sovereign authority was being contested continually. Even as they outlawed the Revolutionary Republican Women and all women's clubs, the legislators exposed deep conflicts within the republican camp about whether the rights of man could be denied to women.

In the short run, the Jacobin leaders tried to eliminate women's institutional power bases by proscribing clubs and popular societies of women and barring them from sessions of the Paris Commune. These restrictions did not silence women's voices. Mixed-sex popular societies in the sections continued to provide channels for women's influence. Immediately after the repressive legislation of October 28, a

---

[47] *Réimpression de l'Ancien Moniteur,* National Convention, Session of 9 Brumaire, Vol. 18, pp. 298–300; translated in Levy, Applewhite, and Johnson, *op. cit.,* pp. 213–217.

deputation from the Fraternal Society of the Two Sexes of the Pan-théon-Français section, led by a woman, came before the section's General Assembly. Citizens protested the presence of women: ". . . a woman does not have the right to speak, to deliberate in assemblies, according to the law."[48] Again in February 1794, the Fraternal Society of the Section Panthéon-Français protested vehemently against accusations in the press that it was a hermaphrodite society that violated nature by offering men and women equal access and rights of participation. Two women officers of the fraternal society signed that protest.[49] A few days earlier, the society's Committee of Purification, composed of women and men, voted to exclude members who argued that women "ought not to have been admitted to deliberate on the affairs of a section or to purify its members"; in the short run, they prevailed, notwithstanding the protest of a woman in the section who argued that women should not be sitting on the Purification Committee, that they were voting illegally.[50]

Women of the popular classes were principal participants in the last great revolutionary uprising, the *journées* of Germinal-Prairial, Year III (1795). However, these insurrections were doomed to failure; by that time, women and men in the sections had lost the popular societies and assemblies that had functioned as the common people's organizational base of influence. In May 1795, the legislature ordered women to remain in their homes and decreed that groups of more than five women in public would be dispersed, forcibly if necessary.[51]

Conclusion

The Napoleonic Code, the French Code of laws completed in 1804, is sometimes offered as evidence that the overtures made by revolutionary women were brave but brief efforts that ultimately worsened conditions for women well into the nineteenth century. Under the

---

[48] Dominique Godineau, "Femmes en citoyenneté: pratiques et politique," *Annales Historiques de la Révolution française*, no. 2 (1995), p. 204.

[49] Robert Barrie Rose, "Symbols, Citizens or Sisterhood: Women and the Popular Movement in the French Revolution. The Beginning of a Tradition," *Australian Journal of Politics and History* 40 (1994), p. 308.

[50] Godineau, *op. cit.*, p. 204, citing from Archives nationales, W 191, 14 pluviôse; Archives, Préfecture de la police, AA 201, 121–139; B.N., MSS, nouvelles acquisitions françaises, 2713.

[51] Dominique Godineau, *Citoyennes Tricôteuses. Les Femmes de peuple à Paris pendant la Révolution française*, Alinea, Aix-en-Provence, 1988, pp. 319–355. This book has been translated as *The Women of Paris and Their French Revolution*, trans. Katherine Streip (Berkeley: University of California Press, 1998).

terms of the code, women could not sign contracts, buy or sell, or maintain bank accounts in their own names. Divorce legal since September 20, 1792, became more difficult. But if we look beyond legal restraints in the code, we recognize that links between women's revolutionary practices of citizenship and principles of universal rights have turned out to be indelible, as well as complex.

A handful of women writers reformulated definitions of citizenship to address women's gender-specific needs and interests in the language of the Declaration of Rights of 1789. Olympe de Gouges, playwright and publicist, drafted a *Declaration of the Rights of Woman.* It appeared just as the first constitution was being ratified in September 1791. Adopting the form and language of the Declaration of the Rights of Man, de Gouges called for full political equality for women, and in addition drafted articles that addressed women's gender-specific struggles to secure property and inheritance rights and to establish the right of the mother to legitimate her children regardless of her marital state. De Gouges had addressed her *Declaration* to Queen Marie Atoinette; she was arrested in 1793, accused of royalism, tried and found guilty by the Revolutionary Tribunal, and guillotined on November 3, 1793. The Dutch-born revolutionary writer Etta Palm d'Aelders addressed the issue of equal rights for women, focusing on marriage laws, educational opportunities, and admission to civil and military positions.[52] Ideas counted in making and legitimating the revolution. Women like De Gouges, d'Aelders, and Anne Félicité Colomb, in roles as journalists, pamphleteers, speechmakers, printers, petitioners, club members, and witnesses, contributed to the ideologies supporting the liberal tradition in France. We suggest that a commonsense logic informed these women's efforts to restate rights so that they addressed gender-specific interests: if women could recognize themselves in the nation, they could grant its government support and legitimacy.

Women and men involved in marching, petitioning, and other political activities that brought them into confrontation with authorities linked these practices to universals; they recast their acts as the nation's expression of its sovereign will and rights. The threat and use of force turned out to be particularly effective in forging links between practices and rights. On June 20, 1792, armed men, women, and children from the radical sections of Paris co-opted the National Guard and scored a symbolic victory over the legislature; on August

---

[52] Etta Palm d'Aelders, *Adresse des citoyennes françoises à l'Assemblée nationale* (n.d.[*Summer, 1791*]); *Archives parlementaires,* 41 (procès-verbal, April 1, 1792) pp. 63–64; both translated in Levy, Applewhite, and Johnson, *op. cit.,* pp. 75–77, 123.

10, they overthrew the constitutional monarchy. All these acts of force prevailed only because the duly constituted authorities in the end accepted these acts as legitimate exercises of the rights and powers of the sovereign nation as these were defined in the Declaration of the Rights of Man.

Links between women's political practices and rights debates were forged not only in Paris but throughout revolutionary France and well beyond its boundaries. Women who founded Jacobin women's clubs in the French departments developed political visions, broad agendas, and practices in the public sphere, including endorsements of the Constitution of 1793, protests against women's political nullity, and demands for the right to vote.[53] In the age of the democratic revolution, the "woman question" was placed squarely on the agenda not only throughout France but also in England, America, the Dutch Republic, Belgium, and elsewhere in the Western world—all revolutionary political cultures in which neighborhoods and communities became caught up in broad democratizing processes and cultural transformations that opened up possibilities for women to claim political identities in the polity, that is, the rights, responsibilities, and powers of citizenship.[54]

The theory of universal rights stands as one of the most vital positive legacies of the French Revolution in the modern world. Because women's ad hoc practices of citizenship were linked to rights issues, the precedent-setting power of these practices was not canceled out by the Jacobins' decrees outlawing women's organized political activities, or by legal restrictions written into the Napoleonic Code, or even by later nineteenth- and twentieth-century exclusionary legislation. Revolutionary women who took up arms, for example, grounded their action in universal claims: the right to self-defense, the right to assemble, the right to free expression, and the right to full political participation. Once such rights have been legislated for some and appropriated and enacted de facto by many, any issue that can be connected to rights is opened up to contestation and remains on the po-

---

[53] Suzanne Desan, "Constitutional Amazons': Jacobin Women's Clubs in the French Revolution," in *Recreating Authority in Revolutionary France*, ed. Bryant T. Ragan and Elizabeth A. Williams, Rutgers University Press, New Brunswick, 1992, ch. 1; Suzanne Desan, "The Family as Cultural Battleground: Religion vs. Republic under the Terror," in *The French Revolution and the Creation of Modern Political Culture*, Vol. 4: *The Terror*, ed. Keith Michael Baker, (Pergamon, Oxford, 1994), pp. 177–193.

[54] Harriet B. Applewhite and Darline G. Levy, eds., *Women and Politics in the Age of the Democratic Revolution*, University of Michigan Press, Ann Arbor, 1990; paperback, 1993.

litical agenda, notwithstanding the force of repressive laws and other sanctions. In fact, in societies in which rights traditions have been established, the burden of proof is on those who wish to exclude specific categories of persons from the enjoyment of rights.

However, along with these liberal principles (like Condorcet's belief that women enjoyed natural and political rights "common to every thinking and sentient being"), legacies of the Enlightenment and the Revolution relating to the woman question included persuasive and persistent formulations of women's biologically and culturally determined incapacity for assuming roles as equals in a world of power and conflict. Viewed critically and historically, rights talk itself, even as it reveals the commonalities of human identity, also masks particular or exclusive interests grounded in class, race, sex, ethnicity, religion, age, and national or national-imperial ideologies. Furthermore, rights claimants must state their claims from a base of historically specific, situated interests; women risk the obstruction of those interests when they invest uncritically in the language of universal rights. All historically situated interests—those of rights legislators and adjudicators and those of rights claimants—must be exposed and addressed if universal rights are to be made operable as guiding principles in actual political cultures—for example, to reshape the nature of political conflict or to maximize equality.

Inevitably, meanings of universal rights, such as the right to self-defense, will change with the changing circumstances of individuals and groups: for the revolutionary generation, women and men, the right of self-defense meant the right to use arms for the protection of person, family, and property; today, at the historical juncture at which we stand, the concept of self-defense might include principles of bodily integrity that enabled the United Nations to define rape as a war crime. It is this expansive nature of rights, that is, the way rights work to narrow exclusions to the vanishing point, to embrace, over time, a plenum of concrete positions, that constitutes their irreplaceable value as an ever receding, ever approachable horizon of women's aspirations as human beings.

In the age of the democratic revolution, women of all social and professional ranks took up positions on fields of power and principle; they demanded recognition as citizens; in the historical conjuncture, these demands necessarily reidentified them as subjects of universal rights. The conquest of a permanent place on those fields of power and principle may turn out to be, for them, the most critically important legacy of the French Revolution.

RURAL COUNTERREVOLUTIONARY WOMEN

Olwen H. Hufton

Olwen H. Hufton (1938–), the daughter of a textile engineer, received the B.A. and Ph.D. from the University of London and has taught at the University of Leicester, Reading University, Harvard University, the European University Institute in Florence, and, since 1997, Oxford University. She is an authority on eighteenth-century social history, especially the poor and women. Her publications include *Bayeux in the Late Eighteenth Century: A Social Study* (1967), *The Poor of Eighteenth-Century France, 1750–1789* (1974), *Europe, Privilege and Protest, 1730–1789* (1980), *Women and the Limits of Citizenship in the French Revolution* (1992), and *The Prospect Before Her; A History of Women in Western Europe, Volume 1, 1500–1800* (1995).

🎩🎩🎩🎩🎩🎩

The history of protest in Paris during the Revolution involves a mixture of the radical and the traditional. Political change was seen in 1789 to open up possibilities that could be used to further, on the one hand, the political aspirations of a de Gouges [for equal rights for women] and, on the other, those of the working masses. Outside the capital, particularly in rural areas, the traditional form of protest was employed to counter radical changes in community and family life imposed from outside.

In much of provincial France, commitment to the Revolution wavered after the heady days of 1789. Away from Paris, in producer France, there existed a large number of people who were first suspicious, and then positively hostile to change. The first to boycott the Revolutionary paper currency and to trigger inflation were peasant women at the markets who refused to hand over basic foodstuffs like

From Olwen Hufton, *The Prospect Before Her: A History of Women in Western Europe, Volume 1, 1500–1800* (London: HarperCollins, 1995), 1: 481–486, 562 note 42 to 563 note 48. Reprinted by permission of HarperCollins Publishers Ltd.

milk and vegetables for anything but coin. In the villages traditional religious practice could have a very firm hold; the replacement of the parish priest who refused to take the oath of loyalty to the government and the changes imposed on the church by the legislation of 1790–1 [the Civil Constitution of the Clergy] could engender resentment of the intrusion of the government in parish life. At this stage much depended on local commitment to their particular parish priest, which was far from universal. The slump in luxury industries, the deliberate destruction of the old agencies of poor relief in small towns and villages without organizing replacements, price fixing which was clearly opposed to the interests of producing France and also to those of towns which were not a priority in the government's provisioning schemes, and mobilization which demanded the young die for a Revolution to which they and their families were far from committed, created a huge pool of dissidence by late 1792.

In this dissidence, baptized by government officials "Counter-Revolution," distinct gender roles were to emerge. Young men were draft dodgers, older men held back on the payment of taxes and tried to evade the government's requisitioning schemes. Many village women from 1790 boycotted state priests and subsequently state cults and, if they were distant from prying town officials, organized clandestine masses. They gathered to say the rosary, that convenient expression of a fortress faith, taught the young to pray and kept their children away from state schools. Against change the counter-revolutionary woman of the villages erected tradition.

After 1795, when the hand of government was conspicuously weakened, Paris politicians were to be made aware of protests which were largely female engineered in many provinces, aimed at restoring patterns of regular Catholic worship destroyed during the Terror. These riots were both conservative and adopted traditional forms of female protest using stereotypical ploys. However, they manifested a deep contempt for the workings of Revolutionary officialdom and in many instances lent the tone to evolving village attitudes to the central government and its policies. The Directory was to learn that a regime which cannot command the respect of its women is in trouble.[1]

During the heady days of the Jacobin dictatorship (1793–4) there had been open scorn for what were interpreted as women's practices, which involved adherence to an old religion and its priesthood.

---

[1]Hufton, *Women and the Limits of Citizenship* (Toronto, 1992), 92–142 and "The Reconstruction of a Church 1796–1801" in G. Lewis and C. Lucas eds., *Beyond the Terror* (Cambridge, 1981), 21–53. S. Desan, *Reclaiming the Sacred: Lay Religion and Popular Politics in Revolutionary France* (Ithaca, 1991).

When dealing with women, officialdom used a vocabulary of dismissive derivatives—*femelles, femelettes, bigotes, bêtes, moutons, légumineuses, fanatiques* (females, little women, bigots, beasts, sheep, vegetables, fanatics).[2] Indeed, it could be argued that officialdom deliberately made a bid for the minds of men over the issue of religious change by converting the notion of Catholic practice into something only sustained by gullible women. Certainly, in support of this thesis, the Jacobins tolerated at the local level gatherings of women to say the rosary and tried, sometimes with tongue in cheek, to convert statues which had been the focal points of women's cults into patriotic symbols by the imposition of a Phrygian cap on their heads or other symbols of Republican commitment. In some cases they blatantly offended village women by a disrespect manifested both towards them, as women, and to their religion.

In the village of Saint Germain de Laval in the Mâconnais in 1795, local Jacobins took a classical nude from a local château and painted a tricolour on her. Having felled as a symbol of obsolete papistry the crucifix which had stood in the village square, they stood the statue in the vacant spot and proclaimed her the goddess of liberty. Days later it began to rain and as the paint started to wash off and to run down her legs, the young guard proclaimed the miracle of the menstruating goddess. The village women, outraged by the tasteless remarks, seized the statue, carried her several miles to the river, washed her and laid her on her side, a purification ceremony which restored her dignity as a female symbol. The next day they broke into the church and reclaimed it for Catholic worship.[3]

This is a striking response to mockery of female dignity and to change imposed in such a way as to slight the women of the community. The balance of shame and honour in the village was destroyed and action by the village women became imperative to restore it. Once restored, it might be hoped that normal or traditional values, in which they were accorded respect, would once again prevail.

Away from civic centres, which were under close scrutiny throughout the Jacobin period, priest sheltering was predominantly the activity of pious and mostly middle-class spinsters and the organization of the clandestine mass was frequently in their hands. After 1796, when the Directory had opened the prison doors and pronounced freedom of worship of all gods or goddesses, but without handing back the parish churches for Catholic worship or permitting

---

[2]Cited by Hufton, *Women and the Limits of Citizenship,* 98–9 and M. Vovelle, *La Révolution contre l'Eglise* (Paris, 1989), 221–6.

[3]Archives Départementales Rhône 42L61. Saint Germain de Laval.

mass to be said by any priest who would not take an oath of loyalty to the government, disturbances began on an extensive scale. Village women assumed the initiative by occupying churches and flouting legislation which prohibited exterior manifestations of public worship (mainly the use of bells). They wrested chalices and sacred vessels from unwilling authorities and rescued dissident priests from prison. On these occasions the menfolk stayed behind or gave subsidiary help. Often the riots, depending on the assessed strength of the opposition, were organized and women from other villages were called in. The ostensibly pregnant and the aged were placed in the forefront of attack and then came the older women as ash carriers and stone throwers, the traditional formation.[4]

Village women in fact soon perfected an effective range of oppositional techniques. The first strategy was a simple collective obstinacy in face of prohibitions. An individual flouting the law could easily be isolated and picked off, whereas the entire female population of a village could have much more effect. In this way officialdom could be forced to cede the keys of churches, for example. The second technique was ridicule of an explicitly sexist variety designed to undermine or embarrass pontificating authority when it sought to enforce state cults. The third was openly flouting an official recognized to have little support from guards in his commitment to government policies. The fourth was refusal to budge on issues where female cooperation was needed, as in the case of schooling or attendance at state cults. The fifth was maintaining the old faith through the rosary and teaching the next generation.

When they encountered opposition in the form of rioting, weary local officialdom, whatever the instructions received from Paris, might not put up much resistance. When admitting defeat, such officials might record a somewhat distorted version of events in order not to be accused of cowardice by their superiors who were anxious to maintain the rule of law. They would exaggerate the numbers of women involved from dozens to hundreds and describe an official's suffering as he was thrown to the ground and his clothes torn. Or they would express a reluctance to spill the blood of silly women with children and would describe matters as best resolved by yielding. By 1796 they also knew that if brought to court the women would be dismissed by royalist judges.

Victory was not, of course, inevitable. The rioting women were fre-

---

[4]M. de Roux, *Histoire de la Révolution à Poitiers et dans la Vienne* (Lyon, 1952), 251 and G. Lefebvre, *Les Paysans du Nord* (Bari, 1959), 874.

quently frustrated by a strategic shifting of imprisoned priests or the disappearance of confiscated chalices. We need to allow constantly for a small overworked force excusing its own inertia and desiring to preserve its face in the community. Nineteenth-century police forces were larger and better equipped, so they were able to be less tolerant of law breakers, whatever their sex. In traditional societies, police forces proceeded more cautiously and on the whole accepted, if reluctantly, that law enforcement reflected the possible not the desirable.

The ultimate aim of the women of the religious riots was the restoration of community solidarity as expressed in communal worship. The women wanted a warm, comforting, personal and familial religion with its own sociability patterns which endorsed the family in its collective celebration of births and marriages and gave the hope of salvation through Christian burial of the dead. This religion, over the centuries, had been structured to provide rites and ritualistic festivals to mark the weeks and the year. The state cults, with their emphasis on reason and liberty, were not only a religious travesty but an irrelevance to the peasant world. Liberty may have been a goddess to replace the old patriarchal God, but she offered nothing in the way of solace and succour. There is nothing rational about the vagaries of life and individual pain and a religion that did not hold out hope to the despairing through prayer and the possibility of change had little to attract them.

The first to seize back Sunday from the Republicans, and to turn their back on the Revolutionary calendar with its dechristianized ten-day week, were peasant women. The first to enter the parish church, even when prohibited by authority from doing so, were village women. Many of them were remarkably indifferent as to who should officiate over their renascent worship provided it was not a priest compromised by having accepted the Revolution. The women looked for non-jurors, those who had not taken an oath of loyalty to the government, and if they could not find such a person, they were content with the services of an educated villager who knew the liturgy and was familiar with the ceremonies, even if he could not, as a layman, administer communion. This circumvention of an officiating priest troubled both the non-juring clergy in exile and those priests who had sworn loyalty to the government and were only too willing to give their services.[5]

What the women wanted was a reversion to normality as they had

---

[5]Hufton, "The Reconstruction of a Church," 38–44.

known it and to the familiar rhythms of parish life. The Revolution had not shaken the bedrock of rural women's faith nor altered their perception of the intrinsic priorities of life, the family, the raising of children, the search for sufficiency, ways of doing. When republican politicians after the Napoleonic coup d'état sought to explain to themselves their failure to capture the minds of the rural masses, some picked out women as the reason for their failure. In particular, they saw the boycotting of state schools and of state religion, the placing of children with former clerics or members of the teaching congregations, as actions which ensured that republicanism was painted to the next generation as the work of the Devil. In this interpretation, the hand that rocked the cradle and guided the child controlled the acculturation process of males as well as females; but it was the moulding of the mind of the female which was the more dangerous because it perpetuated attitudes across generations.[6]

How much truth was there in this interpretation of the failure of the Revolution? The French historian Marcel Marion summarized the reasons for the failure in the following way: "general demoralization, contempt for human life as illustrated in the events of the Revolution, intense economic crisis, extreme poverty, unemployment and the loss of the habits of work, profound social divisions and the weakness of the forces of repression."[7] The return to the church was only one manifestation of contempt for government policy.

So why pick on this as the one cause by which to explain the demise of republicanism? First, the republicans were not prepared to blame themselves. It was an uncomfortable fact that republicanism in power had not worked: the economy had collapsed and the politicians had been able neither to reconcile their differences among themselves nor to control the situation. None of this could be admitted, so they fell back on a traditional scapegoat—woman: unruly, irrational and with the power to control the minds of ensuing generations. This monocausal view was particularly convenient because it kept science and rationality on the side of the Republican politicians and raised a familiar rhetorical spectre. Without ever naming her, the figure of Eve was resurrected to explain why man was kept out of earthly paradise. It was an old, old story, one told many times.

---

[6]The republican Portal spelt out this view in Archives Départementales Haute Loire L371. J. Michelet reiterates the theme in *The Women of the French Revolution* (English trans., Philadelphia, 1855) and T. Zeldin demonstrates its persistence in "The Conflict of Moralities, Confession, Sin and Pleasure in the 19th Century," in *Conflicts in French Society: Anticlericalism, Education and Morals in the Nineteenth Century* (London, 1970).
[7]M. Marion, *Le Brigandage pendant la Révolution* (Paris, 1934), opening chapter.

10
The Directory
(1795–1799)

AFTER the fall of Robespierre, the Convention continued to rule for another fifteen months. Then it was succeeded by the government known as the Directory, which placed power in the hands of a five-man executive and a bicameral legislature.

The dramatic events and personalities before and after the Directory have tended to minimize its attractiveness and reputation. This is clearly shown in the selection from Albert Vandal. In an effort to justify the work of Napoleon Bonaparte as First Consul, he finds it necessary to unleash considerable passion in condemning the preceding regime. Albert Goodwin and Denis Woronoff present a less one-sided view of the Directory. One of the first historians to advance a detailed defense of this regime, Goodwin sees the Directors as advocates of moderate republicanism. Their weaknesses and failures were, he thinks, largely attributable to the actions of misguided predecessors and to such contemporaries as Napoleon and Talleyrand. Moreover, the regime was on the way to solving many of its major problems and was a better government than the military dictatorship that followed. To Woronoff, the Directory was the creation of the republican bourgeoisie and deserves credit for some solid achievements, but fell victim to its own class biases and contradictions.

Who is closer to the truth? Perhaps one can only say that more facts are needed before reaching a conclusion. Or one can argue that all the facts are never in and that it is time to judge whether the Directory came close to any satisfactory standard of what constitutes good, or even acceptable, government. Or one may ask what the realistic alternatives to the Directory were and whether their triumph would have resulted in a better regime.

A SHAMELESS
REGIME

Albert Vandal

Count Albert Vandal (1853–1910), whose father directed the French Post Office during the rule of Napoleon III, trained for the law and then entered public service. But the teaching and writing of history attracted his interest; and he eventually became a professor at the Ecole libre des sciences politiques in Paris. This was one of the few institutions of higher education in the Third Republic that flourished under the aegis of neither the State nor the Church. His great book of diplomatic history, *Napoléon et Alexandre Ier* (1891–1896), was followed by his *Avènement de Bonaparte* (1902–1907), which extolled the beneficent work of Napoleon as First Consul.

🎩🎩🎩🎩🎩🎩

The old order had collapsed; the new order had not yet been established. On domestic matters the Directory had inherited all the faults of the Revolution. Beset by immense difficulties, it found a lasting solution for none. Its burden was heavy, but it was lamentably incapable of bearing it. It could neither restore nor establish anything. It gave to the French neither order nor liberty. . . .

In the spring of 1799, when the direct causes of Napoleon's coup d'état of 18 Brumaire appeared, the chief officials of the revolutionary group were the five Directors—Reubell, La Revellière-Lépeaux, Barras, Merlin, and Treilhard. The well-known corruption of this government has tended to overshadow the violent nature of its rule. After the purging of the great and upright Carnot and of Barthélemy—who had been expelled by their colleagues [in 1797]—the Directory appeared "unspeakably corrupt."[1] This was due to the

From Albert Vandal, *L'Avènement de Bonaparte,* 17th ed. (Paris: Plon, Nourrit, 1912), I, iv, 9–13, 16–18, 21–22, 26–28, 33–34, 70–73, 77. Editors' translation. Wherever possible, the author's citations of sources in footnotes have been clarified.

[1]Eric Magnus Staël-Holstein and Baron Brinkman, *Correspondance diplomatique du Baron de Staël-Holstein et de son successeur . . . le Baron Brinkman . . .* (Paris: Hachette, 1881), p. 369, Brinkman to Sparre.

squalid intrigues swarming around it and to the brazen peculation of its most notorious member [Barras]. Other Directors displayed the traits of dishonest servants rather than of outright robbers. Some did not lack ability. Merlin (of Douai), a remarkable jurist and a very clever prosecutor, excelled in making crime legal; his enemies declared that he was most suited to be "a minister of justice under Louis XI."[2] Treilhard might have rendered valuable service to another regime. La Revellière, completely honest, a visionary bigot, was as weak in mind as he was deformed in body; but the Alsatian Reubell, hard, greedy, cunning, a glutton for work, seems to have been the aggressive leader of the crew.

Although decked out in theatrical costume and provided with a military guard, the Directors usually displayed little extravagance; neither "their mistresses" nor "their carriages" excited comment.[3] They lived side by side in the Luxembourg Palace, which had been divided into five apartments for their use and decorated with carpets, tapestries, and gilt furniture taken from royal palaces. In these sumptuous surroundings, the Directors lived like bourgeois. Carnot's habits were simple; he invited friends familiarly "to take pot-luck; we sit down between four-thirty and five and never eat out."[4] Evenings, La Revellière and his daughter would go to the home of friends, the Thouïns, "to spend a couple of hours in their simple kitchen."[5] Reubell had a reputation for stinginess and a taste for sordid pilfering.[6] Merlin's wife was a frightfully common housewife, as Bonaparte said, a *Madame Angot*.[7] At first the Directors, by an annual deduction

---

[2]From a session of the Council of Five Hundred, 30 Prairial, year VII [June 18, 1799]. [Louix XI, King of France from 1461 to 1483, was noted for his deceitful methods in the pursuit of power.—Eds.]

[3]*Lettres de Charles de Constant,* p. 63.

[4]Letter to Le Coz, quoted in Alfred Roussel, *Un Évêque assermenté (1790–1802); Le Coz: Évêque d'Ille-et-Vilaine* (Paris: Lethielleux, 1888), p. 259.

[5]Louis-Marie de La Revellière-Lépeaux, *Mémoires* (Paris: Plon, Nourrit, 1895), II, 411.

[6]When Reubell retired from the Directory and when the press became free again, the newspapers wrote: "The former Director Reubell, on leaving office, took everything with him—furniture, effects, china belonging to the nation, including a service worth 12,000 francs." The following correction was later inserted: "Citizen Reubell has had those things returned which had been removed from the Luxembourg Palace upon his departure, things which did not belong to him, and of which he had only the temporary use. We are assured, furthermore, that the removal came about neither by his doing nor his orders, but by the action of his sons and the orders of his wife and his sister-in-law." See especially the *Gazette de France,* 5 and 6 Messidor, year VII [June 23 and 24, 1799].

[7]Gaspard Gourgaud, *Journal inédit, de 1815 à 1818* (Paris: Flammarion, 1899), I, 468. [A Madame Angot is a lower-class woman suddenly enriched who retains the coarse

from their salaries, set up a fund to be given to the one who had to retire from office each year—the "kitty" of the Directory. Later, they worked out less legal methods so as not to leave office with empty hands. They also claimed the right to take with them the bourgeois carriages provided for their official use and which would have been too painful to relinquish.

Only Barras showed himself to be ostentatious and magnificent; he was the peacock of the Directory. With flair, he wore the outfit designed by [the painter] David—a full red cloak with a lace collar, a Roman sword, and a hat overladen with plumes. When not at an official function, he usually wore a large blue frock coat and boots.[8] With his chest thrown out and his shoulders back, he resembled, as Bonaparte put it, a "handsome fencing master."[9] His voice was strong and well modulated; in the tumult of the Convention it had rung out like a bell.

He knew how to entertain and to put on a good show. When he threw open his rooms at the Luxembourg Palace the rather mixed company that gathered, moving among "the large armchairs of red velvet trimmed in gold,"[10] were surprised by the series of brilliantly lit gilt rooms. Once again they were happy to encounter luxury, as well as women dressed in filmy elegance and displaying delicate flesh. They believed themselves transported to an Olympus where Mme. Tallien[11] and her rivals played the roles of goddesses in suitable costumes. Barras also entertained in his château of Grosbois, his country house in Suresnes [near Paris]. When he went there in his carriage drawn by cream-colored horses[12] with silver-inlaid harnesses, Parisians remarked that he must have stolen a lot to be able to show off in such splendor. His usual circle included big financiers and speculators, promoters of all types, parasites, questionable people, well-born women with bad reputations, and nobles brought low by the Revolution. He strutted about amidst this corruption and deluded himself that this demi-monde was really high society. He was corrupt to the very core, rotten with vice, unbridled and consummate in his

---

traits of her previous condition. From a comic opera by Ève popular during this period.—Eds.]

[8] Victorine de Chastenay, *Mémoires* (Paris: Plon, Nourrit, 1896–1897), I, 359.

[9] Gourgaud, I, 468.

[10] Chastenay, I, 360.

[11] [The leader of a social set during the Directory noted for its rejection of the prudishness of the earlier years of the revolutionary period.—Eds.]

[12] Edmond and Jules de Goncourt, *Histoire de la société française pendant le Directoire* (Paris: Charpentier [1880]), p. 300.

pleasures, a connoisseur of wine, women, and elegance. All the perfumed profits and the pleasures of power he kept for himself.

A rather easygoing temperament, a taste for munificence, some flexibility of mind, and a rather remarkable political flair distinguished him from his narrowminded colleagues. But whenever his interests and his pleasures were disturbed, he became capable of anything. Ordinarily lazy and sluggish, he regained his native energy for the occasional violent acts which had made him the supporter and the strong man of that faction in the Councils composed of former deputies of the Convention. The shady game of intrigues pleased him even more. Fundamentally treacherous, selling himself to each and deceiving all, a man who enjoyed lying, he had the soul of a whore in the body of a handsome man. La Revellière considered him "ill-bred,"[13] because one could surely see in him the speech and manner of a man who had always lived among bad company. Nevertheless, he retained a certain air, a certain demeanor, that he owed to his origin. No matter how deeply degraded he was, he never departed from "some of the manners customary among men of quality."[14] He gladly played the part of a soldier—it pleased him to be called *citizen general.* Posing as being on extremely friendly terms with the other Directors and eagerly using the intimate form of address with them, he really scorned their pettiness. This déclassé, this gentleman from the Midi [southern France] who had gone bad, disdained the upstarts that the accidents of annual elections gave him as colleagues.

The distinctive feature of all these men was their moral baseness. In them, there was no elevated conception of their duties and rights, no generosity of heart or mind, no willingness to pacify or rally the nation, no compassion for an unhappy France which was enduring so many evils. They governed meanly, stupidly, crudely. Their policy consisted in slashing out sometimes at the Right, sometimes at the Left, and retaining power by these alternate blows. This was the famous seesaw system, which humbled one party only to raise the other. . . .

How did France live under this shameless regime? All the wounds made by the Revolution continued to bleed, and the violent actions of the Directory reopened those that had begun to heal. A France, no longer revolutionary, remained revolutionized, that is, in a state of complete subversion from which a great many evils followed. All of them can be attributed to certain general causes of suffering that

---

[13] La Revellière-Lépeaux, I, 337.

[14] MS Document by Cambacérès. The present Comte de Cambacérès has been so kind as to allow us to consult this valuable document.

were constant and endemic and that oppressed the various regions of France more or less severely.

First, there was the physical disorder. Actually, at the beginning of 1799, some months before the obscure beginnings of the Consulate, large-scale seditious movements were not evident. There had hardly been a time during the Revolution when the government had been held in such contempt and the whole of the country been so manageable. But it was apathy rather than calm, apathy still troubled by thousands of fears, unceasingly assailed by the vexations caused by those in power and by the violence of extremist groups. Although the Directory posed as a government defending the social order and the middle of the road, it could not stop the guerrillas, men of blood and pillage, from oppressing many areas and terrorizing their inhabitants. As late as 1798 there were cruelties in Tours reminiscent of the Terror.[15] And even when the left-wing anarchists, the sans-culottes or *bonnets rouges,* seemed for the moment under control, their presence could still be felt, and people trembled at the thought of a repeat attack. In the bowels of a great many cities and small towns, groups of malevolent men, human slime, secretly plotted a thoroughgoing revolution, a universal abolition of order, babouvism[16] in action. Panic-stricken landlords told each other that sooner or later the agrarian law [splitting up large rural holdings] would come.[17]

At the other extreme swarmed right-wing anarchists, genuine, active anarchists. For the moment, the royalists had given up large-scale armed uprisings, real insurrections. Civil war was splintered into individual actions. Its current form was political brigandage. If Jacobinism was one career for scoundrels and desperate men, highway robbery by royalists was another. . . .

Although this kind of rural terrorism was more or less the common fate of all France, political brigandage centered in certain areas. In the West, *Chouannerie* spread again through nine or ten departments. This large ulcer kept all the surrounding areas irritated and feverish. If we cut obliquely across central France to its southeastern limits, the Bouches-du-Rhône, Vaucluse, Var, and Basses-Alpes departments, we find another *Chouannerie,* that of Provence, a *Chouan-*

---

[15] Jean-Nicolas Dufort, Comte de Cheverny, *Mémoires sur les règnes de Louis XV et Louis XVI et sur la Révolution* (Paris: Plon, Nourrit, 1886), II, 376.

[16] [A reference to the radical revolutionary Babeuf, a proponent of economic equality who was guillotined in 1797.—Eds.]

[17] Dufort, II, 365. Dufort de Cheverny lived in Blésois. His *Memoirs* are valuable. Written by a man free of strong passions, they are almost a day-by-day history of the Revolution in an average department.

nerie whose history has still to be written. Along the entire lower and middle valley of the Rhône River, there were scattered acts of vengeance—Nemesis unchained hovered over this whole murderous region. The Pyrenees region remained in continuous ferment. Along the Cévennes mountains there were remnants of the royalist bands which had made religious war on the Convention and Directory. In most of the other departments brigandage occurred sporadically, appearing as scattered crimes. Even in the vicinity of the capital no road was entirely safe. More than a year after the establishment of the Consulate, a stagecoach was held up at Charenton [a suburb southeast of Paris].[18] Any place that was suitable for ambushes experienced a marked increase in insecurity; it seemed as though the Revolution had spread the Forest of Bondy [a legendary haunt of robbers] everywhere.

Aside from the West, the Midi, and some regions in central France, brigandage almost lost its aspect of counterrevolutionary guerrilla warfare to become simple forays by deserters, vagrants, or *chauffeurs* [robbers who would burn their victims' feet until they revealed where their money was hidden]. Nevertheless, these ruffians tried to give themselves a political coloration by destroying republican symbols and by preferring to attack government officials and buyers of land confiscated from the Church or émigrés. Even in Paris and its suburbs, some royalist commandos, precursors of Cadoudal and his companions, dreamed of abducting or assassinating the Directors.[19] No beneficiary of the Revolution felt completely secure from attack by these armed and vagrant bands.

Against this persistent disorder, from wherever it came, the public authorities were able to do little or nothing. Although innumerable communes were in a state of siege, their means of defense were often lacking; for the continuation of the war kept the largest part of the army out of the country. The rural constabulary was poorly organized and infected by the presence in its ranks of formerly active Jacobins. The units of the National Guard—from which were recruited the flying columns assigned to chase bands of thieves and to organize roundups—were weak and disheartened. The ever changing, unstable civil authorities nowhere constituted a meaningful protective force. . . .

---

[18] MS Papers of General Mortier, Commander of the Seventeenth Division. Archives of Trévise. The Duc de Trévise kindly allowed us to consult these papers.

[19] See the documents cited by André Lebon, *L'Angleterre et l'émigration française de 1794 à 1801* (Paris: Plon, 1882), pp. 265–269. [Cadoudal was a Vendean leader who, in 1803–1804, plotted to assassinate Napoleon.—Eds.]

Wherever government action played a part, the harshest and most thoroughgoing tryanny was added to revolutionary disorder. Whoever was not in armed revolt against the law or did not evade it by subterfuge had to endure its cruelty. Although the revolutionaries during their last years in power spurned the Jacobin label and had not reopened that famous club, they still remained infected by the Jacobin spirit—the urge to persecute. Liberty existed for the Jacobins alone; they denied it to others, while ordering everyone to worship it on his knees; they had made the word divine but forbade the real thing. This is why the French welcomed Bonaparte as a deliverer and so easily exchanged the oppression of wretched despots for a lofty and impartial tyranny.

Among the accepted legends about 18 Brumaire, none is more erroneous than the supposition that it brought the death of liberty. For a long time it was a historical commonplace to represent Bonaparte in the Council of the Five Hundred at Saint-Cloud[20] destroying a genuine legality with one stroke of his sword and drowning out with his drum rolls the last gasps of French liberty. Such solemn nonsense can no longer be repeated in the face of some clearly recognized and understood facts. Bonaparte can be reproached for not having established liberty; he cannot be accused of having destroyed it, for the excellent reason that on his return from Egypt he did not find it anywhere in France. Bonaparte could not suppress something that did not exist.

In the early days of the Directory, amid violent reactionary movements, tension had started to relax and a few liberties were recognized. The death of liberty, however, came not on 18 Brumaire but on 18 Fructidor [September 4, 1797], when the revolutionaries ruthlessly seized dictatorial power again to stop a resurgence of royalism. After this coup d'état against the nation [the people], almost all the liberties constitutionally guaranteed to the French were forcibly snatched away or treacherously withdrawn.

The primary right of a free people is to elect representatives and through them control the management of public affairs. All persons authorized by the constitution to exercise the rights of citizenship should cooperate in this delegation of sovereignty. In the Fructidorian Directory, according to a series of special laws, a whole category of Frenchmen—relatives of émigrés as well as ex-nobles who had not given formal pledges of loyalty to the Revolution—were excluded from the right to vote and to hold office. In addition, the legislature,

---

[20] [The château near Paris where the last act of the coup d'état took place.—Eds.]

twice purged—in Fructidor [September 1797] and in Floréal [May 1798]—did not at all represent a true image of the electorate, which already had been arbitrarily reduced in number. The representation was in essence corrupt and fictitious, a mockery.

Public platforms were available only to those revolutionaries furnished with the government's stamp of approval. The press was servile. After the coup of Fructidor a decree of deportation had been issued against the owners and editors of thirty-five opposition newspapers, a radical method of destroying them. Thereafter, a law of the year V [September 5, 1797], which was renewed in the year VI, submitted all newspapers to supervision by the police, who suppressed them at their pleasure and at their discretion. Public opinion no longer had a channel of expression. Freedom of association and assembly appeared only in the text of the constitution. At any moment arrests arbitrarily carried out and arbitrarily upheld could outrage individual liberty.

Religious liberty existed only in words. After the Terror and the great sacrilegious madness of 1793, the Convention returned to fundamentals and proclaimed religious freedom. The law of 3 Ventôse, year III [February 21, 1795], declared, "The exercise of any religious cult shall not be disturbed, and the Republic will not subsidize any of them." In this way the separation of Church and State replaced the celebrated Civil Constitution of the Clergy, and the Schismatic [Constitutional] Church lost its privileged position. The law declared all cults free of control and placed them on an equal footing before the State. In fact this theoretical freedom was reduced by the Convention to a minimum by the way in which it was regulated. Toward the Christian cults the State called itself neutral and remained hostile.[21] . . .

Sometimes the revolutionaries had to accept strange anomalies. In this France dotted with monasteries falling into ruin and desecrated cloisters, some female religious orders were still permitted to continue—those devoted to helping the poor and caring for the sick. Nothing else could be done, for there was no one to replace them. At the famous Hospital of Beaune in Burgundy, the sisters doffed their four-century-old garb, but managed to keep the hospital a Catholic stronghold. In a rather large number of communes and even right in the middle of Paris—at the Hôtel-Dieu [a large city hos-

---

[21] While speaking of the revolutionaries of the year III, Antonin Debidour was quite right to say: "In general they saw that the separation of Church and State, recently put into effect, was simply a means of destroying the Church." *Histoire des rapports de l'Église et de l'État en France de 1789 à 1870* (Paris: Alcan, 1898), p. 158.

pital]—the sisters, dressed as nurses, furtively continued to serve humanity.[22]

Elsewhere the antireligious mania exceeded all limits, reaching the height of absurdity and ridiculousness. The executive order of 14 Germinal, year IV [April 3, 1796], forbade the selling of fish on what formerly had been called Friday; war was declared on fasting; fish was prohibited as Catholic contraband—to the great distress of our fisheries; in Paris, the oratory was closed in the former Carmelite chapel because the feast of Epiphany had been celebrated there;[23] in Strasbourg a merchant was fined for displaying in his shop more fish than usual on a fast day; and 350 truck gardeners were prosecuted for hallowing Sunday by not bringing their vegetables to market on that day.[24] Such severe measures continued until after Brumaire with local officials acting as the clumsy instruments of the rationalist tyranny. O Reason, what stupidities are committed in thy name! . . .

The Fructidorian Directory kept itself in power by war and victory; it succumbed in a crisis brought on by defeat and aggravated by domestic scandal. After the death of General Hoche and Bonaparte's departure for Egypt, the Directory continued the policy of conquest, or rather of plunder—occupying territories for their money, holding governments for ransom, pillaging the people, making France an object of execration. Rome was invaded. Switzerland was literally sacked. After General Championnet conquered Naples, the Austrians, who had considered the peace of Campo-Formio only a truce, reopened hostilities; the Congress of Rastadt had its bloody epilogue;[25] all of Germany except Prussia seemed ready to fight once more; England supplied ships and subsidies; and finally a Russian army came down from the North. The Second Coalition was formed. Aided everywhere by insurrections, it threatened our conquests and soon our frontiers. Against us was this second kings' war and the first peoples' war.

The Directory ran dreadfully short of money. It had been unable to solve the problems arising from an unprecedented monetary crisis and from the ruin of public finance. No one questioned that there was a deficit, the only issue was its size. The executive listed the figure at 67 million francs, but the Councils tended to reduce the estimate so

---

[22] See especially Léon Lallemand, *La Révolution et les pauvres* (Paris: Picard, 1898), pp. 137–146.

[23] Ludovic Sciout, *Le Directoire* (Paris: Didot, 1895–1897), III, 176.

[24] The documents are cited *ibid.*, III, 390.

[25] [Two of the three French delegates to the Congress, when returning to France in 1799, were murdered by Austrian soldiers.—Eds.]

as to avoid voting new taxes.[26] When the ministers and department heads were questioned, it appeared that the abyss was bottomless. All expedients, all subterfuges, had been tried in turn. Abroad, the conquered territories yielded no more money. At home the taxpayers refused to pay any levies; and the government felt itself unable to force them, since it had not succeeded in establishing a regular method of collection. It fell more and more into the hands of a tremendous gang of exploiters, for whom it was less an accomplice than a victim.

A swarm of suppliers and contractors relentlessly set upon the Republic. Summoned to provide for the needs of the various departments and especially the War Ministry, they turned the regime into an object of cynical speculation. Having to deal with a government that paid irregularly and with light-fingered public employees, they thought only of insuring for themselves excessive guarantees and illegal profits. They billed the state for the graft given to its employees, forced ruinous contracts on it, drained off the little cash that remained in the Treasury's coffers, and delivered only worthless materials.[27] This was the era of gigantic plundering and vile swindles, of massive influence peddling, and of illegal commissions and rebates to lower officials. The era of all kinds of dishonor, the age of mud after the age of blood. This nearly universal plundering found its way into the mainspring of state power an submerged it in a heap of mire; but when the spring had to be used against foreigners, everything had become decayed and rotten.

Our soldiers were without provisions, without shoes, "without

---

[26] According to the recent and learned work of René Stourm, *Les Finances du Consulat* (Paris: Guillaumin, 1902), pp. 270–271, the deficit was 300 million *at the very least.*

[27] A report written after Brumaire by a former minister, General de Beurnonville, gives an idea of the way things were done in the Department of War. "It is, I believe, mathematically provable that the government overpays by more than 50 per cent for all supplies that it receives. . . . Just imagine the path a supplier has to travel. Without the minister's knowledge, he pays an enormous bribe when his contract is signed. Often his contacts take, more or less, 5 or 10 per cent of the profits. In order to put the agreement into effect, the contractor hires his own minions who get rid of the former subcontractors and who, knowing full well that the job is temporary, think only of making a killing. In return for a share of the take, their supervisors become their accomplices. Step by step, all this mounting individual greed raises the costs by fake accounting until they after often double, or more, the value of the actual goods supplied. The State thus finds itself in debt for what it has not received; and it is only by such a system that the contractor is paid back for the sacrifices that he has made to get the contract, for the losses that he has suffered by the manner in which he is paid, and for the delays in the final payment settling the account." Archives of the Ministry of War, MS Correspondance générale, 1799.

pots, kettles, and mess-tins,"[28] without linen for the wounded, and without medicine for the sick. And they had to fight enemies much more redoubtable than those of 1792 and 1793: in Germany Archduke Charles and in Italy the strange Russian general Suvarov, a man who joined to the extravagances of an eccentric the talents of a great leader and the soul of a crusader. With us, politics often determined the assignment of generals. What is more, the excessive length of our line of operations—stretching from Texel [an island north of Amsterdam] to Naples—offered the enemy openings for attack. Together, these causes led to a series of disasters in Germinal, Floréal, and Prairial of the year VII (March to June 1799): Jourdan defeated at Stokach in southern Baden and forced back to the Rhine; Schérer and Moreau defeated in Italy; Lombardy lost; the Cisalpine Republic swept away; Piedmont entered by Suvarov; Naples evacuated; the overthrow of all the governments established by France in Italy. Within France, agitation in the West became more serious; and in the Midi a campaign of brigandage and assassination continued. In the light of these disastrous events, the inability of the Directory stood clearly revealed. The errors and shamefulness of this dictatorship by incompetents appeared in sharp relief. An outcry of disgust and criticism arose in the army. In Paris the muzzled press could say nothing, and the political agitation of the parties continued to operate on a level above the general apathy. Nevertheless, without the Directory noticing the formation of an organized, vocal, and open opposition, the regime collapsed by itself under the weight of its own misdeeds. . . .

In the minds of its civilian authors, the coup d'état of 1799 was to take place for precisely the same reason as had those of 18 Fructidor and 22 Floréal. It was inspired by a passionate desire for political survival. Differing from other coups carried out by men who had nothing to lose and everything to gain, this one was the act of those who had a terrible fear of losing everything. To this motive was added, among some, the honorable desire to purify and regenerate the Republic, to start it at last on a normal course. They wanted to create a true constitutional order in place of the one that Fructidor and Floréal had virtually abolished and they wanted to insure, by a final illegal step, the reign of law.

---

[28] *Le Publiciste,* 6 Thermidor, year VIII [July 25, 1800].

THE LEGEND COMBATED

Albert Goodwin

For biographical information on Albert Goodwin, see
Chapter 4, "Who Was Responsible for the War of 1792?"

🎩🎩🎩🎩🎩🎩

The French Executive Directory which assumed office on 11 Brumaire year IV (2 November 1795), and was destroyed by Bonaparte's
coup d'état of 18 Brumaire year VIII (9 November 1799), has been traditionally regarded by historians as a byword for corruption, governmental incompetence and political instability.[1] Its rule is usually
associated with the financial bankruptcy of 1797, defeats of French
armies in the field, administrative chaos at home and the Directors'
policy of self-perpetuation in office by means of a series of "purifica-
tions" of the elected Assemblies. In 1799 the Directory is supposed to
have been ripe for dissolution and France ready for Bonaparte. It is
the purpose of this paper to suggest that such an interpretation does
not do full justice to the governmental record of the Directory between 1795 and 1799, and that it represents an over-simplification of
the situation in France on the eve of 18 Brumaire.

It is not difficult to see why, in the past, the Directors have been so
harshly treated. The assumption that the Directors were themselves
not exempt from the vices of corruption and immorality characteristic of French society at that date was perhaps unavoidable, especially as the Directory came to be identified in the popular mind with
Barras. This impression of Barras as representative of the general
standards of the Directory, although entirely erroneous, was to some

From Albert Goodwin, "The French Executive Directory—A Revaluation," *History*, n.s.,
22 (December 1937), 201–218. The entire article is reprinted by permission of the author and the editor of *History*. Quotations originally in French have been translated by
the editors.
[1]The chapter on "Brumaire" by H. A. L. Fisher in the *Cambridge Modern History*, VIII
(1904), 665–88, in the main, follows rather closely the opinions of Vandal, but also ex-
presses views which do not altogether accord with them, so that the total effect does
not seem altogether consistent.

extent intelligible. Of the thirteen individuals who at various times held office as Directors, Barras alone succeeded in retaining his position throughout, and he was undoubtedly the most colourful personality of them all. The danger of generalising from the single case of Barras is, however, obvious. Another reason why injustice has been done to the Directory is that French history between 1795 and 1799 has tended to be studied by historians, very largely for the sake of convenience, as a period of *coups d'état.*[2] This approach has had two unfortunate results. On the one hand, it has gained general acceptance for the impression that the age was one of perpetual crisis, thus distracting attention from the more solid achievements of the Directory, and, on the other, it has led to the supposition that it was this series of illegal expedients alone which ensured their survival. It is true that an informed interpretation of the *coups d'état* is essential for the understanding of the period, but due attention should be paid to other factors. Lastly, the reputation of the Directors may have suffered because it has been blackened by the apologists of Robespierre and the admirers of Bonaparte. Between Mathiez,[3] who spent a lifetime in defending the Jacobin leader, and Madelin,[4] equally intent on eulogising Bonaparte, the directors have come in for a good deal of unmerited abuse. Few French historical scholars have been able to free themselves from partisanship in their accounts of the revolution, and the way in which the work of the Directory has been consistently underrated as a means of heightening the contrasts with the immediately preceding or following period is a good illustration of the evils implicit in such zeal. In this way a popular failure to distinguish between Barras and the other Directors, an inadequate historical approach and unconcealed historical bias have combined to enhance the evil repute and minimise the achievements of the Directorate. Recently, however, the researches of French scholars, by making possible a juster appreciation of the record of the Directory, have demonstrated the necessity of re-examining the unfavourable judgments which have often been passed on its rule.

Shortly stated, the usual indictment may be said to be based on

---

[2]Recent examples of this treatment are A. Meynier, *Les coup d'état du Directoire,* 3 vols., and C. Brinton, *A Decade of Revolution 1789–1799,* chap. IX. Brinton, however, takes a much more favourable view of the Directory than most writers. See also Sorel, *L'Europe et la Révolution française,* vol. v, p. 11.

[3]At the time of his death in February 1932 Mathiez was engaged on a detailed study of the Directory the first volume of which, covering the period down to 18 Fructidor, was published in 1934.

[4]See particularly *La France du Directoire; La France de l'Empire; Le Consulat et l'Empire* and *Napoléon.*

four main charges—that the personnel of the Directory was both corrupt and incapable; that its administration of the finances brought the country within measurable distance of ruin; that its foreign policy involved an indefinite postponement of the prospects of a general peace; and, finally, that the government could not even fulfil the first condition of effective rule by securing public order and individual freedom at home. What modifications must be made in these charges in the light of the fuller evidence which is now available?

On the score of venality there is ample authority for the view that the Directors themselves were, with perhaps a single exception, reasonably honest. The corruption of Barras was, of course, notorious and remains indefensible.[5] The evidence against the rest, however, is slight. Certain passages in Thibaudeau's *Memoirs* suggest that Reubell, who for some time virtually controlled Directorial finance, deserved censure,[6] and some suspicion was apparently directed against Merlin de Douai and La Revellière. It is true that Reubell's reputation for financial integrity was not unblemished, since he had suffered disgrace for peculation under the Terror,[7] and he was well known to be avaricious. On the other hand, there is no real evidence against him of corruption while a Director, and it should also be remembered that the Commissions of Inquiry specially appointed by the Councils to investigate his guilt in August 1799 completely exonerated him as well as Merlin and La Revellière.[8] When he retired from the Directory by lot on 16 May 1799, Reubell felt compelled to accept the allowance given by his colleagues as compensation,[9] and he died poor. The rest of the Directors seem never to have been the objects of contemporary criticism on the ground of their dishonesty.

How far is it true to say that the Directors were individually men without ability? For the present purpose it is only necessary to consider the members of the original Directory and three others—François de Neufchâteau, Merlin de Douai and Treilhard. Sieyès may properly be excepted, as his efforts, after he became a Director, were concentrated on the destruction of the constitution of the year III. The others may be disregarded because of the shortness of their period of office—Barthélemy was in power three and a half months, Go-

---

[5]Gohier, President of the Directory on 18 Brumaire, was anxious to rid the government of Barras and thus to make its moral standing unassailable. A. Vandal, *L'Avènenent de Bonaparte,* vol. I, p. 323.

[6]Thibaudeau, *Mémoires,* vol. II, p. 37.

[7]A. Mathiez, *Le Directoire,* p. 44.

[8]Lefebvre, Guyot, Sagnac, *La Révolution française,* p. 457.

[9]Meynier, *Les coups d'état du Directoire,* vol. II, pp. 168–9.

hier less than six months, Ducos and Moulin four and a half months. The usual opinion of the original Directory—"les Pentarques"—is that they were a group of mediocrities. If only the highest standards are applied, such a judgment would not be unfair. But if the ordinary criteria of capacity are accepted, then the Directors must be credited with more than average ability. Mature they were bound to be since article 134 of the constitution insisted that they should be at least forty years of age, and although the manner of their nomination left something to be desired,[10] they were all men of wide experience, most of them with special aptitudes and qualifications for the conduct of the departments of government they controlled. The least remarkable from the point of view of sheer ability were Le Tourneur and Barras. Le Tourneur was entirely devoid of political gifts, and in all matters of policy he followed without question the lead of his school-friend Carnot. He did, however, possess a good knowledge of the technical side of naval affairs. The Directory needed a naval expert, and Le Tourneur admirably filled the gap. Similarly, it would be hard to think of any revolutionary leader, apart from Fouché, better fitted to organise the police than Barras, whose whole life had been spent in intrigue. Nor is it accurate to regard Barras as a political cipher. Especially when resolute action was needed, Barras could be counted on, as he had already shown on 9 Thermidor and 13 Vendémiaire.[11] That he had an eye for talent as well as for beauty is proved by those whose careers he helped to make—Bonaparte and Talleyrand, Saint-Simon and Ouvrard. Luck alone cannot account for his survival till 18 Brumaire.

La Revellière was in many ways a curious mixture, half crank, half fanatic, a botanist, student of Rousseau, high priest of the new revolutionary cult of Theophilanthropy and a believer in the *juste milieu* in politics. A sincere republican, he was consumed with a hatred of priests and aristocrats, and yet he had small liking for the rural or urban proletariat. In foreign policy he was an advocate of the war of propaganda and conquest—an attitude which he had consistently maintained ever since the day he had been the prime mover of the

---

[10] They were the nominees of the former members of the Convention, two-thirds of whom had been re-elected to the new Councils. The procedure for their nomination was that the Council of Five Hundred submitted a list of fifty candidates for whom the Council of Ancients made the final choice. The list drawn up by the Five Hundred consisted of forty-five complete nonentities and the five persons whom they wished to be elected. This manœuvre was completely successful in forcing a group of "hand-picked" Directors on the Ancients. Mathiez, *Le Directoire,* p. 36.

[11] [On both occasions, Barras had organized troops to defend the Convention against armed popular demonstrations.—Eds.]

decree of 19 November 1792 by which the Convention had promised its aid and protection to all nations who wished to recover their liberty. His special sphere in Directorial policy was education, the *fêtes nationales* [patriotic festivals] and manufactures.

Carnot has been aptly described by Mathiez as "almost entirely a man of learning and a patriot." A former member of the Committee of Public Safety, and famous as the "Organiser of Victory," he had been nominated, in place of Sieyès, who had refused to serve as Director, in order to stem the run of French reverses on the Rhine. Carnot was a paragon of executive efficiency, and had real genius in the administration of war. He proved a failure as a Director, and for obvious reasons. He had a biting tongue and alienated his colleagues by his cynicisms. He was a convinced pacifist at a time when both Reubell and La Revellière, for different reasons, were keen supporters of foreign war. He disappointed the expectations of his Jacobin friends by evolving in the direction of the Right.[12] Lastly, although he had little or no talent for politics, he was never satisfied to confine himself to his departmental duties. Still, he can hardly be described as a mediocrity.

There is general agreement that Reubell was a man of great ability.[13] An Alsatian barrister of eminence, he had a good command of modern languages and an encyclopaedic knowledge. He owed his ascendancy over his colleagues to his industry and his strength of will. Utterly devoid of scruple and severely practical, he may be described as the main driving force behind Directorial policy. At one time he maintained a close supervision over the three most important departments of government—justice, finance and foreign affairs. Subsequently, however, he was content to delegate responsibility to ministers of proved capacity, such as Merlin and Ramel, and concentrated his own attention on the conduct of diplomatic affairs. In his sphere he identified himself with the policy of conquest and expansion which he hoped would culminate in the acquisition of the natural frontiers. As Reubell was only eliminated from the Directory by lot in May 1799, his influence upon policy was exerted throughout, and gave it a much-needed continuity.

Of François de Neufchâteau, Merlin and Treilhard, it is only necessary to say that the former was a distinguished administrator whose work as Minister of the Interior conferred lasting benefits on the

---

[12] He took an active part in the suppression of the conspiracy of Babeuf and the Jacobin plot of the year IV [September 1796] at the camp of Grenelle. He was evicted from the Directory along with Barthélemy on 18 Fructidor (4 September 1797), largely because of his moderate and royalist activities.

[13] R. Guyot, *Le Directoire et la Paix*, pp. 45–9.

French state and anticipated many of the Napoleonic reforms, and that Merlin and Treilhard were the leading jurisconsults of the day. Any government which could count on their services might well have considered itself fortunate.

The subject of Directorial finance is both technical and controversial.[14] Here attention can only be directed towards one or two points which serve to modify the severe criticisms usually passed upon it. The two leading events upon which discussion has centred are the collapse of the Assignats in 1796 and the repudiation of two-thirds of the public debt in September 1797. Both these occurrences were, in some ways, regrettable, but, by themselves, do not entail an utter condemnation of the finance of the period. Their full significance does not lie on the surface, and can only be determined by a close study of the financial situation during the Terror and later under the Consulate. Each can, moreover, be interpreted in a way which considerably eases the burden of discredit to be borne by the Directory. The collapse of the Assignats prompted, it is true, an unsuccessful attempt to stabilise the paper currency by means of the *mandats territoriaux* in 1796, but this was followed by a return to a metallic currency without undue deflationary effects—a policy which may be said to have paved the way for that revival of confidence which is so often attributed to the Consulate. Similarly, the bankruptcy of 1797 should not be viewed in isolation, but be regarded as part and parcel of Ramel's economy campaign. Nor should it be overlooked that the bankruptcy itself was not only partial but conditional, and that the final blame for its becoming definite must rest with the Consulate. In fact, the suggested contrast between financial maladministration and chaos under the Directory and financial retrenchment and reform under the Consulate has no real relation to the facts, and should be abandoned. The foundation of the Bank of France in 1800 may have been symptomatic of a new regime, but it was only rendered possible by the financial reforms of the preceding period.

The immediate financial problem to be faced by the Directory was how to arrest the continued fall of the Assignats. One of the last acts of the Convention had been to establish by the law of 21 June 1795 a

---

[14] It is fair to say that M. Marion's standard work *Histoire financière de la France depuis 1715*, vols. III–IV, takes a highly unfavourable view of Directorial finance. Other authorities, however, such as Hawtrey, *Currency and Credit*, Chap. XV, and Pariset, *Études d'histoire révolutionnaire et contemporaine*, pp. 79–134, hold contrary opinions. See also R. Stourm, *Les Finances de l'Ancien Régime et de la Révolution*, vol. 1, pp. 258–446, and the recent study *Les Principes financiers de la Révolution* by J. Barthélemy in *Cahiers de la Révolution française*, vol. vi, pp. 7–44 (1937).

sliding scale of depreciation for contracts and other debts, the value of which was to be fixed according to the quantity of Assignats actually in circulation at the time of the signing of the contract. This experiment failed because it was not applied to all contracts and because the treasury had not a sufficient reserve.[15] The first important proposal made by the Directory was for a forced loan payable in specie, grain, or in Assignats taken at 1 per cent. of their face value (6 December 1795). The manufacture of Assignats was to be discontinued and the plates broken on 21 March following. As the Assignats were worth less than 1 per cent. of their nominal value, and as receipts for payments of the forced loan were to be accepted in payment of direct taxes, this plan really amounted to a timid attempt at deflation and an effort to increase the revenue from taxation.[16] The over-valuation of the Assignats and the lack of specie for their conversion, however, effectually ensured the failure of this scheme.

The next experiment—the issue on 18 March 1796 of *mandats territoriaux*—was devised by the Finance Minister, Ramel-Nogaret. These *mandats* were in effect a new form of paper money which it was hoped would gradually displace the Assignats and be immune from depreciation.[17] To render them attractive to the public they were to entitle the holders to obtain *biens nationaux* [expropriated Church and émigré lands] at the fixed valuation of twenty-two years' purchase of the annual value of 1790.[18] Unfortunately, however, a committee of the Council of Five Hundred made the Assignats convertible into *mandats territoriaux* at one-thirtieth of their nominal value. Thus, although the new facility provided for the acquisition of unsold national property prevented the *mandats* from depreciating immediately, they were bound to collapse eventually because of the over-valuation of the Assignats in terms of the new paper currency.[19] It had been thought that the capitalists would eagerly take up the *mandats* in order to acquire the estates of the Belgian monasteries, but the more cautious of them hesitated to buy property so near to the frontier before the conclusion of a general peace, while the speculators preferred to discredit the *mandats* in order to effect pur-

---

[15] Mathiez, *Le Directoire*, p. 91

[16] Lefebvre, Guyot, Sagnac, *La Révolution française*, p. 319.

[17] R. G. Hawtrey, *Currency and Credit*, p. 256.

[18] Although secured upon the *biens nationaux*, the Assignats had never given holders the right to any particular share of this security. Previously the national lands had been put up for auction and sold to the highest bidder.

[19] G. Pariset, *Études d'histoire révolutionnaire et contemporaine*, p. 84. The 100-livre Assignat was then worth 7 sous, so that 100 livres *mandats* equivalent to 3000 livres Assignats would have been worth only 10 francs.

chases at a later stage at less cost. An additional difficulty was that the new currency was not immediately available, since the government only issued *promesses de mandats.*[20] For these reasons the *mandats* failed to gain general acceptance, and despite the efforts of the government to force their currency, they quickly fell to a discount. In the course of July, August, and September 1796 laws were passed whereby the *mandats* were to be accepted by the government in payment for taxes and in exchange for *biens nationaux* at their market price only. The *mandats* were finally withdrawn from circulation by a law of 4 February 1797. Thus failed the Directory's main effort at stabilisation. The failure was not, however, without its redeeming features, since it at all events prevented the inflation from getting completely out of hand, and it did in fact result in the resumption of a metallic standard.

In its essentials, the "repudiation" of 1797 was a comparatively simple operation. The law of 9 Vendémiaire year VI (30 September 1797) enacted that one-third only of the public debt should be consolidated and entered on the Grand Livre as a sacred charge,[21] and that the capital of the other two-thirds should be redeemed by the issue to stockholders of bearer bonds (*bons des deux tiers mobilisés*). By way of compensation, the state guaranteed that interest payments should in the future be made subject to no deductions as they had been in the past,[22] and that the *bons des deux tiers* should be available for the purchase of national property.

It is clear that many of the contemporary arguments in support of the measure were either specious or merely absurd. Such, for example, was the suggestion that no injustice to fundholders would be involved, since their stock had already lost two-thirds of its value owing to the inflation.[23] Yet repudiation ignored the possibility of a recovery in the value of the public debt and made the former losses irretrievable. Another contention was that the bankruptcy would have a depressing psychological effect on France's enemies, who would be more anxious to sue for peace when they saw the financial burdens of the French state thus lightened. If this view had been cor-

---

[20] Hawtrey, *Currency and Credit*, p. 256; Marion, *Histoire financière*, vol. III, p. 471.

[21] The Great Book or Register of the public debt had been opened by Cambon on 24 May 1793 with the object of consolidating the debt which had been issued under various denominations before the revolution. See *Cahiers de la Révolution française*, vol. vi, pp. 39–40.

[22] In March 1795 the perpetual annuities had been made liable to a stoppage of a tenth and the life annuities to a deduction of a twentieth.

[23] Marion, *Histoire financière*, vol. III, p. 64.

rect, the question was, Why did the Directory stop short of complete repudiation? A much more probable result would have been that the consequent loss of public credit would have prevented France herself from continuing the war. Equally it must be admitted that the bankruptcy demolished the incomes of the rentier class. An example will suffice to show the extent of the injury and to elucidate the actual nature of the operation. A rentier with a capital of 3000 livres invested in the public debt which before September 1797 had given him, at 5 per cent., 150 livres interest, now received 50 livres as interest on one-third of his capital (*tiers consolidé*) and a nominal holding of 2000 livres in *bons des deux tiers mobilisés*. In the final liquidation of 30 Ventôse year IX (21 March 1801), when the two-thirds were converted into perpetual annuities at the rate of ¼ per cent. of their capital value, the 2000 livres would be exchanged for an annuity of 5 livres. The net result was that instead of receiving 150 livres interest, the fundholder received 55 livres, which meant that 63.34 per cent. of his capital had been destroyed.[24] In this way the state repudiated in all nearly 2,000,000,000 livres of public debt.[25] The consequent shock to public credit may be imagined. The spectre of national bankruptcy which had haunted Mirabeau in the early days of the revolution had at last materialised. In M. Barthélemy's words, "The Directory misunderstood the overriding importance of maintaining the government's credit. It thought it could evade economic laws that were inflexible, but in so doing it came to grief. The repudiation of two-thirds of the debt weighed heavily on France's credit for a long time."[26]

It is, however, necessary to say in defence of the consolidation that bankruptcy in France had really been made inevitable by the misguided financial policy of the Constituent Assembly. The issue of the Assignats and the failure to levy sufficient taxation to balance the budgets had compromised the efforts of all subsequent administrations to grapple with financial shortage.[27] The repudiation of 1797 was, in fact, only part of a larger scheme to effect reforms in the French budget. By reducing governmental expenditure from 1,000,000,000 to 616,000,000 livres, Ramel was able, for the first time in the history of revolutionary finance, to establish a balanced budget. Part of this economy was achieved by drastic reductions in the military estimates, but the main saving came from the consolidation of the public debt. The financial end in view was, therefore, sound

---

[24] R. Stourm, *Les Finances de l'Ancien Régime et de la Révolution*, vol. II, p. 342.

[25] G. Pariset, *Études d'histoire révolutionnaire*, p. 86.

[26] *Cahiers de la Révolution française*, vol. vi, p. 44.

[27] R. Stourm, vol. II, p. 341.

enough in the circumstances, although the means were not. Finally, the responsibility for the final liquidation of 21 March 1801 must be borne by the Consulate. The real bankruptcy only came after the Directory had fallen.

One aspect of Directorial finance, also mainly due to Ramel, which deserves more general recognition, was the recasting of the whole system of direct and indirect taxation. Concentrated in the short interval of peace between the preliminaries of Leoben and the war of the Second Coalition [April 1797 to late 1798], these reforms present several points of interest. The new legislation relating to direct taxation was to be one of the most lasting achievements of the revolution, for it survived down to 1914. Some of it was fairly obviously a direct imitation of the younger Pitt's war finance, while the altered arrangements for the assessment and collection of revenue afford one more instance of a reorganisation, the credit for which has been wrongly attributed to the Consulate. Finally, the fresh recourse to indirect taxation, itself a result of inflation, marked a significant reversal of the taxation policy of the early years of the revolution.

The first direct tax to be reorganised was the tax on trade licences (*contribution des patentes*). This had been re-established in 1795, not for fiscal purposes, but as a means of preventing unjustifiable trade practices. Some changes were introduced in the method of its assessment in 1796, and the final adjustments were made by the law of 22 October 1798. The land tax (*contribution foncière*) assumed definitive shape in the law of 23 November 1798, the new tax on doors and windows in that of 24 November. The latter duty, payable in the first case by the owner, but ultimately by the tenant, encountered considerable opposition, on the ground of its English origin. It may be regarded as a first approximation to an income tax, and the manner in which it was first doubled (1 March 1799) and then quadrupled (23 May 1799) as a means of meeting renewed war expenditure may be compared with Pitt's tripling of certain assessed taxes in 1797. Lastly, on 23 December 1798, the *contribution mobilière et personnelle* which was partly a poll tax and partly a tax on movable property was entirely reconstructed. These four direct taxes (subsequently known as *les quatre vieilles*) formed the essential structure of the French taxation system down to the outbreak of the [First] World War.[28] Equally important was the change instituted on 13 November 1798, whereby the assessment and collection of the direct taxes and the adjudications on appeals were removed from the hands of local elected bodies and entrusted to

---

[28] Pariset, *Études d'histoire révolutionnaire*, pp. 87–8.

committees composed entirely of officials and working in the departments under the direct control of a commissioner of the central
government. This fundamental reform was not inaugurated, but only
continued by the Consulate. The only modification subsequently introduced was the change in the name of the officials.[29]

Some of the features of the legislation on direct taxation reappeared
in the revival of the indirect taxes. The very adoption of indirect taxation marked a reaction against the financial policy of the Constituent
Assembly which had relied almost exclusively on direct taxes. Some
of the new duties, such as the highway tolls, imposed on 10 September 1797, were again adopted from England. And hardly less permanent than *les quatre vieilles* were the new mortgage, registration
and stamp duties (November–December 1798).[30] Other indirect taxes
which proved indispensable were those on powder and saltpetre (30
August 1797), on gold and silver ornaments (9 November 1797), play-
ing-cards (30 September 1798) and tobacco (22 November 1798).

A tendency to exaggerate the financial straits of the government
may have inclined historians to accept with greater willingness Sorel's
thesis that continued European war became a necessity to the Directors.[31] The theory is at least plausible. On Sorel's view, war would ensure that the French armies would be occupied and prevented from
interfering in politics at Paris, that the cost of clothing and feeding the
troops would be borne by the foreigner, and that the empty coffers of
the republic would be replenished by the confiscations and forced
contributions levied on the conquered countries. Several unjustifiable assumptions have, however, to be made if this position is to be
upheld. Sorel's assertion that France was "without industry, credit, or
public confidence" is demonstrably false.[32] French industry might
very well have absorbed the returned French armies—they need not
necessarily have been put on half-pay. Nor should generalisations
about the financial resources which the government drew from the
activities of its armies abroad be accepted without caution. It requires
to be proved that the war provided on balance a net income for the
Directory. What figures we have point in the opposite direction.[33]
Moreover, if the main danger to the executive government was felt to

---

[29] Lefebvre, Guyot, Sagnac, p. 442.
[30] Pariset, p. 90.
[31] *L'Europe et la Révolution française,* vol. v, p. 12.
[32] *Ibid.*
[33] In 1795 Cambon estimated the average cost of the war at 2,000,000,000 livres. The
highest figure given for the total extraordinary revenues drawn from abroad is that
of Sciout, who places it at between 1,000,000,000 and 1,500,000,000. Pariset, p. 91.

be the existence of a class of ambitious generals, the real solution would have been not to prolong but to curtail the war, and thus to put an end to the extravagant pretensions and illicit gains of the commanders.[34] There could be little doubt that the country as a whole wanted peace, and the Directors knew it. On *a priori* grounds, therefore, it is conceivable that the problems of peace confronting the Directory would not have been so insuperable as they have been made out.

Nor does the actual diplomacy of the period disprove the contention that the Directors were not averse from the conclusion of a satisfactory peace. The failure of the conference at Lille in July 1797, when [the British representative] Malmesbury had Pitt's instructions to spare no efforts for peace, was not entirely the result of the purge of the moderate party in the *coup d'état* of Fructidor[35] or of the overbearing attitude of the Triumvirate [Barras, Reubell, La Revellière]. The breakdown must be placed at the door of Barras and Talleyrand, whose secret intrigues both before and after Fructidor did so much to prevent the English and French governments from reaching a frank understanding.[36] Malmesbury at the outset agreed to the preliminary conditions put forward by the French agents. Recognition was given to the Republic, the annexation of Belgium and the French treaties of alliance with Holland and Spain. At the same time, however, he excepted secret treaties and made no promise about a "general restoration" of conquered colonies. The French negotiators, Le Tourneur, former Director, Admiral Pléville Le Pelley and Maret, accepted Malmesbury's reservations, although these were quite inconsistent with the public articles of the Spanish treaty and the secret treaty with Holland. This initial ambiguity, with regard to the surrender of Dutch and Spanish colonies, was never explained to the Directory by its representatives.[37] When, therefore, Malmesbury claimed the Cape and Ceylon, the Directory refused to consider his demands. Nevertheless, such was England's desire for peace that the government was even prepared to surrender the colonial conquests without compensation. Meanwhile, as the result of a ministerial reshuffle of 16 July, Talleyrand had become Foreign Minister. His English connections, his hopes of profitable speculative dealings on the London exchange and his sincere desire for peace all inclined Talleyrand to smooth away difficulties. He and

---

[34] Meynier, *Les coups d'état du Directoire*, vol. II, p. 185.
[35] This is the impression given by Dr. Holland Rose in his *Short Life of Pitt*, p. 143.
[36] R. Guyot, *Le Directoire et la Paix*, pp. 431–56.
[37] *Ibid.*, pp. 413–15.

Barras accordingly encouraged Pitt to believe that the French government, in return for hard cash, would not insist on the surrender of the Cape and Ceylon.[38] Pitt consequently did not press the need for immediate concessions on his colleagues, and still reposed considerable faith in the prospects of the triumph of the moderates in Paris.

The precise effect of the *coup d'état* of 18 Fructidor upon the Lille conferences was that Le Tourneur, Maret and Colchen were replaced by Treilhard and Bonnier, who were instructed to present Malmesbury with a virtual ultimatum. It was to the effect that if he had not powers to cede all the English colonial conquests, he was to leave France, and not to return until he had. This new move, so far from being "a raising of the French terms,"[39] marked a reversion to the original demands. The Directory had not been informed that these conditions would be unacceptable from the British point of view, and it is clear that the Directors thought that Fructidor would enable them to impose this settlement. The ultimatum was conceived not as a means to end the peace negotiations, but as a way of exacting the full price from an enemy known to be in great difficulty. Malmesbury, having no authority to make the concessions, left Lille on 17 September with little or no hope of return. The resumption of negotiations was finally prevented by the battle of Camperdown. The Directory has always been strongly criticised by English historians for its failure to close with Pitt's offers, but the responsibility must not be borne entirely by the Directors. It was the secret intrigues of French agents at Lille which stiffened the English resistance before Fructidor, and which, after the *coup d'état,* were the cause of French intransigence.

On the other hand, the approval which, under strong provocation from Bonaparte, the Directors gave to the preliminaries of Leoben and the final treaty of Campo Formio, cannot be regarded as indicative of the pacific views of the Directors. It is fairly certain that those treaties would have been rejected by the Directory if its hands had not been tied, and indeed the best interests of France demanded that Bonaparte's policy should have been set aside. The Directors had, in each case, ample room for dissatisfaction. At Leoben, Bonaparte, anxious to monopolise the credit of having concluded peace, speeded up negotiations in order to prevent the official French negotiator, General Clarke, from arriving in time to share the discussions. In the public ar-

---

[38] Lefebvre, Guyot, Sagnac, p. 363.
[39] H. Rose, *Short Life of Pitt,* p. 143.

ticles of the preliminaries of peace Bonaparte renounced the left bank
of the Rhine, towards the acquisition of which Reubell's foreign policy had been mainly directed, and in the secret articles, by retaining
the Duchy of Milan[40] and suggesting the partition of Venice, he definitely disobeyed his instructions for the first time since the inception
of the Italian campaign.[41] In addition, it is clear that Bonaparte virtually conceded all that Thugut, the Austrian minister, wished to obtain. The principle of the integrity of the Empire was upheld, access
to the Adriatic won, and the surrender by Austria of Belgium and
Milan amply compensated for by her acquisition of part of Venice.
When the articles of Leoben were read to them three of the Directors—Reubell, Barras and La Revellière—declared they were inac-
ceptable, and the Minister of Foreign Affairs—Delacroix—also reported unfavourably on them. Yet on 30 April 1797 Reubell alone
refused to sign the ratification of the preliminaries. The explanation
must be sought in two ways—the Directors were compelled to accept Leoben because the French public, acquainted only with the
public articles, had received the news with an enthusiasm which it
would have been dangerous for the government to have damped,
and, moreover, the rejection of the terms would have entailed an admission that Bonaparte's advance into Austria had an actual fact
placed him in a very serious military position.[42]

These incidents were paralleled by the negotiations at Campo
Formio. Bonaparte withdrew from Austrian territory without waiting
for the ratification of the Leoben preliminaries by his home government, and again ignored his instructions. He had been ordered by the
Directors to renew the war rather than surrender Venice, and also to
insist on the compensation of Austria in Germany. The actual terms
of peace, however, conceded most of the advantages to Austria. As a
result of the exchange of territory, her position was strengthened
both in Italy and Germany,[43] a check was placed on the ambitions of
her rival Prussia, and she had the prospect of still further compen-
sations if France succeeded in wresting the left bank of the Rhine
from the representatives of the Empire in the projected congress at

---

[40] The Directors wished for the cession of Milan to Austria and the acquisition of the
left bank of the Rhine by inducing the Emperor and the German princes to accept
compensation on the right bank.

[41] See the important new work by G. Ferrero, *Aventure: Bonaparte en Italie, 1796–1797*,
passim.

[42] *Ibid.*, pp. 195–6. Owing to shortage of supplies and lack of co-operation from Germany, Bonaparte had been compelled either to treat with the Austrians or to retreat.
He could not have continued the march on Vienna.

[43] Pariset, *La Révolution (1792–1799)*, pp. 369–70.

Rastadt. On the other hand, France deserted her ally Prussia, assumed a share of responsibility for the extinction of Venice, and erected in the Cisalpine Republic an uneasy neighbour whom it would be essential in the future to protect. Once more the Directors submitted, but most unwillingly. They could not afford to forfeit the position they had just won after Fructidor, nor did they wish to see a revival of the European coalition against France, as seemed not unlikely after the failure of the Lille conferences.[44]

The net result of this double surrender on the part of the Directors was to deprive them of the initiative in French foreign policy and to substitute the Italian policy of Bonaparte for that of the natural frontiers as canvassed by Reubell. Moreover, in the years which followed Campo Formio the Directors did much successful work by assimilating the conquered territories in Belgium and on the left bank of the Rhine,[45] by protecting the Italian republics and by exerting further pressure on Great Britain. In fact, for a whole year after Fructidor, French influence on the Continent was virtually unchallenged, and the real reverses suffered by French arms and diplomacy and the revival of the second Coalition must be ascribed not to Directorial incompetence, but to the initiation of the Egyptian expedition—a venture devised by Bonaparte and Talleyrand.[46]

It is less easy to defend the inability of the Directors to secure internal peace and security. Here at least the record of the Directors was one of almost complete failure. This failure, however, only repeated the lapses of monarchical and previous revolutionary governments. Nor should it be overlooked that the task of maintaining public order in the provinces had become immeasurably more difficult under the Directory in consequence of the revival of royalism, the appearance of *chauffage* [bans of roving thieves], and the adoption of conscription (5 September 1798).[47] Conscription was applied at an unfortunate moment—just at the time when the French armies had sustained a series of severe defeats and when the prospect of starvation was greater among the fighting forces than at home. Evasion of the law and desertion both helped to swell the number of brigands, who were able to organise "reigns of terror" in various parts of the country. It is customary to blame the government for having done nothing to face up to these difficulties. A long series of measures designed especially to grapple with brigandage, however,

---

[44] Guyot, *Le Directoire et la Paix,* p. 508.
[45] P. Sagnac, *Le Rhin française pendant la Révolution et l'Empire,* Chap. IV.
[46] See especially E. Dard, *Napoléon et Talleyrand,* pp. 26–30.
[47] A. Vandal, *L'avènement de Bonaparte,* vol. I, p. 18.

affords little support to this criticism. One of the first acts of the Directory after its acceptance of office was to add a seventh ministry—that of general police—to the six ministries provided for in the constitution, and to institute exhaustive inquires into the state of the *garde nationale* and the gendarmie.[48] This investigation revealed defects which were, to some extent, remedied by a law of 17 April 1798 reforming the gendarmerie. Other administrative gaps were filled by the laws prescribing capital punishment for robbery with violence on the high roads and in private houses (15 May 1797), the law enforcing increased penalties against gaolers who connived at the escape of their prisoners (25 September 1797), and the law reforming the personnel of the criminal courts (10 January 1798).[49] It must be admitted that these changes did not effect substantial improvement, but it is evident at least that the problem had been taken in hand. Above all, it should not be forgotten that in the Vendée, where political unrest had been so continuously dangerous to previous revolutionary governments, the problem may be said to have been solved by the Directory.

It only remains to summarise the reasons for thinking that the instability of the Directory has perhaps been exaggerated. This political insecurity has been ascribed partly to the Constitution of the year III, and partly to public hostility to the Directors and the general desire for a strong executive government on the eve of Brumaire. Further investigation, however, seems to be required before this line of argument can be regarded as satisfactory.

For, in the first case, there is something to be said for the view that the main constitutional difficulties of the Directors were in the course of time solved.[50] The necessity of having a majority of at least three to two for the transaction of business may have opened the way to differences of opinion among the Directors,[51] but after Fructidor (4 September 1797) the Triumvirate of Barras, Reubell and La Revellière removed this source of weakness. It was not until Reubell retired on 16 May 1799 and was replaced by Sieyès that this solidarity of the Directors was shaken.[52] Similarly, the lack of any power to dissolve the Councils did not seriously hamper the Directors, since resort could always be had to systematic corruption at the annual

[48] M. Marion, *Le brigandage pendant la Révolution*, p. 68.

[49] M. Marion, *Le brigandage pendant la Révolution*, pp. 105, 106, 113.

[50] M. Deslandres, *Histoire constitutionnelle de la France de 1789 à 1870*, vol. I, pp. 305 seq.

[51] Meynier, vol. III, p. 125.

[52] *Ibid.*, vol. II, p. 5.

election of one-third of the Councils or to a *coup d'état*. Although the right of initiating legislation lay with the Council of Five Hundred, the Directors were not deprived of the power of giving effect to their policy, since the machinery of Directorial messages to the Legislative Assemblies proved an adequate substitute. Moreover, the formal absence of the power of initiation often provided the government with ready-made excuses when public opinion showed itself at all critical. Nor was the tenure of the Directory as a whole or of individual members of it really insecure. The life of the Directory was fixed at five years (Article 137)—a period which exceeded that of the Councils by two years and that of the Assemblies of 1791 and 1793 by three. As only one Director retired annually by lot, the political complexion of the executive could not be effectively altered by the Councils except after a wait of three years, and even then only on the unlikely assumption that the majority in the Councils remained stable. Finally, the substitution of three Consuls for five Directors at Brumaire left the form of the executive government very much the same.

Nor can French public opinion immediately before Brumaire be described as actively hostile to the Directors. The prevailing feeling was one of apathy rather than of antipathy. The initial reforming zeal of the revolutionaries had dwindled, people in the provinces had lost interest in electoral devices, and once the tide of victory against the foreigner had turned in favour of France the cry of *"La patrie en danger"* had lost its meaning. Now, in a situation of this kind the government in actual possession of power is not usually in a weak position, and it is doubtful whether in 1799 there was a general feeling in France that the overthrow of the Directory would do much to improve conditions. Hardly less widespread than apathy was fear—but this fear was of a peculiar kind: it was a fear of extremes, whether royalist or Jacobin. Fortunately for the Directors, the only formidable opposition to their rule came from precisely these two sources. For this reason the Directors had an easy means of prolonging themselves in office by *coups d'état* directed now against the Right, now against the Left. This *politique de bascule* [seesaw political policy] far from being an indication of the essential instability of the government can be regarded as a source of strength. Not only was it effective, it was also consonant with the best interests of the country at large. As the representatives of moderate republicanism, the Directors could in this sense lay claim to a good deal of popular support.

Whether or not Frenchman were willing on the eve of Brumaire to exchange the republican Constitution of the year III for a military dictatorship cannot be decided with certainty. The difficulties encountered with the Council of Five Hundred at St. Cloud on 19 Brumaire, the cries of *"hors la loi"* [outlaw him] which greeted Bonaparte and the well-known sympathies of the Parisian troops, at least make it clear that the Constitution was still regarded as a bulwark against dictatorship.[53] Bonaparte's military prestige had been somewhat tarnished by his abandonment of the army in Egypt[54] and little was known of his political and administrative ability. As a peacemaker, he still enjoyed the reputation he had gained at Leoben and Campo Formio, but Sieyès evidently thought that he would be willing to accept subordinate political office. Perhaps Vandal got nearest to the truth when he said of Bonaparte, "He came to power by taking advantage of his universal prestige and a gigantic misunderstanding." The theory of an "inevitable" military dictatorship has had a long inning; has not the time arrived when it should be abandoned? France in the autumn of 1799 was economically prosperous, the danger of invasion had already been averted, the reforms of Ramel and Neufchâteau were beginning to bear fruit, and the fear of reviving Jacobinism, dating back to the law of the hostages [July 12, 1799], might easily have been dealt with in the usual way. In religious matters it is difficult to believe the persecution of the priests was any more effective in practice than the measures taken to ensure public order, and although the desire for a restoration of the altars may have been pressing, there was a considerable anxiety lest with it there should be associated a return of the church lands.

If Bonaparte had been forty instead of thirty, would he not have remained faithful to his original idea of becoming a Director?

---

[53] Vandal, vol. I, pp. 279, 396.
[54] Gohier, *Mémoires,* vol. I, p. 174.

A REGIME OF CONTRADICTIONS

Denis Woronoff

Denis Woronoff (1939–), a graduate of the École normale supérieure in Paris, taught there and at the École
des hautes études en sciences sociales in Paris. At present he is a professor at the University of Paris. He has
written, among other works, a survey of the Directory,
*La République bourgeoise de Thermidor à Brumaire,
1794–1799* (1972; English translation entitled *The Thermidorean Regime and the Directory, 1794–1799,* 1984), a
massive doctoral thesis on the iron industry during
the Revolution and the Napoleonic Empire, *L'Industrie
sidérurgique en France pendant la Révolution et l'Empire*
(1984), and a survey of French industry since 1500, *Histoire de l'industrie en France: Du XVIe siècle à nos jours*
(1994).

🎩🎩🎩🎩🎩🎩

Recalling 9 Thermidor in his *Mémoires,* [the politician of the Direc-
tory] Thibaudeau quoted the remark of an émigré: "There are no
longer men in France, there are only events." This harsh judgement
is one that many people would apply to the period which separates
the fall of Robespierre from the rise of Bonaparte, a period in which
history seems to have unfolded in a minor key. From these five years
emerges an impression of confused mediocrity, of an interregnum
lacking brilliance. And whether they have been discredited or neglected, the closing stages of the Revolution have hardly won the
favour of historians.

But this drab interlude between two epic periods is crucial for an
understanding of the origins of contemporary France. Behind the in-
coherence, the spectacle and the scandals, one can trace the extra-

From Denis Woronoff, *The Thermidorean Regime and the Directory, 1794–1999,* trans.
Julian Jackson (Cambridge, Eng.: Cambridge University Press, 1984), pp. xix–xx,
192–195. This selection is from an English translation copyright © Maison des sciences
de l'homme and Cambridge University Press 1984 and is reprinted with the permission
of Cambridge University Press and the author.

ordinary tenacity with which the republican bourgeoisie maintained its hold on power. "Respectable" citizens searched ceaselessly for "the means of terminating the Revolution"[1] to their own benefit. They hoped to define, in a set of institutions, in a society, in an ideology, a system which would consolidate and sum up their conquests. That this regime of *"notables"* [influential people] was, in its original form [the Constitution of 1795], only able to survive by means of expedients in no way detracts from the interest and modernity of what was being attempted. The great figures had fallen silent. But would it be too much to claim that after the sound and the fury it becomes easier to distinguish a different form of discourse? Not the language of popular protest, which, outside moments of explosion, reaches us in an increasingly distorted and muffled form, but the language of moderate politicians—of whom Thibaudeau and La Revellière-Lépeaux could be taken as the spokesmen—whose demands, contradictions and indeed very ordinariness were representative of the new dominant classes. One must also be aware of provincial voices. But it remains difficult to know what these were in spite of extensive research which has perhaps concentrated too narrowly on the northern half of the country. Paris retained the initiative and the last word. But as well as similarities of attitude one ought also to pick out time-lags, even discrepancies, which varied depending on the region and the problem. For the relaxation of revolutionary constraints seems to have released powerful centrifugal forces: in many cases the right to make autonomous decisions had been achieved at the local level. As Richard Cobb has written, the country became "communalised" in Year III [1794–1795]; a remark generally valid for the whole of our period [1794–1799]. More than ever, diversity was the hallmark of France. Finally, the political upheavals, the "events" at home and abroad, must not obscure a more secret, because silent, history— that of the underlying forces in society. The Directory was perhaps a period of weakness, but it was also a period rich in political and cultural potential, in transformations, in social tensions. In short, not everything can be reduced to mere spectacle in a period which has been characterised as frivolous in order, perhaps, to evade proper assessment. . . .

The Directory gave way at the first sign of pressure. In fact the regime collapsed above all under the weight of its own contradictions: the contradictions of a liberal system which could only survive

---

[1] To take up the title of the law of 5 Fructidor Year III (22 August 1795) which proposed a new constitution to the French people for their ratification.

by violating its own legality,[2] which needed war—at any rate since Fructidor [the coup d'état of September 4, 1797]—to satisfy the contractors and generals and to provide itself with income, and which, through war, alienated its freedom of manœuvre and justified the accusations of its adversaries at home and abroad. Neither the war nor the Revolution was over; in fact, the Revolution developed yet further. The undisguised domination of the bourgeoisie had developed new awareness among the people. Ultimately it matters little that in the immediate term only a handful of activists had carried out a radical critique of the system. With an impeccable class instinct, the new owners of property had certainly felt the danger. This is why the "anti-anarchist" obsession dominated—paralysed—even the most reflective among them. Was the Directory entirely reassuring on this score? The weakness of its state apparatus stemmed, among other things, from its ambiguous nature: its public servants were both employed by the state and elected. As for the ideological hegemony which would have ensured the domination of the *notables* more effectively than force, the Directory had in this area conducted an interesting but doomed experiment. It was clear that the bourgeois anticlericals were caught in an impasse. Bonaparte came to understand this and drew the appropriate conclusions. Finally, the regime's opponents could plausibly claim that it had itself nurtured a current of social subversion. Had it not on several occasions allowed, if not encouraged, Jacobins, even democrats, to express themselves? These spasmodic upsurges of revolution were full of danger; they risked reviving the popular movement.

Furthermore, the Directory, as a consequence of its imperialist policy, continued to export the Revolution into Europe, gradually weakening old regimes which were already being undermined from within. We know how French expansion rebounded on France politically and economically. It also gave birth, in the conquered territories, to nationalist-revolutionary feelings, which were hardly compatible with the interests of the tutelary power, if not, indeed, directed against them. At the same time the presence of the occupier tended to exacerbate these conflicts and to restore strength to the most traditional sectors of these societies in crisis. But if the foreign policy of the Republic had contradictory consequences, it above all sharpened the

---

[2][This point is much expanded in the article by Lynn Hunt, David Lansky, and Paul Hanson, "The Failure of the Liberal Republic in France, 1795–1799: The Road to Brumaire," *Journal of Modern History* 51 (December 1979), 734–759. The authors argue that the Directory desired a representative government, but would not tolerate the existence of political parties or free elections.—Eds.]

fundamental division which set revolutionary France against monarchical Europe. The Directory thus created for itself irreducible opponents on every front, and led to the inevitable emergence of a regime which could resist this twofold class struggle.

In these circumstances, the regime's longevity is paradoxical. How was it able to survive? One must not underestimate the tenacity of its much-disparaged political class, which, in the image of Barras, fought all the harder since it made no distinction between its own personal interests and the common interest. As long as there appeared to be no alternative solution within a republican framework, these profiteers of the Revolution had no intention of relaxing their grip. But the Directory derived its strength even more from the weakness of its adversaries. On the left, the popular movement did not recover from the disaster of Year III [the Thermidorean repression of the Jacobin and democratic movements]: the new regime benefited from the experience of the Thermidoreans. Its police did not, however, give up the hunt for former leaders of the *journées*. But these were no longer in a position to stir up the people. The movement was atomised, effectively dissolved. The royalist enemy seemed more formidable. The Republic was in danger on at least three occasions: during the summer of 1795 at the moment of the Quiberon landing [a military campaign in Brittany]; between Germinal and Fructidor Year V [March and September 1797] when parliamentary counterrevolution threatened to link up with an armed coup by [General] Pichegru; and finally, during the summer of 1799, when the southwest flared up. But this list reminds us also of the Royalists' numerous failures. Their operations which could have had deadly consequences if they had been better conducted, collapsed through lack of preparation and co-ordination. But such "technical" errors derived ultimately from a political cause: the fundamental heterogeneity of the royalist movement. In each, or almost each, of these operations, one finds elements of internal conflict: Vendémiaire [the Paris insurrection of October 4–6, 1795] was exclusively the work of the constitutional monarchists; the quarrels between Puisaye [commander-in-chief of the royalist expedition] and the absolutists contributed to the Quiberon defeat. Finally, in Year V [1796–1797], the majority in the Councils was paralyzed by dissensions between "white Jacobins" [extreme royalists] and "Feuillants" [moderate royalists]. Above all, the royalist camp was weakened by the extreme positions taken up by the Pretender [the Comte de Provence, the future Louis XVIII]. A more conciliatory attitude would have rallied the majority of the country. On the counter-revolutionary basis of the Verona Manifesto, the monarchy could only hope for a restoration through the defeat of France. This situation left opportunities for the Orléanist party; it is all the more regrettable that the study of this current of opinion has not been properly carried out.

The last adversaries of the Republic were the foreign armies. The Directory's strength rested partly on the quality of the military instrument forged in Year II [1793–1794], partly on the talent of the generals, and partly on the number and on the abnegation of the soldiers. But the divisions within the opposing alliances eased France's task. Prussia's policy in the first coalition [1792–1797], and the rivalries of Austria and Russia in the second [1798–1801], all contributed to the triumph of the Republican government.

After Brumaire the long denigration of the Directory began. Historians have gradually abandoned this black legend in favour of a more balanced study of the period. If the regime founded by the Thermidoreans could not pride itself on numerous successes, it did nonetheless prepare the way for many of the achievements of the Consulate. The reorganisation of the tax system and of the financial administration were begun by [the Minister of Finance] Ramel-Nogaret. François de Neufchâteau [the Minister of the Interior and then Director] contributed to the economic recovery and gave a much-needed stimulus to efforts at innovation. Besides these two areas which are often mentioned, we should add that of the administrative infrastructure. The commissioners of the Directory who watched over the authorities in the *départements* partly held the role which was later taken by the prefects. The regime's evolution in an authoritarian direction in its final phase and the people's lack of enthusiasm for elective office reinforced the powers of these government agents, and thereby its tendency to centralisation. These fragmentary achievements were not enough to enhance the credit of the regime. They were at one and the same time too precarious—at the mercy, therefore, of any change in the economic situation—and too slow to impress contemporaries. For example, the slight take-off in the cotton industry did not compensate for the stagnation of traditional textiles. The improvement of farming techniques had not yet resulted in visible progress. In other words, the reformism of Year VI [1797–1798] had not had time to prove itself. The Consulate inherited schemes which were in the process of fulfilment—and took credit for them. In politics only the short term counts.

The Directory's achievement was not, therefore, insignificant. In spite of the final catastrophe, it had been able to preserve the bourgeois revolution. Taking up once again the aims of the members of the Constituent Assembly, the Thermidoreans had wanted to complete the process of reconstructing the new society for which the previous century had been a preparation. Circumstances and their own weaknesses had prevented them from succeeding. Bonaparte would set about the same task. It would fall to Bonaparte to "terminate the Revolution," to heal the nation.

11
The Revolutionary Legacy:
Positive or Negative?

HISTORIANS agree that the French Revolution transformed France and the rest of Europe, but they disagree about whether it was for better or worse. About its political results, for example, Alexis de Tocqueville claims that it aided future tyrants who took advantage of the passion for equality that the Revolution stimulated. But Albert Mathiez argues that the Revolution's most important legacy was the zest for a democratic way of life among later generations.

As for the Revolution's effects on the propertied classes, Albert Soboul thinks it conferred power on certain strata of the urban and rural bourgeoisie, many of whom were capitalists. This point of view is challenged by Albert Cobban, who finds that the Revolution retarded capitalism and profited a diverse group—lawyers, bureaucrats, and others—in general, conservative landowners from various classes.

In addition what effect did the Revolution have on those of low social status? Albert Soboul claims that peasants gained more than city workers; and Gary Kates argues that Jews achieved emancipation with full citizenship. He attempts to refute Rabbi Arthur Hertzberg's contention that the revolutionaries fostered anti-Semitism by calling for Jews to assimilate. For conflicting interpretations of the experience of women, see Chapter 9 of this book, "Women, Gender, and Politics in Revolution and Counterrevolution: Gains and Losses."

Finally, David Gordon Wright boldly attempts to strike a balance between the good and bad effects of the Revolution. He agrees that it accomplished much that was praiseworthy. For example, he notes that it reorganized and rationalized some of the institutions that still govern France. It proclaimed such universal human rights as religious toleration, trial by jury, and liberty of the press, although sometimes restricting them in practice. It promoted democracy by ending Divine Right Monarchy, proclaiming popular sovereignty, instituting equality before the law, increasing peasant land holdings, and encouraging social mobility. On the other hand, he thinks the costs of the Revolution proved horrendous. Millions died in the civil and foreign wars from 1792 to 1815, with other millions scarred by them and the Reign of Terror. The nation's cultural heritage was harmed by book burnings and the damage done to churches and castles. Moreover, the economy suffered a profound downturn. Finally, revolutionaries came to despise those who disagreed with them and regarded compromise or negotiation as surrender. In turn, the opposition grew more conservative, and they, like the revolutionaries, committed many acts of violence. The French became difficult to govern and remain disunited to this day. Is Wright's survey comprehensive enough? For example, he does not discuss the experience of women and gender issues. Moreover, he goes so far as to characterize the Revolution as a tragedy. Is this too negative a judgment? Should it be considered instead a progressive event with some tragic consequences?

Are all these differences of opinion irreconcilable? Could they be better mediated if one made a distinction concerning the effects of the Revolution on separate sectors of French life? This is what Lynn Hunt does in the following passage:

> In my view the social and economic changes brought about by the Revolution were not revolutionary. Nobles were able to return to their titles and to much of their land. Although considerable amounts of land changed hands during the Revolution, the structure of landholding remained much the same; the rich got richer, and the small peasants consolidated their hold, thanks to the abolition of feudal dues. Industrial capitalism still grew at a snail's pace. . . . In the realm of politics, in contrast, almost everything changed. Thousands of men and even many women gained firsthand experience in the political arena: they talked, read, and listened in new ways; they voted; they joined new organizations; and they marched for their political goals. Revolution became a tradition, and republicanism an enduring option. Afterward, kings could not rule without assemblies, and noble domination of public affairs only provoked more revolution. As a result, France in the nineteenth century had the most bourgeois polity in Europe, even though France was never the leading industrial power. What requires explanation, then, is not the appearance of a new mode of production or economic modernization, but rather the emergence of the political culture of revolution.[1]

Could the differences of opinion be further reduced if one made a distinction between long-term and short-term results? What if one did not treat the Revolution as one event but rather specified which stages in the Revolution had which effects? What if one defined such abstract words as "bourgeois," "capitalist," "class," and "democracy" precisely? Finally, should one study history less to defend and justify one's own social and political philosophy and more to observe and learn about people's behavior as they confront the intractable problems of the human condition?

---

[1]*Politics, Culture, and Class in the French Revolution* (Berkeley: University of California Press, 1984), p. 221.

A POTENTIAL
TYRANT BENEFITED

Alexis De Tocqueville

Alexis de Tocqueville (1805–1859) was descended from an ancient noble family of Normandy and pursued a career as a judge, legislator, and man of letters. During the Second Republic he was Foreign Minister for five months. After Louis Napoleon's coup d'état in 1851, he was imprisoned for a time and retired from public service when released. At least two of his works, *Democracy in America* (1835–1840) and *The Old Regime and the French Revolution* (1856), are regarded as classics. His subtle point of view in both books is not easy to categorize; and scholars still disagree about whether he was, for example, a liberal aristocrat, a conservative democrat, or a Christian conservative. What is clear is that he detested tyranny.

🎩🎩🎩🎩🎩🎩

The French Revolution did not, as has been believed, seek to destroy the sway of religious beliefs. Despite appearances, it was essentially a social and political revolution. Regarding these types of institutions, in no way did it tend to perpetuate and somehow stabilize disorder or to "methodize" anarchy, as one of its leading adversaries has said; but rather it increased the power and rights of public authority. Nor did it, as others have thought, seek to change the character our civilization had until then, nor arrest its progress, nor even alter basically any of the fundamental laws on which our Western society rests. When one separates the Revolution from all the accidents which briefly changed its outward features at different times and in different countries, and when one considers only its essence, then it is clear that the Revolution's sole effect was to abolish those political institutions which for several centuries held total sway over most of the peoples of Europe—institutions which have ordinarily been

From Alexis de Tocqueville, *L'Ancien régime et la Révolution* (3rd ed.; Paris: Lévy, 1857), pp. 53–56, 339–342. Editors' translation.

called by the name feudal—in order to replace them with a more uniform and simpler social and political order having as its foundation
equality of rank.

That alone caused an enormous revolution; for not only were these
ancient feudal institutions still mingled, interwoven so to speak, with
almost all the religious and political laws of Europe, but also these institutions had given rise to a host of ideas, feelings, habits, and customs which were in some way attached to them. A frightful convul-
sion was necessary to destroy and remove all of a sudden from the
social body a portion which was so connected to every organ. That
is why the Revolution appears even greater than it was. It seemed to
destroy everything, for what it destroyed touched everything and
was in some way related to everything.

However radical the Revolution was, it nevertheless introduced
many fewer innovations than is generally supposed. . . . What can
truly be said is that it has entirely destroyed or is in the process of
destroying (for it is still going on) everything from the old society
which derived from aristocratic and feudal institutions, everything
which was connected in some manner with them, everything which
carried in any degree their *slightest* trace. What was conserved from
the old society had always been extraneous to these institutions or
could exist without them. The Revolution was least of all an accidental event. To be sure, it took the world by surprise. However, it was
only the completion of a much longer work, the sudden and violent
termination of a task on which ten generations had worked. Even if
the Revolution had not taken place, the old social edifice would have
crumbled everywhere—in some places sooner, in other places later;
instead of suddenly breaking apart, it would have crumbled piecemeal. By a convulsive and painful effort, the Revolution achieved
suddenly and without transition, precaution, or regard for anything
what would have come about by itself gradually and in the long run.
Such was the Revolution's work.

It is surprising that what seems today so obvious remained then
so perplexing and obscure to the most clear-sighted contemporaries. "You wanted to correct your government's abuses," Burke
said to the French, "but why did you create something new? Why did
you not return to your ancient traditions? Why did you not confine
yourselves to reviving your ancient liberties? Or if you found it impossible to recognize the worn-out features of your forefathers' constitution, why did you not turn your gaze towards us? Here you
would have found again the old common law of Europe." Burke does
not perceive what is right before his eyes. It is precisely the old com-

mon law of Europe that the Revolution seeks to abolish. He completely misses the point—that is exactly the Revolution's real object and nothing else. . . .

Those who have attentively studied France in the eighteenth century . . . have seen the birth and development in her breast of two principal passions that did not grow up simultaneously and did not always tend to the same end.

One, deeper and more long-standing, is the violent and unquenchable hatred of inequality. This hatred was born and fed by the very sight of that inequality; for a long time it has, by a continuous and irresistible force, impelled Frenchmen to seek to destroy all the remaining foundations of medieval institutions and on the cleared ground to build a society where men are as similar, where social positions are as equal, as is humanly possible.

The other passion, more recent and less deeply rooted, inclined them to seek freedom as well as equality.

Near the end of the Old Regime these two passions were sincerely held and appeared equally vigorous. They met at the opening of the Revolution; at that point they mixed and combined for a moment; by contact they kindled each other and then all at once inflamed the heart of France. That was in 1789, a time of inexperience of course, but also of generosity, enthusiasm, virility, and grandeur, an immortal time, a time men's attention will turn to with admiration and respect long after those who have witnessed it and we ourselves have passed away. Frenchmen were then so proud of their cause and of themselves that they believed that they could be both equal and free. They planted, therefore, free institutions everywhere in the midst of democratic institutions. Not only did they reduce to dust the antiquated legislation which separated men into castes, corporate bodies, classes, and which made their legal rights even more unequal than their social positions, but they also destroyed in one blow those other laws—more recently created by royal power—which had deprived the people of personal freedom and which had put the government alongside each Frenchman as his tutor, his guardian, and if necessary his oppressor. As absolute government fell, so did centralization.

But when that vigorous generation which had started the Revolution was destroyed or became weary, as usually happens to any generation which undertakes such ventures; when, following the natural course of such events, the love of liberty flagged and slackened amidst anarchy and dictatorship that was supposedly in the name of the masses, the bewildered nation began to search gropingly for a master; at this point absolute government found available immense facilities for its rebirth and establishment that were easily discovered by the genius [Napoleon] who was going to continue and destroy the Revolution at the same time.

In fact the Old Regime had contained a host of recent institutions which, not being opposed to equality, could easily fit into the new society and which, however, offered despotism some remarkable advantages. These institutions were again sought and found amidst the debris of all the others. Previously these institutions had created habits, passions, and ideas tending to keep men apart and obedient. They were revived and used. Centralization was plucked from the ruins and restored. As it recovered, everything which had previously limited its power remained destroyed; and from the depths of a nation which had just overthrown royalty, arose suddenly a power more extensive, exacting, and absolute than any our kings had wielded. Because people thought only of what they themselves saw and forgot what earlier generations had seen, this enterprise seemed extraordinarily bold and an unprecedented success. The tyrant [Napoleon] fell, but what was really substantial in his work lasted; his government died, his administration continued to live; and ever since, any effort to strike down absolute power has succeeded only in placing the head of Liberty on a servile body.

From the beginning of the Revolution to our own time [1850s], the passion for liberty has over and over again died out, then been reborn, then again died out, then been reborn once again. It will continue that way for a long time, always inexperienced and unruly, easy to discourage, frighten, and vanquish, superficial and fleeting. Meanwhile the passion for equality forever resides in the inner recesses of men's hearts. It had entrenched itself there first, and it is attached to our most cherished feelings. While the passion for liberty is always changing appearance in response to events—decreasing, increasing, becoming stronger, weaker—the other is always the same, always aiming at the same goal with the same obstinate, often blind ardor, ready to sacrifice everything to those who will give it satisfaction; and it provides the government wishing to favor and flatter it the habits, ideas, and laws despotism needs in order to govern.

ALL REPUBLICANS BENEFITED

Albert Mathiez

For biographical information on Albert Mathiez, see
Chapter 6, "Why Terror in 1793–1794?"

꩜꩜꩜꩜꩜꩜

First of all it seems to me, if I am not mistaken, that the French Revolution succeeded only to the extent that it had been prepared:
since it was the work of the bourgeoisie, the bourgeoisie was inevitably the first to profit from it. This wealthy and intellectually superior class was bound to triumph over an impoverished and already half-dispossessed nobility, even though the higher element
among the nobles had made a considerable effort towards the end
of the monarchy to restore itself. It was also bound to triumph over
the people, because the people were still illiterate and had no alternative but to seek their own leaders among the bourgeoisie. The
bourgeoisie alone had a well enough developed class consciousness
to take and keep power.

Furthermore, I am very much struck by the fact that at this time
the democratic artisans took up the struggle only on the political
level, even when that struggle concerned social and economic demands. The guilds were suppressed. The trade unions did not yet
exist. The secret societies of journeymen [*compagnonnages*] were
weakened by their divisions. Strikes were prohibited. It was in the
political clubs and popular societies, as well as in the communes
[municipal governments] and Paris Sections, that the sans-culottes,
mingling with the progressive element among the bourgeoisie, strove
to defend their own interests. They placed all their hopes in winning
political power. In order to take over the state they did not hesitate
to resort to riots, which were organized in the political societies and
which were successful only because an armed force—the National
Guard—worked hand in hand with them. Often the communal au-

From Albert Mathiez, "La Révolution française," *Annales historiques de la Révolution
française* 10 (1933), 19–24. Printed by permission of the editor of the *Annales historiques de la Révolution française*. Editors' translation.

thorities also were their partners. For example, the events of July 14, 1789, were prepared by the electoral assembly that had chosen the Parisian deputies to the Estates General; and that assembly of electors met at the City Hall alongside the official municipal council. Likewise, the insurrection of August 10, 1792, was the work of the Paris Sections and some members of the Commune. The same was true for the coup d'état of May 31, 1793.

After Thermidor [July 27–28, 1794] the bourgeoisie pulled itself together. It purged the National Guard and soon disarmed it; and the riots, no longer backed by the communal authorities, all failed one after the other. The clubs were closed, and the starving and disarmed masses no longer had focal points or bases of support. They drifted aimlessly. It would have been different if the proletariat of that time had succeeded in forming class organizations instead of borrowing its political organizations from the bourgeoisie. When the sans-culottes lost political power, they lost everything.

But the victory of the bourgeoisie was perhaps too perfect. Mercilessly hunted down by the use of emergency laws, the last of the democrats disappeared or took refuge in embittered abstention from politics. The Thermidoreans remained isolated in the midst of a hostile nation.

Most Frenchmen, fed up with politics and crushed by the sufferings of the war, longed only for peace. When voting rights were restored to them, they no longer bothered to fulfill their electoral duties. Politics now interested solely the professional politicians. The ordinary Frenchman spoke of public affairs only with irony and disgust. Dictatorship, which had continued in various guises since 1789 and which maintained itself in power by the several coups d'état of the Directory, compelled people to turn inward. Idealism died among royalists as well as among republicans. Egoism replaced generous aspirations. Bonaparte could emerge to reassure and consolidate the interest groups. In the absence of political liberty, he would assure Frenchmen of their individual rights. In the Napoleonic Code, he would sanctify equality, their dearest possession. He would keep most of the revolutionary institutions while at times amalgamating them with those of the Old Regime, which were restored but adapted. His work would prove so solid that it made any total restoration of the past impossible.

The results of the French Revolution in France and Europe were so great that it can be said without exaggeration that a new era began in the history of the world.

France turned out to be greatly strengthened by the destruction of the Old Regime. No state on the globe was more homogeneous. The suppression of separate orders, corporate bodies, and special privileges, the uniformity of the laws and institutions, the decisive spread of the national language infused the country with enormous force. For a long time it was only in France that the all-powerful state reigned over citizens equal in rights.

A significant part of the individualistic program of the physiocrats was fulfilled. Recognized as an absolute, the right of private property permitted Frenchmen the practice of all economic and civil freedoms. The field was wide open for the expansion of capitalism, and it is not by chance that big capitalists were most of the time ardent revolutionaries.

In principle the Revolution proclaimed that it was for peace. It solemnly renounced conquest, and this spontaneous gesture gained it much sympathy abroad. But revolutionary aims clashed too violently with monarchist aims for peace to be preserved. The war changed the terms of the problem; in order to support it, the kings more and more had to adopt French practices. As early as 1794 the King of Spain confiscated the Church's silver plate. The following year he appropriated the revenue from vacant ecclesiastical benefices, which did not stop him from issuing paper money as well. The Holy Roman Emperor was forced to a similar expedient in Austria. From the third year of the war, with his manpower exhausted, he considered ordering military conscription. Pitt's government survived only by loans. Fortunately, the kings dared not decree universal military service (which had saved France) because, as [the contemporary writer] Mallet du Pan put it, they feared their own subjects almost as much as they feared the enemy.

Victory intoxicated the French. Under the pretext of bringing liberty to their neighbors, they brought conquest based upon the old theory of natural frontiers, a theory which they thus rejuvenated. They became a threat to the liberty of Europe. Napoleonic militarism provoked in reaction the birth of nations which had not yet become conscious of their identity.

The clashes of nationalities, which would fill the nineteenth century, were thus the direct result of the French Revolution. Previous wars had been entirely dynastic. The people had played only a passive role. The new wars would be very different, deploying larger and larger armies conscripted according to the French system of military service, a system gradually extended to the whole nation. In 1793,

France had 1,200,000 men in arms. It was the first time since antiquity that such a force had been assembled. Never before had so national an army been recruited, one which marched into battle not only to defend its independence, but also to impose its political and religious beliefs on others.

In the course of time, as the nineteenth century progressed, the clashes of peoples would become more and more fierce. By opposing each other, the different nationalisms would move farther apart. But at the beginning such was not the case. The conflict was then more social than political. In every country there was a minority, more or less strong, which sympathized with the French ideal and which hoped, more or less secretly, for its victory. The monarchs were forced to make more and more important concessions to this minority in order to prevent it from increasing and winning over their subjects. Thus, the growth of nationalities was accompanied by a liberal movement that little by little brought down the walls of the Old Regime in the states bordering France. Furthermore, nationalists and liberals were recruited in the same social strata. Both belonged to that enlightened bourgeoisie which had reformed France before serving as a model for Europe.

Although tinged with the Voltairian spirit, the French revolutionaries did not originally harbor any hatred for the Church and even less so for religion. On the contrary, they dreamed of using the clergy to defend their political work. Their union with the lower clergy was close. But the Pope's refusal to ratify their religious reforms, the schism of the clergy between those who swore allegiance to the Constitution and those who would not, and the revolutionaries' unsuccessful efforts to restore the broken religious unity pushed them little by little to a policy of conflict with the Church. They eventually secularized the Republic by decreeing the separation of Church and State. Bonaparte's Concordat, designed above all to reassure those who had acquired the nationalized Church lands, could not reestablish the old, intimate union of throne and altar. The registration of vital statistics remained in the hands of civil authorities. Anticlericalism, which had been only a state of mind before 1789, became a program adopted by most liberals throughout Europe.

Likewise, divine right monarchy had suffered irreparable damage from the proclamation of the principles of 1789. The idea of sovereignty had changed its meaning. From the king, it had passed to the people, and the execution of Louis XVI on January 21, 1793, had divested monarchical sovereignty of any supernatural aura. When for the last time Charles X, at his coronation in 1825, was to touch those afflicted with scrofula, this brought forth only derision.[1]

The American Revolution of 1776 had been above all a political revolution. It had respected the privileges of wealth and had established everywhere a regime of limited suffrage. It had not even touched the vestiges of the feudal regime which had survived in some spots. Seigneurial quitrents in New York State, for example, were not suppressed until the middle of the nineteenth century.

The French Revolution was much more thorough. It totally wiped out seigneurial dues and tithes without any indemnity. It nationalized the property of the Church and of the émigrés. It altered regulations on commerce and industry from top to bottom. It was imbued almost from the beginning with an ardent egalitarian spirit which reached its peak in 1793–1794. For the first time, in response to necessities more than to theories, the outlines of a social democracy appeared in the world and sought to cross the barrier between thought and action. This premature attempt failed. But it did not disappear without leaving some trace, at least in the minds of men. The de facto collectivism accomplished by the Terrorist regime—price controls, requisitions, the pooling of the nation's entire resources—served as a model to which social reformers for a century after Babeuf could point.

While the Terror frightened to death the bourgeoisie of the nineteenth century, on the other hand it restored the hopes of the partisans of social justice. It played on their imagination like a grandiose myth, generating devotion and sacrifice. The historian Gabriel Monod, in the preface which he wrote to my *Contributions à l'histoire religieuse de la Révolution,* relates that at Nantes, toward the middle of the last century, the woman at whose home he lodged praised her father, who had welcomed the Revolution enthusiastically and who had in his youth defended it against the Vendeans. He had seen with sorrow the Imperial Regime of Napoleon crush the democratic liberties which had been acquired at such great cost. With each new Revolution, in 1814, in 1830, in 1848, he had believed that the ideal Republic dreamed of in 1793 would reappear. At over ninety years of age he died during Louis Napoleon's Second Empire; and at the moment of death, raising his eyes toward heaven with a look of ecstasy, he murmured: "O sun of '93, am I going to die thus without ever again seeing your rays!" This obscure Breton republican was not an excep-

---

[1] [The king's touch as a way of healing scrofula was a tradition dating from the Middle Ages.—Eds.]

tion. Although the sun of 1793, which had illuminated his youth, had disappeared behind the darkened horizon, he had kept its immortal radiance in the depth of his soul.

In the bitter and difficult march towards progress, men need to be reinvigorated by the sun of hope. The revolutionaries of 1789 drew comfort from the memory of the republics of antiquity or the more recent example of the American Revolution, and this sustained them in their fight. They had read Plutarch's *Lives* and, schooled by it in magnanimity, their courage was inflamed, their faith in the Revolution soared! They imitated the heroes of Greece and Rome and, like them, they gave up their lives. That is why they too were heroes. In their turn, they were for their descendants what Aristides, Brutus, and Cato had been for them—that is, martyrs who witnessed by their life and death what devotion to justice and the sacred love of humanity can achieve. French republicans have faithfully preserved their memory, and in our contemporary history, the Revolution has been the wellspring from which they have drawn their example and fortified their faith.

THE TRIUMPH OF
A NEW BOURGEOISIE

Albert Soboul

For biographical information on Albert Soboul, see Chapter 2, "The Peasants: Mentality and Behavior in 1789."

🎩🎩🎩🎩🎩🎩🎩

The Revolution destroyed the feudal aristocracy; it still has to be made clear to what extent. At the same time it also ruined those sections of the bourgeoisie that were integrated in one way or another into the society of the ancien regime. The Revolution made certain the triumph of capitalist economy based on economic liberty; in this sense, it hastened the ruin of the social categories that were attached to the traditional system of production. But in the realm of agricultural production, the resistance of the poor peasantry was such that capitalism could not win a definitive victory.

The nobility as a social order disappeared. Distinctions between nobles and commons were done away with. The personal seigneurial rights on which the dependence of the peasants was based were abolished after the night of August 4, 1789. Above all the aristocracy was hit in its economic basis. Other feudal rights were finally terminated by the Convention on June 17, 1793. The Revolution attacked the landed property of the nobility. The former seigneurs had to return the communal lands that they had seized, and the property of the émigrés was put on sale in June 1793. As the crisis grew deeper the nobles were gradually excluded from all public positions, civil or military. Exaggeration should be avoided here, however. The nobility was not stripped of its lands altogether nor irrevocably. Only the émigrés had their property confiscated. Many nobles went through the Revolution without great loss and kept their landed properties. Furthermore, fictitious divorces and purchases by straw men enabled some

From Albert Soboul, "Classes and Class Struggles during the French Revolution," *Science & Society* 17 (Summer 1953), 252–257. Reprinted by permission of *Science & Society*.

émigrés to save or recover their lands.[1] In this way a certain section of the old aristocracy held on, and during the 19th century merged with the upper bourgeoisie.

The bourgeoisie of the ancien regime shared the fate of the aristocracy in large measure. The bourgeois who lived "nobly" on their income from the land saw their seigneurial dues and rights vanish. Office holders were ruined by the abolition of the sale of offices. The financial upper bourgeoisie received a mortal blow when stock companies and the farming-out of indirect taxes were abolished. It was hard hit too by the disappearance of the [pre-revolutionary] Bank of Discount as well as by the resumption of price-fixing and controls. Finally, as a measure of the blows the bourgeois revolution struck at certain sections of the bourgeoisie, we must consider the considerable repercussions of inflation on settled fortunes. The traditional bourgeoisie invested its savings in mortgage loans or the public debt rather than in commercial and industrial enterprises. In 1794, the depreciation of the assignats led debtors to get rid of their mortgage debts at little cost. The consolidation of the perpetual and annuity debts [types of government securities] under the Convention, and the two-thirds bankruptcy under the Directory were additional blows. All these facts account for the rallying of the bourgeoisie of the ancien regime to the counter-revolution. It shared the fate of the aristocracy, whose cause it had taken up.

Just as much as the revolutionary bourgeoisie strove for the destruction of the aristocracy, it obstinately sought the ruin of the traditional economic system, which was incompatible with the expansion of capitalist enterprises. After the Ninth of Thermidor [July 27, 1794], economic liberty was inaugurated triumphantly on the ruins of the sans-culotte movement.

This had grave consequences for the traditional lower classes. The abolition of guilds by the Constituent Assembly might have seemed democratic, but it hurt the interests of the master artisans. Thus, at the same time that the material conditions of social life were being transformed, the structure of the traditional lower classes was changing. All the conditions were now present for a broad development of capitalist economy, which would necessarily transform the sans-culottes into a proletariat. The artisans and journeymen had a

---

[1]On what the émigrés were able to recover of their lands, see A. Gain, *La Restauration et les biens des émigrés* (1929). [For how the nobility fared, see a later study by Robert Forster, "The French Revolution and the 'New' Elite, 1800–50," in *The American and European Revolutions, 1776–1848*, ed. Jaroslaw Pelinski (Iowa City: University of Iowa Press, 1980), 182–207.—Eds.]

foreboding of their fate. The latter knew that machinery would increase the chances of unemployment, the former that capitalist concentration would mean the closing of their workshops and make wage earners of them. The Le Chapelier law of 1791, prohibiting "coalition" [labor organizations] and strikes, was an effective means of development for the industrial bourgeoisie.

In the realm of agricultural production, where the resistance of the poor peasantry was more desperate, the bourgeois revolution was less radical in its consequences. It made possible the development of a predominant rural bourgeoisie, but it could not completely destroy the rural community and thereby give free rein to the development of capitalist modes of production.

All the peasantry, whether owners or not, profited by the abolition of seigneurial dues and ecclesiastical tithes. The other agrarian reforms of the Revolution served primarily to strengthen those who were already proprietors. Leaving out the city bourgeoisie, who got into their hands a considerable portion of the national[ized] property, the conditions under which it was sold, particularly the auctions, favored the big farmers and the prosperous peasants. The rural bourgeoisie was strengthened and the moat deepened between them and the poor peasantry.[2]

But the last-named did not emerge from the Revolution as badly disarmed in the face of the triumphant bourgeoisie as the urban sans-culottes were. The poor peasantry did not get from the revolutionary assemblies the restoration or reinforcement of the traditional rural community, as it had desired. But the bourgeois revolution did not destroy it beyond repair; it did not brutally do away with the communal properties and collective customs that formed its economic basis.[3] Both lasted throughout the 19th century and have not entirely disappeared yet [1953]. The law of 1892, still in force, requires the consent of the peasants of the village for the abandonment

---

[2]Despite some timid attempts in 1793, the bourgeoisie that dominated in the revolutionary assemblies was aware of the need for prohibiting access to ownership for the mass of the peasantry, if industrial enterprises were to be developed. See the report presented to the Convention the 27 Fructidor year II [September 13, 1794] by Lozeau, deputy of the Charente-Inférieure, "On the material impossibility of making all Frenchmen landed proprietors and on the bad effects that this change would entail in any case." (*Moniteur,* Vol. XXI, p. 748).

[3]Nevertheless, the revolutionary bourgeoisie was aware of the need of doing away with communal property and collective customs for the sake of the progress of capitalist agriculture. See in this connection the report of Lozeau in Messidor year II [June–July 1794], "On the need for doing away with communal property and on the principles of property in a free country." (*Bibliothèque nationale,* 8^0 Le^{38} 841).

of common pasture. The rural community has thus survived, going through a slow disintegration.

Here some distinctions are necessary. In the regions of large-scale farming, where the farmers were active agents in the capitalist evolution of agriculture, the rural community broke up rapidly, not by dissociating into antagonistic classes (the big farmers were generally city capitalists who were strangers to the rural community) but by losing its substance, as it were. The poor peasants who were proletarianized were to furnish the labor force needed for capitalist agriculture and big industry. In small-scale farming regions the evolution was slower. The rural community was sapped from within by the antagonism between the rural bourgeoisie and the poor peasantry desperately defending its customary rights to use fields and woods. Thus two forms of economy clashed, one archaic, the other new and asserting the individualism of the capitalist producers. The struggle was covert but bitter, marked during the 19th century by agrarian disorders of the traditional type, the last of them, in 1848–51, being by no means the least violent nor the least typical.[4]

The bourgeois revolution was consequently unable to eradicate the traditional forms of agricultural production. It could only enact a compromise whose full significance can be measured by comparing the development of French and English agriculture. Undoubtedly the bourgeois revolution accelerated the capitalist transformation of agriculture; but that development was considerably slowed up by the maintenance of collective customs and by the subdivision of ownership and cultivation. The autonomy of the small producers was kept up for a long time, giving the political development of France, especially under the Third Republic [1870–1940], some of its characteristic traits. If enclosure and concentration had been imposed in France as they were in England, capitalism might have triumphed as completely in the realm of agricultural production as in that of industrial production. The obstinate resistance of the landed aristocracy to any compromise with the bourgeoisie forced the latter to deal gently with the peasantry, even with the poor peasantry.

If we now consider the class which led the Revolution, and basically profited from it, we note that it has been radically changed. The traditional predominance within it of the settled fortunes has been replaced by that of those who direct production and exchange; the

---

[4]See Albert Soboul, "La question paysanne en 1848," in *La Pensée,* 1948, Nos. 18, 19 and 20; "Les troubles agraires de 1848," in *1848 et les Révolutions du XIXe siècle,* 1948, Nos. 180 and 181.

internal equilibrium of the bourgeoisie has been modified. The bourgeoisie of the ancien régime was not totally destroyed, since those of its representatives who had not emigrated kept their lands; but it lost its primacy. A new money bourgeoisie appeared in the forefront, made up of industrial leaders, and the directors of commerce and finance. Equipping, arming and supplying the armies, sale of the national property, exploitation of the conquered countries afforded business men new chances for developing their enterprises. Speculation gave rise to immense fortunes. The bourgeoisie renewed itself by incorporating those "nouveaux riches" who set the tone for the "society" of the Directory. True adventurers of capitalist society, they gave new life to the traditional bourgeoisie by their enterprising spirit and their flair for taking chances. On a lower rung of the bourgeois ladder, circumstances had allowed many tradesmen or artisans to rise into the ranks of the bourgeoisie. It was from this middle level that the new dominant class was soon to recruit the public servants and the members of the liberal professions. The traits of the new bourgeoisie hardened during the Napoleonic period that fused these diverse elements.

At the end of this sketch whose only purpose is to stimulate reflection on the history of the Revolution, several points should be stressed for their educative value.

There are laws of historical development, but they can not be reduced to a mechanical schematism, as some have done by a false application of dialectical materialism. Social classes, even when dominant, are rarely homogeneous; the various sections making them up complicate the interplay of classes in the framework of the general development, sometimes causing autonomous secondary currents, such as the sans-culottes in the bourgeois revolution. Only precise social and economic analysis can account for the place in the class struggle of the various social categories, and disclose the contradictions that may appear between political attitude and an economic position. It will not be forgotten, finally, that as the class struggles develop, they affect and transform the classes engaged in them. The bourgeoisie that profited from the Revolution was no longer the same as the bourgeoisie that started it.

These truths may seen self-evident. They deserve to be recalled nevertheless. History is a dialectical movement. If they are not to deform it by schematization, those who engage in studying it must take into account the complexity that makes its richness, as well as the contradictions that give it its dramatic character.

THE VICTORY OF
CONSERVATIVE
LANDOWNERS

Alfred Cobban

Alfred Cobban (1901–1968) was one of the most eminent twentieth-century British historians. He studied at
Cambridge University, taught at the University of New-
castle-upon-Tyne and the University of London, and
edited the English journal *History.* He wrote an excellent
History of Modern France (new edition; 3 volumes;
1965), several works of political theory, and many
books and articles on the Old Regime and the French
Revolution. His writings include *Edmund Burke and the
Revolt Against the Eighteenth Century* (1929), *Rousseau
and the Modern State* (1934), *In Search of Humanity: The
Role of the Enlightenment in Modern History* (1960), *The
Social Interpretation of the French Revolution* (1964), and
Aspects of the French Revolution (1968). As the following
selection indicates, he was a trenchant critic, who took
independent stands on historical controversies.

🐞🐞🐞🐞🐞🐞

Looking at the economic consequences of the revolution as a whole,
they seem astonishingly small for such a great social and political upheaval. This is what M. Soboul, in spite of his acceptance of the theory of the bourgeois revolution, very frankly recognises. Industrial
production under the Directory, he says, was below that of 1789 in
cotton. The woollen and metallurgy industries were stagnating. Capitalist concentration remained essentially commercial, under capitalists of the old type, employing domestic labour and combining commercial and banking activities with the organisation of manufacture.
Above all, France remained essentially a rural country and its old

agricultural methods continued unchanged.[1] Most statistics in this matter are open to question, but, for what they are worth, the figures for French commerce in 1825, according to Henri Sée, are hardly greater than those of 1788.[2]

This does not entirely settle the question. There is still one final refuge of theory. Capitalist progress during the revolution must not be exaggerated, says M. Soboul. This is rather an under-statement for what seems to have been a period of serious economic decline. However, he continues, the conditions were none the less brought together for the coming great development of capitalist economy.[3] It may seem that this is all a matter of more or less, and that it does not matter fundamentally to what extent the revolution accelerated the growth of a capitalist economy, so long as it did accelerate it. Similarly, the actual effectiveness of corporative restrictions in 1789, and therefore the importance of the legislation of the revolution in liberating trade and industry from the bonds of the *ancien régime,* is only a matter of degree. The effectiveness of the abolition of internal customs is perhaps least open to doubt.

All this is on the assumption that the revolution represented a step forward in the direction of a more developed capitalist economy. According to prevailing social theory steps in history must always be taken forward. I want to suggest the possibility that, at least in some fundamental respects, it may not have been a step forward at all, but rather one backwards, that instead of accelerating the growth of a modern capitalist economy in France, the revolution may have retarded it.

. . . The evidence in respect of trade and industry is that France was worse off in 1815 than she had been in 1789. After two decades of war this was perhaps only to be expected. More important is the fact that such evidence as we have on the organisation of trade and industry suggests that by and large it remained in 1815 what it had been in 1789.[4] The lack of capital investment, which had been one of the factors holding back French industrial development, continued. In Dauphiné, says P. Léon, those with capital to invest preferred to the certain risk of losses in industry, the gains of speculation and of investment in real estate.[5] The peasantry, which held so much of the

---

[1] Albert Soboul, *Précis d'histoire de la Révolution française* (1962), p. 441.
[2] H. Sée, *L'Évolution commerciale et industrielle de la France sous l'ancien régime* (1925), p. 74.
[3] Soboul, *Précis,* p. 475.
[4] For example, in Lyon, Toulouse, Bordeaux.
[5] P. Léon, *La naissance de la grande industrie en Dauphiné* (1954), p. 370.

productive capacity of the country, was still largely self-sufficient and invested its savings in land, which attracted capital to the detriment of both industry and commerce.[6] France was not to know an industrial revolution—apart from isolated and untypical enterprises in a few areas—before the Second Empire [1852–1870]. It is true that the economic history of France is largely unwritten. What I am suggesting is that such researches as have been made give no support to the orthodox theory of the economic effects of the revolution, but on the contrary throw great doubt on it. The revolution, in its economic consequences, seems indeed to have been the kind of revolution we should expect if . . . it was led not by industrialists and merchants, but by *officiers* [office-holders who owned their posts] and professional men.

A Bourgeoisie of Landowners

It must not be supposed, though Georges Lefebvre did,[7] that I am trying to deny the existence of the French Revolution; I merely want to discover what it was. Professor Reinhard has argued that even if we discard the view that the revolution was against "feudalism," still the struggle against seigniorial rights, against the noblesse and against the privileged classes was central to it.[8] This may have been true in the summer of 1789. Is it true of the next ten years? Seigniorial rights were largely eliminated in 1789, and their elimination was completed by the stubborn resistance of the peasantry, despite the reluctance of the revolutionary authorities in Paris, in the course of the following years. Similarly, noblesse was legally brought to an end—even if only for 14 years—in 1789, as the marquis de Ferrières philosophically observed on 20 June 1790. "Noblesse," he writes, "is already destroyed in fact. The abolition of feudal rights and justice, equality in the division of enclosed land, have given it a mortal blow." Do not write to me any longer as M. le marquis, he instructs his wife; and let my daughter and son-in-law stop being called count and countess. He even asks for his family arms in the local church to be obliterated, though, since Ferrières was a cautious man, only with whitewash.[9]

---

[6]F. Crouzet, "Les conséquences économiques de la Révolution à propos d'un inédit de Sir Francis d'Invernois," *Annales historiques de la Révolution française,"* no. 168 (1962), pp. 214–215.

[7]G. Lefebvre, "Le mythe de la Révolution française," *ibid.,* no. 145 (1956).

[8]M. Reinhard, "Sur l'histoire de la Révolution française," *Annales: E.S.C.* (1959), p. 557.

[9]Marquis de Ferrières, *Correspondance inédite 1789, 1790, 1791,* ed. H. Carré (1932), p. 212.

Finally, privileges based on order, heredity and so on were ended by the legislation of 4–11 August 1789. There was no need, then, to continue the revolution to abolish what had already been abolished.

Yet the revolution did continue, and it continued particularly as a struggle against the "aristocrats" and "aristocracy." This was, it is true, a struggle against the counter-revolution, but that is only to say the same thing in different terms. The counter-revolution was led by, and identified with, the aristocrats; it was also a continuation of that *révolte nobiliaire* against the royal government with which the revolutionary movement had begun in 1787–8, and which had been an attempt to set up or—it was believed—revive, aristocratic government. As such it was a political movement, concerned primarily with political power and only secondarily with social privilege. It is not unreasonable, therefore, to expect the opposition to aristocracy also to be mainly political.

An indication of the primarily political nature of the struggle against aristocracy is the actual use of the word. Tom Paine, writing to Edmund Burke from France on 17 January 1790, explains, "The term Aristocrat is used here, similar to the word Tory in America;— it in general means an enemy of the Revolution, and is used without that peculiar meaning formerly affixed to Aristocracy."[10] Nobles could be patriots and if they were such, or often if they were merely discreet and neutral, escaped the label of aristocrats, whereas there were frequent denunciations of bourgeois aristocrats, or, to quote Marat among others, of the *"aristocratie d'argent"* [aristocracy of money].[11] In the Maine [department], we are told, the term aristocrat was employed to designate even simple peasants if they were hostile to the revolution.[12]

The revolution, then, continued as a political struggle against aristocracy—the claim to a monopoly of political power by a small minority of the nation—when the first objectives had been achieved. This is not to assert that it ceased to have any social aims or content, or to deny that removing from power, wealth, influence, and sometimes even life itself, many members, or whole groups, of the socially superior classes, and replacing them in the end with new men—the *"nouveaux messieurs,"* parvenus, founders of the "bourgeois dynasties" of the nineteenth century, was a social as well as a political fact.[13]

---

[10] *The Correspondence of Edmund Burke,* vol. vi, ed. A. Cobban and R. Smith.
[11] *Cf.* L. G. Wickham Legg, *Select Documents of the French Revolution* (1905), I, pp. 171–5.
[12] Paul Bois, *Paysans de l'Ouest* (1960), p. 664, n. 2.
[13] Reinhard, "Sur l'histoire de la Révolution française," p. 561.

How far, apart from the removal of the higher noblesse from their positions of wealth and privilege, there was a permanent change of personnel in the upper ranks of society, however, remains speculative. The bourgeoisie proper of the *ancien régime,* like the noblesse with which it was rapidly becoming assimilated, in some cases survived the storms of the revolution and in some cases went under. The *grande bourgeoisie* of finance, such as the Farmers General, suffered severely, but their place was to be taken by others who differed from them only in being a new first generation of financial wealth, instead of the second or third. The bourgeois who had purchased seigniorial dues lost them, but they kept, and probably added to, their estates; and as owners of land profited by the abolition from which they suffered as owners of dues. The bourgeoisie of *officiers,* M. Soboul says, was ruined by the abolition of venality.[14] This is a point which requires investigation. It was an Assembly containing a large proportion of venal officers which carried out the abolition. The abolition was in fact accompanied by compensation and there are indications that the compensation was sometimes profitably invested in the purchase of Church lands. Moreover, many of the former *officiers* seem subsequently to have obtained salaried judicial and administrative positions not dissimilar from those for the loss of which they had earlier been compensated. The open question is how far the expected compensation was actually paid, but even in the upper ranks of the *ancien régime* bourgeoisie it seems likely, that many survived and prospered, or re-emerged after the revolution, to contribute to the recruitment of the new upper class of nineteenth-century France.

Whether many or few survived from the *ancien régime* bourgeoisie is, however, a minor issue. The important question to ask is what essentially was the constitution of the new ruling class of France that emerged from the revolution. I have already suggested that the revolutionary bourgeoisie was the declining one of venal officers, along with members of the liberal professions, rather than the prospering merchants and industrialists. As M. Reinhard puts the point, "It was these lawyers, these doctors, these *officiers* of lower positions, who captured the posts of executive power."[15] For men of business the revolution was less advantageous: socially and politically they received perhaps even less recognition than before the revolution. The new Napoleonic élite was one of soldiers and bureaucrats.[16] Georges

---

[14] Soboul, *Précis,* p. 478.

[15] Reinhard, "Sur l'histoire de la Révolution française," p. 561.

[16] M. Reinhard, "Élite et noblesse dans la seconde moitié du XVIIIe siècle," *Revue d'histoire moderne et contemporaine,* III (1956).

Lefebvre truly writes of Napoleon that he was essentially a soldier: "His preference was for an agricultural and peasant society; the idea of a society dominated by a capitalist economy was unsympathetic, if not even alien, to him."[17] The effectiveness of his promotion of the economic interests of France, it has been pointed out, is an illusion. Though many historians, and even contemporaries, shared the belief that the industry of Lyon owed much to Napoleon, the Lyonnais merchants did not. One, whose correspondence has been edited, is described as having no words too harsh to use in his criticism of the Emperor and of the toadyism that his policy encouraged.[18] The tendency, which Napoleon shared, to look down on business men, and to exclude them from positions of social prestige or political power, survived well into the nineteenth century. As Michelet said, *"La France n'a pas d'âme marchande"* [France does not have the soul of a shopkeeper].[19]

If the new ruling class was not constituted out of the rising industrial or commercial capitalists, then, how was it composed? Only a few samples have been taken so far, but these, and all other indications, lead in the same direction. An analysis of the 600 *"plus imposés"*—those in the highest tax grade—of the Haute-Garonne [department] in the year X (1801–2) shows that they included in their ranks former nobles and members of *parlements, officiers,* judges and lawyers, but that the new aristocracy of France was above all one of landed proprietors.[20] "It has been said," writes the author of this analysis, "that the First Consul aimed to combine, in the bosom of a new aristocracy, the old noblesse and the industrial and commercial bourgeoisie enriched by the revolution. It seems rather that he aimed to create a new one, whose letters of nobility would be conferred by landed property."[21]

There can be no doubt that the new ruling class was above all one of landowners. These were the local notables. The basis of their wealth and influence was land, their prime aim to increase these by enlarging their estates. Perhaps Taine saw something fundamental in the revolution when he wrote, "Whatever the great words—liberty, equality, fraternity—with which the revolution was

---

[17] G. Lefebvre in *Annales historiques de la Révolution française,* no. 119 (1950), p. 276.

[18] J. Labasse, *La commerce des soies à Lyon sous Napoléon et la crise de 1811* (1957), p. 31.

[19] Cited in R. Bigo, *Les bases historiques de la finance moderne* (1933), p. 4.

[20] P. Bouyoux, "Les 'six cent plus imposés' du département de la Haute-Garonne en l'an X," *Annales du Midi,* t. 70 (1958), pp. 317–27.

[21] *Ibid.*

ornamented, it was essentially a transference of property; that constituted its inmost stay, its prime motive and its historic meaning."[22] Curiously similar was the verdict of Lefebvre in his earlier, more empirical days. After the abolition of privileges, the nobles and *roturiers* [commoners] joined, he wrote, in the same social class. The new bourgeoisie was one of "propriétaires non-exploitants" [absentee landlords.].[23]

This, of course, is one of those broad judgements which can only be given real substance by much detailed research. It raises a host of questions about the changes in ownership of land during the revolution, which cannot at present be answered. Most of the figures for the possession of land before the revolution are robbed of their significance by one simple flaw. The proportions owned by nobles, peasants, clergy, or others, are usually given as percentages of a whole area. Unless we know also how much is good arable land, how much pasture, and how much marsh, woodland or waste, such figures are practically meaningless. The one statement we can safely make is that the proportions of land owned by different classes varied enormously from one part of the country to another; and this doubtless remained true after, as before, the revolution.

It would be interesting to know to what extent, in different parts of the country, the noblesse kept its lands during the revolution, or regained them after temporary loss. It is said that in many departments of the West the noblesse was able to retain or restore its estates almost in their entirety.[24] We know also that there were many purchases of *biens nationaux* [expropriated Church and émigré lands] by nobles, sometimes even on behalf of *émigrés,* but we have very little idea what each section of society—aristocracy and upper bourgeoisie, urban middle class, better-off peasants or poorer ones— gained proportionately from their sale. The difficulty of making any reliable estimate is added to by the fact that the initial purchases were often fictitious or speculative, and subsequent sale, especially to peasants, may have changed the whole situation. Whoever they were, many of the purchasers presumably had a sudden accession of wealth through the difference between the nominal and the real price they paid, which resulted from the fall in value of the assignat. We know that wealthy men in the towns purchased a great deal, but we do not know how far the property they kept was urban, and how

---

[22] H. Taine, *Les origines de la France contemporaine: la Révolution* (10th ed., 1881), I, p. 386.

[23] G. Lefebvre, *Études sur la Révolution française* (1954), p. 238.

[24] Bois, *Paysans de l'Ouest,* pp. 313–14.

far rural, since town property is included along with country.[25] Again, did the area of land in large estates, and the number of such estates, increase or decrease? In one department of the West the decline in the number of noble landowners was accompanied by an increase in the size of estates.[26]

How far was the new landed class recruited from its predecessors of the *ancien régime,* and to what extent from new men risen from lower social ranks? Did revolutionary and Napoleonic armies provide entry tickets to the new aristocracy? Was it, to any important extent, a parish-pump aristocracy of local lawyers and business men who seized the opportunity afforded by the troubles of the revolution to accumulate land or houses and promote themselves to the rank of local notables?

Whatever the answers may be to all these questions, the main argument, that this was a revolution which bequeathed to France a ruling class of landowners, remains unaffected. It was, of course, to some extent a different class and type of landowner from that of the *ancien régime,* and one which possessed more political power than its predecessor. If such a class can be called a bourgeoisie, then this was the revolutionary bourgeoisie. If the latter is capable of being interpreted in such terms as these, at least it gives a great deal more sense to the subsequent history of France. We shall not vainly search for a non-existent industrial revolution, in a country dominated by a landed aristocracy. We shall understand the resistance offered by the landed classes under the Restoration to the attempt of the *émigrés* to come into their own again—now, unfortunately, too often other people's own. We shall see the bourgeois monarchy of Louis Philippe as what its franchise showed it to be—a government by and for landowners.[27] We shall understand the passionate defence of property by the ruling classes of the nineteenth century and their fear of the great centres of urban population, Paris and Lyon. Above all, it will become comprehensible why a revolution should have laid the foundations of such an intensely conservative society as France was to be for the next century and a half. . . .

One object of this study has been to suggest, by providing a positive example, the possibility of an empirical approach to the writing of social history, which will enable it to escape from the rigid patterns of system-makers who have deduced their history from their theories. The relation of social theory to social history should be, it

[25] *Cf.* Lefebvre, *Études,* p. 232.
[26] Bois, *Paysans de l'Ouest,* p. 320.
[27] *Cf.* Sherman Kent, *Electoral Procedure under Louis Philippe* (1937).

seems to me, similar to the relation of political and economic theories respectively to political and economic history. Each of these theoretical disciplines was evolved after consideration of an extensive range of historical experience. Their terminology is therefore relevant to the task of the historian. A particular weakness of most social theory on the contrary, especially from the point of view of its applicability to history, has been its neglect of historical evidence and its almost exclusive dependence on a small range of contemporary material. This not only means that it has developed a language which is inappropriate to past conditions, it also means that it usually deals either with a static situation or else with one involving only very short-term changes. History, on the other hand, requires perspective, which cannot be achieved by concentrating on the developments of a few months or even a few years.

What has been written on the social history of the revolutionary period has suffered from both these defects. It adopted as its model a sociological theory derived from the circumstances of a later age, and it used for the purpose of historical analysis the events of a mere year or two. This interpretation was then projected backwards and forwards, and the histories of the previous and the following centuries were twisted out of shape by the influence of the same arbitrary pattern. To fit in with the theory, eighteenth-century France had to be envisaged as still basically a feudal society, but one which was to become after the revolution predominantly capitalist and industrial, regardless of the facts. Thus Lefebvre could write of "the terrible conditions into which large-scale industry was going to precipitate the working-class in the course of the following decades"[28]— ignoring the terrible conditions, and numbers, of the poor in 1789, which he himself had described, and assuming the appearance in France of a large-scale industry in the early years of the nineteenth century, which his theory required but the facts, alas, repudiated.

If, on the other hand, we look with an open mind on the society that emerged from the revolution, we will be most struck by the permanent elements in the French social pattern. We will see a society with many new elements it is true, but bearing on it like a palimpsest the inadequately effaced writing of the *ancien régime*. The whole development of French society appears in a different light if we recognise that the revolution was a triumph for the conservative, propertied, land-owning classes, large and small. This was one of the factors—of course not the only one—contributing to the economic backwardness of France in the following century. It helps us to see

---

[28] Lefebvre, *Études,* p. 261.

that in the course of the revolution the social hierarchy, modified and based more openly on wealth, particularly landed wealth and political influence, and less on birth and aristocratic connections, was strengthened and re-asserted. Again, it is true that the revolution brought about important humanitarian reforms, and eliminated innumerable traditional barriers to the more unified and politically more efficient modern state: but it also frustrated the movement for a better treatment of the poorest sections of society, both rural and urban, which was manifesting itself in the last years of the *ancien régime*. The agricultural proletariat, says Lefebvre, suffered from the revolution.[29] The charitable activities of the church in the eighteenth century (and these should not be under-estimated) were largely brought to an end; the *biens de charité* were incorporated in the *biens nationaux* in the year II and until 29 fructidor year III [September 15, 1795] went to swell the property of the purchasers of church lands.[30] For the poor, possibly a harsher governmental climate was inaugurated. Whoever won the revolution, they lost.

I am really saying nothing new here, and nothing that the historians in the great revolutionary tradition have not said themselves. But having been said, it has usually been put on one side and forgotten, because the possibility that a revolution of the people—an ambiguous term—might have to be regarded as having had unhappy results for the people themselves could not be contemplated. The revolution was by definition a good thing. If any bad things seemed to be involved in it, then they were not part of it, or did not really exist. The revolution became a Sorelian myth [a slogan calling people to action], as Georges Lefebvre in the end proclaimed.[31] As the heroic age of French republicanism its record must not be sullied. As the mother of revolution to come, to use M. Guérin's phrase, it was to be treated with filial solicitude. It represented an earlier stage on the road that civilisation had to follow. To see it as in any way a diversion, or even a reversal of the one-way traffic dictated by the laws of a great philosophy of history, was too shocking to consider.

Even when evidence that might have led to a different interpretation of the revolution was adduced, it was forced into the preconceived pattern. Lefebvre argues that the economic interpretation of history is given an unduly narrow form when the revolution is re-

---

[29] *Ibid.*, p. 260.

[30] G. Lefebvre, *Paysans du Nord* (1924), pp. 738–40. [*Biens de charité* refer to land or other property held by hospitals or other charitable organizations, the income from which was to be used to succor the poor.—Eds.]

[31] Lefebvre, "Le mythe de la Révolution française," pp. 344–5.

garded as the result simply of the rise of the bourgeoisie. It also came, he says, from the resistance of the privileged to the birth of a new economic order, and the opposition of the least-favoured classes to the coming capitalist society. The grudge of the latter against the aristocracy, he agrees, was not only because the feudal order had always oppressed them, but also because the capitalist spirit was penetrating into the aristocracy itself and rendering it more odious. Most of this is true, though it is not the whole truth; but his conclusion is that though in this way the germination of a new social order provoked hostile reactions, at the same time these favoured its triumph. That this view is a little illogical might not matter, but it also assumes that the new social order hypothesised did in fact triumph.

I have tried to show that the social developments of the revolution are capable of a very different and even an entirely contrary interpretation, that it was not wholly a revolution for, but largely one against, the penetration of an embryo capitalism into French society. Considered as such, it largely achieved its ends. The peasant proprietors in the country, and the lawyers, *rentiers* [persons living off income from property] and men of property in the towns, successfully resisted the new economic trends. The latter, in particular, took control of the revolution and consolidated their régime by the dictatorship of Napoleon. "United to what remained of the old noblesse," says Lefebvre, "it [*the bourgeoisie*] constituted henceforth a landed aristocracy powerful enough to hold down, under its economic dictatorship, that rural democracy which it had in part created."[32]

In so far as capitalist economic developments were at issue, it was a revolution not for, but against, capitalism. This would, I believe, have been recognised long ago if it had not been for the influence of an unhistorical sociological theory. The misunderstanding was facilitated by the ambiguities implicit in the idea of the bourgeoisie. The bourgeois of the theory are a class of capitalists, industrial entrepreneurs and financiers of big business; those of the French Revolution were landowners, *rentiers* and officials, including in their fish-pond a few big fish, many of moderate size, and a host of minnows, who all knew that they swam in the same element, and that without the pervasive influence of the social hierarchy and the maintenance of individual and family property rights against any interference by the state, their way of life, confined, unchanging, conservative, repetitive, would come to an end. The revolution was theirs, and for them at least it was a wholly successful revolution.

---

[32] Lefebvre, *Études*, p. 261.

THE EMANCIPATION OF THE JEWS

Gary Kates

Gary Kates (1952–) received the B.A. from Pitzer College and the Ph.D. from the University of Chicago. He teaches at Trinity University in San Antonio, Texas, and is the author of many articles and two books: *The Cercle Social, The Girondins, and the French Revolution* (1985), and *Monsieur d'Eon Is a Woman: A Tale of Political Intrigue and Sexual Masquerade* (1995). He is also the editor of *The French Revolution: Recent Debates and New Controversies* (1998). His studies of the Revolution are wide ranging, including political history, gender studies, and the role of the Jews.

On 2 January 1792 in the center of the northeastern French town of Nancy, recently elected political leaders gathered to officiate at a new kind of patriotic ceremony. Standing before the town council were fourteen of Nancy's most notable Jews, including the Grand Rabbi, ready to swear an oath of allegiance to the young regime. "The oath that we are about to take," announced Berr Isaac Berr, the lay leader of the local Jewish community, "makes us, thanks to the Supreme Being, and to the sovereignty of the nation, not only men, but French citizens." Never again, they believed, would French Jews be the victims of persecution because of their "religious opinions." Berr, however, made it perfectly clear that he did not believe emancipation meant assimilation. "Each of us will naturally follow the religion of his father," he remarked to his gentile countrymen. "Thus, we can be loyally attached to the Jewish religion and be at the same time

From Gary Kates, "Jews into Frenchmen: Nationality and Representation in Revolutionary France," in *The French Revolution and the Birth of Modernity* ed. Ferenc Fehér (Berkeley: University of California Press, 1990), pp. 103–116. This article is printed by permission of the author and publisher.

good French citizens. Yes, Messieurs, that's what we will become. We swear it to you."[1]

In his response to this avowal, the mayor of Nancy happily welcomed Berr's remarks and declared what he thought to be the fundamental rationale behind Jewish emancipation: "Society must never investigate the beliefs of a citizen. Whatever the form he uses to honor the divinity does not matter so long as he obeys the Laws and serves his country." Then the mayor read the oath, which proclaimed the Jews' loyalty to the nation, to the laws, to the king, and to the Constitution. Each of the Jews responded: "I do swear."

Meanwhile, at Bischheim-au-Saum, a village near Strasbourg, Jews had a more difficult time convincing municipal leaders that they were worthy of emancipation. The town council kept putting off at least five eminent Jews who wanted to take the oath by declaring that every oathtaker must cross himself. That was the only way, the council insisted, that they could be sure that the person was telling the truth. The Jews refused to cross themselves, arguing that it was a violation of their newly won religious freedom. In March 1792, negotiations broke down over this point until both sides appealed to the departmental Directory, a regional authority that spoke on behalf of the central government. The Directory agreed with the Jews, stating that the law required "simply the obligation of taking the civic oath, without prescribing either the form nor the manner in which it will be made." The Directory ordered the town to go ahead with its ceremony.

Because of the controversy, thirty local national guard troops were assigned to the ceremony, which was finally set for 18 April. As the ceremony was beginning, however, there were cries from the crowd, particularly from the national guardsmen, for the Jews to remove their hats. The Jewish leaders refused to do so, claiming that one should never make an oath in God's presence without covering the head. The crowd, of course, argued the reverse, and the municipality was forced to cancel the event, lest it turn into a riot. Once again both sides appealed to the Directory, and once again the Directory sided with the Jews, accusing the town council of obstructing the law. Finally, on 30 April, at the insistence of the Directory, the five most prominent Jews of Bischheim succeeded in swearing allegiance to their country, thereby winning their full political rights.

These ceremonies, the result of the law passed by the Constituent

---

[1]David Feuerwerker, *L'Emancipation des juifs en France de l'Ancien Régime à la fin du Second Empire* (Paris, 1976), pp. 429–441. The account from Bischheim-au-Saum also comes from this source.

Assembly on 27 September 1791 which granted full political rights to Ashkenazic Jews, allow us to examine the ways in which Jewish emancipation was received at the local level. We find leading Jews stubbornly determined to acquire full political rights and equally determined to maintain their religious identity. At the same time, we see French revolutionary leaders insisting on the principles of equality before the law and religious freedom, even at the risk of offending local constituencies. Consequently, ever since these early days of the French Revolution, Jewish emancipation has been seen as something of a watershed in both French and Jewish history. For the French, the law meant that their country was the first modern European nation–state to offer Jews political equality. For the Jews, emancipation meant the beginning of their "Haskalah," the end to the ghetto and centuries of forced separation from gentiles. For both French and Jews, then, Jewish emancipation signaled an entirely new kind of epoch: secular, free, and tolerant.

Yet now, in the midst of the bicentennial celebration of the French Revolution, it has become increasingly difficult to see the emancipation movement in such a sanguine light. The tragic events of our own century have made emancipation at best problematic, and perhaps even irrelevant. From the Dreyfus Affair to the Holocaust, the overriding theme of European Jewry has been its destruction, not its liberation. Berr Isaac Berr pledged that his people would survive as Jews, because it is natural for people to follow "the religion of their fathers." But except for a few very rare families, few French—indeed, few European—Jewish families today can trace their genealogy back to the eighteenth century. Those Jews who did not assimilate were murdered or, if they were lucky, were forced to flee Europe. For many in the generation who lived through the Holocaust, the destruction of European Jewry in this century has made eighteenth-century Jewish emancipation seem like a tragic farce.

Among the most eminent of this generation who share that perspective is Rabbi Arthur Hertzberg. Holder of a Distinguished Chair at Dartmouth, former head of the World Zionist Congress, regular contributor to the "Op-Ed" page of the *New York Times,* as well as to the *New York Review of Books,* Rabbi Hertzberg has established himself as one of the most prominent intellectuals in the American Jewish community, and his book, *The French Enlightenment and the Jews: The Origins of Modern Anti-Semitism,*[2] quickly became the definitive dis-

---

[2]Rabbi Arthur Hertzberg, *The French Enlightenment and the Jews: The Origins of Modern Anti-Semitism* (New York: Columbia University Press, 1968).

cussion of the subject. Its argument is original and disturbing. Until Hertzberg, most writers held the view that modern anti-Semitism was a right-wing phenomenon that surfaced during the late nineteenth century in opposition to the liberal ideas usually associated with the French Revolution. But Hertzberg turned that contention upside down: twentieth-century anti-Semitism, he claimed, is not in conflict with French revolutionary ideology but in fact stems from it. "Modern, secular, anti-Semitism," he wrote, "was fashioned not as a reaction to the Enlightenment and the Revolution, but within the Enlightenment and Revolution themselves."[3] For Hertzberg, Jewish emancipation was the first step in the long march to Auschwitz.

Hertzberg did not simply claim that those who opposed emancipation were anti-Semitic but argued further that even the proemancipation legislators contributed to modern anti-Semitism: they saw emancipation as the only way to assimilate the Jew and rid France of its "Jewish problem." Once Jews lost their communal autonomy and faced the centralized state as individual Frenchmen, Hertzberg claimed, their days were numbered. The hostility of the Jacobins to all religious expression during the Terror offered Hertzberg the proof that he needed.

Hertzberg's argument managed to combine the ideas of three influential Jewish intellectuals: Hannah Arendt, Jacob Talmon, and Asher Ginzberg (better known as Ahad Ha'am). From Arendt's *Origins of Totalitarianism,* Hertzberg gleaned two fundamental concepts: first, that in the modern age the revolutionary left and the radical right are equally repressive. Since revolutionary change most often depends on the coercive power of the centralized state, its impact on the individual is bound to be tyrannical. Second, Arendt claimed that anti-Semitism had played a crucial role in recent European history. "Political developments have driven the Jewish people into the storm center of events," she wrote. The way that Europe treated its Jews could be taken as a bellwether of the quality of European political culture.[4]

Arendt had specifically noted that these features were true only for the contemporary world. She pushed back her analysis to the last decades of the nineteenth century, but no further. Although elsewhere Arendt was later highly critical of the French Revolution, nowhere did she accuse the Jacobins of establishing a totalitarian or

---

[3]*Ibid.,* p. 7.
[4]Hannah Arendt, *The Origins of Totalitarianism* (New York, 1973 [1951]), p. 7. Hertzberg comments on Arendt in *The French Enlightenment,* pp. 6–7.

anti-Semitic state.[5] For her, modern racial anti-Semitism was novel and distinct from older attitudes, preventing any explanation of the Holocaust from reaching back as far as the eighteenth century.

Jacob Talmon's *Origins of Totalitarian Democracy* provided that continuity for Hertzberg. In Jacobinism, Talmon discovered "a vision of society of equal men re-educated by the State in accordance with an exclusive and universal pattern."[6] Like Arendt, Talmon considered the radical left to be as repressive as the right. The Jacobins had acted fanatically, he believed, systematically violating individual liberties on behalf of a messianic ideal. But while Talmon attacked the liberal ideals of the revolutionary left, he ignored Jewish emancipation altogether.

Both Arendt and Talmon, then, sought to discredit the revolutionary left and provide a historical model that justified a more moderate approach to political change. Moreover, like Hertzberg, Arendt and Talmon were both dedicated Zionists, committed in their personal lives to developing an authentic Jewish political culture. Arendt had worked for Youth Aliyah (Jewish immigration to Palestine) programs before World War II and had published articles during the 1940s on Zionist strategy. Talmon moved to Israel after an education in Britain and taught for years at the Hebrew University in Jerusalem. Both, in short, were highly suspicious of the emancipation process as well as the promises of the revolutionary left. But neither of them blamed modern anti-Semitism on the French revolutionary emancipators.[7]

For the notion that the emancipation process *itself* lay at the root of modern anti-Semitism, Hertzberg drew on the writings of Ahad

---

[5]See Hannah Arendt, *On Revolution* (New York, 1963).

[6]J. L. Talmon, *The Origins of Totalitarian Democracy* (New York, 1970 [1952]), p. 250.

[7]For Arendt see Elizabeth Young-Bruehl, *For the Love of the World: A Biography of Hannah Arendt* (New Haven, 1982). Given Talmon's commitment to Zionism and his interest in Jewish history, it is curious that he was silent about Jewish Emancipation. This omission has caused some confusion among his colleagues. On the one hand, Yehoshua Arieli insists that Talmon "perceived the 'Jewish problem' of modern Europe and the modern world as the touchstone, the main indicator and precipitate, of the major trends and problems of modern times, indicating the degree of virulence of the collective neuroses as well as accelerating them." But British political theorist John Dunn is probably closer to the truth when he claims that Talmon's most basic problem was not the Jewish question but rather: "Why exactly is the political character of Communist regimes such an unremitting disaster?" See the articles by Arieli and Dunn in *Totalitarian Democracy and After: International Colloquium in Memory of Jacob L. Talmon* (Jerusalem, 1984), pp. 25, 42. For Talmon's interest in Jewish history and politics see his *The Unique and the Universal* (New York, 1965), and *Israel Among the Nations* (New York, 1970).

Ha'am (1856–1927), the Zionist "secular rabbi" who first began to write in his native Russia during the 1880s and finally moved to Palestine in 1921. Ahad Ha'am had directly attacked France and French Jews for their faith in political emancipation, charging that the Jews' so-called freedom was little more than a mirage. "Their condition may be justly defined as *spiritual slavery under the veil of outward freedom*," he wrote in 1891 (emphasis added). "In reality they accepted this slavery a hundred years ago, together with their 'rights'; but it is only in these evil days that it stands revealed in all its glory." Ahad Ha'am condemned Jews for giving up their separate national identity not so much because he distrusted France, but rather because he did not believe that Jews could maintain a religious identity of any significant value in an epoch in which the broader culture had become almost completely secular. Accepting even the best of circumstances for the emancipated Jew, Ahad Ha'am insisted on asking a nagging question: Why would French Jews choose to remain Jewish "for the sake of certain theoretical beliefs which they no longer hold, or which, if they do really and sincerely maintain them, they might equally hold without this special name, as every non-Jewish Deist has done?"[8]

It is a tribute to Hertzberg's rhetorical skills that he was able to combine distinct arguments from these three thinkers into a powerful interpretation that blamed the tragic events of the twentieth century on the French revolutionary emancipation process itself. "It is strange that he did not even mention the Jewish question during the Revolution," Hertzberg wrote of Talmon.[9]

> Here there can be no doubt whatsoever that the Revolution was "totalitarian." Almost all of those who helped to emancipate the Jews, from [Henri] Grégoire through Robespierre, had in mind some vision of what they ought to be made to become. Talmon's critics may be correct in maintaining that the main body of the revolutionaires, the political center, were willing to leave men to be themselves within the new political order. It was these very people, however, who made demands not only on the public behavior but also on the inner spirit and religion of the Jews. Here the Revolution appeared at its most doctrinaire.

Hertzberg put the blame for modern anti-Semitism on the proemancipators themselves, especially on left-wing deputies who hoped to push France in a more democratic direction. Behind such logic is

---

[8]*Selected Essays of Ahad Ha'Am,* trans. Leon Simon (New York, 1970 [1912]), pp. 177, 184. For Hertzberg on Ahad Ha'am see *The Zionist Idea,* ed. Arthur Hertzberg (New York, 1981 [1959]), pp. 248–277; and Arthur Hertzberg, *Being Jewish in America: The Modern Experience* (New York, 1979), p. xiii.

[9]Hertzberg, *The French Enlightenment,* p. 363.

a clear Zionist agenda. Since the Haskalah, when Jews emerged from their communal autonomy, Western nation–states have faced essentially three choices with regard to their Jewish communities: integration, expulsion, or destruction, or encouraging the establishment of a separate Jewish state. Clearly the French revolutionaries chose the first alternative and, in fact, never seriously contemplated any of the others. The novelty of Hertzberg's argument is that he discredits integration by associating it with expulsion or destruction. Insofar as the French expected Jews to assimilate into French society and culture, they had no respect for Judaism or the Jewish people, he charges. Emancipation was just another way for the French to get rid of their Jews. In this view Zionism was and remains the only response to modernity that is good for Jews.

The problem with Hertzberg's argument is not with his ideology; the notion that Jews are a nation entitled to their own state is certainly legitimate. Rather, it is Hertzberg's understanding of history that is problematic. His interpretation of the French Revolution is highly reductionist. He conflates different phases of the Revolution together, assuming that the achievements of the liberal Constituent Assembly were merely a prelude to the Terror; Hertzberg ignores the differences between the democratic movement of 1790–1792 and the sans-culottes movement of 1793–1794.[10] Worse, by pulling the debates over emancipation out of their proper political context, he distorts the views of the proemancipators as well as the antiemancipators, who were, obviously, more concerned abut the fate of France and her revolution than with Jewish national destiny. Finally, Hertzberg's analysis does an injustice to the Jews themselves. Berr Isaac Berr and hundreds of others who took the loyalty oaths required for full emancipation were not simply fools deceived by their countrymen but patriots who were exploiting a historic opportunity.

Despite these flaws in his analysis, Hertzberg has focused on some genuine historical problems concerning Jewish emancipation which still require attention: given that the Declaration of the Rights of Man and Citizen was passed in August 1789, why did French Jews have to wait two years before being offered full political rights? Why did the proemancipators equate emancipation with assimilation? Why did they have so little respect for the integrity of an autonomous Jewish identity that they expected Jews to dissolve their official communal institutions?

Perhaps the most amazing aspect of Jewish emancipation is that it

---

[10] On the tendency to reduce the French Revolution to the Terror alone, see Ferenc Fehér, *The Frozen Revolution: An Essay on Jacobinism* (Cambridge, 1987), pp. 1–30.

happened at all. French Jews, in fact, constituted only a tiny fraction of French society. Moreover, they were concentrated into relatively few towns. Some 3,500 Sephardic Jews lived in and around Bordeaux, 30,000 Ashkenazic Jews lived in Alsace and Lorraine, and perhaps 500 others lived in Paris.[11] Nor was their participation in the Revolution particularly noteworthy. There were no Jews, to my knowledge, elected to any of the national assemblies during the Revolution. And outside of the debate over their own fate, it is difficult to think of one Jewish writer, journalist, or political activist who played more than the most minor role. It is likely that the vast majority of Frenchmen, including those deputies sitting in the Constituent Assembly, had never met even a handful of Jews, if that many.

These facts have led Eugen Weber to argue that "the Jewish question was a *Jewish* question," that is, of interest only to Jews. "Most normal French," he asserted to a rather dismayed audience at a 1985 conference on the history of Jews in France, have not cared about Jews and don't care to think much about them now. Outside of Alsace, "the French thought about Jews hardly at all. They had other fish to fry."[12] But surely Weber was exaggerating. Otherwise, how do we explain the inordinate amount of attention given to the Jewish issue by the French revolutionaries? No agenda has ever been more full than was the Constituent Assembly's. It had to deal with such crucial issues as the constitution, taxation, and reorganization of the church, and an increasingly recalcitrant king, not to mention their own internal disputes and factions. Many other pressing issues, such as women's rights, were ignored. Certainly it was not imperative that the Constituent Assembly deal with the Jewish question; and at least some deputies did not think it was worth it. "We have even more important matters to deal with," exclaimed the moderate leader Guy Target during one of the debates:

> What we say in regard to the Jews affects only a part of society; but to establish a judiciary, to determine the size and manner of the French army, to establish a financial system, here are three issues that interest the entire kingdom, and which require immediate action.[13]

---

[11] [Sephardic Jews were descended from the Jews of Spain and Portugal exiled by the Spanish Inquisition. Ashkenazic Jews were descended from the Jews who settled in central and eastern Europe after the Babylonian exile.—Eds.]

[12] Eugen Weber, "Reflections on the Jews in France," in Frances Malino and Bernard Wasserstein eds., *The Jews in Modern France* (Hanover and London, 1985), p. 17.

[13] *Archives parlementaires de 1787 à 1860. Recueil complet des débats législatifs et politiques des chambres françaises. Première série (1787 à 1799)*, 88 vols. to date (Paris, 1867–) (hereafter cited as *AP*), 11: 710.

But the Jewish question did not go away. Leaders of the National Assembly kept returning it to the agenda. Even the Paris municipal legislature considered Jewish emancipation very important, though there were only five hundred Jews living in the capital. At one point during the early weeks of 1790, nearly every one of Paris's sixty district assemblies debated the issue and, by an overwhelming majority, urged the National Assembly to fully emancipate all Jews.[14]

Thus Target was off target on one major point: few people treated the debate on the Jews as concerning only "a part of society." Non-Jews chose to address this issue because the emancipation debate was not really about the Jews at all. Since there were so few Jews in France, and since they played little role in the Revolution, they were easily turned into symbols of something else. Various groups and writers, including the Paris Communal Assembly and the national Constituent Assembly, used the issue to test what was then perhaps the most fundamental political question: would the promises inherent in the Declaration of the Rights of Man and Citizen translate into equal political power for all Frenchmen, regardless of status, or would those leading the Revolution stop short of democracy by limiting the political power of certain kinds of people? The debate over Jewish emancipation was thus a debate over what it meant to be a French citizen.

In fact, it has been argued that French Jews did not need emancipation, at least no more so than any other group in France. Although we think of the era before the French Revolution as a bleak period in Jewish history, the status of the Jew was much better in France during the last decades of the Old Regime than in most other European counties. Old Regime society was corporate and particularistic. The law recognized individuals only insofar as they held membership in a legal group. A tailor needed the protection of his guild, a priest his religious order, a merchant his town corporation, and so on. In this respect, Jews were considered legitimate subjects of the king if they were attached to a legally recognized Jewish community. Political life usually consisted of each separate group gaining its own privileges from the royal government at the expense of every other group. As Salo Baron noted sixty years ago, throughout the eighteenth century French Jews were particularly adept at securing special laws for their communities. "Even then they belonged to the privileged minority

---

[14] On Paris see S. Lacroix, "Ce qu'on pensait des juifs à Paris en 1790," *Révolution française* 30 (1898): 91–112.

which included nobles, clergy and urban citizenry."[15] This is perhaps an exaggeration but, at least in terms of legal advantages, the political status of most Jews was greater than that of most peasants. Jewish communities prospered at the pleasure of the royal government and often against the muffled shouts of the peasants who, especially in Alsace and Lorraine, were hostile to Jews. Despite local bigotry, by the eve of the Revolution royal reformers such as Malesherbes were calling for further reform. So long as the central government continued its policy of protecting Jewish interests, French Jews could reasonably expect to be optimistic about the future.

But the French Revolution threw the status of the Jews into confusion. Without their privileged and autonomous communities, Jews were vulnerable to the passions of the local peasants and small shopkeepers. If the new French government became decentralized, Jews might even stand to lose much more than they might gain by the new changes. The Constituent Assembly first discussed the Jewish question on 28 September 1789 because northeastern French Jewish communities had asked for protection from popular violence that had broken out during the summer. The moderate leader Stanislas Clermont-Tonnerre and the radical priest Henri Grégoire urged the Assembly to adopt the following decree:

> The Assembly decrees M. the President to write to the public officials of Alsace that the Jews are under the safeguard of the law and require of the king the protection that they need.[16]

This bill passed with no opposition, and its importance should not be minimized. On the one hand it continued the policies of the old central government of protecting Jews against local persecution and, in that sense, represented no great change for Jews. But insofar as it brought Jews under the same laws as everyone else, it gave them a high degree of civil equality. This was very close to de facto emancipation. Why, then, did it take the Assembly another two years (and hours of tumultuous debate) to go any further?

At about the same time, the Assembly was working out the electoral laws that would operate under the new constitution. Although the Assembly pledged that the constitution and its laws would apply equally to all citizens, they nonetheless made a fundamental distinc-

---

[15] Salo W. Baron, "Ghetto and Emancipation: Shall We Revise the Traditional View?" *The Menorah Journal* 14 (June 1928): 517; Salo W. Baron, "Newer Approaches to Jewish Emancipation," *Diogenes* 29 (Spring 1960): 56–81. For a more general survey see also Feuerwerker, *L'émancipation des juifs,* pp. 3–48.

[16] *AP,* 9: 201.

tion between two kinds of citizens: Active and Passive. Both kinds of citizens were treated equally under the law and held the rights guaranteed in the Declaration of the Rights of Man and Citizen. The difference between them was that only active citizens could vote and hold public office. The most important qualification for active citizenship was wealth: one had to pay a direct tax that amounted to three days' wages for an average worker. In addition, there were gradations of active citizenship. For example, only those who paid an annual tax of about fifty-one livres—a sum well out of reach of most Frenchmen—were eligible for seats in the National Assembly.

Hertzberg and others have ignored the fact that the 28 September 1789 decree effectively transformed Jews into passive citizens. From that day on, no one in the Constituent Assembly denied Jews the basic rights guaranteed in the Declaration of the Rights of Man and Citizen; all agreed, for example, that Jews ought to be free to observe their own religious opinions and should not be forcibly converted. The issue, then, became not one of religious freedom, but rather of the extent to which Jews were qualified to be active citizens. In other words, Hertzberg's claim that "the battle for the Emancipation very nearly failed" needs to be radically qualified: what nearly failed was the attempt to secure the rights of active citizenship for Jews.[17]

Thus when we turn to the debates concerning Jewish rights that took place at the Constituent Assembly on 23–24 December 1789 and 28 January 1790, we find that the bill in question focuses on aspects of active citizenship:[18]

> That non-Catholics, who will have otherwise fulfilled all the conditions prescribed in previous decrees for becoming an elector and eligible [*for public office*] could be elected to all ranks of administration, without exception.

In December this bill passed only when Jews were specifically excluded from it. One month later, a similar bill gave the rights of active citizenship to the Sephardic Jews of Bordeaux and Avignon. But a majority of the Assembly refused to "emancipate" the Ashkenazic Jews of eastern France. Why?

Opposition to offering Jews the right of active citizenship came from three overlapping groups. First were a small core of deputies from Alsace, most notably Jean-Francois Reubell. They clearly echoed the popular anti-Semitism of their region, reflecting a fear of Jewish financial power and, above all else, of usury. Because Jews

---

[17] Hertzberg, *The French Enlightenment*, p. 339.
[18] *AP*, 10: 782.

were concentrated primarily in this part of France, these attitudes were isolated, and this group alone could not have persuaded a majority of their colleagues to vote against Jewish active citizenship.

A second and larger group consisted of clergymen and friends of the church who saw French nationality in religious terms. What concerned the Abbé Maury, for example, was the notion that emancipated Jews could be elected to positions of leadership in what he assumed should be a Christian nation. He thought the prospect of a Jewish judge pronouncing justice on a Christian defendant absurd; for him, the law derived from the sovereign will of a people, 99 percent of whom were Christians. But this did not mean that Maury wished to expel the Jews:

> They must not be persecuted. They are men; they are brothers; and it is an anathema to even consider talking about intolerance. You have already recognized that nothing should be done about their religious opinions, and since then you have assured Jews the broadest protection.[19]

In short, even Maury, among the Constituent Assembly's most conservative and "theocratic" deputies, recognized the importance of the September 1789 decree and was not offended by the idea of Jews living in France as passive citizens; rather, what disturbed him was the possibility of being ruled by them.

Finally, a coalition of conservative deputies wanted to exclude Jews from political life because their goal was to restrict active citizenship to as small a group as possible. These deputies, such as Prince de Broglie, hoped to transform active citizenship into a new kind of aristocracy. Jews, Protestants, actors, urban workers, sansculottes—anyone who was not of the highest class, they felt, should be denied the right to vote and hold office.

These three groups also had in common the belief that French Jews, especially the Ashkenazim in eastern France, constituted a separate nation within France. The differences in language, dress, marriage, and obviously religious rituals made the Jew as different from the Frenchman as an Englishman or Dane. "The Jews collectively are a *corps de nation* [national group] separate from the French," charged Reubell. "They have a distinct role. Thus they can never acquire the status of an Active Citizen."[20] When all was said and done, this was the most effective argument of the antiemancipators, successful enough to retard full emancipation until the final days of the Constituent Assembly.

---

[19] *AP,* 10: 757.
[20] *AP,* 11: 364.

The concept of nationality was extremely important in French revolutionary ideology precisely because it replaced the idea of subjects kept apart by privilege with the notion of citizens brought together through their common national identity. For its leaders, the French Revolution was precisely the act of the French nation repossessing the sovereign state from king and aristocracy. The "people" and the "nation" were often, but not always, considered the same thing. When the people acted according to their self-interest, they were merely a collection of individuals. But when the people shared a common interest, their actions were perceived as expressing the national will.

This definition of nationality, so important for the development of political ideas during the Revolution, is most clearly seen in Sieyès's popular pamphlet, *What Is the Third Estate?* In it, Sieyès described three stages of national development. At first there are a great number of isolated individuals who wish to unite, but they do not yet recognize a common interest. "The second period is characterized by the action of the *common* will. . . . Power exists only in the aggregate. The community needs a common will; without singleness of will it could not succeed in being a willing and acting body." This was the point at which the Revolution occurred. Finally, Sieyès distinguished a future "third period from the second in that it is no longer the *real* common will which is in operation, but a *representative* common will."[21]

Drawing heavily upon Rousseau, Sieyès's ideas were radical because they negated the political legitimacy of all corporate bodies. The Revolution dissolved them all, leaving in their place individuals whose rights were protected by their membership in a nation-state. In this sense "the Jewish question" boiled down to the following problem: Did Jews constitute a nation distinct from the French (and thus were not part of the new sovereign body)? Or were Jewish communities essentially autonomous corporations, like any other in the Old Regime? This was the essential issue that divided proemancipators from their opponents. The antiemancipators believed that during the Old Regime, Jewish communities constituted both corporations and a separate nation. Therefore although the Revolution had dissolved corporations, it still left the nationality problem unresolved. Antiemancipators, such as the Abbé Maury, therefore proposed something of a compromise: in return for the elimination of Jewish corporate autonomy, Jews ought to be given the basic rights

---

[21] Emmanuel Joseph Sieyès, *What Is the Third Estate?*, trans. M. Blondel (London, 1963), pp. 121–122.

of passive citizens. But insofar as their nationality makes them distinct from the sovereign, they should be refused the rights of active citizenship.

The proemancipators constructed their argument around the notion that the Jews of France did not constitute a separate nation but merely a corporation, which, like other corporations, was in dire need of "regeneration." Clermont-Tonnerre offered the best-known version of this position: "One must refuse everything to the Jews as a nation, and give everything to the Jews as individuals. . . . It would be repugnant to have a society of noncitizens in a state, and a nation within a nation."[22] Commenting on the debate, future Girondin chief Jacques-Pierre Brissot predicted that those Jews who were given the rights of active citizens would "lose their particular characteristics." Their "admission to eligibility will regenerate them."[23]

Arthur Hertzberg is correct to see in the proemancipation position the call for an end to Jewish distinctiveness. But he is mistaken in his assertion that this position was the seedbed for anti-Semitism or totalitarianism. The necessity for some kind of "regeneration" stems from the French revolutionary conception of representation. In some representative systems, the deputy is supposed to represent the interests of the majority of voters who elected him. But during the French Revolution, to quote Sieyès again, "every deputy is representing the entire nation."[24] In contrast to the United States, in which legislators represent different interests and constituencies, the French expected their leaders to search only for the one true will of the nation. Any group of deputies who openly represented a particular interest or constituency separate from the national will was considered a dangerous faction. Thus no significant differences could be allowed to arise between a deputy and his constituency, much less between the deputies themselves.

This concept of representation had important implications for the Jews of France. Since granting rights of active citizenship to Jews would make them eligible for various offices, the possibility arose that a Jew could represent a nation that was overwhelmingly Christian, when most of those Christians were ineligible to hold political office. How could a Jewish elector, for example, participate in an election for a bishop (such elections began in late 1790)? Proemanci-

---

[22] *AP,* 10: 754.

[23] *Patriote français,* 24 December 1789, p. 2.

[24] Quoted in Keith Michael Baker, "Representation," in Baker, ed., *The French Revolution and the Creation of Modern Political Culture.* I: *The Political Culture of the Old Regime* (Oxford, 1987), p. 488.

pators such as Sieyès and Grégoire resolved this dilemma by arguing that the Jewish politician should think only about the welfare of the entire nation, relegating his Jewish life strictly to the private sphere. In order for him to adequately represent the true interests of his nation, his own Jewishness, while remaining personally important to him, must have no political significance.

The Ashkenazic Jews did not win their full political rights until the final days of the Constituent Assembly in September 1791. By then the political mood of the country had changed drastically. Many aristocratic deputies had become disgusted by the pace of revolutionary change, and they were fleeing the country. The moderate leaders were less convinced that the king would abide by the new constitution, and they feared that power would fall into the hands of radical republicans. In this new political context, granting Jews the rights to active citizenship no longer seemed so dangerous. Thus when the popular leader Adrien Duport urged his colleagues to "declare relative to the Jews that they can become French Active Citizen," they decreed that all Jews must have the same rights to "becoming Active Citizens" as any other citizen. Thus "emancipation" was equated with active citizenship, while passive citizenship had long ago been assumed by everyone.[25]

These debates over Jewish emancipation do not reveal an anti-Semitic or even a mean-spirited Constituent Assembly. The hypothesis that emancipation itself provided the seedbed for later tragedies turns out to have been based on a distorted view of French revolutionary politics. Insofar as the Jews were concerned, the early French revolutionaries basically carried on the liberal policies of the preceding government. Anti-Semitism was a local affair, confined to northeastern France. The political status of French Jews changed between 1789–1791 because Frenchmen themselves were transformed from subjects of a kingdom to citizens of a nation. If the Constituent Assembly spent many noisy hours over the fate of the Jews, it was because "the Jewish question" raised issues fundamental to their own identity: it helped to define the secular character of the state, the meaning of active and passive citizenship, the nature of representation, and the place of corporate bodies within the new regime. It also gave radical and moderate politicians an issue they could use to fight the power of the church and the aristocracy.

More fundamentally, the debates over Jewish emancipation reveal not a Jewish problem but a problem the *French* had defining nation-

---

[25] *AP,* 31: 372.

ality and representation. Unlike the newly created United States, the French did not conceive of representation in terms of separate interests; only a unitary national will could be the ultimate political expression of French sovereignty. This approach impeded the development of a "loyal opposition," as well as of party politics, and it led France away from political stability. Hertzberg may be correct that this kind of democracy is not good for Jews; indeed, it may not be good for anyone. But this is a political problem and has little to do with anti-Semitism.

Zionist critics distrust the emancipation process because they correctly believe that it represented a renunciation of an autonomous Jewish national destiny. But it is wrong to blame emancipators like Clermont-Tonnerre and Grégoire for what would happen to Jews 150 years later. Worse, it makes fools of those Jews who, since Berr Isaac Berr, have believed in the integrity of the diaspora. In fact, the French Revolution offered French Jews a historic opportunity. Emancipation gave every Jew the *choice* of being Jewish. Participation in the Jewish community was no longer a legal obligation but became instead a moral duty. Only in this context could Jewish identity become a matter of intense personal concern.

STRIKING A BALANCE

David Gordon Wright

David Gordon Wright (1937–1995), the son of textile mill workers, received his B.A. from the University of Manchester and his Ph.D. from the University of Leeds. He taught at the City of Leeds Carnegie College, the Huddersfield Polytechnic in Yorkshire, and the Open University. He wrote several surveys including *Democracy and Reform, 1815–1885* [in Great Britain] (revised edition, 1972), *Napoleon and Europe* (1984), *Popular Radicalism: The [British] Working-Class Experience, 1780–1880* (1988), *Revolution and Terror in France, 1789–1795* (2nd ed., 1990), and *The Great War* [of 1914–1918]: *A Useless Slaughter?* (1991).

It remains difficult to strike a balance between the positive and negative effects of the Revolution. Clearly, the Revolution achieved much that was positive. The work of the National (Constituent) Assembly was remarkable, transforming all France's major institutions and creating a new society and new approaches to the scope of political action, even if it did condone violence and make a hash of the religious settlement. In his didactic and propagandistic *Reflections on the Revolution in France* (1790), Edmund Burke brilliantly argued that it was not possible to destroy a country's institutions and construct a new society from a blank sheet. But the National Assembly proved him wrong, even if the ultimate cost was enormous. A chaotic inheritance of privileges, prejudices and provincial rights was swept away in favour of a new, rationalistic national order, dedicated to the principle that power be entrusted only to those who had been chosen by their fellow citizens, whether they were judges, bishops or National Guard officers. A belief in fundamental natural rights led to religious toleration, civil and political rights for Protestants and Jews, freedom of the press, equality before the law and trial by jury. The declaration

From D. G. Wright, *Revolution and Terror in France, 1789–1795* (2nd ed.; London: Longman, 1990), pp. 108–115, reprinted by permission of Pearson Education Limited.

of the Rights of Man in August 1789 contained a programme that was
largely implemented over the next two years. The administrative reorganisation into departments, clearing away the jumble of jurisdic-
tions which had developed piecemeal over centuries, still survives.

France was therefore transformed in ways which most of its educated citizens, at least, regarded as being for the better. And the Revolution was initially and primarily a movement of the educated and
of intellectuals. The new institutions took root and survived all the
vicissitudes of nineteenth-century France, even if in the short run the
transformation was to tear the country apart and lead to foreign war,
civil war and Terror, as well as the temporary suspension of most of
the "fundamental natural rights." Although the declaration of war in
1792 was a disastrous error, the Convention deserves some credit for
coping with its consequences and constructing the military and administrative machine which defeated the counter-revolution at
home, split the coalition of France's enemies and enabled subsequent French expansion into Europe; although again at terrible cost.

In some other ways the Revolution did not change France all that
much, with the important exception of the sweeping away of seigneurialism, or what the Revolutionaries preferred to call "feudalism."
The nobility were far from being destroyed, for only 1,158 out of
400,000 or so were executed, while 16,431 emigrated, many only temporarily. The majority of noble families remained relatively unaffected materially by the Revolution and Terror, although the loss of
seigneurial rights meant that their status in society was never the
same again. It is true that the noble share of landownership fell, but
the transfer of property during the Revolution was not quite so drastic as one might expect. Those who purchased the *biens nationaux*
[expropriated Church land] and confiscated property of *suspects* and
émigrés usually already possessed land; more often than not they
were the urban bourgeoisie, although many peasants acquired land
during the late 1790s and subsequent decades. Among those who
benefited the most were the financiers, speculators and bureaucrats
who handled the finances of the Republic (and later the Empire).
There was remarkable continuity between the financiers of the *ancien régime,* the Revolution, the Empire and the post-1815 Restoration. Great fortunes, founded on shady speculation by officials and
administrators in the 1790s, not only enriched many bourgeois, but
also some of the nobility whom the Revolution had attempted to dec-
imate. The Church also survived, despite losing nearly half the
parish clergy from death and emigration and suffering untold damage to buildings and property. Having benefited from a considerable
religious revival after Thermidor [July 27–28, 1794], the Roman Cath-

olic Church became the religion of "the majority of Frenchmen" by the 1801 Concordat between Napoleon and the Papacy. Yet neither under the Empire nor the Bourbon restoration did the Church regain the land, wealth, personnel, prestige and respect it had enjoyed under the *ancien régime*.

Divine-Right monarchy had also gone for good. So had the old aristocratic and hierarchical society, for the restorations under Napoleon and Louis XVIII were only partial. After 1795 France possessed a more open and fluid society where careers were accessible to talent and ownership of property was more widely diffused. The power of the press and public opinion could never be completely stifled, even by Napoleon. On the other hand the violence of the Revolution, especially the Terror of the Year II [1793–1794] and the White Terror of the Year III [1794–1795], left France badly divided and difficult to govern. The instability of French administrations in the nineteenth and early twentieth centuries owes a good deal to the antagonisms and tensions created both by the Revolution itself and by the myths which grew up about it after Thermidor.

The Jacobin Republic of 1792–94 provided, for those willing to ignore the violence, a model of a militant minority determined to implement the ideal of the total sovereignty of the people, a model which was to inspire popular agitation—liberal, nationalist and socialist—both in France and abroad, even though there could never be agreement on just what the "sovereignty of the people" implied in practice. It also demonstrated how a revolution can go wrong when the sovereignty of the people comes to mean the government telling people what they ought to want, rather than what they actually did want. In the Thermidorian period, Francois-Nöel Babeuf developed primitive socialist theories whose egalitarianism was to link Jacobinism with nineteenth-century socialism. The "constitutional" Revolution of 1789–91 created a restricted, property-owning political democracy which helped inspire moderate middle-class European liberalism during the following century, especially when such liberals forgot about the howling mobs in the public galleries of the Assembly. The example of the *sans culottes* and the Revolutionary insurrections inspired oppressed peoples to seek their own versions of direct democracy and popular sovereignty.

At the same time it prompted rulers, nobles and clergy to unite in defence of the *status quo ante*. Reforming monarchs and enlightened despots retreated into conservatism, or rather developed it as a doctrine for the first time, fearing that the French epidemic would prove contagious. Whatever the strength of the forces of reaction in both France and Europe after the end of the Revolutionary and Napoleonic

Wars in 1815, there was much that could never be erased. Warfare itself was put on a new footing; the intricate manoeuvring of many eighteenth-century armies had passed away, while armies themselves were larger and suffered much greater casualties. The Revolutionaries had taken the unprecedented step of arming the people.

While the sources of liberal democracy may be sought in the English Revolution of the 1640s and 1688, as well as the American Revolution of 1776–83, the French Revolution in its 1789–92 stage made a further major contribution. The increased power of wealth, as opposed to birth, in industrial society can at least partly be traced back to 1789. And the concept of "revolution" itself, in its modern sense, was also a product of the French Revolution.

There are those who now argue that the Revolution was not worth the costs involved and that, overall, it was a tragedy of gigantic proportions. The first figure to list in the debit column is the two million dead in war and civil war between 1792 and 1815, more, in proportion to population, than in the First World War. Millions more had their lives ruined. Paper money, mass mobilisation and requisitioning during the Terror ruined an economy already shaken by civil and foreign war. To cope with rampant inflation, partly caused by their unrestrained issue of paper money, Revolutionary governments introduced price and wage controls which drove goods off the market, obliged the authorities to requisition food from recalcitrant peasants by force of arms, made bread even scarcer and helped to provoke a rebellion in the Vendée region whose repression involved virtual genocide. Issues of civic loyalty and treason in wartime inflicted yet more suffering on the French people, as small-scale massacres were transformed into official Terror.

Between 1793 and 1794 some 30,000 were killed in the "official" Terror alone and tens of thousands imprisoned without trial in overcrowded, stinking gaols. Jean-Baptiste Carrier, the *représentant* in the rebellious west, turned the Loire into a "national bathtub," drowning prisoners in batches of hundreds at Nantes and reporting to Paris: "We shall turn France into a cemetery rather than fail in her regeneration." Even though the Terror did not last long, its legacy was the reintroduction of the spirit of religious warfare to a country and a continent which had virtually forgotten it. Both politics and war became black-and-white struggles between good and evil, with compromise or negotiation ruled out of court.

The Revolutionaries first introduced and then restricted freedom of the individual, of the press and of association; but they never limited the power of the state or its police. When the Bastille was taken on 14 July 1789 it was found to contain only seven prisoners; five years later the gaols of the Republic bulged with over 400,000 inmates. No sooner was the ink dry on the Declaration of the Rights of Man than the National Assembly set up committees to report on potential counter-revolutionary plots, to open mail, to arrest suspects without warrant and detain them without due process of law. Determined to re-shape humanity, the Revolutionaries re-cast France into new administrative units, replaced local laws by national ones, and attempted to replace local speech and currencies with national means of exchange—French and the *franc*. The metric system, in itself eminently sensible and eventually copied through the world, formed the basis of new national measurements, designed to replace the jungle of weights and measures embedded for centuries in local communities. Although Revolutionary leaders aspired to extend popular primary education, little was done about it, and in 1815 about 5 per cent fewer people could read or sign their names than in 1789.

Not only did the Revolution devour many of its children, as well as many of other people's, but it also destroyed much of France's cultural heritage. The *ancien régime* and its associations had to be eradicated. Noble and monastic libraries were pillaged, confiscated or destroyed. Charters, parchments, manuscripts, books—all were seen as remnants of "feudal oppression" and burned in public ceremonies. Inscriptions, coats of arms, sculptures that recalled "superstition" (that is, Christianity) or the "tyrannical past" were removed, defaced or hammered out in an orgy of destruction. The 231 statues of Strasbourg Cathedral were shattered; so were the 28 thirteenth-century statues of Biblical royalty on the façade of Notre Dame— decapitated on 23 October 1793 under the impression that they represented Kings of France. Rouen Cathedral became blackened from use as a gunpowder factory. Chartres Cathedral escaped "patriotic demolition" only because the contractors judged it would create too much dangerous debris in the narrow streets. But the abbey of Saint-Denis just outside Paris, the traditional burying-place of French monarchs, had its roof stripped, its stained glass shattered and the tombs of 51 Kings and Queens of France desecrated by order of the Convention. Churches, abbeys and castles were demolished by the score. Spires and bell-towers were razed; so were royal *châteaux* and palaces. This destruction marked popular revenge for the repression and humiliation that so many had suffered at the hands of the nobility and clergy before 1789, and to lament such large-scale vandalism is to run the risk of playing down the repressive and unjust aspects of seigneurialism.

No serious historian, however, denies that France's economy suffered severe damage during the Revolution. Population growth slowed after 1789, with France having more spinsters and widows than England because of war deaths. The sale of between 15 and 20 per cent of French land belonging to the Church, *émigrés* and *suspects* more than doubled the number of landowners, but failed to stimulate agricultural productivity. Many of the new owners lacked capital and experience of farming, while agriculture itself was badly affected by labour shortages, fixed prices and depreciating *assignats.* Grain production in 1815 was no higher than in 1789, while there were fewer sheep, cows and horses. During the same period, England's agrarian productivity rose rapidly. So did her industrial lead, as the French concentrated overwhelmingly on the production of war materials. Before 1789, according to François Crouzet, French industry had been able to match that of England. But this was no longer the case during and after the Revolution. Industry was drained of its competitiveness by a quarter-century of revolution and war, being able to survive only under cover of protective tariffs.

Trade also suffered. The war meant maritime blockade, the decline of shipping and the decay of great ports like Nantes, Bordeaux and Marseille. France's road network fell to pieces from neglect and shortage of funds; bridges and tunnels collapsed. Freedom of trade was soon negated by a mass of regulations and restrictions. Bad for business, the Revolutionary years were good only for war contractors, speculators, crooks and smugglers. Nor were Revolutionary governments ever able to solve the financial crisis which had brought down the royal administration. Indeed, the deficit continued to increase and in 1797 the French nation declared itself bankrupt. Whether military glory and the expansion of the French empire under Napoleon were sufficient compensation for so much damage and so many ruined lives seems arguable at the very least.

Yet there are historians on the Left who still emphasise how the peasants, who accounted for 70 per cent of the population in 1789, gained three major benefits which they were to guard jealously over the subsequent century: the end of seigneurialism, eventual access to more land, and a more impartial system of justice. Others point to the fact that the concept of revolution cannot be exorcised or deemed increasingly irrelevant to the modern world, in which gross inequalities and pervasive social injustice produce revolutionary situations. Nor are they happy with revisionist interpretations which play down social and economic causes of the Revolution in favour of political and ideological factors.

While such arguments retain their force, they tend to neglect the experiences of people at the time in favour of posterity, and there seems little doubt that the celebratory tradition of Revolutionary scholarship cannot survive without serious modification. Historians of the counter-revolution have drawn upon a wide range of local studies to demonstrate that most French people were opposed to what was being done in Paris from 1790 onwards. They had revolted against centralisation and the attempt to increase royal state power, but found that Revolutionary centralising policies vastly enhanced the power of the state. While many peasants made material gains, there were many others who proved unwilling to accept either the Civil Constitution of the Clergy or military conscription. If there was a widespread genuinely popular movement during the Revolution, it was not that of the militant *sans culottes;* rather the real popular movement was the counter-revolution, not as expressed in armed risings, which were largely confined to the west and southeast, but in the sense that most ordinary people resented what had happened to them since 1789 and, when circumstances permitted, did not hesitate to take action against local Jacobins and government officials. They certainly did not wish to restore the Bourbons or the *ancien régime,* but wanted simply to be left alone with whatever gains they had made in 1789. What happened after 1790 tended to be resented. Indeed, only the fact that the Revolution was resented by so many of those who had to endure it can explain the vigour and extent of the resistance to successive Revolutionary governments. And the extent of this resistance means that the Revolution was, in the end, a tragedy, and one to be analysed and debated rather than simply celebrated. It may be going too far to argue that the Revolution was a repulsively violent interlude in an otherwise vigorously maturing society. Yet no revolution has been, or ever could be, "one and indivisible." Very few modern historians would unreservedly endorse the view of Charles James Fox that the Revolution was "the greatest event in human history and the best." Revolutions generate hope, energy and Utopian aspirations. At the same time they all too often produce mass bloodshed and a tendency to focus on what men ought to be rather than what they actually are. It was Saint-Just who, defending the excesses of the Terror of 1793–94, defined "humanity" as "the extermination of one's enemies."

When Marie Antoinette went to the scaffold, her once-beautiful hands tied behind her, she accidentally trod on the foot of her executioner and immediately apologised. For the next 180 years the French nation found it impossible to find a universally acceptable substitute for her late husband: "Louis, by the Grace of God, King of France and of Navarre." François Furet's 1978 essay "The French Revolution is over" proved misguided. The bicentenary celebrations and debates showed that the French people are still deeply divided over their "indigestible revolution."

SELECT BIBLIOGRAPHY

1. Aids for Research

Bibliographie annuelle de l'histoire française. Paris: Éditions du CNRS, 1963–.

Bonin, Serge, and Claude Langlois, eds. *Atlas de la Révolution française.* Vol. 1–. Paris: École des hautes études en sciences sociales, 1987–.

Caldwell, Ronald J. *The Era of the French Revolution: A Bibliography of the History of Western Civilization, 1789–1799.* 2 vols. New York: Garland, 1985.

Caron, Pierre. *Manuel pratique pour l'étude de la Révolution française.* New ed. Paris: Picard, 1947.

Censer, Jack R., and Lynn Hunt. *Liberty, Equality, Fraternity: Exploring the French Revolution* [Text and CD Rom]. University Park: The Pennsylvania State University Press, 2001.

Chronique de la Révolution, 1788–1799. Paris: Larousse, 1989.

Fierro, Alfred. *Bibliographie critique des mémoires sur la Révolution écrits ou traduits en français.* Paris: Service des travaux historiques de la ville de Paris, 1988.

French Revolutionary Periodicals [microform]. Leiden: IDC, 2000.

Furet, François, and Mona Ozouf, eds. *Critical Dictionary of the French Revolution.* Trans. Arthur Goldhammer. Cambridge, MA: Harvard University Press, 1989. Orig. 1988.

Godechot, Jacques. *Les Institutions de la France sous la Révolution et L'Empire.* 3rd ed. Paris: Presses universitaires de France, 1985.

Goldstein, Marc Allan, ed. *Social and Political Thought of the French Revolution, 1788–1797: An Anthology of Original Texts Selected, Translated, and Edited with an Introduction and Commentaries on the Texts.* New York: P. Lang, 1997.

Hardman, John, ed. *The French Revolution Sourcebook.* London: Arnold, 1999. Orig. 1981.

Jones, Colin. *The Longman Companion to the French Revolution.* London: Longman, 1988.

Lucas, Colin, ed. *The French Revolution Research Collection and Videodisc.* Boston: G. K. Hall, 1989.

Mason, Laura, and Tracey Rizzo, eds. *The French Revolution: A Document Collection.* Boston: Houghton Mifflin, 1998.

Miravel, Paul, and Raymonde Monnier. *Répertoire des travaux universitaires inédits sur la période révolutionnaire.* Paris: Société des études robespierristes, 1990.

Roberts, John, and John Hardman, eds. *French Revolution Documents.* 2 vols. Oxford: Blackwell, 1966–1973.

Schecter, Ronald, ed. *The French Revolution: The Essential Readings.* Oxford: Blackwell, 2001.

Scott, Samuel F., and Barry Rothaus, eds. *The Historical Dictionary of the*

French Revolution, 1789–1799. 2 vols. Westport, CT: Greenwood Press, 1985.

Soboul, Albert, and others, eds. *Dictionnaire historique de la Révolution française.* Paris: Presses universitaires de France, 1989.

Stewart, John Hall, ed. *A Documentary Survey of the French Revolution.* New York: Macmillan, 1951.

Tulard, Jean, Jean-François Fayard, and Alfred Fierro. *Histoire et dictionnaire de la Révolution française, 1789 à 1799.* Paris: R. Laffont, 1987.

Vovelle, Michel, ed. *Recherches sur la Révolution: Un Bilan des travaux scientifiques du bicentennaire.* Paris: Éditions la Découverte, 1991.

Periodicals
American Historical Review
Annales historiques de la Révolution française
French Historical Studies
French History
Journal of Modern History
Past and Present

2. General Narratives, Surveys, Historiography

Aulard, Alphonse. *The French Revolution: A Political History, 1789–1804.* 4 vols. Trans. Bernard Miall. New York: Charles Scribner's Sons, 1910. Orig. 1901.

Best, Geoffrey, ed. *The Permanent Revolution: The French Revolution and Its Legacy, 1789–1989.* Chicago: University of Chicago Press, 1989. Orig. 1988.

Blanning, T. C. W. *The French Revolution: Class War or Culture Clash?* 2nd ed. New York: St. Martin's Press, 1998.

Blanning, T. C. W., ed. *The Rise and Fall of the French Revolution.* Chicago: University of Chicago Press, 1996.

Bosher, J. F. *The French Revolution.* New York: W. W. Norton, 1988.

Brinton, Crane. *A Decade of Revolution, 1789–1799.* New York: Harper & Row, 1963. Orig. 1934.

Cobban, Alfred. *The Social Interpretation of the French Revolution.* 2nd ed. Cambridge, Eng.: Cambridge University Press, 1999. Orig. 1964.

Comninel, George C. *Rethinking the French Revolution: Marxism and the Revisionist Challenge.* London: Verso, 1987.

Connelly, Owen. *The French Revolution and Napoleonic Era.* 3rd ed. Fort Worth, TX: Harcourt College Publishers, 2000.

Doyle, William. *The Oxford History of the French Revolution.* Oxford: Oxford University Press, 1989.

Forrest, Alan. *The French Revolution.* Oxford: Blackwell, 1995.

Furet, François. *Interpreting the French Revolution.* Trans. Elborg Forster. Cambridge, Eng.: Cambridge University Press, 1981. Orig. 1978.

Furet, François. *Revolutionary France, 1770–1880.* Trans. Antonia Nevill. Oxford: Blackwell, 1992. Orig. 1988.

Furet, François, and Denis Richet. *The French Revolution.* Trans. Stephen Hardman. New York: Macmillan, 1970. Orig. 1965–1966.

Goodwin, Albert, ed. *New Cambridge Modern History.* Vol. VIII: *The American and French Revolutions, 1763–1793.* Cambridge, Eng.: Cambridge University Press, 1965.

Günther, Horst, ed. *Die Französische Revolution: Berichte und Deutungen Deutscher Schriftsteller und Historiker.* Frankfurt am Main: Deutscher Klassiker Verlag, 1985.

Hobsbawm, Eric J. *Echoes of the Marseillaise: Two Centuries Look Back on the French Revolution.* New Brunswick, NJ: Rutgers University Press, 1990.

Jones, Peter M., ed. *The French Revolution in Social and Political Perspective.* London: Arnold, 1996.

Kaplan, Steven L. *Farewell, Revolution: The Historians' Feud: France, 1789/ 1989.* Ithaca, NY: Cornell University Press, 1995.

Kates, Gary, ed. *The French Revolution: Recent Debates and New Controversies.* London: Routledge, 1998.

Lefebvre, Georges. *The French Revolution.* 2 vols. Vol. 1. Trans. Elizabeth Moss Evanson. Vol. 2. Trans. John Hall Stewart and James Friguglietti. New York: Columbia University Press, 1962–1964. Orig. 1951.

Lewis, Gwynne. *The French Revolution: Rethinking the Debate.* London: Routledge, 1993.

Lucas, Colin, ed. *Rewriting the French Revolution.* Oxford: Clarendon Press, 1991.

Mathiez, Albert. *The French Revolution.* Trans. Catherine A. Phillips. New York: Russell & Russell, 1962. Orig. 1927.

Orr, Linda. *Headless History: Nineteenth-Century French Historiography of the Revolution.* Ithaca, NY: Cornell University Press, 1990.

Popkin, Jeremy D. *A Short History of the French Revolution.* 2nd ed. Upper Saddle River, NJ: Prentice Hall, 1998.

Roberts, J.M. *The French Revolution.* 2nd ed. Oxford: Oxford University Press, 1997.

Rudé, George. *The French Revolution.* London: Weidenfeld & Nicholson, 1988.

Schama, Simon. *Citizens: A Chronicle of the French Revolution.* New York, Knopf, 1989.

Schwab, Gail M., and John R. Jeanneney, eds. *The French Revolution of 1789 and its Impact.* Westport, CT: Greenwood Press, 1995.

Soboul, Albert. *La Civilisation et la Révolution française.* 3 vols. Paris: Arthaud, 1970–1983.

Soboul, Albert. *The French Revolution, 1789–1799: From the Storming of the Bastille to Napoleon.* Trans. Alan Forrest and Colin Jones. New York: Vintage Books, 1975. Orig. 1962.

Solé, Jacques. *Questions of the French Revolution.* Trans. Shelly Temchin. New York: Pantheon Books, 1989. Orig. 1988.

Sutherland, Donald M. G. *France, 1789–1815: Revolution and Counterrevolution.* Oxford: Oxford University Press, 1986.

Thompson, James M. *The French Revolution.* Oxford: Oxford University Press, 1978. Orig. 1943.

Tönnesmann, Katja. *Die Zweihundertjahrfeier des Französischen Revolution: Bildrhetorik zwischen Aufklärung und Unterhaltung.* Weimar: VDG, 1999.

Vovelle, Michel, ed. *L'Image de la Révolution française: Communications présentées lors du Congrès mondial pour le bicentenaire de la Révolution, Paris, 6–12 juillet 1989.* 4 vols. Oxford: Pergamon, 1989.

Woloch, Isser. *The New Regime: Transformations of the French Civic Order, 1789–1820s.* New York: W. W. Norton, 1994.

Woloch, Isser, ed. *Revolution and the Meaning of Freedom in the Nineteenth Century.* Stanford, CA: Stanford University Press, 1996.

Wright, David Gordon. *Revolution and Terror in France, 1789–1795.* 2nd ed. London: Longman, 1990.

3. Background of the French Revolution

Adams, Christine, Jack R. Censer, and Lisa Jane Graham, eds. *Visions and Revisions of Eighteenth-Century France.* University Park: The Pennsylvania State University Press, 1997.

Adams, Geoffrey. *The Huguenots and French Opinion, 1685–1787: The Enlightenment Debate on Toleration.* Waterloo, Ontario: Wilford Laurier University Press, 1991.

Andrews, Richard M. *Law, Magistracy and Crime in Old Regime Paris, 1735–1789.* Cambridge, Eng.: Cambridge University Press, 1994.

Baker, Keith Michael. *Inventing the French Revolution: Essays on French Political Culture in the Eighteenth Century.* Cambridge, Eng.: Cambridge University Press, 1990.

Barber, Elinor G. *The Bourgeoisie in 18th Century France.* Princeton, NJ: Princeton University Press, 1955.

Bell, David A. *Lawyers and Citizens: The Making of a Political Elite in Old Regime France.* Oxford: Oxford University Press, 1994.

Bertaud, Jean-Paul. *Les Causes de la Révolution française.* Paris: A. Colin, 1992.

Bien, David. "The Army in the French Enlightenment." *Past and Present* 85 (1979).

Bloch, Marc. *French Rural History: An Essay on its Basic Characteristics.* Trans. Janet Sondheimer. Berkeley: University of Califonia Press, 1966. Orig. 1931.

Bouton, Cynthia A.*The Flour War: Gender, Class, and Community in Late Ancien Régime French Society.* University Park: The Pennsylvania State University Press, 1993.

Braudel, Fernand, and Ernest Labrousse, eds. *Histoire économique et sociale de la France.* Vol. 2: *Les Derniers temps de l'âge seigneurial aux préludes de l'âge industriel (1660–1789).* Paris: Presses universitaires de France, 1970.

Censer, Jack R. *The French Press in the Age of Enlightenment.* London: Routledge, 1994.

Censer, Jack R., and Jeremy Popkin, eds. *Press and Politics in Pre-Revolutionary France.* Berkeley: University of California Press, 1987.

Chartier, Roger. *The Cultural Origins of the French Revolution.* Trans. Lydia G. Cochrane. Durham, NC: Duke University Press, 1991. Orig. 1990.

Chaussinand-Nogaret, Guy. *The French Nobility in the Eighteenth Century: From Feudalism to Enlightenment.* Trans. William Doyle. Cambridge, Eng.: Cambridge University Press, 1985. Orig. 1976. Revised ed. 1990.

Cobban, Alfred. *History of Modern France.* Vol. 1: *1715–1799.* 2nd ed. New York: Penguin, 1963.

Crouzet, François. "England and France in the Eighteenth Century: A Comparative Analysis of Two Economic Growths," in R. M. Hartwell, ed. *The Causes of the Industrial Revolution in England.* London: Methuen, 1967.

Crow, Thomas E. *Painters and Public Life in Eighteenth Century Paris.* New Haven, CT: Yale University Press, 1985.

Darnton, Robert. *The Forbidden Best-Sellers of Pre-Revolutionary France.* New York: W. W. Norton, 1995.

Darnton, Robert. *The Literary Underground of the Old Regime.* Cambridge, MA: Harvard University Press, 1982.

Darnton, Robert, and Daniel Roche, eds. *Revolution in Print: The Press in France, 1775–1800.* Berkeley: University of California Press, 1989.

Doyle, William. *The Ancien Régime.* Basingstoke, Hampshire: Macmillan, 1986.

Doyle, William. *Jansenism: Catholic Resistance to Authority from the Reformation to the French Revolution.* Basingstoke: Macmillan, 2000.

Doyle, William, ed. *Old Regime France.* Oxford: Oxford University Press, 2001.

Doyle, William. *Venality: The Sale of Offices in Eighteenth-Century France.* Oxford: Clarendon Press, 1996.

Echeverria, Durand. *The Maupeou Revolution: A Study in the History of Libertarianism: France, 1770–1774.* Baton Rouge: Louisiana State University Press, 1985.

Farge, Arlette. *Fragile Lives: Violence, Power and Solidarity in Eighteenth-Century Paris.* Trans. Carol Shelton. Cambridge, MA: Harvard University Press, 1993. Orig. 1986.

Farge, Arlette. *Subversive Words: Public Opinion in Eighteenth-Century France.* Trans. Rosemary Morris. University Park: The Pennsylvania State University Press, 1994. Orig. 1992.

Garrioch, David. *Neighbourhood and Community in Paris, 1740–90.* Cambridge, Eng.: Cambridge University Press, 1986.

Gay, Peter. *The Enlightenment: An Interpretation.* 2 vols. New York: Knopf, 1966–1969.

Gelbart, Nina Rattner. *Feminine and Opposition Journalism in Old Regime France: Le Journal des Dames.* Berkeley: University of California Press, 1987.

Goodman, Dena. *The Republic of Letters: A Cultural History of the French Enlightenment.* Ithaca, NY: Cornell University Press, 1994.

Gordon, Daniel. *Citizens Without Sovereignty: Equality and Sociability in French Thought, 1670–1789.* Princeton, NJ: Princeton University Press, 1994.

Goubert, Pierre. *The Ancien Regime: French Society, 1600–1750.* Trans. Steve Cox. New York: Harper & Row, 1974. Orig. 1969–1973.

Gruder, Vivian R. "Whither Revisionism? Political Perspectives on the Ancien Régime." *French Historical Studies* 20 (1996).

Haase-Dubosc, Danielle, and Elaine Viennot. *Femmes et pouvoirs sous l'ancien régime.* Paris: Rivages/Histoire, 1991.

Habermas, Jürgen. *The Structural Transformation of the Public Sphere: An Inquiry into a Category of Bourgeois Society.* Trans. Thomas Burger and Frederick Lawrence. Cambridge, MA: MIT Press, 1989, orig. 1963.

Halévi, Ran. *Les Loges maçonniques dans la France d'ancien régime: Aux Origines de la sociabilité démocratique.* Paris: A. Colin, 1984.

Hampson, Norman. *Will and Circumstance: Montesquieu, Rousseau and the French Revolution.* London: Duckworth, 1983.

Hardman, John. *French Politics, 1774–1789: From the Accession of Louis XVI to the Fall of the Bastille.* London: Longman, 1995.

Higonnet, Patrice. *Sister Republics: The Origins of French and American Republicanism.* Cambridge, MA: Harvard University Press, 1988.

Hufton, Olwen H. *The Poor of Eighteenth-Century France, 1750–1789.* Oxford: Clarendon Press, 1974.

Kafker, Frank A. *The Encyclopedists as a Group.* Vol. 345 of *Studies on Voltaire and the Eighteenth Century.* Oxford: Voltaire Foundation, 1996.

Kaiser, Thomas E. "This Strange Offspring of Philosophie." *French Historical Studies* 15 (1988).

Kaplan, Steven L. *The Bakers of Paris and the Bread Question, 1700–1775.* Durham, NC: Duke University Press, 1996.

Kaplan, Steven L. *The Famine Plot Persuasion in Eighteenth-Century France.* Philadelphia: American Philosophical Society, 1982.

Kaplan, Steven L. *La Fin des corporations.* Trans. Béatrice Vierne. Paris: Fayard, 2001.

Kwass, Michael. *Privilege and the Politics of Taxation in Eighteenth-Century France: Liberté, Égalité, Fiscalité.* Cambridge, Eng.: Cambridge University Press, 2000.

Labrousse, Ernest. *La Crise de l'économie française à la fin de l'ancien régime et au début de la Révolution.* Paris: Presses universitaires de France, 1990. Orig. 1943.

Ladurie, Emmanuel Le Roy. "Rural Revolts and Protest Movements in France from 1675 to 1788." *Studies in Eighteenth-Century Culture* 5 (1976).

Landes, David. "The Statistical Study of French Crises." *Journal of Economic History* 10 (1950).

Le Goff, T. J. A. *France, 1661–1789: An Anatomy of the Ancien Régime.* Oxford: Oxford University Press, 1999.

Levy, Darline Gay. *The Ideas and Careers of Simon-Nicolas-Henri Linguet: A Study in Eighteenth-Century French Politics.* Urbana: University of Illinois Press, 1980.

Manceron, Claude. *The French Revolution.* 5 vols. Trans. Patricia Wolf and Nancy Amphoux. New York: Knopf, 1977–1983 (vols. 1–4); New York: Simon & Schuster, 1989 (vol. 5). Orig. 1972–1987.

Mason, Haydn T., ed. *The Darnton Debate: Books and Revolution in the Eighteenth Century.* Oxford: Voltaire Foundation, 1998.

Maza, Sarah. *Private Lives and Public Affairs: The Causes Célèbres of Prerevolutionary France.* Berkeley: University of California Press, 1993.

McManners, John. *Church and Society in Eighteenth-Century France.* 2 vols. Oxford: Clarendon Press, 1998.

Merrick, Jeffrey. *The Desacralization of the French Monarchy in the Eighteenth Century.* Baton Rouge: Louisiana State University Press, 1990.

Mornet, Daniel. *Les Origines intellectuelles de la Révolution française, 1715–1787.* Lyon: La Manufacture, 1989. Orig. 1933.

Mousnier, Roland. *The Institutions of France Under the Absolute Monarchy, 1598–1789.* Trans. Brian Pearce and Arthur Goldhammer. 2 vols. Chicago: University of Chicago Press, 1979–1984. Orig. 1974–1980.

Murphy, Orville T. *Charles Gravier, Comte de Vergennes: French Diplomacy in the Age of Revolution, 1719–1787.* Albany: SUNY Press, 1982.

Murphy, Orville T. *The Diplomatic Retreat of France and Public Opinion on the Eve of the French Revolution, 1783–1789.* Washington, DC: The Catholic University of America Press, 1998.

Outram, Dorinda, *The Enlightenment.* Cambridge, Eng.: Cambridge University Press, 1995.

Roche, Daniel. *France in the Enlightenment.* Trans. Arthur Goldhammer. Cambridge, MA: Harvard University Press, 1998. Orig. 1993.

Roche, Daniel, ed. *"Journal of My Life" by Jacques-Louis Ménétra.* Trans. Arthur Goldhammer. New York: Columbia University Press, 1986. Orig. 1982.

Roche, Daniel. *The People of Paris: An Essay in Popular Culture in the Eighteenth Century.* Trans. Marie Evans and Gwynne Lewis. Berkeley: University of California Press, 1987. Orig. 1981.

Roche, Daniel. *Les Républicains des lettres: Gens de culture et de Lumières au XVIIIe siècle.* Paris: Fayard, 1988.

Roche, Daniel. *Le Siècle des Lumières en province: Académies et académiciens provinciaux.* 2 vols. Paris: Mouton, 1978.

Sonenscher, Michael. *Work and Wages: Natural Law, Politics, and the Eighteenth-Century French Trades.* Cambridge, Eng.: Cambridge University Press, 1989.

Stone, Bailey. *The French Parlements and the Crisis of the Old Regime.* Chapel Hill: University of North Carolina Press, 1986.

Stone, Bailey. *The Genesis of the French Revolution: A Global-Historical Interpretation.* Cambridge, Eng.: Cambridge University Press, 1994.

Taylor, George V. "Noncapitalist Wealth and the Origins of the French Revolution." *American Historical Review* 72 (1967).

Taylor, George V. "Types of Capitalism in Eighteenth-Century France." *English Historical Review* 79 (1964).

Tocqueville, Alexis de. *The Old Regime and the Revolution.* Eds. François Furet and Françoise Mélanio. Trans. Alan S. Kahan. Vol. 1: *The Complete Text.* Chicago: University of Chicago Press, 1998. Orig. 1856.

Van Kley, Dale, ed. *The French Idea of Freedom: The Old Regime and the Declaration of Rights of 1789.* Stanford, CA: Stanford University Press, 1994.

Van Kley, Dale K. *The Religious Origins of the French Revolution: From Calvin to the Civil Constitution, 1560–1791.* New Haven, CT: Yale University Press, 1996.

Weir, David R. "Les Crises économiques et les origines de la Révolution française." *Annales: Économies, Sociétés, Civilisations* 46 (1991).

Woloch, Isser, ed. *The Peasantry in the Old Regime.* Melbourne, FL: Krieger, 1977.

Wright, Johnson Kent. *A Classical Republican in Eighteenth-Century France: The Political Thought of Mably.* Stanford CA: Stanford University Press, 1997.

Young, Arthur. *Travels in France During the Years 1787, 1788, and 1789.* Cambridge, Eng.: Cambridge University Press, 1950. Orig. 1792.

4. Political History

Aberdam, S., S. Bianchi, and R. Demaude, eds. *Voter, élire pendant la Révolution française, 1789–1799: Guide pour la recherche.* Paris: Éditions du CTHS, 1999.

Andress, David. *Massacre at the Champ de Mars: Popular Dissent and Political Culture in The French Revolution.* Rochester, NY: Boydell & Brewer, 2000.

Applewhite, Harriet B. *Political Alignment in the French National Assembly, 1789–1791.* Baton Rouge: Louisiana State University Press, 1993.

Baczko, Bronislaw. *Ending the Terror: The French Revolution after Robespierre.* Trans. Michael Petheram. Cambridge, Eng.: Cambridge University Press, 1994. Orig. 1989.

Baker, Keith Michael, ed. *The Terror.* Vol. 4: *The French Revolution and the Creation of Modern Political Culture.* Oxford: Pergamon, 1994.

Bienvenu, Richard T., ed. *The Ninth of Thermidor: The Fall of Robespierre.* Oxford: Oxford University Press, 1968.

Blanc, Olivier. *Last Letters: Prisons and Prisoners of the French Revolution, 1793–1794.* Trans. Alan Sheridan. New York: Farrar, Straus & Giroux, 1987. Orig. 1984.

Bouloiseau, Marc. *The Jacobin Republic, 1792–1794.* Trans. Jonathan Mandelbaum. Cambridge, Eng.: Cambridge University Press, 1984. Orig. 1972.

Brinton, Crane. *The Jacobins: An Essay in the New History.* New York: Macmillan, 1930.

Brown, Howard G. "A Discredited Regime: The Directory and Army Contracting." *French History* 4 (1990).

Burley, Peter. *Witness to the Revolution: British and American Commentators in France, 1782–1794.* New York: Weidenfeld & Nicholson, 1989.

Crook, Malcolm. *Elections in The French Revolution: Apprenticeship in Democracy, 1789–1799.* Cambridge, Eng.: Cambridge University Press, 1996.

Doyle, William. *Origins of the French Revolution.* 3rd ed. Oxford: Oxford University Press, 1999.

Edelstein, Melvin. "La Place de la Révolution française dans la politisation des paysans." *Annales historiques de la Révolution française* 62 (1990).

Égret, Jean. *The French Pre-Revolution, 1787–1788.* Trans. Wesley D. Camp. Chicago: University of Chicago Press, 1977. Orig. 1962.

Fayard, Jean-François. *La Justice révolutionnaire: Chronique de la Terreur.* Paris: Laffont, 1987.

Fehér, Ferenc.*The French Revolution: An Essay on Jacobinism.* Cambridge, Eng.: Cambridge University Press, 1987.

Fitzsimmons, Michael P. *The Remaking of France: The National Assembly and the Constitution of 1791.* Cambridge, Eng.: Cambridge University Press, 1994.

Furet, François, and Mona Ozouf, eds. *La Gironde et les Girondins.* Paris: Éditions Payot, 1991.

Furet, François, and Ran Halévi, eds. *Orateurs de la Révolution française.* Vol. 1: *Les Constituants.* Paris: Gallimard, 1989.

Gendron, François. *The Gilded Youth of Thermidor.* Trans. James Cookson. Montreal: McGill-Queens University Press, 1993. Orig. 1979.

"Girondins: Forum." *French Historical Studies* 15 (1988).

Godechot, Jacques. *The Counter Revolution: Doctrine and Action, 1789–1800.* Trans. Salvator Altanasio. Princeton, NJ: Princeton University Press, 1981. Orig. 1961.

Godechot, Jacques. *The Taking of the Bastille: July 14th, 1789.* Trans. Jean Stewart. New York: Charles Scribner's Sons, 1970. Orig. 1965.

Godfrey, James. *Revolutionary Justice: A Study of the Organization, Personnel, and Procedure of the Paris Tribunal, 1793–1795.* Chapel Hill: University of North Carolina Press, 1951.

Greer, Donald. *The Incidence of Emigration during the French Revolution.* Cambridge, MA: Harvard University Press, 1951.

Greer, Donald. *The Incidence of the Terror during the French Revolution: A Statistical Interpretation.* Cambridge, MA: Harvard University Press, 1935.

Gross, Jean-Pierre. *Fair Shares For All: Jacobin Egalitarianism in Practice.* Cambridge, Eng.: Cambridge University Press, 1997.

Gueniffey, Patrice. *La Politique de la Terreur: Essai sur la violence révolutionnaire, 1789–1794.* Paris: Fayard, 2000.

Gueniffey, Patrice. *Le Nombre et la raison: La Révolution française et les élections.* Paris: École des hautes études en sciences sociales, 1993.

Hampson, Norman. *Prelude to the Terror: The Constituent Assembly and the Failure of Consensus, 1789–1791.* Oxford: Blackwell, 1988.

Hesse, Carla. "La Preuve par la lettre: Pratiques juridiques au tribunal révolutionnaire de Paris (1793–1794)." *Annales: Histoire, sciences sociales* 51 (1996).

Higonnet, Patrice. *Goodness Beyond Virtue: Jacobins During the French Revolution.* Cambridge, MA: Harvard University Press, 1998.

Jones, Peter M. *Reform and Revolution in France; The Politics of Transition, 1774–1791.* Cambridge, Eng: Cambridge University Press, 1995.

Jordan, David P. *The King's Trial: The French Revolution vs. Louis XVI.* Berkeley: University of California Press, 1979.

Kates, Gary. *The Cercle Social, the Girondins, and the French Revolution.* Princeton, NJ: Princeton University Press, 1985.

Kelly, George Armstrong. *Victims, Authority, and Terror: The Parallel Deaths of D'Orléans, Custine, Bailly and Malesherbes.* Chapel Hill: University of North Carolina Press, 1982.

Kennedy, Michael L. *The Jacobin Clubs in the French Revolution.* 3 vols. Princeton, NJ: Princeton University Press, 1982–1999.

Lefebvre, Georges. *The Coming of the French Revolution.* Trans. Robert R. Palmer. Princeton, NJ: Princeton University Press, 1947.

Lemay, Edna Hindie, ed. *Dictionnaire des Constituants, 1789–1791.* 2 vols. Oxford: Voltaire Foundation, 1991.

Lemay, Edna Hindie, and Alison Patrick. *Revolutionaries at Work: The Constituent Assembly, 1789–1791.* Oxford: Voltaire Foundation, 1996.

Lyons, Martyn. *France under the Directory.* Cambridge, Eng.: Cambridge University Press, 1984. Orig. 1972.

Margerison, Kenneth. *Pamphlets and Public Opinion: The Campaign for a Union of Orders in the Early French Revolution.* West Lafayette, IN: Purdue University Press, 1998.

Martin, Jean-Clément. *Contre-Révolution et nation en France, 1789–1799.* Paris: Éditions du Seuil, 1998.

Mitchell, C. J. *The French Legislative Assembly of 1791.* Leiden: E. J. Brill, 1988.

Mitchell, Harvey. *The Underground War against Revolutionary France.* Oxford: Clarendon Press, 1965.

Monnier, Raymonde. *L'Espace publique démocratique.* Paris: Éditions Kime, 1994.

Olsen, Mark. "A Failure of Enlightened Politics in the French Revolution: The Société de 1789." *French History* 6 (1992).

Palmer, Robert R. *Twelve Who Ruled: The Year of the Terror in the French Revolution.* Revised ed. Princeton, NJ: Princeton University Press, 1989.

Patrick, Allison. *The Men of the First French Republic: Political Alignments in the National Convention of 1792.* Baltimore: Johns Hopkins University Press, 1972.

Ragan, Bryant T., and Elizabeth A. Williams, eds. *Recreating Authority in Revolutionary France.* New Brunswick, NJ: Rutgers University Press, 1992.

Reichardt, Rolf, and Eberhard Schmitt, eds. *Handbuch politisch-sozialer Grundbegriffe in Frankreich 1680–1820.* Munich: Oldenbourg, 1985–.

Reinhard, Marcel. *La France du Directoire.* 2 vols. Paris: Centre de documentation universitaire, 1956.

Resnick, Daniel. "The Société des Amis des Noirs and the Abolition of Slavery." *French Historical Studies* 7 (1972).

Roberts, James. *The Counter-Revolution in France, 1787–1830.* New York: St. Martin's Press, 1990.

Rose, Robert Barrie. *The Enragés: Socialists of the French Revolution?* London: Methuen, 1968.

Rose, Robert Barrie. *The Making of the Sans-Culottes: Democratic Ideas and Institutions in Paris, 1789–92.* Manchester, Eng.: Manchester University Press, 1983.

Shapiro, Barry M. *Revolutionary Justice in Paris, 1789–90.* Cambridge, Eng.: Cambridge University Press, 1993.

Shapiro, Gilbert, John Markoff, Timothy N. Tackett, and Philip Dawson, eds. *Revolutionary Demands: A Content Analysis of the Cahiers de Doléances of 1789.* Stanford, CA: Stanford University Press, 1998.

Slavin, Morris. *The French Revolution in Miniature: Section Droits-de-l'Homme, 1789–1795.* Princeton, NJ: Princeton University Press, 1984.

Slavin, Morris. *The Hébertistes to the Guillotine: Anatomy of a "Conspiracy" in Revolutionary France.* Baton Rouge : Louisiana State University Press, 1994.

Slavin, Morris. *The Making of an Insurrection: Parisian Sections and the Gironde.* Cambridge, MA: Harvard University Press, 1986.

Soboul, Albert, ed. *Girondins et Montagnards.* Paris: Société des études robespierristes, 1980.

Sonenscher, Michael. "The Nation's Debt and the Birth of the Modern Republic: The French Fiscal Deficit and the Politics of the Revolution of 1789." *History of Political Thought* 18 (1997).

Staum, Martin S. *Minerva's Message: Stabilizing the French Revolution.* Montreal: McGill-Queen's University Press, 1996.

Sydenham, Michael J. *The First French Republic, 1792–1804.* Berkeley: University of California Press, 1974.

Sydenham, Michael J. *The Girondins.* London: University of London Press, 1961.

Tackett, Timothy N. *Becoming a Revolutionary: The Deputies of the French National Assembly and the Emergence of a Revolutionary Culture (1789–1790).* Princeton, NJ: Princeton University Press, 1996.

Troyansky, David G., Alfred Cismaru, and Norwood Andrews, Jr., eds. *The French Revolution in Culture and Society.* Westport, CT: Greenwood Press, 1991.

Van Kley, Dale K. "New Wine in Old Skins: Continuity and Rupture in the Pamphlet Debate of the French Pre-Revolution, 1787–1789." *French Historical Studies* 17 (1991).

Vidalenc, Jean. *Les Émigrés français, 1789–1825.* Caen: Université de Caen, 1963.

Vovelle, Michel. *The Fall of the French Monarchy, 1787–1792.* Trans. Susan Burke. Cambridge, Eng.: Cambridge University Press, 1984. Orig. 1972.

Walzer, Michael, ed. *Regicide and Revolution: Speeches at the Trial of Louis XVI.* 2nd ed. New York: Columbia University Press, 1992.

Whaley, Leigh. "Political Factions and the Second Revolution: The Insurrection of 10 August 1792." *French History* 7 (1993).

Wick, Daniel L. *A Conspiracy of Well-Intentioned Men: The Society of Thirty and the French Revolution.* New York: Garland, 1987.

Woloch, Isser. *Jacobin Legacy: The Democratic Movement Under the Directory.* Princeton, NJ: Princeton University Press, 1970.

Woronoff, Denis. *The Thermidorean Regime and the Directory, 1794–1799.* Trans. Julian Jackson. Cambridge, Eng.: Cambridge University Press, 1984. Orig. 1972.

5. Cultural and Intellectual History

Arrase, Daniel. *The Guillotine and the Terror.* Trans. Christopher Miller. London: Allen Lane/Penguin, 1989. Orig. 1987.

Baecque, Antoine de. *The Body Politic: Corporeal Metaphor in Revolutionary France, 1770–1800.* Trans. Charlotte Mandell. Stanford, CA: Stanford University Press, 1997. Orig. 1993.

Baecque, Antoine de. *La Caricature révolutionnaire.* Paris: Presses du CNRS, 1988.

Baecque, Antoine de. *La Gloire et l'effroi: Sept morts sous la Terreur.* Paris: B. Grasset, 1997.

Baker, Keith Michael, François Furet, Colin Lucas, and Mona Ozouf, eds. *The French Revolution and the Creation of Modern Poitical Culture.* 4 vols. Oxford: Pergamon, 1987–1994.

Bell, David A. "Lingua Populi, Lingua Dei: Language, Religion, and the Origins of French Revolutionary Nationalism." *American Historical Review* 100 (1995).

Bernard-Griffiths, Simone, Marie-Claude Chemin, and Jean Ehrard, eds. *Révolution française et "vandalisme révolutionnaire."* Paris: Universitas, 1992.

Blum, Carol. *Rousseau and the Republic of Virtue: The Language of Politics in the French Revolution.* Ithaca, NY: Cornell University Press, 1986.

Bonnet, Jean-Claude, ed. *La Carmagnole des muses: L'Homme de lettres et l'artiste dans la Révolution.* Paris: A. Colin, 1988.

Bonnet, Jean-Claude, ed. *La Mort de Marat.* Paris: Flammarion, 1986.

Bordes, Philippe. *Le Serment du Jeu de Paume de Jacques-Louis David.* Paris: Éditions de la Réunion des musées nationaux, 1983.

Boroumand, Ladan. *La Guerre des principes: Les Assemblées révolutionnaires face aux droits de l'homme et à la souveraineté de la nation, mai 1789–juillet 1794.* Paris: Éditions de l'École des hautes études en sciences sociales, 1999.

Boyd, Malcolm, ed. *Music and the French Revolution.* Cambridge, Eng.: Cambridge University Press, 1992.

Byrnes, Joseph F. "Celebration of the Revolutionary Festivals Under the Directory: A Failure of Sacrality." *Church History* 63 (1994).

Carlson, Marvin. *The Theatre of the French Revolution.* Ithaca, NY: Cornell University Press, 1966.

Censer, Jack R., ed. *The French Revolution and Inteliectual History.* Chicago: Dorsey Press, 1989.

Censer, Jack R. *Prelude to Power: The Parisian Radical Press, 1789–1791.* Baltimore: Johns Hopkins University Press, 1976.

Chisick, Harvey, ed. *The Press in the French Revolution.* Vol. 237 of *Studies on Voltaire and the Eighteenth Century.* Oxford: Voltaire Foundation, 1991.

Cowans, Jon. *To Speak for the People: Public Opinion and the Problem of Legitimacy in the French Revolution.* London: Routledge, 2001.

Crow, Thomas. *Emulation: Making Artists for Revolutionary France.* New Haven, CT: Yale University Press, 1995.

Cuno, James, ed. *French Caricature and the French Revolution, 1789–1799.*

Chicago: University of Chicago Press for the Grunwald Center for the Graphic Arts, 1988.

Dallet, Sylvie. *La Révolution française et le cinéma*. Paris: Éditions des Quatre–Vents, 1988.

Dallet, Sylvie, and François Gendron. *Filmographie mondiale de la Révolution française*. Montreuil: Centre d'action culturelle de Montreuil, 1989.

Didier, Béatrice. *Écrire la Révolution: 1789–1799*. Paris: Presses universitaires de France, 1989.

Duprat, Catherine. *"Pour l'amour de l'humanité": Le Temps des philanthropes: La Philanthropie parisienne des Lumières à la monarchie de Juillet.* 2 vols. Paris: Éditions du CTHS, 1993.

Fauré, Christine, ed. *Les Déclarations des droits de l'homme de 1789*. New ed. Paris: Éditions Payot, 1992.

Fayet, Joseph. *La Révolution française et la science, 1789–1795*. Paris: M. Rivière, 1960.

Fehér, Ferenc, ed. *The French Revolution and the Birth of Modernity*. Berkeley: University of California Press, 1990.

Frangos, John. *From Housing the Poor to Healing the Sick: The Changing Institution of the Paris Hospitals Under the Old Regime and the Revolution*. Madison, NJ: Fairleigh Dickinson University Press, 1997.

Gauchet, Marcel. *La Révolution des droits de l'homme*. Paris: Gallimard, 1989.

Gauchet, Marcel. *La Révolution des pouvoirs: La Souveraineté, le peuple et la représentation, 1789–1799*. Paris: Gallimard, 1995.

Gelfand, Toby. *Professionalizing Modern Medicine: Paris Surgeons and Medical Science in the 18th Century*. Westport, CT: Greenwood Press, 1980.

Gough, Hugh. *The Newspaper Press in the French Revolution*. Chicago: Dorsey Press, 1988.

Guilhaumou, Jacques. *L'Avènement des porte-parole de la République (1789–1792): Essai de synthèse sur les langages de la Révolution française*. Villeneuve-d'Ascq: Presses universitaires du Septentrion, 1998.

Guilhaumou, Jacques. *La Langue politique et la Révolution française de l'évènement à la raison linguistique*. Paris: Méridiens/Klincksieck, 1989.

Hahn, Roger. *The Anatomy of a Scientific Institution: The Paris Academy of Sciences, 1666–1803*. Berkeley: University of California Press, 1986. Orig. 1971.

Harden, J. David. "Liberty Caps and Liberty Trees." *Past and Present* 146 (1995).

Hemmings, F. W. J. *Culture and Society in France, 1789–1848*. Leicester: Leicester University Press, 1987.

Herding, Klaus, and Rolf Reichardt. *Die Bildpublizistik der Französischen Revolution*. Frankfurt am Main: Suhrkamp, 1989.

Hesse, Carla. *Publishing and Cultural Politics in Revolutionary Paris, 1789–1810*. Berkeley: University of California Press, 1991.

Hunt, Lynn, ed. *The French Revolution and Human Rights: A Brief Documentary History*. Boston: Bedford, 1996.

Hunt, Lynn. *Politics, Culture, and Class in the French Revolution*. Berkeley: University of California Press, 1984.

Julia, Dominique. "Enfance et citoyenneté: Bilan historiographique et perspectives de recherches sur l'éducation et l'enseignement pendant la période révolutionnaire." *Histoire de l'éducation* 45 (1990).

Kennedy, Emmet. *A Cultural History of the French Revolution.* New Haven, CT: Yale University Press, 1989.

Labrosse, Claude, and Pierre Rétat. *Naissance du journal révolutionnaire, 1789.* Lyon: Presses universitaires de Lyon, 1989.

Lajer-Burcharth, Ewa. *Necklines: The Art of Jacques-Louis David After the Terror.* New Haven, CT: Yale University Press, 1999.

Langlois, Claude. *La Caricature contre-révolutionnaire.* Paris: Presses du CNRS, 1988.

Le Cour Grandmaison, Olivier. *Les Citoyennetés en Révolution, 1789–1794.* Paris: Presses universitaires de France, 1992.

Lefevre, Raymond. *Cinéma et Révolution.* Paris: Edilig, 1988.

Leith, James A. *The Idea of Art as Propaganda in France, 1750–1799: A Study in the History of Ideas.* Toronto: University of Toronto Press, 1965.

Leith, James A. *Space and Revolution: Projects For Monuments, Squares, and Public Buildings in France, 1789–1799.* Montreal: McGill-Queen's University Press, 1991.

Lüsebrink, Hans-Jürgen, and Rolf Reichardt. *The Bastille: A History of a Symbol of Despotism and Freedom.* Trans. Norbert Schürer. Durham, NC: Duke University Press, 1997. Orig. 1990.

Maniquis, Robert M. "The French Revolution and the Cinema: Problems in Filmography." *Primary Sources and Original Works* 1(1991).

Mason, Laura. *Singing the French Revolution: Popular Culture and Politics, 1787–1799.* Ithaca, NY: Cornell University Press, 1996.

Mayer, Arno J. *The Furies: Violence and Terror in the French and Russian Revolutions.* Princeton, NJ: Princeton University Press, 2000.

Murray, W. J. *The Right-Wing Press in the French Revolution: 1789–1792.* Woodbridge, Suffolk/Dover, NH: Boydell Press for the Royal Historical Society, 1986.

Olsen, James L. *Royalist Political Thought During the French Revolution.* Westport, CT: Greenwood Press, 1995.

Olsen, Mark. "Enlightened Nationalism in the Early Revolution: The Nation in the Language of the Société de 1789." *Canadian Journal of History* 29(1) 1994.

Ozouf, Mona. *Festivals and the French Revolution.* Trans. Alan Sheridan. Cambridge, MA: Harvard University Press, 1988. Orig. 1976.

Ozouf, Mona. *L'Homme régénéré: Essais sur la Révolution française.* Paris: Gallimard, 1989.

Palmer, Robert R. *The Improvement of Humanity: Education and the French Revolution.* Princeton, NJ: Princeton University Press, 1985.

Parker, Harold Talbot. *The Cult of Antiquity and the French Revolutionaries: A Study in the Development of the Revolutionary Spirit.* New York: Octagon Books, 1965. Orig. 1937.

Popkin, Jeremy D. *Revolutionary News: The Press in France, 1789–1799.* Durham, NC: Duke University Press, 1990.

Popkin, Jeremy D. *The Right Wing Press in France, 1792–1800.* Chapel Hill: University of North Carolina Press, 1980.

Ravel, Jeffrey. *The Contested Parterre: Public Theatre and French Political Culture, 1680–1791.* Ithaca, NY: Cornell University Press, 1999.

Reichardt, Rolf, and Reinhart Koselleck, eds. *Die Französische Revolution als Bruch des gesellschaftlichen Bewusstseins.* Munich, Oldenbourg, 1988.

Rétat, Pierre, ed. *La Révolution du Journal, 1788–1789.* Paris: Éditions du CNRS, 1989.

Scott, William. "The Pursuit of 'Interests' in the French Revolution: A Preliminary Survey." *French Historical Studies* 19 (1996).

Sewell, William H., Jr. *A Rhetoric of Bourgeois Revolution: The Abbé Sieyes and "What is the Third Estate?"* Durham, NC: Duke University Press, 1994.

Tackett, Timothy N. "Conspiracy Obsession in a Time of Revolution: French Elites and the Origins of the Terror," *American Historical Review* 105 (2000).

Talmon, J. L. *The Origins of Totalitarian Democracy* Boulder, CO: Westview, 1985. Orig. 1952.

Taylor, George. *The French Revolution and the London Stage, 1789–1805.* Cambridge, Eng.: Cambridge University Press, 2001.

Thomas, Paul. "The Revolutionary Festival and Rousseau's Quest for Transparency." *History of Political Thought* 18 (1997).

Vess, David. *Medical Revolution in France, 1789–1796.* Gainesville: University Press of Florida, 1975.

Viguerie, Jean de. "Étude sur l'origine et sur la substance du patriotisme révolutionnaire." *Revue historique* 295 (1996).

Vovelle, Michel. *La Découverte de la politique: Géopolitique de la Révolution française.* Paris: Éditions la Découverte, 1993.

Vovelle, Michel. *Ideologies and Mentalities.* Trans. Eamon O'Flaherty. Chicago: University of Chicago Press, 1990. Orig. 1982.

Vovelle, Michel. *Les Images de la Révolution française.* Paris: Publications de la Sorbonne, 1988.

Vovelle, Michel, ed. *La Révolution française: Images et récits: 1789–1799.* 5 vols. Paris: Livre-Club Diderot Messidor, 1986.

Waldinger, Renée, Philip Dawson, and Isser Woloch, eds. *The French Revolution and the Meaning of Citizenship.* Westport, CT: Greenwood Press, 1993.

Weiner, Dora B. *The Citizen-Patient in Revolutionary and Imperial Paris.* Baltimore: Johns Hopkins University Press, 1993.

Welch, Cheryl B. *Liberty and Utility: The French Ideologues and the Transformation of Liberalism.* New York: Columbia University Press, 1984.

Wrigley, Richard. "Transformations of a Revolutionary Emblem: The Liberty Cap in the French Revolution." *French History* 11 (1997).

6. Religious History

Aston, Nigel. *The End of an Elite: French Bishops and the Coming of the Revolution, 1786–1790.* Oxford: Oxford University Press, 1992.

Aston, Nigel. *Religion and Revolution in France, 1780–1804.* Washington, DC: Catholic University of America Press, 2000.

Berkovitz, Jay R. "The French Revolution and the Jews: Assessing the Cultural Impact." *AJS Review* 20 (1995).

Blumenkranz, Bernard, and Albert Soboul, eds. *Les Juifs et la Révolution française: Problèmes et aspirations.* Toulouse: Privat, 1976.

Desan, Suzanne. *Reclaiming the Sacred: Lay Religion and Popular Politics in Revolutionary France.* Ithaca, NY: Cornell University Press, 1990.

Feuerwerker, David. *L'Émancipation des Juifs en France: De l'Ancien Régime à la fin du Second Empire.* Paris: A. Michel, 1976.

Girard, Patrick. *La Révolution française et les juifs.* Paris: R. Laffont, 1989.

Langlois, Claude. "Religion et révolution: Bibliographie critique." *Archives de sciences sociales des religions,* 35 (1990).

Langlois, Claude, and Timothy N. Tackett, "À L'Époque de la Révolution (1770–1839)," in François Lebrun, ed. *Histoire des Catholiques en France: Du XVe siècle à nos jours.* 2nd ed. Paris: Hachette, 1985.

Langlois, Claude, Timothy N. Tackett, and Michel Vovelle. *Atlas de la Révolution française.* Vol. 9: *Religion.* Paris: École des hautes études en sciences sociales, 1996.

Latreille, André. *L'Église catholique et la Révolution française.* 2 vols. New ed. Paris: Éditions du CERF, 1970.

Mathiez, Albert. *Les Origines des cultes révolutionnaires, 1789–1792.* Paris: G. Bellais, 1904.

Mayer, Arno J. "The Perils of Emancipation: Protestants and Jews." *Archives des sciences sociales des religions* 40 (1995).

McManners, John. *The French Revolution and the Church.* Westport, CT: Greenwood Press, 1982. Orig. 1969.

Pierrard, Pierre. *L'Église et la Révolution, 1789–1889.* Paris: Nouvelle cité, 1988.

Plongeron, Bernard, ed. *Pratiques religieuses, mentalités et spiritualités dans l'Europe révolutionnaire (1770–1820).* Turnhout: Brepols, 1988.

Poland, Burdette. *French Protestantism and the French Revolution: A Study in Church and State, Thought and Religion, 1685–1815.* Princeton, NJ: Princeton University Press, 1957.

Schechter, Ronald. "Translating the 'Marseillaise': Biblical Republicanism and the Emancipation of Jews in Revolutionary France." *Past and Present* 143 (1994).

Tackett, Timothy N. *Priest and Parish in Eighteenth-Century France: A Social and Political Study of the Curés in a Diocese of Dauphiné, 1750–1791.* Princeton, NJ: Princeton University Press, 1977.

Tackett, Timothy N. *Religion, Revolution and Regional Culture in Eighteenth-Century France: The Ecclesiastical Oath of 1791.* Princeton, NJ: Princeton University Press, 1986.

Vovelle, Michel. *Religion et Révolution: La Déchristianisation de l'an II.* Paris: Hachette, 1976.

Vovelle, Michel. *The Revolution Against the Church: From Reason to the Supreme Being.* Trans. Alan José. Cambridge, Eng.: Polity Press, 1991. Orig. 1988.

7. Economic History

Aftalion, Florin. *The French Revolution: An Economic Interpretation.* Trans. Martin Thom. Cambridge, Eng.: Cambridge University Press, 1990. Orig. 1987.

Bosher, J. F. *French Finances, 1770–1795: From Business to Bureaucracy.* Cambridge, Eng.: Cambridge University Press, 1970.

Brezis, Elise S., and François Crouzet. "The Role of Assignats During the French Revolution: An Evil or a Rescuer?" *Journal of European Economic History* 24 (1995).

Bruguière, Michel. *Gestionnaires et profiteurs de la Révolution: L'Administration des finances francaises de Louis XVI à Bonaparte.* Paris: O. Orban, 1986.

État, finances et économie pendant la Révolution française. Paris: Comité pour l'histoire économique et financière de la France, 1991.

Gross, Jean-Pierre. "Progressive Taxation and Social Justice in Eighteenth-Century France." *Past and Present* 140 (1993).

Labrousse, Ernest, and Fernand Braudel, eds. *Histoire économique et sociale de la France.* Vol. III: *L'Avènement de l'ère industrielle (1789–années 1800).* Paris: Presses universitaires de France, 1976.

Loutchisky, Ivan. *Propriété paysanne et vente des biens nationaux pendant la Révolution française.* Rev. ed. Paris: CTHS, 1999.

"Révolution de 1789, guerres et croissance économique." *Revue économique* 40 (1989).

Rosenthal, Jean-Laurent. *The Fruits of Revolution: Property Rights, Litigation, and French Agriculture, 1700–1860.* Cambridge, Eng.: Cambridge University Press, 1992.

Sedillot, René. *Le Coût de la Révolution française.* Paris: Perrin 1987.

White, Eugene Nelson. "The French Government and the Politics of Government Finance, 1770–1815." *Journal of Economic History* 55 (1995).

Woronoff, Denis. *L'Industrie sidérurgique en France pendant la Révolution et l'Empire.* Paris: École des hautes études en sciences sociales, 1984.

8. Social History

Ado, Anatoli. *Paysans en révolution: Terre, pouvoir et jacquerie, 1789–1794.* Paris: Société des études robespierristes, 1996.

Andress, David. *French Society in Revolution, 1789–1799.* Manchester, Eng.: Manchester University Press, 1999.

Bertaud, Jean-Paul. *Un Jour, un homme, la Révolution.* Paris: R. Laffont, 1988.

Bertaud, Jean-Paul. *La Vie quotidienne en France au temps de la Révolution (1789–1795).* Paris: Hachette, 1983.

Cobb, Richard. *The People's Armies: The Armées Révolutionnaires, Instrument of Terror in the Departments, April 1793 to Floréal Year II.* Trans. Marianne Elliot. New Haven, CT: Yale University Press, 1987. Orig. 1961–1963.

Cobb, Richard. *The Police and the People: French Popular Protest, 1789–1820.* Oxford: Oxford University Press, 1970.

Cobb, Richard. *Reactions to the French Revolution.* Oxford: Oxford University Press, 1972.

Cobb, Richard, and Colin Jones, eds. *Voices of the French Revolution.* Topsfield, MA: Salem House Publishers, 1988.

Dalby, Jonathan R. *Les Paysans cantaliens et la Révolution française: 1789–1794.* Clermont-Ferrand: Institut d'études du Massif central, 1989.

Fitzsimmons, Michael P. *The Parisian Order of Barristers and the French Revolution.* Cambridge, MA: Harvard University Press, 1987.

Forrest, Alan. *The French Revolution and the Poor.* New York: St. Martin's Press, 1981.

Forster, Robert. "The French Revolution and the 'New Elite,' 1800–1850," in Jaroslaw Pelinski, ed. *The American and European Revolutions, 1776–1848.* Iowa City: University of Iowa Press, 1980.

Garrioch, David. *The Formation of the Parisian Bourgeoisie, 1690–1830.* Cambridge, MA: Harvard University Press, 1996.

Hampson, Norman A. *A Social History of the French Revolution.* Toronto: University of Toronto Press, 1963.

Higonnet, Patrice. *Class, Ideology, and the Rights of Nobles During the French Revolution.* Oxford: Oxford University Press, 1981.

Hunt, David. "Peasant Politics in the French Revolution." *Social History* 9 (1984).

Johnson, Douglas W., ed. *French Society and the Revolution.* Cambridge, Eng.: Cambridge University Press, 1976.

Jones, Peter M. "The 'Agrarian law': Schemes for Land Redistribution During the French Revolution." *Past and Present* 133 (1991).

Jones, Peter M. *The Peasantry in the French Revolution.* Cambridge, Eng.: Cambridge University Press, 1988.

Lefebvre, Georges. *The Great Fear of 1789: Rural Panic in Revolutionary France.* Trans. Joan White. New York: Random House, 1973. Orig. 1932. Revised ed. 1956.

Lefebvre, Georges. *Les Paysans du Nord pendant la Révolution française.* Paris: A. Colin, 1972. Orig. 1924.

Lucas, Colin, ed. *The French Revolution and Social Change.* Oxford: Oxford University Press, 1990.

Markoff, John. *The Abolition of Feudalism: Peasants, Lords, and Legislators in the French Revolution.* University Park: The Pennsylvania State University Press, 1996.

Mathiez, Albert. *La Vie chère et le mouvement social sous la Terreur.* Paris: Payot, 1927.

Patrick, Alison. "The Second Estate in the Constituent Assembly, 1789–1791." *Journal of Modern History* 62 (1990).

Phillips, Roderick. *Family Breakdown in Late Eighteenth-Century France: Divorces in Rouen, 1792–1803.* Oxford: Oxford University Press, 1981.

Ramsey, Clay. *The Ideology of the Great Fear: The Soissonais in 1789.* Baltimore: Johns Hopkins University Press, 1992.

Rudé, George. *The Crowd in the French Revolution.* Oxford: Oxford University Press, 1972. Orig. 1959.

Sewell, William H., Jr. *Work and Revolution in France: The Language of Labor from the Old Regime to 1848.* Cambridge, Eng: Cambridge University Press, 1980.

Soboul, Albert. *Problèmes paysans de la Révolution (1789–1848): Études de l'histoire révolutionnaire.* Paris: Maspero, 1983. Orig. 1976.

Soboul, Albert. *Les Sans-culottes parisiens en l'an II: Mouvement populaire et gouvernement révolutionnaire, 2 juin 1793–9 thermidor an II.* Paris: Clavreuil, 1958. (There are two abridged English translations: *The Parisian Sans-Culottes and the French Revolution, 1793–4.* Trans Gwynne Lewis. Oxford: Clarendon Press, 1964; and *The Sans-Culottes: The Popular Movement and Revolutionary Government, 1793–1794.* Trans. Remy Inglas Hall. Princeton, NJ: Princeton Unviersity Press, 1980.)

Traer, James F. *Marriage and the Family in Eighteenth-Century France.* Ithaca, NY: Cornell University Press, 1980.

Truant, Cynthia Maria. *The Rites of Labor: Brotherhoods of Campagnonnage in Old and New Regime France.* Ithaca, NY: Cornell University Press, 1994.

Williams, Gwynn A. *Artisans and Sans-Culottes: Popular Movements in France and Britain During the French Revolution.* 2nd ed. London: Libris, 1989.

9. Military History

Alder, Ken. *Engineering the Revolution: Arms and Enlightenment in France, 1763–1815.* Princeton, NJ: Princeton University Press, 1997.

Bertaud, Jean-Paul. *The Army of the French Revolution: From Citizen-Soldiers to Instrument of Power.* Trans. Robert R. Palmer. Princeton, NJ: Princeton University Press, 1988. Orig. 1985.

Bertaud, Jean-Paul. *La Vie quotidienne des soldats de la Révolution (1789–1799).* Paris: Hachette, 1985.

Blanning, T. C. W. *The French Revolutionary Wars, 1787–1802.* London: Arnold, 1996.

Blanning, T. C. W. *The Origins of the French Revolutionary Wars.* London: Longman, 1986.

Brown, Howard G. *War, Revolution, and the Bureaucratic State: Politics and Army Administration in France, 1791–1799.* Oxford: Oxford University Press, 1995.

Cormack, William S. *Revolution and Political Conflict in the French Navy, 1789–1794.* Cambridge, Eng.: Cambridge University Press, 1995.

Devlin, Jonathan D. "The Directory and the Politics of Military Command: The Army of the Interior in South-East France." *French History* 4 (1990).

Forrest, Alan. *Conscripts and Deserters: The Army and French Society During the Revolution and Empire.* Oxford: Oxford University Press, 1989.

Forrest, Alan. *The Soldiers of the French Revolution.* Durham, NC: Duke University Press, 1990.

Griffith, Paddy. *The Art of War of Revolutionary France, 1789–1802.* London: Greenhill Books, 1998.

Lynn, John A. *The Bayonets of the Republic: Motivation and Tactics in the Army of Revolutionary France, 1791–1794.* Boulder, CO: Westview Press, 1996. Orig. 1984.

Mahan, Alfred Thayer. *The Influence of Seapower Upon the French Revolution and Empire (1793–1812).* 10th ed. 2 vols. Boston: Little, Brown, 1898.

Martray, Jean. *La Destruction de la marine française par la Révolution.* Paris: France-Empire, 1988.

Quimby, Robert, Sr. *The Background of Napoleonic Warfare.* New York: Columbia University Press, 1957.

Ross, Steven T. *Historical Dictionary of the Wars of the French Revolution.* Lanham, MD: Scarecrow Press, 1998.

Ross, Steven T. *Quest For Victory: French Military Strategy, 1792–1799.* South Brunswick, NJ: A. S. Barnes, 1973.

Scott, Samuel F. *From Yorktown to Valmy: The Transformation of the French Army in an Age of Revolution.* Niwot: University Press of Colorado, 1998.

Scott, Samuel F. *The Response of the Royal Army to the French Revolution: The Role and Development of the Line Army, 1787–1793.* Oxford: Clarendon Press, 1978.

Soboul, Albert. *Les Soldats de l'an II.* Paris: Club français du livre, 1959.

Woloch, Isser. *The French Veteran From the Revolution to the Restoration.* Chapel Hill: University of North Carolina Press, 1979.

10. International History

Amann, Peter, ed. *The Eighteenth-Century Revolution: French or Western?* Boston: D. C. Heath, 1963.

Aymes, Jean-René. "Spain and the French Revolution." *Mediterranean Historical Review* 6 (1991).

Bartlett, Thomas, and others, eds. *The 1798 Rebellion.* Dublin: Four Counts Press, 2000.

Bindman, David. *The Shadow of the Guillotine: Britain and the French Revolution.* London: British Museum Publications, 1989.

Biro, Sidney Seymour. *The German Policy of Revolutionary France: A Study in French Diplomacy During the War of the First Coalition.* 2 vols. Cambridge, MA: Harvard University Press, 1957.

Black, Jeremy. *British Foreign Policy in an Age of Revolutions, 1783–1793.* Cambridge, Eng.: Cambridge University Press, 1994.

Blanning, T. C. W. *The French Revolution in Germany: Occupation and Resistance in the Rhineland, 1792–1802.* Oxford: Clarendon Press, 1983.

Burrows, Simon. *French Exile Journalism and European Politics, 1792–1814.* Rochester, NY: Boydell & Brewer, 2000.

Carpenter, Kirsty. *Refugees of the French Revolution: Émigrés in London, 1789–1802.* Basingstoke: Macmillan, 1999.

Carpenter, Kirsty, and Philip Mansel, eds. *The French Émigrés in Europe and the Struggle Against Revolution, 1789–1814.* Basingstoke: Macmillan, 1999.

Criscuolo, Vittorio. "L'Idée de république chez les Jacobins italiens." *Annales Historiques de la Révolution française.* 296 (1994).

DeConde, Alexander. *The Quasi-War: The Politics and Diplomacy of the Undeclared War With France, 1791–1801.* New York: Charles Scribner's Sons, 1966.

Droz, Jacques. *L'Allemagne et la Révolution.* Paris: Presses universitaires de France, 1949.

Dubois, Laurent. *Les Esclaves de la République: L'Histoire oubliée de la première émancipation, 1789–1794.* Trans. Jean-François Chaix. Paris: Calmann-Lévy, 1998.

Dunn, Susan. *Sister Revolutions: French Lightning, American Light.* New York: Faber & Faber, 1999.

Elliot, Marianne. *Partners in Revolution: The United Irishmen and France.* New Haven, CT: Yale University Press, 1982.

Gaspar, David Barrey. *More Than Chattel: Black Women and Slavery in the Americas.* Bloomington: Indiana University Press, 1996.

Gaspar, David Barrey, and David P. Geggus, eds. *A Turbulent Time: The French Revolution and the Greater Caribbean.* Bloomington: Indiana University Press, 1997.

Geggus, David P. *Slavery, War, and Revolution: The British Occupation of Saint-Domingue, 1793–1798.* Oxford: Clarendon Press, 1982.

Godechot, Jacques. *France and the Atlantic Revolution of the Eighteenth Century, 1770–1799.* Trans. Herbert H. Rowen. New York: Free Press, 1965. Orig. 1963.

Goodwin, Albert. *The Friends of Liberty: The English Democratic Movement in the Age of the French Revolution.* Cambridge, MA: Harvard University Press, 1979.

Hampson, Norman. *The Perfidy of Albion: French Perceptions of England During the Revolution.* Basingstoke: Macmilllan, 1998.

James, C.L.R. *The Black Jacobins: Toussaint L'Ouverture and the San Domingo Revolution.* New ed. London: Allison and Busby, 1980.

Keogh, Dave, and Nicholas Fierlong, eds. *The Women of 1798.* Dublin: Four Counts Press, 1998.

Klaits, Joseph, and Michael H. Haltzel, eds. *The Global Ramifications of the French Revolution.* Cambridge, Eng.: Cambridge University Press, 1994.

Langley, Lester D. *The Americas in the Age of Revolution, 1750–1850.* New Haven, CT: Yale University Press, 1996.

Mason, Haydn T., and William Doyle, eds. *The Impact of the French Revolution on the European Consciousness.* Gloucester: Alan Sutton, 1989.

McFarland, E.W. *Ireland and Scotland in the Age of Revolution: Planting the Green Bough.* Edinburgh: Edinburgh University Press, 1995.

Michalski, Jerzy. "La Révolution française aux yeux d'un roi." *Acta Poloniae Historica* 66 (1992).

Mori, Jennifer. *William Pitt and the French Revolution, 1785–1795.* New York: St. Martin's Press, 1997.

Morris, Marilyn. *The British Monarchy and the French Revolution.* New Haven, CT: Yale University Press, 1998.

Palmer, Robert R. *The Age of the Democratic Revolution: A Political History of*

Europe and America, 1760–1800. 2 vols. Princeton, NJ: Princeton University Press, 1959–1964.

Philp, Mark, ed. *The French Revolution and British Popular Politics.* Cambridge, Eng.: Cambridge University Press, 1991.

Polasky, Janet L. *Revolution in Brussels, 1787–1793.* Hanover, NH: University Press of New England, 1987.

Price, M. "Louis XVI and Gustavus III: Secret Diplomacy and Counter-Revolution," *Historical Journal* 42 (1999).

Rao, Anna Maria. "L'Expérience révolutionnaire italienne." *Annales historiques de la Révolution française* 313 (1998).

Reinalter, Helmüt. *Der Jakobinismus in Mitteleuropa: Eine Einführung.* Stuttgart: Köhlhammer, 1981.

Roider, Karl A., Jr. *Baron Thugut and Austria's Response to the French Revolution.* Princeton, NJ: Princeton University Press, 1987.

Rufer, Alfred. *La Suisse et la Révolution française.* Ed. Jean-René Suratteau. Paris: Société des études robespierristes, 1974.

Savage, Gary. "Favier's Heirs: The French Revolution and the Secret du Roi." *Historical Journal* 41 (1998).

Schama, Simon. *Patriots and Liberators: Revolution in the Netherlands, 1780–1813.* New York: Knopf, 1977.

Schroeder, Paul W. *The Transformation of European Politics 1763–1848.* Oxford: Clarendon Press, 1994.

Shtrange, M. M. *La Révolution française et la société russe.* Trans. Jean Champenois. Moscow: Éditions en langues étrangères, 1960. Orig. 1956.

Sieburg, Heinz-Otto. "The French Revolution as Mirrored in the German Press and in Political Journalism (1789–1801)." *History of European Ideas* 13 (1991).

Sparrow, Elizabeth. *Secret Service: British Agents in France, 1792–1815.* Rochester, NY: Boydell & Brewer, 1999.

Stengers, Jean. "La Révolution Brabançonne: Une Révolution nationale?" *Académie royale de Belgique: Bulletin de la Classe des lettres et des sciences morales et politiques* 3 (1992).

Vincent, Emma. "The Responses of Scottish Churchmen to the French Revolution, 1789–1802." *Scottish Historical Review* 73 (1994).

Wangermann, Ernest. *From Joseph II to the Jacobin Trials: Government Policy and Public Opinion in the Habsburg Dominions in the Period of the French Revolution.* 2nd ed. Oxford: Oxford University Press, 1969.

11. Regional Studies

Balzac, Honoré de. *The Chouans.* Trans. Marion Ayton Crawford. Hammondsworth, Eng: Penguin, 1978. Orig. 1829.

Benoit, Bruno. "Histoire, mémoire, et identité politique: L'Exemple de la Révolution à Lyon." *Annales historiques de la Révolution française* 305 (1996).

Benoit, Bruno, ed. *Ville et Révolution française.* Lyon: Presses universitaires de Lyon, 1994.

Biard, Michel. "Au Coeur des rapports entre Paris et les départements, les représentants en mission (1793–1795). *Cahiers d'histoire: Revue d'histoire critique* 66 (1997).

Blömeke, H. *Revolutionsregierung und Volksbewegung (1793–1794): Die "Terreur" im Departement Seine-et-Marne (Frankreich)*. New York: P. Lang, 1989.

Bossenga, Gail. *The Politics of Privilege: Old Regime and Revolution in Lille.* Cambridge, Eng: Cambridge University Press, 1991.

Brelot, Claude-Isabelle. *Besançon révolutionnaire.* Paris: Les Belles lettres, 1966.

Cawthon, Elizabeth A., and Steven G. Reinhardt, eds. *Essays on the French Revolution: Paris and the Provinces.* College Station: Texas A & M University Press, 1992.

Cobb, Richard. *Paris and Its Provinces, 1792–1802.* Oxford: Oxford University Press, 1975.

Crook, Malcolm. *Toulon in War and Revolution: From the Ancien Régime to the Restoration, 1750–1820.* Manchester, Eng.: Manchester University Press, 1991.

Edmonds, W. D. *Jacobinism and the Revolt of Lyon, 1789–1793.* Oxford: Clarendon Press, 1990.

Forrest, Alan. *The Revolution in Provincial France: Aquitaine, 1789–1799.* Oxford: Clarendon Press, 1996.

Forrest, Alan. *Society and Politics in Revolutionary Bordeaux.* Oxford: Oxford University Press, 1975.

Forrest, Alan, and Peter M. Jones, eds. *Reshaping France: Town, Country and Region During the French Revolution.* Manchester, Eng.: Manchester University Press, 1991.

Gérard, Alain. *"Par principe d'humanité . . . ," La Terreur et la Vendée.* Paris: Fayard, 1999.

Gobry, Ivan. *Joseph Le Bon: La Terreur dans le Nord de la France.* Paris: Mercure de France, 1991.

Godechot, Jacques. *La Révolution française dans le Midi toulousain.* Toulouse: Privat, 1986.

Hanson, Paul R. *Provincial Politics in the French Revolution: Caen and Limoges, 1789–1794.* Baton Rouge: Louisiana State University Press, 1989.

Hartmann, Éric. *La Révolution française en Alsaac et en Lorraine.* Paris: Perrin, 1990.

Hufton, Olwen H. *Bayeux in the Late Eighteenth Century: A Social Study.* Oxford: Clarendon Press, 1967.

Hunt, Lynn. *Revolution and Urban Politics in Provincial France: Troyes and Reims, 1786–1790.* Stanford, CA: Stanford University Press, 1978.

Hutt, M. G. *Chouannerie and Counter-Revolution: Puisaye, the Princes and the British Government in the 1790s.* 2 vols. Cambridge, Eng.: Cambridge University Press, 1983.

Johnson, Hubert C. *The Tide in Revolution: A Study of Regional Political Diversity, 1789–1793.* Princeton, NJ: Princeton University Press, 1986.

Jones, Colin. *Charity and Bienfaisance: The Treatment of the Poor in the Mont-*

pellier Region, 1740–1815. Cambridge, Eng.: Cambridge University Press, 1989.

Kaplow, Jeffrey. *Elbeuf during the Revolutionary Period: History and Social Structure.* Baltimore: Johns Hopkins University Press, 1964.

Kennedy, Michael L. *The Jacobin Club of Marseilles, 1790–1794.* Ithaca, NY: Cornell University Press, 1973.

Laurent, Robert, and G. Gavignaud. *La Révolution française dans le Languedoc méditerranéen.* Toulouse: Privat, 1987.

Lefebvre, Georges. "Urban Society in the Orléanais." *Past and Present* 19 (1961).

Lewis, Gwynne. *The Second Vendée: The Continuity of Counter-Revolution in the Department of the Gard, 1789–1815.* Oxford: Oxford University Press, 1978.

Lewis, Gwynne, and Colin Lucas, eds. *Beyond the Terror: Essays in French Regional and Social History, 1794–1815.* Cambridge, Eng.: Cambridge University Press, 1983.

Lucas, Colin. "The Problem of the Midi in the French Revolution." *Transactions of the Royal Historical Society.* 5th Series, 28 (1975).

Lucas, Colin. *The Structure of the Terror: The Example of Javogues and the Loire.* Oxford: Oxford University Press, 1973.

Lyons, Martyn. *Revolution in Toulouse: An Essay in Provincial Terrorism.* Bern: P. Lang, 1978.

Mansfield, Paul. "The Management of Terror in Montagnard Lyon, Year II." *European History Quarterly* 20 (1990).

Margadant, Ted W. *Urban Rivalries in the French Revolution.* Princeton, NJ: Princeton University Press, 1992.

Martin, Jean-Clément. *La Vendée et la France.* Paris: Seuil, 1987.

McCoy, Rebecca K. "The Société Populaire at Saint-Marie-Aux-Mines: Local Culture and National Identity in an Alsatian Community During the French Revolution." *European History Quarterly* 27 (1997).

McPhee, Peter. "Counter-Revolution in the Pyrenees: Spirituality, Class and Ethnicity in the Haut-Vallespir, 1793–1794." *French History* 7 (1993).

Peterson, Stephen. "The Social Origins of Royalist Political Violence in Directorial Bordeaux." *French History* 10 (1996).

Peyrard, Christine. *Les Jacobins de l'Ouest: Sociabilité révolutionnaire et formes de politisation dans le Maine et la Basse-Normandie, 1789–1799.* Paris: Publications de la Sorbonne, 1996.

Robin, Régine. *La Société française en 1789: Semur-en Auxois.* Paris: Plon, 1970.

Scott, William, *Terror and Repression in Revolutionary Marseilles.* London: Macmillan, 1973.

Secher, Reynald. *Le Génocide franco-français: La Vendée-vengé.* Paris: Presses universitaires de France, 1986.

Sutherland, Donald M. G. *The Chouans: The Social Origins of Popular Counter-Revolution in Upper Brittany, 1770–1796.* Oxford: Oxford University Press, 1982.

Sutherland, Donald M. G. "Noyades and Other Massacres: Reflections on the

Terror in the West." *Consortium on Revolutionary Europe 1750–1850: Proceedings* 23 (1994).
Tilly, Charles. *The Vendée.* New ed. Cambridge, MA: Harvard University Press, 1976.

12. History of Women and Gender

Abray, Jane. "Feminism in the French Revolution." *American Historical Review* 80 (1975).
Applewhite, Harriet Branson, and Darline Gay Levy, eds. *Women and Politics in the Age of the Democratic Revolution.* Ann Arbor: University of Michigan Press, 1990.
Badinter, Elizabeth, ed. *Paroles d'hommes (1790–1795): Condorcet, Prudhomme, Guyomar.* Paris: P.O.L., 1989.
Brive, Marie-France, ed. *Les Femmes et la Révolution française: Actes du colloque international 12–13–14 avril 1989, Université de Toulouse-Le Mirail.* 3 vols. Toulouse: Presses universitaires du Mirail, 1989–1991.
Desan, Suzanne. "Marriage, Religion and Moral Order: The Catholic Critique of Divorce During the Directory," in Renée Waldinger, Philip Dawson, and Isser Woloch, eds. *The French Revolution and the Meaning of Citizenship.* Westport, CT: Greenwood Press, 1993.
Desan, Suzanne. "War Between Brothers and Sisters: Inheritance Law and Gender Politics in Revolutionary France." *French Historical Studies* 20 (1997).
Devance, Louis. "Le Feminisme pendant la Révolution française." *Annales historiques de la Révolution française* 49 (1977).
Duby, Georges, and Michelle Perrot, general eds. *A History of Women in the West.* Trans. Arthur Goldhammer and others. 5 vols. Cambridge, MA: Harvard University Press, 1992–1994. Orig. 1990–1992. Vol 4: Geneviève Fraisse and Michelle Perrot, eds. *Emerging Feminism from Revolution to World War.*
Duhet, Paule-Marie, ed. *Cahiers de doléances des femmes en 1789 et autres textes.* Paris: Des Femmes, 1981.
Duhet, Paule-Marie. *Les Femmes et la Révolution, 1789–1794.* Paris: Juillard, 1971.
Fauré, Christine. *Democracy Without Women: Feminism and the Rise of Liberal Individualism in France.* Trans. Claudia Gorbman and John Berks. Bloomington: Indiana University Press, 1991. Orig. 1985.
Fol, Michel. "Patriotes au féminin: Les Femmes au Club des Jacobins de Bonneville (1792–1794)." *Revue historique* 295 (1996).
Fraisse, Geneviève. *Reason's Muse: Sexual Difference and the Birth of Democracy.* Trans. Jane Marie Todd. Chicago: University of Chicago Press, 1994. Orig. 1989.
Garrioch, David. "The Everyday Lives of Parisian Women and the October Days." *Social History* 24 (1999).
Godineau, Dominique. *The Women of Paris and Their French Revolution.* Trans. Katherine Streip. Berkeley: University of California Press, 1998. Orig. 1988.

Gutwirth, Madelyn. *The Twilight of the Goddesses: Women and Representation in the French Revolutionary Era.* New Brunswick, NJ: Rutgers University Press, 1992.

Harten, Elke, and Hans-Christian Harten, eds. *Femmes, culture, et révolution.* Trans. Bella Chabot, Jeanne Etoré, and Olivier Mannoni. Paris: Des Femmes, 1989. Orig. 1988.

Hesse, Carla. "French Women in Print, 1750–1800: An Essay in Historical Bibliography," in Haydn T. Mason, ed. *The Darnton Debate: Books and Revolution in the Eighteenth Century.* Oxford: Voltaire Foundation, 1998.

Hesse, Carla. "Revolutionary Histories: The Literary Politics of Louise de Kéralio (1758–1822)," in Barbara B. Diefendorf and Carla Hesse, eds. *Culture and Identity in Early Modern Europe (1500–1800).* Ann Arbor: University of Michigan Press, 1993.

Hufton, Olwen H. *The Prospect Before Her: A History of Women in Western Europe,* Vol. 1, *1500–1800.* London: HarperCollins, 1995.

Hufton, Olwen H. *Women and the Limits of Citizenship in the French Revolution.* Toronto: University of Toronto Press, 1992.

Hunt, Lynn, ed. *Eroticism and the Body Politic.* Baltimore: Johns Hopkins University Press, 1991.

Hunt, Lynn. *The Family Romance of the French Revolution.* Berkeley: University of California Press, 1992.

Hunt, Lynn. "Male Virtue and Republican Motherhood," in Keith Michael Baker, ed. *The French Revolution and the Creation of Modern Political Culture* Vol. 4: *The Terror.* Oxford: Pergamon, 1994.

Hunt, Lynn. "Pornography in the French Revolution," in Lynn Hunt, ed. *The Invention of Pornography: Obscenity and the Origins of Modernity, 1500–1800.* New York: Zone Books, 1993.

Kindleberger, Elizabeth R. "Charlotte Corday in Context and Image: A Case Study in the French Revolution and Women's History." *French Historical Studies* 18 (1994).

Landes, Joan B. *Women and the Public Sphere in the Age of the French Revolution.* Ithaca, NY: Cornell University Press, 1988.

Lapied, Martine. "La Place des femmes dans la sociabilité et la vie politique locale en Provence et dans le Comtat Venaissin pendant la Révolution." *Provence historique* 46 (1996).

Levy, Darline Gay. "Women's Revolutionary Citizenship in Action, 1791: Setting the Boundaries," in Renée Waldinger, Philip Dawson, and Isser Woloch, eds. *The French Revolution and the Meaning of Citizenship.* Westport, CT: Greenwood Press, 1993.

Levy, Darline Gay, and Harriet B. Applewhite. "A Political Revolution For Women? The Case of Paris," in Renate Bridenthal, Susan Mosher Stuard and Merry E. Wiesner, eds. *Becoming Visible: Women in European History.* 3rd ed. Boston: Houghton Mifflin, 1998.

Levy, Darline Gay, Harriet B. Applewhite, and Mary Durham Johnson, eds. *Women in Revolutionary Paris, 1789–1795: Selected Documents Translated with Notes and Commentary.* Urbana: University of Illinois Press, 1979.

Melzer, Sara E., and Leslie W. Rabine, eds. *Rebel Daughters: Women and the French Revolution.* Oxford, Eng.: Oxford University Press, 1992.

Montfort, Catherine R., ed. *Literate Women and the French Revolution of 1789.* Birmingham, AL: Summa Publications, 1994.

Outram, Dorinda. *The Body and the French Revolution: Sex, Class and Political Culture.* New Haven, CT: Yale University Press, 1989.

Rose, Robert Barrie. *Tribunes and Amazons: Men and Women of Revolutionary France, 1789–1794.* Sydney: Macleay Press, 1998.

Scott, Joan Wallach. *Only Paradoxes to Offer: French Feminists and the Rights of Man.* Cambridge, MA: Harvard University Press, 1996.

Thomas, Chantal. *The Wicked Queen: The Origins of the Myth of Marie-Antoinette.* Trans. Julie Rose. New York: Zone Books, 1999. Orig. 1989.

Tomaselli, Sylvana. "Responses to the French Revolution." *Gender & History* 7 (1995).

Yalom, Marilyn. *Blood Sisters: The French Revolution in Women's Memory.* New York: Basic Books, 1993. Orig. 1989.

13. Biographies

Badinter, Elizabeth, and Robert Badinter. *Condorcet, 1743–1794: Un Intellectuel en politique.* Paris: Fayard, 1988.

Baker, Keith Michael. *Condorcet: From Natural Philosophy to Social Mathematics.* Chicago: University of Chicago Press, 1975.

Ballard, John R. *Continuity During the Storm: Boissy d'Anglas and the Era of the French Revolution.* Westport, CT: Greenwood Press, 2000.

Barton, H. Arnold. *Count Hans Axel von Fersen: Aristocrat in an Age of Revolution.* Boston: Twayne, 1975.

Bertaud, Jean-Paul. *Camille et Lucile Desmoulins: Un Couple dans la tourmente.* Paris: Presses de la Renaissance, 1986.

Blanc, Olivier. *Olympe de Gouges: Une Femme de liberté.* New ed. Paris: Syros/ Alternatives, 1989.

Bossut, Nicole. *Chaumette, porte-parole des sans-culottes.* Paris: Comité des travaux historiques et scientifiques, 1998.

Bredin, Jean-Denis. *Sieyès, la clé de la Révolution française.* Paris: Éditions de Fallois, 1988.

Bredin, Jean-Denis. *Une Singulière famille: Jacques Necker, Suzanne Necker et Germaine de Staël.* Paris: Fayard, 1999.

Brinton, Crane. *The Lives of Talleyrand.* New York: W. W. Norton, 1963. Orig. 1936.

Césaire, Aimé. *Toussaint L'Ouverture: La Révolution française et le problème colonial.* Paris: Présence africaine, 1981.

Chaussinand-Nogaret, Guy. *Madame Roland: Une Femme en Révolution.* Paris: Seuil, 1985.

Chaussinand-Nogaret, Guy. *Mirabeau.* Paris: Seuil, 1982.

Conner, Clifford D. *Jean-Paul Marat: Scientist and Revolutionary.* Atlantic Highlands, NJ: Humanities, 1997.

Conte, Arthur. *Billaud-Varenne: Géant de la Révolution.* Paris: Orban, 1989.

Cornevin, Marianne. *La Véritable Madame Roland.* Paris: Pygmalion, 1989.

Curtis, Eugene. *Saint-Just: Colleague of Robespierre.* New York: Columbia University Press, 1935.

Égret, Jean. *Necker: Ministre de Louis XVI, 1776–1790.* Paris: Champion, 1975.

Eisenstein, Elizabeth L. *The First Professional Revolutionist: Filippo Michele Buonarroti (1761–1837): A Biographical Essay.* Cambridge, MA: Harvard University Press, 1959.

Ellery, Eloise. *Brissot de Warville: A Study in the History of the French Revolution.* Boston: Houghton Mifflin, 1915.

Forsyth, Murray. *Reason and Revolution: The Political Thought of the Abbé Sieyès.* New York: Holmes & Meier, 1987.

"Forum: Interpreting Brissot." *French Historical Studies* 17 (1991).

Garnier, Jean-Paul. *Barras, le roi du Directoire.* Paris: Perrin, 1970.

Garnier, Robert. *Lazare Hoche, ou l'homme des armes.* Paris: Payot, 1986.

Gershoy, Leo. *Bertrand Barère: A Reluctant Terrorist.* Princeton, NJ: Princeton University Press, 1962.

Gottschalk, Louis R. *Jean Paul Marat: A Study in Radicalism.* Chicago: University of Chicago Press, 1967. Orig. 1927.

Gottschalk, Louis R., and Margaret Maddox. *Lafayette.* 6 vols. Chicago: University of Chicago Press, 1935–1973.

Greenbaum, Louis S. *Talleyrand, Statesman-Priest: The Agent-General of the Clergy and the Church of France at the End of the Old Regime.* Washington, DC: Catholic University of America Press, 1970.

Hampson, Norman. *Danton.* Oxford: Blackwell, 1988.

Hampson, Norman. *The Life and Opinions of Maximilien Robespierre.* Oxford: Blackwell, 1988. Orig. 1974.

Hampson, Norman. *Saint-Just.* Oxford: Blackwell, 1991.

Hardman, John. *Louis XVI.* New Haven, CT: Yale University Press, 1993.

Hardman, John. *Louis XVI, The Silent King.* London: Arnold, 2000.

Haslip, Joan. *Marie Antoinette.* London: Weidenfeld and Nicholson, 1987.

Haydon, Colin, and William Doyle, eds. *Robespierre.* Cambridge, Eng.: Cambridge University Press, 1999.

Homan, Gerlof. *Jean-François Reubell: French Revolutionary, Patriot, and Director, 1747–1807.* The Hague: Nijhoff, 1971.

Jordan, David P. *The Revolutionary Career of Maximilien Robespierre.* Chicago: University of Chicago Press, 1989. Orig. 1985.

Kennedy, Emmet. *A Philosophe in the Age of Revolution: Destutt de Tracy and the Origins of "Ideology."* Philadelphia: American Philosophical Society, 1978.

Kramer, Lloyd S. *Lafayette in Two Worlds: Public Cultures and Personal Identities in an Age of Revolution.* Chapel Hill: University of North Carolina Press, 1996.

Labbé, François. *Anarcharsis Cloots, le Prussien francophile.* Paris: L'Harmatton, 2000.

Lacour-Gayet, Robert. *Calonne: Financier, réformateur, contre-révolutionnaire, 1734–1802.* Paris: Hachette, 1963.

Ladret, Albert. *Saint-Just.* Lyon: Presses universitaires de Lyon, 1989.

Le Guillou, Jean-Marc. *Jacques Roux (1752–1794): L'Annonce faite à la gauche.* Paris: Éditions des Écrivains, 2000.

Lever, Evelyne. *Marie-Antoinette: The Last Queen of France.* Trans. Catherine Temerson. New York: Farrar, Strauss, Giroux, 2000. Orig. 1991.

Lever, Evelyne. *Philippe-Égalité.* Paris: Fayard, 1996.

Lévy-Schneider, Léon. *Le Conventionnel Jeanbon Saint-André.* Paris: Alcan, 1901.

Loomis, Stanley. *The Fatal Friendship: Marie-Antoinette, Count Fersen and the Flight to Varennes.* Garden City, NY: Doubleday, 1972.

Luttrell, Barbara. *Mirabeau.* Carbondale: Southern Illinois University Press, 1990.

Malino, Frances. *A Jew in the French Revolution: The Life of Zalkind Hourwitz.* Oxford: Blackwell, 1996.

May, Gita. *Madame Roland and the Age of Revolution.* New York: Columbia University Press, 1970.

Merrick, Jeffrey, and Dorothy Medlin, eds. *André Morellet (1727–1819) in the Republic of Letters and the French Revolution.* Bern: P. Lang, 1995.

Monnier, Raymonde. *Un Bourgeois sans-culotte: Le Général Santerre.* Paris: La Sorbonne, 1989.

Necheles, Ruth F. *The Abbé Grégoire, 1787–1831: The Odyssey of an Egalitarian.* Westport, CT: Greenwood Press, 1971.

Noack, Paul. *Olympe de Gouges, 1748–1793: Courtisane et militante des droits de la femme, 1748–1793.* Trans. Isabelle Duclos. Paris: Éditions de Fallois, 1993. Orig. 1992.

Plongeron, Bernard. *L'Abbé Grégoire (1750–1831) ou l'arche de la fraternité.* Paris: Letrouzey & Ane, 1989.

Reinhard, Marcel. *Le Grand Carnot.* 2 vols. Paris: Hachette, 1950–1952.

Roberts, Warren. *Jacques-Louis David, Revolutionary Artist.* Chapel Hill: University of North Carolina Press, 1989.

Robison, Georgia. *Revellière-Lepeaux: Citizen Director, 1753–1824.* New York: Columbia University Press, 1938.

Rose, Robert Barrie. *Gracchus Babeuf: The First Revolutionary Communist.* Stanford, CA: Stanford University Press, 1978.

Roudinesco, Elisabeth. *Théroigne de Méricourt: A Melancholic Woman During the French Revolution.* Trans. Martin Thom. New York: Verso, 1991. Orig. 1989.

Rudé, George. *Robespierre: Portrait of a Revolutionary Democrat.* New York: Vintage Press, 1975.

Sydenham, M. J. *Leonard Bourdon. The Career of a Revolutionary, 1754–1807.* Waterloo, Ontario: Wilfred Laurier University Press, 1999.

Thompson, James M. *Leaders of the French Revolution.* Oxford: Blackwell, 1988. Orig. 1929.

Thompson, James M. *Robespierre.* 2 vols. Oxford: Blackwell, 1988. Orig. 1935.

Walter, Gérard. *Hébert et le Père Duchesne* Paris: J. B. Janin, 1946.

Webster, Alison. "J. Barnave: Philosopher of a Revolution." *History of European Ideas* 17 (1993).

14. The Aftermath: Napoleon

Detailed bibliographies are found in the following:

Connelly, Owen. *The French Revolution and Napoleonic Era.* 3rd ed. Fort Worth, TX: Harcourt College Publishers, 2000.

Kafker, Frank A., and James M. Laux, eds. *Napoleon and His Times: Selected Interpretations.* Malabar, FL: Robert E. Krieger, 1989.

ABOUT THE EDITORS

FRANK A. KAFKER is Professor Emeritus of History at the University of Cincinnati. He received the B.A., M.A., and Ph.D. from Columbia University. He has written *The Encyclopedists As a Group: A Collective Biography of the Authors of the Encyclopédie* and, in collaboration with Serena Kafker, *The Encyclopedists as Individuals: A Biographical Dictionary of the Encyclopédie.* Also he has edited *Notable Encyclopedias of the Seventeenth and Eighteenth Centuries: Nine Predecessors of the Encyclopédie* and *Notable Encyclopedias of the Late Eighteenth Century: Eleven Successors of the Encyclopédie.* Among the many journals to which he has contributed articles are *French Historical Studies, Revue d'Histoire Moderne et Contemporaine, Studi Francesi, Eighteenth-Century Studies, British Journal for Eighteenth-Century Studies,* and *Recherches sur Diderot et sur l'Encyclopédie.* With James M. Laux, he edited *Napoleon and His Times: Selected Interpretations* and the journal *French Historical Studies* from 1985 to 1992.

JAMES M. LAUX is Professor Emeritus of History at the University of Cincinnati. He holds a Ph.D. from Northwestern University. He is the translator of *The Right Wing in France,* by R. Rémond, and the author of *In First Gear: The French Automobile Industry to 1914* and *The European Automobile Industry.* He is co-author and translator of *The Automobile Revolution.* His articles have appeared in *French Historical Studies, Le Mouvement Social, Business History, Journal of Transport History, Aerospace Historian, Third Republic, French Review, Political Science Quarterly,* and *Culture Technique.*

DARLINE GAY LEVY is Associate Professor of History at New York University. She received the B.A. from Barnard College and the Ph.D. from Harvard University. She is the author of *The Ideas and Careers of Simon-Nicolas-Henri Linguet: A Study in Eighteenth-Century French Politics* and the co-editor of *Women in Revolutionary Paris, 1789–1795* and *Women and Politics in the Age of the Democratic Revolution.* She is currently completing several volumes: "Stratégies discursives et pouvoir: Le Cas Linguet" (co-author Alain Garoux); the unedited correspondence of Linguet (co-director Alain Garoux); and a co-authored book with Harriet Branson Applewhite, "The Impossible Citizenship: Women, Gender, and Power in Revolutionary Paris," that expands and synthesizes their earlier research on Revolutionary women.